D1065203

AN INTRODUCTION TO THE ANALYSIS OF ALGORITHMS

AN INTRODUCTION TO THE ANALYSIS OF ALGORITHMS

Robert Sedgewick
Princeton University

Philippe Flajolet
INRIA Rocquencourt

ADDISON-WESLEY PUBLISHING COMPANY
Reading, Massachusetts • Menlo Park, California • New York
Don Mills, Ontario • Wokingham, England • Amsterdam • Bonn
Sydney • Singapore • Tokyo • Madrid • San Juan • Milan • Paris

Publishing Partner: **Peter S. Gordon**
Associate Editor: **Deborah Lafferty**
Cover Designer: **Eileen Hoff**
Production: **Editorial Services of New England**
Project Manager: **Penny Stratton,** Editorial Services of New England
Senior Manufacturing Coordinator: **Judy Sullivan**
Senior Production Coordinator: **Marybeth Mooney**

The programs and analyses presented in this book have been included for their instructional value. They have been prepared with care, but are not guaranteed for any particular purpose. The publisher does not offer any warranties or representations, nor does it accept any liabilities with respect to the programs or analytic results.

Library of Congress Cataloging-in-Publication Data

Sedgewick, Robert, 1946 –
An introduction to the analysis of algorithms / Robert Sedgewick, Philippe Flajolet.
512 p. 24 cm.
Includes bibliographical references and index.
ISBN 0-201-40009-X
1. Computer algorithms. I. Flajolet, Philippe. II. Title.
QA76.9.A43S43 1996
005.1—dc20 95-24307
CIP

Reproduced by Addison-Wesley from page description files supplied by the authors.

ISBN 0-201-40009-X
2 3 4 5 6 7 8 9 10-MA-989796

Reprinted with corrections March, 1996.

FOREWORD

PEOPLE who analyze algorithms have double happiness. First of all they experience the sheer beauty of elegant mathematical patterns that surround elegant computational procedures. Then they receive a practical payoff when their theories make it possible to get other jobs done more quickly and more economically.

Mathematical models have been a crucial inspiration for all scientific activity, even though they are only approximate idealizations of real-world phenomena. Inside a computer, such models are more relevant than ever before, because computer programs create artificial worlds in which mathematical models often apply precisely. I think that's why I got hooked on analysis of algorithms when I was a graduate student, and why the subject has been my main life's work ever since.

Until recently, however, analysis of algorithms has largely remained the preserve of graduate students and post-graduate researchers. Its concepts are not really esoteric or difficult, but they are relatively new, so it has taken awhile to sort out the best ways of learning them and using them.

Now, after more than 30 years of development, algorithmic analysis has matured to the point where it is ready to take its place in the standard computer science curriculum. The appearance of this long-awaited textbook by Sedgewick and Flajolet is therefore most welcome. Its authors are not only worldwide leaders of the field, they also are masters of exposition. I am sure that every serious computer scientist will find this book rewarding in many ways.

D. E. Knuth

PREFACE

THIS book is intended to be a thorough overview of the primary techniques used in the mathematical analysis of algorithms. The material covered draws from classical mathematical topics, including discrete mathematics, elementary real analysis, and combinatorics, as well as from classical computer science topics, including algorithms and data structures. The focus is on "average-case" or "probabilistic" analysis, though the basic mathematical tools required for "worst-case" or "complexity" analysis are covered as well.

We assume that the reader has some familiarity with basic concepts in both computer science and real analysis. In a nutshell, the reader should be able to both write programs and prove theorems; otherwise, the book is intended to be self-contained. Ample references to preparatory material in the literature are also provided. A planned companion volume will cover more advanced techniques. Together, the books are intended to cover the main techniques and to provide access to the growing research literature on the analysis of algorithms.

The book is meant to be used as a textbook in a junior- or senior-level course on "Mathematical Analysis of Algorithms." It might also be useful in a course in discrete mathematics for computer scientists, since it covers basic techniques in discrete mathematics as well as combinatorics and basic properties of important discrete structures within a familiar context for computer science students. It is traditional to have somewhat broader coverage in such courses, but many instructors may find the approach here a useful way to engage students in a substantial portion of the material. The book also can be used to introduce students in mathematics and applied mathematics to principles from computer science related to algorithms and data structures.

Supplemented by papers from the literature, the book can serve as the basis for an introductory graduate course on the analysis of algorithms, or as a reference or basis for self-study by researchers in mathematics or computer science who want access to the literature in this field. It also might be of use to students and researchers in combinatorics and discrete mathematics, as a source of applications and techniques.

Despite the large literature on the mathematical analysis of algorithms, basic information on methods and models in widespread use has not been directly accessible to students and researchers in the field. This book aims to address this situation, bringing together a body of material intended to provide the reader with both an appreciation for the challenges of the field and the requisite background for learning the advanced tools being developed to meet these challenges.

Preparation. Mathematical maturity equivalent to one or two years' study at the college level is assumed. Basic courses in combinatorics and discrete mathematics may provide useful background (and may overlap with some material in the book), as would courses in real analysis, numerical methods, or elementary number theory. We draw on all of these areas, but summarize the necessary material here, with reference to standard texts for people who want more information.

Programming experience equivalent to one or two semesters' study at the college level, including elementary data structures, is assumed. We do not dwell on programming and implementation issues, but algorithms and data structures are the central object of our studies. Again, our treatment is complete in the sense that we summarize basic information, with reference to standard texts and primary sources.

Access to a computer system for mathematical manipulation, such as MAPLE or Mathematica, is highly recommended. These systems can relieve one from tedious calculations when checking material in the text or solving exercises.

Related books. Related texts include *The Art of Computer Programming* by Knuth; *Handbook of Algorithms and Data Structure* by Gonnet and Baeza-Yates; *Algorithms* by Sedgewick; *Concrete Mathematics* by Graham, Knuth and Patashnik; and *Introduction to Algorithms* by Cormen, Leiserson, and Rivest. This book could be considered supplementary to each of these, as examined below, in turn.

In spirit, this book is closest to the pioneering books by Knuth. Our focus is on mathematical techniques of analysis, though, whereas Knuth's books are broad and encyclopedic in scope, with properties of algorithms playing a primary role and methods of analysis a secondary role. This book can serve as basic preparation for the advanced results covered and referred to in Knuth's books.

We also cover approaches and results in the analysis of algorithms that have been developed since publication of Knuth's books. Gonnet and

Baeza-Yates's *Handbook* is a thorough survey of such results, including a comprehensive bibliography; it primarily presents results with reference to derivations in the literature. Again, our book provides the basic preparation for access to this literature.

We also strive to keep the focus on covering algorithms of fundamental importance and interest, such as those described in Sedgewick's *Algorithms*, whereas Graham, Knuth, and Patashnik's *Concrete Mathematics* focuses almost entirely on mathematical techniques. This book is intended to be a link between the basic mathematical techniques discussed in Graham, Knuth, and Patashnik and the basic algorithms covered in Sedgewick.

Cormen, Leiserson, and Rivest's *Introduction to Algorithms* is representative of a number of books that provide access to the research literature on "design and analysis" of algorithms, which is normally based on rough worst-case estimates of performance. When more precise results are desired (presumably for the most important methods), more sophisticated models and mathematical tools are required. Cormen, Leiserson, and Rivest focus on *design* of algorithms (usually with the goal of bounding worst-case performance), with analytic results used to help guide the design. Our book, on the other hand, is supplementary to theirs and similar books in that we focus on the *analysis* of algorithms, especially on techniques that can be used to develop detailed results that could be used to predict performance. In this process, we also consider relationships to various classical mathematical tools. Chapter 1 is devoted entirely to developing this context.

This book also lays the groundwork for a companion volume, *Analytic Combinatorics*, a general treatment that places the material here in a broader perspective and develops advanced methods and models that can serve as the basis for new research, not only in average-case analysis of algorithms but also in combinatorics. A higher level of mathematical maturity is assumed for that volume, perhaps at the senior or beginning graduate student level. Of course, careful study of this book is adequate preparation. It certainly has been our goal to make it sufficiently interesting that some readers will be inspired to tackle more advanced material!

How to use this book. Readers of this book are likely to have rather diverse backgrounds in discrete mathematics and computer science. With this in mind, it is useful to be aware the basic structure of book: eight chapters in all, an introductory chapter followed by three chapters emphasizing mathematical methods, then four chapters emphasizing applications in the analysis of algorithms:

INTRODUCTION
- 1. ANALYSIS OF ALGORITHMS

DISCRETE MATHEMATICAL METHODS
- 2. RECURRENCES
- 3. GENERATING FUNCTIONS
- 4. ASYMPTOTIC ANALYSIS

ALGORITHMS AND COMBINATORIAL STRUCTURES
- 5. TREES
- 6. PERMUTATIONS
- 7. STRINGS AND TRIES
- 8. WORDS AND MAPS

Chapter 1 puts the material in the book into perspective, and will help all readers understand the basic objectives of the book and the role of the remaining chapters in meeting those objectives. Chapters 2 through 4 are more oriented towards mathematics, as they cover methods from discrete mathematics, primarily focused on developing basic concepts and techniques. Chapters 5 through 8 are more oriented towards computer science, as they cover properties of combinatorial structures, their relationships to fundamental algorithms, and analytic results.

Though the book is intended to be self-contained, differences in emphasis are appropriate in teaching the material, depending on the background and experience of students and instructor. One approach, more mathematically oriented, would be to emphasize the theorems and proofs in the first part of the book, with applications drawn from Chapters 5 through 8. Another approach, more oriented towards computer science, would be to briefly cover the major mathematical tools in Chapters 2 through 4 and emphasize the algorithmic material in the second half of the book. But our primary intention is that most students should be able to learn new material from both mathematics and computer science in an interesting context by working carefully all the way through the book.

Students with a strong computer science background are likely to have seen many of the algorithms and data structures from the second half of the book but not much of the mathematical material at the beginning;

students with a strong background in mathematics are likely to find the mathematical material familiar but perhaps not the algorithms and data structures. A course covering all of the material in the book could help either group of students fill in gaps in their background while building upon knowledge they already have.

Supplementing the text are lists of references (at the end of each chapter) and several hundred exercises (interspersed throughout the text), to encourage readers to consider the material in the text in more depth and to examine original sources.

Our experience in teaching this material has shown that there are numerous opportunities for instructors to supplement lecture and reading material with computation-based laboratories and homework assignments. The material covered here is an ideal framework for students to develop expertise in a symbolic manipulation system such as Mathematica or MAPLE. Also, the experience of validating the mathematical studies by comparing them against empirical studies can be very valuable for many students.

Acknowledgments. We are very grateful to INRIA, Princeton University, and the National Science Foundation, which have provided the primary support for us to work on this book. Other support has been provided by Brown University, European Community (Alcom Project), Institute for Defense Analyses, Ministère de la Recherche et de la Technologie, Stanford University, Université Libre de Bruxelles, and Xerox Palo Alto Research Center. This book has been many years in the making, so a comprehensive list of people and organizations that have contributed support would be prohibitively long, and we apologize for any omissions.

Don Knuth's influence on our work has been extremely important, as is obvious from the text.

Students in Princeton, Paris, and Providence have provided helpful feedback in courses taught from early versions of this material over the years. We would also like to thank Philippe Dumas; Mordecai Golin and his students San Kuen Chan, Ka Po Lam, Ngok Hing Leung, Derek Ka-Cheong Lueng, and King Shan Lui; Helmut Prodinger; and three anonymous reviewers for their detailed comments on the manuscript.

Corfu R. S.
September 1995 Ph. F.

TABLE OF CONTENTS

NOTATION

$\lfloor x \rfloor$	*floor function* largest integer less than or equal to x
$\lceil x \rceil$	*ceiling function* smallest integer greater than or equal to x
$\{x\}$	*fractional part* $x - \lfloor x \rfloor$
$\lg N$	*binary logarithm* $\log_2 N$
$\ln N$	*natural logarithm* $\log_e N$
$\binom{n}{k}$	*binomial coefficient* number of ways to choose k out of n items
$\left[n \atop k \right]$	*Stirling number of the first kind* number of permutations of n elements that have k cycles
$\left\{ n \atop k \right\}$	*Stirling number of the second kind* number of ways to partition n elements into k nonempty subsets
ϕ	*golden ratio* $(1+\sqrt{5})/2 = 1.61803\cdots$
γ	*Euler's constant* $.57721\cdots$
σ	*Stirling's constant* $\sqrt{2\pi} = 2.50662\cdots$

CHAPTER ONE

ANALYSIS OF ALGORITHMS

MATHEMATICAL studies of the properties of computer algorithms have spanned a broad spectrum, from general complexity studies to specific analytic results. In this chapter, we discuss representative examples of various approaches to studying algorithms. At the same time, these examples allow us to present various classical results from a fundamental and representative problem domain: the study of sorting algorithms.

First, we will consider the general motivations for algorithmic analysis, and relationships among various approaches to studying performance characteristics of algorithms. Next, we discuss computational complexity and consider as an example Mergesort, an "optimal" algorithm for sorting. Following that, we will examine the major components of a full analysis for a sorting algorithm of fundamental practical importance, Quicksort. This includes the study of various improvements to the basic Quicksort algorithm, as well as some examples illustrating how the analysis can help one adjust parameters to improve performance.

This chapter is intended to place our field of study into context among related fields and to set the stage for the rest of the book. In Chapters 2 through 4, our plan is to introduce the basic mathematical concepts needed for the analysis of fundamental algorithms. In Chapters 5 through 8, we consider basic combinatorial properties of fundamental algorithms and data structures. Since there is a close relationship between fundamental methods used in computer science and classical mathematical analysis, we simultaneously consider some introductory material from both areas in this book.

1.1 Why Analyze an Algorithm? There are several answers to this basic question, depending on context: the intended use of the algorithm, the importance of the algorithm in relationship to others from both practical and theoretical standpoints, and the difficulty of analysis and accuracy of the answer required.

The most straightforward reason for analyzing an algorithm is to discover its characteristics in order to evaluate its suitability for various applications or compare it with other algorithms for the same application.

The characteristics of interest are most often the primary resources of time and space, particularly time. Put simply, we want to know how long an implementation of a particular algorithm will run on a particular computer, and how much space it will require. The analysis generally is kept relatively independent of particular implementations—we concentrate instead on obtaining results for essential characteristics of the algorithm that can be used to derive precise estimates of true resource requirements on actual machines.

In practice, achieving independence between an algorithm and characteristics of its implementation might be difficult to arrange. The quality of the implementation and properties of compilers, machine architecture, and other major facets of the programming environment have dramatic effects on performance. We must be cognizant of such effects to be sure the results of analysis are useful. On the other hand, in some cases, analysis of an algorithm can help identify ways for it to take full advantage of the programming environment.

Occasionally, some property other than time or space is of interest, and the focus of the analysis changes accordingly. For example, an algorithm on a machine to drive a circuit wiring device might be studied to determine the total amount of wire used, or an algorithm for a numerical problem might be studied to determine how accurate an answer it can provide. Also, it is sometimes appropriate to address multiple resources in the analysis. For example, an algorithm that uses a large amount of memory may use much less time than an algorithm that gets by with very little memory. Indeed, one prime motivation for doing a careful analysis is to provide accurate information to help in making proper tradeoff decisions in such situations.

The term *analysis of algorithms* has been used to describe two quite different general approaches to putting the study of the performance of computer programs on a scientific basis. We consider these two in turn.

The first, popularized by Aho, Hopcroft, and Ullman [2], concentrates on determining the growth of the worst-case performance of the algorithm (an "upper bound"). A prime goal in such analyses is to determine which algorithms are optimal in the sense that a matching "lower bound" can be proved on the worst-case performance of any algorithm for the same problem. This type of analysis is sometimes called *computational complexity* though that terminology is perhaps more properly reserved for general studies of relationships between problems, algorithms, languages, and machines.

The second approach to the analysis of algorithms, popularized by Knuth [13][14][15][17], concentrates on precisely characterizing the performance of algorithms by determining their best-case, worst-case, and average-case performance using a methodology that can be refined to produce increasingly precise answers when desired. A prime goal in such analyses is to be able to accurately predict the performance characteristics of a particular algorithm when run on a particular computer.

We may view both these approaches as necessary stages in the design and analysis of efficient algorithms. When faced with a new algorithm to solve a new problem, we are interested in developing a rough idea of how well it might be expected to perform and how it might compare to other algorithms for the same problem, even the best possible. Computational complexity studies can provide this. However, so much precision is typically sacrificed in such a rough complexity analysis that it provides little specific information that would allow us to predict performance for an actual implementation or to properly compare one algorithm to another. To be able to do so, we need full details on the implementation, the computer to be used, and, as we see in this book, mathematical properties of the structures manipulated by the algorithm. Computational complexity may be viewed as the first step in an ongoing process of developing a more refined, more accurate analysis; we prefer to use the term *analysis of algorithms* to refer to the whole process, with the goal of providing answers with as much accuracy as necessary.

The analysis of an algorithm can help us understand it better, and can suggest informed improvements. The more complicated the algorithm, the more difficult the analysis. Algorithms tend to become shorter, simpler, and more elegant during the analysis process. More important, the careful scrutiny required for proper analysis often leads to better and more efficient implementations of algorithms. Analysis requires a far more complete understanding of an algorithm than merely producing a working implementation. Indeed, when the results of analytic and empirical studies agree, we become strongly convinced of the validity of the algorithm as well as of the correctness of the process of analysis.

Some algorithms are worth analyzing because their analyses can add to the body of mathematical tools available. Such algorithms may be of limited practical interest but may have properties similar to algorithms of practical interest so that understanding them may help to understand more important methods in the future.

On the other hand, many algorithms (some of intense practical interest, some of little or none) have a complex performance structure with properties of independent mathematical interest. The dynamic element brought to combinatorial problems by the analysis of algorithms leads to challenging, interesting mathematical problems that extend the reach of classical combinatorics to help shed light on properties of computer programs.

To bring these ideas into clearer focus, we next consider in detail some classical results first from the viewpoint of computational complexity and then from the viewpoint of the analysis of algorithms. As a running example to illustrate the different perspectives, we study *sorting algorithms*, which rearrange a list to put it in numerical, alphabetic, or other order. This is an important practical problem that remains the object of widespread study because sorting programs play a central role in many applications.

1.2 Computational Complexity. The prime goal of computational complexity is to classify algorithms according to their performance characteristics. The first step in doing so is to settle upon appropriate mathematical notations for expressing the results:

Definition *Given a function* $f(N)$,

$O(f(N))$ *denotes the set of all* $g(N)$ *such that* $|g(N)/f(N)|$ *is bounded from above as* $N \to \infty$.

$\Omega(f(N))$ *denotes the set of all* $g(N)$ *such that* $|g(N)/f(N)|$ *is bounded from below by a (strictly) positive number as* $N \to \infty$.

$\Theta(f(N))$ *denotes the set of all* $g(N)$ *such that* $|g(N)/f(N)|$ *is bounded from both above and below as* $N \to \infty$.

These notations, adapted from classical number theory, were advocated for use in the analysis of algorithms in a paper by Knuth in 1976 [16]. They have come into widespread use for making mathematical statements about bounds on the performance of algorithms.

The O-notation provides a way to express an upper bound; the Ω-notation provides a way to express a lower bound; and the Θ-notation provides a way to express matching upper and lower bounds. The most common use of the O-notation in mathematics is to express asymptotic approximations—we will consider this in detail in Chapter 4. It is also used more widely than the others in the analysis of algorithms, typically to express a relatively small "error" term in an expression describing the running time of an algorithm. The Ω and Θ notations are directly associated with computational complexity, though similar notations are used in other application areas (see [16]).

For complexity studies, the importance of these notations is that they allow implementation details to be hidden by ignoring constant factors. Since constant factors are being ignored, a side effect of the use of such notations is that derivation of mathematical results using them is simpler than if more precise answers are sought. For example, both the "natural" logarithm $\ln N \equiv \log_e N$ and the "binary" logarithm $\lg N \equiv \log_2 N$ often arise, but they are related by a constant factor, so we can refer to either as being $O(\log N)$ in a complexity analysis.

Exercise 1.1 Show that $f(N) = N \lg N + O(N)$ implies that $f(N) = \Theta(N \log N)$.

As an illustration of the use of these notations to study the performance characteristics of algorithms, we consider methods for sorting a set of numbers in an `array a[1..N]`. The input is the numbers in the array, in arbitrary and unknown order; the output is the same numbers in the array, rearranged in ascending order. This is a well-studied and fundamental problem: we will consider an algorithm for solving it, then show that algorithm to be "optimal" in a precise technical sense.

First, we will show that it is possible to solve the sorting problem efficiently, using a well-known recursive algorithm called Mergesort. Mergesort and nearly all of the algorithms treated in this book are described in detail in Sedgewick [19], so we give only a brief description here. Readers interested in further details on variants of the algorithms, implementations, and applications, are encouraged to consult the books by Cormen, Leiserson, and Rivest [5], Gonnet and Baeza-Yates [8], Knuth [13][14][15], Sedgewick [19], and other sources.

Mergesort divides the array in the middle, sorts the two halves (recursively), and then merges the resulting sorted subfiles together to produce the sorted result. To do so, it uses auxiliary arrays `b` and `c`, as shown in Program 1.1. Invoking this procedure with the call `mergesort(1,N)` will sort the array `a[1..N]`. After the recursive calls, the first sorted half `a[1..m]` is copied over to the auxiliary array `b[1..m-l+1]` and the second sorted half a[m+1..r] is copied over to the second auxiliary array c[1..r-m]. Then the merge is accomplished by moving the smaller of the elements b[i] and c[j] to a[k], incrementing i or j accordingly. The program uses a "sentinel" called max that is assumed to be larger than all the elements, to help accomplish the task of moving the remainder of one of the auxiliary arrays back to a after the other one has been exhausted.

Exercise 1.2 Implement a Mergesort that divides the array into *three* equal parts, sorts them, and does a three-way merge. Empirically compare its running time with standard Mergesort.

Mergesort is prototypical of the well-known *divide-and-conquer* algorithm design paradigm, where a problem is solved by (recursively) solving smaller subproblems and using the solutions to solve the original problem. We will analyze a number of such algorithms in this book. More generally, we will be seeing how the recursive structure of algorithms like Mergesort leads immediately to mathematical descriptions of their performance characteristics.

In the present context, Mergesort is significant because it is guaranteed to be as efficient as any sorting method. To make this claim more

```
procedure mergesort(l, r:  integer);
  var i, j, k, m:  integer;
  begin
  if r-l > 0 then
    begin
      m := (r+l) div 2;
      mergesort(l, m); mergesort(m+1, r);
      for i := 1 to m-l+1 do b[i] := a[l+i-1];
      for j := m+1 to r do c[j-m] := a[j];
      i := 1; j := 1; b[m+1] := max; c[r-m+1] := max;
      for k := l to r do
        if b[i] < c[j]
          then begin a[k] := b[i]; i := i+1 end
          else begin a[k] := c[j]; j := j+1 end;
    end;
  end;
```

Program 1.1 Mergesort

precise, we begin by analyzing the dominant factor in the running time of Mergesort, the number of comparisons that it uses.

Theorem 1.1 (*Mergesort*) *To sort an array of N elements, Mergesort uses $N \lg N + O(N)$ comparisons.*

Proof. If C_N is the number of comparisons that the above program uses to sort N elements, then the number of comparisons to sort the first half is $C_{\lfloor N/2 \rfloor}$, the number of comparisons to sort the second half is $C_{\lceil N/2 \rceil}$, and the number of comparisons for the merge is N (one for each value of the index k). In other words, the number of comparisons for Mergesort is precisely described by the recurrence relation

$$C_N = C_{\lfloor N/2 \rfloor} + C_{\lceil N/2 \rceil} + N \qquad \text{for } N \geq 2 \text{ with } C_1 = 0. \tag{1}$$

To get an indication for the nature of the solution to this recurrence, we consider the case when N is a power of 2:

$$C_{2^n} = 2C_{2^{n-1}} + 2^n \qquad \text{for } n \geq 1 \text{ with } C_1 = 0.$$

Dividing both sides of this equation by 2^n, we find that

$$\frac{C_{2^n}}{2^n} = \frac{C_{2^{n-1}}}{2^{n-1}} + 1 = \frac{C_{2^{n-2}}}{2^{n-2}} + 2 = \frac{C_{2^{n-3}}}{2^{n-3}} + 3 = \ldots = \frac{C_{2^0}}{2^0} + n = n.$$

This proves that $C_N = N \lg N$ when $N = 2^n$; the theorem for general N can be proved by induction from (1). The exact solution turns out to be rather complicated, depending on properties of the binary representation of N. In Chapter 2 we will examine how to solve such recurrences in detail. ■

Exercise 1.3 Develop a recurrence describing the quantity $C_{N+1} - C_N$ and use this to prove that

$$C_N = \sum_{1 \leq k < N} (\lfloor \lg k \rfloor + 2).$$

Exercise 1.4 Prove that $C_N = N\lceil \lg N \rceil + N - 2^{\lceil \lg N \rceil}$.

Exercise 1.5 Analyze the number of comparisons used by the three-way Mergesort proposed in Exercise 1.2.

For most computers, the relative costs of the elementary operations used in the program above will be related by a constant factor, as they are all integer multiples of a basic instruction cycle. Furthermore, the total running time of the program will be within a constant factor of the number of comparisons. Therefore, the running time of Mergesort will be within a constant factor of $N \log N$.

From a complexity standpoint, Mergesort demonstrates that $N \lg N$ is an "upper bound" on the intrinsic difficulty of the sorting problem:

There exists an algorithm that can sort any N-element file in time proportional to $N \log N$.

A full proof of this requires a careful model of the computer to be used in terms of the operations involved and the time they take, but the result holds under rather generous assumptions. We say that the "time complexity of sorting is $O(N \log N)$."

Exercise 1.6 Assume that the running time of Mergesort is $cN \lg N + dN$, where c and d are machine-dependent constants. Show that if we implement the program on a particular machine and observe a running time t_N for some value of N, then we can accurately estimate the running time for $2N$ by $2t_N(1 + 1/\lg N)$, *independent of the machine.*

Exercise 1.7 Implement Mergesort on one or more computers, observe the running time for $N = 50,000$, and predict the running time for $N = 100,000$ as in the previous exercise. Then observe the running time for $N = 100,000$ and calculate the percentage accuracy of the prediction.

The running time of Mergesort as implemented above depends only on the number of elements in the array being sorted, not on the way they are arranged. For many other sorting methods, the running time may vary substantially as a function of the initial ordering of the input. Typically, in complexity studies, we are most interested in worst-case performance, since it can provide a guarantee on the performance characteristics of the algorithm no matter what the input is; and in the analysis of particular algorithms, we are most interested in average-case performance, since it can provide a way to predict performance on "typical" input.

We always seek better algorithms, and a natural question that arises is whether there might be a sorting algorithm with asymptotically better performance than Mergesort. The following classical result from computational complexity says, in essence, that there is not.

Theorem 1.2 (*Complexity of sorting*) *Any comparison-based sorting program must use at least* $\lceil \lg N! \rceil > N \lg N - N/(\ln 2)$ *comparisons for some input.*

Proof. A full proof of this fact may be found in [2] or [15]. Intuitively the result follows from the observation that each comparison can cut down the number of possible arrangements of the elements to be considered by, at most, only a factor of 2. Since there are $N!$ possible arrangements before the sort and the goal is to have just one possible arrangement (the sorted one) after the sort, the number of comparisons must be at least the number of times $N!$ can be divided by 2 before reaching a number less than unity, that is to say $\lceil \lg N! \rceil$. The theorem follows from Stirling's approximation to the factorial function (see the second corollary to Theorem 4.3). ∎

From a complexity standpoint, this result demonstrates that $N \log N$ is a "lower bound" on the intrinsic difficulty of the sorting problem:

All comparison-based sorting algorithms require time proportional to $N \log N$ *to sort some N-element input file.*

This is a general statement about an entire class of algorithms. We say that the "time complexity of sorting is $\Omega(N \log N)$." This is significant because it matches the upper bound of Theorem 1.1, thus showing that Mergesort is optimal in the sense that no algorithm can have a better asymptotic running time. We say that the "time complexity of sorting is $\Theta(N \log N)$." From a computational complexity standpoint, this completes the "solution" of the sorting "problem:" matching upper and lower bounds have been proved.

Again, these results hold under rather generous assumptions, though they are perhaps not as general as it might seem. For example, the results say nothing about sorting algorithms that do not use comparisons. Indeed, there exist sorting methods based on address calculation techniques (such as those discussed in Chapter 8) that run in linear time on average.

Exercise 1.8 Suppose that it is known that each of the items in `a[1..N]` has one of two distinct values. Give a sorting method for such arrays that takes time proportional to N.

Exercise 1.9 Answer the previous exercise for *three* distinct values.

We have omitted many details that relate to proper modeling of computers and programs in the proofs of Theorem 1.1 and Theorem 1.2. The essence of computational complexity is the development of complete models within which the intrinsic difficulty of important problems can be assessed and "efficient" algorithms representing upper bounds matching these lower bounds can be developed. For many important problem domains there is still a significant gap between the lower and upper bounds on asymptotic worst-case performance. Computational complexity provides guidance in the development of new algorithms for such problems. We want algorithms that can lower known upper bounds, but there is no point in searching for an algorithm that performs better than known lower bounds (except perhaps by looking for one that violates conditions of the model upon which a lower bound is based!).

Thus, computational complexity provides a way to classify algorithms according to their asymptotic performance. However, the very process of approximate analysis ("within a constant factor") that extends the applicability of complexity results often limits our ability to accurately predict the performance characteristics of any particular algorithm. More important, complexity is usually based on a worst-case analysis, which can be overly pessimistic and not as helpful in predicting actual performance as an average-case analysis. This is not relevant for optimal algorithms such as Mergesort, but average-case analysis can help us discover that nonoptimal algorithms are sometimes faster in practice, as we will see. Complexity can help us to identify good algorithms, but then it is of interest to refine the analysis to be able to more intelligently compare and improve them. To do so, we need precise knowledge about the performance characteristics of the particular computer being used and mathematical techniques for accurately determining expected instruction execution frequencies. In this book, we concentrate on such techniques.

1.3 Analysis of Algorithms. Though the above analysis of sorting and Mergesort demonstrates the intrinsic "difficulty" of the sorting problem, there are many important questions related to sorting (and to Mergesort) that it does not address at all. How long might an implementation of Mergesort be expected to run on a particular computer? How might its running time compare to other $O(N \log N)$ methods? (There are many.) How does it compare to sorting methods that are fast on average, but perhaps not in the worst case? How does it compare to sorting methods that are not based on comparisons among elements? To answer such questions, a more detailed analysis is required. In this section we briefly describe how such an analysis might be carried out, followed by an example of the application of the analysis to another sorting algorithm, Quicksort.

To analyze an algorithm, we must first identify the resources of primary interest so that the detailed analysis may be properly focused. We describe the process in terms of studying the running time since it is the resource most relevant here. A complete analysis of the running time of an algorithm involves the following steps:

- Implement the algorithm completely.
- Determine the time required for each basic operation.
- Identify unknown quantities that can be used to describe the frequency of execution of the basic operations.
- Develop a realistic model for the input to the program.
- Analyze the unknown quantities, assuming the modelled input.
- Calculate the total running time by multiplying the time by the frequency for each operation, then adding all the products.

The first step in the analysis is to carefully implement the algorithm on a particular computer. We reserve the term *program* to describe such an implementation, so that one algorithm corresponds to many programs. This implementation not only provides a concrete object to study, but also can give useful empirical data to aid in or to check the analysis. Presumably the implementation is designed to make efficient use of resources, but it is a mistake to overemphasize efficiency too early in the process. Indeed, a primary application for the analysis is to provide informed guidance towards better implementations.

The next step is to estimate the time required by each component instruction of the program. This can usually be done very precisely, but it is very dependent on the characteristics of the computer system being used. Another approach is to simply run the program for small input sizes to "estimate" the values of the constants, or do so indirectly in the aggregate, as described in Exercise 1.6. We do not consider this process in detail; rather we focus on the "machine independent" parts of the analysis in this book.

To determine the total running time of the program, it is necessary to study the branching structure of the program in order to express the frequency of execution of the component instructions in terms of unknown mathematical quantities. If the values of these quantities are known, then we can derive the running time of the entire program simply by multiplying the frequency and time requirements of each component instruction and adding these products. Profilers that are part of most programming environments can simplify this task. At the first level of analysis, we concentrate on quantities that have large frequency values or that correspond to large costs; in principle the analysis can be refined to produce a fully detailed answer. We often refer to the "cost" of an algorithm as shorthand for the "value of the quantity in question" when the context allows.

The next step is to model the input to the program, to form a basis for the mathematical analysis of the instruction frequencies. The values of the unknown frequencies are dependent on the input to the algorithm: the input size (usually we name that N) is normally the primary parameter used to express our results, but the order or value of input data items also ordinarily affect the running time, as well. By "model," we mean a precise description of typical inputs to the algorithm. For example, for sorting algorithms, it is normally convenient to assume that the inputs are randomly ordered and distinct, though the programs normally work even when the inputs are not distinct. Another possibility for sorting algorithms is to assume that the inputs are random numbers taken from a relatively large range. These two models can be shown to be nearly equivalent. Most often, we use the simplest available model of "random" inputs, which is often realistic. Several different models can be used for the same algorithm: one model might be chosen to make the analysis as simple as possible; another model might better reflect the actual situation in which the program is to be used.

The last step is to analyze the unknown quantities, assuming the modeled input. For average-case analysis, the quantities can be analyzed individually, then the averages can be multiplied by instruction times and added to give the running time of the whole program. For worst-case analysis, it is usually difficult to get an exact result for the whole program, and so an upper bound is often derived by multiplying worst-case values of the individual quantities by instruction times, then adding.

1.4 Average-Case Analysis. In this book, we concentrate on techniques that are appropriate for deriving results about the average-case performance of algorithms. The mathematical techniques are of course generally applicable to solving a variety of problems related to the performance of algorithms, but we are most interested in being able to make precise statements about resource usage for a "typical" set of inputs.

Elementary probability theory gives a number of different ways to compute the average value of a quantity. While they are quite closely related, it will be convenient for us to explicitly identify two different approaches to compute the mean.

Distributional. Let Π_N be the number of possible inputs of size N and Π_{Nk} be the number of inputs of size N that cause the algorithm to have cost k, so that $\Pi_N = \sum_k \Pi_{Nk}$. Then the probability that the cost is k is Π_{Nk}/Π_N and the expected cost is

$$\frac{1}{\Pi_N}\sum_k k\Pi_{Nk}.$$

The analysis depends on "counting." How many inputs are there of size N and how many inputs of size N cause the algorithm to have cost k? These are the steps to compute the probability that the cost is k, so this approach is perhaps the most direct from elementary probability theory.

Cumulative. Let Σ_N be the total (or cumulated) cost of the algorithm on all inputs of size N. (That is, $\Sigma_N = \sum_k k\Pi_{Nk}$, but the point is that it is not necessary to compute Σ_N in that way.) Then the average cost is simply Σ_N/Π_N. The analysis depends on a less specific counting problem: what is the total cost of the algorithm, on all inputs? We will be using general tools that make this approach very attractive.

The distributional approach gives complete information, which can be used directly to compute the standard deviation and other moments. Indirect (often simpler) methods are also available for computing moments when using the other approaches, as we will see. In this book, we consider both approaches, though our tendency will be towards the cumulative method, which ultimately allows us to consider the analysis of algorithms in terms of combinatorial properties of basic data structures.

Many algorithms solve a problem by recursively solving smaller subproblems and are thus amenable to the derivation of a recurrence relationship that the average cost or the total cost must satisfy. A direct derivation of a recurrence from the algorithm is often a natural way to proceed, as shown in the example in the next section.

No matter how they are derived, we are interested in average-case results because, in the large number of situations where random input is a reasonable model, an accurate analysis can help us:

- Compare different algorithms for the same task.
- Predict time and space requirements for specific applications.
- Compare different computers that are to run the same algorithm.

The average-case results can be compared with empirical data to verify the implementation, the model, and the analysis. The end goal is to gain enough confidence in these that they can be used to predict how the algorithm will perform under whatever circumstances present themselves in particular applications. For example, we may wish to evaluate the possible impact of a new machine architecture on the performance of an important algorithm. Often it is possible to do so through analysis, perhaps before the new architecture comes into existence. Another important example is when an algorithm itself has a parameter that can be adjusted: analysis can show what value is best.

1.5 Example: Analysis of Quicksort. To illustrate this methodology, results are sketched here for a particular algorithm of importance, the Quicksort sorting method. This method was invented in 1962 by C. A. R. Hoare, whose paper [12] is an early and outstanding example in the analysis of algorithms. The analysis is also covered in great detail in Sedgewick [20] (see also [22]); we give highlights here. It is worthwhile to study this

```
procedure quicksort(l, r:  integer);
  var v, t, i, j:  integer;
  begin
  if r >= l then
    begin
      v := a[r]; i := l-1; j := r;
      repeat
        repeat i := i+1 until a[i] >= v;
        repeat j := j-1 until a[j] <= v;
        t := a[i]; a[i] := a[j]; a[j] := t;
      until j <= i;
      a[j] := a[i]; a[i] := a[r]; a[r] := t;
      quicksort(l, i-1);
      quicksort(i+1, r)
    end
  end;
```

Program 1.2 Quicksort

analysis in detail because the sorting method is widely used and the analytic results directly relevant to practice and because the analysis itself is illustrative of many things that we will encounter later in the book. In particular, it turns out that the same analysis applies to the study of basic properties of tree structures, which are of broad interest and applicability. More generally, our analysis of Quicksort is indicative of how we go about analyzing a broad class of recursive programs.

Program 1.2 is an implementation of Quicksort in Pascal. This is a recursive program that sorts the numbers in an `array a[l:r]` by partitioning it into two independent (smaller) parts, then sorting those parts. The recursion terminates when empty subarrays with `r<l` are encountered. Actually, subarrays of size 1 (with `r=l`) are also already "sorted" so nothing need be done in this case as well. We could accomplish this by changing the `r>=l` clause in the `if` statement to `r>l`: we examine below a generalization of this improvement. This kind of change might seem inconsequential at first blush, but, as we will see, the very nature of recursion ensures that the program will be used for a large number of small files, and substantial performance gains can be achieved with simple improvements of this sort.

The partitioning process puts the element that was in the last position in the array (the *partitioning element*) into its correct position, with all smaller elements before it and all larger elements after it. We accomplish this by maintaining two pointers, one scanning from the left, one from the right. The left pointer is incremented until an element larger than the partitioning element is found, the right pointer is decremented until an element smaller than the partitioning element is found. These two elements are exchanged, and the process continues until the pointers meet, which defines where the partitioning element is put. The call `quicksort(1,N)` will sort the array, provided that `a[0]` is set to a value smaller than any other element in the array (in case, for example, the first partitioning element happened to be the smallest element).

There are several ways to implement the general recursive strategy just outlined; the implementation described above is taken from Sedgewick [19] (see also [20]). For the purposes of the present discussion we assume that the `array a` contains randomly ordered, distinct numbers. This is the most convenient model to analyze; it is also possible to study this program under perhaps more realistic models allowing equal numbers [21].

When the input array contains distinct numbers, the pointers always cross with `j=i-1`, but an "extra" exchange is done just before this is detected. The three assignment statements after the outer `repeat` are equivalent to undoing this exchange, then exchanging `a[i]` with `a[r]` to put the partitioning element into position.

After the implementation, the first step in the analysis is to estimate the resource requirements of individual instructions for this program. This is straightforward for any particular computer, and we will omit the details. For example, the "inner loop" instruction

```
repeat i:=i+1 until a[i]>=v
```

might translate, on a typical computer, to assembly language instructions such as the following:

```
LOOP  INC   I,1        # increment i
      CMP   V,A(I)     # compare v with A(i)
      BL    LOOP       # branch if less
```

One iteration of this loop might require four time units (one for each memory reference).

The next step in the analysis is to assign variable names to the frequency of execution of the instructions in the program. Normally there are only a few true variables involved: the frequencies of execution of all the instructions can be expressed in terms of these few. Also, it is desirable to relate the variables to the algorithm itself, not any particular program. For Quicksort, three natural quantities are involved:

A – the number of partitioning stages
B – the number of exchanges
C – the number of comparisons

On a typical computer, the total running time might be about

$$4C + 11B + 35A. \tag{2}$$

The exact values of these coefficients depend on the assembly language program produced by the compiler as well as properties of the machine being used; the values given above are typical. Such expressions are quite useful in comparing different algorithms implemented on the same machine. Indeed, the reason that Quicksort is of practical interest even though

Mergesort is "optimal" is that the cost per comparison (the coefficient of C) is likely to be significantly lower for Quicksort than for Mergesort, which leads to significantly lower running times in typical practical applications.

Theorem 1.3 (*Quicksort*) *To sort an array of N randomly ordered distinct elements, Quicksort uses, on the average:*

$$N \quad \textit{partitioning stages},$$
$$2(N+1)\,(H_{N+1}-1) \approx 2N\ln N - .846N \quad \textit{comparisons, and}$$
$$(N+1)\,(H_{N+1}-5/2)\,/3 + 1/2 \approx .333N\ln N - 1.346N \quad \textit{exchanges.}$$

Proof. First, we note that the exact answers here are expressed in terms of the harmonic numbers

$$H_N = \sum_{1\le k\le N} 1/k,$$

the first of many well-known "special" number sequences that we are likely to encounter in the analysis of algorithms.

As with Mergesort, the analysis of Quicksort involves defining and solving recurrence relations that mirror directly the recursive nature of the program given above. But, in this case, the recurrences must be based on probabilistic statements about the inputs. If C_N is the average number of comparisons to sort N elements, we have $C_0 = 0$ and

$$C_N = N + 1 + \frac{1}{N}\sum_{1\le j\le N}(C_{j-1} + C_{N-j}), \qquad \text{for } N > 0. \tag{3}$$

To get the total average number of comparisons, we add the number of comparisons for the first partitioning stage $(N+1)$ to the number of comparisons used for the subfiles after partitioning. When the partitioning element is the jth largest (which occurs with probability $1/N$ for each $1 \le j \le N$), the subfiles after partitioning are of size $j-1$ and $N-j$.

Now the analysis has been reduced to a mathematical problem (3) that does not depend on properties of the program or the algorithm. This recurrence relation is somewhat more complicated than (1) because the right-hand side depends directly on the history of all the previous values, not just a few. Still, (3) is not difficult to solve: first change j to $N-j+1$ in the second part of the sum to get

$$C_N = (N+1) + \frac{2}{N} \sum_{1 \le j \le N} C_{j-1} \qquad \text{for } N > 0.$$

Then multiply by N and subtract the same formula for $N-1$ to eliminate the sum:

$$NC_N - (N-1)C_{N-1} = 2N + 2C_{N-1} \qquad \text{for } N > 1.$$

Now rearrange terms to get a simple recurrence

$$NC_N = (N+1)C_{N-1} + 2N \qquad \text{for } N > 1.$$

This can be solved by dividing both sides by $N(N+1)$:

$$\frac{C_N}{N+1} = \frac{C_{N-1}}{N} + \frac{2}{N+1} \qquad \text{for } N > 1.$$

Iterating, we are left with the sum

$$\frac{C_N}{N+1} = \frac{C_1}{2} + 2 \sum_{3 \le k \le N+1} 1/k$$

which completes the proof, since $C_1 = 2$.

As implemented above, every element is used for partitioning exactly once, so the number of stages is always N; the average number of exchanges can be found from these results by first calculating the average number of exchanges on the first partitioning stage.

The stated approximations follow from the well-known approximation to the harmonic number $H_N \approx \ln N + .57721\cdots$. We consider such approximations below and in detail in Chapter 4. ■

Exercise 1.10 Give the recurrence for the total number of comparisons used by Quicksort on all $N!$ permutations of N elements.

Exercise 1.11 Prove that the subfiles left after partitioning a random permutation are themselves both random permutations. Then prove that this is *not* the case if, for example, the right pointer is initialized at `j:=r+1` for partitioning.

Exercise 1.12 Follow through the steps above to solve the recurrence

$$A_N = 1 + \frac{2}{N} \sum_{1 \le j \le N} A_{j-1} \qquad \text{for } N > 0.$$

Exercise 1.13 Show that the average number of exchanges used during the first partitioning stage (before the pointers cross) is $(N-2)/6$. (Thus, by linearity of the recurrences, $B_N = \frac{1}{6}C_N - \frac{1}{2}A_N$.)

Figure 1.1 shows how the analytic result of Theorem 1.3 compares to empirical results computed by generating random inputs to the program and counting the comparisons used. The empirical results (1000 trials for each value of N shown) are summarized by a dot at the median and sticks spanning the top and bottom quartile (see [23]); the analytic result is a smooth curve fitting the formula given in Theorem 1.3 with a gray surrounding swath corresponding to the standard deviation, which is discussed when we consider the distribution below. As expected, the fit is extremely good.

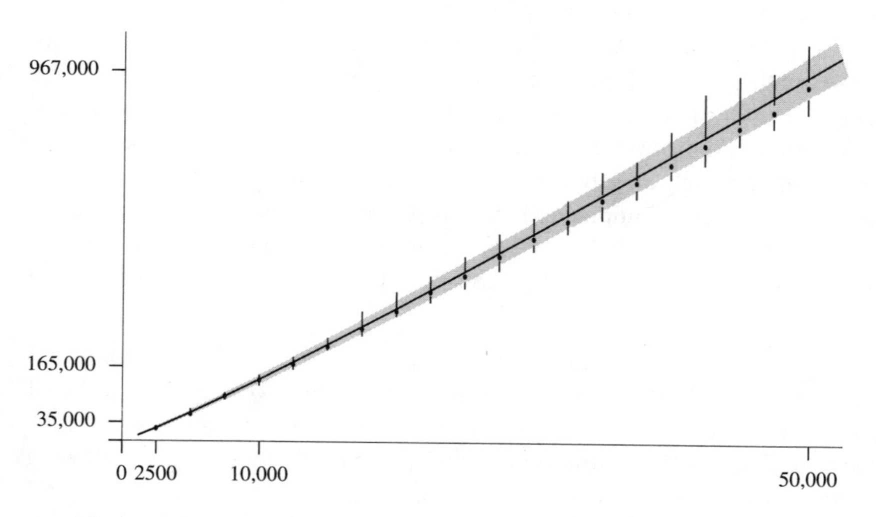

Figure 1.1 Quicksort comparison counts: empirical and analytic

Theorem 1.3 and (2) imply, for example, that Quicksort should take about $11.667N \ln N - 16.810N$ steps to sort a random permutation of N elements for the particular machine described above, and similar formulae for other machines can be derived through an investigation of the properties of the machine as in the discussion preceding (2) and Theorem 1.3. Such formulae can be used to predict (with great accuracy) the running time of Quicksort on a particular machine. More important, they can be used to evaluate and compare variations of the algorithm and provide a quantitative testimony to their effectiveness.

Secure in the knowledge that machine dependencies can be handled with suitable attention to detail, we will generally concentrate on analyzing generic algorithm-dependent quantities, such as "comparisons" and "exchanges," in this book. Not only does this keep our focus on major techniques of analysis, but it also can extend the applicability of the results. For example, a slightly broader characterization of the sorting problem is to consider the items to be sorted as *records* containing other information besides the sort *key*, so that accessing a record might be much more expensive (depending on the size of the record) than doing a comparison (depending on the relative size of records and keys). Then we know from Theorem 1.3 that Quicksort compares keys about $2N \ln N$ times and moves records about $.667N \ln N$ times, and we can compute more precise estimates of costs or compare with other algorithms as appropriate.

The Quicksort program can be improved in several ways to make it the sorting method of choice in many computing environments. A complete analysis can be carried out even for much more complicated improved versions, and expressions for the average running time can be derived that match closely observed empirical times [22]. Of course, the more intricate and complicated the proposed improvement, the more intricate and complicated the analysis. Some improvements can be handled by extending the argument given above, but others require more powerful analytic tools.

Small subfiles. The simplest variant of Quicksort is based on the observation that it is not very efficient for very small files (for example, a file of size 2 can be sorted with one comparison and possibly one exchange), so that a simpler method should be used for smaller subfiles. The following exercises show how the above analysis can be extended to study a hybrid algorithm where "insertion sort" (see §6.6) is used for files of size less than

M. Then, this analysis can be used to help choose the best value of the parameter M.

Exercise 1.14 How many subfiles of size 2 or less are encountered, on the average, when sorting a random file of size N with Quicksort?

Exercise 1.15 If we change the first line in the Quicksort implementation above to

```
if r-l<=M then insertionsort(l,r) else
```

(see §6.6) then the total number of comparisons to sort N elements is described by the recurrence

$$C_N = \begin{cases} N+1+\dfrac{1}{N}\displaystyle\sum_{1\le j\le N}(C_{j-1}+C_{N-j}) & \text{for } N > M; \\ \frac{1}{4}N(N-1) & \text{for } N \le M \end{cases}$$

Solve this exactly as in the proof of Theorem 1.3.

Exercise 1.16 Ignoring small terms (those significantly less than N) in the answer to the previous exercise, find a function $f(M)$ so that the number of comparisons is approximately

$$2N\ln N + f(M)N.$$

Plot the function $f(M)$, and find the value of M that minimizes the function.

Exercise 1.17 As M gets larger, the number of comparisons increases again from the minimum just derived. How large must M get before the number of comparisons exceeds the original number (at $M = 0$)?

Median-of-three Quicksort. A natural improvement to Quicksort is to use sampling: estimate a partitioning element more likely to be near the middle of the file by taking a small sample, then using the median of the sample. For example, if we use just three elements for the sample, then the average number of comparisons required by this "median-of-three" Quicksort is described by the recurrence

$$C_N = N+1+\sum_{1\le k\le N}\frac{(N-k)(k-1)}{\binom{N}{3}}(C_{k-1}+C_{N-k}) \qquad \text{for } N > 3 \quad (4)$$

where $\binom{N}{3}$ is the binomial coefficient that counts the number of ways to choose 3 out of N items. This is true because the probability that the kth smallest element is the partitioning element is now $(N-k)(k-1)/\binom{N}{3}$ (as opposed to $1/N$ for regular Quicksort). We would like to be able to solve recurrences of this nature to be able to determine how large a sample to use and when to switch to insertion sort. However, such recurrences require more sophisticated techniques then the simple ones used so far. In Chapters 2 and 3, we will see methods for developing precise solutions to such recurrences, which allow us to determine the best values for parameters such as the sample size and the cutoff for small subfiles. Extensive studies along these lines have led to the conclusion that median-of-three Quicksort with a cutoff point in the range 10 to 20 achieves close to optimal performance for typical implementations.

Radix-exchange sort. Another variant of Quicksort involves taking advantage of the fact that the keys may be viewed as binary strings. Rather than comparing against a key from the file for partitioning, we partition the file so that all keys with a leading 0 bit precede all those with a leading 1 bit. Then these subfiles can be independently subdivided in the same way using the second bit, and so forth. This variation is referred to as "radix-exchange sort" or "radix Quicksort." How does this variation compare with the basic algorithm? To answer this question, we first have to note that a different mathematical model is required, since keys composed of random bits are essentially different from random permutations. The "random bitstring" model is perhaps more realistic, as it reflects the actual representation, but the models can be proved to be roughly equivalent. (This issue will be discussed in more detail in Chapter 7.) Using a similar argument to the one given above, we can show that the average number of bit comparisons required by this method is described by the recurrence

$$C_N = N + \frac{1}{2^N}\sum_k \binom{N}{k}(C_k + C_{N-k}) \qquad \text{for } N > 1 \text{ with } C_0 = C_1 = 0.$$

This turns out to be a rather more difficult recurrence to solve than the one above—we will see in Chapter 3 how generating functions can be used to transform the recurrence into an explicit formula for C_N, and in Chapters 4 and 7, we will see how to develop an approximate solution.

One limitation to the applicability of this kind of analysis is that all the recurrence relations above depend on the "randomness preservation" property of the algorithm: if the original file is randomly ordered, it can be shown that the subfiles after partitioning are also randomly ordered. The implementor is not so restricted, and many widely used variants of the algorithm do not have this property. Such variants appear to be extremely difficult to analyze. Fortunately (from the point of view of the analyst), empirical studies show that they also perform poorly. Thus, though it cannot be analytically quantified, the requirement for randomness preservation seems to produce more elegant and efficient Quicksort implementations. More important, the versions that preserve randomness do admit to performance improvements that can be fully quantified mathematically, as described above.

Mathematical analysis has played an important role in the development of practical variants of Quicksort and we will see that there is no shortage of other problems to consider where detailed mathematical analysis is an important part of the algorithm design process.

1.6 Asymptotic Approximations. The derivation given above of the average running time of Quicksort yields an exact result, but we also gave a more concise approximate expression in terms of well-known functions that still can be used to compute very accurate numerical results. As we will see, it is often the case that an exact result is not available, or at least an approximation is far easier to derive and interpret. Ideally, our goal in the analysis of an algorithm should be to derive exact results; from a pragmatic point of view, it is perhaps more in line with our general goal of being able to make useful performance predications to strive to derive concise but precise approximate answers.

To do so, we will need to use classical techniques for manipulating such approximations. In Chapter 4, we will examine the Euler-Maclaurin summation formula, which provides a way to estimate sums with integrals. Thus, we can approximate the harmonic numbers by the calculation

$$H_N = \sum_{1\le k\le N} \frac{1}{k} \approx \int_1^N \frac{1}{x}dx = \ln N.$$

But we can be much more precise about the meaning of $\approx$, and we can conclude (for example) that $H_N = \ln N + \gamma + 1/(2N) + O(1/N^2)$ where $\gamma = .57721\cdots$ is a constant known in analysis as Euler's constant. Though the constants implicit in the O-notation are not specified, this formula provides a way to estimate the value of H_N with increasingly improving accuracy as N increases. Moreover, if we want even better accuracy, we can derive a formula for H_N that is accurate to within $O(N^{-3})$ or indeed to within $O(N^{-k})$ for any constant k. Such approximations, called *asymptotic expansions*, are at the heart of the analysis of algorithms, and are the subject of Chapter 4.

The use of asymptotic expansions may be viewed as a compromise between the ideal goal of providing an exact result and the practical requirement of providing a concise approximation. It turns out that we are normally in the situation of, on the one hand, having the ability to derive a more accurate expression if desired, but, on the other hand, not having the desire, because expansions with only a few terms (like the one for H_N above) allow us to compute answers to within several decimal places. We typically drop back to using the $\approx$ notation to summarize results without naming irrational constants, as, for example, in Theorem 1.3.

Moreover, exact results and asymptotic approximations are both subject to inaccuracies inherent in the probabilistic model (usually an idealization of reality) and to stochastic fluctuations. Table 1.1 shows exact, approximate, and empirical values for the running time of Quicksort on random files of various sizes. The exact and approximate values are computed from the formulae given in Theorem 1.3; the "empirical" is a measured average, taken over 100 files consisting of random positive integers less than 10^6; this tests not only the asymptotic approximation that we have discussed, but also the "approximation" inherent in our use of the random permutation model, ignoring equal keys. The analysis of Quicksort when equal keys are present is treated in Sedgewick [21].

file size	*exact solution*	*approximate*	*empirical*
10000	175771	175746	176354
20000	379250	379219	374746
30000	593188	593157	583473
40000	813921	813890	794560
50000	1039713	1039677	1010657
60000	1269564	1269492	1231246
70000	1502729	1502655	1451576
80000	1738777	1738685	1672616
90000	1977300	1977221	1901726
100000	2218033	2217985	2126160

Table 1.1 Average number of comparisons used by Quicksort

Exercise 1.18 How many keys in a file of 10^4 random integers less than 10^6 are likely to be equal to some other key in the file? Run simulations, or do a mathematical analysis (with the help of a system for mathematical calculations), or do both.

Exercise 1.19 Experiment with files consisting of random positive integers less than M for $M = 10000, 1000, 100$ and other values. Compare the performance of Quicksort on such files with its performance on random permutations of the same size. Characterize situations where the random permutation model is inaccurate.

Exercise 1.20 Discuss the idea of having a table similar to Table 1.1 for Mergesort.

In computational complexity, the O-notation is used to supress detail of all sorts: the statement that Mergesort requires $O(N \log N)$ comparisons hides everything but the most fundamental characteristics of the algorithm, implementation, and computer. In the analysis of algorithms, asymptotic expansions provide us with a controlled way to suppress irrelevant details, while preserving the most important information, especially the constant factors involved. The most powerful and general analytic tools produce asymptotic expansions directly, thus often providing simple direct derivations of concise but accurate expressions describing properties of algorithms. Paradoxically, we are sometimes able to use asymptotic estimates to provide *more* accurate descriptions of program performance than might otherwise be available.

1.7 Distributions. In general, probability theory tells us that other facts about the distribution Π_{Nk} of costs are also relevant to our understanding of performance characteristics of an algorithm. Fortunately, for virtually all of the examples that we study in the analysis of algorithms, it turns out that knowing an asymptotic estimate for the average is enough to be able to make reliable predictions. We review a few basic ideas here. Readers not at all familiar with probability theory are referred to any standard text, for example [6].

The full distribution for the number of comparisons used by Quicksort for small N is shown in Figure 1.2. For each value of N, the points $C_{Nk}/N!$ are plotted: the proportion of the inputs for which Quicksort uses k comparisons. Each curve, being a full probability distribution, has area 1. The curves move to the right, since the average $2N \ln N + O(N)$ increases with N. A slightly different view of the same data is shown in Figure 1.3, where the horizontal axes for each curve are scaled to put the mean approximately at the center and shifted slightly to separate the curves. This illustrates that the distribution converges to a "limiting distribution." For many of the problems that we study in this book, not only do limiting distributions like this exist, but also we are able to precisely characterize them. For many other problems, including Quicksort, that is a significant challenge. However, it is very clear that the distribution is *clustered near the mean*. This is commonly the case, and it turns out that we can make precise statements to this effect, and do not need to learn more details about the distribution.

As discussed above, if Π_N is the number of inputs of size N and Π_{Nk} is the number of inputs of size N that cause the algorithm to have cost k, the average cost is given by

$$\mu = \sum_k k\Pi_{Nk}/\Pi_N.$$

The *variance* is defined to be

$$\sigma^2 = \sum_k (k-\mu)^2\Pi_{Nk}/\Pi_N = \sum_k k^2\Pi_{Nk}/\Pi_N - \mu^2.$$

The *standard deviation* σ is the square root of the variance. Knowing the average and standard deviation ordinarily allows us to predict performance reliably. The classical analytic tool that allows this is the *Chebyshev inequality*: the probability that an observation will be more than c multiples of the standard deviation away from the mean is less than $1/c^2$. If the standard deviation is significantly smaller than the mean, then, as N gets large, an observed value is very likely to be quite close to the mean. This is often the case in the analysis of algorithms.

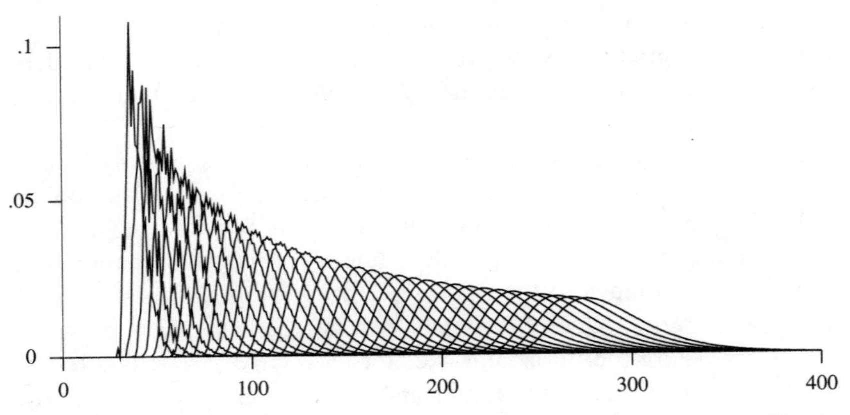

Figure 1.2 Distributions for comparisons in Quicksort, $10 < N \leq 50$

Exercise 1.21 What is the standard deviation of the number of comparisons for the Mergesort implementation given earlier in this chapter?

The standard deviation of the number of comparisons used by Quicksort is $\sqrt{(21-2\pi^2)/3}N \approx .6482776N$ (see §3.12) so, for example, referring to Table 1.1 and taking $c = \sqrt{10}$ in Chebyshev's inequality, we conclude that there is more than a 90% chance that the number of comparisons when $N = 100,000$ is within 205,004 (9.2%) of 2,218,033. This kind of accuracy is certainly adequate for predicting performance.

As N increases, the relative accuracy also increases: for example, the distribution becomes more localized near the peak in Figure 1.3 as N increases. Indeed, Chebyshev's inequality underestimates the accuracy in this situation, as shown in Figure 1.4. This figure plots a histogram showing the number of comparisons used by Quicksort on 10,000 different random files of 1000 elements. The shaded area shows that over 94% of the trials fell within *one* standard deviation of the mean for this experiment.

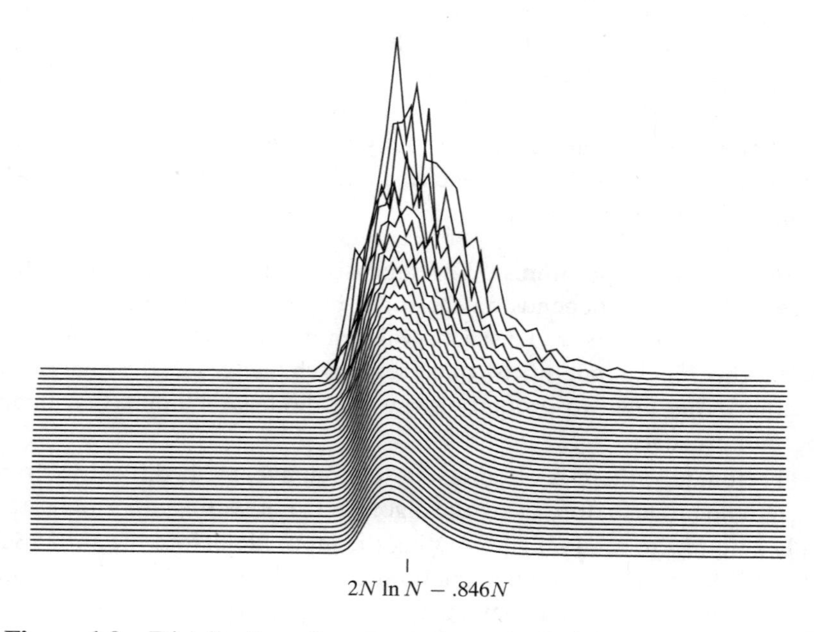

Figure 1.3 Distributions for comparisons in Quicksort, $10 < N \leq 50$ (scaled and translated to center and separate curves)

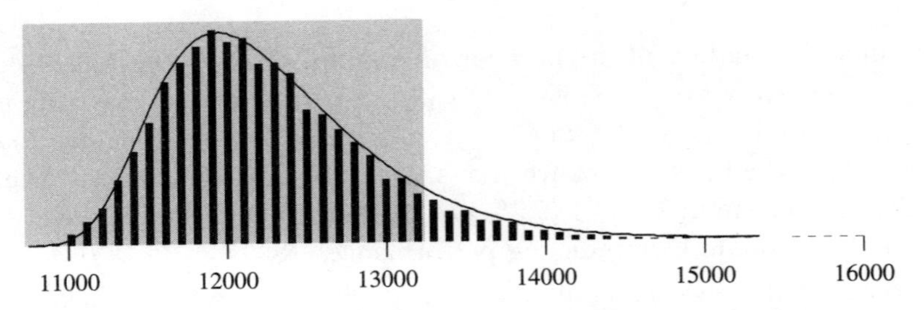

Figure 1.4 Empirical histogram for Quicksort comparison counts (10,000 trials with N=1,000)

For the total running time, we can sum averages (multiplied by costs) of individual quantities, but computing the variance of the total running time is an intricate calculation that we do not bother to do because the variance of the total is asymptotically the same as the largest variance. The fact that the standard deviation is small by comparison to the average for large N explains the observed accuracy of Table 1.1 and Figure 1.1. Cases in the analysis of algorithms where this does not happen are rare, and we normally consider an algorithm "fully analyzed" if we have a precise asymptotic estimate for the average cost and knowledge that the standard deviation is asymptotically smaller.

1.8 Probabilistic Algorithms. The analysis of the average-case performance of Quicksort depends on the input being randomly ordered. This assumption is not likely to be strictly valid in many practical situations. In general, this reflects one of the most serious challenges in the analysis of algorithms: the need to properly formulate models of inputs that might appear in practice.

Fortunately, there is often a way to circumvent this difficulty: "randomize" the inputs before using the algorithm. For sorting algorithms, this simply amounts to randomly permuting the input file before the sort. (See Chapter 6 for a specific implementation of an algorithm for this.) If this is done, then probabilistic statements about performance such as those made above are completely valid and will accurately predict performance in practice, no matter what the input.

Often, it is possible to achieve the same result with less work, by making a random choice (as opposed to a specific arbitrary choice) whenever the algorithm could take one of several actions. For Quicksort, this principle amounts to choosing the element to be used as the partitioning element at random, rather than using the element at the end of the array each time. If this is implemented with care (preserving randomness in the subfiles) then, again, it validates the probabilistic analysis above. (Also, the cutoff for small subfiles should be used, since it cuts down the number of random numbers to generate by a factor of about M.) Other examples of randomized algorithms may be found in [18]. Such algorithms are of interest in practice because they take advantage of randomness to gain efficiency and to avoid worst-case performance with high probability. Moreover, precise probabilistic statements about performance can be made. This further motivates the study of advanced techniques for deriving such results.

THE example of the analysis of Quicksort that we have been considering perhaps illustrates an idealized methodology: not all algorithms can be as smoothly dealt with as this. A full analysis like that above requires a fair amount of effort that should be reserved only for our most important algorithms. Fortunately, as we will see, there are many fundamental methods that do share the basic ingredients that make analysis worthwhile:

- Realistic input models can be specified.
- Mathematical descriptions of performance can be derived.
- Concise, accurate solutions can be developed.
- Results can be used to compare variants and compare with other algorithms, and help adjust values of algorithm parameters.

In this book, we consider a wide variety of such methods, concentrating on mathematical techniques validating the second and third of these points.

Most often, the parts of the methodology outlined above that are program-specific (dependent on the implementation) are skipped, to concentrate either on algorithm design, where rough estimates of the running time may suffice, or on the mathematical analysis, where the formulation and solution of the mathematical problem involved are of most interest. These are the areas involving the most significant intellectual challenge, and deserve the attention that they get.

As we have mentioned above, one important challenge in analysis of algorithms in common use on computers today is to formulate models that realistically represent the input and that lead to manageable analysis problems. We do not dwell on this problem because there is a large class of *combinatorial* algorithms for which the models are natural. In this book, we consider examples of such algorithms and the fundamental structures upon which they operate in some detail. We study permutations, trees, strings, tries, words, and maps because they are all both widely studied combinatorial structures and widely used data structures *and* because "random" structures are both straightforward and realistic.

In Chapters 2 through 4, we will be concentrating on techniques of mathematical analysis that are applicable to the study of the performance of algorithms. This material is important in many applications beyond the analysis of algorithms, but our coverage is developed as preparation for applications later in the book. Then, in Chapters 5 through 8 we will apply these techniques to the analysis of some fundamental combinatorial algorithms, including several of practical interest. Many of these algorithms are of basic importance in a wide variety of computer applications, and so are deserving of the effort involved for detailed analysis. In some cases, algorithms that seem to be quite simple can lead to quite intricate mathematical analyses; in other cases, algorithms that are apparently rather complicated can be dealt with in a straightforward manner. In both situations, analyses can uncover significant differences between algorithms that have direct bearing on the way they are used in practice.

The basic methods that we cover are of course applicable to a much wider class of algorithms and structures than we are able to discuss in this introductory treatment. We do not cover graph algorithms, numerical algorithms, or geometric algorithms in this book, though many such algorithms have been investigated in depth. We also mention only briefly approaches such as amortized analysis and the probabilistic method, which have been successfully applied to the analysis of a number of important algorithms. It is our hope that mastery of the introductory material in this book is good preparation for appreciating such material in the research literature in the analysis of algorithms. Beyond the books by Knuth, Sedgewick, and Aho, Hopcroft, and Ullman cited earlier, other sources of information about the analysis of algorithms and computational complexity are the books by Cormen, Leiserson, and Rivest [5], and by Gonnet and Baeza-Yates [8].

Equally important, we are led to analytic problems of a combinatorial nature that allow us to develop general mechanisms that may help to analyze future, as yet undiscovered, algorithms. The methods that we use are drawn from the classical fields of combinatorics and asymptotic analysis, and we are able to apply classical methods from these fields to treat a broad variety of algorithms in a uniform way. In a companion volume [7], we consider a combinatorial framework allowing the direct derivation of analytic descriptions of algorithm performance, and methods for deriving asymptotic estimates from these descriptions.

In this book, we cover the important fundamental concepts while at the same time developing a context for the more advanced treatment in [7]. Graham, Knuth, and Patashnik [9] is a good source of more material relating to the mathematics that we use; standard references such as Comtet [4] (for combinatorics) and Henrici [11] (for analysis) also have relevant material. Generally, we use elementary combinatorics and real analysis in this book, while [7] involves a more thorough treatment from a combinatorial point of view, and relies on complex analysis for asymptotics.

Our starting point is to study characteristics of fundamental algorithms that are in widespread use, but our primary purpose in this book is to provide a coherent treatment of the combinatorics and analytic methods that we encounter. When appropriate, we consider in detail the mathematical problems that arise naturally and may not apply to any (currently known!) algorithm. In taking such an approach we are led to problems of remarkable scope and diversity. Furthermore, in examples throughout the book we see that the problems we solve are directly relevant to many important applications.

References

1. M. Abramowitz and I. Stegun. *Handbook of Mathematical Functions*, Dover, New York, 1970.
2. A. Aho, J. E. Hopcroft, and J. D. Ullman. *The Design and Analysis of Algorithms*, Addison-Wesley, Reading, MA, 1975.
3. B. Char, K. Geddes, G. Gonnet, B. Leong, M. Monagan, and S. Watt. *Maple V Library Reference Manual*, Springer-Verlag, New York, 1991.
4. L. Comtet. *Advanced Combinatorics*, Reidel, Dordrecht, 1974.

5. T. H. CORMEN, C. E. LEISERSON, AND R. L. RIVEST. *Introduction to Algorithms*, MIT Press, New York, 1990.
6. W. FELLER. *An Introduction to Probability Theory and Its Applications*, John Wiley, New York, 1957.
7. P. FLAJOLET AND R. SEDGEWICK. *Analytic Combinatorics*, in preparation.
8. G. H. GONNET AND R. BAEZA–YATES. *Handbook of Algorithms and Data Structures*, 2nd edition, Addison-Wesley, Reading, MA, 1991.
9. R. GRAHAM, D. E. KNUTH, AND O. PATASHNIK. *Concrete Mathematics*, Addison-Wesley, Reading, MA, 1989.
10. D. H. GREENE AND D. E. KNUTH. *Mathematics for the Analysis of Algorithms*, Birkhäuser, Boston, 1981.
11. P. HENRICI. *Applied and Computational Complex Analysis*, 3 volumes, John Wiley, New York, 1977.
12. C. A. R. HOARE. "Quicksort," *Computer Journal* **5**, 1962, 10–15.
13. D. E. KNUTH. *The Art of Computer Programming. Volume 1: Fundamental Algorithms*, Addison-Wesley, Reading, MA, 1968.
14. D. E. KNUTH. *The Art of Computer Programming. Volume 2: Seminumerical Algorithms*, Addison-Wesley, Reading, MA, 1969.
15. D. E. KNUTH. *The Art of Computer Programming. Volume 3: Sorting and Searching*, Addison-Wesley, Reading, MA, 1973.
16. D. E. KNUTH. "Big Omicron and big Omega and big Theta," *SIGACT News*, April-June 1976, 18–24.
17. D. E. KNUTH. "Mathematical Analysis of Algorithms," *Information Processing 71*, Proceedings of the IFIP Congress, Ljubljana, 1971, 19–27.
18. M. O. RABIN. "Probabilistic algorithms," in *Algorithms and Complexity*, J. F. Traub, ed., Academic Press, New York, 1976, 21–39.
19. R. SEDGEWICK. *Algorithms*, 2nd edition, Addison-Wesley, Reading, MA, 1988.
20. R. SEDGEWICK. *Quicksort*, Garland Publishing, New York, 1980.
21. R. SEDGEWICK. "Quicksort with equal keys," *SIAM Journal on Computing* **6**, 1977, 240–267.
22. R. SEDGEWICK. "Implementing Quicksort programs," *Communications of the ACM* **21**, 1978, 847–856.
23. E. TUFTE. *The Visual Display of Quantitati e Information*, Graphics Press, Chesire, CT, 1987.

24. J. S. VITTER AND P. FLAJOLET, "Analysis of algorithms and data structures," in *Handbook of Theoretical Computer Science A: Algorithms and Complexity*, J. van Leeuwen, ed., Elsevier, Amsterdam, 1990, 431–524.

CHAPTER TWO

RECURRENCE RELATIONS

THE algorithms that we are interested in analyzing normally can be expressed as recursive or iterative procedures, which means that, typically, we can express the cost of solving a particular problem in terms of the cost of solving smaller problems. The most elementary approach to this situation mathematically is to use recurrence relations, as we saw in the Quicksort and Mergesort analyses in the previous chapter. This represents a way to realize a direct mapping from a recursive representation of a program to a recursive representation of a function describing its properties. There are several other ways to do so, though the same recursive decomposition is at the heart of the matter. As we will see in Chapter 3, this is also the basis for the application of generating function methods in the analysis of algorithms.

The development of a recurrence relation describing the performance of an algorithm is already a significant step forward in the analysis, since the recurrence itself carries a great deal of information. Specific properties of the algorithm as related to the input model are encapsulated in a relatively simple mathematical expression. Many algorithms may not be amenable to such a simple description; fortunately, many of our most important algorithms can be rather simply expressed in a recursive formulation, and their analysis leads to recurrences, either describing the average case or bounding the worst case performance. This point is illustrated in Chapter 1 and in many examples in Chapters 5 through 8. In this chapter, we concentrate on fundamental mathematical properties of various recurrences without regard to their origin or derivation. We will encounter many of the types of recurrences seen in this chapter in the context of the study of particular algorithms, and we do revisit the recurrences discussed in Chapter 1, but our focus for the moment is on the recurrences themselves.

First, we examine some basic properties of recurrences and the ways in which they are classified. Then, we examine exact solutions to "first-order" recurrences, where a function of n is expressed in terms of the function evaluated at $n-1$. We also look at exact solutions to higher-order linear recurrences with constant coefficients. Next, we look at a variety of other types of recurrences and examine some methods for deriving approximate solutions to some nonlinear recurrences and recurrences with nonconstant coefficients. Following that, we examine solutions to a class of recurrence of particular importance in the analysis of algorithms: the "divide-and-conquer" class of recurrence. This includes the derivation of and exact solution to the Mergesort recurrence, which involves a connection with the binary representation of integers. We conclude the chapter by looking at general results that apply to the analysis of a broad class of divide-and-conquer algorithms.

All the recurrences that we have considered so far admit to exact solutions. Such recurrences arise frequently in the analysis of algorithms, especially when we use recurrences to do precise counting of discrete quantities. But exact answers may involve irrelevant detail: for example, working with an exact answer like $(2^n-(-1)^n)/3$ as opposed to the approximate answer $2^n/3$ is probably not worth the trouble. In this case, the $(-1)^n$ term serves to make the answer an integer and is negligible by comparison to 2^n; on the other hand we would not want to ignore the $(-1)^n$ term in an exact answer like $2^n(1+(-1)^n)$. It is necessary to avoid the temptations of being overly careless in trading accuracy for simplicity and of being overzealous in trading simplicity for accuracy. We are interested in obtaining approximate expressions that are *both* simple and accurate (even when exact solutions may be available). In addition, we frequently encounter recurrences for which exact solutions simply are not available, but we can estimate the rate of growth of the solution, and, in many cases, derive accurate asymptotic estimates.

Recurrence relations are also commonly called *difference equations* because they may be expressed in terms of the discrete difference operator $\nabla f_n \equiv f_n - f_{n-1}$. They are the discrete analog of ordinary differential equations. Techniques for solving differential equations are relevant because similar techniques often can be used to solve analogous recurrences. In some cases, as we will see in the next chapter, there is an explicit correspondence that allows one to derive the solution to a recurrence from the solution to a differential equation.

There is a large literature on the properties of recurrences because they also arise directly in many areas of applied mathematics. For example, iterative numerical algorithms such as Newton's method directly lead to recurrences, as described in detail in, for example, Bender and Orszag [3].

Our purpose in this chapter is to survey the types of recurrences that commonly arise in the analysis of algorithms and some elementary techniques for deriving solutions. We can deal with many of these recurrence relations in a rigorous, systematic way using *generating functions*, as discussed in detail in the next chapter. We will also consider tools for developing asymptotic approximations in some detail in Chapter 4. In Chapters 5 through 8 we will encounter many different examples of recurrences that describe properties of basic algorithms.

Once we begin to study advanced tools in detail, we will see that recurrences are often not necessarily the most natural mathematical tool to use in the analysis of algorithms. They can introduce complications in the analysis that can be avoided by working at a higher level, using symbolic methods to derive relationships among generating functions, then using direct analysis on the generating functions. This theme is introduced throughout the chapters that follow and treated in detail in [12]. In many cases, it turns out that the simplest and most direct path to solution is to *avoid* recurrences. We point this out not to discourage the study of recurrences, which can be quite fruitful for many applications, but to assure the reader that advanced tools perhaps can provide simple solutions to problems that seem to lead to overly complicated recurrences.

In short, recurrences arise directly in natural approaches to algorithm analysis, and can provide easy solutions to many important problems. Because of our later emphasis on generating function techniques, we give only a brief introduction to techniques that have been developed in the literature for solving recurrences. More information about solving recurrences may be found in standard references, including [3], [4], [6], [14], [15], [16], [21], and [22].

2.1 Basic Properties. In Chapter 1, we encountered the following three recurrences when analyzing Quicksort and Mergesort:

$$C_N = \left(1 + \frac{1}{N}\right)C_{N-1} + 2 \qquad \text{for } N > 1 \text{ with } C_1 = 2. \tag{1}$$

$$C_N = C_{\lfloor N/2 \rfloor} + C_{\lceil N/2 \rceil} + N \qquad \text{for } N > 1 \text{ with } C_1 = 0. \tag{2}$$

$$C_N = N + 1 + \frac{1}{N}\sum_{1 \le j \le N}(C_{j-1} + C_{N-j}) \qquad \text{for } N > 0 \text{ with } C_0 = 0. \tag{3}$$

Each of the equations presents special problems. We solved (1) by multiplying both sides by an appropriate factor; we developed an approximate solution to (2) by solving for the special case $N = 2^n$, then proving a solution for general N by induction; and we transformed (3) to (1) by subtracting it from the same equation for $N - 1$.

Such ad hoc techniques are perhaps representative of the "bag of tricks" approach often required for the solution of recurrences, but the few tricks just mentioned don't apply, for example, to many recurrences that commonly arise, including perhaps the best-known linear recurrence

$$F_n = F_{n-1} + F_{n-2} \qquad \text{for } n > 1 \text{ with } F_0 = 0 \text{ and } F_1 = 1,$$

which defines the Fibonacci sequence $\{0, 1, 1, 2, 3, 5, 8, 13, 21, 34, \ldots\}$. Fibonacci numbers are well studied and actually arise explicitly in the design and analysis of a number of important algorithms. We consider a number of techniques for solving these and other recurrences in this chapter, and we consider other applicable systematic approaches in the next and later chapters.

Recurrences are classified by the way in which terms are combined, the nature of the coefficients involved, and the number and nature of

recurrence type	*typical example*
first-order	
linear	$a_n = na_{n-1} - 1$
nonlinear	$a_n = 1/(1 + a_{n-1})$
second-order	
linear	$a_n = a_{n-1} + 2a_{n-2}$
nonlinear	$a_n = a_{n-1}a_{n-2} + \sqrt{a_{n-2}}$
variable coefficients	$a_n = na_{n-1} + (n-1)a_{n-2} + 1$
tth order	$a_n = f(a_{n-1}, a_{n-2}, \ldots, a_{n-t})$
full-history	$a_n = n + a_{n-1} + a_{n-2} \ldots + a_1$
divide-and-conquer	$a_n = a_{\lfloor n/2 \rfloor} + a_{\lceil n/2 \rceil} + n$

Table 2.1 Classification of recurrences

previous terms used. Table 2.1 lists some of the recurrences that we will be considering, along with representative examples.

Calculating values. Normally, a recurrence provides an efficient way to calculate the quantity in question. In particular, the very first step in attacking any recurrence is to use it to compute small values in order to get a feeling for how they are growing. This can be done by hand for small values, or it is easy to implement a program to compute larger values. For example, Program 2.1 will compute the exact values for the average number of comparisons for Quicksort for all N less than or equal to `Nmax`, corresponding to the recurrence (3) (see Table 1.1). This program uses an array of size `Nmax` to save previously computed values. The temptation to use a purely recursive program based directly on the recurrence should be avoided: computing C_N by computing all the values $C_{N-1}, C_{N-2}, \ldots, C_1$ recursively would be extremely inefficient because many, many values would be unnecessarily recomputed.

We could avoid delving too deeply into the mathematics of the situation if something like Program 2.1 would suffice. We assume that succinct mathematical solutions are more desirable—indeed, one might view the analysis itself as a process that can make Program 2.1 more efficient! At any rate, such "solutions" can be used, for example, to validate analyses. At the other extreme on this continuum would be a brute-force (usually impractical) method for computing the average running time of a program by running it for all possible inputs.

Exercise 2.1 Write recursive and nonrecursive programs to compute values for the Fibonacci recurrence and try to use each to compute F_{20}. Explain the behavior of each program in this case.

Exercise 2.2 How many arithmetic operations are used by Program 2.1 to compute C_{Nmax}?

```
C[0] := 0;
for N := 1 to Nmax do
  begin
    C[N] := N+1;
    for i := 1 to N do C[N] := C[N]+(C[i-1]+C[N-i])/N;
  end;
```

Program 2.1 Computing values (Quicksort recurrence)

Exercise 2.3 Write a recursive program to compute values using the recurrence (1) directly. How does the number of arithmetic operations used by this program compare with Program 2.1(see the previous exercise)?

Exercise 2.4 Estimate how many operations would be required by both recursive and nonrecursive programs to compute values using the recurrences (2), and (3).

Exercise 2.5 Write a program to compare Quicksort, its median-of-three variant, and radix-exchange sort, calculating values from the recurrences given in Chapter 1. For Quicksort, check values against the known solution; for the others, make conjectures about properties of the solution.

Scaling and shifting. An essential property of recurrences is that they depend on their initial values: changing the initial condition in the linear recurrence

$$a_n = f(a_{n-1}) \qquad \text{for } n > 0 \text{ with } a_0 = 1$$

from $a_0 = 1$ to $a_0 = 2$ will change the value of a_n for *all* n (if $f(0) = 0$, the value will be doubled). The "initial" value can be anywhere: if we have

$$b_n = f(b_{n-1}) \qquad \text{for } n > t \text{ with } b_t = 1$$

then we must have $b_n = a_{n-t}$. Changing the initial values is referred to as *scaling* the recurrence; moving the initial values is referred to as *shifting* it. Our initial values are most often directly implied from a problem, but we often use scaling or shifting to simplify the path to the solution. Rather than state the most general form of the solution to a recurrence, we solve a natural form and presume that the solution can be scaled or shifted as appropriate.

Linearity. Linear recurrences with more than one initial value can be "scaled" by changing initial values independently and combining solutions. If $f(x, y)$ is a linear function with $f(0, 0) = 0$, then the solution to

$$a_n = f(a_{n-1}, a_{n-2}) \qquad \text{for } n > 1$$

(a function of the initial values a_0 and a_1) is a_0 times the solution to

$$u_n = f(u_{n-1}, u_{n-2}) \qquad \text{for } n > 1 \text{ with } u_0 = 1 \text{ and } u_1 = 0$$

plus a_1 times the solution to

$$v_n = f(v_{n-1}, v_{n-2}) \qquad \text{for } n > 1 \text{ with } v_0 = 0 \text{ and } v_1 = 1.$$

The condition $f(0,0) = 0$ makes the recurrence *homogeneous*: if there is a constant term in f, then that, as well as the initial values, has to be taken into account. This generalizes in a straightforward way to develop a general solution for any homogeneous linear tth-order recurrence (for any set of initial values) as a linear combination of t particular solutions. We used this procedure in Chapter 1, to solve the recurrence describing the number of exchanges taken by Quicksort, in terms of the recurrences describing the number of comparisons and the number of stages.

Exercise 2.6 Solve the recurrence

$$a_n = a_{n-1} + a_{n-2} \qquad \text{for } n > 1 \text{ with } a_0 = p \text{ and } a_1 = q,$$

expressing your answer in terms of the Fibonacci numbers.

Exercise 2.7 Solve the inhomogeneous recurrence

$$a_n = a_{n-1} + a_{n-2} + r \qquad \text{for } n > 1 \text{ with } a_0 = p \text{ and } a_1 = q,$$

expressing your answer in terms of the Fibonacci numbers.

Exercise 2.8 For f linear, express the solution to the recurrence

$$a_n = f(a_{n-1}, a_{n-2}) \qquad \text{for } n > 1$$

in terms of a_0, a_1, $f(0,0)$ and the solutions to $a_n = f(a_{n-1}, a_{n-2}) - f(0,0)$ for $a_1 = 1, a_0 = 0$ and $a_0 = 1, a_1 = 0$.

2.2 First-Order Recurrences. Perhaps the simplest type of recurrence reduces immediately to a product. The recurrence

$$a_n = x_n a_{n-1} \qquad \text{for } n > 0 \text{ with } a_0 = 1$$

is equivalent to

$$a_n = \prod_{1 \le k \le n} x_k.$$

Thus, if $x_n = n$ then $a_n = n!$ and if $x_n = 2$ then $a_n = 2^n$, and so on.

This transformation is a simple example of *iteration*: apply the recurrence to itself until only constants and initial values are left, then simplify. Iteration also applies directly to the next simplest type of recurrence, much more commonly encountered, which reduces immediately to a sum:

$$a_n = a_{n-1} + y_n \qquad \text{for } n > 0 \text{ with } a_0 = 0$$

is equivalent to

$$a_n = \sum_{1 \le k \le n} y_k.$$

Thus, if $y_n = 1$ then $a_n = n$ and if $y_n = n - 1$ then $a_n = n(n-1)/2$, etc.

Table 2.2 gives a number of commonly encountered discrete sums. A much more comprehensive list may be found in a standard reference such as Graham, Knuth, and Patashnik [14] or Riordan [23].

Exercise 2.9 Solve the recurrence

$$a_n = \frac{n}{n+2} a_{n-1} \qquad \text{for } n > 0 \text{ with } a_0 = 1.$$

Exercise 2.10 Solve the recurrence

$$a_n = a_{n-1} + (-1)^n n \qquad \text{for } n > 0 \text{ with } a_0 = 1.$$

---

geometric series	$\sum_{0 \le k < n} x^k = \frac{1 - x^n}{1 - x}$
arithmetic series	$\sum_{0 \le k < n} k = \frac{n(n-1)}{2} = \binom{n}{2}$
binomial coefficients	$\sum_{0 \le k \le n} \binom{k}{m} = \binom{n+1}{m+1}$
binomial theorem	$\sum_{0 \le k \le n} \binom{n}{k} x^k y^{n-k} = (x+y)^n$
harmonic numbers	$\sum_{1 \le k \le n} \frac{1}{k} = H_n$
sum of harmonic numbers	$\sum_{1 \le k < n} H_k = nH_n - n$
Vandermonde convolution	$\sum_{0 \le k \le n} \binom{n}{k}\binom{m}{t-k} = \binom{n+m}{t}$

Table 2.2 Elementary discrete sums

If we have a recurrence that is not quite so simple, we can often simplify by multiplying both sides of the recurrence by an appropriate factor. We have seen examples of this already in Chapter 1. For example, we solved (1) by dividing both sides by $N+1$, giving a simple recurrence in $C_N/(N+1)$ that transformed directly into a sum when iterated.

Exercise 2.11 Solve the recurrence

$$na_n = (n-2)a_{n-1} + 2 \qquad \text{for } n > 1 \text{ with } a_1 = 1.$$

(*Hint*: Multiply both sides by $n-1$.)

Exercise 2.12 Solve the recurrence

$$a_n = 2a_{n-1} + 1 \qquad \text{for } n > 1 \text{ with } a_1 = 1.$$

(*Hint*: Divide both sides by 2^n.)

Solving recurrence relations (difference equations) in this way is analogous to solving differential equations by multiplying by an integrating factor and then integrating. The factor used for recurrence relations is sometimes called a *summation factor*. Proper choice of a summation factor makes it possible to solve many of the recurrences that arise in practice. For example, an exact solution to the recurrence describing the average number of comparisons used in median-of-three Quicksort was developed by Knuth using such techniques [18] (see also [24]).

Theorem 2.1 (*First-order linear recurrences*) *The recurrence*

$$a_n = x_n a_{n-1} + y_n \qquad \text{for } n > 0 \text{ with } a_0 = 0$$

has the explicit solution

$$a_n = y_n + \sum_{1 \le j < n} y_j x_{j+1} x_{j+2} \ldots x_n.$$

Proof. Dividing both sides by $x_n x_{n-1} \ldots x_1$ and iterating, we have:

$$\begin{aligned} a_n &= x_n x_{n-1} \ldots x_1 \sum_{1 \le j \le n} \frac{y_j}{x_j x_{j-1} \ldots x_1} \\ &= y_n + \sum_{1 \le j < n} y_j x_{j+1} x_{j+2} \ldots x_n. \end{aligned}$$

The same result can be derived by multiplying both sides by $x_{n+1}x_{n+2}\ldots$ (provided it converges) and iterating. ■

For example, the proof of Theorem 2.1 says that we should solve the recurrence

$$C_N = \Big(1 + \frac{1}{N}\Big)C_{N-1} + 2 \qquad \text{for } N > 1 \text{ with } C_1 = 2$$

by dividing both sides by

$$\frac{N+1}{N}\frac{N}{N-1}\frac{N-1}{N-2}\cdots\frac{3}{2}\frac{2}{1} = N + 1,$$

which is precisely what we did in §1.5. Alternatively, the solution

$$2(N+1)(H_{N+1} - 1)$$

follows directly from the explicit form of the solution given in the theorem statement.

Theorem 2.1 is a complete characterization of the transformation from first-order linear recurrences, with constant or nonconstant coefficients, to sums. The problem of solving the recurrence is reduced to the problem of evaluating the sum.

Exercise 2.13 Solve the recurrence

$$a_n = \frac{n}{n+1}a_{n-1} + 1 \qquad \text{for } n > 0 \text{ with } a_0 = 1.$$

Exercise 2.14 Write down the solution to

$$a_n = x_n a_{n-1} + y_n \qquad \text{for } n > t$$

in terms of the x's, the y's, and the initial value a_t.

Exercise 2.15 Solve the recurrence

$$na_n = (n+1)a_{n-1} + 2n \qquad \text{for } n > 0 \text{ with } a_0 = 0.$$

Exercise 2.16 Solve the recurrence

$$na_n = (n-4)a_{n-1} + 12nH_n \qquad \text{for } n > 4 \text{ with } a_n = 0 \text{ for } n \le 4.$$

Exercise 2.17 [Yao] ("Fringe analysis of 2–3 trees") Solve the recurrence

$$A_N = A_{N-1} - \frac{2A_{N-1}}{N} + 2\Big(1 - \frac{2A_{N-1}}{N}\Big) \qquad \text{for } N > 0 \text{ with } A_0 = 0.$$

This recurrence describes the following random process: A set of N elements collect into "2-nodes" and "3-nodes." At each step each 2-node is likely to turn into a 3-node with probability $2/N$ and each 3-node is likely to turn into two 2-nodes with probability $3/N$. What is the average number of 2-nodes after N steps?

2.3 Nonlinear First-Order Recurrences. When a recurrence consists of a nonlinear function relating a_n and a_{n-1}, a broad variety of situations arise, and we cannot expect to have a closed-form solution like Theorem 2.1. In this section we consider a number of interesting cases that do admit to solutions.

Simple convergence. One convincing reason to calculate initial values is that many recurrences with a complicated appearance simply converge to a constant. For example, consider the equation

$$a_n = 1/(1 + a_{n-1}) \qquad \text{for } n > 0 \text{ with } a_0 = 1.$$

This is a so-called continued fraction equation, which is discussed in §2.5. By calculating initial values, we can guess that the recurrence converges to a constant:

n	a_n	$\lvert a_n - (\sqrt{5}-1)/2 \rvert$
1	0.500000000000	0.118033988750
2	0.666666666667	0.048632677917
3	0.600000000000	0.018033988750
4	0.625000000000	0.006966011250
5	0.615384615385	0.002649373365
6	0.619047619048	0.001013630298
7	0.617647058824	0.000386929926
8	0.618181818182	0.000147829432
9	0.617977528090	0.000056460660

Each iteration increases the number of significant digits available by a constant number of digits (about half a digit). This is known as *simple convergence.* If we assume that the recurrence does converge to a constant, we know that the constant must satisfy $\alpha = 1/(1+\alpha)$, or $1 - \alpha - \alpha^2 = 0$, which leads to the solution $\alpha = (\sqrt{5}-1)/2) \approx .6180334$.

Exercise 2.18 Define $b_n = a_n - \alpha$ with a_n and α defined as above. Find an approximate formula for b_n when n is large.

Exercise 2.19 Show that $a_n = \cos(a_{n-1})$ converges and compute $\lim_{n\to\infty} a_n$ to five decimal places.

Quadratic convergence and Newton's method. This well-known iterative method for computing roots of functions can be viewed as a process of calculating an approximate solution to a first-order recurrence (see, for example, [3]). For example, Newton's method to compute the square root of a positive number β is to iterate the formula

$$a_n = \frac{1}{2}\Bigl(a_{n-1} + \frac{\beta}{a_{n-1}}\Bigr) \qquad \text{for } n > 0 \text{ with } a_0 = 1.$$

Changing variables in this recurrence, we can see why the method is so effective. Letting $b_n = a_n - \alpha$, we find by simple algebra that

$$b_n = \frac{1}{2}\frac{b_{n-1}^2 + \beta - \alpha^2}{b_{n-1} + \alpha},$$

so that if $\alpha = \sqrt{\beta}$ we have, roughly, $b_n \approx b_{n-1}^2$. For example, to compute the square root of 2, this iteration gives the following sequence:

n	a_n	$a_n - \sqrt{2}$
1	1.500000000000	0.085786437627
2	1.416666666667	0.002453104294
3	1.414215686275	0.000002123901
4	1.414213562375	0.000000000002
5	1.414213562373	0.000000000000

Each iteration approximately doubles the number of significant digits available. This is a case of so-called quadratic convergence.

Exercise 2.20 Discuss what happens when Newton's method is used to attempt computing $\sqrt{-1}$:

$$a_n = \frac{1}{2}\Bigl(a_{n-1} - \frac{1}{a_{n-1}}\Bigr) \qquad \text{for } n > 0 \text{ with } a_0 \neq 0.$$

Slow convergence. Consider the recurrence

$$a_n = a_{n-1}(1 - a_{n-1}) \qquad \text{for } n > 0 \text{ with } a_0 = \tfrac{1}{2}.$$

In Chapter 5, we will see that similar recurrences play a role in the analysis of the height of "random binary trees." Since the terms in the recurrence decrease and are positive, it is not hard to see that $\lim_{n\to\infty} a_n = 0$. To find the speed of convergence, it is natural to consider $1/a_n$. Substituting, we have

$$\begin{aligned}\frac{1}{a_n} &= \frac{1}{a_{n-1}}\Big(\frac{1}{1-a_{n-1}}\Big)\\ &= \frac{1}{a_{n-1}}(1 + a_{n-1} + a_{n-1}^2 + \ldots)\\ &> \frac{1}{a_{n-1}} + 1.\end{aligned}$$

This telescopes to give $1/a_n > n$, or $a_n < 1/n$. We have thus found that $a_n = O\big(1/n\big)$.

Exercise 2.21 Prove that $a_n = \Theta(1/n)$. Compute initial terms and try to guess a constant c such that a_n is approximated by c/n. Then find a rigorous proof that na_n tends to a constant.

Exercise 2.22 [De Bruijn] Show that the solution to the recurrence

$$a_n = \sin(a_{n-1}) \qquad \text{for } n > 0 \text{ with } a_0 = 1.$$

satisfies $\lim_{n\to\infty} a_n = 0$ and $a_n = O(1/\sqrt{n})$. (*Hint*: consider the change of variable $b_n = 1/a_n$.)

The three cases just considered are particular cases of the form

$$a_n = f(a_{n-1})$$

for some continuous function f. If the a_n converge to a limit α, then necessarily α must be a fixed point of the function, with $\alpha = f(\alpha)$. The three cases above are representative of the general situation: if $0 < |f'(\alpha)| < 1$, the convergence is simple; if $f'(\alpha) = 0$, the convergence is quadratic; and if $|f'(\alpha)| = 1$, the convergence is "slow."

Exercise 2.23 What happens when $f'(\alpha) > 1$?

Exercise 2.24 State sufficient criteria corresponding to the three cases above for local convergence (when a_0 is sufficiently close to α) and quantify the speed of convergence in terms of $f'(\alpha)$ and $f''(\alpha)$.

2.4 Higher-Order Recurrences. Next, we consider recurrences where the right-hand side of the equation for a_n is a linear combination of a_{n-2}, a_{n-3}, etc., as well as a_{n-1} and where the coefficients involved are constants. For a simple example, consider the recurrence

$$a_n = 3a_{n-1} - 2a_{n-2} \qquad \text{for } n > 1 \text{ with } a_0 = 0 \text{ and } a_1 = 1.$$

This can be solved by first observing that $a_n - a_{n-1} = 2(a_{n-1} - a_{n-2})$, an elementary recurrence in the quantity $a_n - a_{n-1}$. Iterating this product gives the result $a_n - a_{n-1} = 2^{n-1}$; iterating the sum for *this* elementary recurrence gives the solution $a_n = 2^n - 1$. We could also solve this recurrence by observing that $a_n - 2a_{n-1} = a_{n-1} - 2a_{n-2}$. These manipulations correspond precisely to factoring the quadratic equation $1 - 3x + 2x^2 = (1 - 2x)(1 - x)$.

Similarly, we can find that the solution to

$$a_n = 5a_{n-1} - 6a_{n-2} \qquad \text{for } n > 1 \text{ with } a_0 = 0 \text{ and } a_1 = 1.$$

is $a_n = 3^n - 2^n$ by solving elementary recurrences on $a_n - 3a_{n-1}$ or $a_n - 2a_{n-1}$.

Exercise 2.25 Give a recurrence that has the solution $a_n = 4^n - 3^n + 2^n$.

These examples illustrate the general form of the solution, and recurrences of this type can be solved explicitly.

Theorem 2.2 (*Linear recurrences with constant coefficients*) *All solutions to the recurrence*

$$a_n = x_1 a_{n-1} + x_2 a_{n-2} + \ldots + x_t a_{n-t} \qquad \text{for } n \geq t$$

can be expressed as linear combination (with coefficients depending on the initial conditions $a_0, a_1, \ldots, a_{t-1}$) of terms of the form $n^j \beta^n$ where β is a root of the "characteristic polynomial"

$$q(z) \equiv z^t - x_1 z^{t-1} - x_2 z^{t-2} - \ldots - x_t$$

and j is such that $0 \leq j < \nu$ if β has multiplicity ν.

Proof. It is natural to look for solutions of the form $a_n = \beta^n$. Substituting, any such solution must satisfy

$$\beta^n = x_1 \beta^{n-1} + x_2 \beta^{n-2} + \ldots + x_t \beta^{n-t} \qquad \text{for } n \geq t$$

or, equivalently,

$$\beta^{n-t} q(\beta) = 0.$$

That is, β^n is a solution to the recurrence for any root β of the characteristic polynomial.

Next, suppose that β is a double root of $q(z)$. We want to prove that $n\beta^n$ is a solution to the recurrence as well as β^n. Again, by substitution, we must have

$$n\beta^n = x_1(n-1)\beta^{n-1} + x_2(n-2)\beta^{n-2} + \ldots + x_t(n-t)\beta^{n-t} \qquad \text{for } n \geq t$$

or, equivalently,

$$\beta^{n-t}((n-t)q(\beta) + \beta q'(\beta)) = 0.$$

This is true, as desired, because $q(\beta) = q'(\beta) = 0$ when β is a double root. Higher multiplicities are treated in a similar manner.

This process provides as many solutions to the recurrence as there are roots of the characteristic polynomial, counting multiplicities. This is the same as the order t of the recurrence. Moreover, these solutions are linearly independent (they have different orders of growth at ∞). Since the solutions of a recurrence of order t form a vector space of dimension t, each solution of our recurrence must be expressible as a linear combination of the particular solutions of the form $n^j\beta^n$. ■

Finding the coefficients. An exact solution to any linear recurrence can be developed from Theorem 2.2 by using the initial values $a_0, a_1, \ldots, a_{t-1}$ to create a system of simultaneous equations that can be solved to yield the constants in the linear combination of the terms that comprise the solution. For example, consider the recurrence

$$a_n = 5a_{n-1} - 6a_{n-2} \qquad \text{for } n \geq 2 \text{ with } a_0 = 0 \text{ and } a_1 = 1.$$

The characteristic equation is $z^2 - 5z + 6 = (z-3)(z-2)$ so

$$a_n = c_0 3^n + c_1 2^n.$$

Matching this formula against the values at $n = 0$ and $n = 1$, we have

$$\begin{aligned} a_0 &= 0 = c_0 + c_1 \\ a_1 &= 1 = 3c_0 + 2c_1. \end{aligned}$$

The solution to these simultaneous equations is $c_0 = 1$ and $c_1 = -1$, so $a_n = 3^n - 2^n$.

Degenerate cases. We have given a method for finding an exact solution for any linear recurrence. The process makes explicit the way in which the full solution is determined by the initial conditions. When the coefficients turn out to be zero and/or some roots have the same modulus, the result can be somewhat counterintuitive, though easily understood in this context. For example, consider the recurrence

$$a_n = 2a_{n-1} - a_{n-2} \qquad \text{for } n \geq 2 \text{ with } a_0 = 1 \text{ and } a_1 = 2.$$

Since the characteristic equation is $z^2 - 2z + 1 = (z-1)^2$ (with a single root, 1, of multiplicity 2), the solution is

$$a_n = c_0 1^n + c_1 n 1^n.$$

Applying the initial conditions

$$\begin{aligned} a_0 &= 1 = c_0 \\ a_1 &= 2 = c_0 + c_1 \end{aligned}$$

gives $c_0 = c_1 = 1$, so $a_n = n + 1$. But if the initial conditions were $a_0 = a_1 = 1$, the solution would be $a_n = 1$, constant instead of linear growth. For a more dramatic example, consider the recurrence

$$a_n = 2a_{n-1} - a_{n-2} + 2a_{n-3} \qquad \text{for } n > 3.$$

Here the solution is

$$a_n = c_0 1^n + c_1(-1)^n + c_2 2^n,$$

and various choices of the initial conditions can make the growth rate of the solution constant, exponential, or fluctuating in sign! This example points out that paying attention to details (initial conditions) is quite important when dealing with recurrences.

Fibonacci numbers. We have already mentioned the familiar sequence $\{0, 1, 1, 2, 3, 5, 8, 13, 21, 34, \ldots\}$ that is defined by the prototypical second-order recurrence

$$F_n = F_{n-1} + F_{n-2} \qquad \text{for } n > 1 \text{ with } F_0 = 0 \text{ and } F_1 = 1.$$

Since the roots of $u^2 - u - 1$ are $\phi = (1+\sqrt{5})/2 = 1.61803\cdots$ and $\widehat{\phi} = (1-\sqrt{5})/2 = -.61803\cdots$ Theorem 2.2 says that the solution is

$$F_N = c_0\phi^N + c_1\widehat{\phi}^N$$

for some constants c_0 and c_1. Applying the initial conditions

$$F_0 = 0 = c_0 + c_1$$
$$F_1 = 1 = c_0\phi + c_1\widehat{\phi}$$

yields the solution

$$F_N = \frac{1}{\sqrt{5}}(\phi^N - \widehat{\phi}^N).$$

Since ϕ is larger than 1 and $\widehat{\phi}$ is smaller than 1 in absolute value, the contribution of the $\widehat{\phi}^N$ term in the above expression for F_N is negligible, and it turns out that F_N is always the nearest integer to $\phi^N/\sqrt{5}$. As N gets large, the ratio F_{N+1}/F_N approaches ϕ, which is well known in mathematics, art, architecture, and nature as the *golden ratio*.

While Theorem 2.2 provides a way to develop complete exact solutions to fixed-degree high-order linear recurrences, we will revisit this topic in Chapters 3 and 4 because the advanced tools there provide convenient ways to get useful results in practice. Theorem 3.3 gives an easy way to compute coefficients, and in particular identify those terms that vanish. Moreover, the phenomenon just observed for Fibonacci numbers generalizes: since the terms $n^j\beta^n$ all grow exponentially, the ones (among those with nonzero coefficient) with largest β will dominate all the others for large n, and among those, the one with largest j will dominate. Generating functions (Theorem 3.3) and asymptotic analysis (Theorem 4.1) provide us with convenient ways to identify the leading term explicitly and evaluate its coefficient for any linear recurrence. This can provide a shortcut to developing a good approximation to the solution in some cases, especially when t is large. For small t, the method described here for getting the exact solution is quite effective.

Exercise 2.26 Explain how to solve an inhomogeneous recurrence of the form

$$a_n = x_1a_{n-1} + x_2a_{n-2} + \ldots + x_ta_{n-t} + r \qquad \text{for } n \ge t.$$

Exercise 2.27 Give initial conditions a_0, a_1 for which the solution to

$$a_n = 5a_{n-1} - 6a_{n-2} \qquad \text{for } n > 1$$

is $a_n = 2^n$. Are there initial conditions for which the solution is $a_n = 2^n - 1$?

Exercise 2.28 Give initial conditions a_0, a_1, and a_2 for which the growth rate of the solution to

$$a_n = 2a_{n-1} - a_{n-2} + 2a_{n-3} \qquad \text{for } n > 2$$

is (*i*) constant, (*ii*) exponential, and (*iii*) fluctuating in sign.

Exercise 2.29 Solve the recurrence

$$a_n = 2a_{n-1} + 4a_{n-2} \qquad \text{for } n > 1 \text{ with } a_1 = 2 \text{ and } a_0 = 1.$$

Exercise 2.30 Solve the recurrence

$$a_n = 2a_{n-1} - a_{n-2} \qquad \text{for } n > 1 \text{ with } a_0 = 0 \text{ and } a_1 = 1.$$

Solve the same recurrence, but change the initial conditions to $a_0 = a_1 = 1$.

Exercise 2.31 Solve the recurrence

$$a_n = a_{n-1} - a_{n-2} \qquad \text{for } n > 1 \text{ with } a_0 = 0 \text{ and } a_1 = 1.$$

Exercise 2.32 Solve the recurrence

$$2a_n = 3a_{n-1} - 3a_{n-2} + a_{n-3} \qquad \text{for } n > 2 \text{ with } a_0 = 0,\ a_1 = 1 \text{ and } a_2 = 2.$$

Exercise 2.33 Find a recurrence describing a sequence for which the order of growth decreases exponentially for odd-numbered terms, but increases exponentially for even-numbered terms.

Exercise 2.34 Give an approximate solution for the "third-order" Fibonacci recurrence

$$F_N^{(3)} = F_{N-1}^{(3)} + F_{N-2}^{(3)} + F_{N-3}^{(3)} \qquad \text{for } N > 2 \text{ with } F_0^{(3)} = F_1^{(3)} = 0 \text{ and } F_2^{(3)} = 1.$$

Compare your approximate result for $F_{20}^{(3)}$ with the exact value.

Nonconstant coefficients. If the coefficients are not constants, then more advanced techniques are needed because Theorem 2.2 does not apply. Typically, generating functions (see Chapter 3) or approximation methods (see below) are called for, but some higher-order problems can be solved with summation factors. For example, the recurrence

$$a_n = na_{n-1} + n(n-1)a_{n-2} \qquad \text{for } n > 1 \text{ with } a_1 = 1 \text{ and } a_0 = 0.$$

can be solved by simply dividing both sides by $n!$, leaving the Fibonacci recurrence in $a_n/n!$, which shows that $a_n = n!F_n$.

Exercise 2.35 Solve the recurrence

$$n(n-1)a_n = (n-1)a_{n-1} + a_{n-2} \qquad \text{for } n > 1 \text{ with } a_1 = 1 \text{ and } a_0 = 1.$$

Symbolic solution. Though no closed form like Theorem 2.2 is available for higher-order recurrences, the result of iterating the general form

$$a_n = s_{n-1}a_{n-1} + t_{n-2}a_{n-2} \qquad \text{for } n > 1 \text{ with } a_1 = 1 \text{ and } a_0 = 0$$

has been studied in some detail. For sufficiently large n, we have

$$\begin{aligned}
a_2 &= s_1,\\
a_3 &= s_2s_1 + t_1,\\
a_4 &= s_3s_2s_1 + s_3t_1 + t_2s_1,\\
a_5 &= s_4s_3s_2s_1 + s_4s_3t_1 + s_4t_2s_1 + t_3s_2s_1 + t_3t_1,\\
a_6 &= s_5s_4s_3s_2s_1 + s_5s_4s_3t_1 + s_5s_4t_2s_1 + s_5t_3s_2s_1 + s_5t_3t_1\\
&\qquad + t_4s_3s_2s_1 + t_4s_3t_1 + t_4t_2s_1,
\end{aligned}$$

and so forth. The number of monomials in the expansion of a_n is exactly F_n, and the expansions have many other properties: they are related to the so-called continuant polynomials that are themselves closely related to continued fractions (see below). Details may be found in Graham, Knuth, and Patashnik [14].

Exercise 2.36 Give a simple algorithm to determine whether or not a given monomial $s_{i_1}s_{i_2}\ldots s_{i_p}t_{j_1}t_{j_2}\ldots t_{j_q}$ appears in the expansion of a_n. How many such monomials are there?

We argue above that for the case of constant coefficients, we are most interested in a derivation of the asymptotic behavior of the leading term because exact solutions, though available, are tedious to use. For the case of nonconstant coefficients, exact solutions are generally not available, so we must be content with approximate solutions for many applications. We now turn to techniques for developing such approximations.

2.5 Methods for Solving Recurrences.

Nonlinear recurrences or recurrences with variable coefficients can normally be solved or approximated through one of a variety of different approaches. We consider a number of such approaches and examples in this section.

We have been dealing primarily with recurrences that admit to exact solutions, at least for some values (in principle). While such problems do arise very frequently in the analysis of algorithms, one certainly can expect to encounter recurrences for which no method for finding an exact solution is known. It is premature to begin treating advanced techniques for working with such recurrences, but we give some guidelines on how to develop accurate approximate solutions and consider several examples. These techniques are useful for learning basic facts about the behavior of recurrences, even if more general or advanced techniques are applicable.

We consider four general methods: *change of variable*, which involves simplifying a recurrence by recasting it in terms of another variable; *repertoire*, which involves working backwards from a given recurrence to find a solution space; *bootstrapping*, which involves developing an approximate solution, then using the recurrence itself to find a more accurate solution, continuing until a sufficiently accurate answer is obtained or no further improvement seems likely; and *perturbation*, which involves studying the effects of transforming a recurrence into a similar, simpler, one with a known solution. The first two of these methods often lead to exact solutions of recurrences; the last two are more typically used to develop approximate solutions.

Change of Variables. Theorem 2.1 actually describes a change of variable: "if we change variables to $b_n = a_n/(x_n x_{n-1} \cdots x_1)$ then b_n satisfies a simple recurrence that reduces to a sum when iterated." We also used a change of variable in the previous section, and in other places earlier in the chapter. More complicated changes of variable can be used to derive exact solutions to formidable-looking recurrences. For instance, consider the nonlinear second-order recurrence

$$a_n = \sqrt{a_{n-1}a_{n-2}} \qquad \text{for } n > 1 \text{ with } a_0 = 1 \text{ and } a_1 = 2.$$

If we take the logarithm of both sides of this equation and make the change of variable $b_n = \lg a_n$, then we find that b_n satisfies

$$b_n = \frac{1}{2}(b_{n-1} + b_{n-2}) \qquad \text{for } n > 1 \text{ with } b_0 = 0 \text{ and } b_1 = 1,$$

a linear recurrence with constant coefficients.

Exercise 2.37 Give exact formulae for b_n and a_n.

Exercise 2.38 Solve the recurrence

$$a_n = \sqrt{1 + a_{n-1}^2} \qquad \text{for } n > 0 \text{ with } a_0 = 0.$$

Our next example arises in the study of register allocation algorithms [11]:

$$a_n = a_{n-1}^2 - 2 \qquad \text{for } n > 0.$$

For $a_0 = 0$ or $a_0 = 2$ the solution is $a_n = 2$ for $n > 1$, and for $a_0 = 1$, the solution is $a_n = -1$ for $n > 1$, but for larger a_0 the dependence on the initial value a_0 is more complicated for this recurrence than for other first-order recurrences that we have seen.

This is a so-called quadratic recurrence, and it is one of the few quadratic recurrences that can be solved explicitly, by change of variables. By setting $a_n = b_n + 1/b_n$, we have the recurrence

$$b_n + \frac{1}{b_n} = b_{n-1}^2 + \frac{1}{b_{n-1}^2} \qquad \text{for } n > 0 \text{ with } b_0 + 1/b_0 = a_0.$$

But this implies that we can solve by making $b_n = b_{n-1}^2$, which iterates immediately to the solution

$$b_n = b_0^{2^n}.$$

By the quadratic equation, b_0 is easily calculated from a_0:

$$b_0 = \frac{1}{2}\Bigl(a_0 \pm \sqrt{a_0^2 - 4}\Bigr).$$

Thus,

$$a_n = \Bigl(\frac{1}{2}\Bigl(a_0 + \sqrt{a_0^2 - 4}\Bigr)\Bigr)^{2^n} + \Bigl(\frac{1}{2}\Bigl(a_0 - \sqrt{a_0^2 - 4}\Bigr)\Bigr)^{2^n}.$$

For $a_0 > 2$, only the larger of the two roots predominates in this expression; the one with the plus sign.

Exercise 2.39 From the above discussion, solve the register allocation recurrence for $a_0 = 3, 4$. Discuss what happens for $a_0 = 3/2$.

Exercise 2.40 Solve the register allocation recurrence for $a_0 = 2 + \epsilon$, where ϵ is an arbitrary fixed positive constant. Give an accurate approximate answer.

Exercise 2.41 Find all values of the parameters α, β, and γ such that $a_n = \alpha a_{n-1}^2 + \beta a_{n-1} + \gamma$ reduces to $b_n = b_{n-1}^2 - 2$ by a linear transformation ($b_n = f(\alpha,\beta,\gamma)a_n + g(\alpha,\beta,\gamma)$). In particular, show that $a_n = a_{n-1}^2 + 1$ does not reduce to this form.

Exercise 2.42 [Melzak] Solve the recurrence

$$a_n = 2a_{n-1}\sqrt{1 - a_{n-1}^2} \qquad \text{for } n > 0 \text{ with } a_0 = \tfrac{1}{2}$$

and with $a_0 = 1/3$. Plot a_6 as a function of a_0 and explain what you observe.

On the one hand, underlying linearity may be difficult to recognize, and finding a change of variable that solves a nonlinear recurrence is no easier than finding a change of variable that allows us to evaluate a definite integral (for example). Indeed, more advanced analysis (iteration theory) may be used to show that most nonlinear recurrences cannot be reduced in this way. On the other hand, a variable change that simplifies a recurrence that arises in practice may not be difficult to find, and a few such changes might lead to a linear form. As illustrated by the register allocation example, such recurrences do arise in the analysis of algorithms.

For another example, consider using change of variables to get an exact solution to a recurrence related to continued fractions.

$$a_n = 1/(1 + a_{n-1}) \qquad \text{for } n > 0 \text{ with } a_0 = 1.$$

Iterating this recurrence gives the sequence

$$\begin{aligned}
a_0 &= 1\\
a_1 &= \frac{1}{1+1} = \frac{1}{2}\\
a_2 &= \frac{1}{1+\dfrac{1}{1+1}} = \frac{1}{1+\dfrac{1}{2}} = \frac{2}{3}\\
a_3 &= \frac{1}{1+\dfrac{1}{1+\dfrac{1}{1+1}}} = \frac{1}{1+\dfrac{2}{3}} = \frac{3}{5}\\
a_4 &= \frac{1}{1+\dfrac{1}{1+\dfrac{1}{1+\dfrac{1}{1+1}}}} = \frac{1}{1+\dfrac{3}{5}} = \frac{5}{8}
\end{aligned}$$

and so on. The Fibonacci numbers may be recognized from the initial values, and the form $a_n = b_{n-1}/b_n$ is certainly suggested: substituting this into the recurrence gives

$$\frac{b_{n-1}}{b_n} = 1 \Big/ \left(1 + \frac{b_{n-2}}{b_{n-1}}\right) \qquad \text{for } n > 1 \text{ with } b_0 = b_1 = 1.$$

Dividing both sides by b_{n-1} gives

$$\frac{1}{b_n} = \frac{1}{b_{n-1} + b_{n-2}} \qquad \text{for } n > 1 \text{ with } b_0 = b_1 = 1,$$

which implies that $b_n = F_{n+1}$, the Fibonacci sequence. This argument generalizes to give a way to express general classes of "continued fraction" representations as solutions to recurrences.

Exercise 2.43 Solve the recurrence

$$a_n = \frac{\alpha a_{n-1} + \beta}{\gamma a_{n-1} + \delta} \qquad \text{for } n > 0 \text{ with } a_0 = 1.$$

Exercise 2.44 Consider the recurrence

$$a_n = 1/(s_n + t_n a_{n-1}) \qquad \text{for } n > 0 \text{ with } a_0 = 1,$$

where $\{s_n\}$ and $\{t_n\}$ are arbitrary sequences. Express a_n as the ratio of two successive terms in a sequence defined by a linear recurrence.

Repertoire. Another path to exact solutions in some cases is the so-called repertoire method, where we use known functions to find a family of solutions similar to the one sought, which can be combined to give the answer. This method primarily applies to linear recurrences, involving the following steps:

- Relax the recurrence by adding an extra functional term.
- Substitute known functions into the recurrence to derive identities similar to the recurrence.
- Take linear combinations of such identities to derive an equation identical to the recurrence.

For example, consider the recurrence

$$a_n = (n-1)a_{n-1} - na_{n-2} + n - 1 \qquad \text{for } n > 1 \text{ with } a_0 = a_1 = 1.$$

We generalize this by introducing a quantity $f(n)$ to the right-hand side, so we want to solve

$$a_n = (n-1)a_{n-1} - na_{n-2} + f(n)$$

for $n > 1$ and $a_0 = a_1 = 1$ with $f(n) = n - 1$. To do so, we inject various possibilities for a_n and look at the resulting $f(n)$ to get a "repertoire" of recurrences that we can solve (forgetting momentarily about initial conditions). For this example, we arrive at the table

a_n	$a_n - (n-1)a_{n-1} + na_{n-2}$
1	2
n	$n-1$
n^2	$n+1$

The first row in this table says that $a_n = 1$ is a solution with $f(n) = 2$ (and initial conditions $a_0 = 1$ and $a_1 = 1$); the second row says that $a_n = n$ is a solution with $f(n) = n - 1$ (and initial conditions $a_0 = 0$ and $a_1 = 1$); and the third row says that $a_n = n^2$ is a solution with $f(n) = n + 1$ (and initial conditions $a_0 = 0$ and $a_1 = 1$). Now, linear combinations of these also give solutions. Subtracting the first row from the third gives the result that means that $a_n = n^2 - 1$ is a solution with $f(n) = n - 1$ (and initial conditions $a_0 = -1$ and $a_1 = 0$). Now we have two (linearly independent) solutions for $f(n) = n-1$, which we combine to get the right initial values, yielding the result $a_n = n^2 - n + 1$.

The success of this method depends on being able to find a set of independent solutions, and on properly handling initial conditions. Intuition or knowledge about the form of the solution can be useful in determining the repertoire. The classic example of the use of this method is in the analysis of an equivalence algorithm by Knuth and Schönhage [20].

For the Quicksort recurrence, we start with

$$a_n = f(n) + \frac{2}{n} \sum_{1 \le j \le n} a_{j-1}$$

for $n > 0$ with $a_0 = 0$. This leads to the repertoire table at the top of the next page.

a_n	$a_n - (2\sum_{0\le j<n} a_j)/n$
1	-1
H_n	$-H_n + 2$
n	1
$\lambda(n+1)$	0
nH_n	$\frac{1}{2}(n-1) + H_n$
$n(n-1)$	$\frac{1}{3}(n^2-1) + n - 1$

Thus $2nH_n + 2H_n + \lambda(n+1) - 2$ is a solution with $f(n) = n+1$; resolving the initial value with $\lambda = 2$ gives the solution

$$2(n+1)H_n - 2n,$$

as expected (see Theorem 1.4). The solution depends on the fifth line in the table, which we are obliged to try because we might expect for other reasons that the solution might be $O(n \log n)$. Note that the repertoire table can conveniently also give the solution for other $f(n)$, as might be required by more detailed analysis of the algorithm.

Exercise 2.45 Solve the Quicksort recurrence for $f(n) = n^3$.

Exercise 2.46 [Greene and Knuth] Solve the Quicksort median-of-three recurrence (see equation (4) in Chapter 1) using the repertoire method. (See [18] or [24] for a direct solution to this recurrence using differencing and summation factors, and see Chapter 3 for a solution using generating functions.)

Bootstrapping. Often we are able to guess the approximate value of the solution to a recurrence. Then, the recurrence itself can be used to place constraints on the estimate that can be used to give a more accurate estimate. Informally, this method involves the following steps:

- Use the recurrence to calculate numerical values.
- Guess the approximate form of the solution.
- Substitute approximate solution back into recurrence.
- Prove tighter bounds on the solution, based on the guessed solution and the substitution.

For illustrative purposes, suppose that we apply this method to the Fibonacci recurrence:

$$a_n = a_{n-1} + a_{n-2} \qquad \text{for } n > 1 \text{ with } a_0 = 0 \text{ and } a_1 = 1.$$

First, we note that a_n is increasing. Therefore, $a_{n-1} > a_{n-2}$ and $a_n > 2a_{n-2}$. Iterating this inequality implies that $a_n > 2^{n/2}$, so we know that a_n has at least an exponential rate of growth. On the other hand, $a_{n-2} < a_{n-1}$ implies that $a_n < 2a_{n-1}$, or (iterating) $a_n < 2^n$. Thus we have proven upper and lower exponentially growing bounds on a_n and we can feel justified in "guessing" a solution of the form $a_n \sim c_0\alpha^n$, with $\sqrt{2} < \alpha < 2$. From the recurrence, we can conclude that α must satisfy $\alpha^2 - \alpha - 1 = 0$, which leads to ϕ and $\widehat{\phi}$. Having determined the value α, we can bootstrap and go back to the recurrence and the initial values to find the appropriate coefficients.

Exercise 2.47 Solve the recurrence

$$a_n = 2/(n + a_{n-1}) \qquad \text{for } n > 0 \text{ with } a_0 = 1.$$

Exercise 2.48 Use bootstrapping to show that median-of-three Quicksort uses $\alpha N \ln N + O(N)$ comparisons and determine the value of α.

Exercise 2.49 [Greene and Knuth] Use bootstrapping to show that the solution to

$$a_n = \frac{1}{n} \sum_{0 \le k < n} \frac{a_k}{n-k} \qquad \text{for } n > 0 \text{ with } a_0 = 1$$

satisfies $n^2 a_n = O(1)$.

Perturbation. Another path to an approximate solution to a recurrence is to solve a simpler related recurrence. This is a general approach to solving recurrences that consists of first studying simplified recurrences obtained by extracting what seems to be dominant parts, solving the simplified recurrence, and then comparing solutions of the original recurrence to those of the simplified recurrence. This technique is akin to a class of methods familiar in numerical analysis, *perturbation methods*. Informally, this method involves the following steps:

- Modify the recurrence slightly to find a known recurrence.
- Change variables to pull out the known bounds and transform into a recurrence on the (smaller) unknown part of the solution.
- Bound or solve the unknown "error" term.

For example, consider the recurrence

$$a_{n+1} = 2a_n + \frac{a_{n-1}}{n^2} \qquad \text{for } n > 1 \text{ with } a_0 = 1 \text{ and } a_1 = 2.$$

It seems reasonable to assume that the last term, because of its coefficient $1/n^2$, only brings a small contribution to the recurrence, so that

$$a_{n+1} \approx 2a_n.$$

Thus a growth of the rough form $a_n \approx 2^n$ is anticipated. To make this precise, we thus consider the simpler sequence

$$b_{n+1} = 2b_n \qquad \text{for } n > 0 \text{ with } b_0 = 1$$

(so that $b_n = 2^n$) and compare the two recurrences by forming the ratio

$$\rho_n = \frac{a_n}{b_n} = \frac{a_n}{2^n}.$$

From the recurrences, we have

$$\rho_{n+1} = \rho_n + \frac{1}{4n^2}\rho_{n-1} \qquad \text{for } n > 0 \text{ with } \rho_0 = 1.$$

Clearly, the ρ_n are increasing. To prove they tend to a constant, note that

$$\rho_{n+1} \le \rho_n\Big(1 + \frac{1}{4n^2}\Big) \qquad \text{for } n \ge 1 \text{ so that} \qquad \rho_{n+1} \le \prod_{k=1}^{n}\Big(1 + \frac{1}{4k^2}\Big).$$

But the infinite product corresponding to the right-hand side converges monotonically to

$$\alpha_0 = \prod_{k=1}^{\infty}\Big(1 + \frac{1}{4k^2}\Big) = 1.46505\cdots.$$

Thus, ρ_n is bounded from above by α_0 and, as it is increasing, it must converge to a constant. We have thus proved that

$$a_n \sim \alpha \cdot 2^n,$$

for some constant $\alpha < 1.46505\cdots$. (In addition, the bound is not too crude as, for instance, $\rho_{100} = 1.44130\cdots$.)

The example above is only a simple one, meant to illustrate the approach. In general, the situation is likely to be more complex, and several steps of iteration of the method may be required, possibly introducing several intermediate recurrences. This relates to bootstrapping, which we have just discussed. Hardships may also occur if the simplified recurrence admits of no closed form expression. The perturbation method is nonetheless an important technique for the asymptotic solution of recurrences.

Exercise 2.50 Find the asymptotic growth of the solution to the "perturbed" Fibonacci recurrence

$$a_{n+1} = (1 + \frac{1}{n})a_n + (1 - \frac{1}{n})a_{n-1} \qquad \text{for } n > 1 \text{ with } a_0 = 0 \text{ and } a_1 = 1.$$

Exercise 2.51 Solve the recurrence

$$a_n = na_{n-1} + n^2 a_{n-2} \qquad \text{for } n > 1 \text{ with } a_1 = 1 \text{ and } a_0 = 0.$$

Exercise 2.52 [Aho and Sloane] The recurrence

$$a_n = a_{n-1}^2 + 1 \qquad \text{for } n > 0 \text{ with } a_0 = 1.$$

satisfies $a_n \sim \lambda\alpha^{2^n}$ for some constants α and λ. Find a convergent series for α and determine α to 50 decimal digits. (*Hint*: consider $b_n = \lg a_n$.)

Exercise 2.53 Solve the following perturbation of the Fibonacci recurrence:

$$a_n = (1 - \frac{1}{n})(a_{n-1} + a_{n-2}) \qquad \text{for } n > 1 \text{ with } a_0 = a_1 = 1.$$

Try a solution of the form $n^\alpha \phi^n$ and identify α.

2.6 Binary Divide-and-Conquer Recurrences and Binary Numbers. Good algorithms for a broad variety of problems have been developed by applying the following fundamental algorithmic design paradigm: "Divide the problem into two subproblems of equal size, solve them recursively, then use the solutions to solve the original problem." Mergesort is a prototype of such algorithms. For example (see the proof of Theorem 1.2 in §1.2), the number of comparisons used by Mergesort is given by the solution to the recurrence

$$C_N = C_{\lfloor N/2 \rfloor} + C_{\lceil N/2 \rceil} + N \qquad \text{for } N > 1 \text{ with } C_1 = 0. \tag{4}$$

This recurrence, and others similar to it, arise in the analysis of a variety of algorithms with the same basic structure as Mergesort. It is normally possible to determine the asymptotic growth of functions satisfying such recurrences, but it is necessary to take special care in deriving exact results, primarily because of the simple reason that a problem of "size" N cannot be divided into equal-sized subproblems if N is odd: the best that can be done is to make the problem sizes differ by one. For large N, this is negligible, but for small N it is noticeable, and, as usual, the recursive structure insures that many small subproblems will be involved.

As we shall soon see, this means that exact solutions tend to have periodicities, sometimes even severe discontinuities, and often cannot be described in terms of smooth functions. For example, Figure 2.1 shows the solution to the Mergesort recurrence (4) and the similar recurrence

$$C_N = 2C_{\lceil N/2 \rceil} + N \qquad \text{for } N > 1 \text{ with } C_1 = 0.$$

The former appears to be relatively smooth; the erratic fractal-based behavior that characterizes the solution to the latter is common in divide-and-conquer recurrences.

Both of the functions illustrated in Figure 2.1 are $\sim N \lg N$ and precisely equal to $N \lg N$ when N is a power of 2. Figure 2.2 is a plot of the same functions with $N \lg N$ subtracted out, to illustrate the periodic behavior of the linear term for both functions. The periodic function associated with Mergesort is quite small in magnitude and continuous,

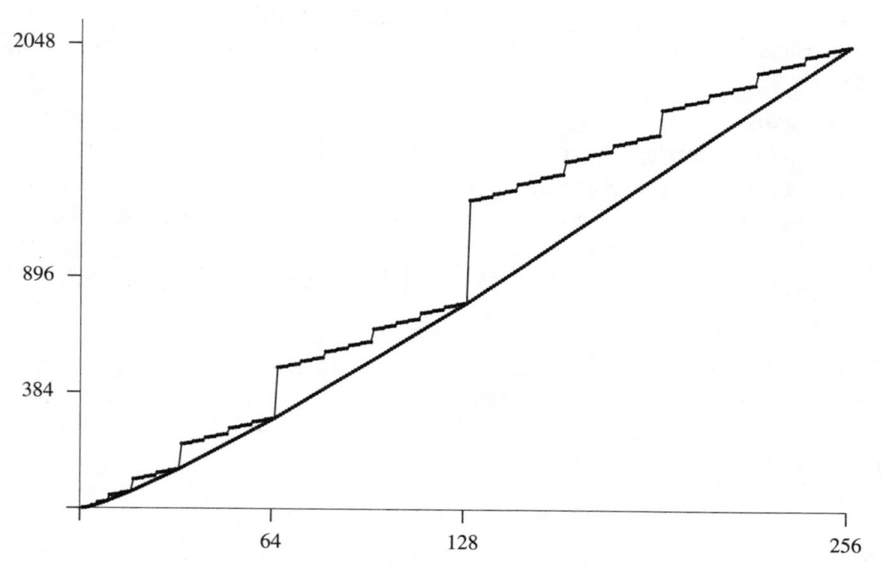

Figure 2.1 Solutions to binary divide-and-conquer recurrences
$C_N = C_{\lfloor N/2 \rfloor} + C_{\lceil N/2 \rceil} + N$ (bottom)
$C_N = C_{\lceil N/2 \rceil} + C_{\lceil N/2 \rceil} + N$ (top)

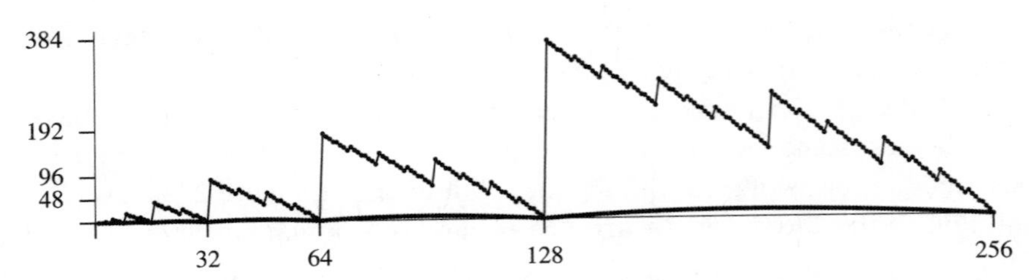

Figure 2.2 Periodic terms in binary divide-and-conquer recurrences
$C_N = C_{\lfloor N/2 \rfloor} + C_{\lceil N/2 \rceil} + N$ (bottom)
$C_N = C_{\lceil N/2 \rceil} + C_{\lceil N/2 \rceil} + N$ (top)

with discontinuities in the derivative at powers of 2; the other function can be relatively large and is essentially discontinuous. Such behavior can be problematic when we are trying to make precise estimates for the purposes of comparing programs, even asymptotically. Fortunately, however, we typically can see the nature of the solutions quite easily when the recurrences are understood in terms of number representations. To illustrate this, we begin by looking at another important algorithm that is a specific instance of a general problem-solving strategy that dates to antiquity.

Binary search. One of the simplest and best-known binary divide-and-conquer algorithms is called *binary search*. Given a fixed set of numbers, we wish to be able to determine quickly whether a given query number is in the set. To do so, we first sort the table. Then, for any query number, the procedure shown in Program 2.1 can be used: look in the middle, then (recursively) use the same method to look in the left half if the number is smaller.

Theorem 2.3 (*Binary search*) *The number of comparisons used during an unsuccessful search with binary search in a table of size N in the worst case is equal to the number of bits in the binary representation of N. Both are described by the recurrence*

$$B_N = B_{\lfloor N/2 \rfloor} + 1 \qquad \text{for } N \geq 2 \text{ with } B_1 = 1,$$

which has the exact solution $B_N = \lfloor \lg N \rfloor + 1$.

Proof. After looking in "the middle," one element is eliminated, and the two halves of the file are of size $\lfloor (N-1)/2 \rfloor$ and $\lceil (N-1)/2 \rceil$. The recurrence is established by checking separately for N odd and N even that the larger of these two is always $\lfloor N/2 \rfloor$. For example, in a table of size 83, both subfiles are of size 41 after the first comparison, but in a table of size 82, one is of size 40 and the other of size 41.

This is equal to the number of bits in the binary representation of N (ignoring leading 0s) because computing $\lfloor N/2 \rfloor$ is precisely equivalent to shifting the binary representation right one bit position. Iterating the recurrence amounts to counting the bits, stopping when the leading 1 bit is encountered.

The number of bits in the binary representation of N is $n+1$ for $2^n \le N < 2^{n+1}$, or, taking logarithms, for $n \le \lg N < n+1$; that is to say, by definition, $n = \lfloor \lg N \rfloor$. ■

The functions $\lg N$ and $\lfloor \lg N \rfloor$ are plotted in Figure 2.3, along with the fractional part $\{\lg N\} \equiv \lg N - \lfloor \lg N \rfloor$.

Exercise 2.54 What is the number of comparisons used during an unsuccessful search with binary search in a table of size N in the *best* case?

Exercise 2.55 Consider a "ternary search" algorithm, where the file is divided into thirds, two comparisons are used to determine where the key could be, and the algorithm applied recursively. Characterize the number of comparisons used by that algorithm in the worst case, and compare to binary search.

Exact solution of Mergesort recurrence. The Mergesort recurrence (2) is easily solved by differencing: if D_N is defined to be $C_{N+1} - C_N$ then D_N

```
function search(l, r, v:  integer):  integer;
  var x:  integer;
  begin
    x := (l+r) div 2;
    if l > r
      then << search unsuccessful >> else
    if v = a[x].key
      then search := x else
    if v < a[x].key
      then search := search(l, x-1, v)
      else search := search(x+1, r, v)
  end;
```

Program 2.2 Binary search

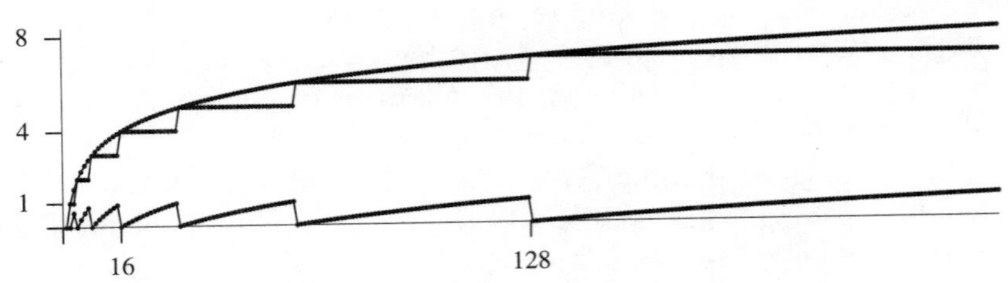

Figure 2.3 $\lg N$ (top); $\lfloor \lg N \rfloor$ (middle); $\{\lg N\}$ (bottom)

satisfies the recurrence

$$D_N = D_{\lfloor N/2 \rfloor} + 1 \qquad \text{for } N \geq 2 \text{ with } D_1 = 0,$$

which iterates to

$$D_N = \lfloor \lg N \rfloor + 2,$$

and, therefore,

$$C_N = N - 1 + \sum_{1 \leq k < N} (\lfloor \lg k \rfloor + 1).$$

There are a number of ways to evaluate this sum to give an exact formula for C_N: as mentioned above it is useful to adopt the approach of noting a relationship to the binary representations of integers. In particular, we just saw that $\lfloor \lg k \rfloor + 1$ is the number of bits in the binary representation of k (ignoring leading 0s), so C_N is precisely the number of bits in the binary representations of all the positive numbers less than N plus $N - 1$.

Theorem 2.4 (*Mergesort*) *The number of comparisons used by Mergesort is equal to $N-1$ plus the number of bits in the binary representations of all the numbers less than N. Both quantities are described by the recurrence*

$$C_N = C_{\lfloor N/2 \rfloor} + C_{\lceil N/2 \rceil} + N \qquad \text{for } N \geq 2 \text{ with } C_1 = 0,$$

which has the exact solution $C_N = N\lfloor \lg N \rfloor + 2N - 2^{\lfloor \lg N \rfloor + 1}$.

Proof. The first part of the theorem is established by the discussion above. Now, all $N - 1$ of the numbers less than N have a rightmost bit; $N - 2$ of them (all except 1) have a second-to-rightmost bit; $N - 4$ of them (all except 1, 2, and 3) have a third-to-rightmost bit; $N-8$ of them have a fourth-to-rightmost bit, etc., so we must have

$$\begin{aligned}C_N &= (N-1)+(N-1)+(N-2)+(N-4)+\cdots+(N-2^{\lfloor \lg N\rfloor})\\ &= (N-1)+N(\lfloor \lg N\rfloor+1)-(1+2+4+\ldots+2^{\lfloor \lg N\rfloor})\\ &= N\lfloor \lg N\rfloor+2N-2^{\lfloor \lg N\rfloor+1}.\end{aligned}$$

As noted above, $\lfloor \lg N\rfloor$ is a discontinuous function with periodic behavior. Also as mentioned, however, C_N itself is continuous, so the discontinuities (but not the periodicities) in the two functions involving $\lfloor \lg N\rfloor$ cancel out. This phenomenon is illustrated in Figure 2.4 and supported by the calculations in the corollary that follows. ■

Corollary $C_N = N\lg N + N\theta(1-\{\lg N\})$, *where* $\theta(x) = 1+x-2^x$ *is a positive function satisfying* $\theta(0)=\theta(1)=0$ *and* $0<\theta(x)<.086$ *for* $0<x<1$.

Proof. Straightforward by substituting the decomposition $\lfloor \lg N\rfloor = \lg N - \{\lg N\}$. The value $.086 \approx 1-\lg e+\lg\lg e$ is calculated by setting the derivative of $\theta(x)$ to zero. ■

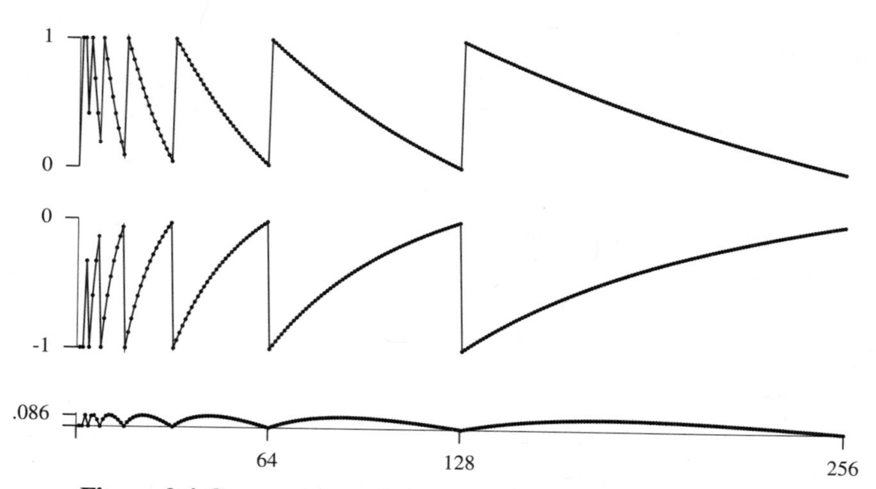

Figure 2.4 Composition of the periodic function $\theta(1-\{\lg N\})$
$1-\{\lg N\}$ (top)
$1-2^{1-\{\lg N\}}$ (middle)
$2-\{\lg N\}-2^{1-\{\lg N\}}$ (bottom)

Exercise 2.56 By considering the rightmost bits, give a direct proof that the number of bits in the binary representations of all the numbers less than N satisfies (4), but with an additive term of $N - 1$ instead of N.

Exercise 2.57 Prove that $N\lfloor \lg N \rfloor + 2N - 2^{\lfloor \lg N \rfloor + 1} = N\lceil \lg N \rceil + N - 2^{\lceil \lg N \rceil}$ for all positive N. (See Exercise 1.4.)

Other properties of binary numbers. Thus, we study properties of binary integers because they naturally model the (binary) decision-making process in many basic algorithms. The quantities encountered above are likely to arise in the analysis of any algorithm that solves a problem by recursively dividing it in two, the way that binary search and Mergesort do, and similar quantities clearly will arise in other divide-and-conquer schemes. To complete our study of binary divide-and-conquer recurrences, we consider two more properties of the binary representation of numbers that frequently arise in the analysis of algorithms.

Definition *Given an integer N, define the* population count *function ν_N to be the number of 1s in the binary representation of N and the* cumulated population count *function P_N to be the number of 1s in the binary representations of all the numbers less than N.*

Definition *Given an integer N, define the* ruler *function ψ_N to be the number of trailing 1s in the binary representation of N and the* cumulated ruler *function R_N to be the number of trailing 1s in the binary representations of all the numbers less than N.*

Table 2.3 gives the values of the functions for $N \le 16$. The reader may find it instructive to try to compute values of these functions for larger N. For example, the binary representation of 83 is 1010011, so $\nu_{83} = 4$ and

N	1	2	3	4	5	6	7	8	9	10	11	12	13	14	15
	0001	0010	0011	0100	0101	0110	0111	1000	1001	1010	1011	1100	1101	1110	1111
ν_N	1	1	2	1	2	2	3	1	2	2	3	2	3	3	4
P_N	0	1	2	4	5	7	9	12	13	15	17	20	22	25	28
ψ_N	1	0	2	0	1	0	3	0	1	0	2	0	1	0	4
R_N	0	1	1	3	3	4	4	7	7	8	8	10	10	11	11

Table 2.3 Ruler and population count functions

$\psi_{83} = 2$. The cumulated values

$$P_N \equiv \sum_{0 \le j < N} \nu_j \quad \text{and} \quad R_N \equiv \sum_{0 \le j < N} \psi_j$$

are less easily computed. For example, $P_{84} = 215$ and $R_{84} = 78$.

It is not hard to see, for example, that

$$P_{2^n} = n2^{n-1} \text{ and } R_{2^n} = 2^n - 1$$

and that

$$P_N = \frac{1}{2} N \lg N + O(N) \text{ and } R_N = N + O(\lg N),$$

but exact representations or more precise asymptotic estimates are difficult to derive, as indicated by the plot of $P_N - (N \lg N)/2$ in Figure 2.5.

As noted above, functions of this type satisfy recurrences that are simply derived but can differ markedly, even when describing the same quantity. For example, considering the leftmost bits, we see that $2^{\lfloor \lg N \rfloor}$ of the numbers less than N start with 0 and the rest start with 1, so we have

$$P_N = P_{2^{\lfloor \lg N \rfloor}} + (N - 2^{\lfloor \lg N \rfloor}) + P_{N - 2^{\lfloor \lg N \rfloor}}.$$

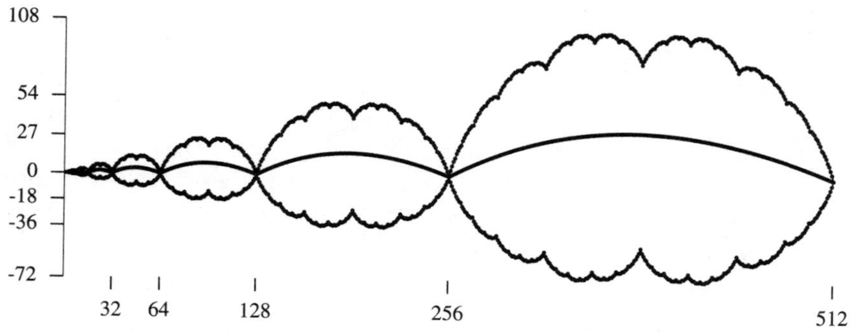

Figure 2.5 Periodic and fractal terms in bit counting
$\{\#$ 1 bits in numbers less than $N\} - (N \lg N)/2$ (top)
$\{\#$ 0 bits in numbers less than $N\} - (N \lg N)/2$ (bottom)
$\{\#$ bits in numbers less than $N\} - N \lg N$ (middle)

But also, considering the rightmost bit, it is clear that

$$P_N = P_{\lfloor N/2 \rfloor} + P_{\lceil N/2 \rceil} + \lfloor N/2 \rfloor \qquad \text{for } N > 1 \text{ with } P_1 = 0.$$

This is similar to the Mergesort recurrence, which is associated with counting all the bits less than N (there should be about half as many 1 bits), but the function is remarkably different. (Compare Figure 2.5 with Figure 2.2.) The function counting the number of 0 bits is similar: both are fractal in behavior, but they cancel out to get the periodic but continuous function that we have seen before (see Figure 2.2). Delange [7] studied the function P_N in some detail, and expressed it in terms of a function that is nowhere differentiable.

Other recurrences. Binary search and Mergesort are typical "binary divide-and-conquer" algorithms; they illustrate how natural such algorithms are to develop and the characteristics of potential solutions. The examples that we have given and the relationships to properties of the binary representations of numbers that we have seen make it clear that we could develop more precise solutions for other, similar, recurrences along the lines we have been discussing, mindful of the fact that precise results may be elusive (or less useful than we might like) because of fractal-like behavior of the functions involved, even in the leading term. Table 2.4 shows a number of recurrences that commonly arise, along with approximate solutions derived from the general theorems given in the next section. In the table, $a_{N/2}$ means "$a_{\lfloor N/2 \rfloor}$ or $a_{\lceil N/2 \rceil}$," $2a_{N/2}$ means "$a_{N/2} + a_{N/2}$," and so forth—in the next section we discuss the fact that minor variations of this sort do not affect the asymptotic results given in Table 2.4 (though they do prevent us from giving more general estimates).

Normally, applications involving such recurrences involve worst-case results, as in Theorem 2.5 and Theorem 2.6, but if the subproblems are independent and still "random" after the divide step, then these results can also yield expected costs for some problems.

It is worth recognizing that it is only a small step from these properties of numbers to properties of bitstrings that are certainly more combinatorial in nature. For example, suppose that we wanted to know the average length of the longest string of consecutive 0s in a random bitstring, say, to enable certain optimizations in designing an arithmetic unit. Is this a property of the number, or the bits that represent it? Such questions lead immediately to more generally applicable combinatorial studies, which we will consider in Chapter 7.

We encounter functions of this type frequently in the analysis of algorithms, and it is worthwhile to be cognizant of their relationship to simple properties of binary numbers. Beyond divide-and-conquer algorithms, these functions also arise, of course, in the direct analysis of arithmetic algorithms on numbers represented in binary. A famous example of this is the analysis of the expected length of the carry propagation chain in an adder, a problem dating back to von Neumann that was completely solved by Knuth [19]. These results relate directly to analyses of fundamental algorithms on strings, as we will see in Chapter 7. Binary divide-and-conquer recurrences and properties of their solutions are studied in more detail by Allouche and Shallit [2] and by Flajolet and Golin [9].

Exercise 2.58 Give recurrences for the functions plotted in Figure 2.5.

Exercise 2.59 Derive recurrences for R_N similar to those given above for P_N.

$a_N = a_{N/2} + 1$	$\lg N + O(1)$
$a_N = a_{N/2} + N$	$2N + O(\lg N)$
$a_N = a_{N/2} + N \lg N$	$\Theta(N \lg N)$
$a_N = 2a_{N/2} + 1$	$\Theta(N)$
$a_N = 2a_{N/2} + \lg N$	$\Theta(N)$
$a_N = 2a_{N/2} + N$	$N \log N + O(N)$
$a_N = 2a_{N/2} + N \lg N$	$\frac{1}{2} N \lg N^2 + O(N \log N)$
$a_N = 2a_{N/2} + N \lg^{\delta-1} N$	$\delta^{-1} N \lg^{\delta} N + O(N \lg^{\delta-1} N)$
$a_N = 2a_{N/2} + N^2$	$2N^2 + O(N)$
$a_N = 3a_{N/2} + N$	$\Theta(N^{\lg 3})$
$a_N = 4a_{N/2} + N$	$\Theta(N^2)$

Table 2.4 Binary divide-and-conquer recurrences and solutions

Exercise 2.60 Plot the solution to the recurrence

$$A_N = A_{\lfloor N/2 \rfloor} + A_{\lceil N/2 \rceil} + \lfloor \lg N \rfloor \qquad \text{for } N \geq 2 \text{ with } A_1 = 0,$$

for $1 \leq N \leq 512$.

Exercise 2.61 Plot the solution to the recurrence

$$B_N = 3B_{\lceil N/2 \rceil} + N \qquad \text{for } N \geq 2 \text{ with } B_1 = 0,$$

for $1 \leq N \leq 512$.

Exercise 2.62 Plot the solution to

$$D_N = D_{\lceil N/2 \rceil} + D_{\lceil N/2 \rceil} + C_N \qquad \text{for } N > 1 \text{ with } D_1 = 0$$

where C_N is the solution to

$$C_N = C_{\lceil N/2 \rceil} + C_{\lceil N/2 \rceil} + N \qquad \text{for } N > 1 \text{ with } C_1 = 0.$$

Consider the variants of this problem derived by changing $\lceil N/2 \rceil$ to $\lfloor N/2 \rfloor$ in each of the terms.

Exercise 2.63 Take the binary representation of N, reverse it, and interpret the result as an integer, $\rho(N)$. Show that $\rho(N)$ satisfies a divide-and-conquer recurrence. Plot its values for $1 \leq N \leq 512$ and explain what you see.

Exercise 2.64 What is the average length of the initial string of 1s in the binary representation of a number less that N, assuming all such numbers equally likely?

Exercise 2.65 What is the average length of the initial string of 1s in a random bitstring of length N, assuming all such strings equally likely?

Exercise 2.66 What is the average and the variance of the length of the initial string of 1s in a (potentially infinite) sequence of random bits?

Exercise 2.67 What is the total number of carries made when a binary counter increments N times, from 0 to N?

2.7 General Divide-and-Conquer Recurrences. More generally, efficient algorithms and upper bounds in complexity studies are very often derived by extending the divide-and-conquer algorithmic design paradigm along the following lines: "Divide the problem into smaller (perhaps overlapping) subproblems, solve them recursively, then use the solutions to solve the original problem." A variety of "divide-and-conquer" recurrences arise that depend on the number and relative size of subproblems, the extent to which they overlap, and the cost of recombining them for the solution. It is normally possible to determine the asymptotic growth of functions satisfying such recurrences, but, as above, the periodic and fractal nature of functions that are involved make it necessary to specify details carefully.

In pursuit of a general solution, we start with the recursive formula

$$a(x) = \alpha a(x/\beta) + f(x) \qquad \text{for } x > 1 \text{ with } a(x) = 0 \text{ for } x \le 1$$

defining a *function* over the positive real numbers. In essence, this corresponds to a divide-and-conquer algorithm that divides a problem of size x into α subproblems of size x/β and recombines at a cost of $f(x)$. Here $a(x)$ is a function defined for positive real x, so that $a(x/\beta)$ is well defined. In most applications, α and β will be integers, though we do not use that fact in developing the solution. We do insist that $\beta > 1$, of course.

For example, consider the case where $f(x) = x$ and we restrict ourselves to the integers $N = \beta^n$. In this case, we have

$$a_{\beta^n} = \alpha a_{\beta^{n-1}} + \beta^n \qquad \text{for } n > 0 \text{ with } a_1 = 0.$$

Dividing both sides by α^n and iterating (that is, applying Theorem 2.1) we have the solution

$$a_{\beta^n} = \alpha^n \sum_{1 \le j \le n} \left(\frac{\beta}{\alpha}\right)^j.$$

Now, there are three cases: if $\alpha > \beta$, the sum converges to a constant; if $\alpha = \beta$, it evaluates to n; and if $\alpha < \beta$, the sum is dominated by the latter terms and is $O(\beta/\alpha)^n$. Since $\alpha^n = (\beta^{\log_\beta \alpha})^n = (\beta^n)^{\log_\beta \alpha}$, this means that the solution to the recurrence is $O(N^{\log_\beta \alpha})$ when $\alpha > \beta$, $O(N \log N)$ when $\alpha = \beta$, and $O(N)$ when $\alpha < \beta$. Though this solution only holds for $N = \beta^n$, it illustrates the overall structure encountered in the general case.

Theorem 2.5 (*Divide-and-conquer functions*) *If the function $a(x)$ satisfies the recurrence*

$$a(x) = \alpha a(x/\beta) + x \qquad \text{for } x > 1 \text{ with } a(x) = 0 \text{ for } x \le 1.$$

then

$$\begin{aligned} &\text{if } \alpha < \beta \qquad a(x) \sim \frac{\beta}{\beta - \alpha} x \\ &\text{if } \alpha = \beta \qquad a(x) \sim x \log_\beta x \\ &\text{if } \alpha > \beta \qquad a(x) \sim \frac{\alpha}{\alpha - \beta} \left(\frac{\beta}{\alpha}\right)^{\{\log_\beta \alpha\}} x^{\log_\beta \alpha}. \end{aligned}$$

Proof. The basic idea, which applies to all divide-and-conquer recurrences, is to iterate the recurrence until the initial conditions are met for the subproblems. Here, we have

$$\begin{aligned} a(x) &= x + \alpha a(x/\beta) \\ &= x + \alpha\frac{x}{\beta} + \alpha a(x/\beta^2) \\ &= x + \alpha\frac{x}{\beta} + \alpha^2\frac{x}{\beta^2} + \alpha a(x/\beta^3) \end{aligned}$$

and so on. After $t = \lfloor \log_\beta x \rfloor$ iterations, the term $a(x/\beta^t)$ that appears can be replaced by 0 and the iteration process terminates. This leaves an exact representation of the solution:

$$a(x) = x\Big(1 + \frac{\alpha}{\beta} + \ldots + \frac{\alpha^t}{\beta^t}\Big).$$

Now, as above, three cases can be distinguished. First, if $\alpha < \beta$ then the sum converges and

$$a(x) \sim x\sum_{j\ge 0}\Big(\frac{\alpha}{\beta}\Big)^j = \frac{\beta}{\beta-\alpha}x.$$

Second, if $\alpha = \beta$ then each of the terms in the sum is 1 and the solution is simply

$$a(x) = x(\lfloor \log_\beta x \rfloor + 1) \sim x\log_\beta x.$$

Third, if $\alpha > \beta$ then the last term in the sum predominates, so that

$$\begin{aligned} a(x) &= x\Big(\frac{\alpha}{\beta}\Big)^t\Big(1 + \frac{\beta}{\alpha} + \ldots + \frac{\beta^t}{\alpha^t}\Big) \\ &\sim x\frac{\alpha}{\alpha-\beta}\Big(\frac{\alpha}{\beta}\Big)^t. \end{aligned}$$

As above, the periodic behavior of the expression in the third case can be isolated by separating the integer and fractional part of $\log_\beta x$ and writing $t \equiv \lfloor \log_\beta x \rfloor = \log_\beta x - \{\log_\beta x\}$. This gives

$$x\Big(\frac{\alpha}{\beta}\Big)^t = x\Big(\frac{\alpha}{\beta}\Big)^{\log_\beta x}\Big(\frac{\alpha}{\beta}\Big)^{-\{\log_\beta x\}} = x^{\log_\beta \alpha}\Big(\frac{\beta}{\alpha}\Big)^{\{\log_\beta x\}},$$

since $\alpha^{\log_\beta x} = x^{\log_\beta \alpha}$. This completes the proof.

For $\alpha \leq \beta$, the periodic behavior is not in the leading term, but for $\alpha > \beta$, the coefficient of $x^{\log_\beta \alpha}$ is a periodic function of $\log_\beta x$ that is bounded and oscillates between $\alpha/(\alpha - \beta)$ and $\beta/(\alpha - \beta)$. ■

Figure 2.6 illustrates how the relative values of α and β affect the asymptotic growth of the function. Boxes in the figures correspond to problem sizes for a divide-and-conquer algorithm. The top diagram, where a problem is split into two subproblems, each a third the size of the original, shows how the performance is linear because the problem sizes go to 0 exponentially fast. The middle diagram, where a problem is split into three subproblems, each a third the size of the original, shows how the total problem size is well balanced so a "log" multiplicative factor is needed. The last diagram, where a problem is split into four subproblems, each a third the size of the original, shows how the total problem size grows exponentially, so the total is dominated by the last term. This shows the asymptotic growth and is representative of what happens in general situations.

To generalize this to the point where it applies to practical situations, we need to consider other $f(x)$ and less restrictive subdivision strategies than precisely equal subproblem sizes (which will allow us to move back to

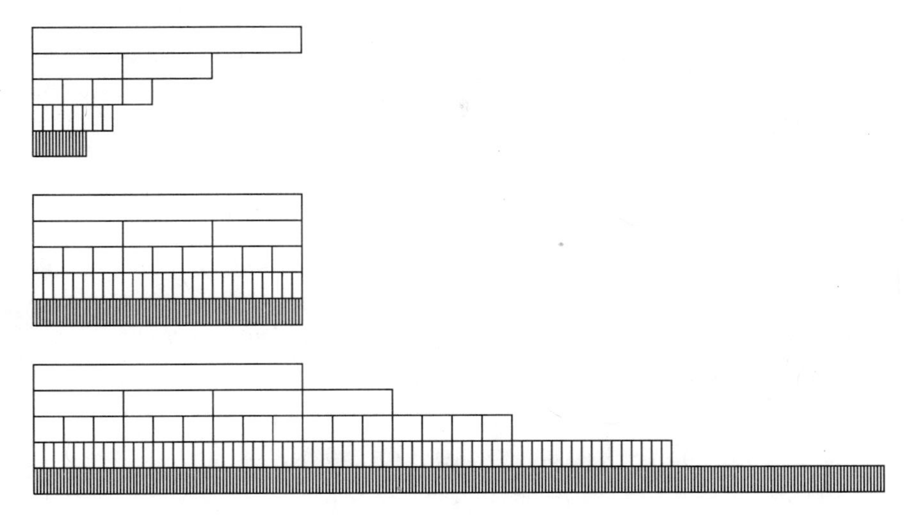

Figure 2.6 Divide-and-conquer for $\beta = 3$ and $\alpha = 2, 3, 4$

recurrences on integers). For other $f(x)$, we proceed precisely as above: at the top level we have one problem of cost $f(x)$, then we have α problems of cost $f(x/\beta)$, then α^2 problems of cost $f(x/\beta^2)$, etc., so the total cost is

$$f(x) + \alpha f(x/\beta) + \alpha^2 f(x/\beta^2) + \cdots .$$

As above, there are three cases: if $\alpha > \beta$, the later terms in the sum dominate; if $\alpha = \beta$, the terms are roughly equal; and if $\alpha < \beta$, the early terms dominate. Some "smoothness" restrictions on the function f are necessary to derive a precise answer. For example, if we restrict f to be of the form $x^\gamma(\log x)^\delta$—which actually represents a significant portion of the functions that arise in complexity studies—an argument similar to that given above can be used to show that

$$\begin{aligned} &\text{if } \gamma < \log_\beta \alpha && a(x) \sim c_1 x^\gamma (\log x)^\delta \\ &\text{if } \gamma = \log_\beta \alpha && a(x) \sim c_2 x^\gamma (\log x)^{\delta+1} \\ &\text{if } \gamma > \log_\beta \alpha && a(x) = \Theta(x^{\log_\beta \alpha}) \end{aligned}$$

where c_1 and c_2 are appropriate constants that depend on α, β, and γ.

Exercise 2.68 Give explicit formulae for c_1 and c_2. Start by doing the case $\delta = 0$.

Intuitively, we expect the same kind of result even when the subproblems are almost, but not necessarily exactly, the same size. Indeed, we are bound to consider this case because "problem sizes" must be integers: of course, dividing a file whose size is odd into two parts gives subproblems of almost, but not quite, the same size. Moreover, we expect that we need not have an exact value of $f(x)$ in order to estimate the growth of $a(x)$. Of course we are also interested in functions that are defined only on the integers. Putting these together, we get a result that is useful for the analysis of a variety of algorithms.

Theorem 2.6 (*Divide-and-conquer sequences*) *If a divide-and-conquer algorithm works by dividing a problem of size n into β parts, each of size $n/\alpha + O(1)$, and solving the subproblems independently with additional cost $f(n)$ for dividing and combining, then if $f(n) = \Theta(n^\gamma(\log n)^\delta)$, the total cost is given by*

$$\begin{aligned} &\textit{if } \gamma < \log_\beta \alpha && a_n = \Theta(n^\gamma (\log n)^\delta) \\ &\textit{if } \gamma = \log_\beta \alpha && a_n = \Theta(n^\gamma (\log n)^{\delta+1}) \\ &\textit{if } \gamma > \log_\beta \alpha && a_n = \Theta(n^{\log_\beta \alpha}). \end{aligned}$$

Proof. The general strategy is the same as above: iterate the recurrence until the initial conditions are satisfied, then collect terms. The calculations involved are rather intricate and are omitted. Details may be found in Flajolet and Sedgewick [13]. ■

In complexity studies, a more general formulation is often used, since less specific information about $f(n)$ may be available. Under suitable conditions on the smoothness of $f(n)$, it can be shown that

$$\begin{aligned} &\text{if } f(n) = O(n^{\log_\beta \alpha - \epsilon}) && a_n = \Theta(n^{\log_\beta \alpha}) \\ &\text{if } f(n) = \Theta(n^{\log_\beta \alpha}) && a_n = \Theta(n^{\log_\beta \alpha} \log n) \\ &\text{if } f(n) = \Omega(n^{\log_\beta \alpha + \epsilon}) && a_n = \Theta(f(n)). \end{aligned}$$

This result is primarily due to Bentley, Haken, and Saxe [4]; a full proof of a similar result may also be found in [5]. This type of result is normally used to prove upper bounds and lower bounds on asymptotic behavior of algorithms, by choosing $f(n)$ to bound true costs appropriately. In this book, we are normally interested in deriving more accurate results for specific $f(n)$.

Exercise 2.69 Plot the periodic part of the solution to the recurrence

$$a_N = 3a_{\lfloor N/3 \rfloor} + N \qquad \text{for } N > 2 \text{ with } a_1 = a_2 = a_3 = 1$$

for $1 \le N \le 512$.

Exercise 2.70 Answer the previous question for the other possible ways of dividing a problem of size N into three parts with the size of each part either $\lfloor N/3 \rfloor$ or $\lfloor N/3 \rfloor$.

Exercise 2.71 Give an asymptotic solution to the recurrence

$$a(x) = \alpha a_{x/\beta} + 2^x \qquad \text{for } x > 1 \text{ with } a(x) = 0 \text{ for } x \le 1.$$

Exercise 2.72 Give an asymptotic solution to the recurrence

$$a_N = a_{3N/4} + a_{N/4} + N \qquad \text{for } N > 2 \text{ with } a_1 = a_2 = a_3 = 1.$$

Exercise 2.73 Give an asymptotic solution to the recurrence

$$a_N = a_{N/2} + a_{N/4} + N \qquad \text{for } N > 2 \text{ with } a_1 = a_2 = a_3 = 1.$$

Exercise 2.74 Consider the recurrence

$$a_n = a_{f(n)} + a_{g(n)} + a_{h(n)} + 1 \qquad \text{for } n > t \text{ with } a_n = 1 \text{ for } n < t$$

with the constraint that $f(n) + g(n) + h(n) = n$. Prove that $a_n = \Theta(n)$.

Exercise 2.75 Consider the recurrence

$$a_n = a_{f(n)} + a_{g(n)} + 1 \qquad \text{for } N > t \text{ with } a_n = 1 \text{ for } n < t$$

with $f(n) + g(n) = n - h(n)$. Give the smallest value of $h(n)$ for which you can prove that $a_n/n \to 0$ as $n \to \infty$.

RECURRENCE relations correspond naturally to iterative and recursive programs, and they can serve us well in a variety of applications in the analysis of algorithms, so we have surveyed in this chapter the types of recurrence relations that can arise and some ways of coping with them. Understanding an algorithm sufficiently well to be able to develop a recurrence relation describing an important performance characteristic is often an important first step in analyzing it. Given a recurrence relation, we can often compute or estimate needed parameters for practical applications even if an analytic solution seems too difficult to obtain.

There is a large literature on "difference equations" and recurrences, from which we have tried to select useful and relevant tools, techniques and examples. There are general and essential mathematical tools for dealing with recurrences, but finding the appropriate path to solving a particular recurrence is often challenging. Nevertheless, a careful analysis can lead to understanding of the essential properties of a broad variety of the recurrences that arise in practice. We calculate values of the recurrence to get some idea of its rate of growth; try telescoping (iterating) it to get an idea of the asymptotic form of the solution; perhaps look for a summation factor, change of variable, or repertoire suite that can lead to an exact solution; or apply an approximation technique such as bootstrapping or perturbation to estimate the solution.

Computational complexity studies often depend on solving recurrences for estimating and bounding the performance characteristics of algorithms. Specifically, the "divide-and-conquer" recurrences at the end of the chapter arise particularly frequently in the computational complexity literature. Most such recurrences have a similar structure, which reflects the degree of balance in the algorithm design. They also are closely related to properties of number systems, and thus tend to exhibit fractal-like behavior when carefully analyzed. Approximate bounds such as those we have seen are appropriate (and widely used) for deriving upper bounds in complexity proofs, but not necessarily for analyzing the performance of algorithms, because they do not always provide sufficiently accurate information to allow us to predict performance. We can often get more precise estimates in situations where we have more precise information about $f(n)$ and the divide-and-conquer method, though we must be cognizant that periodicities and possible fractal behaviors will be involved in solutions.

Our discussion has been exclusively devoted to recurrences on one index N. We defer discussion of multivariate and other types of recurrences until we have developed more advanced tools for solving them.

Recurrences arise in a natural way in the study of performance characteristics of algorithms. As we develop detailed analyses of complicated algorithms, we encounter rather complex recurrences to be solved. In the next chapter, we introduce generating functions, which are fundamental to the analysis of algorithms. Not only can they help us solve recurrences, but also they have a direct connection to algorithms at a high level, allowing us to leave the detailed structure described by recurrences below the surface for many applications.

References

1. A. V. AHO AND N. J. A. SLOANE. "Some doubly exponential sequences," *Fibonacci Quarterly* **11**, 1973, 429–437.
2. J.-P. ALLOUCHE AND J. SHALLIT. "The ring of k-regular sequences," *Theoretical Computer Science* **98**, 1992, 163–197.
3. C. M. BENDER AND S. A. ORSZAG. *Ad anced Mathematical Methods for Scientists and Engineers*, McGraw-Hill, New York, 1978.
4. J. L. BENTLEY, D. HAKEN, AND J. B. SAXE. "A general method for solving divide-and-conquer recurrences," *SIGACT News*, Fall 1980, 36–44.
5. T. H. CORMEN, C. E. LEISERSON, AND R. L. RIVEST. *Introduction to Algorithms*, MIT Press, New York, 1990.
6. N. G. DE BRUIJN. *Asymptotic Methods in Analysis*, Dover Publications, New York, 1981.
7. H. DELANGE. "Sur la fonction sommatoire de la fonction somme des chiffres," *L'enseignement Mathématique* **XXI**, 1975, 31–47.
8. P. FLAJOLET AND M. GOLIN. "Exact asymptotics of divide–and–conquer recurrences," in *Automata, Languages, and Programming*, A. Lingas,

R. Karlsson, and S. Carlsson, ed., Lecture Notes in Computer Science #700, Springer Verlag, Berlin, 1993, 137–149.

9. P. Flajolet and M. Golin. "Mellin transforms and asymptotics: the mergesort recurrence," *Acta Informatica* **31**, 1994, 673–696.
10. P. Flajolet, P. Grabner, and P. Kirschenhofer. "Mellin Transforms and asymptotics: digital sums," *Theoretical Computer Science* **123**, 1994, 291–314.
11. P. Flajolet, J.-C. Raoult, and J. Vuillemin. "The number of registers required to evaluate arithmetic expressions," *Theoretical Computer Science* **9**, 1979, 99–125.
12. P. Flajolet and R. Sedgewick. *Analytic Combinatorics*, in preparation.
13. P. Flajolet and R. Sedgewick. "Asymptotic behavior of divide-and-conquer recurrences," in preparation.
14. R. L. Graham, D. E. Knuth, and O. Patashnik. *Concrete Mathematics*, Addison-Wesley, Reading, MA, 1988.
15. D. H. Greene and D. E. Knuth. *Mathematics for the Analysis of Algorithms*, Birkhäuser, Boston, 1981.
16. P. Henrici. *Applied and Computational Complex Analysis*, 3 volumes, John Wiley, New York, 1977.
17. D. E. Knuth. *The Art of Computer Programming. Volume 2: Seminumerical Algorithms*, Addison-Wesley, Reading, MA, 1969.
18. D. E. Knuth. *The Art of Computer Programming. Volume 3: Sorting and Searching*, Addison-Wesley, Reading, MA, 1973.
19. D. E. Knuth. "The average time for carry propagation," *Indagationes Mathematicae* **40**, 1978, 238–242.
20. D. E. Knuth and A. Schönhage. "The expected linearity of a simple equivalence algorithm," *Theoretical Computer Science* **6**, 1978, 281–315.
21. G. Lueker. "Some techniques for solving recurrences," *Computing Surveys* **12**, 1980, 419–436.
22. Z. A. Melzak. *Companion to concrete mathematics*, John Wiley, New York, 1968.
23. J. Riordan. *Combinatorial Identities*, John Wiley, New York, 1968.
24. R. Sedgewick. "The analysis of quicksort programs," *Acta Informatica* **7**, 1977, 327–355.
25. A. Yao. "On random 2–3 trees," *Acta Informatica* **9**, 1978, 159–170.

CHAPTER THREE

GENERATING FUNCTIONS

IN this chapter we introduce the central concept that we use in the average-case analysis of algorithms: generating functions. This mathematical material is so fundamental to the rest of the book that we shall concentrate on presenting a synopsis somewhat apart from applications, though we do draw some examples from properties of algorithms.

After defining the basic notions of "ordinary" generating functions and "exponential" generating functions, we begin with a description of the use of generating functions to solve recurrence relations, including a discussion of necessary mathematical tools. For both ordinary and exponential generating functions, we survey many elementary functions that arise in practice, and consider their basic properties and ways of manipulating them. We discuss a number of examples, including a detailed look at solving the Quicksort median-of-three recurrence from Chapter 1.

We next consider in detail the role that generating functions can play in enumerating combinatorial structures, culminating in an introduction to the "symbolic method" that allows us to develop relationships between objects being analyzed and associated generating functions. To illustrate these concepts, we consider examples from Chapters 5 through 8, including the well-known example of counting binary trees. In this context, we examine the Lagrange inversion theorem, which is a nice complement to the symbolic method for problems with a recursive structure.

We normally are interested not just in counting combinatorial structures, but also analyzing their properties. We look at how to use "bivariate" generating functions for this purpose, and how this relates to the use of "probability" generating functions.

The chapter concludes with a discussion of various special types of generating functions that can arise in applications in the analysis of algorithms.

One goal of the previous chapters was to convince the reader of the essential role played by recurrences in the analysis of algorithms; one goal of this chapter is to convince the reader not only that many basic recurrences can easily be solved with the use of generating functions, but also that generating functions play such an essential role that recurrences themselves often can be bypassed! Generating functions are more than a technical tool used to solve recurrences and compute moments—they are a necessary and natural link between the algorithms that are our objects of study and analytic methods that are necessary to discover their properties. Generating functions serve both as a combinatorial tool to facilitate counting and as an analytic tool to develop precise estimates for quantities of interest.

We illustrate this throughout the book with examples of direct derivations using generating functions for combinatorial properties that are often too complicated to be conveniently described with recurrence relations. These methods are also a starting point for the more general combinatorial techniques developed in [3].

Because of their central role throughout the book, we describe basic properties and techniques for manipulating generating functions in some detail and provide a catalog of the most important ones in this chapter, for reference. We introduce a substantial amount of material, with examples from combinatorics and the analysis of algorithms, though our treatment of each particular topic is relatively concise. Fuller discussion of these topics may be found in our coverage of various applications in Chapters 5 through 8 and in the other references listed at the end of the chapter, primarily [1], [4], [5], and [17].

3.1 Ordinary Generating Functions. As we saw in the previous chapter, our goal in the analysis of algorithms is to derive specific expressions for the values of terms in a sequence of quantities $a_0, a_1, a_2, \ldots$ that measure some performance parameter. In this chapter we see the benefits of working with a single mathematical object that represents the whole sequence.

Definition *Given a sequence* $a_0, a_1, a_2, \ldots, a_k, \ldots$*, the function*

$$A(z) = \sum_{k \geq 0} a_k z^k$$

is called the ordinary generating function (OGF) of the sequence. We use the notation $[z^k]A(z)$ *to refer to the coefficient* a_k*.*

Some elementary generating functions and their corresponding sequences are given in Table 3.1. We discuss below how to derive these functions and various ways to manipulate them. The OGFs in Table 3.1 are fundamental

$1, 1, 1, 1, \ldots, 1, \ldots$	$\dfrac{1}{1-z} = \sum_{N\ge0} z^N$
$0, 1, 2, 3, 4, \ldots, N, \ldots$	$\dfrac{z}{(1-z)^2} = \sum_{N\ge1} Nz^N$
$0, 0, 1, 3, 6, 10, \ldots, \binom{N}{2}, \ldots$	$\dfrac{z^2}{(1-z)^3} = \sum_{N\ge2} \binom{N}{2} z^N$
$0, \ldots, 0, 1, M+1, \ldots, \binom{N}{M}, \ldots$	$\dfrac{z^M}{(1-z)^{M+1}} = \sum_{N\ge M} \binom{N}{M} z^N$
$1, M, \binom{M}{2} \ldots, \binom{M}{N}, \ldots, M, 1$	$(1+z)^M = \sum_{N\ge0} \binom{M}{N} z^N$
$1, M+1, \binom{M+2}{2}, \binom{M+3}{3}, \ldots$	$\dfrac{1}{(1-z)^{M+1}} = \sum_{N\ge0} \binom{N+M}{N} z^N$
$1, 0, 1, 0, \ldots, 1, 0, \ldots$	$\dfrac{1}{1-z^2} = \sum_{N\ge0} z^{2N}$
$1, c, c^2, c^3, \ldots, c^N, \ldots$	$\dfrac{1}{1-cz} = \sum_{N\ge0} c^N z^N$
$1, 1, \frac{1}{2!}, \frac{1}{3!}, \frac{1}{4!}, \ldots, \frac{1}{N!}, \ldots$	$e^z = \sum_{N\ge0} \dfrac{z^N}{N!}$
$0, 1, \frac{1}{2}, \frac{1}{3}, \frac{1}{4}, \ldots, \frac{1}{N}, \ldots$	$\ln \dfrac{1}{1-z} = \sum_{N\ge1} \dfrac{z^N}{N}$
$0, 1, 1+\frac{1}{2}, 1+\frac{1}{2}+\frac{1}{3}, \ldots, H_N, \ldots$	$\dfrac{1}{1-z} \ln \dfrac{1}{1-z} = \sum_{N\ge1} H_N z^N$
$0, 0, 1, 3(\frac{1}{2}+\frac{1}{3}), 4(\frac{1}{2}+\frac{1}{3}+\frac{1}{4}), \ldots$	$\dfrac{z}{(1-z)^2} \ln \dfrac{1}{1-z} = \sum_{N\ge0} N(H_N - 1) z^N$

Table 3.1 Elementary ordinary generating functions

and arise frequently in the analysis of algorithms. Each sequence can be described in many ways (with simple recurrence relations, for example), but we will see below that there are significant advantages to representing them directly with generating functions.

The sum in the definition may or may not converge—for the moment we ignore questions of convergence, for two reasons. First, the manipulations that we perform on generating functions are typically well-defined formal manipulations on power series, even in the absence of convergence. Second, the sequences that arise in our analyses are normally such that convergence is assured, at least for some (small enough) z. In a great many applications in the analysis of algorithms, we are able to exploit formal relationships between power series and the algorithms under scrutiny to derive explicit formulae for generating functions in the first part of a typical analysis; and we are able to learn analytic properties of generating functions in detail (convergence plays an important role in this) to derive explicit formulae describing fundamental properties of algorithms in the second part of a typical analysis.

Given generating functions $A(z) = \sum_{k\geq 0} a_k z^k$ and $B(z) = \sum_{k\geq 0} b_k z^k$ that represent the sequences $\{a_0, a_1, \ldots, a_k, \ldots\}$ and $\{b_0, b_1, \ldots, b_k, \ldots\}$, we can perform a number of simple transformations to get generating functions for other sequences. Several such operations are shown in Table 3.2. Examples of the application of these operations may be found in relationships among entries in Table 3.1.

Theorem 3.1 (*OGF operations*) *If two sequences* $a_0, a_1, \ldots, a_k, \ldots$ *and* $b_0, b_1, \ldots, b_k, \ldots$ *are represented by the OGFs* $A(z) = \sum_{k\geq 0} a_k z^k$ *and* $B(z) = \sum_{k\geq 0} b_k z^k$, *then the operations given in Table 3.2 produce OGFs that represent the indicated sequences. In particular:*

$$\begin{array}{rll} A(z)+B(z) & \textit{is the OGF for} & a_0+b_0, a_1+b_1, a_2+b_2, \ldots \\ zA(z) & \textit{is the OGF for} & 0, a_0, a_1, a_2, \ldots \\ A'(z) & \textit{is the OGF for} & a_1, 2a_2, 3a_3, \ldots \\ A(z)B(z) & \textit{is the OGF for} & a_0b_0, a_0b_1+a_1b_0, a_0b_2+a_1b_1+a_2b_0, \ldots \end{array}$$

Proof. Most of these are elementary and can be verified by inspection. The *convolution* operation (and the *partial sum* special case) are easily

$$A(z) = \sum_{n\geq 0} a_n z^n \qquad a_0, a_1, a_2, \ldots, a_n, \ldots,$$

$$B(z) = \sum_{n\geq 0} b_n z^n \qquad b_0, b_1, b_2, \ldots, b_n, \ldots,$$

right shift

$$zA(z) = \sum_{n\geq 1} a_{n-1} z^n \qquad 0, a_0, a_1, a_2, \ldots, a_{n-1}, \ldots,$$

left shift

$$\frac{A(z) - a_0}{z} = \sum_{n\geq 0} a_{n+1} z^n \qquad a_1, a_2, a_3, \ldots, a_{n+1}, \ldots,$$

index multiply (differentiation)

$$A'(z) = \sum_{n\geq 0} (n+1) a_{n+1} z^n \qquad a_1, 2a_2, \ldots, (n+1)a_{n+1}, \ldots,$$

index divide (integration)

$$\int_0^z A(t)dt = \sum_{n\geq 1} \frac{a_{n-1}}{n} z^n \qquad 0, a_0, \frac{a_1}{2}, \frac{a_2}{3} \ldots, \frac{a_{n-1}}{n}, \ldots,$$

scaling

$$A(\lambda z) = \sum_{n\geq 0} \lambda^n a_n z^n \qquad a_0, \lambda a_1, \lambda^2 a_2, \ldots, \lambda^n a_n, \ldots,$$

addition

$$A(z) + B(z) = \sum_{n\geq 0} (a_n + b_n) z^n \qquad a_0 + b_0, \ldots, a_n + b_n, \ldots,$$

difference

$$(1 - z)A(z) = a_0 + \sum_{n\geq 1} (a_n - a_{n-1}) z^n \qquad a_0, a_1 - a_0, \ldots, a_n - a_{n-1}, \ldots,$$

convolution

$$A(z)B(z) = \sum_{n\geq 0} \Big(\sum_{0\leq k\leq n} a_k b_{n-k} \Big) z^n \qquad a_0 b_0, a_1 b_0 + a_0 b_1, \ldots, \sum_{0\leq k\leq n} a_k b_{n-k}, \ldots,$$

partial sum

$$\frac{A(z)}{1 - z} = \sum_{n\geq 0} \Big(\sum_{0\leq k\leq n} a_k \Big) z^n \qquad a_1, a_1 + a_2, \ldots, \sum_{0\leq k\leq n} a_k, \ldots,$$

Table 3.2 Operations on ordinary generating functions

proved by manipulating the order of summation:

$$\begin{aligned}A(z)B(z) &= \sum_{i\geq 0} a_i z^i \sum_{j\geq 0} b_j z^j \\ &= \sum_{i,j\geq 0} a_i b_j z^{i+j} \\ &= \sum_{n\geq 0}\Big(\sum_{0\leq k\leq n} a_k b_{n-k}\Big) z^n.\end{aligned}$$

Taking $B(z) = 1/(1-z)$ in this formula gives the partial sum operation. The convolution operation plays a special role in generating function manipulations, as we shall see. ■

Corollary *The OGF for the harmonic numbers is*

$$\sum_{N\geq 1} H_N z^N = \frac{1}{1-z}\ln\frac{1}{1-z}.$$

Proof. Start with $1/(1-z)$ (the OGF for $1, 1, \ldots, 1\ldots$), integrate (to get the OGF for $0, 1, 1/2, 1/3, \ldots, 1/k, \ldots$), and multiply by $1/(1-z)$. Similar examples may be found in relationships among entries in Table 3.1. ■

Readers unfamiliar with generating functions are encouraged to work the following exercises to gain a basic facility for applying these transformations.

Exercise 3.1 Find the OGFs for each of the following sequences:

$$\{2^{k+1}\}_{k\geq 0}, \qquad \{k2^{k+1}\}_{k\geq 0}, \qquad \{kH_k\}_{k\geq 1}, \qquad \{k^3\}_{k\geq 2}.$$

Exercise 3.2 Find $[z^N]$ for each of the following OGFs:

$$\frac{1}{(1-3z)^4}, \qquad (1-z)^2\ln\frac{1}{1-z}, \qquad \frac{1}{(1-2z^2)^2}.$$

Exercise 3.3 Differentiate the OGF for harmonic numbers to verify the last line of Table 3.1.

Exercise 3.4 Prove that

$$\sum_{1\leq k\leq N} H_k = (N+1)(H_{N+1} - 1).$$

Exercise 3.5 By factoring

$$\frac{z^M}{(1-z)^{M+1}}\ln\frac{1}{1-z}$$

in two different ways (and performing the associated convolutions), prove a general identity satisfied by the harmonic numbers and binomial coefficients.

Exercise 3.6 Find the OGF for

$$\Big\{\sum_{0<k<n} \frac{1}{k(n-k)}\Big\}_{n>1}.$$

Generalize your answer.

Exercise 3.7 Find the OGF for $\{H_k/k\}_{k\geq 1}$.

Exercise 3.8 Find $[z^N]$ for each of the following OGFs:

$$\frac{1}{1-z}\Big(\ln\frac{1}{1-z}\Big)^2 \qquad \text{and} \qquad \Big(\ln\frac{1}{1-z}\Big)^3.$$

Use the notation

$$H_N^{(2)} \equiv 1 + \frac{1}{2^2} + \frac{1}{3^2} + \ldots + \frac{1}{N^2}$$

for the "generalized harmonic numbers" that arise in these expansions.

Such elementary manipulations suffice to derive many of the sequences that we encounter in the analysis of algorithms, though more advanced tools are needed for many algorithms. From this point forward, it should become very clear that the analysis of algorithms revolves around the twin questions of determining an explicit formula for the generating function of a sequence and, conversely, determining an exact formula for members of the sequence from the generating-function representation. We will see many examples of this below and in Chapters 5 through 8.

Formally, we could use any kernel family of functions $w_k(z)$ to define a "generating function"

$$A(z) = \sum_{k\geq 0} a_k w_k(z)$$

that encapsulates a sequence $a_0, a_1, \ldots, a_k, \ldots$. Though we focus almost exclusively on the kernels z^k and $z^k/k!$ (see next section) in this book, other types do occasionally arise in the analysis of algorithms; we mention them briefly at the end of this chapter.

3.2 Exponential Generating Functions. Some sequences are more conveniently handled by a generating function that involves a normalizing factor:

Definition *Given a sequence $a_0, a_1, a_2, \ldots, a_k, \ldots$, the function*

$$A(z) = \sum_{k\geq 0} a_k \frac{z^k}{k!}$$

is called the exponential generating function (EGF) of the sequence. We use the notation $k![z^k]A(z)$ to refer to the coefficient a_k.

$1, 1, 1, 1, \ldots, 1, \ldots$	$e^z = \sum_{N\geq 0} \frac{z^N}{N!}$
$0, 1, 2, 3, 4, \ldots, N, \ldots$	$ze^z = \sum_{N\geq 1} \frac{z^N}{(N-1)!}$
$0, 0, 1, 3, 6, 10, \ldots, \binom{N}{2}, \ldots$	$\frac{1}{2}z^2e^z = \frac{1}{2}\sum_{N\geq 2} \frac{z^N}{(N-2)!}$
$0, \ldots, 0, 1, M+1, \ldots, \binom{N}{M}, \ldots$	$\frac{1}{M!}z^Me^z = \frac{1}{M!}\sum_{N\geq M} \frac{z^N}{(N-M)!}$
$1, 0, 1, 0, \ldots, 1, 0, \ldots$	$\frac{1}{2}(e^z + e^{-z}) = \sum_{N\geq 0} \frac{1+(-1)^N}{2}\frac{z^N}{N!}$
$1, c, c^2, c^3, \ldots, c^N, \ldots$	$e^{cz} = \sum_{N\geq 0} \frac{c^N z^N}{N!}$
$0, 1, \frac{1}{2}, \frac{1}{3}, \ldots, \frac{1}{N+1}, \ldots$	$\frac{e^z - 1}{z} = \sum_{N\geq 0} \frac{z^N}{(N+1)!}$
$1, 2, 6, 24, \ldots, N!, \ldots$	$\frac{1}{1-z} = \sum_{N\geq 0} \frac{N!z^N}{N!}$

Table 3.3 Elementary exponential generating functions

The EGF for $\{a_k\}$ is nothing more than the OGF for $\{a_k/k!\}$, but it arises in combinatorics and the analysis of algorithms for a specific and simple reason. Suppose that the coefficients a_k represent a count associated with a structure of k items. Suppose further that the k items are "labelled" so that each has a distinct identity. In some cases, the labelling is relevant (and EGFs are appropriate); in other cases it is not (and OGFs are appropriate). The factor of $k!$ accounts for all the arrangements of the labelled items that become indistinguishable if they are unlabelled. We will consider this in more detail in §3.9 when we look at the "symbolic method" for associating generating functions and combinatorial objects; for the moment, we offer this explanation simply as justification for considering properties of EGFs in detail. They are well studied because they arise in many other applications as well.

Table 3.3 gives a number of elementary exponential generating functions that we will be encountering later in the book, and Table 3.4 gives some of the basic manipulations on EGFs. Note that the shift left/right operations for EGFs are the same as the index multiply/divide operations for OGFs (see Table 3.2) and vice versa. As with OGFs, application of the basic operations from Table 3.4 on the basic functions in Table 3.3 yields a large fraction of the EGFs that arise in practice, and the reader is encouraged to work the exercises below to become familiar with these functions. Also as with OGFs, we can easily establish the validity of the basic operations:

Theorem 3.2 (*EGF operations*) *If two sequences* $a_0, a_1, \ldots, a_k, \ldots$ *and* $b_0, b_1, \ldots, b_k, \ldots$ *are represented by the EGFs* $A(z) = \sum_{k\geq 0} a_k z^k/k!$ *and* $B(z) = \sum_{k\geq 0} b_k z^k/k!$, *then the operations given in Table 3.4 produce EGFs that represent the indicated sequences. In particular,*

$$A(z) + B(z) \quad \textit{is the EGF for} \quad a_0 + b_0, a_1 + b_1, a_2 + b_2 \ldots$$

$$A'(z) \quad \textit{is the EGF for} \quad a_1, a_2, a_3 \ldots$$

$$zA(z) \quad \textit{is the EGF for} \quad 0, a_1, 2a_2, 3a_3, \ldots$$

$$A(z)B(z) \quad \textit{is the EGF for} \quad a_0b_0, a_0b_1 + a_1b_0, a_0b_2 + 2a_1b_1 + a_2b_0, \ldots$$

Proof. As for Theorem 3.1, these are elementary and can be verified by inspection with the possible exception of binomial convolution, which is

$$A(z) = \sum_{n\geq 0} a_n \frac{z^n}{n!} \qquad a_0, a_1, a_2, \ldots, a_n, \ldots,$$

$$B(z) = \sum_{n\geq 0} b_n \frac{z^n}{n!} \qquad b_0, b_1, b_2, \ldots, b_n, \ldots,$$

right shift (integration)

$$\int_0^z A(t)dt = \sum_{n\geq 1} a_{n-1} \frac{z^n}{n!} \qquad 0, a_0, a_1, \ldots, a_{n-1}, \ldots,$$

left shift (differentiation)

$$A'(z) = \sum_{n\geq 0} a_{n+1} \frac{z^n}{n!} \qquad a_1, a_2, a_3, \ldots, a_{n+1}, \ldots,$$

index multiply

$$zA(z) = \sum_{n\geq 0} n a_{n-1} \frac{z^n}{n!} \qquad 0, a_0, 2a_1, 3a, \ldots, na_{n-1}, \ldots,$$

index divide

$$(A(z) - A(0))/z = \sum_{n\geq 1} \frac{a_{n+1}}{n+1} \frac{z^n}{n!} \qquad a_1, \frac{a_2}{2}, \frac{a_3}{3} \ldots, \frac{a_{n+1}}{n+1}, \ldots,$$

addition

$$A(z) + B(z) = \sum_{n\geq 0} (a_n + b_n) \frac{z^n}{n!} \qquad a_0 + b_0, \ldots, a_n + b_n, \ldots,$$

difference

$$A'(z) - A(z) = \sum_{n\geq 0} (a_{n+1} - a_n) \frac{z^n}{n!} \qquad a_1 - a_0, a_2 - a_1, \ldots, a_{n+1} - a_n, \ldots,$$

binomial convolution

$$A(z)B(z) = \sum_{n\geq 0} \Big(\sum_{0\leq k\leq n} \binom{n}{k} a_k b_{n-k} \Big) \frac{z^n}{n!}$$

$$a_0 b_0, a_1 b_0 + a_0 b_1, \ldots, \sum_{0\leq k\leq n} \binom{n}{k} a_k b_{n-k}, \ldots,$$

binomial sum

$$e^z A(z) = \sum_{n\geq 0} \Big(\sum_{0\leq k\leq n} \binom{n}{k} a_k \Big) \frac{z^n}{n!}$$

$$a_0, a_0 + a_1, \ldots, \sum_{0\leq k\leq n} \binom{n}{k} a_k, \ldots,$$

Table 3.4 Operations on exponential generating functions

easily verified with OGF convolution:

$$A(z)B(z) = \sum_{n\geq 0} \sum_{0\leq k\leq n} \frac{a_k}{k!} \frac{b_{n-k}}{(n-k)!} z^n$$
$$= \sum_{n\geq 0} \sum_{0\leq k\leq n} \binom{n}{k} a_k b_{n-k} \frac{z^n}{n!}.$$

■

Exercise 3.9 Find the EGFs for each of the following sequences:

$$\{2^{k+1}\}_{k\geq 0}, \qquad \{k2^{k+1}\}_{k\geq 0}, \qquad \{k^3\}_{k\geq 2}.$$

Exercise 3.10 Find the EGFs for $1, 3, 5, 7, \ldots$ and $0, 2, 4, 6, \ldots$.

Exercise 3.11 Find $N![z^N]A(z)$ for each of the following EGFs:

$$A(z) = \frac{1}{1-z} \ln \frac{1}{1-z}, \qquad A(z) = \Bigl(\ln \frac{1}{1-z}\Bigr)^2, \qquad A(z) = e^{z+z^2}.$$

Exercise 3.12 Show that

$$N![z^N]e^z \int_0^z \frac{1-e^{-t}}{t} dt = H_N.$$

(*Hint*: Form a first-order ordinary differential equation for the EGF $H(z) = \sum_{N\geq 0} H_N z^N/N!$.)

It is not always clear whether an OGF or an EGF will lead to the most convenient solution to a problem: sometimes one will lead to a trivial solution and the other to difficult technical problems; other times either will work well. For many of the combinatorial and algorithmic problems that we encounter, the choice of whether to use OGFs or EGFs comes naturally from the structure of the problem. Moreover, interesting questions arise from an analytic standpoint: for example, can we automatically convert from the OGF for a sequence to the EGF for the same sequence, and vice versa? (Yes, by the Laplace transform: see Exercise 3.14.) In this book, we will consider many examples involving applications of both OGFs and EGFs.

Exercise 3.13 Given the EGF $A(z)$ for a sequence $\{a_k\}$, find the EGF for the sequence

$$\Big\{ \sum_{0 \le k \le N} N! \frac{a_k}{k!} \Big\}.$$

Exercise 3.14 Given the EGF $A(z)$ for a sequence $\{a_k\}$, show that the OGF for the sequence is given by

$$\int_0^\infty A(zt)e^{-t}dt,$$

if the integral exists. Check this for sequences that appear in both Table 3.1 and Table 3.3.

3.3 Generating Function Solution of Recurrences. Next, we examine the role that generating functions can play in the solution of recurrence relations, the second step in a classical approach to the analysis of algorithms: after a recurrence relationship describing some fundamental property of an algorithm is derived, generating functions can be used to solve the recurrence. Some readers may be familiar with this approach because of its widespread use and its basic and fundamental nature, though we will see later that it is often possible to avoid the recurrence and work with generating functions directly.

Generating functions provide a mechanical method for solving many recurrence relations. Given a recurrence describing some sequence $\{a_n\}_{n \ge 0}$, we can often develop a solution by carrying out the following steps:

- Multiply both sides of the recurrence by z^n and sum on n.
- Evaluate the sums to derive an equation satisfied by the OGF.
- Solve the equation to derive an explicit formula for the OGF.
- Express the OGF as a power series to get expressions for the coefficients (members of the original sequence).

The same method applies for EGFs, where we multiply by $z^n/n!$ and sum on n in the first step. Whether OGFs or EGFs are more convenient depends on the recurrence.

The most straightforward example of this method is its use in solving linear recurrences with constant coefficients (see Chapter 2).

Trivial linear recurrence. To solve the recurrence

$$a_n = a_{n-1} + 1 \qquad \text{for } n \ge 1 \text{ with } a_0 = 0$$

we first multiply by z^n and sum to get

$$\sum_{n\geq 1} a_n z^n = \sum_{n\geq 1} a_{n-1} z^n + \frac{z}{1-z}.$$

In terms of the generating function $A(z) = \sum_{n\geq 0} a_n z^n$, this equation says

$$A(z) = zA(z) + \frac{z}{1-z}$$

or $A(z) = z/(1-z)^2$, and $a_n = n$, as expected.

Simple exponential recurrence. To solve the recurrence

$$a_n = 2a_{n-1} + 1 \qquad \text{for } n \geq 1 \text{ with } a_0 = 1$$

we proceed as above to find that the generating function $A(z) = \sum_{n\geq 0} a_n z^n$ satisfies

$$A(z) - 1 = 2zA(z) + \frac{z}{1-z},$$

which simplifies to

$$A(z) = \frac{1}{(1-z)(1-2z)}.$$

From Table 3.1 we know that $1/(1-2z)$ is the generating function for the sequence $\{2^n\}$, and from Table 3.2 we know that multiplying by $1/(1-z)$ corresponds to taking partial sums:

$$a_n = \sum_{0\leq k\leq n} 2^k = 2^{n+1} - 1.$$

Partial fractions. An alternative method for finding the coefficients in the above problem that is instructive preparation for more difficult problems is to use the *partial fractions* expansion for $A(z)$. By factoring the denominator, the generating function can be expressed as the sum of two fractions

$$\frac{1}{(1-z)(1-2z)} = \frac{c_0}{1-2z} + \frac{c_1}{1-z}$$

where c_0 and c_1 are constants to be determined. Cross-multiplying, we see that these constants must satisfy the simultaneous equations

$$\begin{aligned} c_0 + c_1 &= 1 \\ -c_0 - 2c_1 &= 0 \end{aligned}$$

so $c_0 = 2$ and $c_1 = -1$. Therefore,

$$[z^n]\frac{1}{(1-z)(1-2z)} = [z^n]\Big(\frac{2}{1-2z} - \frac{1}{1-z}\Big) = 2^{n+1} - 1.$$

This technique can be applied whenever we have a polynomial in the denominator, and leads to a general method for solving high-order linear recurrences that we discuss below.

Fibonacci numbers. The generating function $F(z) = \sum_{k\geq 0} F_k z^k$ for the Fibonacci sequence

$$F_n = F_{n-1} + F_{n-2} \qquad \text{for } n > 1 \text{ with } F_0 = 0 \text{ and } F_1 = 1$$

satisfies

$$F(z) = zF(z) + z^2F(z) + z.$$

This implies that

$$F(z) = \frac{z}{1-z-z^2} = \frac{1}{\sqrt{5}}\Big(\frac{1}{1-\phi z} - \frac{1}{1-\widehat{\phi}z}\Big)$$

by partial fractions, since $1-z-z^2$ factors as $(1-z\phi)(1-z\widehat{\phi})$ where

$$\phi = \frac{1+\sqrt{5}}{2} \qquad \text{and} \qquad \widehat{\phi} = \frac{1-\sqrt{5}}{2}$$

are the reciprocals of the roots of $1-z-z^2$. Now the series expansion is straightforward from Table 3.4:

$$F_n = \frac{1}{\sqrt{5}}(\phi^n - \widehat{\phi}^n).$$

Of course, this strongly relates to the derivation given in Chapter 2. We examine this relationship in general terms next.

Exercise 3.15 Find the EGF for the Fibonacci numbers.

High-order linear recurrences. Generating functions make explicit the "factoring" process described in Chapter 2 to solve high-order recurrences with constant coefficients. Factoring the recurrence corresponds to factoring the polynomial that arises in the denominator of the generating function, which leads to a partial fraction expansion and an explicit solution. For example, the recurrence

$$a_n = 5a_{n-1} - 6a_{n-2} \qquad \text{for } n > 1 \text{ with } a_0 = 0 \text{ and } a_1 = 1$$

implies that the generating function $a(z) = \sum_{n\geq 0} a_n z^n$ is

$$a(z) = \frac{z}{1-5z+6z^2} = \frac{z}{(1-3z)(1-2z)} = \frac{1}{1-3z} - \frac{1}{1-2z}$$

so that we must have $a_n = 3^n - 2^n$.

Exercise 3.16 Use generating functions to solve the following recurrences:

$$a_n = -a_{n-1} + 6a_{n-2} \qquad \text{for } n > 1 \text{ with } a_0 = 0 \text{ and } a_1 = 1;$$
$$a_n = 11a_{n-2} - 6a_{n-3} \qquad \text{for } n > 2 \text{ with } a_0 = 0 \text{ and } a_1 = a_2 = 1;$$
$$a_n = 3a_{n-1} - 4a_{n-2} \qquad \text{for } n > 1 \text{ with } a_0 = 0 \text{ and } a_1 = 1;$$
$$a_n = a_{n-1} - a_{n-2} \qquad \text{for } n > 1 \text{ with } a_0 = 0 \text{ and } a_1 = 1.$$

In general, the explicit expression for the generating function is the ratio of two polynomials; then partial fraction expansion involving roots of the denominator polynomial leads to an expression in terms of powers of roots. A precise derivation along these lines can be used to obtain a proof of Theorem 2.2.

Theorem 3.3 (*OGFs for linear recurrences*) *If a_n satisfies the recurrence*

$$a_n = x_1 a_{n-1} + x_2 a_{n-2} + \ldots + x_t a_{n-t}$$

for $n \geq t$, then the generating function $a(z) = \sum_{n\geq 0} a_n z^n$ is a rational function $a(z) = f(z)/g(z)$, where the denominator polynomial is $g(z) = 1 - x_1 z - x_2 z^2 - \ldots - x_t z^t$ and the numerator polynomial is determined by the initial values $a_0, a_1, \ldots, a_{t-1}$.

Proof. The proof follows the general paradigm for solving recurrences described at the beginning of this section. Multiplying both sides of the recurrence by z^n and summing for $n \geq t$ yields

$$\sum_{n\geq t} a_n z^n = x_1 \sum_{n\geq t} a_{n-1} z^n + \cdots + x_t \sum_{n\geq t} a_{n-t} z^n.$$

The left-hand side evaluates to $a(z)$ minus the generating polynomial of the initial values; the first sum on the right evaluates to $za(z)$ minus a polynomial, and so forth. Thus $a(z)$ satisfies

$$a(z) - u_0(z) = \big(x_1 z a(z) - u_1(z)\big) + \ldots + \big(x_t z^t a(z) - u_t(z)\big),$$

where the polynomials $u_0(z), u_1(z), \ldots, u_t(z)$ are of degree at most $t-1$ with coefficients depending only on the initial values $a_0, a_1, \ldots, a_{t-1}$. This functional equation is linear.

Solving the equation for $a(z)$ gives the explicit form $a(z) = f(z)/g(z)$, where $g(z)$ has the form announced in the statement and

$$f(z) \equiv u_0(z) - u_1(z) - \ldots - u_t(z)$$

depends solely on the initial values of the recurrence and has degree less than t. ■

The general form immediately implies an alternate formulation for the dependence of $f(z)$ on the initial conditions, as follows. We have $f(z) = a(z)g(z)$ and we know that the degree of f is less than t. Therefore, we must have

$$f(z) = g(z) \sum_{0 \le n < t} a_n z^n \pmod{z^t}.$$

This gives a shortcut to computing the coefficients of $f(z)$, which provides a quick exact solution to many recurrences.

Simple example. To solve the recurrence

$$a_n = 2a_{n-1} + a_{n-2} - 2a_{n-3} \qquad \text{for } n > 2 \text{ with } a_0 = 0 \text{ and } a_1 = a_2 = 1$$

we first compute

$$g(z) = 1 - 2z - z^2 + 2z^3 = (1-z)(1+z)(1-2z)$$

then, using the initial conditions, write

$$\begin{aligned} f(z) &= (z + z^2)(1 - 2z - z^2 + 2z^3) \pmod{z^3} \\ &= (z - z^2) = z(1-z). \end{aligned}$$

This gives

$$a(z) = \frac{f(z)}{g(z)} = \frac{z}{(1+z)(1-2z)} = \frac{1}{3}\Big(\frac{1}{1-2z} - \frac{1}{1-z}\Big),$$

so that $a_n = \frac{1}{3}(2^n - (-1)^n)$.

Cancellation. In the above recurrence, the $1-z$ factor canceled, so there was no constant term in the solution. Consider the same recurrence with different initial conditions:

$$a_n = 2a_{n-1} + a_{n-2} - 2a_{n-3} \qquad \text{for } n > 2 \text{ with } a_0 = a_1 = a_2 = 1.$$

The function $g(z)$ is the same as above, but now we have

$$\begin{aligned} f(z) &= (1 + z + z^2)(1 - 2z - z^2 + 2z^3) \pmod{z^3} \\ &= (1 - z - 2z^2) = (1 - 2z)(1 + z). \end{aligned}$$

In this case, we have cancellation to a trivial solution: $a(z) = f(z)/g(z) = 1/(1-z)$ and $a_n = 1$ for all $n \geq 0$. The initial conditions can have drastic effects on the eventual growth rate of the solution by leading to cancellation of factors in this way.

We adopt the convention of factoring $g(z)$ in the form

$$g(z) = (1 - \beta_1 z) \cdot (1 - \beta_2 z) \cdots (1 - \beta_n z)$$

since it is slightly more natural in this context. Note that if a polynomial $g(z)$ satisfies $g(0) = 1$ (which is usual when $g(z)$ is derived from a recurrence as above), then the product of its roots is 1, and the $\beta_1, \beta_2, \ldots, \beta_n$ in the equation above are simply the inverses of the roots. If $q(z)$ is the "characteristic polynomial" of Theorem 2.2, we have $g(z) = z^t q(1/z)$, so the β's are the roots of the characteristic polynomial.

Complex roots. All the manipulations that we have been doing are valid for complex roots, as illustrated by the recurrence

$$a_n = 2a_{n-1} - a_{n-2} + 2a_{n-3} \qquad \text{for } n > 2 \text{ with } a_0 = 1,\ a_1 = 0, \text{ and } a_2 = -1.$$

This gives

$$g(z) = 1 - 2z + z^2 - 2z^3 = (1 + z^2)(1 - 2z)$$

and

$$f(z) = (1 - z^4)(1 - 2z) \pmod{z^4} = (1 - 2z),$$

so

$$a(z) = \frac{f(z)}{g(z)} = \frac{1}{1+z^2} = \frac{1}{2}\Big(\frac{1}{1-iz} - \frac{1}{1+iz}\Big),$$

and $a_n = \frac{1}{2}(i^n + (-i)^n)$. From this, it is easy to see that a_n is 0 for n odd, 1 when n is a multiple of 4, and -1 when n is even but not a multiple of 4 (this also follows directly from the form $a(z) = 1/(1+z^2)$). For the initial conditions $a_0 = 1$, $a_1 = 2$, and $a_2 = 3$, we get $f(z) = 1$, so the solution grows like 2^n, but with periodic varying terms caused by the complex roots.

Multiple roots. When multiple roots are involved, we finish the derivation with the expansions given on the second and third lines of Table 3.1. For example, the recurrence

$$a_n = 5a_{n-1} - 8a_{n-2} + 4a_{n-3} \qquad \text{for } n > 2 \text{ with } a_0 = 0,\ a_1 = 1, \text{ and } a_2 = 4$$

gives

$$g(z) = 1 - 5z + 8z^2 - 4z^3 = (1-z)(1-2z)^2$$

and

$$f(z) = (z + 4z^2)(1 - 5z + 8z^2 - 4z^3) \pmod{z^3} = z(1-z),$$

so $a(z) = z/(1-2z)^2$ and $a_n = n2^{n-1}$ from Table 3.1.

These examples illustrate a straightforward general method for developing exact solutions to linear recurrences:

- Derive $g(z)$ from the recurrence.
- Compute $f(z)$ from $g(z)$ and the initial conditions.
- Eliminate common factors in $f(z)/g(z)$.
- Use partial fractions to represent $f(z)/g(z)$ as a linear combination of terms of the form $(1-\beta z)^{-j}$.
- Expand each term in the partial fractions expansion, using

$$[z^n](1-\beta z)^{-j} = \binom{n+j-1}{j-1}\beta^n.$$

In essence, this process amounts to a constructive proof of Theorem 2.2.

Exercise 3.17 Solve the recurrence

$$a_n = 5a_{n-1} - 8a_{n-2} + 4a_{n-3} \qquad \text{for } n > 2 \text{ with } a_0 = 1,\ a_1 = 2, \text{ and } a_2 = 4.$$

Exercise 3.18 Solve the recurrence

$$a_n = 2a_{n-2} - a_{n-4} \qquad \text{for } n > 4 \text{ with } a_0 = a_1 = 0 \text{ and } a_2 = a_3 = 1.$$

Exercise 3.19 Solve the recurrence

$$a_n = 6a_{n-1} - 12a_{n-2} + 18a_{n-3} - 27a_{n-4} \quad \text{for } n > 4$$

with $a_0 = 0$ and $a_1 = a_2 = a_3 = 1$.

Exercise 3.20 Solve the recurrence

$$a_n = 3a_{n-1} - 3a_{n-2} + a_{n-3} \qquad \text{for } n > 2 \text{ with } a_0 = a_1 = 0 \text{ and } a_2 = 1.$$

Solve the same recurrence with the initial condition on a_1 changed to $a_1 = 1$.

Exercise 3.21 Solve the recurrence

$$a_n = -\sum_{1 \le k \le t} \binom{t}{k} (-1)^k a_{n-k} \qquad \text{for } n \ge t \text{ with } a_0 = \cdots = a_{t-2} = 0 \text{ and } a_{t-1} = 1.$$

Solving the Quicksort recurrence with an OGF. When coefficients in a recurrence are polynomials in the index n, then the implied relationship constraining the generating function is a differential equation. As an example, let us revisit the basic recurrence from Chapter 1 describing the number of comparisons used by Quicksort:

$$NC_N = N(N+1) + 2\sum_{1 \le k \le N} C_{k-1} \qquad \text{for } N \ge 1 \text{ with } C_0 = 0. \tag{1}$$

We define the generating function

$$C(z) = \sum_{N \ge 0} C_N z^N \tag{2}$$

and proceed as described above to get a functional equation that $C(z)$ must satisfy. First, multiply both sides of (1) by z^N and sum on N to get

$$\sum_{N \ge 1} NC_N z^N = \sum_{N \ge 1} N(N+1) z^N + 2 \sum_{N \ge 1} \sum_{1 \le k \le N} C_{k-1} z^N.$$

Now, we can evaluate each of these terms in a straightforward manner. The left-hand side is $zC'(z)$ (differentiate both sides of (2) and multiply by z) and the first term on the right is $2z/(1-z)^3$ (see Table 3.1). The remaining term, the double sum, is a partial sum convolution (see Table 3.2) that evaluates to $zC(z)/(1-z)$. Therefore, our recurrence relationship corresponds to a differential equation on the generating function

$$C'(z) = \frac{2}{(1-z)^3} + 2\frac{C(z)}{1-z}. \tag{3}$$

We obtain the solution to this differential equation by solving the corresponding homogeneous equation $\rho'(z) = 2\rho(z)/(1-z)$ to get an "integration factor" $\rho(z) = 1/(1-z)^2$. This gives

$$((1-z)^2C(z))' = (1-z)^2C'(z) - 2(1-z)C(z)$$
$$= (1-z)^2\Big(C'(z) - 2\frac{C(z)}{1-z}\Big) = \frac{2}{1-z}.$$

Integrating, we get the result

$$C(z) = \frac{2}{(1-z)^2}\ln\frac{1}{1-z}. \qquad (4)$$

Theorem 3.4 (*Quicksort OGF*) *The a erage number of comparisons used by Quicksort for a random permutation is gi en by*

$$C_N = [z^N]\frac{2}{(1-z)^2}\ln\frac{1}{1-z} = 2(N+1)(H_{N+1}-1).$$

Proof. The above discussion yields the explicit expression for the generating function, which completes the third step of the general procedure for solving recurrences with OGFs given at the beginning of §3.2. To extract coefficients, differentiate the generating function for the harmonic numbers. ■

This method for solving recurrences with OGFs, while quite general, certainly cannot be relied upon to give solutions for all recurrence relations: various examples from the end of Chapter 2 can serve testimony to that. For some problems, it may not be possible to evaluate the sums to a simple form; for others, an explicit formula for the generating function can be difficult to derive; and for others, the expansion back to power series can present the main obstacle. However, there are many recurrences that might seem at first glance to be intractable which we can in fact solve with generating functions.

Exercise 3.22 Use generating functions to solve the recurrence

$$na_n = (n-2)a_{n-1} + 2 \qquad \text{for } n > 1 \text{ with } a_1 = 1.$$

Exercise 3.23 [Greene and Knuth] Solve the recurrence

$$na_n = (n+t-1)a_{n-1} \qquad \text{for } n > 0 \text{ with } a_0 = 1.$$

Exercise 3.24 Solve the recurrence

$$a_n = n + 1 + \frac{t}{n}\sum_{1\le k\le n} a_{k-1} \qquad \text{for } n \ge 1 \text{ with } a_0 = 0$$

for $t = 2-\epsilon$ and $t = 2+\epsilon$, where ϵ is a small positive constant.

3.4 Expanding Generating Functions. Given an explicit functional form for a generating function, we would like a general mechanism for finding the associated sequence. This process is called "expanding" the generating function, as we take it from a compact functional form into an infinite series of terms. As we have seen in the preceding examples, we can handle many functions with algebraic manipulations involving the basic identities and transformations given in Tables 3.1–3.4. But where do the elementary expansions in Table 3.1 and Table 3.3 originate?

The *Taylor theorem* permits us to expand a function $f(z)$ given its derivatives at 0:

$$f(z) = f(0) + f'(0)z + \frac{f''(0)}{2!}z^2 + \frac{f'''(0)}{3!}z^3 + \frac{f''''(0)}{4!}z^4 + \ldots.$$

Thus, by calculating derivatives, we can, in principle, find the sequence associated a with given generating function.

Exponential sequence. Since all the derivatives of e^z are e^z, the easiest application of Taylor's theorem is the fundamental expansion

$$e^z = 1 + z + \frac{z^2}{2!} + \frac{z^3}{3!} + \frac{z^4}{4!} + \ldots.$$

Geometric sequence. From Table 3.1, we know that the generating function for the sequence $\{1, c, c^2, c^3, \ldots\}$ is $(1 - cz)^{-1}$. The kth derivative of $(1 - cz)^{-1}$ is $k!c^k(1 - cz)^{-k-1}$, which is simply $k!c^k$ when evaluated at $z = 0$, so Taylor's theorem verifies that the expansion of this function is given by

$$\frac{1}{1 - cz} = \sum_{k \geq 0} c^k z^k,$$

as stated in Table 3.1.

Binomial theorem. The kth derivative of the function $(1 + z)^x$ is

$$x(x-1)(x-2)\cdots(x-k+1)(1+z)^{x-k},$$

so by Taylor's theorem, we get a generalized version of the binomial theorem known as *Newton's formula*:

$$(1+z)^x = \sum_{k \geq 0} \binom{x}{k} z^k,$$

where the binomial coefficients are defined by

$$\binom{x}{k} \equiv x(x-1)(x-2)\cdots(x-k+1)/k!.$$

A particularly interesting case of this is

$$\frac{1}{\sqrt{1-4z}} = \sum_{k\geq 0}\binom{2k}{k}z^k,$$

which follows from the identity

$$\begin{aligned}\binom{-1/2}{k} &= \frac{-\frac{1}{2}(-\frac{1}{2}-1)(-\frac{1}{2}-2)\cdots(-\frac{1}{2}-k+1)}{k!}\\ &= \frac{(-1)^k}{2^k}\frac{1\cdot 3\cdot 5\cdots(2k-1)}{k!}\frac{2\cdot 4\cdot 6\cdots 2N}{2^k k!}\\ &= \frac{(-1)^k}{4^k}\binom{2k}{k}.\end{aligned}$$

An expansion closely related to this plays a central role in the analysis of algorithms, as we will see in §3.8 and Chapter 5.

Exercise 3.25 Use Taylor's theorem to find the expansions of the following functions:

$$\sin(z), \qquad 2^z, \qquad ze^z.$$

Exercise 3.26 Use Taylor's theorem to verify that the coefficients of the series expansion of $(1-az-bz^2)^{-1}$ satisfy a second-order linear recurrence with constant coefficients.

Exercise 3.27 Use Taylor's theorem to verify directly that

$$H(z) = \frac{1}{1-z}\ln\frac{1}{1-z}$$

is the generating function for the harmonic numbers.

Exercise 3.28 Find an expression for

$$[z^n]\frac{1}{\sqrt{1-z}}\ln\frac{1}{1-z}.$$

(*Hint*: Expand $(1-z)^{-\alpha}$ and differentiate with respect to α.)

Exercise 3.29 Find an expression for

$$[z^n]\Big(\frac{1}{1-z}\Big)^t \ln\frac{1}{1-z} \qquad \text{for integer } t > 0.$$

In principle, we can always compute generating function coefficients by direct application of Taylor's theorem, but the process can become too complex to be helpful. Most often, we expand a generating function by decomposing it into simpler parts for which expansions are known, as we have done for several examples above, including the use of convolutions to expand the generating functions for binomial coefficients and the harmonic numbers and the use of partial fraction decomposition to expand the generating function for the Fibonacci numbers. Indeed, this is the *method of choice*, and we will be using it extensively throughout this book. For specific classes of problems, other tools are available to aid in this process—for example the *Lagrange inversion theorem*, which we will examine in detail later in this chapter.

Moreover, for problems that do not seem amenable to expansion by decomposition, there exists something even better than a "general tool" for expanding generating functions to derive succinct representations for coefficients—a tool for directly deriving asymptotic estimates of coefficients, which allows us to ignore irrelevant detail. Though the general method involves complex analysis and is beyond the scope of this book, our use of partial fractions expansions for linear recurrences is based on the same intuition. For example, the partial fraction expansion of the Fibonacci numbers immediately implies that the generating function $F(z)$ does not converge when $z = 1/\phi$ or $z = 1/\widehat{\phi}$. But it turns out that these "singularities" completely determine the asymptotic growth of the coefficients F_N. In this case, we are able to verify by direct expansion that the coefficients grow as ϕ^N (to within a constant factor). It is possible to state general conditions under which coefficients grow in this way and general mechanisms for determining other growth rates. By analyzing singularities of generating functions, we are very often able to reach our goal of deriving accurate estimates of the quantities of interest without having to resort to detailed expansions. This topic is discussed in §4.10, and in detail in [3].

But there are a large number of sequences for which the generating functions are known and for which simple algebraic manipulations of the generating function can yield simple expressions for the quantities of interest. Basic generating functions for classic combinatorial sequences are discussed in further detail in this chapter, and Chapters 5 through 8 are devoted to building up a repertoire of familiar functions that arise in the analysis of combinatorial algorithms. We will proceed to discuss and consider detailed manipulations of these functions, secure in the knowledge that we have powerful tools available for getting the coefficients back, when necessary.

3.5 Transformations with Generating Functions. Generating functions succinctly represent infinite sequences. Often, their importance lies in the fact that simple manipulations on equations involving the generating function can lead to surprising relationships involving the underlying sequences that otherwise might be difficult to derive. Several basic examples of this follow.

Vandermonde's convolution. This identity relating binomial coefficients (see Chapter 2),

$$\sum_k \binom{r}{k}\binom{s}{N-k} = \binom{r+s}{N},$$

is trivial to derive as it is the convolution of coefficients that express the functional relation

$$(1+z)^r(1+z)^s = (1+z)^{r+s}.$$

Similar identities can be derived in abundance from more complicated convolutions.

Quicksort recurrence. Multiplying OGFs by $(1-z)$ corresponds to differencing the coefficients, as stated in Table 3.2, and as we saw in Chapter 1 (without remarking on it) in the Quicksort recurrence. Other transformations were involved to get the solution. Our point here is that these various manipulations are more easily done with the generating function representation than with the sequence representation. We will examine this in more detail later in this chapter.

Fibonacci numbers. The generating function for Fibonacci numbers can be written

$$F(z) = \frac{z}{1-y} \qquad \text{with } y = z + z^2.$$

Expanding this in terms of y, we have

$$F(z) = z\sum_{N\geq 0} y^N = z\sum_{N\geq 0}(z+z^2)^N$$
$$= \sum_{N\geq 0}\sum_k \binom{N}{k} z^{N+k+1}.$$

But F_N is simply the coefficient of z^N in this, so we must have

$$F_N = \sum_k \binom{N-k-1}{k},$$

a well-known relationship between Fibonacci numbers and diagonals in Pascal's triangle.

Binomial transform. If $a^n = (1-b)^n$ for all n, then, obviously, $b^n = (1-a)^n$. Surprisingly, this generalizes to arbitrary sequences: given two sequences $\{a_n\}$ and $\{b_n\}$ related according to the equation

$$a_n = \sum_k \binom{n}{k}(-1)^k b_k,$$

we know from Table 3.4 that the associated generating functions satisfy $B(-z) = e^z A(z)$. But then, of course, $A(-z) = e^z B(z)$, which implies that

$$b_n = \sum_k \binom{n}{k}(-1)^k a_k.$$

We will see more examples of such manipulations in ensuing chapters.

Exercise 3.30 Show that

$$\sum_k \binom{2k}{k}\binom{2N-2k}{N-k} = 4^N.$$

Exercise 3.31 What recurrence on $\{C_N\}$ corresponds to multiplying both sides of the differential equation (3) for the Quicksort generating function by $(1-z)^2$?

Exercise 3.32 Suppose that an OGF satisfies the differential equation

$$A'(z) = -A(z) + \frac{A(z)}{1-z}.$$

What recurrence does this correspond to? Multiply both sides by $(1-z)$ and set coefficients equal to derive a different recurrence, then solve that recurrence. Compare this path to the solution with the method of directly finding the OGF and expanding.

Exercise 3.33 What identity on binomial coefficients is implied by the convolution

$$(1+z)^r(1-z)^s = (1-z^2)^s(1+z)^{r-s}$$

where $r > s$?

Exercise 3.34 Prove that

$$\sum_{0\le k\le t}\binom{t-k}{r}\binom{k}{s} = \binom{t+1}{r+s+1}.$$

Exercise 3.35 Use generating functions to evaluate $\sum_{0\le k\le N} F_k$.

Exercise 3.36 Use generating functions to find a sum expression for $[z^n]\dfrac{z}{(1-e^z)}$.

Exercise 3.37 Use generating functions to find a sum expression for $[z^n]\dfrac{1}{(2-e^z)}$.

Exercise 3.38 [Dobinski, cf. Comtet] Prove that

$$n![z^n]e^{e^z-1} = e^{-1}\sum_{k\ge 0}\frac{k^n}{n!}.$$

Exercise 3.39 Prove the binomial transform identity using OGFs. Let $A(z)$ and $B(z)$ be related by

$$B(z) = \frac{1}{1-z}A\Bigl(\frac{z}{z-1}\Bigr),$$

then use the change of variable $z = y/(y-1)$.

Exercise 3.40 Prove the binomial transform identity directly, *without* using generating functions.

Exercise 3.41 [Faà di Bruno's formula, cf. Comtet] Let $f(z) = \sum_n f_n z^n$ and $g(z) = \sum_n g_n z^n$. Express $[z^n]f(g(z))$ using the multinomial theorem.

3.6 Functional Equations on Generating Functions. In the analysis of algorithms, recursion in an algorithm (or recurrence relationships in its analysis) very often leads to functional equations on the corresponding generating functions. We have seen some cases where we can find an explicit solution to the functional equation and then expand to find the coefficients. In other cases, we may be able to use the functional equation to determine the asymptotic behavior without ever finding an explicit form for the generating function, or to transform the problem to a similar form that can be more easily solved. We offer a few comments on the different types of functional equations in this section, along with some exercises and examples.

Linear. The generating function for the Fibonacci numbers is the prototypical example here:

$$f(z) = zf(z) + z^2 f(z) + z.$$

The linear equation leads to an explicit formula for the generating function, which perhaps can be expanded. But *linear* here just refers to the function itself appearing only in linear combinations—the coefficients and consequent formulae could be arbitrarily complex.

Nonlinear. More generally, it is typical to have a situation where the generating function can be shown to be equal to an arbitrary function of itself, not necessarily a linear function. Famous examples of this include the GF for the Catalan numbers, which is defined by the functional equation

$$f(z) = zf(z)^2 + 1$$

and the GF for trees, which satisfies the functional equation

$$f(z) = ze^{f(z)}.$$

The former is discussed in some detail below and the latter in Chapter 5. Depending on the nature of the nonlinear function, it may be possible to derive an explicit formula for the generating function algebraically. Later in the chapter, we will examine a general tool known as the Lagrange inversion theorem, which can also be used to extract coefficients in many such cases.

Differential. The equation might involve derivatives of the generating function. We have already seen an example of this with Quicksort,

$$f'(z) = \frac{2}{(1-z)^3} + 2\frac{f(z)}{1-z},$$

and will see a more detailed example below. Our ability to find an explicit formula for the generating function is of course directly related to our ability to solve the differential equation.

Compositional. In still other cases, the functional equation might involve linear or nonlinear functions on the *arguments* of the generating function of interest, as in the following examples from the analysis of algorithms:

$$f(z) = e^{z/2} f(z/2)$$

$$f(z) = z + f(z^2 + z^3).$$

The first is related to binary tries and radix-exchange sort (see Chapter 7), and the second counts 2–3 trees (see Chapter 5). Clearly, we could concoct arbitrarily complicated equations, and there is no assurance that solutions are readily available. Some general tools for attacking such equations are treated in [3].

These examples give some indication of what we can expect to encounter in the use of generating functions in the analysis of algorithms. We will be examining these and other functional equations on generating functions throughout the book. Often, such equations are a dividing line where detailed study of the algorithm leaves off and detailed application of analytic tools begins. However difficult the solution of the functional equation might appear, it is important to remember that we can use such equations to learn properties of the underlying sequence.

As with recurrences, the technique of *iteration*, simply applying the equation to itself successively, can often be useful in determining the nature of a generating function defined by a functional equation. For example, consider an EGF that satisfies the functional equation

$$f(z) = e^z f(z/2).$$

Then, provided that $f(0) = 1$, we must have

$$\begin{aligned} f(z) &= e^z e^{z/2} f(z/4) \\ &= e^z e^{z/2} e^{z/4} f(z/8) \\ &\;\vdots \\ &= e^{z+z/2+z/4+z/8+\dots} \\ &= e^{2z}. \end{aligned}$$

This proves that 2^n is the solution to the recurrence

$$f_n = \sum_k \binom{n}{k} \frac{f_k}{2^k} \qquad \text{for } n > 0 \text{ with } f_0 = 1.$$

Technically, we need to justify carrying out the iteration indefinitely, but the solution is easily verified from the original recurrence.

Exercise 3.42 Show that the coefficients f_n in the expansion

$$e^{z+z^2/2} = \sum_{n\geq 0} f_n \frac{z^n}{n!}$$

satisfy the second-order linear recurrence $f_n = f_{n-1} + (n-1)f_{n-2}$. (*Hint*: Find a differential equation satisfied by the function $f(z) = e^{z+z^2/2}$.)

Exercise 3.43 Solve

$$f(z) = e^{-z} f\Big(\frac{z}{2}\Big) + e^{2z} - 1$$

and, assuming that $f(z)$ is an EGF, derive the corresponding recurrence and solution.

Exercise 3.44 Find an explicit formula for the OGF of the sequence satisfying the divide-and-conquer recurrence

$$f_{2n} = f_{2n-1} + f_n \qquad \text{for } n > 1 \text{ with } f_0 = 0;$$

$$f_{2n+1} = f_{2n} \qquad \text{for } n > 0 \text{ with } f_1 = 1.$$

Exercise 3.45 Iterate the following functional equation to obtain an explicit formula for $f(z)$:

$$f(z) = 1 + zf\Big(\frac{z}{1+z}\Big).$$

Exercise 3.46 [Polya] Given $f(z)$ defined by the functional equation

$$f(z) = \frac{z}{1 - f(z^2)},$$

find explicit expressions for $a(z)$ and $b(z)$ with $f(z) = a(z)/b(z)$.

Exercise 3.47 Prove that there is only one power series of the form $f(z) = \sum_{n\geq 1} f_n z^n$ that satisfies $f(z) = \sin(f(z))$.

Exercise 3.48 Derive an underlying recurrence from the functional equation for 2–3 trees and use the recurrence to determine how many 2–3 trees of 100 nodes there are.

3.7 Solving the Quicksort Median-of-Three Recurrence with OGFs. As a detailed example of manipulating functional equations on generating functions, we revisit the recurrence given in §1.5 that describes the average number of comparisons taken by the median-of-three Quicksort. This recurrence would be difficult to handle without generating functions:

$$C_N = N + 1 + \sum_{1\leq k\leq N} \frac{(N-k)(k-1)}{\binom{N}{3}} (C_{k-1} + C_{N-k}) \qquad \text{for } N > 2$$

with $C_0 = C_1 = C_2 = 0$. We use $N+1$ as the number of comparisons required to partition N elements for convenience in the analysis. The actual cost depends on how the median is computed and other properties of the implementation, but it will be within a small additive constant of $N+1$. Also, the initial condition $C_2 = 0$ (and the implied $C_3 = 4$) is used for convenience in the analysis, though different costs are likely in actual implementations. As in §1.5, we can account for such details by taking linear combinations of the solution to this recurrence and other, similar, recurrences such as the one counting the number of partitioning stages (the same recurrence with cost 1 instead of $N+1$).

We follow through the standard steps for solving recurrences with generating functions. Multiplying by $N(N-1)(N-2)$ and removing the symmetry in the sum, we have

$$N(N-1)(N-2)C_N = (N+1)N(N-1)(N-2) + 12\sum_{1\le k\le N}(N-k)(k-1)C_{k-1}.$$

Then, multiplying both sides by z^{N-3} and summing on N eventually leads to the differential equation:

$$C'''(z) = \frac{24}{(1-z)^5} + 12\frac{C'(z)}{(1-z)^2}. \qquad (5)$$

One cannot always hope to find explicit solutions for high-order differential equations, but this one is in fact of a type that can be solved explicitly. First, multiply both sides by $(1-z)^3$ to get

$$(1-z)^3C'''(z) = 12(1-z)C'(z) + \frac{24}{(1-z)^2}. \qquad (6)$$

Now, in this equation the degree equals the order of each term. Such a differential equation is known in the theory of ordinary differential equations as an *Euler equation*. We can decompose it by rewriting it in terms of an operator that both multiplies and differentiates. In this case, we define the operator

$$\Psi C(z) \equiv (1-z)\frac{d}{dz}C(z),$$

which allows us to rewrite (6) as

$$\Psi(\Psi+1)(\Psi+2)C(z) = 12\Psi C(z) + \frac{24}{(1-z)^2}.$$

Collecting all the terms involving Ψ into one polynomial and factoring, we have

$$\Psi(\Psi+5)(\Psi-2)C(z) = \frac{24}{(1-z)^2}.$$

The implication of this equation is that we can solve for $C(z)$ by successively solving three first-order differential equations:

$$\Psi U(z) = \frac{24}{(1-z)^2} \qquad \text{or} \qquad U'(z) = \frac{24}{(1-z)^3},$$

$$(\Psi+5)T(z) = U(z) \qquad \text{or} \qquad T'(z) = -5\frac{T(z)}{1-z} + \frac{U(z)}{1-z},$$

$$(\Psi-2)C(z) = T(z) \qquad \text{or} \qquad C'(z) = 2\frac{C(z)}{1-z} + \frac{T(z)}{1-z}.$$

Solving these first-order differential equations exactly as for the simpler case given above, we arrive at the solution.

Theorem 3.5 (*Median-of-three Quicksort*) *The a erage number of comparisons used by the median-of-three Quicksort for a random permutation is gi en by*

$$C_N = \frac{12}{7}(N+1)(H_{N+1} - \frac{23}{14}) \qquad \textit{for } N \geq 6.$$

Proof. Continuing the discussion above, we solve the differential equations to get the result

$$U(z) = \frac{12}{(1-z)^2} - 12;$$

$$T(z) = \frac{12}{7}\frac{1}{(1-z)^2} - \frac{12}{5} + \frac{24}{35}(1-z)^5;$$

$$C(z) = \frac{12}{7}\frac{1}{(1-z)^2}\ln\frac{1}{1-z} - \frac{54}{49}\frac{1}{(1-z)^2} + \frac{6}{5} - \frac{24}{245}(1-z)^5.$$

Expanding this expression for $C(z)$ (ignoring the last term) gives the result (see the exercises in §3.1). The leading term in the OGF differs from the OGF for standard Quicksort only by a constant factor. ∎

We can translate the decomposition into $U(z)$ and $T(z)$ into recurrences on the corresponding sequences. Consider the generating functions $U(z) = \sum U_N z^N$ and $T(z) = \sum T_N z^N$. In this case, manipulations on generating functions do correspond to manipulations on recurrences, but the tools used are more generally applicable and somewhat easier to discover and apply than would be a direct solution of the recurrence. Furthermore, the solution with generating functions can be used in the situation when a larger sample is used. Further details may be found in [8] or [12].

Besides serving as a practical example of the use of generating functions, this rather detailed example illustrates how precise mathematical statements about performance characteristics of interest can be used to help choose proper values for controlling parameters of algorithms (in this case, the size of the sample). For instance, the above analysis shows that we save about 14% of the cost of comparisons by using the median-of-three variant for Quicksort, and a more detailed analysis, taking into account the extra costs (primarily, the extra exchanges required because the partitioning element is nearer the middle), shows that bigger samples lead to marginal further improvements.

Exercise 3.49 Show that $(1-z)^t C^{(t)}(z) = \Psi(\Psi+1)\ldots(\Psi+t+1)C(z)$.

Exercise 3.50 Find the average number of exchanges used by median-of-three Quicksort.

Exercise 3.51 Find the number of comparisons and exchanges used, on the average, by Quicksort when modified to use the median of *fi e* elements for partitioning.

Exercise 3.52 [Euler] Discuss the solution of the differential equation

$$\sum_{0\le j\le r} (1-z)^{r-j} \frac{d^j}{dz^j} f(z) = 0$$

and the inhomogeneous version where the right-hand side is of the form $(1-z)^\alpha$.

Exercise 3.53 [van Emden, cf. Knuth] Show that, when the median of a sample of $(2t+1)$ elements is used for partitioning, the number of comparisons used by Quicksort is

$$\frac{1}{H_{2t+2} - H_{t+1}} N \ln N + O(N).$$

3.8 Counting with Generating Functions. Above, we have concentrated on describing generating functions as analytic tools for solving recurrence relationships. This is only part of their significance—they also provide

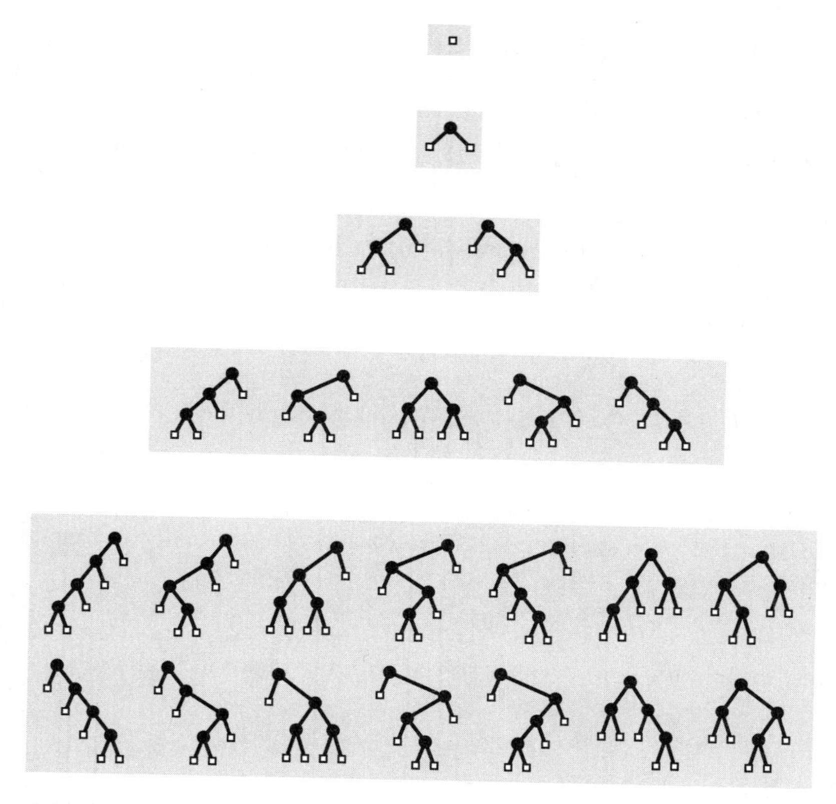

Figure 3.1 All binary trees with 1, 2, 3, 4, and 5 external nodes

a way to count combinatorial objects systematically. The "combinatorial objects" may be data structures being operated upon by algorithms, so this process plays a fundamental role in the analysis of algorithms as well.

Our first example is a classical combinatorial problem that also corresponds to a fundamental data structure that will be considered in Chapter 5 and in several other places in the book. A *binary tree* is a structure defined recursively to be either a single *external node* or an *internal node* that is connected to two binary trees, a *left subtree* and a *right subtree*. Figure 3.1 shows the binary trees with five or fewer nodes. Binary trees appear in many problems in combinatorics and the analysis of algorithms: for example, if internal nodes correspond to two-argument arithmetic operators and external nodes correspond to variables, then binary trees correspond to arithmetic expressions. The question at hand is, how many binary trees are there with N external nodes?

Counting binary trees. One way to proceed is to define a recurrence. Let T_N be the number of binary trees with $N+1$ external nodes. From Figure 3.1 we know that $T_0 = 1$, $T_1 = 1$, $T_2 = 2$, $T_3 = 5$, and $T_4 = 14$. Now, we can derive a recurrence from the recursive definition: if the left subtree in a binary tree with $N+1$ external nodes has k external nodes (there are T_{k-1} different such trees), then the right subtree must have $N-k+1$ external nodes (there are T_{N-k} possibilities), so T_N must satisfy

$$T_N = \sum_{1 \le k \le N} T_{k-1} T_{N-k} \qquad \text{for } N > 0 \text{ with } T_0 = 1.$$

This is a simple convolution: multiplying by z^N and summing on N, we find that the corresponding OGF must satisfy the nonlinear functional equation

$$T(z) = zT(z)^2 + 1.$$

This formula for $T(z)$ is easily solved with the quadratic equation:

$$zT(z) = \frac{1}{2}(1 \pm \sqrt{1-4z}).$$

To get equality when $z = 0$, we take the solution with a minus sign.

Theorem 3.6 (*OGF for binary trees*) *The number of binary trees with $N+1$ external nodes is given by the Catalan numbers:*

$$T_N = [z^{N+1}]\frac{1-\sqrt{1-4z}}{2} = \frac{1}{N+1}\binom{2N}{N}.$$

Proof. The explicit representation of the OGF is derived above. To extract coefficients, use the binomial theorem with exponent $\frac{1}{2}$ (Newton's formula):

$$zT(z) = -\frac{1}{2}\sum_{N \ge 1}\binom{\frac{1}{2}}{N}(-4z)^N.$$

Setting coefficients equal gives

$$\begin{aligned}T_N &= -\frac{1}{2}\binom{\frac{1}{2}}{N+1}(-4)^{N+1}\\ &= -\frac{1}{2}\frac{\frac{1}{2}(\frac{1}{2}-1)(\frac{1}{2}-2)\ldots(\frac{1}{2}-N)(-4)^{N+1}}{(N+1)!}\\ &= \frac{1\cdot 3\cdot 5\cdots(2N-1)\cdot 2^N}{(N+1)!}\\ &= \frac{1}{N+1}\frac{1\cdot 3\cdot 5\cdots(2N-1)}{N!}\frac{2\cdot 4\cdot 6\cdots 2N}{1\cdot 2\cdot 3\cdots N}\\ &= \frac{1}{N+1}\binom{2N}{N}.\end{aligned}$$

■

As we will see in Chapter 5, every binary tree has exactly one more external node than internal node, so the Catalan numbers T_N also count the binary trees with N internal nodes. In the next chapter, we will see that the approximate value is $T_N \approx 4^N/N\sqrt{\pi N}$.

Counting binary trees (direct). There is a simpler way to determine the explicit expression for the generating function above, that gives more insight into the intrinsic utility of generating functions for counting. We define $\mathcal{T}$ to be the set of all binary trees, and adopt the notation $|t|$ to represent, for $t \in \mathcal{T}$, the number of internal nodes in t. Then we have the following derivation:

$$\begin{aligned}T(z) &= \sum_{t\in\mathcal{T}} z^{|t|}\\ &= 1 + \sum_{t_L\in\mathcal{T}}\sum_{t_R\in\mathcal{T}} z^{|t_L|+|t_R|+1}\\ &= 1 + zT(z)^2\end{aligned}$$

The first line is an alternate way to express $T(z)$ from its definition. Each tree with exactly k external nodes contributes exactly 1 to the coefficient of z^k, so the coefficient of z^k in the sum "counts" the number of trees with k internal nodes. The second line follows from the recursive definition of binary trees: either a binary tree has no internal nodes (which accounts for the 1), or it can be decomposed into two independent binary trees whose internal nodes comprise the internal nodes of the original tree, plus one for the root. The third line follows because the index variables t_L and t_R are independent. Readers are advised to study this fundamental example carefully—we will be seeing many other similar examples throughout the book.

Exercise 3.54 Modify the above derivation to derive directly the generating function for the number of binary trees with N external nodes.

Changing a dollar (Polya). A classical example of counting with generating functions, due to Polya, is to answer the following question: "How many ways are there to change a dollar, using pennies, nickels, dimes, quarters, and fifty-cent coins?" Arguing as in the direct counting method for binary trees, we find that the generating function is given by

$$D(z) = \sum_{p,n,d,q,f\geq 0} z^{p+5n+10d+25q+50f}.$$

The indices of summation p, n, d, etc., are the number of pennies, nickels, dimes, etc., used. Each configuration of coins that adds up to k cents clearly contributes exactly 1 to the coefficient of z^k, so this is the desired generating function. But the indices of summation are all independent in this expression for $D(z)$, so we have

$$\begin{aligned} D(z) &= \sum_p z^p \sum_n z^{5n} \sum_d z^{10d} \sum_q z^{25q} \sum_f z^{50f} \\ &= \frac{1}{(1-z)(1-z^5)(1-z^{10})(1-z^{25})(1-z^{50})}. \end{aligned}$$

By setting up the corresponding recurrence, or by using a computer algebra system, we find that $[z^{100}]D(z) = 292$.

Exercise 3.55 Discuss the form of an expression for $[z^N]D(z)$.

Exercise 3.56 Write an efficient computer program that can compute $[z^N]D(z)$, given N.

Exercise 3.57 Show that the generating function for the number of ways to express N as a linear combination (with integer coefficients) of powers of 2 is

$$\prod_{k\geq 1} \frac{1}{1-z^{2^k}}.$$

Exercise 3.58 [Euler] Show that

$$\frac{1}{1-z} = (1+z)(1+z^2)(1+z^4)(1+z^8)\cdots.$$

Give a closed form for the product of the first t factors. This identity is sometimes called the "computer scientist's identity." Why?

Exercise 3.59 Generalize the previous exercise to base 3.

Exercise 3.60 Express $[z^N](1-z)(1-z^2)(1-z^4)(1-z^8)\cdots$ in terms of the binary representation of N.

Binomial distribution. How many binary sequences of length N have exactly k bits that are 1 (and $N-k$ bits that are 0)? Let $\mathcal{B}_N$ denote the set of all binary sequences of length N and $\mathcal{B}_{Nk}$ denote the set of all binary sequences of length N with the property that k of the bits are 1. Now we consider the generating function for the quantity sought:

$$B_N(z) = \sum_k |\mathcal{B}_{Nk}| z^k.$$

But we can note that each binary string b in $\mathcal{B}_N$ with exactly k 1s contributes exactly 1 to the coefficient of z^k and rewrite the generating function so that it "counts" each string:

$$B_N(z) \equiv \sum_{b \in \mathcal{B}_N} z^{\{\#\text{ of 1 bits in } b\}} = \sum_{b \in \mathcal{B}_{Nk}} z^k \left(= \sum_k |\mathcal{B}_{Nk}| z^k \right).$$

Now the set of all strings of N bits with k 1s can be formed by taking the union of the set of all strings with $N-1$ bits and k 1s (adding a 0 to the beginning of each string) and the set of all strings with $N-1$ bits and $k-1$ 1s (adding a 1 to the beginning of each string). Therefore,

$$\begin{aligned} B_N(z) &= \sum_{b \in \mathcal{B}_{(N-1)k}} z^k + \sum_{b \in \mathcal{B}_{(N-1)(k-1)}} z^k \\ &= B_{N-1}(z) + zB_{N-1}(z) \end{aligned}$$

so $B_N(z) = (1+z)^N$. Expanding this function with the binomial theorem yields the expected answer $|\mathcal{B}_{Nk}| = \binom{N}{k}$.

To summarize informally, we can use the following method to "count" with generating functions:

- Write down a general expression for the GF involving a sum indexed over the combinatorial objects to be counted.
- Decompose the sum in a manner corresponding to the structure of the objects, to derive an explicit formula for the GF.
- Express the GF as a power series to get expressions for the coefficients.

As we saw when introducing generating functions for the problem of counting binary trees at the beginning of the previous section, an alternative approach is to use the objects' structure to derive a recurrence, then use GFs to solve the recurrence. For simple examples, there is little reason to choose one method over the other, but for more complicated problems, the direct method just sketched can avoid tedious calculations that sometimes arise with recurrences. We will be seeing many examples of this later in the book. More important, this leads to a powerful general approach. In the next section, we introduce a framework within which the first steps of this procedure are almost automatic. The last step, extracting coefficients from the explicit expression for the generating function, is of course the same as for solving recurrences.

3.9 The Symbolic Method. The functional equation for binary trees is quite simple, and the question arises whether an even more direct derivation is available. Indeed, the similarity between the recursive definition of trees and the quadratic equation of the OGF is striking. In this section we show this similarity to be not coincidental, but essential: we can interpret

$$T(z) = 1 + zT(z)^2$$

as meaning "a binary tree consists either of an empty tree or of a node and two binary trees."

The approach that we use for this has two primary features: first, it is symbolic, using only a few algebraic rules to manipulate symbolic information. Some authors emphasize this by actually using symbolic diagrams rather than variables like z in the generating formulae. Second, it directly mirrors the way in which we define the structure. We generate the structures, as opposed to dissecting them for analysis.

Unlabelled objects. When counting with generating functions as in the previous section, we are considering classes of combinatorial objects, with a notion of "size" defined for each object. For a class $\mathcal{A}$, we denote the number of members of the class of size n by a_n. Then we are interested in the OGF

$$A(z) = \sum_{n\geq 0} a_n z^n = \sum_{a\in\mathcal{A}} z^{|a|}.$$

Given two classes $\mathcal{A}$ and $\mathcal{B}$ of combinatorial objects, we can combine them with a "disjoint union" operation $\mathcal{A} + \mathcal{B}$ that gives the class consisting of disjoint copies of the members of $\mathcal{A}$ and $\mathcal{B}$, and by a "Cartesian product" operation $\mathcal{A} \times \mathcal{B}$ that gives the class of ordered pairs of objects, one from $\mathcal{A}$ and one from $\mathcal{B}$. The following theorem provides a simple correspondence between these operations on pairs of classes of combinatorial objects and their associated generating functions. These can be used to derive functional relationships on generating functions directly from constructive definitions of the objects.

Theorem 3.7 (*OGFs, symbolic method*) *Let $\mathcal{A}$ and $\mathcal{B}$ be classes of combinatorial objects. If $A(z)$ is the OGF that enumerates $\mathcal{A}$ and $B(z)$ is the OGF that enumerates $\mathcal{B}$, then:*

$A(z) + B(z)$ *is the OGF that enumerates $\mathcal{A} + \mathcal{B}$*

$A(z)B(z)$ *is the OGF that enumerates $\mathcal{A} \times \mathcal{B}$*

$\dfrac{1}{1 - A(z)}$ *is the OGF that enumerates sequences of objects from $\mathcal{A}$.*

Proof. The first part of the proof is trivial. If a_n is the number of objects of size n in $\mathcal{A}$ and b_n is the number of objects of size n in $\mathcal{B}$, then $a_n + b_n$ is the number of objects of size n in $\mathcal{A} + \mathcal{B}$.

To prove the second part, note that, for every k from 0 to n, we can pair any of the a_k objects of size k from $\mathcal{A}$ with any of the b_{n-k} objects of size $n - k$ from $\mathcal{B}$ to get an object of size n in in $\mathcal{A} \times \mathcal{B}$. Thus, the number of objects of size n in $\mathcal{A} \times \mathcal{B}$ is

$$\sum_{0 \le k \le n} a_k b_{n-k},$$

a simple convolution that implies the stated result. Alternatively,

$$\sum_{\gamma \in \mathcal{A} \times \mathcal{B}} z^{|\gamma|} = \sum_{\alpha \in \mathcal{A}} \sum_{\beta \in \mathcal{B}} z^{|\alpha| + |\beta|} = A(z)B(z).$$

The result for sequences follows from the representation

$$\epsilon + \mathcal{A} + \mathcal{A}^2 + \mathcal{A}^3 + \mathcal{A}^4 + \ldots$$

of the class of sequences of objects from $\mathcal{A}$, where ϵ denotes the empty sequence. From the first two parts of the theorem, the generating function that enumerates this class is

$$1 + A(z) + A(z)^2 + A(z)^3 + A(z)^4 + \ldots = \frac{1}{1 - A(z)}. \qquad \blacksquare$$

Exercise 3.61 Give a proof of the second part of Theorem 3.7 using the combinatorial form of the OGFs, as in the "direct" derivation for binary trees given above.

For a simple example of this, let $\mathcal{A}$ be the class consisting of the null object ϵ of size zero and $\mathcal{B}$ be the class comprised of two objects of size one: $\{0,1\}$. Then $A(z) = 1$, $B(z) = 2z$, and the OGF for the combinatorial class $\{\epsilon, 0, 1\}$ is $1 + 2z$. Note that ϵ, the null object, with OGF 1, is quite different from ϕ, the empty class, with OGF 0. Now let $\mathcal{B}$ be the set of all binary strings. A binary string is either empty or corresponds precisely to an ordered pair consisting of a 0 or a 1 followed by a binary string. Symbolically,

$$\mathcal{B} = \epsilon + \{0,1\} \times \mathcal{B}.$$

Theorem 3.7 allows us to translate directly from this symbolic form to a functional equation satisfied by the generating function. We have

$$B(z) = 1 + 2zB(z),$$

so $B(z) = 1/(1-2z)$ and $B_N = 2^N$, as expected. Alternatively, we may view $\mathcal{B}$ as being formed of sequences over the binary alphabet $\{0,1\}$ whose OGF is simply $2z$, so that $B(z) = 1/(1-2z)$ by the sequence rule of Theorem 3.7.

A more interesting, but similar example is to consider binary strings with no two consecutive 0 bits. Such strings are either ϵ, a single 0, or 1 or 01 followed by a string with no two consecutive 0 bits. Symbolically,

$$\mathcal{G} = \epsilon + \{0\} + \{1, 01\} \times \mathcal{G}.$$

Again, Theorem 3.7 allows us to translate this immediately into a formula for the generating function $G(z)$ that enumerates such strings:

$$G(z) = 1 + z + (z + z^2)G(z).$$

Thus we have $G(z) = (1+z)/(1-z-z^2)$, which leads directly to the result that the number of strings of length N with no two consecutive 0 bits is $F_N + F_{N+1} = F_{N+2}$, a Fibonacci number.

Still another way to look at binary strings is to define the number of 1 bits as the size parameter, so that we can interpret $1 + z$ as the OGF for the class $\{0,1\}$. Then $(1+z)^2$ is the OGF for the class $\{00, 01, 10, 11\}$, and so on, and $(1+z)^N$ is the OGF for the number of 1 bits in the binary strings of length N.

Returning to binary trees, we have the symbolic formula

$$\mathcal{T} = \{\square\} + \{\bullet\} \times \mathcal{T} \times \mathcal{T}.$$

To count internal nodes, we translate $\{\square\}$ to 1 and $\{\bullet\}$ to z to get

$$T(z) = 1 + zT(z)^2,$$

the functional equation defining the Catalan numbers that we have derived. As we will see in Chapter 5, the simplicity of the symbolic approach in studying properties of various types of trees is compelling, especially by comparison with analyses using recurrences.

Theorem 3.7 is called a "translation theorem" because it gives a direct translation from symbolic formulae defining structures to generating functions enumerating them. There are a number of other operations that we use to build combinatorial structures besides the *union*, *Cartesian product*, and *sequence* operations corresponding to Theorem 3.7. Examples include *set of* or *multiset of*. We will see more examples of these in Chapter 5, and they are covered thoroughly in [3].

Exercise 3.62 Let $\mathcal{B}$ be defined as the collection of all finite subsets of $\mathcal{A}$. If $A(z)$ and $B(z)$ are the OGFs of $\mathcal{A}$ and $\mathcal{B}$, show that

$$B(z) = \prod_{n\geq 1}(1+z^n)^{A_n} = \exp\Big(A(z) - \frac{1}{2}A(z^2) + \frac{1}{3}A(z^3) - \ldots\Big).$$

Exercise 3.63 Let $\mathcal{B}$ be defined as the collection of all finite multisets of $\mathcal{A}$ (subsets with repetitions allowed). If $A(z)$ and $B(z)$ are the OGFs of $\mathcal{A}$ and $\mathcal{B}$, show that

$$B(z) = \prod_{n\geq 1}\frac{1}{(1-z^n)^{A_n}} = \exp\Big(A(z) + \frac{1}{2}A(z^2) + \frac{1}{3}A(z^3) + \ldots\Big).$$

Labelled objects. A primary feature of the preceding discussion is that the individual items from which the combinatorial objects are assembled are indistinguishable. An alternative paradigm is to assume that the individual items *are* distinguishable—that they are *labelled* and that, therefore, the order in which items appear when assembled to make combinatorial objects is significant. Labelled objects are normally enumerated by exponential generating functions. We will illustrate basic principles with a simple example here, then we will study labelled objects in detail in Chapters 5 and 6.

To be specific, if a combinatorial structure consists of N atomic items (sometimes called "atoms"), we consider their labels to be the integers 1 to N. Objects where the labels are in different order in the structure are considered to be different.

Above, we described ways to assemble unlabelled structures by means of operations like "sum" and "Cartesian product." Here, we are going to define analogous constructions suitable for labelled objects. The primary difference is that, when two objects are combined, it is necessary to relabel in a consistent manner so that only the labels 1 to N appear if the resulting object has size N. In particular, this makes the "product" operation for combinatorial classes more complicated, but actually we have translation theorems that are quite similar to Theorem 3.7.

Cycles and permutations. The simplest labelled structure is the *permutation*, which we have already referred to in the analysis of sorting algorithms. A permutation is a sequential arrangement of labelled items. For example, we write `2 1 3` to represent the sequential arrangement where the item with label `2` is first, the item with label `1` is second, and the item with label `3` is third. There are $N!$ different sequential arrangements of N labelled items, so the EGF for permutations is

$$\sum_{p\in\mathcal{P}}\frac{z^{|p|}}{|p|!}=\sum_{n\geq 0}N!\frac{z^N}{N!}=\frac{1}{1-z}.$$

As a more instructive example, we will consider the combinatorial class consisting of "sets of cycles" of labelled items. This example seems somewhat more abstract than the bitstrings example above, but it is actually nothing more than another way of looking at permutations. We will see in Chapter 6 that cycles and permutations are directly relevant to the analysis of a number of fundamental algorithms, and the approach that we use for analysis extends to help solve problems that would otherwise be quite difficult to solve.

A labelled *cycle* is an arrangement of labelled items into a cyclic order. For example, we write `(1 2 3)` to represent a cyclic order where the item with label `2` follows the item with label `1`, the item with label `3` follows the item with label `2`, *and* the item with label `1` follows the item with label `3`. Thus, `(1 2 3)` represents the same structured object as `(2 3 1)`, but is *not* the same as `(2 1 3)`.

Exercise 3.64 Prove that the number of labelled cycles of n items is $(n-1)!$.

A *set* of cycles is simply a collection of such objects, with the order among the objects not significant. We are interested in knowing how many sets of cycles of N items there are (and various other properties, as we will see in Chapter 6). Table 3.5 enumerates all the sets of cycles for $N = 2, 3, 4$.

As with unlabelled objects such as trees, we need ways to combine classes of labelled objects. The "disjoint union" operation is essentially the same, but the "product" operation involves relabelling. An example will help to make this clear: suppose that we want to make a structured two-cycle object from the cycles `(1)` and `(1 3 2)`. The simplest structure is a sequential arrangement, a cycle with one item followed by a cycle with three items. The result has four items, and so needs the labels 1 through 4. There are four different ways to do so in a "consistent" manner that preserves order among the labels in the constituent cycles:

```
(1) (2 4 3)     (2) (1 4 3)     (3) (1 4 2)     (4) (1 3 2)
```

The singleton cycle can be labelled with one of the four possible labels—for each choice, the 3-cycle can be labelled in just one way with the remain-

```
(1)(2)      (1)(2)(3)     (1)(2)(3)(4)     (1)(2) (3 4)
 (1 2)      (1) (2 3)      (1) (2 3 4)     (1)(3) (2 4)
            (2) (1 3)      (2) (1 3 4)     (1)(4) (2 3)
            (3) (1 2)      (3) (1 2 4)     (2)(3) (1 4)
             (1 2 3)       (4) (1 2 3)     (2)(4) (1 3)
             (1 3 2)       (1) (2 4 3)     (3)(4) (1 2)
                           (2) (1 4 3)      (1 2 3 4)
                           (3) (1 4 2)      (1 2 4 3)
                           (4) (1 3 2)      (1 3 2 4)
                           (1 2) (3 4)      (1 3 4 2)
                           (1 3) (2 4)      (1 4 2 3)
                           (1 4) (2 3)      (1 4 3 2)
```

Table 3.5 All labelled sets of cycles of items ($n = 2, 3, 4$)

ing labels. Similarly, there are six different ways to make a sequential arrangement of two labelled cycles from two copies of `(1 2)`:

```
(1 2) (3 4)     (1 3) (2 4)     (1 4) (2 3)
(2 3) (1 4)     (2 4) (1 3)     (3 4) (1 2)
```

Generalizing this leads to a "product" operation for two classes $\mathcal{A}$ and $\mathcal{B}$ of labelled objects $\mathcal{A} \star \mathcal{B}$ that gives the class of ordered pairs of objects, one from $\mathcal{A}$ and one from $\mathcal{B}$ *relabelled in all consistent ways*.

Next, consider building structured objects by forming *sets* of objects. In the example above, when two 2-cycles were combined into a two-cycle sequential arrangement, each set of two labelled cycles appeared twice in the enumeration, because the order of the cycles is immaterial when we want to combine them as sets. There are just three different ways to make a set of two labelled cycles from two copies of `(1 2)`:

```
(1 2) (3 4)     (1 3) (2 4)     (1 4) (2 3)
```

In general, if there are k identical components in a sequential arrangement and we relabel them in all possible ways, each set of components appears $k!$ times, because we "forget" about the order between components. Equivalently, the number of sets can be computed by dividing the number of sequential arrangements by $k!$.

Symbolic method for labelled objects. This discussion makes it clear that, again, we have a translation theorem:

Theorem 3.8 (*EGFs, symbolic method*) *Let $\mathcal{A}$ and $\mathcal{B}$ be classes of labelled combinatorial objects. If $A(z)$ is the EGF that enumerates $\mathcal{A}$ and $B(z)$ is the EGF that enumerates $\mathcal{B}$, then:*

$$A(z) + B(z) \quad \textit{is the EGF that enumerates } \mathcal{A} + \mathcal{B}$$

$$A(z)B(z) \quad \textit{is the EGF that enumerates } \mathcal{A} \star \mathcal{B}$$

$$\frac{1}{1 - A(z)} \quad \textit{is the EGF that enumerates sequences of objects from } \mathcal{A}$$

$$e^{A(z)} \quad \textit{is the EGF that enumerates sets of objects from } \mathcal{A}.$$

Proof. The first part of the proof is the same as for Theorem 3.7.

To prove the second part, note that, for every k from 0 to n, we can pair any of the a_k objects of size k from $\mathcal{A}$ with any of the b_{n-k} objects of size $n-k$ from $\mathcal{B}$ to get an object of size n in in $\mathcal{A}\star\mathcal{B}$. The relabellings can be done in $\binom{n}{k}$ ways (simply choose the labels; the order is determined). Thus, the number of objects of size n in $\mathcal{A}\star\mathcal{B}$ is

$$\sum_{0\le k\le n}\binom{n}{k}a_k b_{n-k},$$

again, a simple convolution.

The result for sequences is the same as for Theorem 3.7, and the result for sets follows from the symbolic formula

$$\epsilon + \mathcal{A} + \mathcal{A}^2/2! + \mathcal{A}^3/3! + \mathcal{A}^4/4! + \ldots.$$

where $\mathcal{A}^2 = \mathcal{A}\star\mathcal{A}$, $\mathcal{A}^3 = \mathcal{A}\star\mathcal{A}\star\mathcal{A}$, etc. ■

Now, returning to our example, since the number of labelled cycles of size n is $(n-1)!$ (see Exercise 3.63), the associated EGF is

$$\sum_{n\ge1}\frac{z^n}{n} = \ln\frac{1}{1-z}.$$

Then, Theorem 3.8 says that the EGF that enumerates labelled sets of cycles is

$$\exp\Bigl(\ln\frac{1}{1-z}\Bigr) = \frac{1}{1-z}.$$

That is the number of labelled sets of cycles of n items is precisely $n!$, the number of permutations. This is a fundamental result. As we will see in Chapter 6, there certainly are easier ways to prove it, but the structure of this proof will lead us easily to solutions for considerably more difficult problems.

This brief introduction only scratches the surface of what is known about the symbolic method, which is one of the cornerstones of modern combinatorial analysis. Much more information may be found in Goulden and Jackson [5] or Stanley [14]. In [3], we give a thorough treatment of the method in the context of the analysis of algorithms (see also [16]). The theory is sufficiently complete that it has been embodied in a computer program that can automatically determine generating functions for a structure from a simple recursive definition, as described in Flajolet, Salvy, and Zimmerman [2]. In this book, we present basic structures and their properties, with some pointers forward to [3] when the symbolic method might apply.

The symbolic method summarized by Theorem 3.7 and Theorem 3.8 works for an ever-expanding set of structures, though it cannot naturally solve all problems: some combinatorial objects just have too much internal "cross-structure" to be amenable to this treatment. But it is a method of choice for combinatorial structures that have a nice decomposable form, such as trees (Chapter 5), the example *par excellence*; permutations (Chapter 6); strings (Chapter 7); and words or maps (Chapter 8). When the method does apply, it can succeed spectacularly, especially in allowing quick analysis of variants of basic structures. For many of the basic structures in Chapters 5 through 8, we will give more than one derivation, as we have done with binary trees and with bitstrings, in order to develop facility with basic tools, maintain some consistency with the literature, and cover cases where the application of the symbolic method has not been worked out. We will see a large number of examples that will help develop an appreciation for the underlying combinatorial origin of simple relationships among generating functions.

3.10 Lagrange Inversion. The symbolic method makes it plain that we often are faced with extracting coefficients from generating functions that are implicitly defined through functional equations. The following general tool is available for this task, and is of particular importance in connection with tree enumeration.

Theorem 3.9 (*Lagrange inversion theorem*) *If a generating function* $A(z) = \sum_{n\geq 0} a_n z^n$ *satisfies the functional equation* $z = f(A(z))$, *where* $f(z)$ *satisfies* $f(0) = 0$ *and* $f'(0) \neq 0$, *then*

$$a_n \equiv [z^n]A(z) = \frac{1}{n}[u^{n-1}]\Big(\frac{u}{f(u)}\Big)^n.$$

Also,

$$[z^n](A(z))^m = \frac{m}{n}[u^{n-m}]\Big(\frac{u}{f(u)}\Big)^n.$$

and

$$[z^n]g(A(z)) = \frac{1}{n}[u^{n-1}]g'(u)\Big(\frac{u}{f(u)}\Big)^n.$$

Proof. Omitted; see, for example, [1]. There is a vast literature on this formula, dating back to the eighteenth century. ■

The *functional inverse* of a function f is the function f^{-1} that satisfies $f^{-1}(f(z)) = f(f^{-1}(z)) = z$. Applying f^{-1} to both sides of the equation $z = f(A(z))$, we see that the function $A(z)$ is the functional inverse of $f(z)$. The Lagrange theorem is a general tool for inverting power series, in this sense. Its surprising feature is to provide a direct relation between the coefficients of the functional inverse of a function and the powers of that function. In the present context, it is a very useful tool for extracting coefficients for implicit functions. Below we give a number of examples that emphasize the formal manipulations but only sketch the nature of the applications (various tree enumeration problems). More definitive statements about the applications are a primary concern of Chapters 5 and 8.

Binary trees. Let $T^{[2]}(z) = zT(z)$ be the OGF for binary trees, counted by external nodes. Rewriting the functional equation $T^{[2]}(z) = z + T^{[2]}(z)^2$ as

$$z = T^{[2]}(z) - T^{[2]}(z)^2,$$

we can apply Lagrange inversion with $f(u) = u - u^2$. This gives the result

$$[z^n]T^{[2]}(z) = \frac{1}{n}[u^{n-1}]\Big(\frac{u}{u-u^2}\Big)^n = \frac{1}{n}[u^{n-1}]\Big(\frac{1}{1-u}\Big)^n.$$

Now, from Table 3.1, we know that

$$\frac{u^{n-1}}{(1-u)^n} = \sum_{k\geq n-1}\binom{k}{n-1}u^k$$

so that, considering the term $k = 2n-2$,

$$[u^{n-1}]\Big(\frac{1}{1-u}\Big)^n = \binom{2n-2}{n-1} \quad \text{and therefore} \quad [z^n]T^{[2]}(z) = \frac{1}{n}\binom{2n-2}{n-1},$$

as expected.

Ternary trees. One way to generalize binary trees is to consider trees with more than two children per node. For example, *ternary trees* are trees where every node is either external or has three subtrees (left, middle, and right). The sequence of counts for ternary trees with n external nodes for $n = 1, 2, 3, 4, 5, 6, 7, \ldots$ is $1, 0, 1, 0, 3, 0, 3, \ldots$. With the symbolic method, we can immediately derive the functional equation

$$z = T^{[3]}(z) - T^{[3]}(z)^3,$$

Proceeding as in §3.8 for binary trees does not succeed easily because this is a cubic equation, not a quadratic. But applying Lagrange inversion with $f(u) = u - u^3$ immediately gives the result

$$[z^n]T^{[3]}(z) = \frac{1}{n}[u^{n-1}]\Big(\frac{1}{1-u^2}\Big)^n.$$

Proceeding in the same manner as above, we know from Table 3.1 that

$$\frac{u^{2n-2}}{(1-u^2)^n} = \sum_{k \ge n-1} \binom{k}{n-1} u^{2k}$$

so that, considering the term $2k = 3n - 3$ (which only exists when n is odd), we find that

$$[z^n]T^{[3]}(z) = \frac{1}{n}\binom{(3n-3)/2}{n-1}$$

for n odd, 0 for n even.

Forests of binary trees. Another way to generalize binary trees is to consider sets of them, or so-called forests. A *k-forest* of binary trees is simply an ordered sequence of k binary trees. By Theorem 3.7, the OGF for k-forests is just $(zT(z))^k$, where $T(z)$ is the OGF for binary trees, and by Lagrange inversion (using the second case in Theorem 3.9), the number of k-forests of binary trees with n external nodes is therefore

$$[z^n]\Big(\frac{1-\sqrt{1-4z}}{2}\Big)^k = \frac{k}{n}\binom{2n-k-1}{n-1}.$$

These numbers are also known as the *ballot numbers*, for reasons made clear in Chapter 7.

Labelled trees. Consider the functional equation

$$C(z) = ze^{C(z)}.$$

This well-known functional equation is satisfied by the exponential generating function for general (labelled unordered) trees (see Chapter 5). Lagrange inversion with $f(u) = ue^{-u}$ immediately gives

$$[z^n]C(z) = \frac{1}{n}[u^{n-1}]e^{un} = \frac{1}{n}\frac{n^{n-1}}{(n-1)!} = \frac{n^{n-1}}{n!}.$$

The function $C(z)$ is known as the *Cayley* function.

Exercise 3.65 Find $[z^n]A(z)$ when $A(z)$ is defined by the functional equation

$$z = \frac{A(z)}{1 - A(z)}.$$

Exercise 3.66 Find $[z^n]e^{\alpha C(z)}$ where $C(z)$ is the Cayley function.

Exercise 3.67 ("Abel's binomial theorem.") Use the result of the previous exercise and the identity $e^{(\alpha+\beta)C(z)} = e^{\alpha C(z)}e^{\beta C(z)}$ to prove that

$$(\alpha+\beta)(n+\alpha+\beta)^{n-1} = \alpha\beta\sum_k \binom{n}{k}(k+\alpha)^{k-1}(n-k+\beta)^{n-k-1}.$$

Exercise 3.68 What is the functional inverse of $e^z - 1$? What do we get in terms of power series by applying Lagrange inversion?

Exercise 3.69 Find the number of 4-ary trees, where every node is either external or has a sequence of four subtrees.

Exercise 3.70 Find the number of n-node 3-forests of ternary trees.

3.11 Probability Generating Functions. An application of generating functions that is directly related to the analysis of algorithms is their use for manipulating probabilities, to simplify the calculation of averages and variances.

Definition *Gi en a random ariable X that takes on only nonnegati e integer alues, with* $p_k \equiv Pr\{X = k\}$, *the function* $P(u) = \sum_{k\ge 0} p_k u^k$ *is called the probability generating function (PGF) for the random ariable.*

We have been assuming basic familiarity with computing averages and standard deviations for random variables in the discussion in §1.7 and in the examples of average-case analysis of algorithms that we have examined, but we review the definitions here because we will be doing related calculations in this and the next section.

Definition *The* expected value *of X, or $E(X)$, (also known as the* mean value *of X) is defined to be $\sum_{k\geq 0} kp_k$. In terms of $r_k \equiv Pr\{X \leq k\}$, this is equivalent to $E(X) = \sum_{k\geq 0}(1 - r_k)$. The* variance *of X, or $var(X)$, is defined to be $\sum_{k\geq 0}(k - E(X))^2 p_k$. The* standard deviation *of X is defined to be $\sqrt{var(X)}$.*

Probability generating functions are important because they can provide a way to find the average and the variance without tedious calculations involving discrete sums.

Theorem 3.10 (*Mean and variance from PGFs*) *Given a PGF $P(z)$ for a random variable X, the expected value of X is given by $P'(1)$ with variance $P''(1) + P'(1) - P'(1)^2$.*

Proof. If $p_k \equiv \Pr\{X = k\}$, then

$$P'(1) = \sum_{k\geq 0} kp_k u^{k-1}|_{u=1} = \sum_{k\geq 0} kp_k,$$

the expected value, by definition. Similarly, noting that $P(1) = 1$, the stated result for the variance follows directly from the definition:

$$\begin{aligned}\sum_{k\geq 0}(k - P'(1))^2 p_k &= \sum_{k\geq 0} k^2 p_k - 2\sum_{k\geq 0} kP'(1)p_k + \sum_{k\geq 0} P'(1)^2 p_k \\ &= \sum_{k\geq 0} k^2 p_k - P'(1)^2 \\ &= P''(1) + P'(1) - P'(1)^2.\end{aligned}$$ ■

The quantity $E(X^r) = \sum_k k^r p_k$ is known as the *rth moment* of X. The expected value is the first moment and the variance is the difference between the second moment and the square of the first.

Composition rules such as the theorems given in §3.9 for enumeration through the symbolic method translate into statements about combining PGFs for independent random variables. For example, if $P(u), Q(u)$ are probability generating functions for independent random variables X and Y, then $P(u)Q(u)$ is the probability generating function for $X + Y$. Moreover, the average and variance of the distribution represented by the product of two probability generating functions is the sum of the individual averages and variances.

Exercise 3.71 Give a simple expression for var(X) in terms of $r_k = \Pr\{X \le k\}$.

Exercise 3.72 Define mean(P) $\equiv P'(1)$ and var(P) $\equiv P''(1) + P'(1) - P'(1)^2$. Prove that mean($PQ$) = mean($P$) + mean($Q$) and var($PQ$) = var($P$) + var($Q$) for any differentiable functions P and Q with $P(1) = Q(1) = 1$, not just PGFs.

Uniform discrete distribution. Given an integer $n > 0$, suppose that X_n is a random variable that is equally likely to take on each of the integer values $0, 1, 2, \ldots, n-1$. Then the probability generating function for X_n is

$$P_n(u) = \frac{1}{n} + \frac{1}{n}u + \frac{1}{n}u^2 + \cdots + \frac{1}{n}u^{n-1},$$

the expected value is

$$P_n'(1) = \frac{1}{n}(1 + 2 + \cdots + (n-1)) = \frac{n-1}{2},$$

and, since

$$P_n''(1) = \frac{1}{n}(1\cdot 2 + 2\cdot 3 + \cdots + (n-2)(n-1)) = \frac{1}{6}(n-2)(n-1),$$

the variance is

$$P_n''(1) + P_n'(1) - P_n'(1)^2 = \frac{n^2-1}{12}.$$

Exercise 3.73 Verify the above results from the closed form

$$P_n(u) = \frac{1-u^n}{n(1-u)},$$

using l'Hôpital's rule to compute the derivatives at 1.

Exercise 3.74 Find the PGF for the random variable that counts the number of leading 0s in a random binary string, and use the PGF to find the mean and standard deviation.

Binomial distribution. Consider a random string of N independent bits, where each bit is 0 with probability p and 1 with probability $q = 1 - p$. We can argue that the probability that exactly k of the N bits are 0 is

$$\binom{N}{k} p^k q^{N-k},$$

so the corresponding PGF is

$$P_N(u) = \sum_{0 \le k \le N} \binom{N}{k} p^k q^{N-k} u^k = (pu + q)^N.$$

Alternatively, we could observe that PGF for 0s in a single bit is $(pu + q)$ and the N bits are independent, so the PGF for the number of 0s in the N bits is $(pu+q)^N$. Now, the average number of 0s is $P'(1) = pN$ and the variance is $P''(1) + P'(1) - P'(1)^2 = pqN$, etc. We can make these calculations easily without ever explicitly determining individual probabilities.

One cannot expect to be so fortunate as to regularly encounter the full decomposition into independent PGFs that characterized the previous example. In this case, the count of the number of structures 2^N trivially factors into N simple factors. Since this quantity appears as the denominator in calculating the average, it is not surprising that the numerator decomposes as well. Conversely, if the count does not factor in this way, as for example in the case of the Catalan numbers, then we might not expect to find easy independence arguments like these. This is our primary reason for emphasizing the use of cumulative and bivariate generating functions, not PGFs, in the analysis of algorithms (see the next section).

Quicksort distribution. Let $Q_N(u)$ be the PGF for the number of comparisons used by Quicksort. We can apply the composition rules for PGFs to show that function to satisfy the functional equation

$$Q_N(u) = \frac{1}{N} \sum_{1 \le k \le N} u^{N+1} Q_{k-1}(u) Q_{N-k}(u).$$

Though using this equation to find an explicit expression for $Q_N(u)$ appears to be quite difficult, it does provide a basis for calculation of the moments. For example, differentiating and evaluating at $u = 1$ leads directly to the standard Quicksort recurrence that we addressed in §3.3. Note that the PGF corresponds to a sequence indexed by the number of comparisons; the OGF that we used to solve (1) in §3.3 is indexed by the number of elements in the file. In the next section we will see how to treat both with just one double generating function.

Though it would seem that probability generating functions are natural tools for the average-case analysis of algorithms (and they are), we generally give this point of view less emphasis than the approach of analyzing parameters of combinatorial structures, for reasons that will become more clear in the next section. When dealing with discrete structures, the two approaches are formally related if not equivalent, but counting is more natural and allows for more flexible manipulations.

3.12 Bivariate Generating Functions. In the analysis of algorithms, we are normally interested not just in counting structures of a given size, but also in knowing values of various parameters relating to the structures. The symbolic method also extends to this situation.

We use *bivariate* generating functions for this purpose. These are functions of two variables that represent doubly indexed sequences: one index for the problem size, one for the value of the parameter being analyzed. Bivariate generating functions allow us to capture both indices with just one generating function, of two variables.

Definition *Given a doubly indexed sequence* $\{a_{nk}\}$, *the function*

$$A(u,z)=\sum_{n\ge0}\sum_{k\ge0}a_{nk}u^kz^n$$

is called the bivariate generating function (BGF) of the sequence. We use the notation $[u^kz^n]A(u,z)$ *to refer to* a_{nk}; $[z^n]A(u,z)$ *to refer to* $\sum_{k\ge0}a_{nk}u^k$; *and* $[u^k]A(u,z)$ *to refer to* $\sum_{n\ge0}a_{nk}z^n$.

As appropriate, a BGF may need to be made "exponential" by dividing by $n!$. Thus the exponential BGF of $\{a_{nk}\}$ is

$$A(u,z)=\sum_{n\ge0}\sum_{k\ge0}a_{nk}u^k\frac{z^n}{n!}.$$

Most often, we use BGFs to count parameter values in combinatorial structures as follows. For $p\in\mathcal{P}$, where $\mathcal{P}$ is a class of combinatorial structures, let *cost*(p) be a function that gives the value of some parameter defined for each structure. Then our interest is in the BGF

$$P(u,z)=\sum_{p\in\mathcal{P}}u^{\{\mathrm{cost}(p)\}}z^{|p|}=\sum_{n\ge0}\sum_{k\ge0}p_{nk}u^kz^n.$$

where p_{nk} is the number of structures of size n and cost k. We also write

$$P(u,z)=\sum_{n\ge0}p_n(u)z^n\quad\text{where}\quad p_n(u)=[z^n]A(u,z)=\sum_{k\ge0}p_{nk}u^k$$

to separate out all the costs for the structures of size n, and

$$P(u,z)=\sum_{k\geq 0} q_k(z)u^k \quad \text{where} \quad q_k(z)=[u^k]A(u,z)=\sum_{n\geq 0} p_{nk}z^n$$

to separate out all the structures of cost k. Also, note that

$$P(1,z)=\sum_{p\in\mathcal{P}} z^{|p|}=\sum_{n\geq 0} p_n(1)z^n=\sum_{k\geq 0} q_k(z)$$

is the ordinary generating function that enumerates $\mathcal{P}$.

Of primary interest is the fact that $p_n(u)/p_n(1)$ is the PGF for the random variable representing the cost, if all structures of size n are taken as equally likely. Thus, knowing $p_n(u)$ and $p_n(1)$ allows us to compute average cost and other moments, as described in the previous section. BGFs provide a convenient framework for such computations, based on counting and analysis of cost parameters for combinatorial structures.

Binomial distribution. Let $\mathcal{B}$ be the set of all binary strings, and consider the "cost" function for a binary string to be the number of 1 bits. In this case, $\{a_{nk}\}$ is the number of n-bit binary strings with k 1s, so the associated BGF is

$$P(u,z)=\sum_{n\geq 0}\sum_{k\geq 0}\binom{n}{k}u^k z^n=\sum_{n\geq 0}(1+u)^n z^n=\frac{1}{1-(1+u)z}.$$

As in §3.8, it will be instructive to consider an alternate derivation, which is more closely related to the symbolic method, to illustrate the basic approach used for a number of similar derivations throughout the book. We begin with the definition

$$P(u,z)\equiv\sum_{b\in\mathcal{B}} u^{\{\text{\# of 1-bits in } b\}}z^{|b|}.$$

Every binary string b is either empty or consists of a single bit (either 0 or 1) followed by a binary string b'. This leads to the decomposition

$$\begin{aligned}P(u,z)&=1+\sum_{b'\in\mathcal{B}} u^{\{\text{\# of 1 bits in } b'\}}z^{1+|b'|}+\sum_{b'\in\mathcal{B}} u^{1+\{\text{\# of 1 bits in } b'\}}z^{1+|b'|}\\&=1+zP(u,z)+uzP(u,z).\end{aligned}$$

Solving for $P(u,z)$ gives the same closed-form expression as above. As usual, a simple relationship like this among generating functions can be explained with the symbolic method: this corresponds to defining a binary string as empty or a single bit followed by a binary string: the BGF for a 0 bit is z and the BGF for a 1 bit is uz. These observations, combined with translation theorems like those in the previous section for BGFs, would give the result directly. Also as mentioned in §3.8, a third alternative is to use a "sequence" construction to argue that the BGF for the number of 1 bits in sequences of bits is

$$P(u,z) = \sum_{N\ge 0}(z+uz)^N = \frac{1}{1-(1+u)z}.$$

Expanding, we see immediately that

$$p_n(u) = (1+u)^n \quad \text{and} \quad q_k(z) = z^k/(1-z)^{k+1}.$$

Of course,

$$[u^k]p_n(u) = [z^n]q_k(z) = \binom{n}{k},$$

as expected.

We certainly do not need the general mechanisms being discussed here for such trivial tasks as counting 1s in binary strings, but it is helpful to use an easy problem like this as a running example to help the reader check the definitions and understand the concepts. Later in this section and in numerous places in Chapters 5 through 8, we will be using these mechanisms to help solve more difficult problems.

BGF expansions. Separating out the structures of size n as $[z^n]P(u,z) = p_n(u)$ is often called the "horizontal" expansion of the BGF. This comes from the natural representation of the full BGF expansion as a two-dimensional table, with powers of u increasing in the horizontal direction and powers of z increasing in the vertical direction. For example, the BGF for the binomial distribution may be written as follows:

$$\begin{aligned}
&z^0(u^0)+\\
&z^1(u^0+u^1)+\\
&z^2(u^0+2u^1+u^2)+\\
&z^3(u^0+3u^1+3u^2+u^3)+\\
&z^4(u^0+4u^1+6u^2+4u^3+u^4)+\\
&z^5(u^0+5u^1+10u^2+10u^3+5u^4+u^5)+\ldots.
\end{aligned}$$

Or, proceeding vertically through such a table, we can collect $[u^k]P(u, z) = q_k(z)$. For the binomial distribution, this gives

$$\begin{aligned}
&u^0(z^0 + z^1 + z^2 + z^3 + z^4 + z^5 + \ldots)+\\
&u^1(z^1 + 2z^2 + 3z^3 + 4z^4 + 5z^5 + \ldots)+\\
&u^2(z^2 + 3z^3 + 6z^4 + 10z^5 \ldots)+\\
&u^3(z^3 + 4z^4 + 10z^5 + \ldots)+\\
&u^4(z^4 + 5z^5 + \ldots)+\\
&u^5(z^5 + \ldots) + \ldots,
\end{aligned}$$

the so-called vertical expansion of the BGF. As we will see, these alternate representations are important in the analysis of algorithms, especially when explicit expressions for the full BGF are not available.

Calculating moments "horizontally." With these notations, calculations of probabilities and moments are straightforward. Differentiating with respect to u and evaluating at $u = 1$, we find that

$$p'_n(1) = \sum_{k\geq 0} kp_{nk}.$$

The partial derivative with respect to u of $P(z, u)$ evaluated at $u = 1$ is the generating function for this quantity. Now, $p_n(1)$ is the number of members of $\mathcal{P}$ of size n. If we consider all members of $\mathcal{P}$ of size n to be equally likely, then the probability that a structure of size n has cost k is $p_{nk}/p_n(1)$ and the average cost of a structure of size n is $p'_n(1)/p_n(1)$.

Definition *Let $\mathcal{P}$ be a class of combinatorial structures with BGF $P(u, z)$. Then the function*

$$\left.\frac{\partial P(u, z)}{\partial u}\right|_{u=1} = \sum_{p\in\mathcal{P}} cost(p) z^{|p|}$$

is defined to be the cumulative generating function *(CGF) for the class. Also, let $\mathcal{P}_n$ denote the class of all the structures of size n in $\mathcal{P}$. Then the sum*

$$\sum_{p\in\mathcal{P}_n} cost(p)$$

is defined to be the cumulated cost *for the structures of size n.*

This terminology is justified since the cumulated cost is precisely the coefficient of z^n in the CGF. The cumulated cost is sometimes referred to as the *unnormalized mean*, since the true mean is obtained by "normalizing," or dividing by the number of structures of size n.

Theorem 3.11 (*BGFs and average costs*) *Given a BGF $P(u, z)$ for a class of combinatorial structures, the average cost for all structures of a given size is given by the cumulated cost divided by the number of structures, or*

$$\frac{[z^n]\dfrac{\partial P(u,z)}{\partial u}\Big|_{u=1}}{[z^n]P(1,z)}.$$

Proof. The calculations are straightforward, following directly from the observation that $p_n(u)/p_n(1)$ is the associated PGF, then applying Theorem 3.10. ■

The importance of the use of BGFs and Theorem 3.11 is that the average cost can be calculated by extracting coefficients *independently* from

$$\frac{\partial P(u,z)}{\partial u}\Big|_{u=1} \qquad \text{and} \qquad P(1,z)$$

and dividing. For more compact notation, we often write the partial derivative as $P_u(1, z)$. The standard deviation can be calculated in a similar manner. These notations and calculations are summarized in Table 3.5.

For the example given above involving the binomial distribution, the number of binary strings of length n is

$$[z^n]\frac{1}{1-(1+u)z}\Big|_{u=1} = [z^n]\frac{1}{(1-2z)} = 2^n,$$

and the cumulated cost (number of 1 bits in all n-bit binary strings) is

$$[z^n]\frac{\partial}{\partial u}\frac{1}{1-(1+u)z}\Big|_{u=1} = [z^n]\frac{z}{(1-2z)^2} = n2^{n-1},$$

so the average number of 1 bits is thus $n/2$. Or, starting from $p_n(u) = (1+u)^n$, the number of structures is $p_n(1) = 2^n$ and the cumulated cost is $p'_n(1) = n2^{n-1}$. Or, we can compute the average by arguing directly that the number of binary strings of length n is 2^n and the number of 1 bits in all binary strings of length n is $n2^{n-1}$, since there are a total of $n2^n$ bits, half of which are 1 bits.

$$P(u,z) = \sum_{p\in\mathcal{P}} u^{\{\text{cost}(p)\}} z^{|p|} = \sum_{n\geq 0}\sum_{k\geq 0} p_{nk}u^k z^n = \sum_{n\geq 0} p_n(u)z^n = \sum_{k\geq 0} q_k(z)u^k.$$

GF of costs for structures of size n	$[z^n]P(u,z) \equiv p_n(u)$
GF enumerating structures with cost k	$[u^k]P(u,z) \equiv q_k(z)$
cumulative generating function (CGF)	$\left.\dfrac{\partial P(u,z)}{\partial u}\right\vert_{u=1} \equiv q(z)$ $= \sum_{k\geq 0} kq_k(z)$
number of structures of size n	$[z^n]P(1,z) = p_n(1)$
cumulated cost	$[z^n]\left.\dfrac{\partial P(u,z)}{\partial u}\right\vert_{u=1} = \sum_{k\geq 0} kp_{nk}$ $= p_n'(1)$ $= [z^n]q(z)$
average cost	$\dfrac{[z^n]\left.\dfrac{\partial P(u,z)}{\partial u}\right\vert_{u=1}}{[z^n]P(1,z)} = \dfrac{p_n'(1)}{p_n(1)}$ $= \dfrac{[z^n]q(z)}{p_n(1)}$
variance	$\dfrac{p_n''(1)}{p_n(1)} + \dfrac{p_n'(1)}{p_n(1)} - \left(\dfrac{p_n'(1)}{p_n(1)}\right)^2$

Table 3.6 Calculating moments from a bivariate generating function

Exercise 3.75 Calculate the variance for the number of 1 bits in a random binary string of length n, using Table 3.6 and $p_n(u) = (1+u)^n$, as shown above.

Calculating moments "vertically." Alternatively, the cumulated cost may be calculated using the vertical expansion:

$$[z^n]\sum_{k\geq 0} kq_k(z) = \sum_{k\geq 0} kp_{nk}.$$

Corollary *The cumulated cost is also equal to*

$$[z^n]\sum_{k\geq 0}(P(1,z) - r_k(z)) \qquad \textit{where} \qquad r_k(z) \equiv \sum_{0\leq j\leq k} q_j(z).$$

Proof. The function $r_k(z)$ is the generating function for all structures with cost no greater than k. Since $r_k(z) - r_{k-1}(z) = q_k(z)$, the cumulated cost is

$$[z^n]\sum_{k\geq 0} k(r_k(z) - r_{k-1}(z)),$$

which telescopes to give the stated result. ∎

As k increases in this sum, initial terms cancel (all small structures have cost no greater than k), so this representation lends itself to asymptotic approximation. We will return to this topic in detail in Chapter 5, where we first encounter problems for which the vertical formulation is appropriate.

Exercise 3.76 Verify from the vertical expansion that the mean for the binomial distribution is $n/2$ by first calculating $r_k(z)$ as described above.

Leaves in binary trees. For a more interesting example of the use of BGFs, we will consider the problem of determining the average number of internal nodes in a binary tree of size n with both children external. Such nodes are called *lea es*. From inspection of Figure 3.1 (see §3.8), we see that the total numbers of such nodes for $n = 0, 1, 2, 3,$ and 4 are $0, 1, 2, 6,$ and 20. Dividing by the Catalan numbers, the associated averages are $0, 1, 1, 6/5$ and $10/7$. In terms of the BGF

$$T(u,z) = \sum_{t\in\mathcal{T}} u^{\{\text{leaves}(t)\}} z^{|t|}$$

the trees in Figure 3.1 correspond to the terms

$$(u^0)z^0+$$
$$(u^1)z^1+$$
$$(u^1+u^1)z^2+$$
$$(u^1+u^1+u^2+u^1+u^1)z^3+$$
$$(u^1+u^1+u^2+u^1+u^1+u^2+u^2+u^1+u^1+u^2+u^1+u^1+u^2+u^2)z^4.$$

This "two-dimensional" aspect of the situation underscores the utility of BGFs for the analysis. We have one variable z to keep track of one dimension (the size) and another variable u to keep track of the other dimension (the cost). Adding these terms, we know that

$$T(u,z) = 1 + uz^1 + 2uz^2 + (4u + u^2)z^3 + (8u + 6u^2)z^4 + \ldots.$$

Checking small values, we find that

$$T(1,z) = 1 + z^1 + 2z^2 + 5z^3 + 14z^4 + \ldots$$

and

$$T_u(1,z) = z^1 + 2z^2 + 6z^3 + 20z^4 + \ldots$$

as expected. The functional equation

$$T(u,z) = 1 + uz + zT(u,z)^2 - z$$

follows from the symbolic method (the z is subtracted to avoid accounting twice for the tree of size 1). Strictly speaking, we need a translation theorem to justify writing this equation (see [3] for such theorems), but we could also verify the equation or derive it with a direct argument with the generating function like the one given above for deriving the Catalan numbers. Of course, setting $u = 1$ gives a familiar functional equation, since $T(1,z)$ is the OGF for the Catalan numbers. Now, differentiating with respect to u and evaluating at $u = 1$ gives

$$\begin{aligned} T_u(1,z) &= z + 2zT(1,z)T_u(1,z) \\ &= \frac{z}{1 - 2zT(1,z)} \\ &= \frac{z}{\sqrt{1-4z}}. \end{aligned}$$

Thus, we have shown that the average number of internal nodes with both nodes external in a binary tree of size n is

$$\frac{[z^n]\dfrac{z}{\sqrt{1-4z}}}{\dfrac{1}{n+1}\dbinom{2n}{n}} = \frac{\dbinom{2n-2}{n-1}}{\dfrac{1}{n+1}\dbinom{2n}{n}} = \frac{(n+1)n}{2(2n-1)}$$

(see §3.4 and §3.8), which tends to $n/4$ in the limit. About $1/4$ of the internal nodes in a binary tree are leaves.

Exercise 3.77 Find the average number of internal nodes in a binary tree of size n with both children internal.

Exercise 3.78 Find the average number of internal nodes in a binary tree of size n with one child internal and one child external.

Exercise 3.79 Find an explicit formula for $T(u, z)$ and compute the variance of the number of leaves in binary trees.

Quicksort distribution. We have studied the average-case analysis of the running time of Quicksort in some detail in §1.5 and §3.3, so it will be instructive to examine that analysis, including calculation of the variance, from the perspective of BGFs. We begin by considering the exponential BGF

$$Q(u,z) = \sum_{N\ge 0}\sum_{k\ge 0} q_{Nk} u^k \frac{z^N}{N!}$$

where q_{Nk} is the cumulative count of the number of comparisons taken by Quicksort on all permutations of N elements. Now, because there are $N!$ permutations of N elements, this is actually a "probability" BGF: $[z^N]Q(u,z)$ is nothing other than the PGF $Q_N(u)$ introduced at the end of the previous section. As we will see in several examples in Chapter 6, this relationship between exponential BGFs and PGFs of course holds whenever we study properties of permutations. Therefore, by multiplying both sides of the recurrence from §3.10

$$Q_N(u) = \frac{1}{N}\sum_{1\le k\le N} u^{N+1} Q_{k-1}(u) Q_{N-k}(u).$$

by z^N and summing on N, we can derive the functional equation

$$\frac{\partial}{\partial z} Q(u,z) = u^2 Q^2(u, zu) \quad \text{with} \quad Q(u,0) = 1$$

that must be satisfied by the BGF. This carries enough information to allow us to compute the moments of the distribution.

Theorem 3.12 (*Quicksort variance*) *The variance of the number of comparisons used by Quicksort is*

$$7N^2 - 4(N+1)^2 H_N^{(2)} - 2(N+1)H_N + 13N \sim N^2\Big(7 - \frac{2\pi^2}{3}\Big).$$

Proof. This calculation is sketched in the above discussion and the following exercises, and is perhaps best done with the help of a computer algebra system. The asymptotic estimate follows from the approximations $H_N \sim \ln N$ (see the first corollary to Theorem 4.3) and $H_N^{(2)} \sim \pi^2/6$ (see Exercise 4.58). This result is due to Knuth [8]. ■

As discussed in §1.7, the standard deviation ($\approx .65N$) is asymptotically smaller than the average value ($\approx 2N\ln N - .846N$). This means that the observed number of comparisons when Quicksort is used to sort a random permutation (or when partitioning elements are chosen randomly) should be close to the mean with high probability, more so as N increases.

Exercise 3.80 Confirm that

$$q^{[1]}(z) \equiv \frac{\partial}{\partial u} Q(u,z)\,\Big|_{u=1} = \frac{1}{(1-z)^2}\ln\frac{1}{1-z}$$

and show that

$$\begin{aligned} q^{[2]}(z) \equiv \frac{\partial^2}{\partial u^2} Q(u,z)\,\Big|_{u=1} &= \frac{6}{(1-z)^3} + \frac{8}{(1-z)^3}\ln\frac{1}{1-z} + \frac{8}{(1-z)^3}\ln^2\frac{1}{1-z} \\ &\quad - \frac{6}{(1-z)^2} - \frac{12}{(1-z)^2}\ln\frac{1}{1-z} - \frac{4}{(1-z)^2}\ln^2\frac{1}{1-z} \end{aligned}$$

Exercise 3.81 Extract the coefficient of z^N in $q^{[2]}(z) + q^{[1]}(z)$ and verify the exact expression for the variance given in Theorem 3.12. (See Exercise 3.8.)

The analysis of leaves in binary trees and the analysis of the number of comparisons taken by Quicksort are representative of numerous other examples, which we will see in Chapters 5 through 8, of the use of bivariate generating functions in the analysis of algorithms. As our examples here have illustrated, one reason for this is our ability to use symbolic arguments to encapsulate properties of algorithms and data structures in relationships among their generating functions. As also illustrated by our examples, another reason for this is the convenient framework provided by BGFs for computing moments, particularly the average.

binomial coefficients	$\frac{1}{1-z-uz} = \sum_{n,k\geq 0} \binom{n}{k} u^k z^n$
	$\frac{z^k}{(1-z)^{k+1}} = \sum_{n\geq k} \binom{n}{k} z^n$
	$(1+u)^n = \sum_{k\geq 0} \binom{n}{k} u^k$
Stirling numbers of the first kind	$\frac{1}{(1-z)^u} = \sum_{n,k\geq 0} \left[{n \atop k} \right] u^k \frac{z^n}{n!}$
	$\frac{1}{k!}\left(\ln \frac{1}{1-z}\right)^k = \sum_{n\geq 0} \left[{n \atop k} \right] \frac{z^n}{n!}$
	$u(u+1)\ldots(u+n-1) = \sum_{k\geq 0} \left[{n \atop k} \right] u^k$
Stirling numbers of the second kind	$e^{u(e^z-1)} = \sum_{n,k\geq 0} \left\{ {n \atop k} \right\} u^k \frac{z^n}{n!}$
	$\frac{1}{k!}(e^z-1)^k = \sum_{n\geq 0} \left\{ {n \atop k} \right\} \frac{z^n}{n!}$
	$\frac{z^k}{(1-z)(1-2z)\ldots(1-kz)} = \sum_{n\geq k} \left\{ {n \atop k} \right\} z^n$
Bernoulli numbers	$\frac{z}{(e^z-1)} = \sum_{n\geq 0} B_n \frac{z^n}{n!}$
Catalan numbers	$\frac{1-\sqrt{1-4z}}{2z} = \sum_{n\geq 0} \frac{1}{n+1}\binom{2n}{n} z^n$
harmonic numbers	$\frac{1}{1-z} \ln \frac{1}{1-z} = \sum_{n\geq 1} H_n z^n$
factorials	$\frac{1}{1-z} = \sum_{n\geq 0} n! \frac{z^n}{n!}$
Fibonacci numbers	$\frac{z}{1-z-z^2} = \sum_{n\geq 0} F_n z^n$

Table 3.7 Classic “special” generating functions

3.13 Special Functions. We have already encountered a number of "special" sequences of numbers—such as the harmonic numbers, the Fibonacci numbers, binomial coefficients, and $N!$—that are intrinsic to the problems under examination and that appear in so many different applications that they are worthy of study on their own merit. In this section, we briefly consider several more such sequences.

We define these sequences in Table 3.7 as the coefficients in the generating functions given. Alternatively, there are combinatorial interpretations that could serve to define these sequences, but we prefer to have the generating function serve as the definition to avoid biasing toward any particular application. We may view these generating functions as adding to our tool kit of "known" functions—these particular ones have appeared so frequently that their properties are quite well understood.

The primary heritage of these sequences is from combinatorics: each of them "counts" some basic combinatorial object, some of which are briefly described below. For example, $N!$ is the number of permutations of N objects, and H_N is the average number of times we encounter a value larger than all previously encountered when proceeding from left to right through a random permutation (see Chapter 6). We will avoid a full survey of the combinatorics of the special numbers, concentrating instead on those that play a role in fundamental algorithms and in the basic structures discussed in Chapters 5 through 8. Much more information about the special numbers may be found, for example, in the books by Comtet [1], by Graham, Knuth, and Patashnik [4], and by Goulden and Jackson [5]. The sequences also arise in analysis. For example, we can use them to translate from one way to represent a polynomial to another. We mention a few examples below but avoid considering full details.

The analysis of algorithms perhaps adds a new dimension to the study of special sequences: we resist the temptation to define the special sequences in terms of basic performance properties of fundamental algorithms, though it would be possible to do so for each of them, as discussed in Chapters 5 through 8. In the meantime, it is worthwhile to become familiar with these sequences because they arise so frequently—either directly, when we study algorithms that turn out to be processing fundamental combinatorial objects, or indirectly, when we are led to one of the generating functions below. Whether or not we are aware of a specific combinatorial connection, well-understood properties of these generating functions are often exploited in the analysis of algorithms. Chapters 5 through 8 will cover many more details about these sequences with relevance to specific algorithms.

Binomial coefficients. We have already been assuming that the reader is familiar with properties of these special numbers: the number $\binom{n}{k}$ counts the number of ways to choose k objects out of n, without replacement; they are the coefficients that arise when the polynomial $(1+x)^n$ is expanded in powers of x. As we have seen, binomial coefficients appear often in the analysis of algorithms, for example, when Quicksort is improved by first choosing a sample.

Stirling numbers. There are two kinds of Stirling numbers; they can be used to convert back and forth between the standard representation of a polynomial and a representation using so-called falling factorial powers $x^{\underline{k}} = x(x-1)(x-2)\dots(x-k+1)$:

$$x^{\underline{n}} = \sum_k \begin{bmatrix} n \\ k \end{bmatrix} (-1)^{n-k} x^k \qquad \text{and} \qquad x^n = \sum_k \begin{Bmatrix} n \\ k \end{Bmatrix} x^{\underline{k}}.$$

Stirling numbers have combinatorial interpretations similar to those for binomial coefficients: $\left\{ {n \atop k} \right\}$ is the number of ways to divide a set of n objects into k nonempty subsets; and $\left[{n \atop k} \right]$ is the number of ways to divide n objects into k nonempty cycles. We have touched on the $\left[{n \atop k} \right]$ Stirling distribution already in §3.9 and will cover it in detail in Chapter 6. The $\left\{ {n \atop k} \right\}$ Stirling distribution makes an appearance in Chapter 8, in our discussion of the coupon collector problem.

Bernoulli numbers. The sequence with EGF $z/(e^z-1)$ arises in a number of combinatorial applications. For example, we need these numbers if we want to write down an explicit expression for the sum of the tth powers of the integers less than N, as a standard polynomial in N. We can deduce first few terms in the sequence by setting coefficients of z equal in

$$z = \Bigl(B_0 + B_1 z + \frac{B_2}{2} z^2 + \frac{B_3}{6} z^3 + \dots\Bigr)\Bigl(z + \frac{z^2}{2} + \frac{z^3}{6} + \dots\Bigr).$$

This gives $B_0 = 1$, then $B_1 + B_0/2 = 0$ so $B_1 = -1/2$, then $B_2 + B_1/2 + B_0/6 = 0$ so $B_2 = 1/6$, etc. If we let

$$S_{Nt} = \sum_{0 \le k < N} k^t,$$

then the EGF is given by

$$S_N(z) = \sum_{t\geq 0}\sum_{0\leq k<N} k^t\frac{z^t}{t!} = \sum_{0\leq k<N} e^{kz} = \frac{e^{Nz}-1}{e^z-1}.$$

This is now a convolution of "known" generating functions, from which the explicit formula

$$S_{Nt} = \frac{1}{t+1}\sum_{0\leq k\leq t}\binom{t+1}{k}B_k N^{t+1-k}$$

follows. We have

$$\sum_{1\leq k\leq N} k = \frac{N^2}{2}+\frac{N}{2} = \frac{N(N+1)}{2},$$

$$\sum_{1\leq k\leq N} k^2 = \frac{N^3}{3}+\frac{N^2}{2}+\frac{N}{6} = \frac{N(N+1)(2N+1)}{6},$$

$$\sum_{1\leq k\leq N} k^3 = \frac{N^4}{4}+\frac{N^3}{2}+\frac{N^2}{4} = \frac{N^2(N-1)^2}{4},$$

and in general

$$\sum_{1\leq k\leq N} k^t \sim \frac{N^{t+1}}{t+1}.$$

Beyond this basic use, Bernoulli numbers play an essential role in the Euler-Maclaurin summation formula (which is discussed in §4.5) and they arise naturally in other applications in the analysis of algorithms. For example, they appear in the generating functions for a family of algorithms related to the digital trees discussed in Chapter 7.

Bernoulli polynomials. The polynomials

$$B_m(x) = \sum_k \binom{m}{k} B_k x^{m-k}$$

that appear above have the EGF

$$\sum_{m\geq 0} B_m(x)\frac{z^m}{m!} = \frac{z}{e^z-1}e^{xz}$$

from which a number of interesting properties can be proven. For example, differentiating this EGF gives the identity

$$B_m'(x) = mB_{m-1}(x) \qquad \text{for } m > 1.$$

Our primary interest in the Bernoulli polynomials is an analytic application for approximating integrals—the Euler-Maclaurin summation formula—that we will examine in detail in the next chapter.

Exercise 3.82 Give closed-form expressions for the following:

$$\sum_{n,k\geq 0}\binom{n}{k}u^k\frac{z^n}{n!} \qquad \sum_{n,k\geq 0}k!\begin{bmatrix}n\\k\end{bmatrix}u^k\frac{z^n}{n!} \qquad \sum_{n,k\geq 0}k!\left\{\begin{matrix}n\\k\end{matrix}\right\}u^k\frac{z^n}{n!}.$$

Exercise 3.83 Prove from the generating function that

$$\binom{n}{k} = \binom{n-1}{k} + \binom{n-1}{k-1}.$$

Exercise 3.84 Prove from the generating function that

$$\begin{bmatrix}n\\k\end{bmatrix} = (n-1)\begin{bmatrix}n-1\\k\end{bmatrix} + \begin{bmatrix}n-1\\k-1\end{bmatrix}.$$

Exercise 3.85 Prove from the generating function that

$$\left\{\begin{matrix}n\\k\end{matrix}\right\} = k\left\{\begin{matrix}n-1\\k\end{matrix}\right\} + \left\{\begin{matrix}n-1\\k-1\end{matrix}\right\}.$$

Exercise 3.86 Prove that $B_m(0) = B_m(1) = B_m$ for all $m > 1$.

Exercise 3.87 Prove from the generating function that B_k is zero for k odd, $k \geq 3$.

Other types of generating functions. As mentioned at the beginning of the chapter, kernel functions other than z^k and $z^k/k!$ lead to other types of generating functions. For example, using k^{-z} as the kernel function gives *Dirichlet generating functions* (DGFs), which play an important role in number theory and in the analysis of several algorithms. These are best understood as functions of complex z, so their analytic properties are beyond the scope of this book. Nevertheless, we mention them to motivate the utility of other kernels and illustrate the kinds of formal manipulations that can arise. The Dirichlet generating function for $1, 1, 1, \ldots$ is

$$\zeta(z) = \sum_{k\geq 1}\frac{1}{k^z},$$

the Riemann zeta function. This function plays a central role in analytic number theory.

In the analysis of algorithms, Dirichlet generating functions normally represent number-theoretic properties of sequences and are expressed in terms of the zeta function. For example,

$$\zeta(z)^2 = \sum_{k\geq 1}\frac{1}{k^z}\sum_{j\geq 1}\frac{1}{j^z} = \sum_{k\geq 1}\sum_{j\geq 1}\frac{1}{(kj)^z} = \sum_{N\geq 1}\sum_{j \text{ divides } N}\frac{1}{N^z} = \sum_{N\geq 1}\frac{d_N}{N^z}$$

where d_N is the number of divisors of N. In other words, $\zeta(z)^2$ is the Dirichlet generating function for $\{d_N\}$.

Dirichlet generating functions turn out to be especially useful when we need to work with the binary representation of numbers. For example, we can easily find the DGF for the characteristic sequence for the even numbers:

$$\sum_{\substack{N\geq 1\\ N \text{ even}}}\frac{1}{N^z} = \sum_{N\geq 1}\frac{1}{(2N)^z} = \frac{1}{2^z}\zeta(z).$$

Again, while these formal manipulations are interesting, the analytic properties of these functions in the complex plane are an important facet of their use in the analysis of algorithms. Details may be found in [3] or [8].

By using other kernels—such as $z^k/(1-z^k)$ (Lambert), $\binom{z}{k}$ (Newton), or $z^k/(1-z)(1-z^2)\ldots(1-z^k)$ (Euler)—we obtain other types of generating functions that have proved over the centuries to have useful properties in analysis. Such functions arise occasionally in the analysis of algorithms, and exploration of their properties is fascinating. We mention them in passing but we do not consider them in detail because they do not play the central role that OGFs and EGFs do. Much more information on these can be found in [4], [6], [9], and [15].

Exercise 3.88 Show that, for any $k \geq 0$, the DGF for the characteristic sequence of numbers whose binary representation ends in k 0s is $\zeta(z)/2^{kz}$.

Exercise 3.89 Find the DGF for the function ψ_N, the number of trailing 0s in the binary representation of N.

Exercise 3.90 Find the DGF for the characteristic function of $\{N^2\}$.

Exercise 3.91 Prove that

$$\sum_k \frac{z^k}{1-z^k} = \sum_N d_N z^N,$$

where d_N is the number of divisors of N.

GENERATING functions have long been used in combinatorics, probability theory, and analytic number theory; hence a rich array of mathematical tools have been developed that turn out to be germane to the analysis of algorithms. We use generating functions both as *combinatorial* tools to aid in the process of precisely accounting for quantities of interest and as *analytic* tools to yield solutions. As such, their role in the analysis of algorithms is central.

We have introduced generating functions as a tool to solve the recurrences that arise in the analysis of algorithms in order to emphasize their direct relationship to the quantity being studied (running time, or other characteristic parameter, as a function of problem size). But we have also noted that a recurrence is simply one characterization of a sequence; the corresponding generating function itself is another. For many problems it is the case that direct arguments can yield explicit expressions for generating functions and recurrences can be avoided entirely. This is the basis of the symbolic method, and this theme is developed in examples in the chapters that follow and formalized in [3].

We want to understand the structures that we are analyzing sufficiently well that we can apply the symbolic method to derive functional equations on generating functions that correspond to structural definitions. When this is the case, we are able to derive all manner of information about the structures. More important, we can analyze and compare countless varieties of structures that are defined in a similar manner.

In this book, we often give classical derivations both for consistency with the literature and to allow the reader to gain experience with the kinds of generating functions that arise in the analysis of algorithms. But we stress that simple functional relationships among these functions can, in most cases, be explained in a systematic and straightforward manner through the symbolic method.

The second major reason for the importance of GFs is their analytical role. Using the generating function representation, we are often able to transform a problem to see how the sequence of interest is expressed in terms of classical special number sequences. If an exact representation is not available, the generating function representation positions us to employ powerful mathematical techniques based on properties of functions of a complex variable in order to learn properties of our algorithms. For a great many of the kinds of functions that arise in the analysis of algorithms, we can find precise estimates of asymptotic behavior of coefficients by expansion in terms of classical functions. If not, we can be secure that complex asymptotic methods are available for extracting estimates of the asymptotic values of coefficients, as discussed briefly in Chapter 4 and in detail in [3].

Ordinary, exponential, and bivariate generating functions provide a fundamental framework that enables us to develop a systematic approach to analyzing a large number of the fundamental structures that play a central role in the design of algorithms. With the additional help of the asymptotic methods to be developed in the next chapter, we are able to use the tools to develop results that we can use to predict the performance characteristics of a variety of important and useful algorithms. This theme will be developed in detail in Chapters 5 through 8.

References

1. L. Comtet. *Ad anced Combinatorics*, Reidel, Dordrecht, 1974.
2. P. Flajolet, B. Salvy, and P. Zimmerman. "Automatic average–case analysis of algorithms," *Theoretical Computer Science* **79**, 1991, 37–109.
3. P. Flajolet and R. Sedgewick. *Analytic Combinatorics*, in preparation.
4. R. L. Graham, D. E. Knuth, and O. Patashnik. *Concrete Mathematics*, Addison-Wesley, Reading, MA, 1989.
5. I. Goulden and D. Jackson. *Combinatorial Enumeration*, John Wiley, New York, 1983.
6. G. H. Hardy. *Di ergent Series*, Oxford University Press, 1947.
7. D. E. Knuth. *The Art of Computer Programming. Volume 1: Fundamental Algorithms*, Addison-Wesley, Reading, MA, 1968.
8. D. E. Knuth. *The Art of Computer Programming. Volume 3: Sorting and Searching*, Addison-Wesley, Reading, MA, 1973.
9. N. E. Nörlund. *Vorlesungen über Differenzenrechnung*, Chelsea Publishing Company, New York, 1954.
10. G. Polya, R. E. Tarjan, and D. R. Woods. *Notes on Introductory Combinatorics*, Birkhäuser, Boston, 1983.
11. J. Riordan. *Introduction to Combinatorial Analysis*, Princeton University Press, Princeton, NJ, 1980.

12. R. SEDGEWICK. “The analysis of quicksort programs,” *Acta Informatica* **7**, 1977, 327–355.
13. R. SEDGEWICK. *Quicksort*, Garland Publishing, New York, 1980.
14. R. P. STANLEY. *Enumerative Combinatorics*, Wadsworth & Brooks/Cole, 1986.
15. R. P. STANLEY. “Generating functions,” in *Studies in Combinatorics*, (M.A.A. Studies in Mathematics, **17**, G. C. Rota, ed.), The Mathematical Association of America, 1978, 100–141.
16. J. S. VITTER AND P. FLAJOLET. “Analysis of algorithms and data structures,” in *Handbook of Theoretical Computer Science A: Algorithms and Complexity*, J. van Leeuwen, ed., Elsevier, Amsterdam, 1990, 431–524.
17. H. WILF. *Generatingfunctionology*, Academic Press, San Diego, 1990.

CHAPTER FOUR

ASYMPTOTIC APPROXIMATIONS

OUR initial general orientation in the analysis of algorithms is towards deriving *exact* mathematical results. However, such exact solutions may not be always available, or if available they may be too unwieldy to be of much use. In this section, we will examine some methods of deriving approximate solutions to problems or of approximating exact solutions; as a result, we may modify our primary orientation to be towards deriving *concise* and *precise* estimates of quantities of interest.

In a manner similar to Chapter 3, our primary goal in this chapter is to provide an overview of the basic properties of asymptotic expansions, methods of manipulating them, and a catalog of those that we encounter most often in the analysis of algorithms. At times, this may seem to take us rather far from the analysis of algorithms, though we continue to draw examples and exercises directly from problems introduced in relation to specific algorithms in Chapter 1, and to set the groundwork for studying a broad variety of algorithms in Chapters 5 through 8. As we have been doing, we focus in this chapter on methods from real analysis. Asymptotic methods using complex analysis are a primary topic of [11], and the principle upon which they are based is briefly discussed in §4.10.

We have seen that the analysis of computer algorithms involves tools from discrete mathematics, leading to answers most easily expressed in terms of discrete functions (such as harmonic numbers or binomial coefficients) rather than more familiar functions from analysis (such as logarithms or powers). However, it is generally true that these two types of functions are closely related, and one reason to do asymptotic analysis is to "translate" between them.

Generally, a problem carries a notion of "size" and we are interested in approximations that become more accurate as the size becomes large. By the nature of the mathematics and the problems that we are solving, it is also often true that our answers, if they are to be expressed in terms of a single parameter N, will be (primarily) expressed in terms of asymptotic series in N and $\log N$. These series are not necessarily convergent (indeed, they are often divergent), but the initial terms give very accurate estimates for many quantities that arise in the analysis of algorithms. Our general approach will be to convert quantities to such series, then manipulate them in well-defined ways.

One motivation for considering asymptotic methods is simply to find a convenient way to calculate good approximations to specific values for quantities of interest. Another motivation is to get all our quantities in a canonical form so that we can compare and combine them easily. For example, as we saw in Chapter 1, it is helpful to know that the number of comparisons taken by Quicksort approaches $2NH_N$ as compared to the optimal $\lg N!$, but it is more useful to know that both are proportional to $N \lg N$ with coefficient $1.4421\cdots$ for the former and 1 for the latter, and that even more accurate estimates are available.

For another example, in §6.6 we encounter a simple sorting algorithm whose average running time depends on the quantity $N4^{N-1}/\binom{2N}{N}$. This is a concise exact result, but to estimate the running time of the algorithm, we might want to know the value of the quantity for, say, $N = 1000$. Using the formula to compute the value for large N is not a straightforward task, since it involves dividing two very large numbers or rearranging the computation to avoid doing so. In this chapter, we will see how to show that this quantity is very close to $N\sqrt{\pi N}/4$, which evaluates to $14,012$ for $N = 1000$ and is only about a hundredth of a percent off the exact value, which is about $14,014$. More important, as above, the way in which the value of the quantity grows as N grows is clearly indicated by the approximate result (for example, we know by inspection that the value associated with $100N$ is about 1000 times the value associated with N), making it easier to compare the approximate result with similar results for other algorithms or other versions of the same algorithm.

Another important reason for working with approximate values is that they can substantially simplify symbolic calculations that might be involved in the analysis for many problems, allowing derivation of concise answers that might otherwise not be available. We touched upon this in Chapter 2 when discussing the solution of recurrences by solving similar, simpler, recurrences and estimating the error. Asymptotic analysis gives a systematic approach to aid in such arguments.

A primary topic of the chapter is our treatment of methods for computing approximate values of sums for which exact evaluation may be difficult or impossible. Specifically, we consider how to evaluate sums by approximating them with integrals using the *Euler-Maclaurin summation formula.* We also will look at the *Laplace method* for evaluating sums by adjusting the range of summation to make different approximations applicable in different parts of the range.

We consider several examples of the application of these concepts to find approximate values of some of the special number sequences introduced in Chapter 3 and other quantities that are likely to appear in the analysis of algorithms. In particular, we consider in some detail the *Ramanujan-Knuth Q-function* and related distributions, which arise frequently in the analysis. Then, we consider limits of the binomial distribution under various circumstances. The *normal approximation* and the *Poisson approximation* are classical results that are very useful in the analysis of algorithms and also provide excellent examples of the application of tools developed in this chapter.

The standard reference on these topics is the book by De Bruijn [6], which certainly should be read by anyone with a serious interest in asymptotic analysis. A recent survey by Odlyzko [18] also provides a great deal of information and a wealth of examples. Specific information about the normal and Poisson approximations may be found, for example, in Feller [8]. Detailed coverage of many of the topics that we consider may also be found in [2], [12], [13], [15], [19], and other references listed at the end of this chapter. Methods based on complex analysis are covered in detail in [11].

4.1 Notation for Asymptotic Approximations. The following notations, which date back at least to the beginning of the century, are widely used for making precise statements about the approximate value of functions:

Definition *Given a function $f(N)$, we write*

$g(N) = O(f(N))$

if and only if $|g(N)/f(N)|$ is bounded from above as $N \to \infty$,

$g(N) = o(f(N))$

if and only if $g(N)/f(N) \to 0$ as $N \to \infty$,

$g(N) \sim f(N)$

if and only if $g(N)/f(N) \to 1$ as $N \to \infty$.

The O- and o-notations provide ways to express upper bounds (with o being the stronger assertion), and the $\sim$-notation provides a way to express asymptotic equivalence. The O-notation here coincides with the definition given in Chapter 1 for use in our discussion on computational complexity.

A variety of similar notations and definitions have been proposed. A reader interested in pursuing implications may wish to read the discussion in [6] or [12].

Exercise 4.1 Show that

$$N/(N+1) = O(1), \quad 2^N = o(N!), \quad \text{and} \quad \sqrt[N]{e} \sim 1.$$

Exercise 4.2 Show that

$$\frac{N}{N+1} = 1 + O\Big(\frac{1}{N}\Big) \quad \text{and} \quad \frac{N}{N+1} \sim 1 - \frac{1}{N}.$$

Exercise 4.3 Show that $N^\alpha = o(N^\beta)$ if $\alpha < \beta$.

Exercise 4.4 Show that, for r fixed,

$$\binom{N}{r} = \frac{N^r}{r!} + O(N^{r-1}) \quad \text{and} \quad \binom{N+r}{r} = \frac{N^r}{r!} + O(N^{r-1}).$$

Exercise 4.5 Show that $\log N = o(N^\epsilon)$ for all $\epsilon > 0$.

Exercise 4.6 Show that

$$\frac{1}{2+\ln N} = o(1) \quad \text{and} \quad \frac{1}{2+\cos N} = O(1) \quad \text{but not } o(1).$$

As we will see below, it is not usually necessary to directly apply the definitions to determine asymptotic values of quantities of interest, because the O-notation makes it possible to develop approximations using a small set of basic algebraic manipulations.

The same notations are used when approximating functions of real or complex variables near any given point. For example, we say that

$$\frac{1}{1+x} = \frac{1}{x} - \frac{1}{x^2} + \frac{1}{x^3} + O\Big(\frac{1}{x^4}\Big) \quad \text{as} \quad x \to \infty$$

and

$$\frac{1}{1+x} = 1 - x + x^2 - x^3 + O(x^4) \quad \text{as} \quad x \to 0.$$

A more general definition of the O-notation that encompasses such uses is obtained simply by replacing $N \to \infty$ by $x \to x_0$ in the definition above, and specifying any restrictions on x (for example, whether it must be integer, real, or complex). The limiting value x_0 is usually 0 or ∞, but it could be any value whatever. It is usually obvious from the context what set of numbers and what limiting value is of interest, so we normally drop the qualifying "$x \to x_0$" or "$N \to \infty$." Of course, the same remarks apply to the o and $\sim$ notations.

In the analysis of algorithms, we avoid direct usages such as "the average value of this quantity is $O\big(f(N)\big)$" because this gives scant information for the purpose of predicting performance. Instead, we strive to use the O-notation to bound "error" terms that have far smaller values than the main, or "leading" term. Informally, we expect that the terms involved should be so small as to be negligible for large N.

O-approximations. We say that $g(N) = f(N) + O(h(N))$ to indicate that we can approximate $g(N)$ by calculating $f(N)$ and that the error will be within a constant factor of $h(N)$. As usual with the O-notation, the constant involved is unspecified, but the assumption that it is not large is often justified. As discussed below, we normally use this notation with $h(N) = o(f(N))$.

o-approximations. A stronger statement is to say that $g(N) = f(N) + o(h(N))$ to indicate that we can approximate $g(N)$ by calculating $f(N)$ and that the error will get smaller and smaller compared to $h(N)$ as N gets larger. An unspecified function is involved in the rate of decrease, but the assumption that it is never large numerically (even for small N) is often justified.

$\sim$-approximations. The notation $g(N) \sim f(N)$ is used to express the weakest nontrivial o-approximation $g(N) = f(N) + o(f(N))$.

These notations are useful because they can allow suppression of unimportant details without loss of mathematical rigor or precise results. If a more accurate answer is desired, one can be obtained, but most of the detailed calculations are suppressed otherwise. We will be most interested in methods that allow us to keep this "potential accuracy," producing answers that could be calculated to arbitrarily fine precision if desired.

Exponentially small terms. When logarithms and exponentials are involved, it is worthwhile to be cognizant of "exponential differences" and avoid calculations that make truly negligible contributions to the ultimate answer of interest. For example, if we know that the value of a quantity is $2N + O\big(\log N\big)$ then we can be reasonably confident that $2N$ is within a few percent or a few thousandths of a percent of the true value when

N is a thousand or a million, and that it may not be worthwhile to find the coefficient of $\log N$ or sharpen the expansion to within $O(1)$. Similarly, an asymptotic estimate of $2^N + O(N^2)$ is quite sharp. On the other hand, knowing that a quantity is $2N \ln N + O(N)$ might not be enough to estimate it within a factor of 2, even when N is a million. To highlight exponential differences, sometimes we refer informally to a quantity as being *exponentially small* if it is smaller than any negative power of N, that is, $O(1/N^M)$ for any positive M. Typical examples of exponentially small quantities are e^{-N}, $e^{-\log^2 N}$, and $(\log N)^{-\log N}$.

Exercise 4.7 Prove that e^{-N^ϵ} is exponentially small for any positive constant ϵ. (That is, given ϵ, prove that $e^{-N^\epsilon} = O(N^{-M})$ for any fixed $M > 0$.)

Exercise 4.8 Prove that $e^{-\log^2 N}$ and $(\log N)^{-\log N}$ are exponentially small.

Exercise 4.9 If $\alpha < \beta$, show that α^N is exponentially small relative to β^N. For $\beta = 1.2$ and $\alpha = 1.1$, find the absolute and relative errors when $\alpha^N + \beta^N$ is approximated by β^N, for $N = 10$ and $N = 100$.

Exercise 4.10 Show that the product of an exponentially small quantity and any polynomial in N is an exponentially small quantity.

Exercise 4.11 Find the most accurate expression for a_n implied by each of the following recurrence relationships:

$$a_n = 2a_{n/2} + O(n)$$
$$a_n = 2a_{n/2} + o(n)$$
$$a_n \sim 2a_{n/2} + n.$$

In each case assume that $a_{n/2}$ is taken to be shorthand notation for $a_{\lfloor n/2 \rfloor} + O(1)$.

Exercise 4.12 Using the definitions from Chapter 1, find the most accurate expression for a_n implied by each of the following recurrence relationships:

$$a_n = 2a_{n/2} + O(n)$$
$$a_n = 2a_{n/2} + \Theta(n)$$
$$a_n = 2a_{n/2} + \Omega(n).$$

In each case assume that $a_{n/2}$ is taken to be shorthand notation for $a_{\lfloor n/2 \rfloor} + O(1)$.

Exercise 4.13 Let $\beta > 1$ and take $f(x) = x^\alpha$ with $\alpha > 0$. If $a(x)$ satisfies the recurrence

$$a(x) = a(x/\beta) + f(x) \qquad \text{for } x \geq 1 \text{ with } a(x) = 0 \text{ for } x < 1$$

and $b(x)$ satisfies the recurrence

$$b(x) = b(x/\beta + c) + f(x) \qquad \text{for } x \ge 1 \text{ with } b(x) = 0 \text{ for } x < 1$$

prove that $a(x) \sim b(x)$ as $x \to \infty$. Extend your proof to apply to a broader class of functions $f(x)$.

Asymptotics of linear recurrences. Linear recurrences provide an illustration of the way that asymptotic expressions can lead to substantial simplifications. We have seen in §2.4 and §3.3 that any linear recurrent sequence $\{a_n\}$ has a rational OGF and is a linear combination of terms of the form $\beta^n n^j$. Asymptotically speaking, it is clear that only a few terms need be considered, because those with larger β exponentially dominate those with smaller β (see Exercise 4.9). For example, we saw in §2.3 that the exact solution to

$$a_n = 5a_{n-1} - 6a_{n-2}, \qquad n > 1; \quad a_0 = 0 \text{ and } a_1 = 1$$

is $3^n - 2^n$, but the approximate solution 3^n is accurate to within a thousandth of a percent for $n > 25$. In short, we need keep track only of terms associated with the largest absolute value or modulus.

Theorem 4.1 (*Asymptotics for linear recurrences*) *Assume that a rational generating function $f(z)/g(z)$, with $f(z)$ and $g(z)$ relatively prime and $g(0) \ne 0$, has a unique pole $1/\beta$ of smallest modulus (that is, $g(1/\alpha) = 0$ and $\alpha \ne \beta$ implies that $|1/\alpha| > |1/\beta|$, or $|\alpha| < |\beta|$). Then, if the multiplicity of $1/\beta$ is ν, we have*

$$[z^n]\frac{f(z)}{g(z)} \sim C\beta^n n^{\nu-1} \quad \textit{where} \quad C = \nu\frac{(-\beta)^\nu f(1/\beta)}{g^{(\nu)}(1/\beta)}.$$

Proof. From the discussion in §3.3, $[z^n]f(z)/g(z)$ can be expressed as a sum of terms, one associated with each root $1/\alpha$ of $g(z)$, that is of the form $[z^n]c_0(1-\alpha z)^{-\nu_\alpha}$, where ν_α is the multiplicity of α. For all α with $|\alpha| < |\beta|$, such terms are exponentially small relative to the one associated with β because

$$[z^n]\frac{1}{(1-\alpha z)^{\nu_\alpha}} = \binom{n+\nu_\alpha-1}{\nu_\alpha-1}\alpha^n$$

and $\alpha^n n^M = o(\beta^n)$ for any nonnegative M (see Exercise 4.10).

Therefore, we need only consider the term associated with β:

$$[z^n]\frac{f(z)}{g(z)} \sim [z^n]\frac{c_0}{(1-\beta z)^\nu} \sim c_0\binom{n+\nu-1}{\nu-1}\beta^n \sim \frac{c_0}{(\nu-1)!}n^{\nu-1}\beta^n$$

(see Exercise 4.4) and it remains to determine c_0. Since $(1-\beta z)$ is not a factor of $f(z)$, this computation is immediate from l'Hôpital's rule:

$$c_0 = \lim_{z\to 1/\beta}(1-\beta z)^\nu \frac{f(z)}{g(z)} = f(1/\beta)\frac{\lim\limits_{z\to 1/\beta}(1-\beta z)^\nu}{\lim\limits_{z\to 1/\beta} g(z)} = f(1/\beta)\frac{\nu!(-\beta)^\nu}{g^{(\nu)}(1/\beta)}. \quad \blacksquare$$

For recurrences leading to $g(z)$ with a unique pole of smallest modulus, this gives a way to determine the asymptotic growth of the solution, including computation of the coefficient of the leading term. If $g(z)$ has more than one pole of smallest modulus, then, among the terms associated with such poles, the ones with highest multiplicity dominate (but not exponentially). This leads to a general method for determining the asymptotic growth of the solutions to linear recurrences, a modification of the method for exact solutions given at the end of §3.3.

- Derive $g(z)$ from the recurrence.
- Compute $f(z)$ from $g(z)$ and the initial conditions.
- Eliminate common factors in $f(z)/g(z)$. This could be done by factoring both $f(z)$ and $g(z)$ and cancelling, but full polynomial factorization of the functions is not required, just computation of the greatest common divisor.
- Identify terms associated with poles of highest multiplicity among those of smallest modulus.
- Determine the coefficients, using Theorem 4.1. As indicated above, this gives very accurate answers for large n because the terms neglected are exponentially small by comparison with the terms kept.

This process leads immediately to concise, precise approximations to solutions for linear recurrences. For example, consider the recurrence

$$a_n = 2a_{n-1} + a_{n-2} - 2a_{n-3}, \qquad n > 2; \quad a_0 = 0, a_1 = a_2 = 1.$$

We found in §3.3 that the generating function for the solution is

$$a(z) = \frac{f(z)}{g(z)} = \frac{z}{(1+z)(1-2z)}.$$

Here $\beta = 2$, $\nu = 1$, $g'(1/2) = -3$, and $f(1/2) = 1/2$, so Theorem 4.1 tells us that $a_n \sim 2^n/3$, as before.

Exercise 4.14 Use Theorem 4.1 to find an asymptotic solution to the recurrence

$$a_n = 5a_{n-1} - 8a_{n-2} + 4a_{n-3} \qquad \text{for } n > 2 \text{ with } a_0 = 1,\ a_1 = 2, \text{ and } a_2 = 4.$$

Solve the same recurrence with the initial conditions on a_0 and a_1 changed to $a_0 = 1$ and $a_1 = 2$.

Exercise 4.15 Use Theorem 4.1 to find an asymptotic solution to the recurrence

$$a_n = 2a_{n-2} - a_{n-4} \qquad \text{for } n > 4 \text{ with } a_0 = a_1 = 0 \text{ and } a_2 = a_3 = 1.$$

Exercise 4.16 Use Theorem 4.1 to find an asymptotic solution to the recurrence

$$a_n = 3a_{n-1} - 3a_{n-2} + a_{n-3} \qquad \text{for } n > 2 \text{ with } a_0 = a_1 = 0 \text{ and } a_2 = 1.$$

Exercise 4.17 [Miles, cf. Knuth] Show that the polynomial $z^t - z^{t-1} - \ldots - z - 1$ has t distinct roots and that exactly one of the roots has modulus greater than 1, for all $t > 1$.

Exercise 4.18 Give an approximate solution for the "tth-order Fibonacci" recurrence

$$F_N^{[t]} = F_{N-1}^{[t]} + F_{N-2}^{[t]} + \ldots + F_{N-t}^{[t]} \qquad \text{for } N \geq t$$

with $F_0^{[t]} = F_1^{[t]} = \ldots = F_{t-2}^{[t]} = 0$ and $F_{t-1}^{[t]} = 1$.

Exercise 4.19 [Schur] Show that the number of ways to change an N-denomination bill using coin denominations $d_1, d_2, \ldots, d_t$ with $d_1 = 1$ is asymptotic to

$$\frac{N^{t-1}}{d_1 d_2 \ldots d_t (t-1)!}.$$

(See Exercise 3.55.)

4.2 Asymptotic Expansions. As mentioned above, we prefer the equation $f(N) = c_0 g_0(N) + O(g_1(N))$ with $g_1(N) = o(g_0(N))$ to the equation $f(N) = O(g_0(N))$ because it provides the constant c_0, and therefore allows us to provide specific estimates for $f(N)$ that improve in accuracy as N gets large. If $g_0(N)$ and $g_1(N)$ are relatively close, we might wish to find a constant associated with g_1 and thus derive a "more accurate" expression: if $g_2(N) = o(g_1(N))$, we write $f(N) = c_0 g_0(N) + c_1 g_1(N) + O(g_2(N))$. For example, the expression $2N \ln N + (2\gamma - 2)N + O(\log N)$ allows us to make far more accurate estimates of the average number of comparison required for Quicksort than the expression $2N \ln N + O(N)$ for practical values of N, and adding the $O(\log N)$ and $O(1)$ terms provide even more accurate estimates, as shown in Table 4.1.

The concept of an *asymptotic expansion*, developed by Poincaré (cf. [6]), generalizes this notion:

Definition *Given a sequence of functions* $\{g_k(N)\}_{k\geq 0}$ *with* $g_{k+1}(N) = o(g_k(N))$ *for* $k \geq 0$,

$$f(N) \sim c_0 g_0(N) + c_1 g_1(N) + c_2 g_2(N) + \ldots$$

is called an asymptotic series for f, *or an asymptotic expansion of* f. *The asymptotic series represents the collection of formulae*

$$\begin{aligned}
f(N) &= O(g_0(N)) \\
f(N) &= c_0 g_0(N) + O(g_1(N)) \\
f(N) &= c_0 g_0(N) + c_1 g_1(N) + O(g_2(N)) \\
f(N) &= c_0 g_0(N) + c_1 g_1(N) + c_2 g_2(N) + O(g_3(N)) \\
&\vdots
\end{aligned}$$

and the $g_k(N)$ *are referred to as an asymptotic scale.*

Each additional term that we take from the asymptotic series gives a more accurate asymptotic estimate. Full asymptotic series are available for many functions commonly encountered in the analysis of algorithms, and we primarily consider methods that could be extended, in principle, to provide asymptotic expansions describing quantities of interest. We can use the $\sim$-notation to simply drop information on error terms or we can use the O-notation or the o-notation to provide more specific information.

N	$2(N+1)(H_{N+1}-1)$	$2N\ln N$	$+(2\gamma-2)N$	$+2(\ln N+\gamma)+1$
10	44.43	46.05	37.59	44.35
100	847.85	921.03	836.47	847.84
1000	12,985.91	13,815.51	12,969.94	12,985.91
10000	175,771.70	184,206.81	175,751.12	175,771.70

Table 4.1 Asymptotic estimates for Quicksort comparison counts

This is an extension of the definition of $\sim$ given at the beginning of §4.1. The earlier use normally would involve just one term on the right-hand side, whereas the current definition calls for a series of (decreasing) terms.

Indeed, we primarily deal with *finite* expansions, not (infinite) asymptotic series, and use, for example, the notation

$$f(N) \sim c_0 g_0(N) + c_1 g_1(N) + c_2 g_2(N)$$

to refer to a finite expansion with the implicit error term $o(g_2(N)$. Most often, we use finite asymptotic expansions of the form

$$f(N) = c_0 g_0(N) + c_1 g_1(N) + c_2 g_2(N) + O(g_3(N)),$$

obtained by simply truncating the asymptotic series. In practice, we generally use only a few terms (perhaps three or four) for an approximation, since the usual situation is to have an asymptotic scale that makes later terms extremely small in comparison to early terms for large N. For the Quicksort example shown in Table 4.1, the "more accurate" formula $2N \ln N + (2\gamma - 2)N + 2\ln N + 2\gamma + 1$ gives an absolute error less than .1 already for $N = 10$.

Exercise 4.20 Extend Table 4.1 to cover the cases $N = 10^5$ and 10^6.

The full generality of the Poincaré approach allows asymptotic expansions to be expressed in terms of *any* infinite series of functions that decrease (in a o-notation sense). However, we are most often interested in a very restricted set of functions: indeed, we are very often able to express approximations in terms of decreasing powers of N when approximating functions as N increases. Other functions occasionally are needed, but we normally will be content with an asymptotic scale consisting of terms of decreasing series of products of powers of N, $\log N$, iterated logarithms such as $\log\log N$, and exponentials.

When developing an asymptotic estimate, it is not necessarily clear how many terms should be carried in the expansion to get the desired accuracy in the result. For example, frequently we need to subtract or divide quantities for which we only have asymptotic estimates, so cancellations might occur that necessitate carrying more terms. Typically, we carry three or four terms in an expansion, perhaps redoing the derivation to streamline it or to add more terms once the nature of the result is known.

Taylor expansions. Taylor series are the source of many asymptotic expansions: each (infinite) Taylor expansion gives rise to an asymptotic series as $x \to 0$.

Table 4.2 gives asymptotic expansions for some of the basic functions, derived from truncating Taylor series. These expansions are classical, and follow immediately from the Taylor theorem. In the sections that follow, we describe methods of manipulating asymptotic series using these expansions. Other similar expansions follow immediately from the generating functions given in the previous chapter. The first four expansions serve as the basis for many of the asymptotic calculations that we do (actually, the first three suffice, since the geometric expansion is a special case of the binomial expansion).

For a typical example of the use of Table 4.2, consider the problem of finding an asymptotic expansion for $\ln(N-2)$ as $N \to \infty$. We do so by

exponential	$e^x = 1 + x + \frac{x^2}{2} + \frac{x^3}{6} + O(x^4)$
logarithmic	$\ln(1+x) = x - \frac{x^2}{2} + \frac{x^3}{3} + O(x^4)$
binomial	$(1+x)^k = 1 + kx + \binom{k}{2}x^2 + \binom{k}{3}x^3 + O(x^4)$
geometric	$\frac{1}{1-x} = 1 + x + x^2 + x^3 + O(x^4)$
trigonometric	$\sin(x) = x - \frac{x^3}{6} + \frac{x^5}{120} + O(x^7)$
	$\cos(x) = 1 - \frac{x^2}{2} + \frac{x^4}{24} + O(x^6)$

Table 4.2 Asymptotic expansions derived from Taylor series ($x \to 0$)

pulling out the leading term, writing

$$\ln(N-2) = \ln N + \ln(1 - \frac{2}{N}) = \ln N - \frac{2}{N} + O\Big(\frac{1}{N^2}\Big).$$

That is, in order to use Table 4.2, we find a substitution ($x = -2/N$) with $x \to 0$.

Or, we can use more terms of the Taylor expansion to get a more general asymptotic result. For example, the expansion

$$\ln(N + \sqrt{N}) = \ln N + \frac{1}{\sqrt{N}} - \frac{1}{2N} + O\Big(\frac{1}{N^{3/2}}\Big)$$

follows from factoring out $\ln N$, then taking $x = 1/\sqrt{N}$ in the Taylor expansion for $\ln(1+x)$. This kind of manipulation is typical, and we will see many examples below.

Exercise 4.21 Expand $\ln(1 - x + x^2)$ as $x \to 0$, to within $O(x^4)$.

Exercise 4.22 Give an asymptotic expansion for $\ln(N^\alpha + N^\beta)$, where α and β are positive constants with $\alpha > \beta$.

Exercise 4.23 Give an asymptotic expansion for $\dfrac{N}{N-1}\ln\dfrac{N}{N-1}$.

Exercise 4.24 Estimate the value of $e^{.1} + \cos(.1) - \ln(.9)$ to within 10^{-4}, without using a calculator.

Exercise 4.25 Show that

$$\frac{1}{9801} = 0.000102030405060708091011\cdots47484950\cdots$$

to within 10^{-100}. How many more digits can you predict? Generalize.

Nonconvergent asymptotic series. Any convergent series leads to a full asymptotic approximation, but it is very important to note that the converse is *not* true—an asymptotic series may well be divergent. For example, we might have a function

$$f(N) \sim \sum_{k\ge 0} \frac{k!}{N^k}$$

implying (for example) that

$$f(N) = 1 + \frac{1}{N} + \frac{2}{N^2} + \frac{6}{N^3} + O\Big(\frac{1}{N^4}\Big)$$

even though the infinite sum does not converge. Why is this allowed? If we take any fixed number of terms from the expansion, then the equality implied from the definition is meaningful, as $N \to \infty$. That is, we have an infinite collection of better and better approximations, but the point at which they start giving useful information gets larger and larger.

Stirling's formula. The most celebrated example of a divergent asymptotic series is *Stirling's formula*, which begins as follows:

$$N! = \sqrt{2\pi N}\left(\frac{N}{e}\right)^N\left(1 + \frac{1}{12N} + \frac{1}{288N^2} + O\left(\frac{1}{N^3}\right)\right).$$

In §4.6 we show how this formula is derived, using a method that gives a full (but divergent!) series in decreasing powers of N. The fact that the series is divergent is of little concern in practice because the first few terms give an extremely accurate estimate, as shown in Table 4.3 and discussed in further detail below. Now, the constant implicit in the O-notation means that, strictly speaking, such a formula does not give complete information about a specific value of N, since the constant is arbitrary (or unspecified). In principle, one can always go to the source of the asymptotic series and prove specific bounds on the constant to overcome this objection. For example, it is possible to show that

$$N! = \sqrt{2\pi N}\left(\frac{N}{e}\right)^N\left(1 + \frac{\theta_N}{12N}\right).$$

N	$N!$	$\sqrt{2\pi N}\left(\frac{N}{e}\right)^N\left(1 + \frac{1}{12N} + \frac{1}{288N^2}\right)$	*absolute error*	*relative error*
1	1	1.002183625	.0022	10^{-2}
2	2	2.000628669	.0006	10^{-3}
3	6	6.000578155	.0006	10^{-4}
4	24	24.00098829	.001	10^{-4}
5	120	120.0025457	.002	10^{-4}
6	720	720.0088701	.009	10^{-4}
7	5040	5040.039185	.039	10^{-5}
8	40320	40320.21031	.210	10^{-5}
9	362880	362881.3307	1.33	10^{-5}
10	3628800	3628809.711	9.71	10^{-5}

Table 4.3 Accuracy of Stirling's formula for $N!$

for all $N > 1$ where $0 < \theta_N < 1$ (see, for example, [1]). As in this example, it is normally safe to assume that the constants implicit in the O-notation are small and forgo the development of precise bounds on the error. Typically, if more accuracy is desired, the next term in the asymptotic series will eventually provide it, for large enough N.

Exercise 4.26 Use the nonasymptotic version of Stirling's formula to give a bound on the error made in estimating $N4^{N-1}/\binom{2N}{N}$ with $N\sqrt{\pi N}/4$.

Absolute error. As defined above, a finite asymptotic expansion has only one O-term, and we will discuss below how to perform various standard manipulations that preserve this property. If possible, we strive to express the final answer in the form $f(N) = g(N)+O(h(N))$, so that the unknown error represented by the O-notation becomes negligible in an absolute sense as N increases (which means that $h(N) = o(1)$). In an asymptotic series, we get more accurate estimates by including more terms in $g(N)$ and taking smaller $h(N)$. For example, Table 4.4 shows how adding terms to the asymptotic series for the harmonic numbers gives more accurate estimates. We show how this series is derived below. Like Stirling's formula, it is a divergent asymptotic series.

Relative error. We can always express estimates in the alternative form $f(N) = g(N)(1 + O(h(N)))$, where $h(N) = o(1)$. In some situations, we have to be content with an absolute error that may increase with N. The relative error decreases as N increases, but the absolute error is not necessarily "negligible" when trying to compute $f(N)$. We often encounter this type of estimate when $f(N)$ grows exponentially. For example, Table 4.3 shows the absolute and relative error in Stirling's formula. The logarithm

N	H_N	$\ln N$	$+\gamma$	$+\frac{1}{2N}$	$+\frac{1}{12N^2}$
10	2.9289683	2.3025851	2.8798008	2.9298008	2.9289674
100	5.1873775	4.6051702	5.1823859	5.1873859	5.1873775
1000	7.4854709	6.9077553	7.4849709	7.4854709	7.4854709
10000	9.7876060	9.2103404	9.7875560	9.7876060	9.7876060
100000	12.0901461	11.5129255	12.0901411	12.0901461	12.0901461
1000000	14.3927267	13.8155106	14.3927262	14.3927267	14.3927267

Table 4.4 Asymptotic estimates of the harmonic numbers

of Stirling's expansion gives an asymptotic series for $\ln N!$ with very small absolute error, as shown in Table 4.5.

We normally use the "relative error" formulation only when working with quantities that are exponentially large in N, like $N!$ or the Catalan numbers. In the analysis of algorithms, such quantities typically appear at intermediate stages in the calculation; then operations such as dividing two such quantities or taking the logarithm takes us back into the realm of absolute error for most quantities of interest in applications.

This situation is normal when we use the cumulative counting method for computing averages. For example, to find the number of leaves in binary trees in Chapter 3, we counted the total number of leaves in all trees, then divided by the Catalan numbers. In that case, we could compute an exact result, but for many other problems, it is typical to divide two asymptotic estimates. Indeed, this example illustrates a primary reason for using asymptotics. The average number of nodes satisfying some property in a tree of, say, 1000 nodes will certainly be less than 1000, and we may be able to use generating functions to derive an exact formula for the number in terms of Catalan numbers and binomial coefficients. But computing that number (which might involve multiplying and dividing numbers like 2^{1000} or 1000!) might be a rather complicated chore without asymptotics. In the next section, we show basic techniques for manipulating asymptotic expansions that allow us to derive accurate asymptotic estimates in such cases.

Table 4.6 gives asymptotic series for special number sequences that are encountered frequently in combinatorics and the analysis of algorithms. Many of these approximations are derived below as examples of manipulating and deriving asymptotic series. We refer to these expansions frequently later in the book because the number sequences themselves arise

N	$\ln N!$	$(N+\frac{1}{2})\ln N - N + \ln\sqrt{2\pi} + \dfrac{1}{12N}$	*error*
10	15.104413	15.104415	10^{-6}
100	363.739375556	363.739375558	10^{-11}
1000	5912.128178488163	5912.128178488166	10^{-15}
10000	82108.9278368143533455	82108.9278368143533458	10^{-19}

Table 4.5 Absolute error in Stirling's formula for $\ln N!$

factorials (Stirling's formula)

$$N! = \sqrt{2\pi N}\Big(\frac{N}{e}\Big)^N\Big(1 + \frac{1}{12N} + \frac{1}{288N^2} + O\Big(\frac{1}{N^3}\Big)\Big)$$

$$\ln N! = \Big(N + \frac{1}{2}\Big)\ln N - N + \ln\sqrt{2\pi} + \frac{1}{12N} + O\Big(\frac{1}{N^3}\Big)$$

harmonic numbers

$$H_N = \ln N + \gamma + \frac{1}{2N} - \frac{1}{12N^2} + O\Big(\frac{1}{N^4}\Big)$$

binomial coefficients

$$\binom{N}{k} = \frac{N^k}{k!}\Big(1 + O\Big(\frac{1}{N}\Big)\Big) \quad \text{for } k = O(1)$$

$$= \frac{2^{N/2}}{\sqrt{\pi N}}\Big(1 + O\Big(\frac{1}{N}\Big)\Big) \quad \text{for } k = \frac{N}{2} + O(1)$$

normal approximation to the binomial distribution

$$\binom{2N}{N-k}\frac{1}{2^{2N}} = \frac{e^{-k^2/N}}{\sqrt{\pi N}} + O\Big(\frac{1}{N^{3/2}}\Big)$$

Poisson approximation to the binomial distribution

$$\binom{N}{k}p^k(1-p)^{N-k} = \frac{\lambda^k e{-}\lambda}{k!} + o(1) \quad \text{for } p = \lambda/N$$

Stirling numbers of the first kind

$$\begin{bmatrix} N \\ k \end{bmatrix} \sim \frac{(N-1)!}{(k-1)!}(\ln N)^{k-1} \quad \text{for } k = O(1)$$

Stirling numbers of the second kind

$$\begin{Bmatrix} N \\ k \end{Bmatrix} \sim \frac{k^N}{k!} \quad \text{for } k = O(1)$$

Bernoulli numbers

$$B_{2N} = (-1)^N\frac{(2N)!}{(2\pi)^{2N}}(-2 + O(4^{-N}))$$

Catalan numbers

$$T_N \equiv \frac{1}{N+1}\binom{2N}{N} = \frac{4^N}{\sqrt{\pi N^3}}\Big(1 + O\Big(\frac{1}{N}\Big)\Big)$$

Fibonacci numbers

$$F_N = \frac{\phi^N}{\sqrt{5}} + O(\phi^{-N}) \quad \text{where } \phi = \tfrac{1+\sqrt{5}}{2}$$

Table 4.6 Asymptotic expansions for special numbers ($N \to \infty$)

naturally when studying properties of algorithms, and the asymptotic expansions therefore provide a convenient way to accurately quantify performance characteristics and appropriately compare algorithms.

Exercise 4.27 Assume that the constant C implied in the O-notation is less than 10 in absolute value. Give specific bounds for H_{1000} implied by the absolute formula $H_N = \ln N + \gamma + O(1/N)$ and by the relative formula $H_N = \ln N(1 + O(1/\log N))$.

Exercise 4.28 Assume that the constant C implied in the O-notation is less than 10 in absolute value. Give specific bounds for the 10th Catalan number implied by the relative formula

$$\frac{1}{N+1}\binom{2N}{N} = \frac{4^N}{\sqrt{\pi N^3}}\Bigl(1 + O\Bigl(\frac{1}{N}\Bigr)\Bigr).$$

Exercise 4.29 Suppose that $f(N)$ admits a convergent representation

$$f(N) = \sum_{k\geq 0} a_k N^{-k}$$

for $N \geq N_0$ where N_0 is a fixed constant. Prove that

$$f(N) = \sum_{0\leq k<M} a_k N^{-k} + O(N^{-M})$$

for any $M > 0$.

Exercise 4.30 Construct a function $f(N)$ such that $f(N) \sim \sum_{k\geq 0} \frac{k!}{N^k}$.

4.3 Manipulating Asymptotic Expansions. We use asymptotic series, especially finite expansions, not only because they provide a succinct way to express approximate results with some control on accuracy, but also because they are relatively easy to manipulate, and allow us to perform complicated operations while still working with relatively simple expressions. The reason for this is that we rarely insist on maintaining the full asymptotic series for the quantity being studied, only the first few terms of the expansion, so that we are free to discard less significant terms each time we perform a calculation. In practice, the result is that we are able to get accurate expressions describing a wide variety of functions in a canonical form involving only a few terms.

Basic properties of the O-notation. A number of elementary identities, easily proven from the definition, facilitate manipulating expressions involving O-notation. These are intuitive rules, some of which we have been implicitly using already. We use an arrow to indicate that any expression containing the left-hand side of one of these identities can be simplified by using the corresponding right-hand side, on the right-hand side of an equation:

$$
\begin{aligned}
f(N) &\to O(f(N)) \\
cO(f(N)) &\to O(f(N)) \\
O(cf(N)) &\to O(f(N)) \\
f(N) - g(N) = O(h(N)) &\to f(N) = g(N) + O(h(N)) \\
O(f(N))O(g(N)) &\to O(f(N)g(N)) \\
O(f(N)) + O(g(N)) &\to O(g(N)) \qquad \text{if } f(N) = O(g(N)).
\end{aligned}
$$

It is not strictly proper to use the O-notation on the left-hand side of an equation. We do often write expressions like $N^2+N+O(1) = N^2+O(N) = O(N^2)$ to avoid cumbersome formal manipulations with notations like the arrow used above, but we would not use the equations $N = O(N^2)$ and $N^2 = O(N^2)$ to reach the absurd conclusion $N = N^2$.

The O-notation actually makes possible a wide range of ways of describing any particular function, but it is common practice to apply these rules to write down simple canonical expressions without constants. We write $O(N^2)$, never $NO(N)$ or $2O(N^2)$ or $O(2N^2)$, even though these are all equivalent. It is conventional to write $O(1)$ for an unspecified constant, never something like $O(3)$. Also, we write $O(\log N)$ without specifying the base of the logarithm (when it is a constant), since specifying the base amounts to giving a constant that is irrelevant because of the O-notation.

The manipulation of asymptotic expansions generally reduces in a straightforward manner to the application of one of several basic operations, which we consider in turn. In the examples, we will normally consider series with one, two, or three terms (not counting the O-term). Of course, the methods apply to longer series, as well.

Exercise 4.31 Prove or disprove the following, for $N \to \infty$:

$$e^N = O(N^2), \quad e^N = O(2^N), \quad 2^{-N} = O\Big(\frac{1}{N^{10}}\Big), \quad \text{and} \quad N^{\ln N} = O\big(e^{(\ln N)^2}\big).$$

Simplification. The main principle that we must be cognizant of when doing asymptotics is that an asymptotic series is only as good as its O-term, so anything smaller (in an asymptotic sense) may as well be discarded. For example, the expression $\ln N + O(1)$ is mathematically equivalent to the expression $\ln N + \gamma + O(1)$, but simpler.

Substitution. The simplest and most common asymptotic series derive from substituting appropriately chosen variable values into Taylor series expansions such as those in Table 4.2, or into other asymptotic series. For example, by taking $x = -1/N$ in the geometric series

$$\frac{1}{1-x} = 1 + x + x^2 + O(x^3) \qquad \text{as } x \to 0$$

we find that

$$\frac{1}{N+1} = \frac{1}{N} - \frac{1}{N^2} + O\Big(\frac{1}{N^3}\Big) \qquad \text{as } N \to \infty.$$

Similarly,

$$e^{1/N} = 1 + \frac{1}{N} + \frac{1}{2N^2} + \frac{1}{6N^3} + \cdots + \frac{1}{k!N^k} + O\Big(\frac{1}{N^{k+1}}\Big).$$

Exercise 4.32 Give an asymptotic expansion for $e^{1/(N+1)}$ to within $O(N^{-3})$.

Factoring. In many cases, the "approximate" value of a function is obvious upon inspection, and it is worthwhile to rewrite the function making this explicit in terms of relative or absolute error. For example, the function $1/(N^2 + N)$ is obviously very close to $1/N^2$ for large N, which we can express explicitly by writing

$$\begin{aligned}\frac{1}{N^2+N} &= \frac{1}{N^2}\frac{1}{1+1/N}\\ &= \frac{1}{N^2}\Big(1 + \frac{1}{N} + O\Big(\frac{1}{N^2}\Big)\Big)\\ &= \frac{1}{N^2} + \frac{1}{N^3} + O\Big(\frac{1}{N^4}\Big).\end{aligned}$$

If we are confronted with a complicated function for which the approximate value is not immediately obvious, then a short trial-and-error process might be necessary.

Multiplication. Multiplying two asymptotic series is simply a matter of doing the term-by-term multiplications, then collecting terms. For example,

$$\begin{aligned}(H_N)^2 &= \Bigl(\ln N + \gamma + O\Bigl(\frac{1}{N}\Bigr)\Bigr)\Bigl(\ln N + \gamma + O\Bigl(\frac{1}{N}\Bigr)\Bigr)\\ &= \Bigl((\ln N)^2 + \gamma\ln N + O\Bigl(\frac{\log N}{N}\Bigr)\Bigr)\\ &\quad + \Bigl(\gamma\ln N + \gamma^2 + O\Bigl(\frac{1}{N}\Bigr)\Bigr)\\ &\quad + \Bigl(O\Bigl(\frac{\log N}{N}\Bigr) + O\Bigl(\frac{1}{N}\Bigr) + O\Bigl(\frac{1}{N^2}\Bigr)\Bigr)\\ &= (\ln N)^2 + 2\gamma\ln N + \gamma^2 + O\Bigl(\frac{\log N}{N}\Bigr).\end{aligned}$$

In this case, the product has less absolute asymptotic "accuracy" than the factors—the result is only accurate to within $O(\log N/N)$. This is normal, and we typically need to begin a derivation with asymptotic expansions that have more terms than desired in the result. Often, we use a two-step process: do the calculation, and if the answer does not have the desired accuracy, express the original components more accurately and repeat the calculation.

Exercise 4.33 Calculate $(H_N)^2$ to within $O(1/N)$, then to within $o(1/N)$.

For another example, we estimate N factorial squared:

$$\begin{aligned}N!N! &= \Bigl(\sqrt{2\pi N}\Bigl(\frac{N}{e}\Bigr)^N(1 + O\Bigl(\frac{1}{N}\Bigr)\Bigr)^2\\ &= 2\pi N\Bigl(\frac{N}{e}\Bigr)^{2N}\Bigl(1 + O\Bigl(\frac{1}{N}\Bigr)\Bigr)\end{aligned}$$

since

$$\Bigl(1 + O\Bigl(\frac{1}{N}\Bigr)\Bigr)^2 = 1 + 2O\Bigl(\frac{1}{N}\Bigr) + O\Bigl(\frac{1}{N^2}\Bigr) = 1 + O\Bigl(\frac{1}{N}\Bigr).$$

Division. To compute the quotient of two asymptotic series, we typically factor and rewrite the denominator in the form $1/(1-x)$ for some symbolic expression x that tends to 0, then expand as a geometric series, and multiply. For example, to compute an asymptotic expansion of $\tan x$, we can divide the series for $\sin x$ by the series for $\cos x$, as follows:

$$\begin{aligned}
\tan x = \frac{\sin x}{\cos x} &= \frac{x - x^3/6 + O(x^5)}{1 - x^2/2 + O(x^4)} \\
&= \Bigl(x - x^3/6 + O(x^5)\Bigr)\frac{1}{1 - x^2/2 + O(x^4)} \\
&= \Bigl(x - x^3/6 + O(x^5)\Bigr)(1 + x^2/2 + O(x^4)) \\
&= x + x^3/3 + O(x^5).
\end{aligned}$$

Exercise 4.34 Derive an asymptotic expansion for $\cot x$ to $O(x^4)$.

Exercise 4.35 Derive an asymptotic expansion for $x/(e^x - 1)$ to $O(x^5)$.

For another example, consider approximating the middle binomial coefficients $\binom{2N}{N}$. We divide the series

$$(2N)! = 2\sqrt{\pi N}\Bigl(\frac{2N}{e}\Bigr)^{2N}\Bigl(1 + O\Bigl(\frac{1}{N}\Bigr)\Bigr)$$

by (from above)

$$N!N! = 2\pi N\Bigl(\frac{N}{e}\Bigr)^{2N}(1 + O\Bigl(\frac{1}{N}\Bigr))$$

to get the result

$$\binom{2N}{N} = \frac{2^{2N}}{\sqrt{\pi N}}\Bigl(1 + O\Bigl(\frac{1}{N}\Bigr)\Bigr).$$

Multiplying this by $1/(N+1) = 1/N - 1/N^2 + O(1/N^3)$ gives the approximation for the Catalan numbers in Table 4.6.

Exponentiation/logarithm. Writing $f(x)$ as $\exp\{\ln(f(x))\}$ is often a convenient start for doing asymptotics involving powers or products. For example, an alternate way to derive the asymptotics of the Catalan numbers using the Stirling approximation is to write

$$\begin{aligned}
\frac{1}{N+1}\binom{2N}{N} &= \exp\{\ln((2N)!) - 2\ln N! - \ln(N+1)\} \\
&= \exp\Bigl\{\Bigl(2N + \frac{1}{2}\Bigr)\ln(2N) - 2N + \ln\sqrt{2\pi} + O\Bigl(\frac{1}{N}\Bigr) \\
&\qquad - 2\Bigl(N + \frac{1}{2}\Bigr)\ln N + 2N - 2\ln\sqrt{2\pi} + O\Bigl(\frac{1}{N}\Bigr) \\
&\qquad - \ln N + O\Bigl(\frac{1}{N}\Bigr)\Bigr\} \\
&= \exp\Bigl\{\Bigl(2N + \frac{1}{2}\Bigr)\ln 2 - \frac{3}{2}\ln N - \ln\sqrt{2\pi} + O\Bigl(\frac{1}{N}\Bigr)\Bigr\}
\end{aligned}$$

which is again equivalent to the approximation in Table 4.6 for the Catalan numbers.

Exercise 4.36 Carry out the expansion for the Catalan numbers to within $O(N^{-4})$ accuracy.

Exercise 4.37 Calculate an asymptotic expansion for $\binom{3N}{N}/(N+1)$.

Exercise 4.38 Calculate an asymptotic expansion for $(3N)!/(N!)^3$.

Another standard example of the exp/log manipulation is the following approximation for e:

$$\begin{aligned}\Bigl(1+\frac{1}{N}\Bigr)^N &= \exp\Bigl\{N\ln\Bigl(1+\frac{1}{N}\Bigr)\Bigr\}\\ &= \exp\Bigl\{N\Bigl(\frac{1}{N}+O\Bigl(\frac{1}{N^2}\Bigr)\Bigr)\Bigr\}\\ &= \exp\Bigl\{1+O\Bigl(\frac{1}{N}\Bigr)\Bigr\}\\ &= e+O\Bigl(\frac{1}{N}\Bigr).\end{aligned}$$

The last step of this derivation is justified below. Again, we can appreciate the utility of asymptotic analysis by considering how to compute the value of this expression when (say) N is a million or a billion.

Exercise 4.39 What is the approximate value of $\Bigl(1-\dfrac{\lambda}{N}\Bigr)^N$?

Exercise 4.40 Give a three-term asymptotic expansion of $\Bigl(1-\dfrac{\ln N}{N}\Bigr)^N$.

Exercise 4.41 Suppose that interest on a bank account is "compounded daily," that is, $1/365$ of the interest is added to the account each day, for 365 days. How much more interest is paid in a year on an account with \$10,000, at a 10% interest rate compounded daily, as opposed to the \$1,000 that would be paid if interest were paid once a year?

Composition. From substitution into the expansion of the exponential it is obvious that

$$e^{1/N}=1+\frac{1}{N}+O\Bigl(\frac{1}{N^2}\Bigr),$$

but this is slightly different from

$$e^{O(1/N)}=1+O\Bigl(\frac{1}{N}\Bigr),$$

which was assumed in the two derivations just given. In this case, substituting $O(1/N)$ into the expansion of the exponential is still valid:

$$e^{O(1/N)} = 1 + O\Big(\frac{1}{N}\Big) + O\Big(\Big(O\Big(\frac{1}{N}\Big)\Big)^2\Big)$$
$$= 1 + O\Big(\frac{1}{N}\Big).$$

Since we usually deal with relatively short expansions, we can often develop simple asymptotic estimates for functions with a rather complicated appearance, just by power series substitution. Specific conditions governing such manipulations are given in [7].

Exercise 4.42 Simplify the asymptotic expression $\exp\{1+1/N+O(1/N^2)\}$ without losing asymptotic accuracy.

Exercise 4.43 Find an asymptotic estimate for $\ln(\sin((N!)^{-1}))$ to within $O(1/N^2)$.

Exercise 4.44 Show that $\sin(\tan(1/N)) \sim 1/N$ and $\tan(\sin(1/N)) \sim 1/N$. Then find the order of growth of $\sin(\tan(1/N)) - \tan(\sin(1/N))$.

Exercise 4.45 Find an asymptotic estimate for H_{T_N}, where T_N is the Nth Catalan number, to within $O(1/N)$.

Inversion. Suppose that we have an asymptotic expansion

$$y = x + c_2x^2 + c_3x^3 + O(x^4).$$

We omit the constant term and the coefficient of the linear term to simplify calculations. This expansion can be transformed into an equation expressing x in terms of y through a bootstrapping process similar to that used to estimate approximate solutions to recurrences in Chapter 2. First, we clearly must have

$$x = O(y)$$

because $x/y = x/(x + c_2x^2 + O(x^3))$ is bounded as $x \to 0$. Substituting into the original expansion, this means that $y = x + O(y^2)$, or

$$x = y + O(y^2).$$

Substituting into the original expansion again, we have $y = x + c_2(y + O(y^2))^2 + O(y^3)$, or

$$x = y - c_2y^2 + O(y^3).$$

Each time we substitute back into the original expansion, we get another term. Continuing, we have $y = x + c_2(y - c_2y^2 + O(y^3))^2 + c_3(y - c_2y^2 + O(y^3))^3 + O(y^4)$, or

$$x = y - c_2y^2 + (2c_2^2 - c_3)y^3 + O(y^4).$$

Exercise 4.46 Let a_n be defined as the unique positive root of the equation

$$n = a_n e^{a_n}$$

for $n > 1$. Find an asymptotic estimate for a_n, to within $O\big(1/(\log n)^3\big)$.

Exercise 4.47 Give the reversion of the power series

$$y = c_0 + c_1x + c_2x^2 + c_3x^3 + O(x^4).$$

(*Hint*: Take $z = (y - c_0)/c_1$.)

4.4 Asymptotic Approximations of Finite Sums. Frequently, we are able to express a quantity as a finite sum, and therefore we need to be able to accurately estimate the value of the sum. As we saw in Chapter 2, some sums can be evaluated exactly, but in many more cases, exact values are not available. Also, it may be the case that we only have estimates for the quantities themselves being summed.

In [6], De Bruijn considers this topic in some detail. He outlines a number of different cases that frequently arise, oriented around the observation that it is frequently the case that the terms in the sum vary tremendously in value. We briefly consider some elementary examples in this section, but concentrate on the *Euler-Maclaurin formula*, a fundamental tool for estimating sums with integrals. We show how the Euler-Maclaurin formula gives asymptotic expansions for the harmonic numbers and factorials (Stirling's formula).

We consider a number of applications of Euler-Maclaurin summation throughout the rest of this chapter, particularly concentrating on summands involving classical "bivariate" functions exemplified by binomial coefficients. As we will see, these applications are predicated upon estimating summands differently in different parts of the range of summation, but they ultimately depend on estimating a sum with an integral by means of Euler-Maclaurin summation. Many more details on these and related topics may be found in [2], [3], [6], [12], and [19].

Bounding the tail. When the terms in a finite sum are rapidly decreasing, an asymptotic estimate can be developed by approximating the sum with an infinite sum and developing a bound on the size of the infinite tail. The following classical example, which counts the number of permutations that are "derangements" (see Chapter 6), illustrates this point:

$$N!\sum_{0\le k\le N}\frac{(-1)^k}{k!} = N!e^{-1} - R_N \quad\text{where}\quad R_N = N!\sum_{k>N}\frac{(-1)^k}{k!}.$$

Now we can bound the tail R_N by bounding the individual terms:

$$|R_N| < \frac{1}{N+1} + \frac{1}{(N+1)^2} + \frac{1}{(N+1)^3} + \ldots = \frac{1}{N}$$

so that the sum is $N!e^{-1} + O(1/N)$. In this case, the convergence is so rapid that it is possible to show that the value is always equal to $N!e^{-1}$ rounded to the nearest integer.

The infinite sum involved converges to a constant, but there may be no explicit expression for the constant. However, the rapid convergence normally means that it is easy to calculate the value of the constant with great accuracy. The following example is related to sums that arise in the study of tries (see Chapter 7):

$$\sum_{1\le k\le N}\frac{1}{2^k-1} = \sum_{k\ge 1}\frac{1}{2^k-1} - R_N, \quad\text{where}\quad R_N = \sum_{k>N}\frac{1}{2^k-1}.$$

In this case, we have

$$0 < R_N < \sum_{k>N}\frac{1}{2^{k-1}} = \frac{1}{2^{N-1}}$$

so that the constant $1 + 1/3 + 1/7 + 1/15 + \ldots = 1.6066\cdots$ is an extremely good approximation to the finite sum. It is a trivial matter to calculate the value of this constant to any reasonable desired accuracy.

Using the tail. When the terms in a finite sum are rapidly increasing, the last term often suffices to give a good asymptotic estimate for the whole sum. For example,

$$\sum_{0\le k\le N} k! = N!\Bigl(1 + \frac{1}{N} + \sum_{0\le k\le N-2}\frac{k!}{N!}\Bigr) = N!\Bigl(1 + O\Bigl(\frac{1}{N}\Bigr)\Bigr).$$

The latter equality follows because there are $N-1$ terms in the sum, each less than $1/(N(N-1))$.

Exercise 4.48 Give an asymptotic estimate for $\sum_{1\le k\le N} 1/(k^2 H_k)$.

Exercise 4.49 Give an asymptotic estimate for $\sum_{0\le k\le N} 1/F_k$.

Exercise 4.50 Give an asymptotic estimate for $\sum_{0\le k\le N} 2^k/(2^k+1)$.

Exercise 4.51 Give an asymptotic estimate for $\sum_{0\le k\le N} 2^{k^2}$.

Approximating sums with integrals. More generally, we expect that we should be able to estimate the value of a sum with an integral and to take advantage of the wide repertoire of known integrals.

What is the magnitude of the error made when we use

$$\int_a^b f(x)dx \quad \text{to estimate} \quad \sum_{a\le k<b} f(k)?$$

The answer to this question depends on how "smooth" the function $f(x)$ is. Essentially, in each of the $b-a$ unit intervals between a and b, we are using $f(k)$ to estimate $f(x)$. Letting

$$\delta_k = \max_{k\le x<k+1} |f(x)-f(k)|$$

denote the maximum error in each interval, we can get a rough approximation to the total error:

$$\sum_{a\le k<b} f(k) = \int_a^b f(x)dx + \Delta, \qquad \text{with } |\Delta| \le \sum_{a\le k<b} \delta_k.$$

If the function is monotone increasing or decreasing over the whole interval $[a,b]$, then the error term telescopes to simply $\Delta \le |f(a)-f(b)|$. For example, for the harmonic numbers, this gives the estimate

$$H_N = \sum_{1\le k\le N} \frac{1}{k} = \int_1^N \frac{1}{x}dx + \Delta = \ln N + \Delta$$

with $|\Delta| \le 1-1/N$, an easy proof that $H_N \sim \ln N$; and for $N!$ this gives the estimate

$$\ln N! = \sum_{1\le k\le N} \ln k = \int_1^N \ln x\,dx + \Delta = N\ln N - N + 1 + \Delta$$

with $|\Delta| \le \ln N$ for $\ln N!$, an easy proof that $\ln N! \sim N \ln N - N$. The accuracy in these estimates depends on the care taken in approximating the error.

More precise estimates of the error terms depend on the derivatives of the function f. Taking these into account leads to an asymptotic series derived using the *Euler-Maclaurin summation formula*, one of the most powerful tools in asymptotic analysis.

4.5 Euler-Maclaurin Summation. In the analysis of algorithms, we approximate sums with integrals in two distinct ways. In the first case, we have a function defined on a fixed interval, and we evaluate a sum corresponding to sampling the function at an increasing number of points along the interval, with smaller and smaller step sizes, with the difference between the sum and the integral converging to zero. This is akin to classical Riemann integration. In the second case, we have a fixed function and a fixed discrete step size, so the interval of integration gets larger and larger, with the difference between the sum and the integral converging to a constant. We consider these two cases separately, though they both embody the same basic method, which dates back to the eighteenth century.

General form for Euler-Maclaurin summation formula. The method is based on integration by parts, and involves Bernoulli numbers (and Bernoulli polynomials), which are described in §3.13. We start from the formula

$$\int_0^1 g(x)dx = \Big(x - \frac{1}{2}\Big)g(x)\,\Big|_0^1 - \int_0^1 \Big(x - \frac{1}{2}\Big)g'(x)dx,$$

which is obtained by partial integration of $g(x)$ with the "clever" choice of the integration constant in $x - \frac{1}{2} = B_1(x)$. Using this formula with $g(x) = f(x + k)$, we get

$$\int_k^{k+1} f(x)dx = \frac{f(k+1) + f(k)}{2} - \int_k^{k+1} \Big(\{x\} - \frac{1}{2}\Big)f'(x)dx$$

where, as usual, $\{x\} \equiv x - \lfloor x \rfloor$ denotes the fractional part of x. Taking all values of k greater than or equal to a and less than b and summing these formulae gives

$$\int_a^b f(x)dx = \sum_{a \le k \le b} f(k) - \frac{f(a) + f(b)}{2} - \int_a^b \Big(\{x\} - \frac{1}{2}\Big)f'(x)dx$$

because $f(k)$ appears in two formulae for each value of k except a and b. Thus, rearranging terms, we have a precise relationship between a sum and the corresponding integral:

$$\sum_{a\le k\le b} f(k) = \int_a^b f(x)dx + \frac{f(a)+f(b)}{2} + \int_a^b \Bigl(\{x\} - \frac{1}{2}\Bigr) f'(x)dx.$$

To know how good an approximation this is, we need to be able to develop a bound for the integral at the end. We could do so by developing an absolute bound as at the end of the previous section, but it turns out that we can iterate this process, often leaving a very small error term because the derivatives of $f(x)$ tend to get smaller and smaller (as functions of N) and/or because the polynomial in $\{x\}$ that is also involved in the integral becomes smaller and smaller.

Theorem 4.2 (*Euler-Maclaurin summation formula, first form*) *Let $f(x)$ be a function defined on an interval $[\,a,b\,]$ with a and b integers, and suppose that the derivatives $f^{(i)}(x)$ exist and are continuous for $1 \le i \le 2m$, where m is a fixed constant. Then*

$$\sum_{a\le k\le b} f(k) = \int_a^b f(x)dx + \frac{f(a)+f(b)}{2} + \sum_{1\le i\le m} \frac{B_{2i}}{(2i)!} f^{(2i-1)}(x)\Big|_a^b + R_m,$$

where B_{2i} are the Bernoulli numbers and R_m is a remainder term satisfying

$$|R_m| \le \frac{|B_{2m}|}{(2m)!}\int_a^b |f^{(2m)}(x)|dx < \frac{4}{(2\pi)^{2m}}\int_a^b |f^{(2m)}(x)|dx.$$

Proof. We continue the argument above, using integration by parts and basic properties of the Bernoulli polynomials. For any function $g(x)$ that is differentiable in $[0,1)$ and any $i>0$, we can integrate $g(x)B'_{i+1}(x)$ by parts to get

$$\int_0^1 g(x)B'_{i+1}(x)dx = B_{i+1}(x)g(x)\Big|_0^1 - \int_0^1 g'(x)B_{i+1}(x)dx.$$

Now, from §3.13, we know that $B'_{i+1}(x) = (i+1)B_i(x)$ so, dividing by $(i+1)!$, we get a recurrence relation:

$$\int_0^1 g(x)\frac{B_i(x)}{i!}dx = \frac{B_{i+1}(x)}{(i+1)!}g(x)\Big|_0^1 - \int_0^1 g'(x)\frac{B_{i+1}(x)}{(i+1)!}dx.$$

Now, starting at $i = 0$ and iterating, this gives, formally,

$$\int_0^1 g(x)dx = \frac{B_1(x)}{1!}g(x)\Big|_0^1 - \frac{B_2(x)}{2!}g'(x)\Big|_0^1 + \frac{B_3(x)}{3!}g''(x)\Big|_0^1 - \ldots$$

where the expansion can be pushed arbitrarily far for functions that are infinitely differentiable. More precisely, we stop the iteration after m steps, and also note that $B_1(x) = x - \frac{1}{2}$ and $B_i(0) = B_i(1) = B_i$ for $i > 1$ with $B_i = 0$ for i odd and greater than 1 (see Exercises 3.86 and 3.87) to get the formula

$$\int_0^1 g(x)dx = \frac{g(0) + g(1)}{2} - \sum_{1 \le i \le m} \frac{B_{2i}}{(2i)!} g^{2i-1}(x)\Big|_0^1 - \int_0^1 g^{2m}(x)\frac{B_{2m}(x)}{(2m)!}dx.$$

Substituting $g(x) = f(x + k)$ and summing for $a \le k < b$, this telescopes to the stated result with remainder term

$$|R_m| = \int_a^b \Big|\frac{B_{2m}(\{x\})}{(2m)!} f^{(2m)}(x)\Big| dx$$

in the same way as above. The stated bound on the remainder term follows from asymptotic properties of the Bernoulli numbers. (See De Bruijn [6] or Graham, Knuth, and Patashnik [12] for more details.) ■

For example, taking $f(x) = e^x$, the left-hand side is $(e^b - e^a)/(e - 1)$, and all the derivatives are the same on the right-hand side, so we can divide through by $e^b - e^a$ and increase m to confirm that $1/(e - 1) = \sum_k B_k/k!$.

Since the Bernoulli numbers grow to be quite large, this formula is a often a *di ergent* asymptotic series, typically used with small values of m. The first few Bernoulli numbers $B_0 = 1$, $B_1 = -1/2$, $B_2 = 1/6$, $B_3 = 0$, and $B_4 = -1/30$ suffice for typical applications of Theorem 4.2. We write the simpler form

$$\sum_{a \le k \le b} f(k) = \int_a^b f(x)dx + \frac{1}{2}f(a) + \frac{1}{2}f(b) + \frac{1}{12}f'(x)\Big|_a^b - \frac{1}{720}f'''(x)\Big|_a^b + \ldots$$

with the understanding that the conditions of the theorem and the error bound have to be checked for the approximation to be valid.

Taking $f(x) = x^t$, the derivatives and remainder term vanish for large enough m, confirming the Bernoulli numbers as coefficients in expressing sums of powers of integers. We have

$$\sum_{1\le k\le N} k = \frac{N^2}{2} + \frac{N}{2} = \frac{N(N+1)}{2},$$

$$\sum_{1\le k\le N} k^2 = \frac{N^3}{3} + \frac{N^2}{2} + \frac{N}{6} = \frac{N(N+1)(2N+1)}{6},$$

and so forth, precisely as in §3.13.

Exercise 4.52 Use Euler-Maclaurin summation to determine the coefficients when $\sum_{1\le k\le N} k^t$ is expressed as a sum of powers of N (see §3.13).

Corollary *If h is an infinitely differentiable function, then*

$$\sum_{0\le k\le N} h(k/N) \sim N\int_0^1 h(x)dx + \frac{1}{2}(h(0)+h(1)) + \sum_{i\ge 1} \frac{B_{2i}}{(2i)!}\frac{1}{N^{2i-1}} h^{(2i-1)}(x)\Big|_0^1.$$

Proof. Apply Theorem 4.2 with $f(x) = h(x/N)$. ∎

Dividing by N gives a Riemann sum relative to h. In other words, this corollary is a refinement of

$$\lim_{N\to\infty} \frac{1}{N} \sum_{0\le k\le N} h(k/N) = \int_0^1 h(x)dx.$$

Euler-Maclaurin summation will be effective for obtaining asymptotic expansions for related sums of this type, such as, for example

$$\sum_{0\le k\le N} h(k^2/N).$$

We will be seeing applications of this shortly.

Exercise 4.53 Develop an asymptotic expansion for

$$\sum_{0\le k\le N} \frac{1}{1+k/N}.$$

Exercise 4.54 Show that

$$\sum_{0\le k\le N}\frac{1}{1+k^2/N^2}=\frac{\pi N}{4}+\frac{3}{4}-\frac{1}{24N}+O\Big(\frac{1}{N^2}\Big).$$

As stated, Theorem 4.2 will not provide sufficiently accurate estimates when the interval of summation/integration grows and the step size is fixed. For example, if we try to estimate

$$H_k=\sum_{1\le k\le N}\frac{1}{k}\qquad\text{with}\qquad\int_a^b f(x)dx$$

we encounter a difficulty because the difference between the sum and the integral tends to an unknown constant as $N\to\infty$. Next, we turn to a form of Euler-Maclaurin summation that addresses this problem.

Discrete form of Euler-Maclaurin summation. Taking $a=1$ and $b=N$ in the discussion preceding Theorem 4.2 gives

$$\int_1^N f(x)dx=\sum_{1\le k\le N}f(k)-\frac{1}{2}(f(1)+f(N))-\int_1^N\Big(\{x\}-\frac{1}{2}\Big)f'(x)dx.$$

This formula relates the sum and the integral up to a constant factor if $f'(x)$ has a fast enough decay to 0 as $N\to\infty$. In particular, if the quantity

$$C_f=\frac{1}{2}f(1)+\int_1^\infty\Big(\{x\}-\frac{1}{2}\Big)f'(x)dx$$

exists, it defines the *Euler-Maclaurin constant* of f, and we have proved that

$$\lim_{N\to\infty}\Big(\sum_{1\le k\le N}f(k)-\int_1^N f(x)dx-\frac{1}{2}f(N)\Big)=C_f.$$

Taking $f(x)=1/x$, gives an approximation for the harmonic numbers. The Euler-Maclaurin constant for this case is known plainly as *Euler's constant*:

$$\gamma=\frac{1}{2}-\int_1^\infty\Big(\{x\}-\frac{1}{2}\Big)\frac{dx}{x^2}.$$

Thus

$$H_N=\ln N+\gamma+o(1).$$

The constant γ is approximately $.57721\cdots$ and is not known to be a simple function of other fundamental constants.

Taking $f(x) = \ln x$ gives Stirling's approximation to $\ln N!$. In this case, the Euler-Maclaurin constant is

$$\int_1^\infty \Bigl(\{x\} - \frac{1}{2}\Bigr)\frac{dx}{x}.$$

This constant *does* turn out to be a simple function of other fundamental constants: it is equal to $\ln\sqrt{2\pi} - 1$. We will see one way to prove this in §4.7. The value $\sigma = \sqrt{2\pi}$ is known as *Stirling's constant*. It arises frequently in the analysis of algorithms and many other applications. Thus

$$\ln N! = N\ln N - N + \frac{1}{2}\ln N + \ln\sqrt{2\pi} + o(1).$$

When the Euler-Maclaurin constant is well defined, pursuing the analysis to obtain more terms in the asymptotic series is relatively easy. Summarizing the discussion above, we have shown that

$$\sum_{1\le k\le N} f(k) = \int_1^N f(x)dx + \frac{1}{2}f(N) + C_f - \int_N^\infty \Bigl(\{x\} - \frac{1}{2}\Bigr) f'(x)dx.$$

Now, repeatedly integrating the remaining integral by parts, in the same fashion as above, we get an expansion involving Bernoulli numbers and higher order derivatives. This often leads to a complete asymptotic expansion because it is a common fact that the high-order derivatives of functions of smooth behavior get smaller and smaller at ∞.

Theorem 4.3 (*Euler-Maclaurin summation formula, second form*) *Let $f(x)$ be a function defined on the interval $[1,\infty)$ and suppose that the derivatives $f^{(i)}(x)$ exist and are absolutely integrable for $1 \le i \le 2m$, where m is a fixed constant. Then*

$$\sum_{1\le k\le N} f(k) = \int_1^N f(x)dx + \frac{1}{2}f(N) + C_f + \sum_{1\le k\le m} \frac{B_{2k}}{(2k)!} f^{(2k-1)}(N) + R_m,$$

where C_f is a constant associated with the function and R_{2m} is a remainder term satisfying

$$|R_{2m}| = O\Bigl(\int_N^\infty |f^{(2m)}(x)|dx\Bigr).$$

Proof. By induction, extending the argument in the discussion above. Details may be found in [6] or [12]. ■

Corollary *The harmonic numbers admit a full asymptotic expansion in descending powers of N:*

$$H_N \sim \ln N + \gamma + \frac{1}{2N} - \frac{1}{12N^2} + \frac{1}{120N^4} - \cdots.$$

Proof. Take $f(x) = 1/x$ in Theorem 4.3, use the constant γ discussed above and note that the remainder term is of the same order as the last term in the sum, to show that

$$H_N = \ln N + \gamma + \frac{1}{2N} - \sum_{1\le k<M} \frac{B_{2k}}{2kN^{2k}} + O\Big(\frac{1}{N^{2m}}\Big)$$

for any fixed m, which implies the stated result. ■

Corollary *(Stirling's formula.) The functions* $\ln N!$ *and* $N!$ *admit a full asymptotic expansion in descending powers of N:*

$$\ln N! \sim (N + \frac{1}{2}) \ln N - N + \ln\sqrt{2\pi} + \frac{1}{12N} - \frac{1}{360N^3} + \cdots$$

and

$$N! \sim \sqrt{2\pi N}\Big(\frac{N}{e}\Big)^N \Big(1 + \frac{1}{12N} + \frac{1}{288N^2} - \frac{139}{5140N^3} + \cdots\Big).$$

Proof. Take $f(x) = \ln x$ in Theorem 4.3 and argue as above to develop the expansion for $\ln N!$. As mentioned above, the first derivative is not absolutely integrable, but the Euler-Maclaurin constant exists, so Theorem 4.3 clearly holds. The expansion for $N!$ follows by exponentiation and basic manipulations discussed in §4.3. ■

Corollary *The Catalan numbers admit a full asymptotic expansion in descending powers of N:*

$$\frac{1}{N+1}\binom{2N}{N} \sim \frac{4^N}{N\sqrt{\pi N}}\Big(1 - \frac{9}{8N} + \frac{145}{128N^2} - \cdots\Big).$$

Proof. This follows from elementary manipulations with the asymptotic series for $(2N)!$ and $N!$. Many of the details are given in the examples in §4.3. ■

Euler-Maclaurin summation is a general tool, which is useful only subject to the caveats that the function must be "smooth" (as many derivatives must exist as terms in the asymptotic series desired), and we must be able to calculate the integral involved. The asymptotic expansions just given for factorials, harmonic numbers, and Catalan numbers play a central role in the analysis of many fundamental algorithms, and the method arises in many other applications.

Exercise 4.55 Evaluate γ to 10 decimal places.

Exercise 4.56 Show that the generalized (second-order) harmonic numbers admit the asymptotic expansion

$$H_N^{(2)} \equiv \sum_{1\le k\le N} \frac{1}{k^2} \sim \frac{\pi^2}{6} - \frac{1}{N} + \frac{1}{2N^2} - \frac{1}{6N^3} + \ldots.$$

Exercise 4.57 Derive an asymptotic expansion for

$$H_N^{(3)} \equiv \sum_{1\le k\le N} \frac{1}{k^3}$$

to within $O(N^3)$.

Exercise 4.58 Use Euler-Maclaurin summation to estimate

$$\sum_{1\le k\le N} \sqrt{k}, \qquad \sum_{1\le k\le N} \frac{1}{\sqrt{k}}, \qquad \text{and} \qquad \sum_{1\le k\le N} \frac{1}{\sqrt[3]{k}}$$

to within $O(1/N^2)$.

Exercise 4.59 Derive full asymptotic expansions for

$$\sum_{1\le k\le N} \frac{(-1)^k}{k} \qquad \text{and} \qquad \sum_{1\le k\le N} \frac{(-1)^k}{\sqrt{k}}.$$

4.6 Bivariate Asymptotics. Many of the most challenging problems that we face in approximating sums have to do with so-called bivariate asymptotics, where the summands depend both on the index of summation and on the "size" parameter that describes asymptotic growth. Suppose that the two parameters are named k and N, respectively, as we have done many times. Now, the relative values of k and N and the rate at which they grow certainly dictate the significance of asymptotic estimates. For a simple example of this, note that the function $k^N/k!$ grows exponentially as $N \to \infty$ for fixed k, but is exponentially small as $k \to \infty$ for fixed N.

In the context of evaluating sums, we generally need to consider all values of k less than N (or some function of N), and therefore we are interested in developing accurate asymptotic estimates for as large a range of k as possible. Evaluating the sum eliminates the k and leaves us back in the univariate case. In this section we will conduct a detailed examination of some bivariate functions of central importance in the analysis of algorithms: Ramanujan functions and binomial coefficients. In subsequent sections, we will see how the estimates developed here are used to obtain asymptotic approximations to sums involving these functions, and how these relate to applications in the analysis of algorithms.

Ramanujan distributions. Our first example concerns a distribution that was first studied by Ramanujan (see [4]) and later, because it arises in so many applications in the analysis of algorithms, by Knuth [16]. As we will see in Chapter 8, the performance characteristics of a variety of algorithms depend on the function

$$Q(N) \equiv \sum_{1 \le k \le N} \frac{N!}{(N-k)!N^k}.$$

This is also well known in probability theory as the *birthday function*: $Q(N)+1$ is the expected trials needed to find two people with the same

$N \downarrow$ $k \to$	1	2	3	4	5	6	7	8	9	10
2	1	.5000								
3	1	.6667	.2222							
4	1	.7500	.3750	.0938						
5	1	.8000	.4800	.1920	.0384					
6	1	.8333	.5556	.2778	.0926	.0154				
7	1	.8571	.6122	.3499	.1499	.0428	.0061			
8	1	.8750	.6563	.4102	.2051	.0769	.0192	.0024		
9	1	.8889	.6914	.4609	.2561	.1138	.0379	.0084	.0009	
10	1	.9000	.7200	.5040	.3024	.1512	.0605	.0181	.0036	.0004

Table 4.7 Ramanujan Q-distribution $\dfrac{N!}{(N-k)!N^k}$

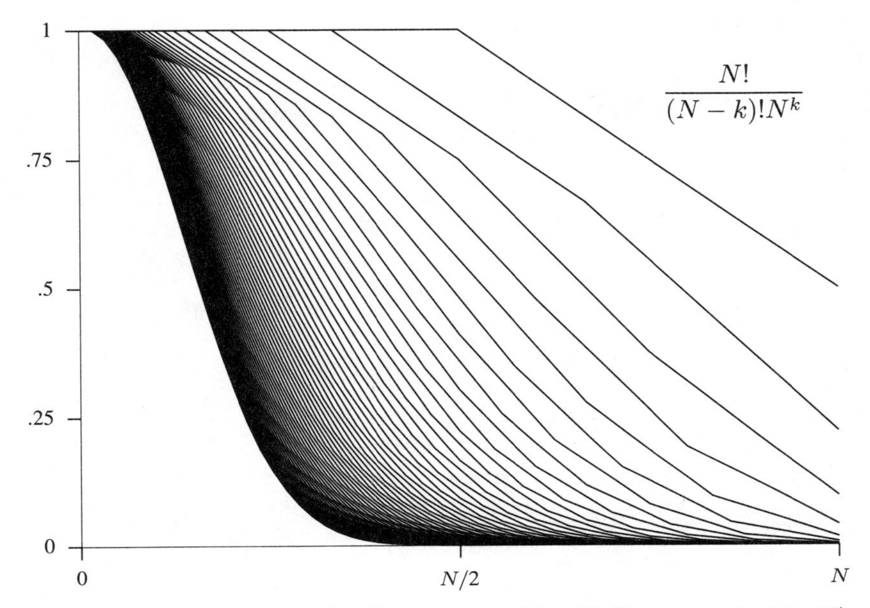

Figure 4.1 Ramanujan Q-distribution, $2 \le N \le 60$ (k-axes scaled to N)

birthday (when the year has N days). The summand is tabulated for small values of N and k in Table 4.7 and plotted in Figure 4.1. In the figure, separate curves are given for each value of N, with successive values of k connected by straight lines. The k-axis for each curve is scaled so that the curve fills the whole figure. In order to be able to estimate the value of the sum, we first need to be able to estimate the value of the summand accurately for *all* values of k, as N grows.

Theorem 4.4 (*Ramanujan Q-distribution*) *As $N \to \infty$, the following (relative) approximation holds for $k = o(N^{2/3})$:*

$$\frac{N!}{(N-k)!N^k} = e^{-k^2/(2N)}\Bigl(1 + O\Bigl(\frac{k}{N}\Bigr) + O\Bigl(\frac{k^3}{N^2}\Bigr)\Bigr).$$

In addition, the following (absolute) approximation holds for all k:

$$\frac{N!}{(N-k)!N^k} = e^{-k^2/(2N)} + O\Bigl(\frac{1}{\sqrt{N}}\Bigr).$$

Proof. The relative error bound is proved with the "exp/log" technique given in §4.3. We write

$$\begin{aligned}\frac{N!}{(N-k)!N^k} &= \frac{N(N-1)(N-2)\dots(N-k+1)}{N^k}\\ &= 1\cdot\Bigl(1-\frac{1}{N}\Bigr)\Bigl(1-\frac{2}{N}\Bigr)\cdots\Bigl(1-\frac{1}{N}\Bigr)\\ &= \exp\Bigl\{\ln\Bigl(1-\frac{1}{N}\Bigr)\Bigl(1-\frac{2}{N}\Bigr)\cdots\Bigl(1-\frac{1}{N}\Bigr)\Bigr\}\\ &= \exp\Bigl\{\sum_{1\le j<k}\ln\Bigl(1-\frac{j}{N}\Bigr)\Bigr\}.\end{aligned}$$

Now, for $k = o(N)$, we can apply the approximation

$$\ln(1+x) = x + O(x^2) \quad \text{with } x = -j/N$$

from Table 4.2 and evaluate the sum:

$$\begin{aligned}\frac{N!}{(N-k)!N^k} &= \exp\Bigl\{\sum_{1\le j<k}\Bigl(-\frac{j}{N}+O\Bigl(\frac{j^2}{N^2}\Bigr)\Bigr)\Bigr\}\\ &= \exp\Bigl\{-\frac{k(k-1)}{2N}+O\Bigl(\frac{k^3}{N^2}\Bigr)\Bigr\}.\end{aligned}$$

Finally, for $k = o(N^{2/3})$ we can use the approximation $e^x = 1+O(x)$ from Table 4.2 to get the stated relative approximation.

We need to carry both O-terms to cover the range in values of k. The $O(k^3/N^2)$ term is not sufficient by itself because, for example, it is $O(1/N^2)$ for $k = O(1)$, when $O(1/N)$ is called for. The $O(k/N)$ term is not sufficient by itself because, for example, it is $O(1/N^{2/5})$ for $k = O(N^{3/5})$, when $O(1/N^{1/5})$ is called for. This illustrates the care that is necessary in bivariate asymptotics.

To develop the absolute error bound, we first consider the case where k is "small," say $k \le k_0$ where k_0 is the nearest integer to $N^{3/5}$. The relative approximation certainly holds, and we have

$$\frac{N!}{(N-k)!N^k} = e^{-k^2/(2N)} + e^{-k^2/(2N)}O\Bigl(\frac{k}{N}\Bigr) + e^{-k^2/(2N)}O\Bigl(\frac{k^3}{N^2}\Bigr).$$

Now, the second term is $O(1/\sqrt{N})$ because we can rewrite it in the form $xe^{-x^2}O(1/\sqrt{N})$ and $xe^{-x^2} = O(1)$ for all $x \ge 0$. Similarly, the third term is of the form $x^3e^{-x^2}O(1/\sqrt{N})$ and is $O(1/\sqrt{N})$ because $x^3e^{-x^2} = O(1)$ for all $x \geq 0$.

Next, consider the case where k is "large," or $k \geq k_0$. The argument just given shows that

$$\frac{N!}{(N-k_0)!N^{k_0}} = e^{-\sqrt[5]{N}/2} + O\Big(\frac{1}{\sqrt{N}}\Big).$$

The first term is exponentially small, and the coefficients decrease as k increases, so this implies that

$$\frac{N!}{(N-k)!N^k} = O\Big(\frac{1}{\sqrt{N}}\Big)$$

for $k \geq k_0$. But $\exp\{-k^2/(2N)\}$ is also exponentially small for $k \geq k_0$, so the absolute error bound in the statement holds for $k \geq k_0$.

The above two paragraphs establish the absolute error bound for all $k \geq 0$. The cutoff point $N^{3/5}$ is not particularly critical in this case: it need only be small enough that the relative error bound hold for smaller k (slightly smaller than $N^{2/3}$) and large enough that the terms be exponentially small for larger k (slightly larger than $\sqrt{N}$). ■

Corollary *For all k and N,* $\dfrac{N!}{(N-k)!N^k} \leq e^{-k(k-1)/(2N)}$.

Proof. Use the inequality $\ln(1-x) \leq -x$ instead of the asymptotic estimate in the derivation above. ■

N ↓ k →	1	2	3	4	5	6	7	8	9
2	.6667	.3333							
3	.7500	.4500	.2250						
4	.8000	.5333	.3048	.1524					
5	.8333	.5952	.3720	.2067	.1033				
6	.8571	.6429	.4286	.2571	.1403	.0701			
7	.8750	.6806	.4764	.3032	.1768	.0952	.0476		
8	.8889	.7111	.5172	.3448	.2122	.1212	.0647	.0323	
9	.9000	.7364	.5523	.3823	.2458	.1475	.0830	.0439	.0220

Table 4.8 Ramanujan R-distribution $\dfrac{N!N^k}{(N+k)!}$

A virtually identical set of arguments apply to another function studied by Ramanujan, the so-called *R-distribution*. This function is tabulated for small values of N and k in Table 4.8 and plotted in Figure 4.2. We include a detailed statement of the asymptotic results for this function as well, for reasons that will become clear later.

Theorem 4.5 (*Ramanujan R-distribution*) *As $N \to \infty$, the following (relative) approximation holds for $k = o(N^{2/3})$:*

$$\frac{N!N^k}{(N+k)!} = e^{-k^2/(2N)}\Bigl(1 + O\Bigl(\frac{k}{N}\Bigr) + O\Bigl(\frac{k^3}{N^2}\Bigr)\Bigr).$$

In addition, the following (absolute) approximation holds for all k:

$$\frac{N!N^k}{(N+k)!} = e^{-k^2/(2N)} + O\Bigl(\frac{1}{\sqrt{N}}\Bigr).$$

Proof. After the first step, the proof is virtually identical to the proof for the Q-distribution:

$$\begin{aligned}
\frac{N!N^k}{(N-k)!} &= \frac{N^k}{(N+k)(N+k-1)\ldots(N+1)} \\
&= \frac{1}{\Bigl(1+\dfrac{k}{N}\Bigr)\Bigl(1+\dfrac{k-1}{N}\Bigr)\cdots\Bigl(1+\dfrac{1}{N}\Bigr)} \\
&= \exp\Bigl\{-\sum_{1\le j\le k}\ln\Bigl(1+\frac{j}{N}\Bigr)\Bigr\} \\
&= \exp\Bigl\{\sum_{1\le j\le k}\Bigl(-\frac{j}{N}+O\Bigl(\frac{j^2}{N^2}\Bigr)\Bigr)\Bigr\} \\
&= \exp\Bigl\{-\frac{k(k+1)}{2N}+O\Bigl(\frac{k^3}{N^2}\Bigr)\Bigr\} \\
&= e^{-k^2/(2N)}\Bigl(1+O\Bigl(\frac{k}{N}\Bigr)+O\Bigl(\frac{k^3}{N^2}\Bigr)\Bigr).
\end{aligned}$$

The absolute error bound follows as for the Q-distribution. ∎

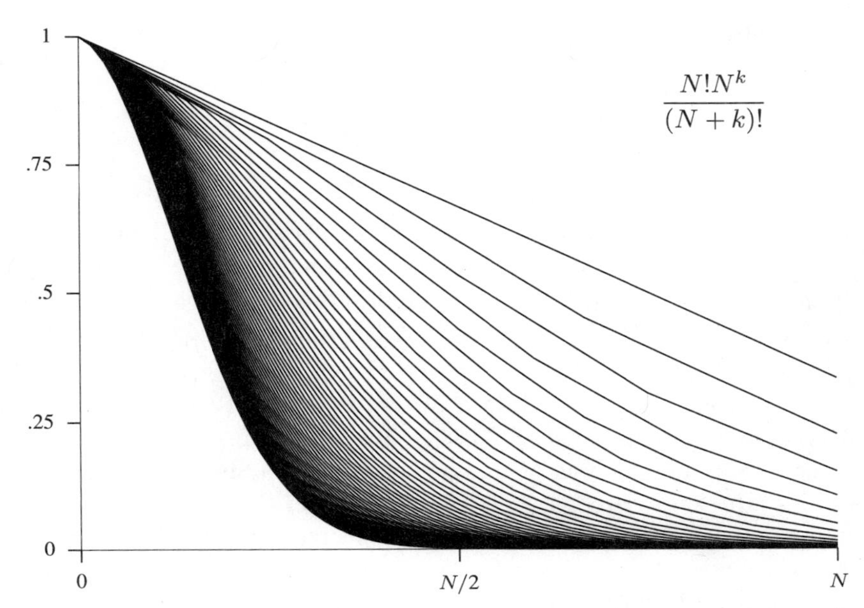

Figure 4.2 Ramanujan R-distribution, $2 \le N \le 60$ (k-axes scaled to N)

Corollary *For all k and N with $k \le N$,* $\dfrac{N!N^k}{(N+k)!} \le e^{-k(k+1)/(4N)}$.

Proof. Use the inequality $-\ln(1+x) \le -x/2$ (valid for $0 \le x \le 1$) instead of the asymptotic estimate in the derivation above. ∎

Exercise 4.60 Prove that $\dfrac{N!N^k}{(N+k)!} \ge e^{-k(k+1)/(2N)}$ for all k and N.

We will return to the Ramanujan distributions for several applications later in this chapter. Before doing so, however, we turn attention to a bivariate distribution that plays an even more central role in the analysis of algorithms, the familiar *binomial distribution.* It turns out that the development of asymptotic approximations for the Ramanujan distributions given above encapsulates the essential aspects of approximating the binomial distribution.

Exercise 4.61 Use Stirling's formula for $\ln N!$ to prove the relative bounds for the Ramanujan Q- and R-distributions given in the two theorems above.

Binomial distribution. Given N random bits, the probability that exactly k of them are 0 is the familiar *binomial distribution*, also known as the *Bernoulli distribution*:

$$\frac{1}{2^N}\binom{N}{k} = \frac{1}{2^N}\frac{N!}{k!(N-k)!}.$$

The interested reader may consult Feller's classic text [8] or any of a number of standard references for basic information on properties of this distribution and applications in probability theory. Since it appears frequently in the analysis of algorithms, we summarize many of its important properties here.

Table 4.9 gives exact values of the binomial distribution for small N and approximate values for larger N. As usual, one motivation for doing asymptotic analysis of this function is the desire to compute such values. The value of $\binom{10000}{5000}/2^{5000}$ is about .007979, but one would not compute that by first computing 10000!, then dividing by 5000!, etc. Indeed, this distribution has been studied for three centuries, and the motivation for finding easily computed approximations was present before computers arrived on the scene.

Exercise 4.62 Write a program to compute exact values of the binomial distribution to single-precision floating point accuracy.

N ↓ $k \rightarrow$	0	1	2	3	4	5	6	7	8	9
1	.5000	.5000								
2	.2500	.5000	.2500							
3	.1250	.3750	.3750	.1250						
4	.0625	.2500	.3750	.2500	.0625					
5	.0312	.1562	.3125	.3125	.1562	.0312				
6	.0156	.0938	.2344	.3125	.2344	.0938	.0156			
7	.0078	.0547	.1641	.2734	.2734	.1641	.0547	.0078		
8	.0039	.0312	.1094	.2188	.2734	.2188	.1094	.0312	.0039	
9	.0020	.0176	.0703	.1641	.2461	.2461	.1641	.0703	.0176	.0020

Table 4.9 Binomial distribution $\binom{N}{k}/2^N$

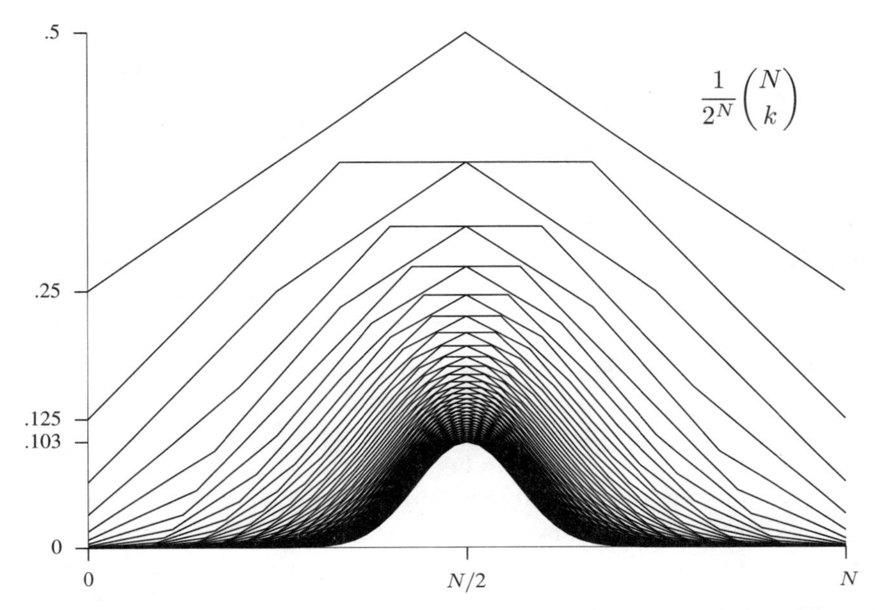

Figure 4.3 Binomial distribution, $2 \le N \le 60$ (k-axes scaled to N)

We have already computed the approximate value of the middle binomial coefficients:

$$\binom{2N}{N} = \frac{2^{2N}}{\sqrt{\pi N}}\Bigl(1 + O\Bigl(\frac{1}{N}\Bigr)\Bigr).$$

That is, the middle entries in Table 4.9 decrease like $1/\sqrt{N}$. How does the distribution behave for other values of k? Figure 4.3 shows a scaled version of the distribution that gives some indication, and a precise asymptotic analysis is given below.

The limiting curve is the familiar "bell curve" described by the normal probability density function $e^{-x^2/2}/\sqrt{2\pi}$. The top of the curve is at $\binom{N}{\lfloor N/2 \rfloor}/2^N \sim 1/\sqrt{\pi N/2}$, which is about .103 for $N = 60$.

Our purpose here is to analyze properties of the bell curve, using the asymptotic tools that we have been developing. The results that we present are classical, and play a central role in probability and statistics. Our interest in these results stems not only from the fact that they are directly useful in the analysis of many algorithms, but also from the fact that the techniques used to develop asymptotic estimates for the binomial distribution are of direct use in a plethora of similar problems that arise in the analysis of algorithms. For a treatment of the normal approximation in the context of probability and statistics, see, for example, Feller [8].

Figure 4.3 makes it plain that the most significant part of the curve is near the center—as N increases, the values near the edge become negligible. This is intuitive from the probabilistic model that we started with: we expect the number of 0s and 1s in a random bitstream to be about equal, and the probability that the bits are nearly all 0 or nearly all 1 to become vanishingly small as the size of the bitstream increases. We now turn to quantifying such statements more precisely.

Normal approximation. Since the significant values of the binomial distribution are near the center, it is convenient to rewrite it and consider estimating $\binom{2N}{N-k}/2^{2N}$. This is symmetric about $k = 0$ and decreases as $|k|$ increases from 0 to N. This is an important step in working with any distribution: putting the largest terms at the beginning and the small terms in the tails makes it more convenient to bound the tails and concentrate on the main terms, particularly when using the approximation in evaluating sums, as we will see below.

As it turns out, we have already seen the basic methods required to prove the classic *normal approximation* to the binomial distribution:

Theorem 4.6 (*Normal approximation*) *As $N \to \infty$, the following (relative) approximation holds for $k = o(N^{3/4})$:*

$$\frac{1}{2^{2N}}\binom{2N}{N-k} = \frac{e^{-k^2/N}}{\sqrt{\pi N}}\Big(1 + O\Big(\frac{1}{N}\Big) + O\Big(\frac{k^4}{N^3}\Big)\Big).$$

In addition, the following (absolute) approximation holds for all k:

$$\frac{1}{2^{2N}}\binom{2N}{N-k} = \frac{e^{-k^2/N}}{\sqrt{\pi N}} + O\Big(\frac{1}{N^{3/2}}\Big).$$

Proof. If we write

$$\frac{1}{2^{2N}}\binom{2N}{N-k} = \frac{1}{2^{2N}}\frac{(2N)!}{N!N!}\frac{N!}{(N-k)!N^k}\frac{N!N^k}{(N+k)!}$$

we see that the binomial distribution is precisely the product of

$$\frac{1}{2^{2N}}\binom{2N}{N} = \frac{1}{\sqrt{\pi N}}\Big(1 + O\Big(\frac{1}{N}\Big)\Big),$$

the Ramanujan Q-distribution, and the Ramanujan R-distribution (!!). Accordingly, we can obtain a relative approximation accurate to $O(k^3/N^2)$ by simply multiplying the asymptotic estimates for these quantities (given in Theorem 4.4, Theorem 4.5, and the third corollary to Theorem 4.3) to get the result. However, taking an extra term in the derivation leads to cancellation that gives more accuracy. As in the proofs of Theorem 4.4 and Theorem 4.5, we have:

$$\begin{aligned}
\frac{N!}{(N-k)!N^k}\frac{N!N^k}{(N+k)!} &= \exp\Bigl\{\sum_{1\le j<k}\ln\Bigl(1-\frac{j}{N}\Bigr)-\sum_{1\le j\le k}\ln\Bigl(1+\frac{j}{N}\Bigr)\Bigr\}.\\
&= \exp\Bigl\{\sum_{1\le j<k}\Bigl(-\frac{j}{N}-\frac{j^2}{2N^2}+O\Bigl(\frac{j^3}{N^3}\Bigr)\Bigr)\\
&\qquad -\sum_{1\le j\le k}\Bigl(\frac{j}{N}-\frac{j^2}{2N^2}+O\Bigl(\frac{j^3}{N^3}\Bigr)\Bigr)\Bigr\}\\
&= \exp\Bigl\{-\frac{k(k-1)}{2N}-\frac{k(k+1)}{2N}+O\Bigl(\frac{k^2}{N^2}\Bigr)+O\Bigl(\frac{k^4}{N^3}\Bigr)\Bigr\}\\
&= \exp\Bigl\{-\frac{k^2}{N}+O\Bigl(\frac{k^2}{N^2}\Bigr)+O\Bigl(\frac{k^4}{N^3}\Bigr)\Bigr\}\\
&= e^{-k^2/N}\Bigl(1+O\Bigl(\frac{k^2}{N^2}\Bigr)+O\Bigl(\frac{k^4}{N^3}\Bigr)\Bigr).
\end{aligned}$$

The improved accuracy results from cancellation of the j^2/N^2 terms in the sums. The $O(k^2/N^2)$ term can be replaced by $O(1/N)$ because k^2/N^2 is $O(1/N)$ if $k \le \sqrt{N}$ and $O(k^4/N^3)$ if $k \ge \sqrt{N}$.

The same procedure as in the proof of Theorem 4.4 can be used to establish the absolute error bound for all $k \ge 0$, and by symmetry in the binomial coefficients, it holds for all k. ■

This is the normal approximation to the binomial distribution: the function $e^{-k^2/N}/\sqrt{\pi N}$ is the well-known "bell curve" at the bottom of Figure 4.3. Most of the curve is within plus or minus a small constant times $\sqrt{N}$ of the mean, and the tails decay exponentially outside that range. Typically, when working with the normal approximation, we need to make use of both of these facts.

Corollary *For all k and N,* $\displaystyle\frac{1}{2^{2N}}\binom{2N}{N-k} \le e^{-k^2/(2N)}$.

Proof. Note that $\binom{2N}{N}/2^{2N} < 1$, and multiply the bounds in the Corollaries to Theorem 4.4 and Theorem 4.5. ■

This kind of result is often used to bound the tail of the distribution in the following manner. Given $\epsilon > 0$, we have, for $k > \sqrt{2N^{1+\epsilon}}$,

$$\frac{1}{2^{2N}}\binom{2N}{N-k} \le e^{-(2N)^\epsilon}.$$

That is, the tails of the distribution are exponentially small when k grows slightly faster than $\sqrt{N}$.

Exercise 4.63 Carry out the normal approximation to $O(1/N^2)$ for the case $k = \sqrt{N} + O(1)$.

Exercise 4.64 Plot the smallest k for which the binomial probabilities are greater than .001 as a function of N.

Poisson approximation. In slightly more general form, the binomial distribution gives the probability of k successes in N independent trials, each having a probability p of success:

$$\binom{N}{k} p^k (1-p)^{N-k}.$$

As we discuss in detail in Chapter 8, this is often studied in terms of the "occupancy distribution" when N balls are distributed into M urns. Taking $p = 1/M$, the probability that exactly k balls fall into a particular urn (for instance, the first urn) is

$$\binom{N}{k}\left(\frac{1}{M}\right)^k\left(1-\frac{1}{M}\right)^{N-k}.$$

The "balls-and-urns" model is classical (see, for example, [8]), and it also turns out to be directly applicable to a variety of fundamental algorithms that are in widespread use, as we will see in Chapters 7 and 8.

Whenever M is a constant, the distribution can still be approximated by a normal distribution centered at Np, as verified in Exercise 4.67 and illustrated in Figure 4.4, for $p = 1/5$.

The case where M varies with N is of special interest. In other words, we take $p = 1/M = \lambda/N$, where λ is a constant. This corresponds to performing N trials each of which has a small (λ/N) probability of success. We thus expect an average of λ trials to succeed.

The probability law corresponding to this (in the asymptotic limit) is called the *Poisson law*. It applies when we want to describe the collective

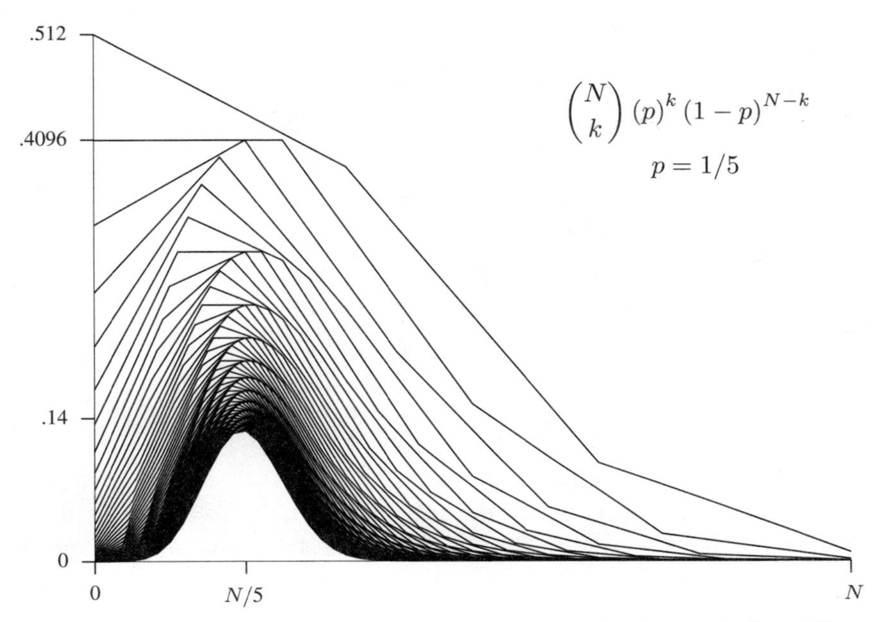

Figure 4.4 Binomial distribution, $3 \le N \le 60$ (k-axes scaled to N)

behavior of a large number of "agents," each with a small probability of being "active," "successful," or somehow otherwise distinguished. One of the very first applications of the Poisson law (due to Von Bortkiewicz in the nineteenth century) was to characterize the number of cavalrymen killed by horse kicks in the Prussian Army. Since then, it has been used to describe a large variety of situations, from radioactive decay to bomb hits on London (cf. [8]). In the present context, the Poisson law describes the situation of any given urn (e.g., the first one) in the balls-and-urns model.

Theorem 4.7 (*Poisson approximation*) *For fixed λ, $N \to \infty$ and all k*

$$\binom{N}{k}\left(\frac{\lambda}{N}\right)^k\left(1-\frac{\lambda}{N}\right)^{N-k} = \frac{\lambda^k e^{-\lambda}}{k!} + o(1).$$

In particular, for $k = O(N^{1/2})$

$$\binom{N}{k}\left(\frac{\lambda}{N}\right)^k\left(1-\frac{\lambda}{N}\right)^{N-k} = \frac{\lambda^k e^{-\lambda}}{k!}\left(1+O\left(\frac{1}{N}\right)+O\left(\frac{k}{N}\right)\right).$$

Proof. Rewriting the binomial coefficient in yet another form,

$$\binom{N}{k}\left(\frac{\lambda}{N}\right)^k\left(1-\frac{\lambda}{N}\right)^{N-k} = \frac{\lambda^k}{k!}\frac{N!}{(N-k)!N^k}\left(1-\frac{\lambda}{N}\right)^{N-k},$$

we see that the Ramanujan Q-distribution again appears. Combining the result of Theorem 4.4 with

$$\begin{aligned}\left(1-\frac{\lambda}{N}\right)^{N-k} &= \exp\Big\{(N-k)\ln\Big(1-\frac{\lambda}{N}\Big)\Big\}\\ &= \exp\Big\{(N-k)\Big(-\frac{\lambda}{N}+O\Big(\frac{1}{N^2}\Big)\Big)\Big\}\\ &= e^{-\lambda}\Big(1+O\Big(\frac{1}{N}\Big)+O\Big(\frac{k}{N}\Big)\Big)\end{aligned}$$

we get the stated relative error bound.

To prove the first part of the theorem (the absolute error bound), observe that for $k > \sqrt{N}$ (and λ fixed) both the Poisson and the binomial terms are exponentially small, and in particular $o(1)$. ■

$N \downarrow$ $k \rightarrow$	0	1	2	3	4	5	6	7	8	9
4	.0039	.0469	.2109	.4219	.3164					
5	.0102	.0768	.2304	.3456	.2592	.0778				
6	.0156	.0938	.2344	.3125	.2344	.0938	.0156			
7	.0199	.1044	.2350	.2938	.2203	.0991	.0248	.0027		
8	.0233	.1118	.2347	.2816	.2112	.1014	.0304	.0052	.0004	
9	.0260	.1171	.2341	.2731	.2048	.1024	.0341	.0073	.0009	
10	.0282	.1211	.2335	.2668	.2001	.1029	.0368	.0090	.0014	.0001
11	.0301	.1242	.2329	.2620	.1965	.1031	.0387	.0104	.0019	.0002
12	.0317	.1267	.2323	.2581	.1936	.1032	.0401	.0115	.0024	.0004
13	.0330	.1288	.2318	.2550	.1912	.1033	.0413	.0124	.0028	.0005
14	.0342	.1305	.2313	.2523	.1893	.1032	.0422	.0132	.0031	.0006
100	.0476	.1471	.2252	.2275	.1706	.1013	.0496	.0206	.0074	.0023
∞	.0498	.1494	.2240	.2240	.1680	.1008	.0504	.0216	.0027	.0009

Table 4.10 Binomial distribution $\binom{N}{k}\left(\frac{3}{N}\right)^k\left(1-\frac{3}{N}\right)^{N-k}$, tending to Poisson distribution $3^k e^{-3}/k!$.

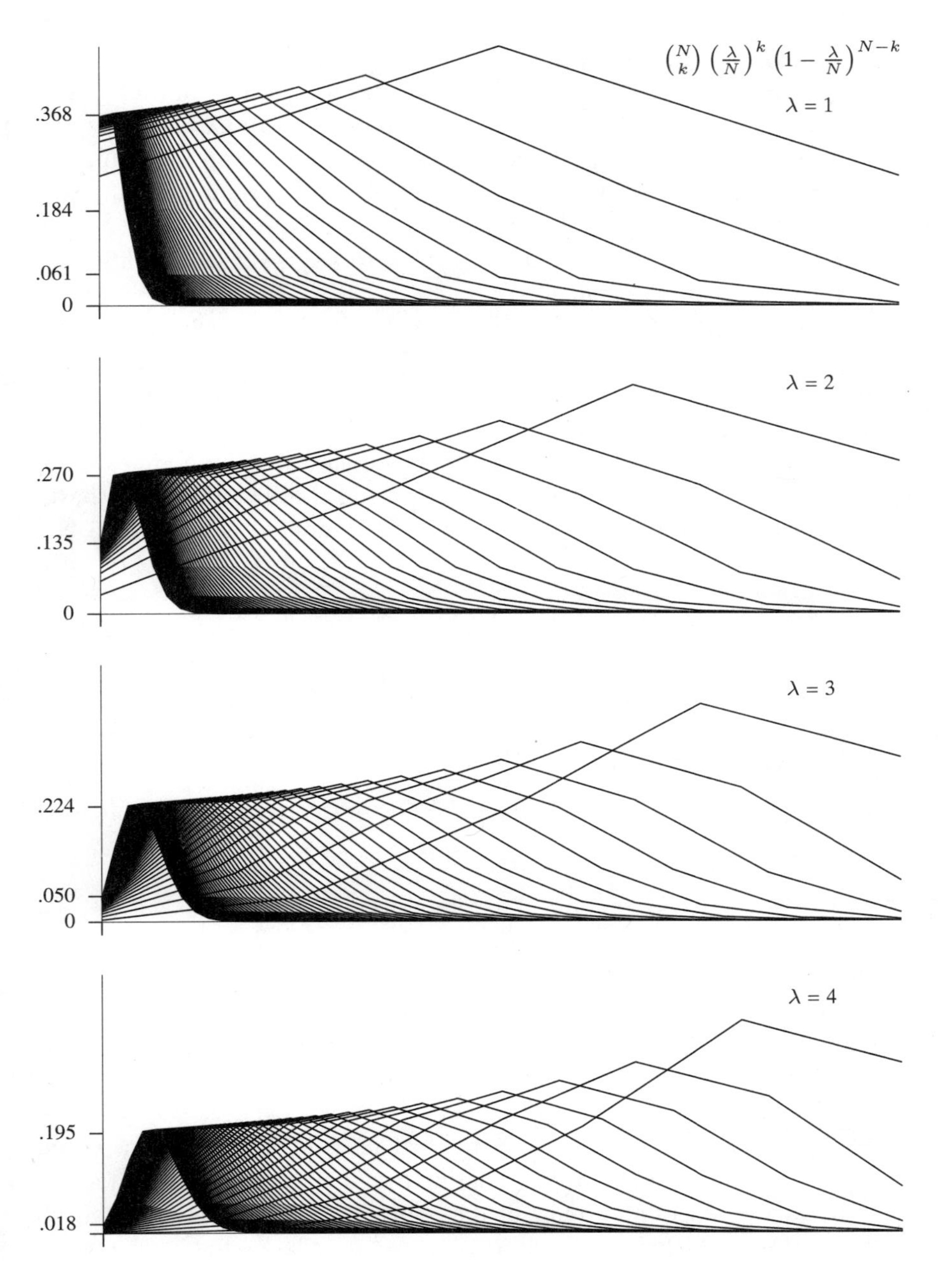

Figure 4.5 Binomial distributions, $3 \leq N \leq 60$ with $p = \lambda/N$, tending to Poisson distributions $\lambda^k e^{-\lambda}/k!$ (k-axes scaled to N)

As k grows, the $\lambda^k/k!$ term grows until $k = \lfloor\lambda\rfloor$, then becomes very small very quickly. As with the normal approximation, a bound on the tail can easily be derived by working through the above derivation, using inequalities rather than the O-notation. Figure 4.5 shows how the distribution evolves for small fixed λ as N grows. Table 4.10 gives the binomial distribution and Poisson approximation for $\lambda = 3$. The approximation is a fairly accurate estimate for the binomial distribution whenever probabilities are relatively small, even for small N.

The function $\lambda^k e^{-\lambda}/k!$ is the *Poisson distribution*, which, as mentioned above, models many stochastic processes. The PGF of this distribution is $e^{\lambda(z-1)}$, whence both the mean and the variance are λ. See Feller [8] for more details.

The Poisson approximation to the binomial distribution appears frequently in the analysis of algorithms, for example, in the analysis of hashing algorithms and other problems involving random maps, as described in Chapter 8.

Exercise 4.65 Give an asymptotic approximation to $\binom{N}{pN}p^{pN}(1-p)^{N-pN}$.

Exercise 4.66 Give an asymptotic approximation to $\binom{N}{k}p^k(1-p)^{N-k}$ for p fixed. (*Hint*: Shift so that the largest terms in the distribution are at $k = 0$.)

Exercise 4.67 Give an asymptotic approximation of the binomial distribution for the case where $p = \lambda/\sqrt{N}$.

Exercise 4.68 Give an asymptotic approximation of the binomial distribution for the case where $p = \lambda/\ln N$.

4.7 Laplace Method. In the theorems of the previous section, we saw that different bounds are appropriate for different parts of the range for bivariate distributions. When estimating sums across the whole range, we want to take advantage of our ability to get accurate estimates of the summand in various different parts of the range. On the other hand, it is certainly more convenient if we can stick to a single function across the entire range of interest.

In this section, we discuss a general method that allows us to do both, the *Laplace method* for estimating the value of sums and integrals. We frequently encounter sums in the analysis of algorithms that can be estimated with this approach. Generally, we are also taking advantage of our ability to approximate sums with integrals in such cases. Full discussion of this method and many examples may be found in Bender and Orszag [2] or De Bruijn [6].

In short, the method is centered around the following three steps for evaluating sums:

- restrict the range to an area that contains the largest summands.
- approximate the summand and bound the tails.
- extend the range and bound the new tails, to get a simpler sum.

Figure 4.6 illustrates the method in a schematic manner. Actually, when approximating sums, the functions involved are all step functions; usually a "smooth" function makes an appearance at the end, in an application of the Euler-Maclaurin formula.

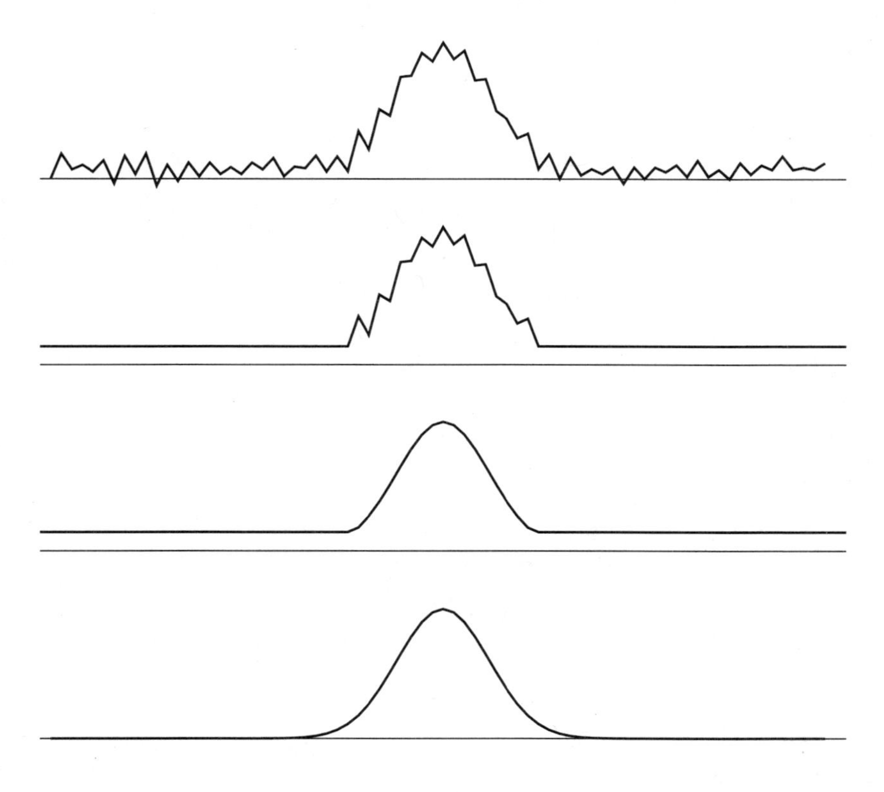

Figure 4.6 Laplace method: bound tails, approximate, and extend

A typical case of the application of the Laplace method is the evaluation of the Ramanujan Q-function that we introduced at the beginning of the previous section. As mentioned above, it is of interest in the analysis of algorithms because it arises in many applications, including hashing algorithms, random maps, equivalence algorithms, and analysis of memory cache performance (see Chapter 8).

Theorem 4.8 (*Ramanujan Q-function*) *As* $N \to \infty$,

$$Q(N) \equiv \sum_{1 \le k \le N} \frac{N!}{(N-k)!N^k} = \sqrt{\pi N/2} + O(1).$$

Proof. Neither of the estimates given in Theorem 4.4 is useful across the entire range of summation, so we have to restrict each to the portion of the range to which they apply. More precisely, we define k_0 to be an integer that is $o(N^{2/3})$ and divide the sum into two parts:

$$\sum_{1 \le k \le N} \frac{N!}{(N-k)!N^k} = \sum_{1 \le k \le k_0} \frac{N!}{(N-k)!N^k} + \sum_{k_0 < k \le N} \frac{N!}{(N-k)!N^k}.$$

We approximate the two parts separately, using the different restrictions on k in the two parts to advantage. For the first (main) term, we use the relative approximation in Theorem 4.4. For the second term (the tail), the restriction $k > k_0$ and the fact that the terms are decreasing imply that they are all exponentially small, as discussed in the proof of Theorem 4.4. Putting these two observations together, we have shown that

$$Q(N) = \sum_{1 \le k \le k_0} e^{-k^2/(2N)} \left(1 + O\left(\frac{k}{N}\right) + O\left(\frac{k^3}{N^2}\right)\right) + \Delta.$$

Here we use Δ as a notation to represent a term that is exponentially small, but otherwise unspecified. Moreover, $\exp(-k^2/(2N)$ is *also* exponentially small for $k > k_0$ and we can add the terms for $k > k_0$ back in, so we have

$$Q(N) = \sum_{k \ge 1} e^{-k^2/(2N)} + O(1).$$

Essentially, we have replaced the tail of the original sum by the tail of the approximation, which is justified because both are exponentially small. We leave the proof that the error terms contribute an absolute error that is

$O(1)$ as an exercise below, because it is a slight modification of the proof for the main term, which is discussed in the next paragraph. Of course, the $O(1)$ also absorbs the exponentially small terms.

The remaining sum is the sum of values of the function $e^{x^2/2}$ at regularly spaced points with step $1/\sqrt{N}$. Thus, the Euler-Maclaurin theorem provides the approximation

$$\sum_{k\geq 1} e^{-k^2/(2N)} = \sqrt{N}\int_0^\infty e^{-x^2/2}dx + O(1).$$

The value of this integral is well known to be $\sqrt{\pi/2}$. Substituting into the above expression for $Q(N)$ gives the stated result. ■

Note that, in this case, the large terms occur for small values of k, so that we had only one tail to take care of. In general, as depicted in Figure 4.6, the dominant terms occur somewhere in the middle of the range, so that both left and right tails have to be treated.

Exercise 4.69 By applying Euler-Maclaurin summation to the functions $xe^{-x^2/2}$ and $x^3e^{-x^3/2}$, show that

$$\sum_{1\leq k\leq k_0} e^{-k^2/(2N)}O\Big(\frac{k}{N}\Big) \qquad \text{and} \qquad \sum_{1\leq k\leq k_0} e^{-k^2/(2N)}O\Big(\frac{k^3}{N^2}\Big)$$

are both $O(1)$.

The Q-function takes on several forms; also Knuth defines two related functions, the P-function and the R-function (which is a sum of the R-distribution that we considered above). These, along with the asymptotic estimates given by Knuth, are shown in Table 4.11. Note that

$$Q(N)+R(N) = \sum_k \frac{N!}{k!}\frac{N^k}{N^N} = \frac{N!}{N^N}e^N = \sqrt{2\pi N} + \frac{1}{6}\sqrt{\frac{\pi}{2N}} + O\Big(\frac{1}{N}\Big)$$

by Stirling's approximation.

Exercise 4.70 Show that

$$P(N) = \sum_{k\geq 0}\frac{(N-k)^k(N-k)!}{N!} = \sqrt{\pi N/2} + O(1)$$

Exercise 4.71 Find a direct argument showing that $R(N) - Q(N) \sim 2/3$.

$$
\begin{aligned}
Q(N) &= \sum_{1\le k\le N} \frac{N!}{(N-k)!N^k} \\
&= \sum_{1\le k\le N} \prod_{1\le j<k} \Bigl(1-\frac{j}{N}\Bigr) = \sum_{1\le k\le N} \Bigl(1-\frac{1}{N}\Bigr)\Bigl(1-\frac{2}{N}\Bigr)\ldots\Bigl(1-\frac{k-1}{N}\Bigr) \\
&= \sum_{0\le k<N} \frac{N!}{k!}\frac{N^k}{N^N} \\
&= \sum_k \binom{N}{k}\frac{k!}{N^k} - 1 \\
&= \sqrt{\frac{\pi N}{2}} - \frac{1}{3} + \frac{1}{12}\sqrt{\frac{\pi}{2N}} + O\Bigl(\frac{1}{N}\Bigr)
\end{aligned}
$$

$$
\begin{aligned}
P(N) &= \sum_{0\le k\le N} \frac{(N-k)^k (N-k)!}{N!} \\
&= \sum_{1\le k\le N} \prod_{1\le j<k} \Bigl(\frac{N-k}{N-j}\Bigr) \\
&= \sum_{0\le k<N} \frac{k!}{N!}\frac{k^N}{k^k} \\
&= \sum_k \frac{(N-k)^k}{k!\binom{N}{k}} \\
&= \sqrt{\frac{\pi N}{2}} - \frac{2}{3} + \frac{11}{24}\sqrt{\frac{\pi}{2N}} + O\Bigl(\frac{1}{N}\Bigr)
\end{aligned}
$$

$$
\begin{aligned}
R(N) &= \sum_{k\ge 0} \frac{N!N^k}{(N+k)!} \\
&= \sum_{1\le k\le N} \prod_{1\le j<k} \Bigl(\frac{N}{N+j}\Bigr) \\
&= \sum_{k\ge N} \frac{N!}{k!}\frac{N^k}{N^N} \\
&= \sqrt{\frac{\pi N}{2}} + \frac{1}{3} + \frac{1}{12}\sqrt{\frac{\pi}{2N}} + O\Bigl(\frac{1}{N}\Bigr)
\end{aligned}
$$

Table 4.11 Ramanujan P-, Q-, and R-functions

4.8 "Normal" Examples from the Analysis of Algorithms. The analysis of several algorithms depends on the evaluation of a sum that is similar to the binomial distribution:

$$\sum_k F(k)\binom{2N}{N-k}\Big/\binom{2N}{N}.$$

As long as $F(k)$ is reasonably well behaved, such a sum can be estimated accurately using the Laplace method and the Euler-Maclaurin formula (Theorem 4.2). We consider this sum in some detail because it is representative of many similar problems that arise in the analysis of algorithms and because it provides a good vehicle for further illustrating the Laplace method.

The nature of the applications involving various $F(k)$ is only briefly sketched here, since the applications are described fully in the cited sources, and we will cover related basic concepts in the chapters that follow. Our purpose here is to provide a concrete example of how asymptotic methods can give accurate estimates for complex expressions that arise in practice. Such sums are sometimes called *Catalan sums* as they arise in connection with tree enumerations and Catalan numbers, as we will see in Chapter 5. They also occur in connection with path enumerations and merging algorithms, as we will see in Chapter 6.

2-ordered sequences. A sequence of numbers is said to be *2-ordered* if the numbers in the odd positions are in ascending order and the numbers in the even positions are in ascending order. Taking a pair of ordered sequences and "shuffling" them (alternate taking one number from each sequence) gives a 2-ordered sequence. In Chapters 6 and 7, we will examine the combinatorial properties of such sequences. Analysis of a number of merging and sorting methods leads to the study of properties of 2-ordered sequences. Taking $F(k) = k^2$ in the Catalan sum gives the average number of *inversions* in a 2-ordered sequence, which is proportional to the average running time of a simple sorting method for the sequence.

Batcher's odd-even merge. Another example involves a sorting method due to Batcher (see [16] and [20]) that is suitable for hardware implementation. Taking $F(k) = k \log k$ gives the leading term in the running time for this method, and a more accurate analysis is possible, involving a much more complicated $F(k)$.

For $F(k) = 1$, we immediately have the result $4^N/\binom{2N}{N}$, which we have already shown to be asymptotic to $\sqrt{\pi N}$. Similarly, for $F(k) = k$ and $F(k) = k^2$, it is also possible to derive an exact value for the sum as a linear combination of a few binomial coefficients, then develop asymptotic estimates using Stirling's approximation. The methods of this section come into play when $F(k)$ is more complicated, as in the analysis of Batcher's method. The primary assumption that we make about $F(k)$ is that it is bounded by a polynomial.

As discussed in the proof of Theorem 4.6, we are working with the product of the Ramanujan Q-distribution and R-distribution:

$$\frac{\binom{2N}{N-k}}{\binom{2N}{N}} = \frac{\dfrac{(2N)!}{(N-k)!(N+k)!}}{\dfrac{(2N)!}{N!N!}}$$

$$= \frac{N!N!}{(N-k)!(N+k)!} = \frac{N!}{(N-k)!N^k}\frac{N!N^k}{(N+k)!}.$$

Thus we can use the results derived during the proof of Theorem 4.6 and its corollary in an application of the Laplace method for this problem. Choosing the cutoff point $k_0 = \sqrt{2N^{1+\epsilon}}$ for a small constant $\epsilon > 0$, we have the approximations

$$\frac{N!N!}{(N-k)!(N+k)!} = \begin{cases} e^{-k^2/N}\Bigl(1+O\Bigl(\dfrac{1}{N^{1-2\epsilon}}\Bigr)\Bigr) & \text{for } k < k_0 \\ O\Bigl(e^{-(2N)^\epsilon}\Bigr) & \text{for } k \ge k_0. \end{cases}$$

This is the basic information that we need for approximating the summand and then using the Laplace method. As above, we use the first part of this to approximate the main contribution to the sum and the second part to bound the tails:

$$\sum_k \frac{\binom{2N}{N-k}}{\binom{2N}{N}} F(k) = \sum_{|k|\le k_0} F(k)e^{-k^2/N}\Bigl(1+O\Bigl(\frac{1}{N^{1-2\epsilon}}\Bigr)\Bigr) + \Delta$$

where, again, Δ represents an exponentially small term. As above, we can add the tails back in because $\exp(-k^2/N)$ is also exponentially small for $k > k_0$, which leads to:

Theorem 4.9 (*Catalan sums*) *If $F(k)$ is bounded by a polynomial, then*

$$\sum_k F(k)\binom{2N}{N-k}\Big/\binom{2N}{N} = \sum_k e^{-k^2/N}F(k)\Big(1+O\Big(\frac{1}{N^{1-2\epsilon}}\Big)\Big)+\Delta,$$

where Δ denotes an exponentially small error term.

Proof. See the discussion above. The condition on F is required to keep the error term exponentially small. ∎

If the sequence $\{F(k)\}$ is the specialization of a real function $F(x)$ that is sufficiently smooth, then the sum is easily approximated with the Euler-Maclaurin formula. In fact, the exponential and its derivatives vanish very quickly at ∞, so all the error terms vanish there, and, under suitable conditions on the behavior of F, we expect to have

$$\sum_{-\infty<k<\infty} F(k)\binom{2N}{N-k}\Big/\binom{2N}{N} = \int_{-\infty}^{\infty} e^{-x^2/N}F(x)dx\Big(1+O\Big(\frac{1}{N^{1-2\epsilon}}\Big)\Big).$$

A similar process works for one-sided sums, where k is restricted to be, say, nonnegative, leading to integrals that are similarly restricted.

Stirling's constant. Taking $F(x) = 1$ gives a familiar integral that leads to the expected solution $\sqrt{\pi N}$. Indeed, this constitutes a derivation of the value of Stirling's constant, as promised in §4.5: we know that the sum is equal to $4^N/\binom{2N}{N}$, which is asymptotic to $\sigma\sqrt{N/2}$ by the same elementary manipulations we did in §4.3, but leaving σ as an unknown in Stirling's formula. Taking $N\to\infty$, we get the result $\sigma = \sqrt{2\pi}$.

Other examples. The average number of inversions in a 2-ordered file is given by the one-sided version (that is, $k \ge 0$) of the Catalan sum with $F(x) = x^2$. This integral is easily evaluated (integration by parts) to give the asymptotic result $N\sqrt{\pi N}/4$. For Batcher's merging method, we use the one-sided sum with $F(x) = x\lg x + O(x)$ to get the estimate

$$\int_0^{\infty} e^{-x^2/N} x\lg x\,dx + O(N).$$

The substitution $t = x^2/N$ transforms the integral to another well-known integral, the "exponential integral function," with the asymptotic result

$$\frac{1}{4}N\lg N + O(N).$$

It is not easy to get a better approximation for $F(x)$, and it turns out that complex analysis can be used to get a more accurate answer, as described in [20]. These results are summarized in Table 4.12.

Exercise 4.72 Find an asymptotic estimate for $\displaystyle\sum_{k\geq 0}\binom{N}{k}^3$.

Exercise 4.73 Find an asymptotic estimate for $\displaystyle\sum_{k\geq 0}\frac{N!}{(N-2k)!k!2^k}$.

Exercise 4.74 Find an asymptotic estimate for $\displaystyle\sum_{k\geq 0}\binom{N-k}{k}^2$.

4.9 "Poisson" Examples from the Analysis of Algorithms. Several other basic algorithms lead to the evaluation of sums where the largest terms are at the beginning, with an eventual exponential decrease. This kind of sum is more like the Poisson distribution with $\lambda < 1$. An example of such a sum is

$$\sum_k \binom{N}{k}\frac{f(k)}{2^k}$$

where, for example, $f(k)$ is a fast-decreasing function.

For an example, we consider the radix-exchange sorting method mentioned in Chapter 1, which is closely related to the "trie" data structure in

$F(k)$	$\displaystyle\sum_{k\geq 0}F(k)\binom{2N}{N-k}\Big/\binom{2N}{N}$
1	$\sim\dfrac{\sqrt{\pi N}}{2}$
k	$\dfrac{N}{2}$
$k\lg k$	$\sim\dfrac{N\lg N}{4}$
k^2	$N4^{N-1}\Big/\binom{2N}{N}\sim\dfrac{\sqrt{\pi N^3}}{4}$

Table 4.12 Catalan sums

Chapter 7. Below we show that the solution to the recurrence describing the number of bit inspections in radix-exchange sorting involves the "trie sum"

$$S_N = \sum_{j\geq 0}\left(1 - \left(1 - \frac{1}{2^j}\right)^N\right).$$

Expanding the binomial gives sums of terms of the form shown above with $f(k) = (-1)^k$, $(-1/2)^k$, $(-1/4)^k$, $(-1/8)^k$, and so forth. Precise evaluation of this sum is best done with complex analysis, but a very good estimate is easy to obtain from the approximation

$$1 - \left(1 - \frac{1}{2^j}\right)^N \sim 1 - e^{-N/2^j}.$$

We can show that the approximation is good to within $O(1/N)$ for $j < \lg N$ and that both sides are very small for large $j >> \lg N$, so it is elementary to show that

$$S_N = \sum_{j\geq 0}(1 - e^{-N/2^j}) + o(1).$$

By splitting the range of summation into three parts, it is not difficult to get a good estimate for this sum. As shown in Figure 4.7, the summand is near 1 for small j, near 0 for large j, and in transition from 1 to 0 for j

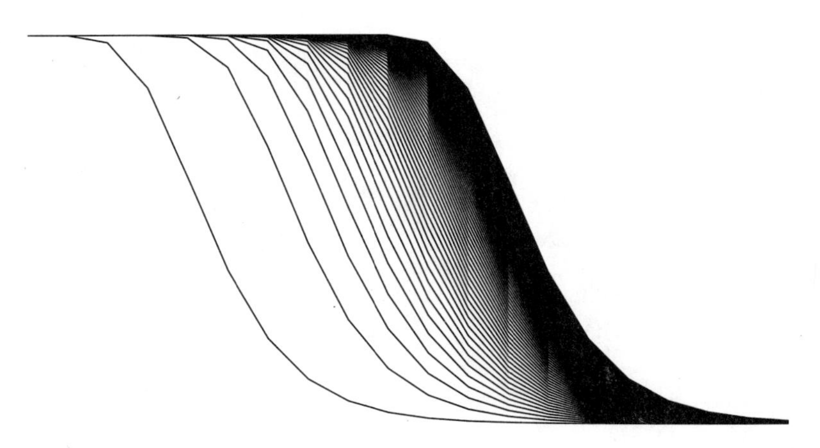

Figure 4.7 Asymptotic behavior of the terms in $\sum_{j\geq 0}(1 - e^{-N/2^j})$

near $\lg N$. More precisely, for $j < (1-\epsilon)\lg N$, the summand is very close to 1; for $j > (1+\epsilon)\lg N$ it is very close to 0; and for j in between the bounds, the sum is certainly between 0 and 1. This argument proves that, up to smaller order terms, the sum is between $(1-\epsilon)\lg N$ and $(1+\epsilon)\lg N$ for any ϵ; a more careful choice of the bounds will show that the sum is $\sim \lg N$:

Theorem 4.10 (*Trie sum*) *As* $N \to \infty$,

$$S_N = \sum_{j\geq 0}\Bigl(1 - \Bigl(1 - \frac{1}{2^j}\Bigr)^N\Bigr) = \lg N + O(\log\log N).$$

Proof. Use bounds of $\lg N \pm \ln\ln N$ in the argument above. A more detailed argument can be used to show that $S_N = \lg N + O(1)$. We will analyze the function $S_N - \lg N$ in some detail in Chapter 7. ∎

Corollary *The average number of bit inspections used by radix-exchange sort is* $N\lg N + O(N)$.

Proof. As discussed in §1.5 this quantity satisfies the recurrence

$$C_N = N + \frac{2}{2^N}\sum_k \binom{N}{k} C_k \qquad \text{for } N > 1 \text{ with } C_0 = 0 \text{ and } C_1 = 0.$$

Multiplying by z^N and summing on N leaves a straightforward convolution that simplifies to demonstrate that the EGF $\sum_{N\geq 0} C_N z^N/N!$ must satisfy the functional equation

$$C(z) = ze^z - z + 2e^{z/2}C(z/2).$$

As we might expect, this equation is also available via the symbolic method [10]. Iterating the equation, we find that

$$\begin{aligned}
C(z) &= ze^z - z + 2e^{z/2}C(z/2)\\
&= ze^z - z + 2e^{z/2}\Bigl(\frac{z}{2}e^{z/2} - \frac{z}{2} + 2e^{z/4}C(z/4)\Bigr)\\
&= z(e^z - 1) + z(e^z - e^{z/2}) + 4e^{3z/4}C(z/4)\\
&= z(e^z - 1) + z(e^z - e^{z/2}) + z(e^z - e^{3z/4}) + 8e^{7z/8}C(z/8)\\
&\;\;\vdots\\
&= z\sum_{j\geq 0}\Bigl(e^z - e^{(1-2^{-j})z}\Bigr)
\end{aligned}$$

and therefore

$$C_N = N![z^N]C(z) = N\sum_{j\ge 0}\left(1-\left(1-\frac{1}{2^j}\right)^{N-1}\right).$$

Thus we have $C_N = NS_{N-1}$, and the claimed result is established. ∎

As discussed further in Chapter 7, the linear term oscillates in value. This is perhaps not surprising because the algorithm deals with bits and has the "binary divide-and-conquer" flavor of some of the algorithms discussed in §2.6. It presents significant analytic challenges nonetheless, which are best met by complex analysis methods.

Exercise 4.75 Find an asymptotic estimate for $\sum_{0\le j\le N}\left(1-\frac{1}{2^j}\right)^N$.

Exercise 4.76 Find an asymptotic estimate for $\sum_{j\ge 0}(1-e^{-N/j^t})$ for $t > 1$.

4.10 Generating Function Asymptotics. The symbolic method makes it possible to analyze a large number of complicated combinatorial problems in terms of generating functions. As we have shown in many examples, we can often expand these generating functions and approximate the combinatorial sums expressing the coefficients. However, we certainly encounter many generating functions for which such direct expansion is not feasible. We present here a direct approach that can be highly effective even for complicated generating functions.

Radius-of-convergence bounds. First, we note that knowledge of the *radius of convergence* of a generating function provides information on the rate of growth of its coefficients, as has been known since Euler and Cauchy.

Theorem 4.11 (*Radius-of-convergence bound*) *Let $f(z)$ be a power series that has radius of convergence $R > 0$. Then*

$$[z^n]f(z) = O(r^{-n})$$

for any positive $r < R$.

Proof. Take any r such that $0 < r < R$ and let $f_n = [z^n]f(z)$. The series $\sum_n f_n r^n$ converges; hence its general term $f_n r^n$ tends to zero and in particular is bounded from above by a constant. ∎

For example, the Catalan generating function converges for $|z| < 1/4$ since it involves $(1-4z)^{1/2}$ and the binomial series $(1+u)^{1/2}$ converges for $|u| < 1$. This gives us the bound

$$[z^n]\frac{1-\sqrt{1-4z}}{2} = O((4+\epsilon)^n)$$

for any ϵ, a weaker form of what derives from Stirling's formula.

The bounds of Theorem 4.11 can be strengthened in the case of combinatorial generating functions. More generally, let $f(z)$ have positive coefficients; then

$$[z^n]f(z) \le \min_{x\in(0,R)} \frac{f(x)}{x^n}.$$

This follows simply from $f_n x^n \le f(x)$, as $f_n x^n$ is just one term in a convergent sum of positive quantities. In particular, we will make use of this very general bounding technique in Chapter 6, where we will discuss permutations with restricted cycle lengths.

Exercise 4.77 Prove that there exists a constant C such that

$$[z^n]\exp(z/(1-z)) = O(\exp(C\sqrt{n})).$$

Exercise 4.78 Establish similar bounds for the OGF of integer partitions

$$[z^n]\prod_{k\ge1}(1-z^k)^{-1}.$$

Asymptotic analysis of coefficients. We can often derive not only upper bounds but also asymptotic equivalents from direct consideration of generating functions. We have already seen a particular instance of this in §4.1, in the context of our discussion of rational generating functions. For instance, if $g(z)$ is a polynomial and r is an integer, then the partial fraction decomposition yields

$$[z^n]\frac{g(z)}{(1-z)^r} \sim g(1)\binom{n+r-1}{n} \sim g(1)\frac{n^{r-1}}{(r-1)!},$$

provided of course $g(1) \ne 0$. A much more general result actually holds:

Theorem 4.12 (*Radius-of-convergence approximation*) *Let $g(z)$ have radius of convergence strictly larger than 1 and assume that $g(1) \neq 0$. For any real $\alpha \notin \{0, -1, -2, \ldots\}$, there holds*

$$[z^n]\frac{g(z)}{(1-z)^\alpha} \sim g(1)\binom{n+\alpha-1}{n}.$$

Proof. Let $g(z)$ have radius of convergence $> r$ where $r > 1$. We know that $g_n \equiv [z^n]g(z) = O(r^{-n})$ from our first theorem, and in particular the sum $\sum_n g_n$ converges to $g(1)$ geometrically fast.

It is then a simple matter to analyze the convolution:

$$\begin{aligned}[z^n]\frac{g(z)}{(1-z)^\alpha} &= g_0\binom{n+\alpha-1}{n} + g_1\binom{n+\alpha-2}{n-1} + \cdots + g_n\binom{\alpha-1}{0} \\ &= \binom{n+\alpha-1}{n}\Bigl(g_0 + g_1(\frac{n}{n+\alpha-1}) \\ &\qquad + g_2\frac{n(n-1)}{(n+\alpha-1)(n+\alpha-2)} \\ &\qquad + g_3\frac{n(n-1)(n-2)}{(n+\alpha-1)(n+\alpha-2)(n+\alpha-3)} + \cdots\Bigr).\end{aligned}$$

The term of index j in this sum is simply

$$g_j\frac{n(n-1)\cdots(n-j+1)}{(n+\alpha-1)(n+\alpha-2)\cdots(n+\alpha-j)},$$

which tends to g_j when $n \to +\infty$. From this, we deduce that

$$[z^n]g(z)(1-z)^{-\alpha} \sim \binom{n+\alpha-1}{n}(g_0 + g_1 + \cdots g_n) \sim g(1)\binom{n+\alpha-1}{n},$$

since the partial sums $g_0 + \cdots + g_n$ converge to $g(1)$ geometrically fast. ∎

Exercise 4.79 Give a detailed proof of the assertions above.

For various specific values of α, more detailed asymptotic bounds are easy to derive. From the Euler-Maclaurin formula, the binomial coefficient $\binom{n+\alpha-1}{n}$ is $O(n^{\alpha-1})$, and the constant is known, as well (see Exercise 4.80). For example, we have already seen (in §3.4) that

$$\binom{n-1/2}{n} = (-1)^n\binom{-1/2}{n} = \binom{2n}{n} \Big/ 4^n \sim \frac{1}{\sqrt{\pi n}}.$$

A famous example of the application of this technique (see Comtet [5]) is to the function

$$f(z) = \frac{e^{z/2+z^2/4}}{\sqrt{1-z}}$$

that is the EGF of the so-called 2-regular graphs. It involves a numerator $g(z) = \exp(z/2 + z^2/4)$ that has radius of convergence clearly equal to ∞. Thus Theorem 4.12 gives *immediately*

$$[z^n]f(z) \sim \frac{e^{3/4}}{\sqrt{\pi n}}.$$

With results such as Theorem 4.12, the asymptotic form of coefficients is directly "transferred" from elements like $(1-z)^{-\alpha}$ (called "singular elements") that play a role very similar to partial fraction elements in the analysis of rational functions. The way that the asymptotic form of coefficients can be read off so easily is quite remarkable. Again, we will see more examples of this in connection with permutations in Chapter 6.

Theorem 4.12 naturally applies in many contexts where we encounter products of generating functions with different radii of convergence. It is only the simplest of a whole set of similar results originating with Darboux in the last century (see [5] and [22]), and further developed by Pólya and Szegő, Bender, and others [3][9]. These methods are discussed in detail in [11]; unlike what we could do here, their full development requires the theory of functions of a complex variable. This approach to asymptotics is called *singularity analysis*.

Exercise 4.80 Prove that

$$[z^n]\binom{n+\alpha-1}{n} \sim \frac{n^{\alpha-1}}{\Gamma(\alpha)},$$

for some constant $\Gamma(\alpha)$. (*Hint*: Use Euler-Maclaurin summation.) The "constant" $\Gamma(\alpha)$ is actually the well-known *Gamma function* that generalizes the factorial function beyond the integers; see [21].

Exercise 4.81 Prove that a full asymptotic expansion can be derived under the conditions of Theorem 4.12.

Exercise 4.82 Extend the method to the analysis of

$$[z^n]g(z)\log\frac{1}{1-z} \quad \text{and} \quad [z^n]\frac{g(z)}{1-z}\log\frac{1}{1-z}.$$

ASYMPTOTIC methods play an essential role in the analysis of algorithms. Without asymptotics we might be left with hopelessly complex exact answers or hopelessly difficult closed-form solutions to evaluate. With asymptotics, we can focus on those parts of the solution that contribute most to the answer. This extra insight from the analysis also plays a role in the algorithm design process: when seeking to improve the performance of an algorithm, we focus on precisely those parts of the algorithm that lead to the terms we focus on in the asymptotic analysis.

Understanding distinctions among the various notations that are commonly used in asymptotic analysis is critically important. We have included many elementary exercises and examples in this chapter to help illustrate such distinctions, and the reader is urged to study them carefully. Proper use of elementary definitions and manipulations can greatly simplify asymptotic formulas.

As with GFs, a good deal of the basic material for asymptotic analysis follows from combining well-known classical expansions, for generating functions associated with well-known special numbers such as Stirling numbers, harmonic numbers, geometric series, and binomial coefficients. Algebraic manipulations and simplification also play an important role. Indeed, the ability to suppress detail in such calculations makes the asymptotic representation very attractive.

We considered in detail the use of these methods to derive two of the most important approximations to the binomial distribution: normal and Poisson. We also considered the related functions that were studied by Ramanujan and Knuth that appear in the analysis of many algorithms. Not only are these approximations extremely useful in the analysis of algorithms, but they also are prototypical of the kind of manipulations that arise often.

We have concentrated on so-called elementary methods, from real analysis. Proficiency in elementary methods is important, especially simplifying complicated asymptotic expressions, refining estimates, approximating sums with integrals, and bounding tails, including the Laplace method. Better understanding of asymptotic analysis relies on understanding of properties of functions in the complex plane. Surprisingly, powerful methods derive from only a few basic properties, especially singularities of generating functions. We have given a general idea of the basic method, which is considered in detail in [11]. Advanced techniques often cannot be avoided in detailed asymptotics, since complex values appear in answers. In particular, we see many examples where an oscillating phenomenon appears as the function under study grows. This seems surprising, until we recall that it appears in our most fundamental algorithms, including divide-and-conquer methods such as Mergesort or methods involving binary representation of integers. Complex analysis provides a simple way to explain such phenomena.

We can conclude this chapter in a similar fashion to the previous chapters: the techniques given here can take us reasonably far in studying important properties of fundamental computer algorithms. They play a crucial role in our treatment of algorithms associated with trees, permutations, strings, and maps in Chapters 5 through 8.

References

1. M. ABRAMOWITZ AND I. STEGUN. *Handbook of Mathematical Functions*, Dover, New York, 1970.
2. C. M. BENDER AND S. A. ORSZAG. *Ad anced Mathematical Methods for Scientists and Engineers*, McGraw-Hill, New York, 1978.
3. E. A. BENDER. "Asymptotic methods in enumeration," *SIAM Re iew* **16**, 1974, 485–515.
4. B. C. BERNDT. *Ramanujan's Notebooks, Parts I and II*, Springer-Verlag, Berlin, 1985 and 1989.
5. L. COMTET. *Ad anced Combinatorics*, Reidel, Dordrecht, 1974.
6. N. G. DE BRUIJN. *Asymptotic Methods in Analysis*, Dover, New York, 1981.
7. A. ERDÉLYI. *Asymptotic Expansions*, Dover, New York, 1956.
8. W. FELLER. *An Introduction to Probability Theory and Its Applications*, John Wiley, New York, 1957.
9. P. FLAJOLET AND A. ODLYZKO. "Singularity analysis of generating functions," *SIAM Journal on Discrete Mathematics* **3**, 1990, 216–240.
10. P. FLAJOLET, M. REGNIER, AND D. SOTTEAU. "Algebraic methods for trie statistics," *Annals of Discrete Mathematics* **25**, 1985, 145–188.
11. P. FLAJOLET AND R. SEDGEWICK. *Analytic Combinatorics*, in preparation.
12. R. L. GRAHAM, D. E. KNUTH, AND O. PATASHNIK. *Concrete Mathematics*, Addison-Wesley, Reading, MA, 1989.

13. D. H. GREENE AND D. E. KNUTH. *Mathematics for the Analysis of Algorithms*, Birkhäuser, Boston, 1981.
14. PETER HENRICI. *Applied and Computational Complex Analysis*, 3 volumes, John Wiley, New York, 1977.
15. D. E. KNUTH. *The Art of Computer Programming. Volume 1: Fundamental Algorithms*, Addison-Wesley, Reading, MA, 1968.
16. D. E. KNUTH. *The Art of Computer Programming. Volume 3: Sorting and Searching*, Addison-Wesley, Reading, MA, 1973.
17. D. E. KNUTH. "Big Omicron and big Omega and big Theta," *SIGACT News*, April-June 1976, 18–24.
18. A. ODLYZKO. "Asymptotic enumeration methods," in *Handbook of Combinatorics*, R. Graham, M. Grötschel, and L. Lovász, eds., North Holland, 1995.
19. F. W. J. OLVER. *Asymptotics and Special Functions*, Academic Press, New York, 1974.
20. R. SEDGEWICK. "Data movement in odd-even merging," *SIAM Journal on Computing* **7**, 1978, 239–272.
21. E. T. WHITTAKER AND G. N. WATSON. *A Course of Modern Analysis*, 4th edition, Cambridge University Press, Cambridge (England), 1927 (reprinted 1973).
22. H. WILF. *Generatingfunctionology*, Academic Press, San Diego, 1990.

CHAPTER FIVE

TREES

TREES are fundamental structures that arise implicitly and explicitly in many practical algorithms, and it is important to understand their properties in order to be able to analyze these algorithms. Many algorithms construct trees explicitly; in other cases trees assume significance as models of programs, especially recursive programs. Indeed, trees are the quintessential nontrivial recursively defined objects: a tree is either empty or a root node connected to a sequence (or a multiset) of trees. We will examine in detail how the recursive nature of the structure leads directly to recursive analyses based upon generating functions.

We begin with *binary trees*, a particular type of tree first introduced in Chapter 3. Binary trees have many useful applications and are particularly well suited to computer implementations. We then consider properties of trees in general, including their close relationship to binary trees. Trees and binary trees are also directly related to several other combinatorial structures such as paths in lattices, triangulations, and ruin sequences. We discuss several different ways to represent trees, not only because alternate representations often arise in applications, but also because an analytic argument often may be more easily understood when based upon an alternate representation.

We consider binary trees both from a purely combinatorial point of view (where we enumerate and examine properties of all possible different structures) and from an algorithmic point of view (where the structures are built and used by algorithms, with the probability of occurrence of each structure induced by the input). The former is important in the analysis of recursive structures and algorithms, and the most important instance of the latter is a fundamental algorithm called *binary tree search*. Binary trees and binary tree search are so important in practice that we study their properties in considerable detail, expanding upon the approach begun in Chapter 3.

As usual, after considering enumeration problems, we move on to analysis of parameters. We focus on the analysis of *path length*, a basic parameter of trees that is natural to study and useful to know about, and we consider *height* and some other parameters as well. Knowledge of basic facts about path length and height for various kinds of trees is crucial for us to be able to understand a variety of fundamental computer algorithms. Our analysis of these problems is prototypical of the relationship between classical combinatoric and modern algorithmic studies of fundamental structures, a recurring theme throughout this book.

As we will see, the analysis of path length flows naturally from the basic tools that we have developed, and generalizes to provide a way to study a broad variety of tree parameters. On the other hand, the analysis of height presents significant technical challenges and requires a large fraction of the major tools that we covered in Chapters 2 through 4. Though there is not necessarily any relationship between the ease of describing a problem and the ease of solving it, this disparity in ease of analysis is somewhat surprising at first look, because both parameters have simple recursive descriptions that are quite similar.

As discussed in Chapter 3, the "symbolic method" from classical combinatorics can unify the study of tree enumeration problems and analysis of tree parameters, leading to very straightforward solutions for many otherwise unapproachable problems. For best effect, this requires a certain investment in some basic combinatorial machinery (see [13]), so we provide direct analytic derivations for many of the important problems considered in this chapter, along with informal descriptions of how results can be explained by symbolic arguments. Detailed study of this chapter might also be characterized as an exercise in appreciating the value of the symbolic method.

We then consider a number of different types of trees, and some classical combinatorial results about properties of trees, moving from the specifics of the binary tree to the general notion of a tree as an acyclic connected graph. Our goal is to provide access to results from an extensive literature on the combinatorial analysis of trees, while at the same time providing the groundwork for a host of algorithmic applications.

5.1 Binary Trees. In Chapter 3, we encountered *binary trees*, perhaps the simplest type of tree. Binary trees are made up of two different types of nodes that are attached together according to a simple recursive definition:

Definition *A* binary tree *is either an external node or an internal node attached to an ordered pair of binary trees called the left subtree and the right subtree of that node.*

Usually, external nodes are used to represent empty binary trees. As such, they serve as placeholders. Unless in a context where both types are being considered, we refer to the internal nodes of a tree simply as the "nodes" of the tree. We normally consider the subtrees of a node to be connected to the node with two links, the left link and the right link.

Figure 5.1 shows three binary trees, and the 14 binary trees with four internal nodes (and five external nodes) are drawn in Figure 5.2. By definition, each internal node has exactly two links; by convention, we draw the subtrees of each node below the node on the page, and represent the links as lines connecting nodes. Each node has exactly one link "to" it, except the node at the top, a distinguished node called the *root*. It is customary to borrow terminology from family trees: the nodes directly below a node are called its *children*; nodes farther down are called *descendants*; the node directly above each node is call its *parent*; nodes farther up are called *ancestors*. External nodes have no children and the root has no parent.

Lemma *The number of external nodes in any binary tree is exactly one greater than the number of internal nodes.*

Proof. Let e be the number of external nodes and i the number of internal nodes. We count the links in the tree in two different ways. Each internal node has exactly two links "from" it, so the number of links is $2i$. But the number of links is also $i + e - 1$, since each node but the root has exactly on link "to" it. Equating these two gives $2i = i + e - 1$, or $i = e - 1$. ∎

Exercise 5.1 Develop an alternative proof of this result using induction.

We have already considered the problem of enumerating binary trees: the following basic result is described in detail in Chapters 3 and 4.

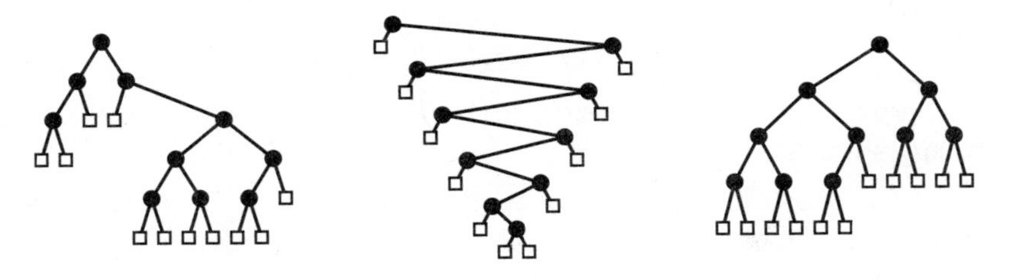

Figure 5.1 Three binary trees

Theorem 5.1 (*Enumeration of binary trees*) *The number of binary trees with N internal nodes and $N+1$ external nodes is given by the Catalan numbers:*

$$T_N = \frac{1}{N+1}\binom{2N}{N} = \frac{4^N}{\sqrt{\pi N^3}}\Bigl(1 + O\Bigl(\frac{1}{N}\Bigr)\Bigr).$$

Proof. We briefly restate the proof given in §3.8. Let $\mathcal{T}$ represent the set of all binary trees, with associated ordinary generating function

$$T(z) = \sum_{t \in \mathcal{T}} z^{|t|} = \sum_{N \geq 0} T_N z^N.$$

That is, $T_N = [z^N]T(z)$ is the number of binary trees with N internal nodes. Also, $zT(z)$ is the OGF for trees counted by external nodes, since $[z^N]zT(z) = T_{N-1}$ is the number of binary trees with N external nodes.

A binary tree is either an external node or an internal node attached to an ordered pair of binary trees, so the symbolic method tells us that

$$\mathcal{T} = \{\square\} + \{\bullet\} \times \mathcal{T} \times \mathcal{T}.$$

This translates directly to the functional equation

$$T(z) = 1 + zT(z)^2.$$

(Note that counting by external nodes gives the equivalent form $zT(z) = z + (zT(z))^2$.) Solving with the quadratic formula and expanding with the binomial theorem, we get

$$zT(z) = \frac{1}{2}(1 - \sqrt{1-4z}) = -\frac{1}{2}\sum_{N \geq 1}\binom{\frac{1}{2}}{N}(-4z)^N.$$

Setting coefficients equal gives the Catalan numbers

$$T_N = -\frac{1}{2}\binom{\frac{1}{2}}{N+1}(-4)^{N+1} = \frac{1}{N+1}\binom{2N}{N}.$$

The approximation follows directly from Stirling's approximation (see the corollaries to Theorem 4.3). ■

In Chapter 3, we also looked at related problems, such as enumerating forests of binary trees, counting leaves, and so forth. In this chapter, we will use similar tools on more complicated problems, to discover other interesting properties of binary trees and other types of trees.

Figure 5.2 Binary trees with four internal nodes

We count trees by internal nodes from now on. For binary trees, this is strictly equivalent by the lemma above; some other types of trees have no external nodes.

Exercise 5.2 What proportion of the binary trees with N internal nodes have both subtrees of the root nonempty? For $N = 4$, the answer is $4/14$ (see Figure 5.2).

Exercise 5.3 What proportion of the binary trees with $2N + 1$ internal nodes have N internal nodes in each of the subtrees of the root?

5.2 Trees and Forests. In a binary tree, no node has more than two children. This characteristic makes it obvious how to represent and manipulate such trees in computer implementations, and it relates naturally to "divide-and-conquer" algorithms that divide a problem into two subproblems. However, in many applications (and in more traditional mathematical usage), we need to consider *general* trees:

Definition *A* tree *(also called a* general tree*) is a node (called the root) connected to a sequence of disjoint trees. Such a sequence is called a* forest.

We use the same nomenclature as for binary trees: the subtrees of a node are its children, a root node has no parents, and so forth. Trees are more appropriate models than binary trees for certain computations.

All the trees of five nodes are shown in Figure 5.3. The fact that the number of such trees is the same as the number of binary trees with four internal nodes is no coincidence. Actually, it is well known that general trees are closely related combinatorially to binary trees. Below, we examine a construction that establishes this relationship, but first, we consider an analytic proof based on the symbolic method.

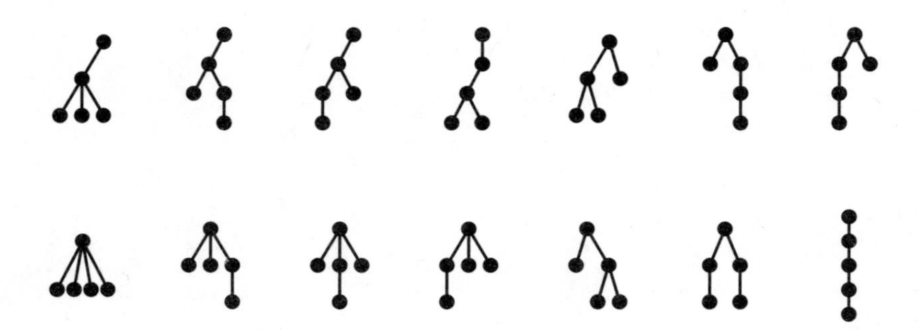

Figure 5.3 Trees with five nodes

Theorem 5.2 (*Enumeration of general trees*) *Let G_N be the number of general trees with N nodes. Then G_N is exactly equal to the number of binary trees with $N-1$ internal nodes and is gi en by the Catalan numbers:*

$$G_N = T_{N-1} = \frac{1}{N}\binom{2N-2}{N-1}.$$

Proof. Consider the generating function

$$G(z) = \sum_{g \in \mathcal{G}} z^{|g|}$$

where $\mathcal{G}$ is the set of all trees. Then, since a tree can have any number of subtrees, which are also trees, we have

$$\begin{aligned} G(z) &= \sum_{k \ge 0} \sum_{g_1 \in \mathcal{G}} \cdots \sum_{g_k \in \mathcal{G}} z^{|g_1|+\cdots+|g_k|+1} \\ &= z \sum_{k \ge 0} (G(z))^k \\ &= \frac{z}{1 - G(z)}. \end{aligned}$$

Thus $G(z) - G(z)^2 = z$ and therefore $G(z) = zT(z)$, since both functions satisfy the same functional equation. That is, the number of trees with N nodes is equal to the number of binary trees with N external nodes, which is the number of binary trees with $N-1$ internal nodes. ∎

This result is also easily available through the symbolic method. A forest is either empty or a sequence of trees:

$$\mathcal{F} = \epsilon + \mathcal{G} + (\mathcal{G} \times \mathcal{G}) + (\mathcal{G} \times \mathcal{G} \times \mathcal{G}) + (\mathcal{G} \times \mathcal{G} \times \mathcal{G} \times \mathcal{G}) + \ldots$$

which translates directly (see Theorem 3.7) into

$$F(z) = 1 + G(z) + G(z)^2 + G(z)^3 + G(z)^4 + \ldots = \frac{1}{1 - G(z)}.$$

The obvious one-to-one correspondence between forests and trees (cut off the root) means that $zF(z) = G(z)$, which leads again to the functional equation for the Catalan OGF.

Exercise 5.4 Find the proportion of trees (asymptotically) for which the root has t children, for $t = 1$, 2, and 3.

Rotation correspondence. There is an easily constructed one-to-one correspondence between forests and binary trees, so that a binary tree could be used on a computer to represent a forest. This correspondence, called the *rotation correspondence*, or the "first child, next sibling" representation, is illustrated in Figure 5.4. Given a forest, it can be represented by a binary tree as follows: the root of the binary tree is the root of the first tree in the forest; its right link points to the representation of the remainder of the forest (not including the first tree); its left link points to the representation for the forest comprising the subtrees of the root of the first tree. In other words, each node has a left link to its first child and a right link to its next sibling in the forest. For the figure, the nodes in the binary tree appear to be placed by rotating the general tree clockwise.

Exercise 5.5 Describe how a given binary tree is represented as a forest.

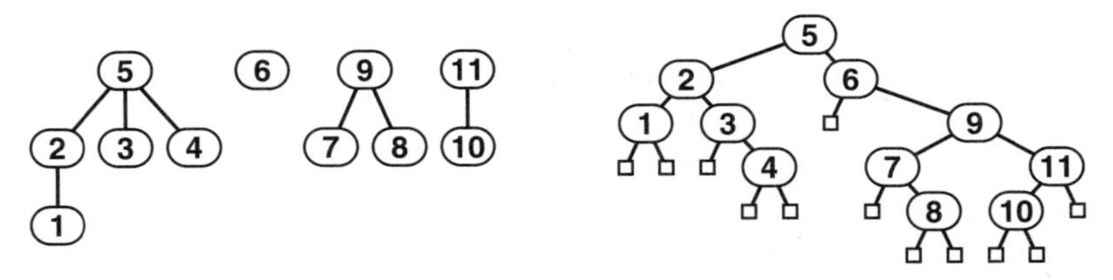

Figure 5.4 Rotation correspondence between trees and binary trees

5.3 Properties of Trees. Trees arise naturally in a variety of computer applications. Our primary notion of *size* is generally taken to be the number of nodes for general trees and, depending on context, the number of internal nodes or the number of external nodes for binary trees. For the analysis of algorithms, we are primarily interested in two basic properties of trees of a given size: *path length* and *height.*

We often speak of the *level* of a node in a tree: the root is at level 0, children of the root are at level 1, and in general, children of a node at level k are at level $k+1$. Another way of thinking of the level is as the distance (number of links) we have to traverse to get from the root to the node. We are particularly interested in the sum of the distances from each node to the root:

Definition *Given a tree t, the* path length *is the sum of the levels of each of the nodes in t and the* height *is the maximum level among all the nodes of the tree.*

We use the notation $|t|$ to refer to the number of nodes in a tree t, the notation $\pi(t)$ to refer to the path length, and the notation $\eta(t)$ to refer to the height. These definitions hold for forests as well. In addition, the path length of a forest is the sum of the path lengths of the constituent trees and the height of a forest is the maximum of the heights of the constituent trees.

Definition *Given a binary tree t, the* internal path length *is the sum of the levels of each of the internal nodes in t, the* external path length *is the sum of the levels of each of the external nodes in t, and the* height *is the maximum level among all the external nodes of the tree.*

We use the notation $\pi(t)$ to refer to the internal path length of a binary tree, $\xi(t)$ to refer to the external path length, and $\eta(t)$ to refer to the height. We use $|t|$ to refer to the number of internal nodes in a binary tree unless specifically noted in contexts where it is more appropriate to count by external nodes or all nodes.

Definition *In general trees,* leaves *are defined to be the nodes with no children at all. In binary trees, the leaves are defined to be the (internal) nodes with both children external.*

The binary tree on the right in Figure 5.4 has height 5, internal path length 25, and external path length 47, with 4 leaves; the forest on the left has height 2 and path length 8, with 7 leaves.

Recursive definitions. It is often convenient to work with recursive definitions for tree parameters. In a binary tree t, the parameters we have defined are all 0 if t is an external node; otherwise if the root of t is an internal node and the left and right subtrees, respectively, are denoted by t_l and t_r, we have following recursive formulae:

$$\begin{aligned}|t| &= |t_l| + |t_r| + 1\\ \pi(t) &= \pi(t_l) + \pi(t_r) + |t| - 1\\ \xi(t) &= \xi(t_l) + \xi(t_r) + |t| + 1\\ \eta(t) &= 1 + \max(\eta(t_l), \eta(t_r)).\end{aligned}$$

These are easily seen to be equivalent to the definitions above. First, the internal node count of a binary tree is the sum of the node counts for its subtrees plus 1 (the root). Second, the internal path length is the sum of the internal path lengths of the subtrees plus $|t| - 1$ because each of the $|t| - 1$ nodes in the subtrees is moved down exactly one level when the subtrees are attached to the tree. The same argument holds for external path length, noting that there are $|t|+1$ external nodes in the two subtrees of a binary tree with $|t|$ internal nodes. The result for height again follows from the fact that the levels of all the nodes in the subtrees are increased by exactly 1.

Exercise 5.6 Give recursive formulations describing path length and height in general trees.

Exercise 5.7 Give recursive formulations for the number of leaves in binary trees and in general trees.

These definitions will serve as the basis for deriving functional equations on associated generating functions when we analyze the parameters below. Also, they can be used for inductive proofs about relationships among the parameters.

Lemma *Path lengths in any binary tree t satisfy* $\xi(t) = \pi(t) + 2|t|$.

Proof. Subtract the equation $\pi(t) = \pi(t_l) + \pi(t_r) + |t| - 1$ from the equation $\xi(t) = \xi(t_l) + \xi(t_r) + |t| + 1$. The lemma follows directly by induction. ■

Path length and height are not independent parameters: if the height is very large, then so must be the path length, as shown by the following bounds, which are relatively crude, but useful.

Lemma *The height and internal path length of any nonempty binary tree t satisfy the inequalities*

$$\frac{\pi(t)}{|t|} \le \eta(t) \le \sqrt{2\pi(t)} + 1.$$

Proof. This follows from straightforward bounds on the path length, given the height. If $\eta(t) = 0$ then $\pi(t) = 0$ and the stated inequalities hold. Otherwise, we must have $\pi(t) < |t|\eta(t)$, since the level of each internal node must be strictly smaller than the height. Furthermore, there is at least one internal node at each level less than the height, so we must have $\pi(t) \ge \sum_{0\le i<\eta(t)} i$. Hence $2\pi(t) \ge \eta(t)^2 - \eta(t) \ge (\eta(t)-1)^2$ (subtract the quantity $\eta(t)-1$, which is nonnegative, from the right-hand side), and thus $\eta(t) \le \sqrt{2\pi(t)} + 1$. Combining these two inequalities gives the stated result. ∎

In the analysis of algorithms, we are particularly interested in knowing the *average* values of these parameters, for various types of "random" trees. One of our primary topics of discussion for this chapter is how these quantities relate to fundamental algorithms and how we can determine their expected values. Figures 5.5 and 5.6 give some indication of how these differ for different types of trees. Figure 5.5 is a random binary tree, when each binary tree is considered to be equally likely to occur. Figure 5.6 is a random forest, where each forest is equally likely to occur. Each figure also has a plot of the number of nodes at each level, which makes it easy to calculate the height (number of levels) and path length (sum over i of i times the number of nodes at level i). The random binary tree clearly has larger values for both path length and height than the random forest. One of the prime objectives of this chapter is to quantify these and similar observations, precisely.

Exercise 5.8 Prove that the height of a binary tree with N external nodes has to be at least $\lg N$.

Exercise 5.9 [Kraft equality] Let k_j be the number of external nodes at level j in a binary tree. The sequence $\{k_0, k_1, \ldots, k_h\}$ (where h is the height of the tree) describes the *profile* of the tree. Show that a vector of integers describes the profile of a binary tree if and only if $\sum_j 2^{-k_j} = 1$.

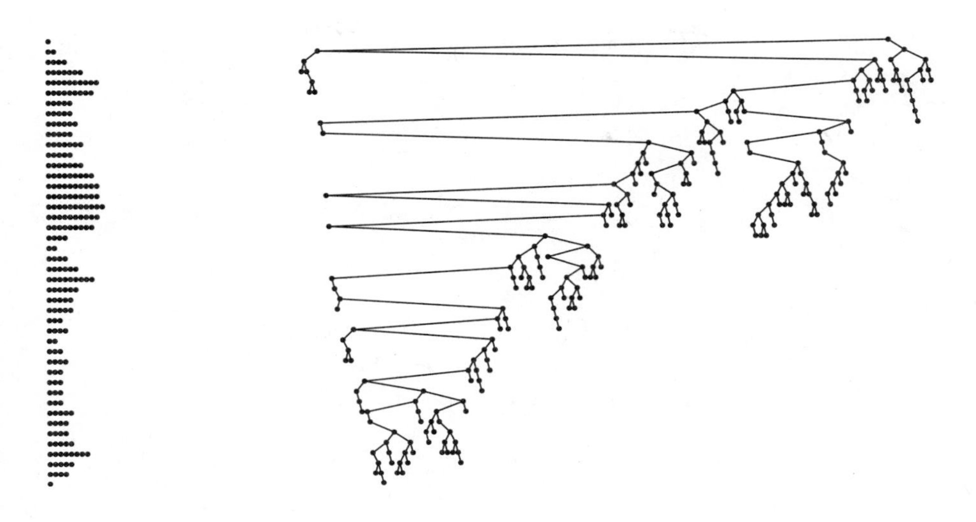

Figure 5.5 A random binary tree with 256 internal nodes

Exercise 5.10 Give tight upper and lower bounds on the path length of a general tree with N nodes.

Exercise 5.11 Give tight upper and lower bounds on the internal and external path lengths of a binary tree with N internal nodes.

Exercise 5.12 Give tight upper and lower bounds on the number of leaves in a binary tree with N nodes.

5.4 Tree Algorithms. Trees are relevant to the study of analysis of algorithms not only because they implicitly model the behavior of recursive programs but also because they are involved explicitly in many basic algorithms that are widely used. We will briefly describe a few of the most fundamental such algorithms here. This brief description certainly cannot do justice to the general topic of the utility of tree structures in algorithm design, but we can indicate that the study of tree parameters such as path length and height provides the basic information needed to analyze a host of important algorithms.

Traversal. In a computer representation, one of the fundamental operations on trees is *traversal*: systematically processing each of the nodes

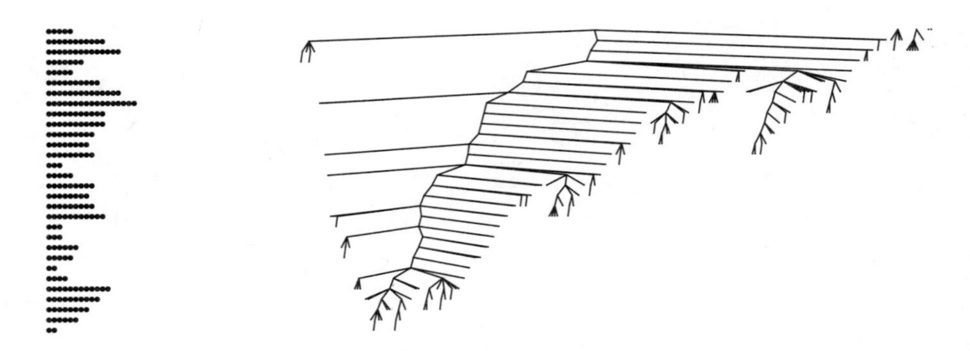

Figure 5.6 A random forest with 256 nodes

of the tree. This operation also is of interest combinatorially, as it represents a way to establish a correspondence between (two-dimensional) tree structures and various (one-dimensional) linear representations.

The recursive nature of trees gives rise to a simple recursive procedure for traversal. We "visit" the root of the tree and recursively "visit" the subtrees. Depending on whether we visit the root before, after, or (for binary trees) in between the subtrees, we get one of three different traversal methods:

To visit all the nodes of a tree in *preorder*:
- visit the root
- visit the subtrees (in preorder)

To visit all the nodes of a tree in *postorder*:
- visit the subtrees (in postorder)
- visit the root

To visit all the nodes of a binary tree in *inorder*:
- visit the left subtree (in inorder)
- visit the root
- visit the right subtree (in inorder)

Program 5.1 is an implementation of preorder traversal of binary trees. In these methods, "visiting" the root might imply any procedure at all that should be systematically applied to nodes in the tree. Different procedures might be appropriate for different types of nodes, for example, external nodes in binary trees.

When a recursive procedure call is executed, a *pushdown stack* is used to save the current "environment," to be restored upon return from the procedure. The maximum amount of memory used by the pushdown stack when traversing a tree is directly proportional to tree height. Though this memory usage may be hidden from the programmer in this case, it certainly is an important performance parameter, and we are interested in analyzing tree height.

Another way to traverse a tree is called *level order*: first list all the nodes on level 0 (the root), then list all the nodes on level 1, left to right, then list all the nodes on level 2 (left to right), and so on. This method is not suitable for implementation as a recursive program, but it is easily implemented nonrecursively just as above using a queue (first-in-first-out data structure) instead of a stack.

Tree traversal algorithms are fundamental and widely applicable. For many more details about them and relationships among recursive and nonrecursive implementations, see Knuth [21] or Sedgewick [29].

Expression evaluation. Consider arithmetic expressions consisting of *operators* such as $+$, $-$, $*$, and $/$, and *operands*, denoted by numbers or letters. Such expressions are typically parenthesized to indicate precedence between operations. Expressions can be represented as binary trees called *parse trees*. For example, consider the case where an expression uses only binary operators. Such an expression corresponds to a binary tree, with operators in the internal nodes and operands in the external nodes, as

```
procedure traverse(x:  link);
  begin
  if x <> NIL then
    begin
    visit (x^.key);
    traverse (x^.left);
    traverse (x^.right)
    end
  end;
```

Program 5.1 Preorder traversal of a binary tree

shown in Figure 5.7, which depicts the parse tree for the expression

$$((x + y) * z) - (w + ((a - (v + y))/((z + y) * x))).$$

Given a parse tree, we can use a simple recursive program to compute the value of the corresponding expression: (recursively) evaluate the two subtrees, then apply the operator to the computed values. Evaluation of an external node gives the current value of the associated variable. This program is equivalent to a tree traversal such as Program 5.1. As with tree traversal, the space consumed by this program will be proportional to the tree height.

Typically, expression tree evaluation is done directly as described above in an interpreter, but also indirectly in code produced by a compiler. That is, a compiler might have the job of first building an expression tree associated with part of a program, then converting an expression tree into a list of instructions for evaluating an expression at execution time. The instructions used are close to machine instructions, for example, involving binary arithmetic operations using machine registers. This translation corresponds to "code generation," and typically leads to the *register allocation* problem. For example, the following code might be produced for the tree in Figure 5.7:

```
r1 ← x+y
r2 ← r1*z
r3 ← v+y
r4 ← a-r3
r5 ← z+y
r6 ← r5*x
r7 ← r4/r6
r8 ← w+r7
r9 ← r2-r8
```

This type of code can easily be translated into machine code. In a typical situation, the temporary variables r1 through r2 might correspond to machine registers, a (limited) machine resource for holding results of arithmetic operations, and we might want to minimize the number of registers used. For example, we could replace the last two instructions above by the instructions

```
r7 ← w+r7
r7 ← r2-r7
```

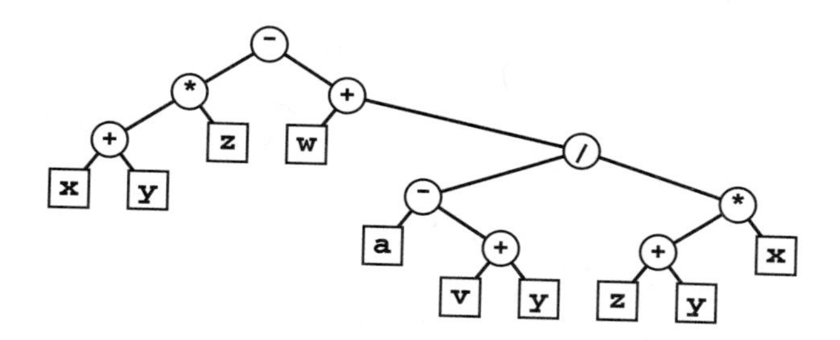

Figure 5.7 Tree representation of an arithmetic expression

and use two fewer registers. Similar savings are available at other parts of the expression. The minimum number of registers needed to evaluate an expression is a tree parameter of direct practical interest. This quantity is bounded from above by tree height, but it is quite different. (For example, the degenerate binary tree where all nodes but one have exactly one null link has height N but the corresponding expression can be evaluated with one register.) Expression evaluation is of importance in its own right, but it is also indicative of the importance of trees in the process of translating computer programs from higher-level languages to machine languages. Compilers generally first "parse" programs into tree representations, then process the tree representation.

Exercise 5.13 What is the minimum number of registers needed to evaluate the expression in Figure 5.7?

Exercise 5.14 Give the binary tree corresponding to the expressions $((a+b)*d$ and $((a+b)*(d-e)*(f+g))-h*i$. Also give the preorder, inorder, and postorder traversals of those trees.

Exercise 5.15 An expression where operators have varying numbers of operands corresponds to a tree, with operands in leaves and operators in nonleaves. Give the preorder and postorder traversals of the tree corresponding to the expression $((a^2+b+c)*(d^4-e^2)*(f+g+h))-i*j$, then give the binary tree representation of that tree and the preorder, inorder, and postorder traversals of the binary tree.

For these and many other applications, we are interested in the path length and height of trees. To consider the average value of such parameters, of course, we need to specify a model defining what is meant by a "random" tree. For tree traversal and expression manipulation, it is customary to use the empirical model where all trees are taken equally likely. Thus, for these applications, we study so-called *Catalan models*, where each of the T_N binary trees of size N or general trees of size $N+1$ are taken with equal probability. This is not the only possibility—in many situations, the trees are induced by external data, and other models of randomness are appropriate. Next, we consider a particularly important example of this.

5.5 Binary Search Trees. One of the most important applications of binary trees is the *binary tree search* algorithm, a method that uses binary trees explicitly to provide an efficient solution to a fundamental problem that arises in numerous applications. The analysis of binary tree search illustrates the distinction between models where all trees are equally likely to occur and models where the underlying distribution is nonuniform. The juxtaposition of these two is one of the essential concepts of this chapter.

The *dictionary*, *symbol table*, or simply *search* problem is a fundamental one in computer science: a set of keys (perhaps with associated information) is to be organized so that efficient searches can be made for particular keys. The binary search method discussed in §2.6 is one basic method for solving this problem, but it requires a preprocessing step where all the keys are first put into sorted order.

A binary tree structure can be used to provide a more fliexible solution to the dictionary problem, by incrementally building a tree with a key in each node and keeping things arranged so that the key in every node is not smaller than any key in the left subtree and not larger than any key in the right subtree. Any set of N distinct keys can be assigned in a unique way to the nodes of any N-node binary tree in this way. For example, Figure 5.8 shows three different binary search trees containing the set of integers `23 26 31 41 44 53 58 59 93 97`.

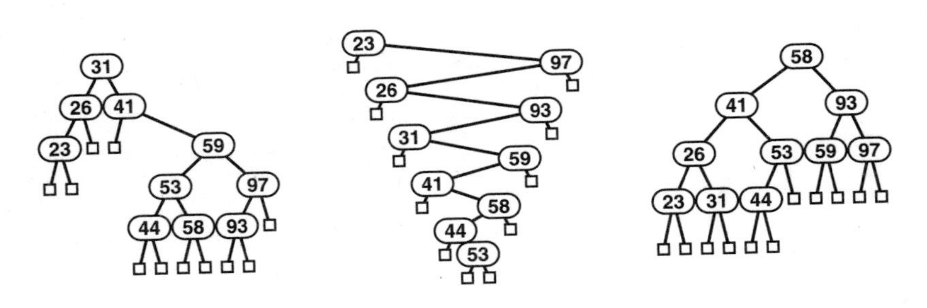

Figure 5.8 Three binary search trees

Definition *A* binary search tree *is a binary tree with keys associated with the internal nodes, satisfying the constraint that the key in every node is greater than or equal to all the keys in its left subtree and less than or equal to all the keys in its right subtree.*

If we assume that the keys have been put into a binary search tree, then Program 5.2 gives a solution to the dictionary problem using a simple recursive implementation of a "search" procedure that determines whether of not a given key is somewhere in the binary search tree. To search for a node with a key `v`, terminate the search (unsuccessfully) if the tree is empty and terminate the search (successfully) if the key in the root node is `v`. Otherwise, look in the left subtree if `v` is less than the key in the root node and look in the right subtree if `v` is greater than they key in the root node. Given a binary search tree, it is a simple matter to verify that Program 5.2 returns a node containing a key `v` if and only if there is one in the tree; otherwise it returns `NIL`. In general there are many binary search trees associated with any particular set of keys; the algorithm works properly for any of them.

To construct a binary search tree, we add keys one by one to an initially empty tree, using a recursive strategy. To insert a new node into an empty tree, create the node, make its left and right pointers `NIL`, and return the pointer to the node. (We use the value `NIL` to represent all external nodes.) If the tree is nonempty, insert the key into the left subtree if it is less than the key at the root, and into the right subtree if it is greater than the key at the root. This is equivalent to doing an unsuccessful search for the key, then inserting a new node containing the key in place of the external node where the search ends. Program 5.3 is an implementation

```
function search(v: integer, x: link): link;
  begin
  if x = NIL search := NIL else
  if v = x^.key then search := x else
  if v < x^.key then search(x^.left)
                else search(x^.right)
  end;
```

Program 5.2 Binary tree search

of this method. This implementation assumes that the key is not in the tree; another alternative is to mix the search and insert functions.

Since each call on `search` in both programs leads to at most one recursive call, it is straightforward to develop equivalent nonrecursive implementations, with no stack required. More details on binary search tree implementations may be found in Knuth [22] or Sedgewick [29] or any elementary textbook on algorithms and data structures.

For example, if the key `30` were to be inserted into the tree on the left in Figure 5.8, a new node would be created as the right child of `26`. The shape of the tree and the number of steps required to build it and search using it are dependent on the order in which the keys are inserted. For example, the tree on the left in Figure 5.8 results if the keys are inserted into an initially empty tree in the order

```
31 26 23 41 59 53 44 58 97 93,
```

and the tree on the right results if the keys are inserted in the order

```
58 41 93 26 53 59 97 23 31 44.
```

The key at the root must appear first; otherwise any ordering where the keys in the left subtree and the keys in the right subtree are intermixed,

```
function insert(v:  integer, x:  link):  link
  begin
  if x = NIL then
    begin
    new(x); x^.left := NIL; x^.r := NIL; x^.key := v;
    end;
  else
    begin
    if v < x^.key
        then x^.left := insert(v, x^.left)
        else x^.right := insert(v, x^.right)
    end;
  return x;
  end;
```

Program 5.3 Binary tree insertion

but appear in the same relative order, will give the same tree. If the keys are inserted in the order

```
23 26 31 41 44 53 58 59 93 97,
```

then a degenerate tree, with no leaves, results. The middle tree in Figure 5.8 is another example of a degenerate tree.

Ignoring equal keys, we may think of constructing a tree from a permutation of the keys in its nodes. In general, many different permutations may map to the same tree. Figure 5.9 shows the mapping between the permutations of four elements and the trees of four nodes. Thus, for example, it is not true that each tree is equally likely to occur if keys are inserted in random order into an initially empty tree. Indeed, it is fortunately the case that the more "balanced" tree structures, for which search and construction costs are low, are more likely to occur than tree structures for which the costs are high. In the analysis, we will quantify this.

Some trees are more expensive to construct than others. In the worst case, a degenerate tree, $i-1$ internal nodes are examined to insert the ith node for each i between 1 and N, so a total of $N(N-1)/2$ nodes

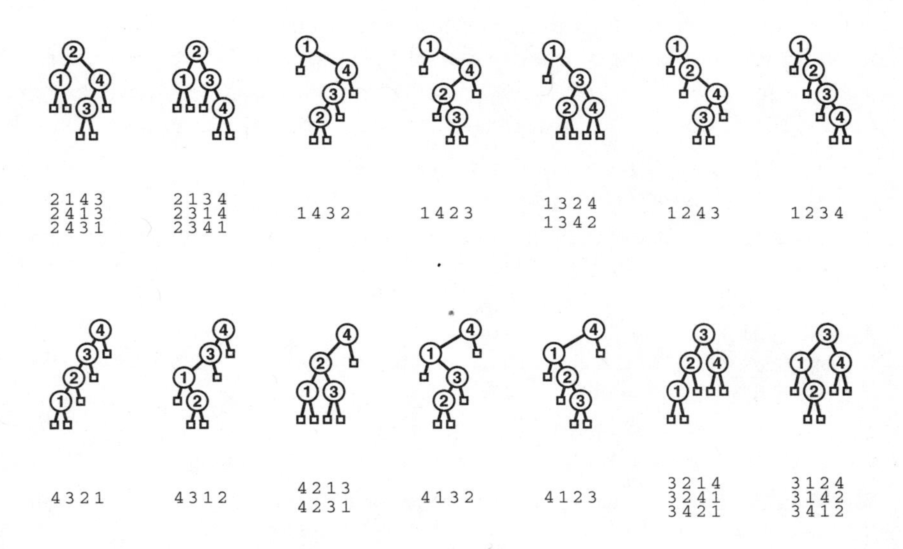

Figure 5.9 Binary search trees with four nodes

are examined in order to construct the tree. In the best case, the middle node will be at the root for every subtree, with about $N/2$ nodes in each subtree, so the standard divide-and-conquer recurrence $T_N = 2T_{N/2} + N$ holds, which implies that a total of about $N \lg N$ steps are required to construct the tree (see §2.6).

The cost of constructing a particular tree is directly proportional to its internal path length, since nodes are not moved once inserted, and the level of a node is exactly the number of nodes required to insert it. Thus, the cost of constructing a tree is the same for each of the insertion sequences that could lead to its construction. We could obtain the average construction cost by adding, for all $N!$ permutations, the internal path length of the resulting tree (the cumulated cost) and then dividing by $N!$. The cumulated cost also could be computed by adding, for all trees, the product of the internal path length and the number of permutations that lead to the tree being constructed. This is the average internal path length that we expect after N random insertions into an initially empty tree, but it is *not* the same as the average internal path length of a random binary tree, under the Catalan model where all trees are equally likely. It requires a separate analysis. We will consider the Catalan tree case in the next section and the binary search tree case in §5.7.

Many other useful operations are easily defined on binary search trees. For example, an inorder traversal gives the keys in sorted order, a useful side benefit in many applications. For a more detailed treatment or further discussion of practical issues, see Knuth [22] or Sedgewick [29].

Exercise 5.16 Give all the key insertion sequences that result in the construction of each of the trees in Figure 5.8.

Exercise 5.17 Show that two different key insertion sequences cannot give the same degenerate tree structure. If all $N!$ key insertion sequences are equally likely, what is the probability that a degenerate tree structure will result?

Exercise 5.18 For $N = 2^n - 1$, what is the probability that a perfectly balanced tree structure (all 2^n external nodes on level n) will be built, if all $N!$ key insertion sequences are equally likely?

Exercise 5.19 Which five-node binary search tree shapes are most likely to occur if five distinct keys are inserted into random order into an initially empty tree?

Exercise 5.20 Show that the preorder traversal of a binary search tree could be the input key sequence that built the tree. That is, traversing a binary search tree in preorder and inserting the keys into an initially empty tree results in the original tree. Is the same true for postorder and/or level order? Prove your answer.

5.6 Average Path Length in Catalan Trees. To begin our analysis of tree parameters, we consider the model where each tree is equally likely to occur. To avoid confusion with other models, we add the modifier *Catalan* to refer to random trees under this assumption, since the probability that a particular tree occurs is the inverse of a Catalan number. As mentioned in §5.4, this model is reasonable for applications such as expression evaluation, and the combinatorial tools developed in Chapter 3 are directly applicable in the analysis.

Binary Catalan trees. What is the *average* (internal) path length of a binary tree with N internal nodes, if each N-node tree is considered to be equally likely? Our analysis of this important question is prototypical of the general approach to analyzing parameters of combinatorial structures that we introduced in Chapter 3:

- Define a bivariate generating function (BGF), with one variable marking the size of the tree and the other marking the internal path length.
- Derive a functional equation satisfied by the BGF, or its associated cumulative generating function (CGF).
- Extract coefficients to derive the result.

We will start with a recurrence-based argument for the second step, though we know from Chapter 3 that a direct generating-function-based argument is often available for such problems. We show both the detailed argument (here) and the simple argument (in the next subsection) to further emphasize this point.

To begin, we observe that the probability that the left subtree has k nodes (and the right subtree has $N-k-1$ nodes) in a random binary Catalan tree with N nodes is T_kT_{N-k-1}/T_N (where $T_N = \binom{2N}{N} \,/\, (N+1)$ is the Nth Catalan number). The denominator is the number of possible N-node trees and the numerator counts the number of ways to make an N-node tree by using any tree with k nodes on the left and any tree with $N-k-1$ nodes on the right. We refer to this probability distribution as the *Catalan distribution*.

Figure 5.10 shows the Catalan distribution as N grows. One of the striking facts about the distribution is that the probability that one of the subtrees is empty tends to a constant as N grows: it is $2T_{N-1}/T_N \sim 1/2$. Indeed, about half the nodes in a "random" binary tree are likely to have an empty subtree, so such trees are not particularly well balanced.

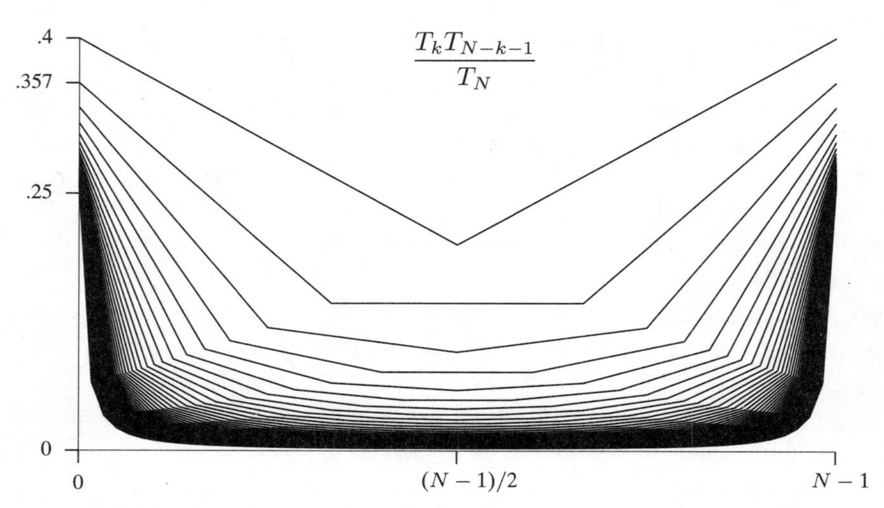

Figure 5.10 Catalan distribution (subtree sizes in random binary trees) (k-axes scaled to N)

Using the Catalan distribution, we can analyze path length using a recurrence very much like the one that we have studied for Quicksort: The average internal path length in a random binary Catalan tree is described by the recurrence

$$Q_N = N - 1 + \sum_{1 \le k \le N} \frac{T_{k-1}T_{N-k}}{T_N}(Q_{k-1} + Q_{N-k}) \qquad \text{for } N > 0$$

with $Q_0 = 0$. The argument underlying this recurrence is general, and can be used to analyze random binary tree structures under other models of randomness, by substituting other distributions for the Catalan distribution. For example, as discussed below, the analysis of binary search trees leads to the uniform distribution (each subtree size occurs with probability $1/N$) and the recurrence becomes like the Quicksort recurrence of Chapter 1.

Theorem 5.3 (*Path length in binary trees*) *The average internal path length in a random binary tree with N internal nodes is*

$$\frac{(N+1)4^N}{\binom{2N}{N}} - 3N - 1 = N\sqrt{\pi N} - 3N + O(\sqrt{N}).$$

Proof. We develop a BGF as in §3.12: First, the probability generating function $Q_N(u) = \sum_{k\geq 0} q_{Nk}u^k$ with q_{Nk} the probability that k is the total internal path length satisfies the recurrence relation

$$Q_N(u) = u^{N-1} \sum_{1\leq k\leq N} \frac{T_{k-1}T_{N-k}}{T_N} Q_{k-1}(u)Q_{N-k}(u) \quad \text{for } N > 0$$

with $Q_0(u) = 1$. To simplify this recurrence, we move to an enumerative approach, where we work with $p_{Nk} = T_N q_{Nk}$ (the number of trees of size N with internal path length k) instead of the probabilities. These satisfy, from the above recurrence,

$$\sum_{k\geq 0} p_{Nk}u^k = u^{N-1} \sum_{1\leq k\leq N} \sum_{r\geq 0} p_{(k-1)r}u^r \sum_{s\geq 0} p_{(N-k)s}u^s \quad \text{for } N > 0.$$

To express this in terms of the bivariate generating function

$$P(u,z) = \sum_{N\geq 0} \sum_{k\geq 0} p_{Nk}u^k z^N,$$

we multiply the above by z^N and sum on N to get

$$\begin{aligned}
P(u,z) &= \sum_{N\geq 1} \sum_{1\leq k\leq N} \sum_{r\geq 0} p_{(k-1)r}u^r \sum_{s\geq 0} p_{(N-k)s}u^s z^N u^{N-1} + 1 \\
&= z\sum_{k\geq 0} \sum_{r\geq 0} p_{kr}u^r (zu)^k \sum_{N\geq k} \sum_{s\geq 0} p_{(N-k)s}u^s (zu)^{N-k} + 1 \\
&= z\sum_{k\geq 0} \sum_{r\geq 0} p_{kr}u^r (zu)^k \sum_{N\geq 0} \sum_{s\geq 0} p_{Ns}u^s (zu)^N + 1 \\
&= zP(u,zu)^2 + 1.
\end{aligned}$$

Below we will also see a simple direct argument for this equation. Now, we can use Theorem 3.11 to get the desired result: setting $u = 1$ gives the familiar functional equation for the generating function for the Catalan numbers, so $P(1,z) = T(z) = (1 - \sqrt{1-4z})/(2z)$. The partial derivative $P_u(1,z)$ is the generating function for the cumulative total if we add the internal path lengths of all binary trees. From Theorem 3.11, the average that we seek is $[z^N]P_u(1,z)/[z^N]P(1,z)$.

Differentiating both sides of the functional equation for the BGF with respect to u (using the chain rule for partial derivatives) gives

$$P_u(u,z) = 2zP(u,zu)(P_u(u,zu) + zP_z(u,zu))$$

Evaluating this at $u = 1$ gives a functional equation for the CGF:

$$P_u(1,z) = 2zT(z)(P_u(1,z) + zT'(z))$$

which yields the solution

$$P_u(1,z) = \frac{2z^2T(z)T'(z)}{1 - 2zT(z)}.$$

Now, $T(z) = (1 - \sqrt{1-4z})/(2z)$, so $1 - 2zT(z) = \sqrt{1-4z}$ and $zT'(z) = -T(z) + 1/\sqrt{1-4z}$. Substituting these gives the explicit expression

$$zP_u(1,z) = \frac{z}{1-4z} - \frac{1-z}{\sqrt{1-4z}} + 1,$$

which expands to give the stated result. ■

This result is illustrated by the large random binary tree in Figure 5.5: asymptotically, a large tree roughly fits into a $\sqrt{N}$-by-$\sqrt{N}$ square.

Direct combinatorial argument for BGF. The proof of Theorem 5.3 involves the bivariate generating function

$$P(u,z) = \sum_{N\ge 0}\sum_{k\ge 0} p_{Nk}u^k z^N$$

where p_{Nk} is the number of trees with N nodes and internal path length k. As we know from Chapter 3, this may be expressed equivalently as

$$P(u,z) = \sum_{t\in\mathcal{T}} u^{\pi(t)} z^{|t|}.$$

Now the recursive definitions in §5.3 lead immediately to

$$P(u,z) = \sum_{t_l\in\mathcal{T}}\sum_{t_r\in\mathcal{T}} u^{\pi(t_l)+\pi(t_r)+|t_l|+|t_r|} z^{|t_l|+|t_r|+1} + 1.$$

The number of nodes is 1 plus the number of nodes in the subtrees, and the internal path length is the sum of the internal path lengths of the subtrees plus 1 for each node in the subtrees. Now, this double sum is easily rearranged to make two independent sums:

$$\begin{aligned}P(u,z) &= z\sum_{t_l\in\mathcal{T}} (zu)^{|t_l|}u^{\pi(t_l)} \sum_{t_r\in\mathcal{T}} (zu)^{|t_r|}u^{\pi(t_r)} + 1\\ &= zP(u,zu)^2 + 1,\end{aligned}$$

as before. The reader may wish to study this example carefully, to appreciate both its simplicity and its subtleties. It is also possible to directly derive equations of this form via the symbolic method (see [13]).

Cumulative generating function. Yet another path to the same result is to derive the functional equation for the CGF directly. We define the CGF

$$C_T(z) \equiv P_u(1,z) = \sum_{t\in\mathcal{T}} \pi(t)z^{|t|}.$$

The average path length is $[z^n]C_T(z)/[z^n]T(z)$. In precisely the same manner as above, the recursive definition of binary trees leads immediately to

$$\begin{aligned} C_T(z) &= \sum_{t_l\in\mathcal{T}}\sum_{t_r\in\mathcal{T}} (\pi(t_l)+\pi(t_r)+|t_l|+|t_r|)z^{|t_l|+|t_r|+1} \\ &= 2zC_T(z)T(z) + 2z^2T(z)T'(z), \end{aligned}$$

which is the same as the functional equation derived for Theorem 5.3.

Exercise 5.21 Derive this directly from the recurrence for path length.

The three derivations just considered are based on the same combinatorial decomposition of binary trees, but the CGF suppresses the most detail and is certainly the preferred method for finding the average. The contrast between the complex recurrence given in the proof to Theorem 5.3 and this "two-line" derivation of the same result given here is typical, and we will see many other problems throughout this book where the amount of detail suppressed using CGFs is considerable.

General Catalan trees. Proceeding in the same manner, BGFs can be used to find the expected path length in a random general tree.

Theorem 5.4 (*Path length in general trees*) *The average internal path length in a random general tree with N internal nodes is*

$$\frac{N}{2}\left(\frac{4^{N-1}}{\binom{2N-2}{N-1}} - 1\right) = \frac{N}{2}(\sqrt{\pi N} - 1) + O(\sqrt{N}).$$

Proof. Proceed as above:

$$\begin{aligned} Q(u,z) &\equiv \sum_{t\in\mathcal{G}} \pi(t)z^{|t|} \\ &= \sum_{k\geq 0}\sum_{t_1\in\mathcal{G}}\cdots\sum_{t_k\in\mathcal{G}} u^{\pi(t_1)+\cdots+\pi(t_k)+|t_1|+\ldots+|t_k|}z^{|t_1|+\ldots+|t_k|+1} \\ &= z\sum_{k\geq 0} Q(u,zu)^k \\ &= \frac{z}{1-Q(u,zu)}. \end{aligned}$$

Setting $u = 1$, we see that $Q(1, z) = G(z) = zT(z) = (1 - \sqrt{1-4z})/2$ is the Catalan generating function, which enumerates general trees, as we found in §5.2. Differentiating the BGF derived above with respect to u and evaluating at $u = 1$ gives the CGF

$$C_G(z) \equiv Q_u(1, z) = \frac{zC_G(z) + z^2G'(z)}{(1 - G(z))^2}.$$

This simplifies to give

$$C_G(z) = \frac{1}{2}\frac{z}{1-4z} - \frac{1}{2}\frac{z}{\sqrt{1-4z}}.$$

As above, we use Theorem 3.11 and compute $[z^N]C_G(z)/[z^N]G(z)$, which immediately leads to the stated result. ∎

Readers not yet convinced of the utility of BGFs and CGFs are invited to go through the exercise of deriving this result from a recurrence.

Exercise 5.22 Justify directly the equation given in the proof of Theorem 5.4 for the CGF for path length in general trees (as we did for binary trees).

Exercise 5.23 Use the rotation correspondence between general trees and binary trees to derive the average path length in random general trees from the corresponding result on random binary trees.

5.7 Path Length in Binary Search Trees. The analysis of path length in binary search trees is actually the study of a property of *permutations*, not trees, since we start with a random permutation. In Chapter 6, we discuss properties of permutations as combinatorial objects in some detail. We consider the analysis of path length in BSTs here not only because it is interesting to compare it with the analysis just given for random trees, but also because we have already done all the work, in Chapters 1 and 3.

Figure 5.9 indicates—and the analysis proves—that the binary search tree insertion algorithm maps more permutations into the more balanced trees with small internal path length than to the less balanced trees with large internal path length. Binary search trees are widely used because they accommodate intermixed searches, insertions, and other operations in a uniform and flexible manner, and they are primarily useful because the search itself is efficient. In the analysis of the costs of any searching algorithm, there are two quantities of interest: the *construction cost* and the *search cost*, and, for the latter, it is normally appropriate to consider separately the cases where the search is successful or unsuccessful. In the case of binary search trees, these cost functions are closely related to path length.

Construction cost. We assume that a binary search tree is built by successive insertions, drawing from a random source of keys (for example, independent and uniformly distributed random numbers between 0 and 1). This implies that all $N!$ key orderings are equally likely, and is thus equivalent to assuming that the keys are a random permutation of the integers 1 to N. Now, observe that the trees are formed by a splitting process: the first key inserted becomes the node at the root, then the left and right subtrees are built independently. The probability that the kth smallest of the N keys is at the root is $1/N$ (independent of k), in which case subtrees of size $k-1$ and $N-k$ are built on the left and right, respectively. The total cost of building the subtrees is one larger for each node (a total of $k-1+N-k=N-1$) than if the subtree were at the root, so we have the recurrence

$$C_N = N - 1 + \frac{1}{N} \sum_{1 \le k \le N} (C_{k-1} + C_{N-k}) \qquad \text{for } N > 0 \text{ with } C_0 = 0.$$

Of course, as mentioned in §5.5, this recurrence also describes the average internal path length for binary search trees. And, this is the recurrence solved in Chapter 1 for the number of comparisons taken by Quicksort, except with $N-1$ instead of $N+1$.

Thus, we actually already have done the analysis of the cost of constructing a binary search tree, in §1.5 and in §3.12.

Theorem 5.5 (*Construction cost of BSTs*) *The average number of comparisons involved in the process of constructing a binary search tree by inserting N distinct keys in random order into an initially empty tree (the average internal path length of a random binary search tree) is*

$$2(N+1)(H_{N+1} - 1) - 2N \approx 1.386N \lg N - 2.846N$$

with variance asymptotic to $(7 - 2\pi^2/3)N^2$.

Proof. From the discussion above, the solution for the average follows directly from the proof and discussion of Theorem 1.2.

The variance follows precisely as in the proof of Theorem 3.12. Define the BGF

$$Q(u,z) = \sum_{p \in \mathcal{P}} \frac{u^{\xi(p)} z^{|p|}}{|p|!}$$

where $\mathcal{P}$ denotes the set of all permutations and $\xi(p)$ denotes the internal path length of the binary search tree constructed when the elements of p are inserted into an initially empty tree using the standard algorithm. By virtually the same computation as in §3.12, this BGF must satisfy the functional equation

$$\frac{\partial}{\partial z} Q(u,z) = Q^2(u, zu) \quad \text{with} \quad Q(u,0) = 1.$$

This differs from the corresponding equation for Quicksort only in that it lacks a u^2 factor (which originates in the difference between $N+1$ and $N-1$ in the recurrences). Computing the variance is done just as in §3.12, with exactly the same result (the u^2 factor does not contribute to the variance). ∎

Thus, a "random" binary search tree costs only about 40% more than a perfectly balanced tree. Figure 5.11 shows a large random binary search tree, which is quite well balanced by comparison with Figure 5.5, a "random" tree under the assumption that all trees are equally likely.

The relationship to the Quicksort recurrence highlights a fundamental reason why trees are important to study in the analysis of algorithms: recursive programs involve implicit tree structures. For example, the tree on the left in Figure 5.8 can also be viewed as a precise description of the process of sorting the keys with Program 1.2: we view the key at the root as the partitioning element; the left subtree as a description of the sorting of the left subfile; and the right subtree as a description of the sorting of

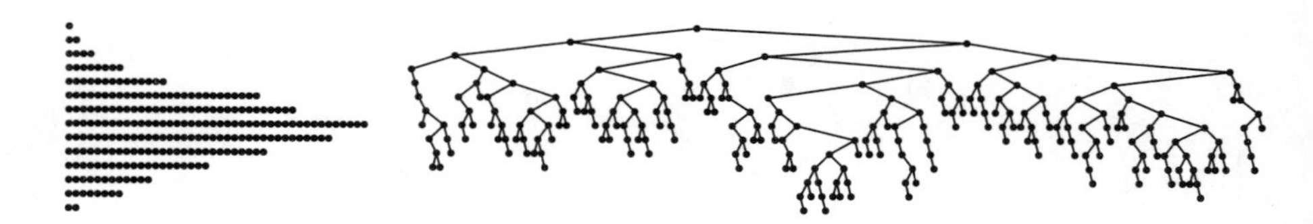

Figure 5.11 A binary search tree built from 256 randomly ordered keys

the right subfile. Binary trees could also be used to describe the operation of Mergesort, and other types of trees are implicit in the operation of other recursive programs.

Exercise 5.24 For each of the trees in Figure 5.8, give permutations that would cause Program 1.2 to partition as described by the tree.

Search costs. A *successful search* is a search where a previously inserted key is found. We assume that each key in the tree is equally likely to be sought. An *unsuccessful search* is a search for a key that has *not* been previously inserted. That is, the key sought is not in the tree, so the search terminates at an external node. We assume that each external node is equally likely to be reached. For example, this is the case for each search in our model, where new keys are drawn from a random source.

We want to analyze the costs of searching in the tree, apart from its construction. This is important in applications because we normally expect a tree to be involved in a very large number of search operations, and the construction costs are insignificant compared to the search costs for many applications. To do the analysis, we adopt the probabilistic model that the tree was built by random insertions and that the searches are "random" in the tree, as described in the previous paragraph. Both costs are directly related to path length.

Theorem 5.6 (*Search costs in BSTs*) *In a random binary search tree of* N *nodes, the average cost of a successful search is* $2H_N - 3 - 2H_N/N$ *and the average cost of an unsuccessful search is* $2H_{N+1} - 2$. *In both cases, the variance is* $2H_N + O(1)$.

Proof. The number of comparisons needed to find a key in the tree is exactly one greater than the number that was needed to insert it, since keys never move in the tree. Thus, the result for successful search is obtained by dividing the cost of constructing the tree (the internal path length, given in Theorem 5.5) by N and adding 1.

Since the level of an external node is precisely the cost of reaching it during an unsuccessful search, the average cost of an unsuccessful search is exactly the external path length divided by $N + 1$, so the stated result follows directly from the first lemma in §5.3 and Theorem 5.5.

The variances require a different kind of calculation, which is discussed below. ■

Analysis with PGFs. The proof of Theorem 5.6 is a convenient application of previously derived results to give average costs; however, it does not give a way to calculate, for example, the standard deviation.

This is true because of differences in the probabilistic models. For internal path length (construction cost), there are $N!$ different possibilities to be accounted for, while for successful search cost, there are $N{\cdot}N!$ possibilities. Internal path length is a quantity that varies between $N \lg N$ and N^2 (roughly), while successful search cost varies between 1 and N. For a particular tree, we get the *average* successful search cost by dividing the internal path length by N, but characterizing the *distribution* of search costs is another matter. For example, the probability that the successful search cost is 1 is $1/N$, which is not at all related to the probability that the internal path length is N, which is 0 for $N > 1$.

Exercise 5.25 What is the probability that the successful search cost is 2?

Exercise 5.26 Construct a random 1000-node binary search tree by inserting 1000 random keys into an initially empty tree, then do 10,000 random searches in that tree and plot a histogram of the search costs, for comparison with Figure 1.4.

Exercise 5.27 Do the previous exercise, but generate a new tree for each trial.

Probability generating functions (PGFs, see §3.11) provide an alternate derivation for search costs and also can allow calculation of moments. For example, the PGF for the cost of an unsuccessful search satisfies

$$p_N(u) = \Big(\frac{N-1}{N+1} + \frac{2u}{N+1}\Big)p_{N-1}(u),$$

since the Nth insertion contributes 1 to the cost of an unsuccessful search if the search terminates at one of its two external nodes, which happens with probability $2/(N+1)$; or 0 otherwise. Differentiating and evaluating at 1 gives a simple recurrence for the average that telescopes directly to the result of Theorem 5.6, and the variance follows in a similar manner. These calculations are summarized in the exercises that follow.

Exercise 5.28 [Lynch, cf. Knuth] By calculating $p_N''(1) + p_N'(1) - p'(1)^2$. show that the variance of unsuccessful search cost is $2H_{N+1} - 4H_{N+1}^{(2)} + 2$.

Exercise 5.29 [Knott, cf. Knuth] Using a direct argument with PGFs, find the average and variance for the cost of a *successful* search.

Exercise 5.30 Express the PGF for successful search in terms of the PGF for unsuccessful search. Use this to express the average and variance for successful search in terms of the average and variance for unsuccessful search.

5.8 Additive Parameters of Random Trees. The CGF-based method that we used above to analyze path length in Catalan trees and binary search trees generalizes to cover a large class of parameters that are defined additively over subtrees. Specifically, define an *additive parameter* to be any parameter whose cost function satisfies the linear recursive schema

$$c(t) = e(t) + \sum_{s} c(s)$$

where the sum is over all the subtrees of the root of t. The function e is called the "toll," the portion of the cost associated with the root. The following table gives examples of cost functions and associated tolls:

toll function $e(t)$	*cost function* $c(t)$
1	size $\vert t \vert$
$\vert t \vert - 1$	internal path length
$\delta_{\vert t \vert 1}$	number of leaves

We normally take the toll function to be 0 for the empty binary tree.

It is possible to develop a fully general treatment of the average-case analysis of any additive parameter for both of the Catalan tree models and for the BST model. Indeed, this encompasses all the theorems about properties of trees that we have seen to this point.

Theorem 5.7 (*Additive parameters in random trees*) *Let $C_T(z)$, $C_G(z)$, and $C_B(z)$ be the CGFs of an additive tree parameter $c(t)$ for the binary Catalan, general Catalan, and binary search tree models, respectively, and let $E_T(z)$, $E_G(z)$, and $E_B(z)$ be the CGFs for the associated toll function $e(t)$. (For the binary search tree case, use exponential CGFs.) These functions are related by the equations*

$$C_T(z) = \frac{E_T(z)}{\sqrt{1-4z}} \quad \textit{(binary Catalan trees)}$$

$$C_G(z) = \frac{1}{2}E_G(z)\Bigl(1 + \frac{1}{\sqrt{1-4z}}\Bigr) \quad \textit{(general Catalan trees)}$$

$$C_B(z) = \frac{1}{(1-z)^2}\Bigl(E_B(0) + \int_0^z (1-x)^2 E_B'(x)dx\Bigr) \quad \textit{(binary search trees).}$$

Proof. The proofs follow precisely the same lines as the arguments that we have given for path length.

First, let $\mathcal{T}$ be the set of all binary Catalan trees. Then, just as in §5.6, we have

$$\begin{aligned} C_T(z) &\equiv \sum_{t\in\mathcal{T}} c(t)z^{|t|} \\ &= \sum_{t\in\mathcal{T}} e(t)z^{|t|} + \sum_{t_l\in\mathcal{T}}\sum_{t_r\in\mathcal{T}} (c(t_l)+c(t_r))z^{|t_l|+|t_r|+1} \\ &= E_T(z) + 2zT(z)C_T(z), \end{aligned}$$

where $T(z) = (1-\sqrt{1-4z})/(2z)$ is the OGF for the Catalan numbers T_N. This leads directly to the stated result.

Next, for general Catalan trees, let $\mathcal{G}$ be the set of trees. Again, just as in §5.6, we have

$$\begin{aligned} C_G(z) &\equiv \sum_{t\in\mathcal{G}} c(t)z^{|t|} \\ &= \sum_{t\in\mathcal{G}} e(t)z^{|t|} + \sum_{k\ge 0}\sum_{t_1\in\mathcal{G}}\cdots\sum_{t_k\in\mathcal{G}} (c(t_1)+\cdots+c(t_k))z^{|t_1|+\ldots+|t_k|+1} \\ &= E_G(z) + z\sum_{k\ge 0} kC_G(z)G^{k-1}(z) \\ &= E_G(z) + \frac{zC_G(z)}{(1-G(z))^2} \end{aligned}$$

where $G(z) = zT(z) = (1-\sqrt{1-4z})/2$ OGF for the Catalan numbers T_{N-1}, enumerating general trees. Again, substituting this and simplifying leads directly to the stated result.

For binary search trees, we let c_N and e_N denote the expected values of $c(t)$ and $e(t)$ over random BSTs of size N, respectively. Then the exponential CGFs $C(z)$ and $E(z)$ are the same as the OGFs for these sequences, and we follow the derivation in §3.3. We have the recurrence

$$c_N = e_N + \frac{2}{N}\sum_{1\le k\le N} c_{k-1} \qquad \text{for } N\ge 1 \text{ with } c_0 = e_0$$

which leads to the differential equation

$$C_B'(z) = E_B'(z) + 2\frac{C_B(z)}{1-z} \qquad \text{with } C_B(0) = E_B(0)$$

which can be solved precisely as in §3.3 to yield the stated solution. ■

Corollary *The mean alues of the additi e parameters are gi en by*

$$[z^N]C_T(z)/T_N \qquad \textit{(binary Catalan trees)}$$
$$[z^N]C_G(z)/T_{N-1} \qquad \textit{(general Catalan trees)}$$
$$[z^N]C_B(z) \qquad \textit{(binary search trees)}.$$

Proof. These follow directly from the definitions and Theorem 3.11. ■

This vastly generalizes the counting and path length analyses that we have done and permits us to analyze many important parameters. The counting and path length results that we have derived in the theorems earlier in this chapter all follow from a simple application of this theorem. For example, to compute average path length in binary Catalan trees, we have

$$E_T(z) = 1 + \sum_{t \in \mathcal{T}} (|t| - 1)z^{|t|} = 1 + zT'(z) - T(z)$$

and therefore

$$C_T(z) = \frac{zT'(z) - T(z) + 1}{\sqrt{1 - 4z}}.$$

which is equivalent to the expression derived in the proof of Theorem 5.3.

Leaves. As an example of the use of Theorem 5.7 for a new problem, we consider the analysis of the average number of leaves for each of the three models. This is representative of an important class of problems related to memory allocation for recursive structures. For example, in a binary tree, if space is at a premium, we need not keep pointers in leaves: instead, we can be mark them as leaves (with one bit, no pointers), using so-called variant records. How much space is saved in this way? The answer to this question depends on the tree model: determining the average number of leaves is a straightforward application of Theorem 5.7, using $e(t) = \delta_{|t|1}$ and therefore $E_T(z) = E_G(z) = E_B(z) = z$.

First, for binary Catalan trees, we have $C_T(z) = z/\sqrt{1 - 4z}$. This matches the result derived in §3.12.

Second, for general Catalan trees, we have

$$C_G(z) = \frac{z}{2} + \frac{z}{2\sqrt{1 - 4z}},$$

which leads to the result that the average is $N/2$ exactly for $N > 1$.

Third, for binary search trees, we get

$$C_B(z) = \frac{1}{3}\frac{1}{(1-z)^2} + \frac{1}{3}(z-1),$$

so the mean number of leaves is $(N+1)/3$ for $N > 1$.

Corollary *For $N > 1$, the average number of leaves is given by*

$$\frac{N(N+1)}{2(2N-1)} \sim \frac{N}{4} \quad \textit{in a random binary Catalan tree with } N \textit{ nodes}$$

$$\frac{N}{2} \quad \textit{in a random general Catalan tree with } N \textit{ nodes}$$

$$\frac{N+1}{3} \quad \textit{in a binary search tree built from } N \textit{ random keys.}$$

Proof. See the discussion above. ∎

These techniques are obviously quite useful in analyzing algorithms involving trees, and they apply in some other situations, as well. For example, in Chapter 6, we also use these techniques to analyze properties of permutations, via a correspondence with trees (see §6.5).

Exercise 5.31 Find the average number of children of the root in a random Catalan tree of N nodes. (From Figure 5.3, the answer is 2 for $N = 5$.)

Exercise 5.32 In a random Catalan tree of N nodes, find the proportion of nodes with one child.

Exercise 5.33 In a random Catalan tree of N nodes, find the proportion of nodes with k children for $k = 2, 3$, and higher.

Exercise 5.34 Internal nodes in binary trees fall into one of three classes: they have either two, one, or zero external children. What fraction of the nodes are of each type, in a random binary Catalan tree of N nodes?

Exercise 5.35 Answer the previous question for random binary search trees.

Exercise 5.36 Set up BGFs for the number of leaves and estimate the variance for each of the three random tree models.

Exercise 5.37 Prove relationships analogous to those in Theorem 5.7 for BGFs.

5.9 Height. What is the average height of a tree? Path length analysis (using the second lemma in §5.3) suggests lower and upper bounds of order $N^{1/2}$ and $N^{3/4}$ for Catalan trees (either binary or general) and of order $\log N$ and $\sqrt{N \log N}$ for binary search trees. Developing more precise estimates for the average height turns out to be a more difficult question to answer, even though the recursive definition of height is as simple as the recursive definition of path length. The height of a tree is 1 plus the maximum of the heights of the subtrees, and the path length of a tree is 1 plus the sum of the path lengths of the subtrees plus the number of nodes in the subtrees. As we have seen, the latter decomposition can correspond to "constructing" trees from subtrees, and additivity is mirrored in the analysis (by the linearity of the cost GF equations). No such treatment applies to the operation of taking the maximum over subtrees.

Generating functions for binary Catalan trees. We begin with the problem of finding the height of a binary Catalan tree. Attempting to proceed as for path length, we start with the bivariate generating function

$$P(u, z) = \sum_{N \geq 0} \sum_{h \geq 0} P_{Nh} u^h z^N = \sum_{t \in \mathcal{T}} u^{\eta(t)} z^{|t|}.$$

Now the recursive definition of height leads to

$$P(u, z) = \sum_{t_l \in \mathcal{T}} \sum_{t_r \in \mathcal{T}} u^{\max(\eta(t_l), \eta(t_r))} z^{|t_l| + |t_r| + 1}.$$

For path length, we were able to rearrange this into independent sums, but the "max" precludes this.

On the other hand, using the "vertical" formulation for bivariate sequences that is described in §3.12, we can derive a simple functional equation. Let $\mathcal{T}_h$ be the class of binary Catalan trees of height no greater than h, and

$$T^{[h]}(z) = \sum_{t \in \mathcal{T}_h} z^{|t|}.$$

Proceeding in precisely the same manner as for enumeration gives a simple functional equation for $T^{[h]}(z)$: any tree with height no greater than $h+1$ is either empty or a root node and two subtrees with height no greater than h, so

$$\begin{aligned} T^{[h+1]}(z) &= 1 + \sum_{t_L \in \mathcal{T}_h} \sum_{t_R \in \mathcal{T}_h} z^{|t_L| + |t_R| + 1} \\ &= 1 + z T^{[h]}(z)^2. \end{aligned}$$

This result is also available via the symbolic method: it corresponds to the symbolic equation

$$\mathcal{T}_{h+1} = \{\Box\} + \{\bullet\} \times \mathcal{T}_h \times \mathcal{T}_h.$$

Iterating this recurrence, we have

$$\begin{aligned}
T^{[0]}(z) &= 1\\
T^{[1]}(z) &= 1 + z\\
T^{[2]}(z) &= 1 + z + 2z^2 + z^3\\
T^{[3]}(z) &= 1 + z + 2z^2 + 5z^3 + 6z^4 + 6z^5 + 4z^6 + z^7\\
&\vdots\\
T^{[\infty]}(z) &= 1 + z + 2z^2 + 5z^3 + 14z^4 + 42z^5 + 132z^6 + \ldots = T(z).
\end{aligned}$$

The reader may find it instructive to check these against the initial values for the small trees given in Figure 3.1. Now, the corollary to Theorem 3.11 tells us that the cumulated cost (the sum of the heights of all trees of N nodes) is given by

$$[z^N]\sum_{h\geq 0}(T(z) - T^{[h]}(z)).$$

But now our analytic task is much harder. Rather than estimating coefficients in an expansion on one function for which we have a defining functional equation, we need to estimate coefficients in an entire series of expansions of functions defined by interrelated functional equations. This turns out to be an extremely challenging task for this particular problem.

Theorem 5.8 (*Binary tree height*) *The average height of a random binary Catalan tree with N nodes is $2\sqrt{\pi N} + O(N^{1/4+\epsilon})$ for any $\epsilon > 0$.*

Proof. Omitted, though see the comments above. Details may be found in Flajolet and Odlyzko [10]. ■

Average height of Catalan trees. For general Catalan trees, the problem of determining the average height is still considerably more difficult than analyzing path length, but we can sketch the solution. (*Warning*: This "sketch" involves a combination of many of the advanced techniques from Chapters 2 through 4, and should be approached with caution by novice readers.)

First, we construct $\mathcal{G}_{h+1}$, the set of trees of height $\le h+1$, by

$$\mathcal{G}_{h+1} = \{\bullet\} \times (\epsilon + \mathcal{G}_h + (\mathcal{G}_h \times \mathcal{G}_h) + (\mathcal{G}_h \times \mathcal{G}_h \times \mathcal{G}_h) + (\mathcal{G}_h \times \mathcal{G}_h \times \mathcal{G}_h \times \mathcal{G}_h) + \ldots)$$

which translates by the symbolic method to

$$G^{[h+1]}(z) = z(1 + G^{[h]}(z) + G^{[h]}(z)^2 + G^{[h]}(z)^3 + G^{[h]}(z)^4 + \ldots) = \frac{z}{1 - G^{[h]}(z)}.$$

Iterating this recurrence, we see that

$$\begin{aligned}
G^{[0]}(z) &= z \\
G^{[1]}(z) &= z\frac{1}{1-z} \\
G^{[2]}(z) &= \frac{z}{1 - \dfrac{z}{1-z}} = z\frac{1-z}{1-2z} \\
G^{[3]}(z) &= \frac{z}{1 - \dfrac{z}{1 - \dfrac{z}{1-z}}} = z\frac{1-2z}{1-3z+z^2} \\
&\vdots \\
G^{[\infty]}(z) &= z + z^2 + 2z^3 + 5z^3 + 14z^5 + 42z^6 + 132z^7 + \ldots = zT(z)
\end{aligned}$$

These are rational functions with enough algebraic structure that we can derive exact enumerations for the height and obtain asymptotic estimates.

Theorem 5.9 (*Catalan tree height GF*) *The number of Catalan trees with $N+1$ nodes and height greater than or equal to $h-1$ is*

$$G_{N+1} - G_{N+1}^{[h-2]} = \sum_{k\ge1}\left(\binom{2N}{N+1-kh} - 2\binom{2N}{N-kh} + \binom{2N}{N-1-kh}\right).$$

Proof. From the basic recurrence and initial values given above, it is not hard to verify that $G^{[h]}(z)$ can be expressed in the form $G^{[h]}(z) =$

$zF_{h+1}(z)/F_{h+2}(z)$ where $F_h(z)$ is a family of polynomials

$$\begin{aligned}F_0(z) &= 0\\ F_1(z) &= 1\\ F_2(z) &= 1\\ F_3(z) &= 1 - z\\ F_4(z) &= 1 - 2z\\ F_5(z) &= 1 - 3z + z^2\\ F_6(z) &= 1 - 4z + 3z^2\\ F_7(z) &= 1 - 5z + 6z^2 - z^3\\ &\vdots\end{aligned}$$

that satisfy the recurrence

$$F_{h+2}(z) = F_{h+1}(z) - zF_h(z) \qquad \text{for } h \geq 0 \text{ with } F_0(z) = 0 \text{ and } F_1(z) = 1.$$

These functions are sometimes called *Fibonacci polynomials*, because they generalize the Fibonacci numbers, to which they reduce when $z = -1$.

When z is kept fixed, the Fibonacci polynomial recurrence is simply a linear recurrence with constant coefficients (see §2.4). Thus its solutions are expressible in terms of the solutions

$$\beta = \frac{1+\sqrt{1-4z}}{2} \quad \text{and} \quad \widehat{\beta} = \frac{1-\sqrt{1-4z}}{2}$$

of the characteristic equation $y^2 - y + z = 0$. Solving precisely as we did for the Fibonacci numbers in §2.4, we find that

$$F_h(z) = \frac{\beta^h - \widehat{\beta}^h}{\beta - \widehat{\beta}} \quad \text{and therefore} \quad G^{[h]}(z) = z\frac{\beta^{h+1} - \widehat{\beta}^{h+1}}{\beta^{h+2} - \widehat{\beta}^{h+2}}.$$

Notice that the roots are closely related to the Catalan GF:

$$\widehat{\beta} = G(z) = zT(z) \quad \text{and} \quad \beta = z/\widehat{\beta} = z/G(z) = 1/T(z).$$

Also, we have the identities

$$z = \beta(1-\beta) = \widehat{\beta}(1-\widehat{\beta}).$$

In summary, the GF for trees of bounded height satisfies the nice formula

$$G^{[h]}(z) = 2z\frac{(1+\sqrt{1-4z})^{h+1} - (1-\sqrt{1-4z})^{h+1}}{(1+\sqrt{1-4z})^{h+2} - (1-\sqrt{1-4z})^{h+2}},$$

and a little algebra shows that

$$G(z) - G^{[h]}(z) = \sqrt{1-4z}\frac{u^{h+2}}{1-u^{h+2}}$$

where $u \equiv \widehat{\beta}/\beta = G^2(z)/z$. This is a function of $G(z)$, which is implicitly defined by $z = G(z)(1-G(z))$, so the Lagrange inversion theorem (Theorem 3.9 in §3.10) applies, leading (after some calculation) to the stated result for $[z^{N+1}](G(z) - G^{[h-2]}(z))$. ■

Corollary *The average height of a random Catalan tree with N nodes is* $\sqrt{\pi N} + O(1)$.

Proof Sketch. By the corollary to Theorem 3.11, the average height is given by

$$\sum_{h\ge 1}\frac{[z^N](G(z) - G^{[h-1]}(z))}{G_N}.$$

For Theorem 5.9, this reduces to three sums that are very much like Catalan sums, and can be treated in a manner similar to the proof of Theorem 4.9. From asymptotic results on the tails of the binomial coefficients (the corollary to Theorem 4.6), the terms are exponentially small for large h. We have

$$[z^N](G(z) - G^{[h-1]}(z)) = O\big(N4^N e^{-(\log^2 N)}\big),$$

for $h > \sqrt{N}\log N$ by applying tail bounds to each term in the binomial sum in Theorem 5.9. This already shows that the expected height is itself $O\big(N^{1/2}\log N\big)$.

For smaller values of h, the normal approximation of Theorem 4.6 applies nicely. Using the approximation termwise as we did in the proof of Theorem 4.9, it is possible to show that

$$\frac{[z^N](G(z) - G^{[h-1]}(z))}{G_N} \sim H(h/\sqrt{N})$$

where

$$H(x) \equiv \sum_{k\geq 1}(4k^2x^2 - 2)e^{-k^2x^2}.$$

Like the trie sum diagrammed in Figure 4.7, the function $H(h/\sqrt{N})$ is close to 1 when h is small and close to 0 when h is large, with a transition from 1 to 0 when h is close to $\sqrt{N}$. Then, the expected height is approximately

$$\sum_{h\geq 1} H(h/\sqrt{N}) \sim \sqrt{N}\int_0^{\infty} H(x)dx \sim \sqrt{\pi N}$$

by Euler-Maclaurin summation and by explicit evaluation of the integral.

In the last few steps, we have ignored the error terms, which must be kept suitably uniform. As usual for such problems, this is not difficult because the tails are exponentially small, but we leave the details for the exercises below. Full details for a related but different approach to proving this result are given in De Bruijn, Knuth, and Rice [7]. ■

This analysis is the hardest nut that we are cracking in this book. It combines techniques for solving linear recurrences and continued fractions (Chapter 2), generating function expansions, especially by the Lagrange inversion theorem (Chapter 3), and binomial approximations and Euler-Maclaurin summations (Chapter 4). While we recognize that many readers may not be expected to follow a proof of this scope and complexity without very careful study, we have sketched the derivation in some detail because height analysis is extremely important to understanding basic properties of trees. Still, this sketch allows us to appreciate (*i*) that analyzing tree height is not an easy task, but (*ii*) that it is *possible* to do so, using the basic techniques that we have covered in Chapters 2 through 4.

Exercise 5.38 Prove that $F_{h+1}(z) = \sum_j \binom{h-j}{j}(-z)^j$.

Exercise 5.39 Show the details of the expansion of $G(z) - G^{[h-2]}(z)$ with the Lagrange inversion theorem.

Exercise 5.40 Provide a detailed proof of the corollary, including proper attention to the error terms.

Exercise 5.41 Draw a plot of the function $H(x)$.

Height of binary search trees. For binary search trees built from random permutations, the problem of finding the average height is also quite difficult. Since the average path length is $O(N \log N)$, we would expect the average height of a binary search tree to be $\sim c \log N$, for some constant c; this is in fact the case.

Theorem 5.10 (*Binary search tree height*) *The expected height of a binary search tree built from N random keys is $\sim c \log N$, where $c \approx 4.31107...$ is the solution $c > 2$ of $c \ln(2e/c) = 1$.*

Proof. Omitted; see Devroye [8] or Mahmoud [24]. ∎

Though the complete analysis is at least as daunting as the Catalan tree height analysis given above, it is easy to derive functional relationships among the generating functions. Let $q_N^{[h]}$ be the probability that a BST built with N random keys has height no greater than h. Then, using the usual splitting argument, and noting that the subtrees have height no greater than $h-1$, we have the recurrence

$$q_N^{[h]} = \frac{1}{N} \sum_{1 \le k \le N} q_{k-1}^{[h-1]} q_{N-1-k}^{[h-1]},$$

which leads immediately to the schema

$$\frac{d}{dz} q^{[h]}(z) = (q^{[h-1]}(z))^2.$$

Stack height. Tree height appears frequently in the analysis of algorithms. Fundamentally, it measures not only the size of the stack needed to traverse a tree, but also the space used when a recursive program is executed. For example, in the expression evaluation algorithm discussed above, the tree height $\eta(t)$ measures the maximum depth reached by the recursive stack when the expression represented by t is evaluated. Similarly, the height of a binary search tree measures the maximum stack depth reached by a recursive inorder traversal to sort the keys, or the implicit stack depth used when a recursive Quicksort implementation is used.

Tree traversal and other recursive algorithms also can be implemented without using recursion by directly maintaining a pushdown stack (last-in-first-out data structure). When there is more than one subtree to visit, we save all but one on the stack; when there are no subtrees to visit, we pop the stack to get a tree to visit. This uses fewer stack entries than are required in a stack supporting a recursive implementation, because nothing is put on the stack if there is only one subtree to visit.

(A technique called *end recursion removal* is sometimes used to get equivalent performance for recursive implementations.) The maximum stack size needed when a tree is traversed using this method is a tree parameter called the *stack height*, which is similar to height. It can be defined by the recursive formula:

$$s(t) = \begin{cases} 0, & \text{if } t \text{ is an external node;} \\ s(t_l), & \text{if } t_r \text{ is an external node;} \\ s(t_r), & \text{if } t_l \text{ is an external node;} \\ 1 + \max(s(t_l), s(t_r)) & \text{otherwise.} \end{cases}$$

Because of the rotation correspondence, it turns out that the stack height of binary Catalan trees is essentially distributed like the height of general Catalan trees. Thus, the average stack height for binary Catalan trees is also studied by De Bruijn, Knuth, and Rice [7], and shown to be $\sim \sqrt{\pi N}$.

Exercise 5.42 Find a relationship between the stack height of a binary tree and the height of the corresponding forest.

Register allocation. When the tree represents an arithmetic expression, the minimum number of registers needed to evaluate the expression can be described by the recursive formula:

$$r(t) = \begin{cases} 0, & \text{if } t \text{ is an external node;} \\ r(t_l), & \text{if } t_r \text{ is an external node;} \\ r(t_r), & \text{if } t_l \text{ is an external node;} \\ 1 + r(t_l), & \text{if } r(t_l) = r(t_r); \\ \max(r(t_l), r(t_r)) & \text{otherwise.} \end{cases}$$

The average value of this quantity was studied by Flajolet, Raoult, and Vuillemin [12] and by Kemp [20]. Though this recurrence seems quite similar to the corresponding recurrences for height and stack height, the solution is *not* $O(\sqrt{N})$ in this case, but rather $\sim (\lg N)/2$.

5.10 Summary of Average-Case Results on Properties of Trees. We have discussed three different tree structures (binary trees, trees, and binary search trees) and two basic parameters (path length and height), giving a total of six theorems describing the average values of these parameters in these structures. Each of these results is fundamental, and it is worthwhile to consider them in concert with one another. As indicated in §5.8, the basic analytic methodology for these parameters extends to cover a wide variety of properties of trees, and we can place new problems in proper context by examining relationships among these parameters and tree models. At the same time, we briefly sketch the history of these results, which are summarized in Tables 5.1 and 5.2. For brevity in this section, we refer to binary Catalan trees simply as "binary trees," Catalan trees as "trees," and binary search trees as "BSTs," recognizing that a prime objective in the long series of analyses that we have discussed has been to justify these distinctions in terminology and quantify differences in the associated models of randomness.

Figures 5.6, 5.5, and 5.11 show a random forest (random tree not including the root), binary tree, and binary search tree, respectively. These reinforce the analytic information given in Tables 5.1 and 5.2: height for binary trees and trees are similar (and proportional to $\sqrt{N}$), with trees about half as high as binary trees; and paths in binary search trees are much shorter (proportional to $\log N$). The probability distribution imposed on binary search tree structures is biased toward trees with short paths.

Perhaps the easiest problem on the list is the analysis of path length in binary search trees. This is easily available with elementary methods, and dates at least back to the invention of Quicksort in 1960 [19]. The variance for tree construction costs (the same as the variance for Quicksort) was evidently first published by Knuth [22]; Knuth indicates that recurrence relations describing the variance and results about search costs were known in the 1960s. By contrast, the analysis of the average height of binary search trees is a quite challenging problem, and was the last problem on the list to be completed, by Devroye in 1986 [8][9].

	functional equation on GF	*asymptotic estimate of* $[z^N]$
tree	$Q(u,z) = \dfrac{z}{1 - Q(z, zu)}$	$\dfrac{N}{2}\sqrt{\pi N} - \dfrac{N}{2} + O(\sqrt{N})$
binary tree	$Q(u,z) = zQ(u,zu)^2 + 1$	$N\sqrt{\pi N} - 3N + O(\sqrt{N})$
BST	$\dfrac{\partial}{\partial z}Q(u,z) = Q(z,zu)^2$	$2N \ln N + (2\gamma - 4)N + O(\log N)$

Table 5.1 Expected path length of trees

Path length in random trees and random binary trees is also not difficult to analyze, though it is best approached with generating-function based or symbolic combinatorial tools. With such an approach, analysis of this parameter (and other additive parameters) is not much more difficult than counting.

The central role of tree height in the analysis of computer programs based on trees and recursive programs was clear as such programs came into widespread use, but it was equally clear that the analysis of nonadditive parameters in trees such as height can present significant technical challenges. The analysis of the height of trees (and stack height for binary trees)—published in 1972 by De Bruijn, Knuth, and Rice [7]—showed that such challenges could be overcome, with known analytic techniques, as we have sketched in §5.9. Still, developing new results along these lines can be a daunting task, even for experts. For example, the analysis of height of binary trees was not completed until 1982, by Flajolet and Odlyzko [10].

The analyses of path length and height in random trees are worthy of careful study because they illustrate the power of generating functions, and the contrasting styles in analysis that are appropriate for "additive" and "nonadditive" parameters in recursive structures. As we will see in the next section, trees relate directly to a number of classical problems in probability and combinatorics, so some of the problems that we consider have a distinguished heritage, tracing back a century or two. But the motivation for developing precise asymptotic results for path length and height as we have been doing certainly can be attributed to the importance of trees in the analysis of algorithms (see Knuth [7][21][22]).

	functional equation on GF	*asymptotic estimate of mean*
tree	$q^{[h+1]}(z) = \dfrac{z}{1 - q^{[h]}(z)}$	$\sqrt{\pi N} + O(1)$
binary tree	$q^{[h+1]}(z) = z(q^{[h]}(z))^2 + 1$	$2\sqrt{\pi N} + O(N^{1/4+\epsilon})$
BST	$\dfrac{d}{dz}q^{[h+1]}(z) = (q^{[h]}(z))^2$	$(4.3110\cdots)\ln N + o(\log N)$

Table 5.2 Expected height of trees

5.11 Representations of Trees and Binary Trees. Trees and binary trees may be viewed as two specific ways to represent the same combinatorial objects (which are enumerated by the Catalan numbers), because of the rotation correspondence. A number of other ways to represent them arise (for example, see Read [28]), some of which are summarized here.

Parenthesis systems. Each forest with N nodes corresponds to a set of N pairs of parentheses: from the definition, there is a sequence of trees, each consisting of a root and a sequence of subtrees with the same structure. If we consider that each tree should be enclosed in parentheses, then we are led immediately to a representation that uses only parentheses: for each tree in the forest, write a left parenthesis, followed by the parenthesis system for the forest comprising the subtrees (determined recursively), followed by a right parenthesis. For example, the forest at the left in Figure 5.4 can be represented by

```
( ( ( ) ) ( ) ( ) ) ( ) ( ( ) ( ) ) ( ( ) ) .
```

The relationship between this and the tree structure is easily seen by writing parentheses at the levels corresponding to the root nodes of the tree they enclose, as follows:

```
(                 ) ( ) (         ) (     )
  (     ) ( ) ( )         ( ) ( )     ( )
    ( )
```

Collapsing this structure gives the parenthesis system representation.

Cast in terms of tree traversal methods, we can find the parenthesis system corresponding to a tree by recursively traversing the tree, writing "`(`" when going "down" an edge and "`)`" when going "up" an edge. Equivalently, we may regard "`(`" as corresponding to "start a recursive call" and "`)`" as corresponding to "finish a recursive call."

In this representation, we are describing only the shape of the tree, not any information that might be contained in the nodes—next we consider representations that are appropriate if nodes may have an associated key or other additional information.

Space-efficient representations of tree shapes. The parenthesis system encodes a tree of size N with a sequence of $2N+O(1)$ bits. This is appreciably lower than standard representations of trees with pointers. Actually, it comes close to the information-theoretic optimum encoding length, the logarithm of the Catalan numbers:

$$\lg T_N = 2N - O(\log N).$$

Such representations of tree shapes are useful in applications where very large trees must be stored (e. g., index structures in databases) or transmitted (e. g., representations of Huffman trees; see Sedgewick [29]).

Preorder and postorder representations of trees. It is straightforward to extend the parenthesis system to include information at the nodes. As with tree traversal, the information at the root can be listed either before the subtrees (preorder) or after the subtrees (postorder). Thus the preorder representation of the forest on the left in Figure 5.4 is

```
( 5 ( 2 (1) ) (3) (4) ) (6) ( 9 (7) (8) ) ( 11 (10) )
```

and the postorder representation is

```
( ( (1) 2 ) (3) (4) 5 ) (6) ( (7) (8) 9 ) ( (10) 11 ).
```

When we discuss refinements below, we do so in terms of preorder, though of course the representations are essentially equivalent, and the refinements apply to postorder as well.

Preorder degree representation. Another way to represent the shape of the forest in Figure 5.4 is the string of integers

```
3 1 0 0 0 0 2 0 0 1 0.
```

This is simply a listing of the numbers of children of the nodes, in preorder. To see why it is a unique representation, it is simpler to consider the same sequence, but subtracting 1 from each term:

```
2 0 -1 -1 -1 -1 1 -1 -1 0 -1.
```

Moving from left to right, this can be divided into subsequences that have the property that (*i*) the sum is of the numbers in the subsequence is -1, and (*ii*) the sum of any prefix of the numbers in the subsequence is greater than or equal to -1. Delimiting the subsequences by parentheses, we have

```
( 2 0 -1 -1 -1 ) ( -1 ) ( 1 -1 -1 ) ( 0 -1 ).
```

This gives a correspondence to parenthesis systems: each of these subsequences corresponds to a tree in the forest. Deleting the first number in each sequence and recursively decomposing gives the parenthesis system. Now, each parenthesized sequence of numbers not only sums to -1 but also has the property that the sum of any prefix is nonnegative. It is straightforward to prove by induction that conditions (*i*) and (*ii*) are necessary and sufficient to establish a direct correspondence between sequences of integers and trees.

Binary tree traversal representations. Binary tree representations are simpler because of the marked distinction between external (degree 0) and internal (degree 2) nodes. Consider the expression tree of Figure 5.7. The familiar representation is to list the subtrees, parenthesized, with the key associated with the root in between:

```
((x + y) * z) - (w + ((a - (v + y)) / ((z + y) * x)))).
```

This is called *inorder* or *infix* when referring specifically to arithmetic expressions. It corresponds to an inorder tree traversal where we write "`(`," then traverse the left subtree, then write the key at the root, then traverse the right subtree, then write "`)`."

Representations corresponding to preorder and postorder traversals can be defined in an analogous manner. But for preorder and postorder, parentheses are not needed: external (operands) and internal (operators) nodes are identified; thus the preorder node degree sequence is implicit in the representation, which determines the tree structure, in the same manner as discussed above. Thus, the preorder, or *prefix*, listing of the above sequence is

```
- * + x y z + w / - a + v y * + z y x,
```

and the postorder, or *postfix*, listing is

```
x y + z * w a v y + - z y + x * / + -.
```

Exercise 5.43 Given an (ordered) tree, consider its representation as a binary tree using the rotation correspondence. Discuss the relationship between the preorder and postorder representations of the ordered tree and the preorder, inorder, and postorder representations of the corresponding binary tree.

Gambler's ruin and lattice paths. For binary trees, nodes have either two or zero children. If we list, for each node, one less than the number of children, in preorder, then we get either $+1$ or -1, which we abbreviate simply as $+$ or $-$. Thus a binary tree can be uniquely represented as a string of $+$ and $-$ symbols. The tree in Figure 5.7 is

$$+ + + - - - + - + + - + - - + + - - - .$$

This encoding is a special case of the preorder degree representation. Which strings of $+$ and $-$ symbols correspond to binary trees?

Gambler's ruin sequences. These strings correspond exactly to the following situation. Suppose that a gambler starts with \$0 and makes a \$1 bet. If he loses, he has \$$-1$ and is ruined, but if he wins, he has \$1 and bets again. The plot of his holdings is simply the plot of the partial sums of the plus-minus sequence (number of pluses minus number of minuses). Any path that does not cross the \$0 point (except at the last step) represents a possible path to ruin for the gambler, and such paths are also in direct correspondence with binary trees. Given a binary tree, we produce the corresponding path as just described: it is a gambler's ruin path by the same inductive reasoning as we used above to prove the validity of the preorder degree representation of ordered trees. Given a gambler's ruin path, it can be divided in precisely one way into two subpaths with the same characteristics by deleting the first step and splitting the path at the *first* place that it hits the \$0 axis. This division (inductively) leads to the corresponding binary tree.

Ballot problems. A second way of looking at this situation is to consider an election where the winner has $N+1$ votes and the loser has N votes. A plus-minus sequence then corresponds to the set of ballots, and plus-minus sequences corresponding to binary trees are those where the winner is never behind as the ballots are counted.

Paths in a lattice. A third way of looking at the situation is to consider paths in an N-by-N square lattice that proceed from the upper left corner down to the lower right corner using "right" and "down" steps. There are $\binom{2N}{N}$ such paths, but only one out of every $N+1$ starts "right" and does not cross the diagonal, because there is a direct correspondence between such paths and binary trees, as shown in Figure 5.12. This is obviously a graph of the gambler's holdings (or of the winner's margin as the ballots

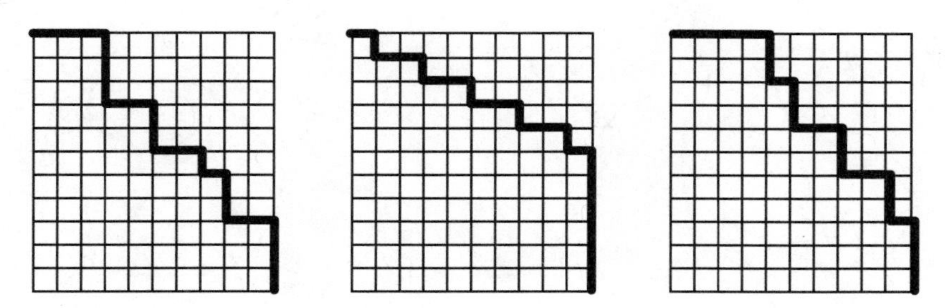

Figure 5.12 Lattice-path representations of binary trees in Figure 5.1

are counted) rotated 45 degrees. It also is a graph of the stack size if the corresponding tree is traversed in preorder.

We will study properties of these *gambler's ruin sequences*, or *ballot sequences* in Chapters 6 and 7. They turn out to be relevant in the analysis of sorting and merging algorithms (see §6.6), and they can be studied using general tools related to string enumeration (see §7.5).

Exercise 5.44 Find and prove the validity of a correspondence between N-step gambler's ruin paths and ordered forests of $N-1$ nodes.

Exercise 5.45 How many N-bit binary strings have the property that the number of ones in the first k bits does not exceed the number of zeros, for all k?

Exercise 5.46 Compare the parenthesis representation of an ordered forest to the plus-minus representation of its associated binary tree. Explain your observation.

Exercise 5.47 Show from the plus-minus representation that both breadth-first search (i. e., level order, saving unvisited nodes on a queue) and depth-first search (i. e., preorder, saving unvisited nodes on a stack) for a binary tree use the same amount of space.

Planar subdivision representations. We mention another classical correspondence because it is so well known in combinatorics: the "triangulated N-gon" representation, shown in Figure 5.13 for the binary tree at the left in Figure 5.1. Given an N-gon, how many ways are there to divide it into triangles with noncrossing "diagonal" lines connecting vertices? The answer is the Catalan numbers, because of the direct correspondence with binary trees. This application marked the first appearance of Catalan numbers, in the work of Euler and Segner in 1753, about a century before Catalan himself. The correspondence is plain from Figure 5.13: given a triangulated N-gon, put an internal node on each diagonal and one (the

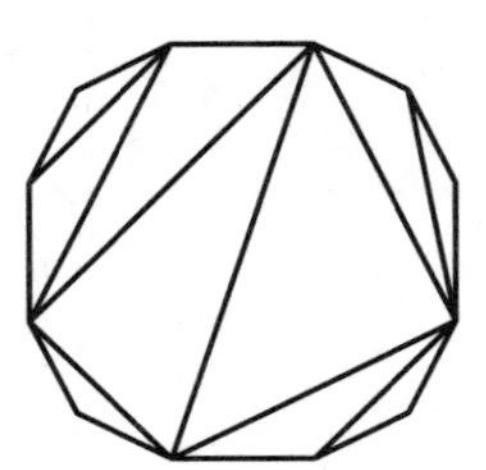
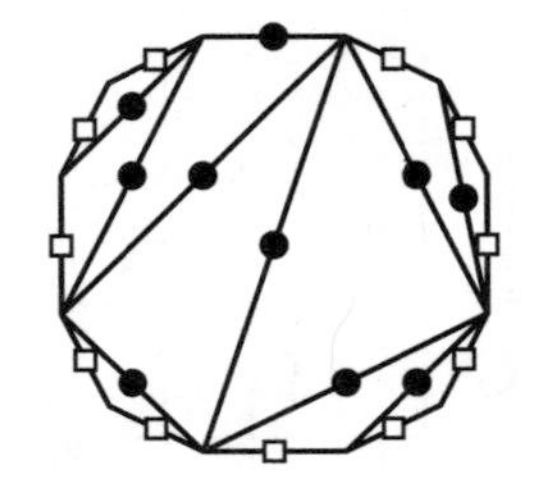
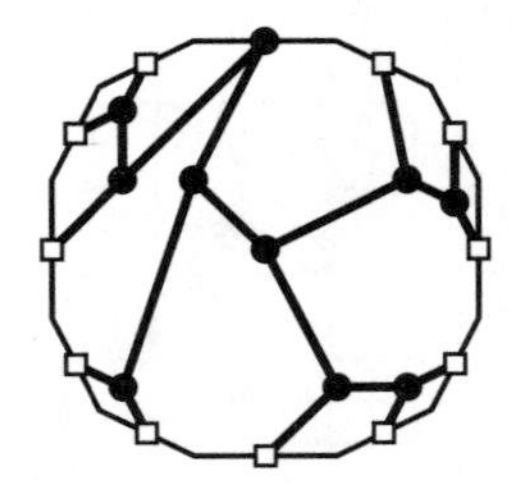

Figure 5.13 Binary tree corresponding to a triangulated N-gon

root) on one exterior edge and an external node on each remaining exterior edge. Then connect the root to the other two nodes in its triangle and continue connecting in the same way down to the bottom of the tree.

This particular correspondence is classical in combinatorics, and there are similar planar subdivisions that have been more recently developed and are of importance in the design and analysis of some geometric algorithms. For example, the *2D-tree* data structure (see Sedgewick [29]) is based on dividing a rectangular region in the plane with horizontal lines, then further dividing the resulting regions with vertical lines, and so on, continuing to divisions as fine as desired, alternating horizontal and vertical lines. This recursive division corresponds to a tree representation. Such structures can be used to subdivide multidimensional spaces for point location and other applications.

Figure 5.14 summarizes the most well-known tree representations discussed above, for five-node trees. We dwell on these representations because Catalan numbers appear frequently in combinatorics and—since they enumerate a very basic data structure—the analysis of algorithms, as well. Properties of a particular algorithm are often more clearly seen in one of the equivalent representations than in another.

Exercise 5.48 Show that Figure 5.17 corresponds to the parenthesis system

(( ) ( )) ((( ) ( )) ( ) (( ) ( )) (( ) ( ) ( ))) ((( ) ( )) ( ) ( )) .

Exercise 5.49 Give a method for representing a tree with a subdivided rectangle when the ratio of the height to the width of any rectangle is between α and $1/\alpha$ for constant $\alpha > 1$. Find a solution for α as small as you can.

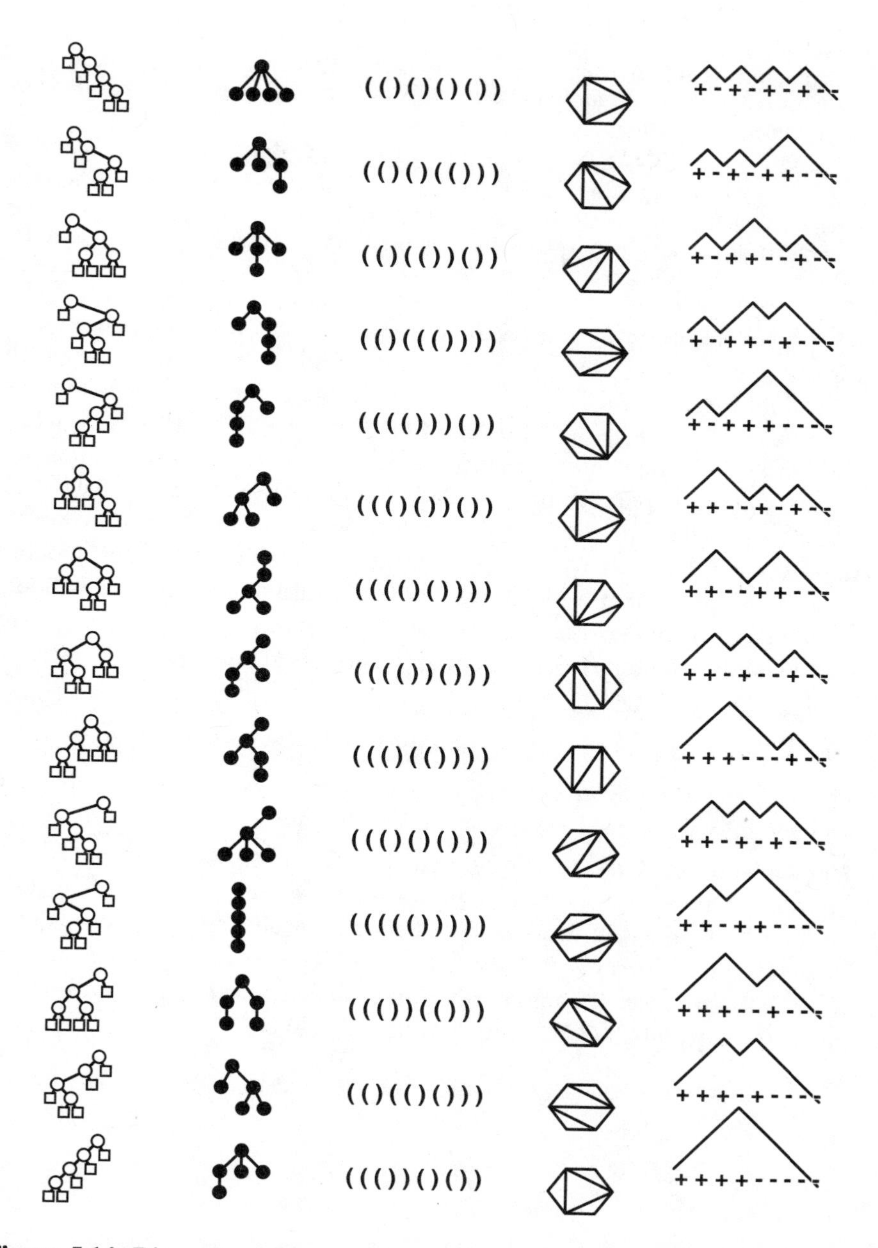

Figure 5.14 Binary trees, trees, parentheses, triangulations, ruin sequences

Exercise 5.50 There is an obvious correspondence where left-right symmetry in triangulations is reflected in left-right symmetry in trees. What about rotations? Is there any relationship among the N trees corresponding to the N rotations of an asymmetric triangulation?

Exercise 5.51 Consider strings of N integers with two properties: first, if $k > 1$ is in the string, then so is $k - 1$, and second, some larger integer must appear somewhere between any two occurrences of any integer. Show that the number of such strings of length N is described by the Catalan numbers, and find a direct correspondence with trees or binary trees.

5.12 Unordered Trees. An essential aspect of the definition of trees and forests given above is the notion of a *sequence* of trees: the order in which individual trees appear is considered significant. Indeed, the trees that we have been considering are also called *ordered* trees. This is natural when we consider various computer representations or, for example, when we draw a tree on paper, because we must somehow put down one tree after another—forests with trees in differing orders *look* different. However, there are applications where the sequence is actually irrelevant and the intrinsic graph structure of the tree is of central importance. We will see examples of such algorithms as we consider the basic definitions, then we will consider enumeration problems for unordered trees.

Definition *An* unordered tree *is a node (called the root) attached to a multiset of unordered trees. (Such a multiset is called an unordered forest.)*

Figure 5.15 shows two forests (the nodes happen to be labelled) that are equivalent when considered as unordered forests.

Rooted unordered trees. As an example of an algorithm where rooted unordered trees occur naturally, we consider the *union-find* problem: give an algorithm that will process a sequence of equivalence relations on N distinct items, returning 0 if the two items were already equivalent, 1 if this relation reduces the number of equivalence classes by 1. For example, given 16 items labelled A through O, the sequence

$$A \equiv B \quad A \equiv C \quad B \equiv C \quad O \equiv M \quad J \equiv I \quad E \equiv D$$

$$O \equiv N \quad G \equiv A \quad E \equiv F \quad B \equiv D \quad O \equiv P \quad F \equiv A$$

should result in the sequence

```
1  1  0  1  1  1  1  1  1  1  1  0
```

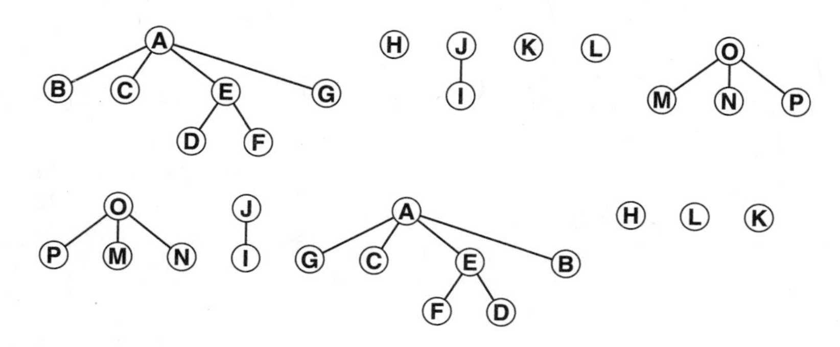

Figure 5.15 Two representations of the same rooted (unordered) forest

of return values, because the first two instructions make A, B, and C equivalent, then the third finds B and C to be already equivalent, etc.

Program 5.4 gives a solution to this problem that uses an explicit "parent link" representation of unordered forests. The forest is represented as an array: the entry corresponding to each node is the index of its father in the tree containing them (0 for roots). The algorithm considers the roots to "represent" all nodes in the trees. Given a node, its corresponding root can be found simply by following parent links until a 0 is found; given an edge, the roots corresponding to the two constituent edges are found. If both nodes correspond to the same root, then they belong to the same equivalence class, and the new relation is redundant; otherwise the relation connects heretofore disconnected components. The

```
function find(x, y:  integer; uf:  boolean):  boolean;
  var i, j:  integer;
  begin
  i := x; while dad[i] > 0 do i := dad[i];
  j := y; while dad[j] > 0 do j := dad[j];
  if uf and (i<>j) then dad[j] := i;
  find := (i<>j)
  end;
```

Program 5.4 Union-find

forest in Figure 5.15 is the one built for the example given above. The shape of the forest depends on the relations seen so far and the order in which they are presented.

The algorithm moves up through the tree and never examines the subtrees of a node (or even tests how many there are). Combinatorially, the union-find algorithm is a mapping from permutations of relations to unordered forests. Program 5.4 is quite simple, and a variety of improvements to the basic idea have been suggested and analyzed. The key point to note now is that the order of appearance of children of a node is not significant to the algorithm, or to the internal representation of the associated tree—these algorithms provide an example of unordered trees naturally occurring in a computation.

Unrooted ("free") trees. Still more general is the concept of a tree where no root node is distinguished. To properly define "unrooted, unordered trees," which are also commonly called "free trees" or just "trees," it is convenient to move from the general to the specific, starting with *graphs*, the fundamental structure underlying all combinatorial objects based on sets of nodes and connections between them.

Definition *A* graph *is a set of nodes together with a set of edges that connect pairs of distinct nodes (with at most one edge connecting any pair of nodes).*

We can envision starting at some node and "following" an edge to the constituent node for the edge, then following an edge to another node, and so on. The shortest sequence of edges leading from one node to another in this way is called a *simple path*. A graph is *connected* if there is a simple path connecting any pair of nodes. A simple path from a node back to itself is called a *cycle*.

Every tree is a graph; which graphs are trees? It is well known that any one of the following four conditions are necessary and sufficient to ensure that a graph G with N nodes is an (unrooted unordered) tree:

(*i*) G has $N-1$ edges and no cycles.

(*ii*) G has $N-1$ edges and is connected.

(*iii*) Exactly one simple path connects each pair of vertices in G.

(*iv*) G is connected, but does not remain connected if any edge is removed.

That is, we could use any one of these conditions to define free trees.

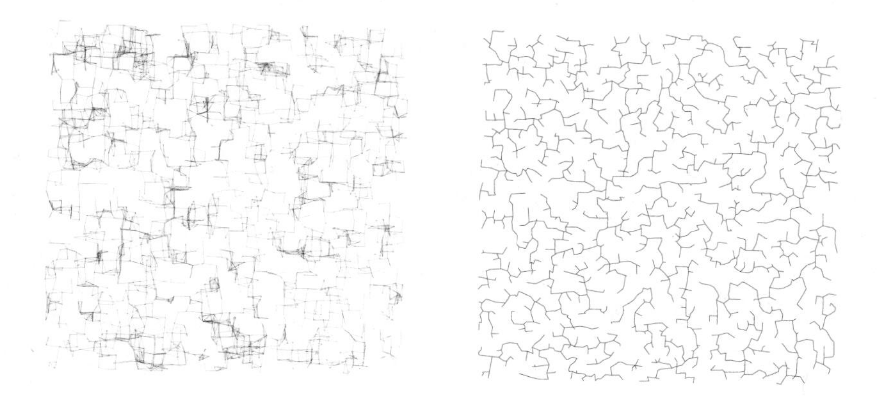

Figure 5.16 A large graph and one of its spanning trees

As an example of an algorithm where free trees arise in a natural way, consider perhaps the most basic question that we can ask about a graph: is it connected, or not? That is, is there some path connecting every pair of vertices? If so, then there is a minimal set of edges comprising such paths called the *spanning tree* of the graph. If the graph is not connected, then there is a spanning forest, one tree for each connected component. Figure 5.16 gives an example of a spanning tree of a large graph.

Definition *A* spanning tree *of a graph of N ertices is a set of $N-1$ of the edges of the graph that form a tree.*

By the basic properties of trees, the spanning tree must include all of the nodes, and its existence demonstrates that all pairs of nodes are connected by some path. The spanning tree is an unrooted, unordered tree.

One well-known algorithm for finding the spanning tree is *Kruskal's algorithm*: considering each edge in turn, check to see if adding the next edge to the set comprising the partial spanning tree built so far would cause a cycle. If not, add it to the spanning tree and go on to consider the next edge. When the set has $N-1$ edges in it, the edges represent an unordered, unrooted tree; indeed, it is a spanning tree for the graph. One way to implement Kruskal's algorithm is to use the union-find algorithm given above for the cycle test. Many other algorithms for finding spanning trees have been devised and analyzed. But the key point to note now is that Kruskal's algorithm is an example of free trees naturally occurring in a computation.

The combinatorics literature contains a vast amount of material on the theory of graphs, including many textbooks; and the computer science literature contains a vast amount of material about algorithms on graphs, also including many textbooks. Full coverage of this material is of course beyond the scope of this book, but understanding the simpler structures and algorithms that we do cover is good preparation for addressing more difficult questions about properties of random graphs and the analysis of algorithms on graphs. Examples of graph problems where the techniques we have been considering apply directly may be found in [13] and the classical reference Harary and Plamer [18]. We will consider some special families of graphs again in Chapter 8, but let us return now to our study of various types of trees.

Exercise 5.52 How many of the $2^{\binom{N}{2}}$ graphs on N labelled vertices are free trees?

Exercise 5.53 For each of the four properties listed above, show that the other three are implied. (This is 12 exercises in disguise!)

Tree hierarchy. The four major types of trees that we have defined form a hierarchy, as summarized and illustrated in Table 5.3. (*i*) The *free tree* is the most general, simply an acyclic connected graph. (*ii*) The *rooted tree* has a distinguished root node. (*iii*) The *ordered tree* is a rooted tree where the order of the subtrees of a node is significant. (*iv*) The *binary tree* is an ordered tree with the further restriction that every node has degree 0 or 2. In the nomenclature that we use, the adjective describes the characteristic that separates each type of tree from the one above it in the hierarchy. It is also common to use nomenclature that separates each type from the one *below* it in the hierarchy. Thus, we sometimes refer to free trees as unrooted trees, rooted trees as unordered trees, and ordered trees as general Catalan trees.

A few more words on nomenclature are appropriate because of the variety of terms found in the literature. Ordered trees are often called *plane* trees and unordered trees are referred to as *nonplane* trees. The term *plane* is used because the structures can be transformed to one another with continuous operations in the plane. Though this terminology is widely used, we prefer *ordered* because of its natural implications with regard to computer representations. The term *oriented* in Table 5.3 refers to the fact that the root is distinguished, so there is an orientation of the edges towards the root; we prefer to use the term *rooted* if it is not obvious from the context that there is a root involved.

As the definitions get more restrictive, the number of trees that are regarded as different gets larger, so, for a given size, there are more rooted trees than free trees, more ordered trees than rooted trees, and more binary trees than ordered trees. It turns out that the ratio between the number of rooted trees and the number of free trees is proportional to N; the corresponding ratio of ordered trees to rooted trees grows exponentially with N; and the ratio of binary trees to ordered trees is a constant. The rest of this section is devoted to a derivation of analytic results that quantify these distinctions. The enumeration results are summarized in Table 5.4.

Figure 5.17 is an illustration of the hierarchy for trees with five nodes. The 14 different five-node ordered trees are depicted in the figure, and they are further organized into equivalence classes using small shaded and larger open rectangles. There are 9 different five-node rooted trees (those

	other names	*basic properties*	*identical trees*	*different trees*
free tree	unrooted tree tree	connected, no cycles	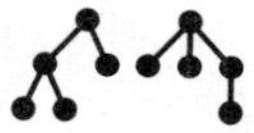	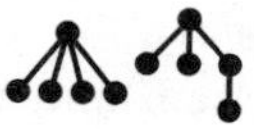
rooted tree	planted tree oriented tree unordered tree	root node specified	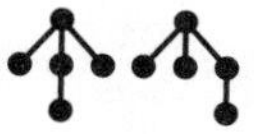	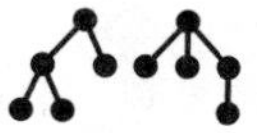
ordered tree	planar tree Catalan tree tree	node order significant	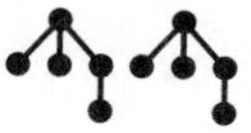	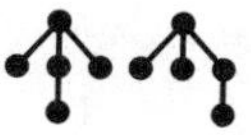
binary tree	binary Catalan tree	left, right subtrees		

Table 5.3 Summary of tree nomenclature

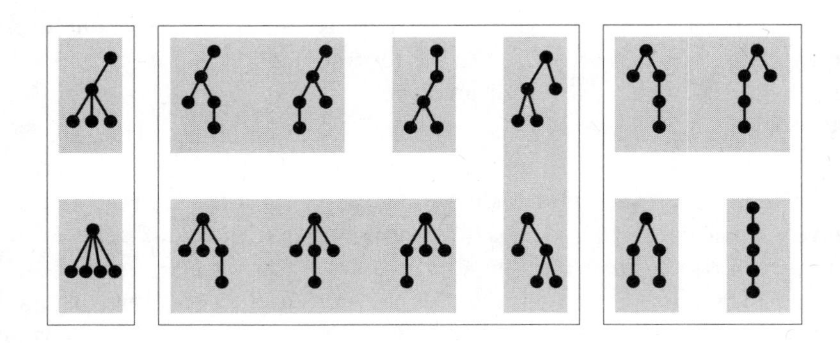

Figure 5.17 Trees with five nodes (ordered, unordered, and unrooted)

in shaded rectangles are identical as rooted trees) and 3 different five-node free trees (those enclosed in large rectangles are identical as free trees). It is amusing to note that, as a hierarchy, this representation itself could be represented as a tree (see Exercise 5.48). Note that the counts just given for Figure 5.17 correspond to the fourth column ($N = 5$) in Table 5.4.

From a combinatorial point of view, we perhaps might be more interested in free trees because they differentiate structures at the most essential level. From the point of view of computer applications, we are perhaps more interested in binary trees and ordered trees because they have the property that the standard computer representation uniquely determines the tree, and in rooted trees because they are the quintessential recursive structure. In this book, we consider all these types of trees not only

	2	3	4	5	6	7	8	9	10	N
free	1	1	2	3	6	11	23	47	106	$\sim c_1\alpha^N/N^{5/2}$
rooted	1	2	4	9	20	48	115	286	719	$\sim c_2\alpha^N/N^{3/2}$
ordered	1	2	5	14	42	132	429	1430	4862	$\sim c_3 4^N/N^{3/2}$
binary	2	5	14	42	132	429	1430	4862	16796	$\sim (4c_3)4^N/N^{3/2}$

$\alpha \approx 2.9558$, $c_1 \approx .5350$, $c_2 \approx .4399$, $c_3 = 1/4\sqrt{\pi} \approx .1410$

Table 5.4 Enumeration of unlabelled trees

because they all arise in important computer algorithms but also because their analysis illustrates nearly the full range of analytic techniques that we present. But we maintain our algorithmic bias, by reserving the word *tree* for ordered trees, which arise in perhaps the most natural way in computer applications. Combinatorics texts more typically reserve the unmodified "tree" to describe unordered or free trees.

Exercise 5.54 Which free tree structure on six nodes appears most frequently among all ordered trees on six nodes? (Figure 5.17 shows that the answer for five nodes is the tree in the middle.)

Exercise 5.55 Answer the previous exercise for seven, eight, and more nodes, going as high as you can.

In binary tree search and other algorithms that use binary trees, we directly represent the ordered pair of subtrees with an ordered pair of links to subtrees. Similarly, a typical way to represent the subtrees in general Catalan trees is an ordered list of links to subtrees. There is a one-to-one correspondence between the trees and their computer representation. Indeed, in §5.11, we considered a number of different ways to represent trees and binary trees in an unambiguous manner. The situation is different when it comes to representing rooted trees and free trees, where we are faced with several ways to represent the same tree. This has many implications in algorithm design and analysis. A typical example is the "tree isomorphism" problem: given two different tree representations, determine whether or not they represent the same rooted tree, or the same free tree. In the analysis of algorithms, of course, the *number* of representations of each tree is likely to have an impact on the study of such algorithms.

The first challenge in analyzing algorithms that use trees is to find a probabilistic model that realistically approximates the situation at hand. Are the trees random? Is the tree distribution induced by some external randomness? How does the tree representation affect the algorithm and analysis? These lead to a host of analytic problems. For example, the "union-find" problem mentioned above has been analyzed using a number of different models (see Knuth and Schönhage [23]). We can assume that the sequence of equivalence relations are random node pairs, or that they correspond to random edges from a random forest, and so on. As we have seen with binary search trees and binary Catalan trees, the fundamental recursive decomposition leads to similarities in the analysis, but the induced distributions lead to significant differences in the analysis.

For various applications we may be interested in values of parameters that measure fundamental characteristics of the various types of trees, so we are faced with a host of analytic problems to consider. The enumeration results are classical (see [18], [27], and [21]), and are summarized in Table 5.4. Discussion of the derivation of some of these results is given below. Functional equations on the generating functions are easily available through the symbolic method, but asymptotic estimates of coefficients are slightly beyond the scope of this book, in some cases. More details may be found in [13].

Exercise 5.56 Give an efficient algorithm that takes as input a set of edges that represents a tree and produces as output a parenthesis system representation of that tree.

Exercise 5.57 Give an efficient algorithm that takes as input a set of edges that represents a tree and produces as output a binary tree representation of that tree.

Exercise 5.58 Give an efficient algorithm that takes as input two binary trees and determines whether or not they are different when considered as unordered trees.

Exercise 5.59 [cf. Aho, Hopcroft, and Ullman] Give an efficient algorithm that takes as input two parenthesis systems and determines whether or not they represent the same rooted tree.

Counting rooted unordered trees. Let $\mathcal{U}$ be the set of all rooted (unordered) trees with associated OGF

$$U(z) = \sum_{u \in \mathcal{U}} z^{|u|} = \sum_{N \geq 0} U_N z^N,$$

where U_N is the number of rooted trees with N nodes. Since each rooted tree comprises a root and a multiset of rooted trees, we can also express this generating function as an infinite product, in two ways:

$$U(z) = z \prod_{u \in \mathcal{U}} (1 - z^{|u|})^{-1} = z \prod_{N} (1 - z^N)^{-U_N}.$$

The first product is a simple application of the "multiset" construction associated with the symbolic method (see Exercise 3.62): for each tree u, the term $(1 - z^{|u|})^{-1}$ allows for the presence of an arbitrary number of occurrences of u in the set. The second product follows by grouping the U_N terms corresponding to the trees with N nodes.

Theorem 5.11 (*Enumeration of rooted unordered trees*) *The OGF that enumerates unordered trees satisfies the functional equation*

$$U(z) = z\exp\Bigl\{U(z) + \frac{1}{2}U(z^2) + \frac{1}{3}U(z^3) + \ldots\Bigr\}.$$

Asymptotically,

$$U_N \equiv [z^N]U(z) \sim c\alpha^N/N^{3/2}$$

where $c \approx 0.4399237$ *and* $\alpha \approx 2.9557649$.

Proof. Continuing the discussion above, take the logarithm of both sides:

$$\begin{aligned}\ln\frac{U(z)}{z} &= -\sum_{N\ge1} U_N \ln(1-z^N)\\ &= \sum_{N\ge1} U_N (z^N + \frac{1}{2}z^{2N} + \frac{1}{3}z^{3N} + \frac{1}{4}z^{4N} + \ldots)\\ &= U(z) + \frac{1}{2}U(z^2) + \frac{1}{3}U(z^3) + \frac{1}{4}U(z^4) + \ldots.\end{aligned}$$

The stated functional equation follows by exponentiating both sides.

The asymptotic analysis is beyond the scope of this book. It depends on complex analysis methods related to the direct generating function asymptotics that we introduced in Chapter 4. Details may be found in [13], [18], and [27]. ■

This result tells us several interesting lessons. First, the OGF admits no explicit form in terms of elementary functions of analysis. However, is is fully determined by the functional equation. Indeed, the same reasoning shows that the OGF of trees of height $\le h$ satisfies

$$U^{[0]}(z) = z; \quad U^{[h+1]}(z) = z\exp\{U^{[h]}(z) + \frac{1}{2}U^{[h]}(z^2) + \frac{1}{3}U^{[h]}(z^3) + \ldots\}.$$

Moreover, $U^{[h]}(z) \to U(z)$ as $h \to \infty$, and both series agree to $h+1$ terms. This provides a way to compute an arbitrary number of initial values:

$$U(z) = z + z^2 + 2z^3 + 4z^4 + 9z^5 + 20z^6 + 48z^7 + 115z^8 + 286z^9 + \ldots.$$

It is also noteworthy that a precise asymptotic analysis can be effected even though the OGF admits no closed form. Actually, this analysis is the historical source of the so-called Darboux-Polya method of asymptotic enumeration, which we introduced briefly in §4.10. Polya in 1937 realized in this way the asymptotic analysis of a large variety of tree types (see Polya and Read [27], a translation of Polya's classic paper), especially models of chemical isomers of hydrocarbons, alchohols, and so forth.

Exercise 5.60 Write a program to compute all the values of U_N that are smaller than the maximum representable integer in your machine, using the method suggested in the text. Estimate how many (unlimited precision) arithmetic operations would be required for large N, using this method.

Exercise 5.61 [cf. Harary-Palmer] Show that

$$NU_{N+1} = \sum_{1 \le k \le N} \Bigl(kU_k \sum_{k \le kl \le N} T_{N+1-kl} \Bigr)$$

and deduce that U_N can be determined in $O(N^2)$ arithmetic operations. (*Hint*: Differentiate the functional equation.)

Exercise 5.62 Give a polynomial-time algorithm to generate a random rooted tree of size N.

Counting free trees. Without a root to fix upon, the combinatorial argument is somewhat more sophisticated, though it has been known at least since 1889 (see Harary and Palmer [18]). The asymptotic estimate can be derived via a generating function argument, using the asymptotic formula for rooted trees just derived. We leave the details for exercises.

Exercise 5.63 Show that the number of rooted trees of N nodes is bounded below by the number of free trees of N nodes and bounded above by N times the number of free trees of N nodes. (Thus, the exponential order of growth of the two quantities is the same.)

Exercise 5.64 Let $F(z)$ be the OGF for free trees. Show that

$$F(z) = U(z) - \frac{1}{2}U(z)^2 + \frac{1}{2}U(z^2).$$

Exercise 5.65 Derive the asymptotic formula for free trees given in Table 5.4, using the formula given in Theorem 5.11 for rooted (unordered) trees and the previous exercise.

5.13 Labelled Trees. The counting results above assume that the nodes in the trees are indistinguishable. If, on the contrary, we assume that the nodes have distinct identities, then there are many more ways to organize them into trees. For example, different trees result when different nodes are used for the root. As above, the number of "different" trees increases when we consider the order of subtrees significant and when we specify a root. We speak of "labels" as a combinatorial device to distinguish nodes. This of course has nothing to do with keys in binary search trees, which are applications data associated with nodes.

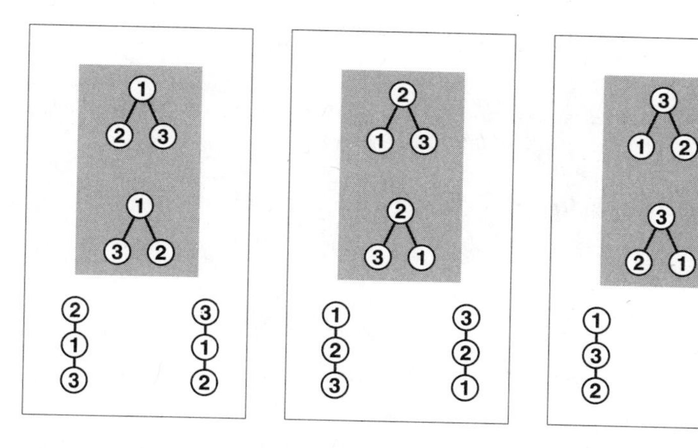

Figure 5.18 Labelled trees with three nodes (ordered, unordered, and unrooted)

The different types of labelled trees are illustrated in Figure 5.18, which corresponds to Figure 5.17. All the trees are different rooted, ordered, and labelled trees; those in shaded rectangles are isomorphic as unordered labelled trees, and those in large rectangles are isomorphic as unrooted, unordered labelled trees. As usual, we are interested in knowing how many labelled trees there are, of each of the types that we have considered. Table 5.5 gives small values and asymptotic estimates for the counts of the various labelled trees. The second column ($N = 3$) in Table 5.4 corresponds to the trees in Figure 5.18.

As discussed in Chapter 3, EGFs are the appropriate tool for approaching the enumeration of labelled trees, not just because there are so many more possibilities, but also because the basic combinatorial manipu-

	2	3	4	5	6	7	N
ordered	2	12	120	1680	46656	665280	$\frac{(2N-2)!}{(N-1)!}$
rooted	2	9	64	625	7976	117649	N^{N-1}
free	1	3	16	125	1296	16807	N^{N-2}

Table 5.5 Enumeration of labelled trees

lations that we use on labelled structures are naturally understood through EGFs.

Exercise 5.66 Which tree of four nodes has the most different labellings? Answer this question for five, six, and more nodes, going as high as you can.

Counting ordered labelled trees. Let $\mathcal{L}$ be the set of ordered (rooted) labelled trees with EGF

$$L(z) = \sum_{\ell \in \mathcal{L}} \frac{z^{|\ell|}}{\ell!} = \sum_{N \geq 0} L_N \frac{z^N}{N!},$$

where L_N is the number of trees with N nodes. An ordered labelled forest is either empty or an unordered sequence of ordered labelled trees, so by the symbolic method we have

$$\begin{aligned} L(z) &= z(1 + L(z) + L(z)^2 + L(z)^3 + \ldots + L(z)^k + \ldots) \\ &= \frac{z}{1 - L(z)}. \end{aligned}$$

This is virtually the same argument as that used above for ordered (unlabelled) trees, but we are now working with EGFs (Theorem 3.8) for labelled objects, where before we were using OGFs for unlabelled objects (Theorem 3.7). Thus

$$L(z) = \frac{1 - \sqrt{1 - 4z}}{2}$$

and the number of ordered rooted labelled trees with N nodes is given by

$$N![z^N]L(z) = N!\frac{1}{N}\binom{2N-2}{N-1} = \frac{(2N-2)!}{(N-1)!}.$$

Another way to interpret this result is via a combinatorial correspondence: an unlabelled tree is determined by a preorder traversal, and any of the $N!$ permutations can be used with preorder traversal to assign labels to an ordered tree with N nodes, so the number of labelled trees is just $N!$ times the number of unlabelled trees. Such an argument is clearly general. For ordered trees, the labelled and unlabelled varieties are closely related and their counts differ only by a factor of $N!$.

Counting unordered labelled trees. Unordered (rooted) labelled trees are also called *Cayley trees*, because they were enumerated by A. Cayley, in the nineteenth century. Let C be the set of all Cayley trees with associated EGF

$$C(z) = \sum_{|c| \in C} \frac{z^{|c|}}{|c|!} = \sum_{N \geq 0} C_N \frac{z^N}{N!},$$

where C_N is the number of Cayley trees with N nodes. A Cayley forest is either empty or a set of k Cayley trees bearing distinct labels. So, by the symbolic method we have

$$\begin{aligned} C(z) &= z\Bigl(1 + C(z) + \frac{C(z)^2}{2!} + \frac{C(z)^3}{3!} + \ldots + \frac{C(z)^k}{k!} + \ldots\Bigr) \\ &= ze^{C(z)}. \end{aligned}$$

This differs from the argument above in only one way: when order is not significant, $(C(z))^k$ counts each forest $k!$ times, so we divide by $k!$.

Theorem 5.12 (*Enumeration of unordered labelled trees*) *The OGF that enumerates unordered labelled trees satisfies the functional equation*

$$C(z) = ze^{C(z)}.$$

The number of such trees of size N is

$$C_N = N![z^N]C(z) = N^{N-1}$$

and the number of unordered k-forests of such trees is

$$C_N^{[k]} = N![z^N]\frac{(C(z))^k}{k!} = \binom{N-1}{k-1} N^{N-k}.$$

Proof. This functional equation can be solved explicitly with Lagrange inversion (see §3.10), which immediately yields the stated results. ■

Combinatorially, it is obvious that, for unordered labelled trees, the number of rooted trees of N nodes is just N times the number of unrooted trees: each unrooted tree corresponds to precisely N rooted trees, just by identifying each of the nodes as the root. Thus the number of labelled free trees is N^{N-2}.

For reference, the enumeration generating functions for both unlabelled trees and labelled trees are given in Table 5.6. The values of the coefficients for labelled trees are given in Table 5.5.

Exercise 5.67 Find a way to represent labelled rooted trees with $(N-1)$-tuples of positive integers less than N. That is, there are N^{N-1} such N-tuples and an equal number of such trees: find a one-to-one correspondence. (*Hint*: Associate nodes with parents.)

Exercise 5.68 Show that the EGF that enumerates labelled free trees is equal to $C(z) - C(z)^2/2$.

5.14 Other Types of Trees. It is often convenient to place various local and global restrictions on trees, for example, to suit requirements of a particular application or to try rule out degenerate cases. From a combinatorial standpoint, any restriction corresponds to a new class of tree, and a new set of problems need to be solved to enumerate the trees and to learn their statistical properties. In this section, we catalog many well-known and widely used special types of trees, for reference. Examples are drawn in Figure 5.19, and definitions are given in the discussion below. (*Note on nomenclature*: In this section, we use $T(z)$ to denote the OGF for various generalizations of the Catalan OGF to emphasize similarities in the analysis, while sparing the reader from excessive notational baggage.)

Definition *A* t-ary tree *is either an external node or an internal node attached to an ordered sequence of* t *subtrees, all of which are* t*-ary trees.*

This is the natural generalization of binary trees that we considered as an example when looking at Lagrange inversion in Chapter 3. We insist that

	unlabelled (OGF)	*labelled (EGF)*
ordered	$G(z) = \dfrac{z}{1 - G(z)}$	$L(z) = \dfrac{z}{1 - L(z)}$
rooted	$U(z) = z \exp\{\sum_{i \geq 1} U(z^i)/i\}$	$C(z) = ze^{C(z)}$
free	$U(z) - U(z)^2/2 + U(z^2)/2$	$C(z) - C(z)^2/2$

Table 5.6 Tree enumeration generating functions

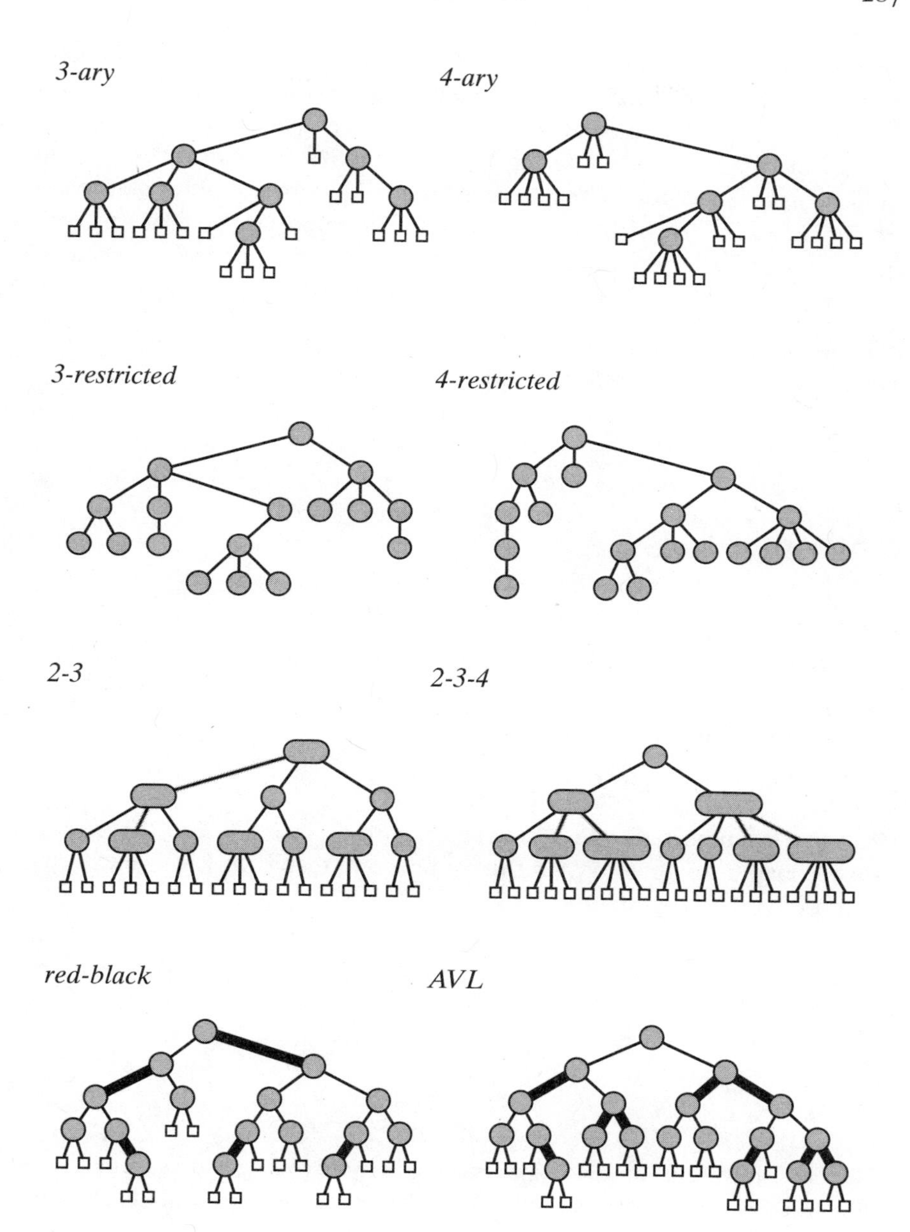

Figure 5.19 Examples of various other types of trees

every node have exactly t descendants. These trees are normally considered to be ordered—this matches a computer representation where t links are reserved for each node, to point to its descendants. In some applications, keys might be associated with internal nodes; in other cases internal nodes might correspond to sequences of $t-1$ keys; in still other cases data might be associated with external nodes. One important tree of this type is the *quad tree*, where information about geometric data is organized by decomposing an area into four quadrants, proceeding recursively.

Theorem 5.13 (*Enumeration of t-ary trees*) *The OGF that enumerates t-ary trees (by external nodes) satisfies the functional equation*

$$T(z) = z + (T(z))^t.$$

The number of t-ary trees with N internal nodes and $(t-1)N+1$ external nodes is

$$\frac{1}{(t-1)N+1}\binom{tN}{N} \sim c_t(\alpha_t)^N/N^{3/2}$$

where $\alpha_t = t^t/(t-1)^{t-1}$ and $c_t = 1/\sqrt{(2\pi)(t-1)^3/t}$.

Proof. We use Lagrange inversion, in a similar manner as for the solution given in §3.11 for the case $t = 3$. By the symbolic method, the OGF with size measured by external nodes satisfies

$$T(z) = z + T(z)^3.$$

This can be subjected to the Lagrange theorem, since $z = T(z)(1-T(z)^2)$, so we have an expression for the number of trees with $2N+1$ external nodes (N internal nodes):

$$\begin{aligned}[z^{2N+1}]T(z) &= \frac{1}{2N+1}[u^{2N}]\frac{1}{(1-u^2)^{2N+1}}\\ &= \frac{1}{2N+1}[u^{N}]\frac{1}{(1-u)^{2N+1}}\\ &= \frac{1}{2N+1}\binom{3N}{N}.\end{aligned}$$

This is equivalent to the expression given in §3.11, and it generalizes immediately to give the stated result. The asymptotic estimate also follows directly when we use the same methods as for the Catalan numbers (see §4.3). ■

Exercise 5.69 Find the number of k-forests with a total of N internal nodes.

Exercise 5.70 Derive the asymptotic estimate given in Theorem 5.13 for the number of t-ary trees with N internal nodes.

Definition *A t-restricted tree is a node (called the root) containing links to t or fewer t-restricted trees.*

The difference between these and t-ary trees is that not every internal node must have t links. This has direct implications in the computer representation: for t-ary trees, we might as well reserve space for t links in all internal nodes, but t-restricted trees might be better represented as binary trees, using the standard correspondence. Again, we normally consider these to be ordered, though we might also consider unordered and/or unrooted t-restricted trees. Every node is linked to at most $t+1$ other nodes in a t-restricted tree, as shown in Figure 5.19.

The case $t = 2$ corresponds to the so-called *Motzkin numbers*, for which we can get an explicit expression for the OGF $M(z)$ by solving the quadratic equation. We have

$$M(z) = z(1 + M(z) + M(z)^2)$$

so that

$$M(z) = \frac{1 - z - \sqrt{1 - 2z - 3z^2}}{2z} = \frac{1 - z - \sqrt{(1+z)(1-3z)}}{2z}.$$

Now, Theorem 4.11 provides an immediate proof that $[z^N]M(z)$ is $O(3^N)$, and methods from complex asymptotics yield the more accurate asymptotic estimate $3^N/\sqrt{3/4\pi N^3}$. Actually, with about the same amount of work, we can derive a much more general result.

Theorem 5.14 (*Enumeration of t-restricted trees*) *Let $\theta(u) = 1 + u + u^2 + \ldots + u^t$. The OGF that enumerates t-restricted trees satisfies the functional equation*

$$T(z) = z\theta(T(z))$$

and the number of t-restricted trees is

$$[z^N]T(z) = [u^{n-1}](\theta(u))^n \sim c_t \alpha_t^N / N^{3/2}$$

where ρ is the smallest positive root of $\theta(\rho) - \rho\theta'(\rho) = 0$ and the constants α_t and c_t are given by $\alpha_t = \theta'(\rho)$ and $c_t = \sqrt{\theta(\rho)/2\pi\theta''(\rho)}$.

Proof. The first parts of the theorem are immediate from the symbolic method and Lagrange inversion. The asymptotic result requires singularity analysis, using an extension of Theorem 4.12 (see [13]).

This result follows from a theorem proved by Meir and Moon in 1978 [25], and it actually holds for a large class of polynomials $\theta(u)$ of the form $1 + a_1 u + a_2 u^2 + \ldots$, subject to the constraint that the coefficients are positive and that a_1 and at least one other coefficient are nonzero. ■

The asymptotic estimates of the number of t-restricted trees for small t are given in the following table:

	t	c_t	α_t
	2	.4886025119	3.0
	3	.2520904538	3.610718613
$c_t \alpha_t^N / N^{3/2}$	4	.1932828341	3.834437249
	5	.1691882413	3.925387252
	6	.1571440515	3.965092635
	∞	.1410473965	4.0

For large t, the values of α_t approaches 4, which is perhaps to be expected, since the trees are then like general Catalan trees.

Exercise 5.71 Use the identity $1 + u + u^2 + \ldots + u^t = (1 - u^{t+1})/(1 - u)$ to find a sum expression for the number of t-restricted trees with N nodes.

Exercise 5.72 Write a program that, given t, will compute the number of t-restricted trees for all values of N for which the number is smaller than the maximum representable integer in your machine.

Exercise 5.73 Find the number of "even" t-restricted trees, where all nodes have an even number of, and less than t, children.

Height-restricted trees. Other types of trees involve restrictions on height. Such trees are important because they can be used as binary search tree replacements that provide a guaranteed $O(\log N)$ search time. This was first shown in 1960 by Adel'son-Vel'skii and Landis [1], and such trees have been widely studied since (for example, see Bayer and McCreight [3] or Guibas and Sedgewick [17]). Balanced trees are of practical interest because they combine the simplicity and flexibility of binary tree search and insertion with good worst-case performance. They are often used for very large database applications, so asymptotic results on performance are of direct practical interest.

Definition *An* AVL tree *of height 0 or height* -1 *is an external node; an AVL tree of height* $h > 0$ *is an internal node linked to a left and a right subtree, both of height* $h-1$ *or* $h-2$.

Definition *A* B-tree *of height 0 is an external node; a B-tree of order* M *and height* $h > 0$ *is an internal node connected to a sequence of between* $\lceil M/2 \rceil$ *and* M *B-trees of order* M *and height* $h-1$.

B-trees of order 3 and 4 are normally called 2-3 trees and 2-3-4 trees, respectively. Several methods, known as *balanced tree* algorithms, have been devised using these and similar structures, based on the general theme of mapping permutations into tree structures that are guaranteed to have no long paths. More details, including relationships among the various types, are given by Guibas and Sedgewick [17], who also show that many of the structures (including AVL trees and B-trees) can be mapped into binary trees with marked edges, as in Figure 5.19.

Exercise 5.74 Without solving the enumeration problem in detail, try to place the following classes of trees in increasing order of their cardinality for large N: 3-ary, 3-restricted, 2-3, and AVL.

Exercise 5.75 Build a table giving the number of AVL and 2-3 trees with fewer than 15 nodes that are different when considered as unordered trees.

Balanced tree structures illustrate the variety of tree structures that arise in applications. They lead to a host of analytic problems of interest and they fall at various points along the continuum between purely combinatoric structures and partially "algorithmic" structures. None of the binary tree structures have been precisely analyzed under random insertions for statistics such as path length, despite their importance. It is even challenging to enumerate them (for example, see Aho and Sloane [2] or Flajolet and Odlyzko [11]).

For each of these types of structures, we are interested in knowing how many essentially different structures there are of each size, plus statistics about various important parameters. For some of the structures, developing functional equations for enumeration is relatively straightforward, because they are recursively defined. (Some of the balanced tree structures cannot even be easily defined and analyzed recursively, but rather need to be defined in terms of the algorithm that maps permutations into them.) As with tree height, the functional equation is only a starting point, and further analysis of these structures turns out to be quite difficult. Functional equations on generating functions for several of the types we have discussed are given in Table 5.7.

Exercise 5.76 Prove the functional equations on the generating functions for AVL and 2-3 trees given in Table 5.7.

More important, just as we analyzed both binary trees (uniformly distributed) and binary search trees (binary trees distributed as constructed from random permutations by the algorithm), we often need to know statistics on various classes of trees according to a distribution induced by an algorithm that transforms some other combinatorial object into a tree structure, which leads to more analytic problems. That is, several of the basic tree structures that we have defined serve many algorithms. We used the term *binary search tree* to distinguish the combinatorial object (the binary tree) from the algorithm that maps permutations into it; balanced tree and other algorithms need to be distinguished in a similar manner.

tree type (size measure)	*functional equation on generating function*
3-ary (external nodes)	$T(z) = z + T(z)^3$
3-ary (internal nodes)	$T(z) = 1 + zT(z)^3$
3-restricted (nodes)	$T(z) = z(1 + T(z) + T(z)^2 + T(z)^3)$
AVL of height h (internal nodes)	$A_h(z) = \begin{cases} 1 & h < 0 \\ 1 & h = 0 \\ zA_{h-1}(z)^2 + 2zA_{h-1}(z)A_{h-2}(z) & h > 0 \end{cases}$
2-3 of height h (external nodes)	$B_h(z) = \begin{cases} z & h = 0 \\ B_{h-1}(z^2 + z^3) & h > 0 \end{cases}$

Table 5.7 Generating functions for other types of trees

Indeed, AVL trees, B-trees, and other types of search trees are *primarily* of interest when distributed as constructed from random permutations. The "each tree equally likely" combinatorial objects have been studied both because the associated problems are more amenable to combinatorial analysis and because knowledge of their properties may give some insight into solving problems that arise when analyzing them as data structures. Even so, the basic problem of just enumerating the balanced tree structures is still quite difficult (for example, see [26]). None of the associated algorithms have been analyzed under the random permutation model, and the average-case analysis of balanced tree algorithms is one of the outstanding problems in the analysis of algorithms.

Figure 5.20 gives some indication of the complexity of the situation. It shows the distribution of the subtree sizes in random AVL trees (all trees equally likely) and may be compared with Figure 5.10, the corresponding figure for Catalan trees. The corresponding figure for BSTs is a series of straight lines, at height $1/N$. Where Catalan trees have an asymptotically constant probability of having a fixed number of nodes in a subtree for any tree size N, the balance condition for AVL trees means that small subtrees cannot occur for large N. Indeed, we might expect the trees to be "balanced" in the sense that the subtree sizes might cluster near the middle for large N. This does seem to be the case for some N, but it also is true that for some other N, there are *two* peaks in the distribution, which means that a large fraction of the trees have significantly fewer than half of the nodes on one side or the other. Indeed, the distribution exhibits an oscillatory behavior, roughly between these two extremes. An analytic expression describing this has to account for this oscillation and so may not be as concise as we would like. Presumably, similar effects are involved when balanced trees are built from permutations in searching applications, but this has not yet been shown.

TREES are pervasive in the algorithms we consider, either as explicit structures or as models of recursive computations. Much of our knowledge of properties of our most important algorithms can be traced to properties of trees.

We will encounter other types of trees in later chapters, but they all share an intrinsic recursive nature that makes their analysis natural using generating functions as above: the recursive structure leads directly to an equation that yields a closed-form expression or a recursive formulation

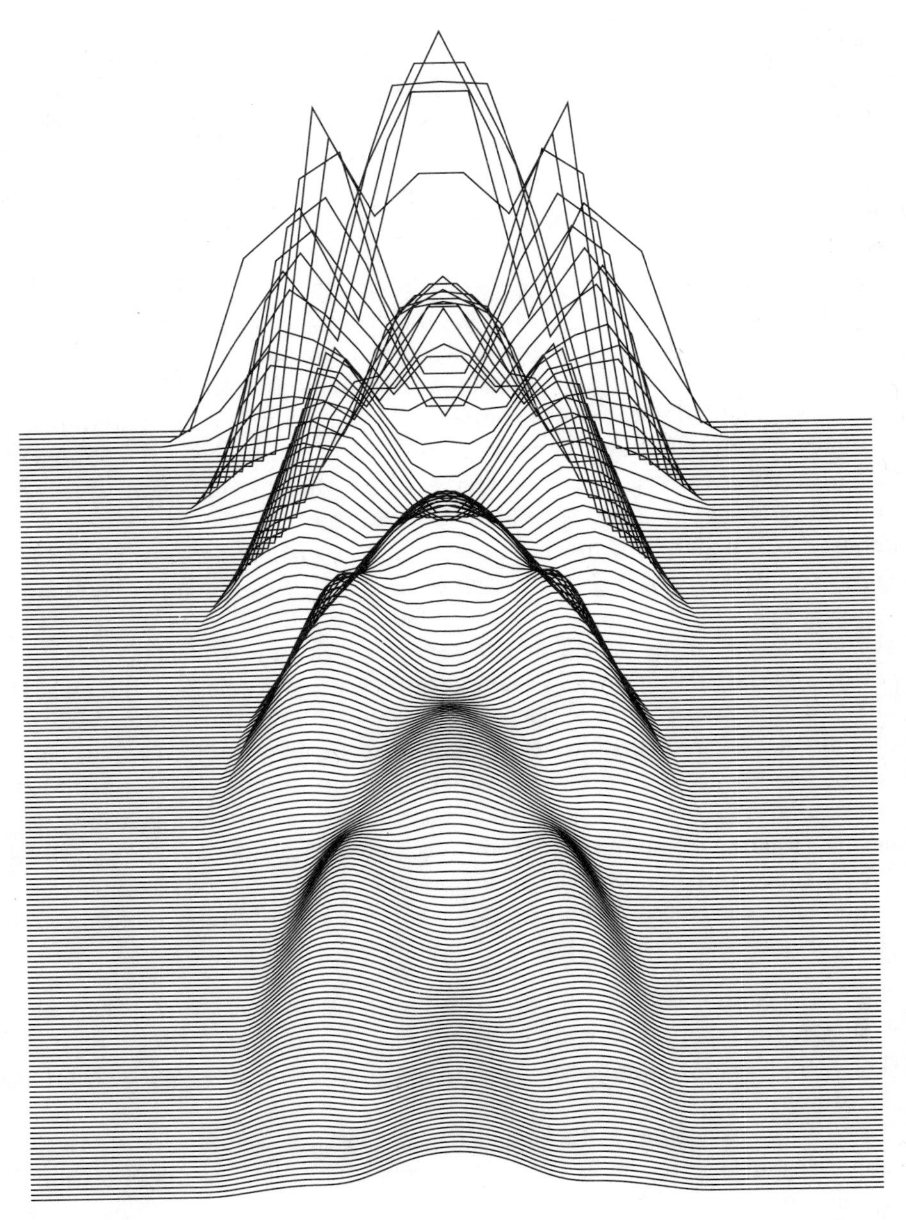

Figure 5.20 AVL distribution (subtree sizes in random AVL trees) (scaled and translated to separate curves)

for the generating function. The second part of the analysis, extracting the desired coefficients, requires advanced techniques for some types of trees.

The distinction exhibited by comparing the analysis of tree path length with tree height is essential. Generally, we can describe combinatorial parameters recursively, but "additive" parameters such as path length are much simpler to handle than "nonadditive" parameters such as height, simply because generating function constructions that correspond to combinatorial constructions can be exploited directly in the former case.

Our first theme in this chapter has been to reveal the extensive history of the analysis of trees as combinatorial objects. In recent years, general techniques have been found that help to unify some of the classical results and make it possible to learn characteristics of arbitrarily complicated new tree structures. We discuss this in detail and give examples in [13]. Certainly many important problems remain to be solved. For example, accurate results about one of the most basic of tree parameters, tree height, have only recently been derived.

Beyond classical combinatorics and specific applications in algorithmic analysis, we have endeavored to show how algorithmic applications lead to a host of new mathematical problems that have an interesting and intricate structure in their own right. The binary search tree algorithm is prototypical of many of the problems that we know how to solve: an algorithm transforms some input combinatorial object (permutations, in the case of binary search trees) into some form of tree. Then we are interested in analyzing the combinatorial properties of trees, not under the uniform model, but under the distribution induced by the transformation. Knowing detailed properties of the combinatorial structures that arise and studying effects of such transformations are the bases for our approach to the analysis of algorithms.

References

1. G. Adel'son-Vel'skii and E. Landis. *Doklady Akademii Nauk SSR* **146**, 1962, 263–266. English translation in *Soviet Math* **3**.
2. A. V. Aho and N J. A. Sloane. "Some doubly exponential sequences," *Fibonacci Quarterly* **11**, 1973, 429–437.
3. R. Bayer and E. McCreight. "Organization and maintenance of large ordered indexes," *Acta Informatica* **3**, 1972, 173–189.
4. B. Bollobás. *Random Graphs*, Academic Press, London, 1985.

5. L. Comtet. *Advanced Combinatorics*, Reidel, Dordrecht, 1974.
6. T. H. Cormen, C. E. Leiserson, and R. L. Rivest. *Introduction to Algorithms*, MIT Press, New York, 1990.
7. N. G. De Bruijn, D. E. Knuth, and S. O. Rice. "The average height of planted plane trees," in *Graph Theory and Computing*, R. C. Read, ed., Academic Press, New York, 1971.
8. L. Devroye. "A note on the expected height of binary search trees," *Journal of the ACM* **33**, 1986, 489–498.
9. L. Devroye. "Branching processes in the analysis of heights of trees," *Acta Informatica* **24**, 1987, 279–298.
10. P. Flajolet and A. Odlyzko. "The average height of binary trees and other simple trees," *Journal of Computer and System Sciences* **25**, 1982, 171–213.
11. P. Flajolet and A. Odlyzko. "Limit distributions for coefficients of iterates of polynomials with applications to combinatorial enumerations," *Mathematical Proceedings of the Cambridge Philosophical Society* **96**, 1984, 237–253.
12. P. Flajolet, J.-C. Raoult, and J. Vuillemin. "The number of registers required to evaluate arithmetic expressions," *Theoretical Computer Science* **9**, 1979, 99–125.
13. P. Flajolet and R. Sedgewick. *Analytic Combinatorics*, in preparation.
14. R. Graham, D. E. Knuth, and O. Patashnik. *Concrete Mathematics*, Addison-Wesley, Reading, MA, 1989.
15. G. H. Gonnet and R. Baeza–Yates. *Handbook of Algorithms and Data Structures*, 2nd edition, Addison-Wesley, Reading, MA, 1991.
16. I. Goulden and D. Jackson. *Combinatorial Enumeration*, John Wiley, New York, 1983.
17. L. Guibas and R. Sedgewick. "A dichromatic framework for balanced trees," in *Proceedings 19th Annual IEEE Symposium on Foundations of Computer Science*, 1978, 8–21.
18. F. Harary and E. M. Palmer. *Graphical Enumeration*, Academic Press, New York, 1973
19. C. A. R. Hoare. "Quicksort," *Computer Journal* **5**, 1962, 10–15.
20. R. Kemp. "The average number of registers needed to evaluate a binary tree optimally," *Acta Informatica* **11**, 1979, 363–372.

21. D. E. Knuth. *The Art of Computer Programming. Volume 1: Fundamental Algorithms*, Addison-Wesley, Reading, MA, 1968.
22. D. E. Knuth. *The Art of Computer Programming. Volume 3: Sorting and Searching*, Addison-Wesley, Reading, MA, 1973.
23. D. E. Knuth and A. Schönhage. "The expected linearity of a simple equivalence algorithm," *Theoretical Computer Science* **6**, 1978, 281–315.
24. H. Mahmoud. *E olution of Random Search Trees*, John Wiley, New York, 1992.
25. A. Meir and J. W. Moon. "On the altitude of nodes in random trees," *Canadian Journal of Mathematics* **30**, 1978, 997–1015.
26. A. M. Odlyzko. "Periodic oscillations of coefficients of power series that satisfy functional equations," *Ad ances in Mathematics* **44**, 1982, 180–205.
27. G. Polya and R. C. Read. *Combinatorial Enumeration of Groups, Graphs, and Chemical Compounds*, Springer-Verlag, New York, 1987. (English translation of original paper in *Acta Mathematica* **68**, 1937, 145–254.)
28. R. C. Read. "The coding of various kinds of unlabelled trees," in *Graph Theory and Computing*, R. C. Read, ed., Academic Press, New York, 1971.
29. R. Sedgewick. *Algorithms*, 2nd edition, Addison-Wesley, Reading, MA, 1988.
30. J. S. Vitter and P. Flajolet, "Analysis of algorithms and data structures," in *Handbook of Theoretical Computer Science A: Algorithms and Complexity*, J. van Leeuwen, ed., Elsevier, Amsterdam, 1990, 431–524.

CHAPTER SIX

PERMUTATIONS

COMBINATORIAL algorithms often deal only with the relative order of a linear array of N elements; thus we can view them as operating on the numbers 1 through N in some order. Such an ordering is called a *permutation*, a familiar combinatorial object with a wealth of interesting properties. We first encountered permutations in Chapter 1, where we discussed the analysis of two important comparison-based sorting algorithms using random permutations as an input model. In this chapter, we survey combinatorial properties of permutations, show how they relate in a natural way to fundamental sorting algorithms, and consider average-case analysis, using probability, cumulative, and bivariate generating functions.

We cover the analysis of basic sorting methods such as insertion sort, selection sort, and bubble sort, and discuss a variety of other algorithms that are of importance in practice, including Shellsort, priority queue algorithms, and rearrangement algorithms. The correspondence between these methods and basic properties of permutations is perhaps to be expected, but it underscores the importance of fundamental combinatorial mechanisms in the analysis of algorithms.

We begin the chapter by defining several of the most important properties of permutations and considering some examples as well as some relationships between them. We consider both properties that arise immediately when analyzing basic sorting algorithms and properties that are of independent combinatorial interest.

Following this, we consider different ways to represent permutations, particularly representations implied by inversions and cycles and a two-dimensional representation that exposes relationships between a permutation and its inverse. This representation also helps define explicit relationships between permutations, binary search trees, and "heap-ordered trees" and reduces the analysis of certain properties of permutations to the study of properties of trees.

Next, we consider enumeration problems on permutations, where we want to count permutations satisfying certain properties. Such problems can be attacked in a straightforward manner using generating functions (including the symbolic method on labelled objects). Specifically, we consider properties related to the "cycle structure" of the permutations in some detail.

Following the same general structure as Chapter 5, we proceed next to analysis of parameters. For trees, we considered path length, height, number of leaves and other parameters. For permutations, we consider properties such as the number of runs and the number of inversions, many of which can be easily analyzed. As usual, we are interested in the expected "cost" of permutations under various measures relating to their properties, assuming all permutations equally likely. This can sometimes be computed by finding an explicit expression for the number of permutations of length N with cost k, though we emphasize shortcuts based on generating functions, like the use of CGFs.

We consider the analysis of parameters in the context of two fundamental sorting methods, insertion sort and selection sort, and their relationship to two fundamental characteristics of permutations, inversions and left-to-right minima. We show how CGFs lead to relatively straightforward analyses of these algorithms. We also consider the problem of permuting an array in place and its relationship to the cycle structure of permutations. Some of these analyses lead to familiar generating functions for special numbers from Chapter 3, for example, Stirling and harmonic numbers.

Problems analogous to height in trees will also be discussed in this chapter, including the problems of finding the average length of the shortest and longest cycles in a random permutation. As with tree height, we can set up functional equations on indexed "vertical" generating functions, but asymptotic estimates are best developed using more advanced tools.

The study of properties of permutations illustrates that there is a fine dividing line indeed between trivial and difficult problems in the analysis of algorithms. Some of the problems that we consider can be easily solved with elementary arguments; other (similar) problems are not elementary but can be studied with generating functions and the asymptotic methods we have been considering; still other (still similar) problems require advanced complex analysis or probabilistic methods.

6.1 Basic Properties of Permutations. Permutations may be represented in many ways. The most straightforward is simply a rearrangement of the numbers 1 through N, as in the following example.

index	1	2	3	4	5	6	7	8	9	10	11	12	13	14	15
permutation	9	14	4	1	12	2	10	13	5	6	11	3	8	15	7

One way to think of a permutation is as a specification of a rearrangement: "1 goes to 9, 2 goes to 14, 3 goes to 4," and so on. Obviously, there are $N!$ different permutations of N elements. There are a number of basic characteristics of permutations that not only are of inherent interest from a combinatorial standpoint, but also are of importance in the study of a number of important algorithms. In this section, we define these properties and give some basic results; in later sections we will discuss how the results are derived and relate them to the analysis of algorithms.

We will be studying inversions, left-to-right minima and maxima, cycles, rises, runs, falls, peaks, valleys, and increasing subsequences in permutations; inverses of permutations; and special types of permutations called involutions and derangements. These are all explained, in terms of a permutation $p_1 p_2 p_3 \ldots p_N$ of the integers 1 to N, in the definitions and text below, also with reference to the sample permutation above.

Definition *An* inversion *is a pair $i < j$ with $p_i > p_j$. If q_j is the number of $i < j$ with $p_i > p_j$, then $q_1 q_2 \ldots q_N$ is called the* inversion table *of $p_1 p_2 \ldots p_N$. We use the notation $\sigma(p)$ to denote the number of inversions in a permutation p, the sum of the entries in the inversion table.*

The sample permutation given above has 49 inversions, as evidenced by adding the elements in its inversion table.

index	1	2	3	4	5	6	7	8	9	10	11	12	13	14	15
permutation	9	14	4	1	12	2	10	13	5	6	11	3	8	15	7
inversion table	0	0	2	3	1	4	2	1	5	5	3	9	6	0	8

By definition, the entries in the inversion table $q_1 q_2 \ldots q_N$ of a permutation satisfy $0 \le q_j < j$ for all j from 1 to N. As we will see in §6.3, a unique permutation can be constructed from any sequence of numbers satisfying these constraints. That is, there is a 1-1 correspondence between inversion tables of size N and permutations of N elements (and there are $N!$ of each). That correspondence will be exploited later in this chapter in the analysis of basic sorting methods such as insertion sort and bubble sort.

Definition *A* left-to-right maximum *is an index i with $p_j < p_i$ for all $j < i$. We use the notation $\lambda(p)$ to refer to the number of left-to-right maxima in a permutation p.*

The first element in every permutation is a left-to-right maximum; so is the largest element. If the largest element is the first, then it is the only left-to-right maximum; otherwise there are at least two (the first and the largest). In general, there could be as many as N left-to-right maxima (in the permutation `1 2 ... N`). There are three in the sample permutation given above, at positions 1, 2, and 14. Note that each left-to-right maximum corresponds to a zero in the inversion table (no larger elements to the left), so counting left-to-right maxima in permutations is the same as counting zeros in inversion tables. Left-to-right minima and right-to-left minima and maxima are defined analogously. In probability theory, left-to-right maxima are also known as *records* because they represent new "record" high values that are encountered when moving from left to right through the permutation.

Exercise 6.1 Explain how to compute left-to-right minima, right-to-left minima, and right-to-left maxima from the inversion table.

Definition *A* cycle *is an index sequence* $i_1 i_2 \ldots i_t$ *with* $p_{i_1} = i_2$, $p_{i_2} = i_3$, $\ldots$, $p_{i_t} = i_1$. *We use the notation* $(\, i_1 \; i_2 \; \ldots i_t \,)$ *to specify a cycle. An element in a permutation of length N belongs to a unique cycle of length from 1 to N; permutations of length N are comprised of sets of from 1 to N cycles. A* derangement *is a permutation with no cycles of length 1.*

Our sample permutation is made up of four cycles (one of which is of length 1) and is not a derangement.

index	1	2	3	4	5	6	7	8	9	10	11	12	13	14	15
permutation	9	14	4	1	12	2	10	13	5	6	11	3	8	15	7
cycles	(1 9 5 12 3 4)					(2 14 15 7 10 6)						(8 13)		(11)	

This might be read as "1 goes to 9 goes to 5 goes to 12 goes to 3 goes to 4 goes to 1," and so on. The longest cycle in this permutation is of length 6 (there are two such cycles); the shortest is of length 1. There are t equivalent ways to list any cycle of length t, and the cycles comprising a permutation may be themselves listed in any order. That is, as combinatorial objects, permutations are equivalent to the "sets of cycles" that we examined in §3.9.

If we choose to list the largest element in each cycle (the *cycle leaders*) first and then take the cycles in increasing order of their leaders, then we get a canonical form that has an interesting property: *the parentheses are unnecessary*, since each left-to-right maximum in the canonical form corresponds to a new cycle.

cycles	(1 9 5 12 3 4) (2 14 15 7 10 6) (8 13) (11)
canonical form	11 12 3 4 1 9 5 13 8 15 7 10 6 2 14

This constitutes a combinatorial proof that cycles and left-to-right maxima are identically distributed for random permutations, a fact we also will verify analytically in this chapter. In combinatorics, this is known as "Foata's correspondence," or the "fundamental correspondence."

Exercise 6.2 How many different ways are there to write the sample permutation in cycle notation?

Exercise 6.3 How many permutations of $2n$ elements have exactly two cycles, each of length n? How many have n cycles, each of length 2?

Exercise 6.4 Which permutations of n elements have the maximum number of different representations with cycles?

Definition *The* inverse *of a permutation* $p_1 \ldots p_N$ *is the permutation* $q_1 \ldots q_N$ *with* $q_{p_i} = p_{q_i} = i$. *An* involution *is a permutation that is its own inverse:* $p_{p_i} = i$.

For our sample permutation, the 1 is in position 4, the 2 in position 6, the 3 in position 12, the 4 in position 3, and so forth.

index	1	2	3	4	5	6	7	8	9	10	11	12	13	14	15
permutation	9	14	4	1	12	2	10	13	5	6	11	3	8	15	7
inverse	4	6	12	3	9	10	15	13	1	7	11	5	8	2	14

By the definition, every permutation has a unique inverse, and the inverse of the inverse is the original permutation. The following example of an involution and its representation in cycle form expose the important properties of involutions.

index	1	2	3	4	5	6	7	8	9	10	11	12	13	14	15
involution	9	2	12	4	7	10	5	13	1	6	11	3	8	15	14

cycles (1 9) (2) (3 12) (4) (5 7) (6 10) (8 13) (11) (14 15)

Clearly, a permutation is an involution if and only if all its cycles are of length 1 or 2. Determining a precise estimate for the number of involutions of length N turns out to be an interesting problem that illustrates many of the tools that we consider in this book.

Definition *A* rise *is an occurrence of* $p_i < p_{i+1}$. *A* fall *is an occurrence of* $p_{i-1} > p_i$. *A* run *is a maximal increasing contiguous subsequence in the permutation. A* peak *is an occurrence of* $p_{i-1} < p_i > p_{i+1}$. *A* valley *is an occurrence of* $p_{i-1} > p_i < p_{i+1}$. *A* double rise *is an occurrence of* $p_{i-1} < p_i < p_{i+1}$. *A* double fall *is an occurrence of* $p_{i-1} > p_i > p_{i+1}$. *We use the notation* $\alpha(p)$ *to refer to the number of rises in a permutation* p.

In any permutation, the number of rises plus the number of falls is the length minus 1. The number of runs is one greater than the number of falls, since every run except the last one in a permutation must end with a fall. These facts and others are clear if we consider a representation of $N-1$ plus signs and minus signs corresponding to the sign of the difference between successive elements in the permutation; falls correspond to + and rises correspond to -.

permutation	9	14	4	1	12	2	10	13	5	6	11	3	8	15	7
rises/falls		–	+	+	–	+	–	–	+	–	–	+	–	–	+

This representation tells us that there are eight rises and six falls. Also, the plus signs mark the ends of runs (except the last), so there are seven runs. Double rises, valleys, peaks, and double falls correspond to occurrences of – – , + –, – + , and + + (respectively). This permutation has three double rises, five valleys, four peaks, and one double fall.

Definition *An* increasing subsequence *in a permutation is an increasing sequence of indices* $i_1, i_2, \ldots, i_k$ *with* $p_{i_1} < p_{i_2} < \ldots < p_{i_k}$.

By convention, the empty subsequence is considered to be "increasing." Thus, the increasing permutation `1 2 3 ... N` has 2^N increasing subsequences, one corresponding to every set of the indices, and the decreasing permutation `N N-1 N-2 ... 1` has just $N+1$ increasing subsequences. We may account for the increasing subsequences in a permutation in a manner similar to inversions: we keep a table $s_1 s_2 \ldots s_N$ with s_i the number of increasing subsequences that begin at position i. Our sample permutation has 9 increasing subsequences starting at position 1, 2 starting at position 2, and so forth.

index	1	2	3	4	5	6	7	8	9	10	11	12	13	14	15
permutation	9	14	4	1	12	2	10	13	5	6	11	3	8	15	7
subseq. table	9	2	33	72	4	34	5	2	8	7	2	5	2	1	1

For example, the fifth entry in this table corresponds to the four increasing subsequences 12, 12 13, 12 15, and 12 13 15. Adding the entries in this table (plus one for the empty subsequence) shows that the number of increasing subsequences in our sample permutation is 188.

Exercise 6.5 Write a program that computes the number of increasing subsequences in a given permutation in polynomial time.

Table 6.1 enumerates all of these properties for all of the permutations of four elements, and Table 6.2 gives their values for several random permutations of nine elements. Close examination of Tables 6.1 and 6.2 will reveal characteristics of these various properties of permutations and relationships among them that we will be proving in this chapter. For example, we have already mentioned that the distribution for the number of left-to-right maxima is the same as the distribution for the number of cycles.

perm.	*subseqs.*	*invs.*	*l-r max*	*cycles*	*max cyc.*	*runs*	*inv. table*	*inverse*
1234	15	0	4	4	1	1	0000	1234
1243	13	1	3	3	2	2	0001	1243
1324	12	1	3	3	2	2	0010	1324
1342	9	2	3	2	3	2	0002	1423
1423	9	2	2	2	3	2	0011	1342
1432	7	3	2	3	3	3	0012	1432
2134	11	1	3	2	3	2	0100	2134
2143	9	2	2	2	2	3	0101	2143
2314	9	2	3	2	3	2	0020	3124
2341	8	3	3	1	4	2	0003	4123
2413	7	4	2	1	4	2	0013	3142
2431	6	4	2	2	3	3	0013	4132
3124	8	1	2	2	3	2	0010	2314
3142	7	3	2	1	4	3	0002	2413
3214	7	3	2	3	2	3	0120	3214
3241	6	4	2	2	3	3	0003	4213
3412	6	4	2	2	2	2	0022	3412
3421	5	5	2	1	4	3	0023	4312
4123	8	3	1	1	4	2	0111	2341
4132	7	4	1	2	3	3	0112	2431
4213	6	4	1	2	3	3	0122	3142
4231	5	5	1	3	2	3	0113	4231
4312	5	5	1	1	4	3	0122	3421
4321	4	6	1	2	2	4	0123	4321

Table 6.1 Basic properties of all permutations of four elements

Intuitively, we would expect rises and falls to be equally likely, so that there should be about $N/2$ of each in a random permutation of length N. Similarly, we would expect about half the elements to the left of each element to be larger, so the number of inversions should be about $\sum_{1\le i\le N} i/2$, which is about $N^2/4$. We will see how to quantify these arguments precisely, to compute other moments for these quantities, and to study left-to-right minima and cycles using similar techniques.

Of course, if we ask more detailed questions, then we are led to more difficult analytic problems. For example, what proportion of permutations are involutions? Derangements? How many permutations have no cycles with more than three elements? How many have no cycles with fewer than three elements? What is the average value of the *maximum* element in the inversion table? What is the expected number of increasing subsequences in a permutation? What is the average length of the longest cycle in a permutation? The longest run? Such questions arise in the study of specific algorithms and have also been addressed in the combinatorics literature.

In this chapter, we answer many of these questions. Some of the average-case results that we will develop are summarized in Table 6.3. Some of these analyses are quite straightforward, but others require more advanced tools, as we will see when we consider the use of generating functions to derive these and other results throughout this chapter. We also will consider relationships to sorting algorithms in some detail.

6.2 Algorithms on Permutations.

Permutations, by their very nature, arise directly or indirectly in the analysis of a wide variety of algorithms. Permutations specify the way data objects are ordered, and many algorithms need to process data in some specified order. Typically, a complex

permutation	*invs.*	*l-r max.*	*cycles*	*runs*	*max. cyc.*	*inv. table*	*inverse*
961534872	21	1	2	6	7	012233127	395642871
412356798	4	5	5	3	4	011100001	234156798
732586941	19	3	4	6	3	012102058	932846157
236794815	15	5	2	3	7	000003174	812693475
162783954	13	5	4	5	4	001003045	136982457
259148736	16	3	2	4	4	000321253	418529763

Table 6.2 Basic properties of some random permutations of nine elements

algorithm will invoke a sorting procedure at some stage, and the direct relationship to sorting algorithms is motivation enough for studying properties of permutations in detail. We also consider a number of related examples.

Sorting. As we saw in Chapter 1, we very often assume that the input to a sorting method is a list of randomly ordered records with distinct keys. Keys in random order will in particular be produced by any process that draws them *independently* from an arbitrary continuous distribution. This makes the analysis of sorting methods essentially equivalent to the analysis of properties of permutations. Beginning with the comprehensive coverage in Knuth [10], there is a vast literature on this topic (see, for example, the bibliography in Gonnet and Baeza-Yates [5]). There are a broad variety of sorting algorithms, appropriate for differing situations, and the analysis of algorithms has played an essential role in our understanding of their comparative performance. In this chapter, we will study direct connections between some of the most basic properties of permutations and some fundamental elementary sorting methods.

Exercise 6.6 Let a_1, a_2, and a_3 be "random" numbers between 0 and 1 produced independently as values of a random variable X satisfying the continuous distribution $F(x) = \Pr\{X \le x\}$. Show that the probability of the event $a_1 < a_2 < a_3$ is $1/3!$. Generalize to any ordering pattern and any number of keys.

Rearrangement. As mentioned above, one way to think of a permutation is as a specification of a rearrangement to be made. This leads to a direct connection with the practice of sorting. Sorting algorithms are often imple-

	2	3	4	5	6	7	*exact average*	*asymptotic estimate*
permutations	2	6	24	120	720	5040	1	1
inversions	1	9	72	600	5400	52920	$N(N-1)/4$	$\sim N^2/4$
l-r maxima	3	11	50	274	1764	13068	H_N	$\sim \ln N$
cycles	3	11	50	274	1764	13068	H_N	$\sim \ln N$
rises	6	36	48	300	2160	17640	$(N-1)/2$	$\sim N/2$
incr. subseqs.	5	27	169	1217	7939	72871	$\sum_{k\ge0}\binom{N}{k}/k!$	$O(e^{\sqrt{N}})$

Table 6.3 Cumulative counts and averages for properties of permutations

mented to refer to the array being sorted indirectly: rather than moving elements around to put them in order, we compute the permutation that would put the elements in order. Virtually any sorting algorithm can be implemented in this way: for the methods we have seen, we maintain an "index" array `p[1]...p[N]` that will contain the permutation. Initially, we set `p[i]=i`, then we modify the sorting code to refer to `a[p[i]]` instead of `a[i]` for any comparison, but to refer to `p` instead of `a` when doing any data movement. These changes ensure that, at any point during the execution of the algorithm, `a[p[1]], a[p[2]], ..., a[p[N]]` is identical to `a[1], a[2], ..., a[N]` in the original algorithm.

For example, if a sorting method is used in this way to put the sample input file

index	1	2	3	4	5	6	7	8	9	10	11	12	13	14	15
keys	29	41	77	26	58	59	97	82	12	44	63	31	53	23	93

into increasing order, it produces the permutation

index	1	2	3	4	5	6	7	8	9	10	11	12	13	14	15
permutation	9	14	4	1	12	2	10	13	5	6	11	3	8	15	7

as the result. One way of interpreting this is as instructions that the original input can be printed out (or accessed) in sorted order by first printing out the ninth element (12), then the fourteenth (23), then the fourth (26), then the first (29), etc. In the present context, we note that the permutation computed is the inverse of the permutation that represents the initial ordering of the keys, for our example the permutation

```
4  6  12  3  9  10  15  13  1  7  11  5  8  2  14 .
```

That is, sorting amounts to computing the inverse of a permutation.

If an output array `b[1]...b[N]` is available, the program that actually finishes a sort is trivial:

```
for i := 1 to N do b[i] := a[p[i]].
```

For sorting applications where data movement is expensive (for example, when records are much larger than keys) this change can be very important. If space is not available for the output array, it is still possible to do the rearrangement "in place"—we will examine an algorithm for doing so later in this chapter.

It is amusing to note that, of course, the result of the sort can be an involution. For example, the permutation

```
9  2  12  4  7  10  5  13  1  6  11  3  8  15  11
```

not only represents the initial ordering of the input file

```
58  23  77  29  44  59  31  82  12  41  63  26  53  97  93
```

but also is the permutation that specifies how to rearrange the file to sort it. That is, the permutation can be interpreted in two ways: not only is it the case that 58 is the ninth smallest element, 23 the second smallest, 77 the twelfth smallest, and so on, but also it is the case that the ninth element in the file (12) is the smallest, the second element (26) is the second smallest, the twelfth element (29) is the third smallest, and so on.

Randomization. If the assumption that the inputs are not randomly ordered is not necessarily justified, we can use the method shown in Program 6.1 to create a random ordering, and then sort the array. This *randomization technique* assumes a procedure that can produce a "random" integer in a given range (such programs are well studied; see Knuth [9]). Each of the $N!$ orderings of the input is equally likely to occur: the ith time through the loop, any one of i distinct rearrangements could happen, for a grand total of $2 \cdot 3 \cdot 4 \cdot \ldots \cdot N = N!$. As mentioned in Chapter 1, from the standpoint of the analysis of algorithms, randomizing the order of the inputs in this way turns any sorting algorithm into a "probabilistic algorithm" whose performance characteristics are precisely described by the average-case results that we study. Indeed, this is one of the very first probabilistic algorithms, as it was proposed for Quicksort by Hoare in 1960 (see Chapter 1).

```
for i := 2 to N do
  begin
  t := randominteger(1, i);
  v := a[t]; a[t]  := a[i]; a[i]:= v;
  end
```

Program 6.1 Randomly permuting an array

Priority queues. It is not always necessary that an algorithm rearrange its inputs into sorted order before it examines any of them. Another widely used option is to develop a data structure, consisting of records with keys, that supports two operations: *insert* a new item into the data structure and *remove smallest*, which retrieves the record with the smallest key from the data structure. Such a data structure is called a *priority queue*. Priority queue algorithms are closely related to sorting algorithms: for example, we could use any priority queue algorithm to implement a sorting algorithm simply by inserting all the records, then removing them all. (They will come out in increasing order.) But priority queue algorithms are much more general, and they are widely used, both because the insert and remove operations can be intermixed, and because several other operations can be supported as well. The study of the properties of sophisticated priority queue algorithms is among the most important and most challenging areas of research in the analysis of algorithms. In this chapter, we will examine the relationship between a fundamental priority queue structure (heap-ordered trees), and binary search trees, which is made plain by the association of both with permutations.

6.3 Representations of Permutations. While it is normally most convenient to represent permutations as we have been doing—as rearrangements of the numbers 1 through N—many other ways to represent permutations are often appropriate. We will see that various different representations can show relationships among basic properties of permutations and can expose essential properties germane to some particular analysis or algorithm. Since there are $N!$ different permutations of N elements, any set of $N!$ different combinatorial objects might be used to represent permutations—we will examine several useful ones in this section.

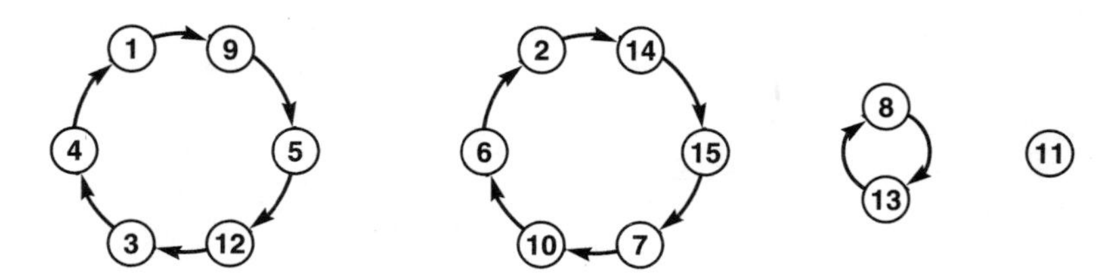

Figure 6.1 Graph representation of a permutation

Cycle structure. Considering a permutation $p_1p_2 \dots p_N$ as a function mapping i to p_i leads immediately to a representation as a graph, as shown in Figure 6.1. This representation is of interest because it makes the cycle structure obvious. Also, the corresponding structure for general functions has many interesting properties, which we will study in Chapter 8.

Linear representation. The fundamental correspondence between a permutation and the canonical form of its cycle structure representation defines a "representation" of permutations: as discussed in the previous section, we can represent a permutation by writing its cycles in a canonical linear form, obtained by identifying the "cycle leader" (the largest element) for each cycle, then writing each cycle in the order where its cycle leader appears first, putting the cycles in increasing order of their cycle leaders:

permutation	9	14	4	1	12	2	10	13	5	6	11	3	8	15	7
cycle form	11	12	3	4	1	9	5	13	8	15	7	10	6	2	14

Exercise 6.7 We could also put the cycles in increasing order of their smallest elements, writing the smallest element in the cycle first. Give this representation for our sample permutation.

Exercise 6.8 Write a program that will compute the canonical cycle representation corresponding to a given permutation.

Exercise 6.9 Write a program that will compute the permutation corresponding to a given canonical cycle representation.

Inversion tables. A one-to-one correspondence between permutations and lists of N integers $q_1q_2 \dots q_N$ with $0 \le q_i < i$ is easy to establish. Given a permutation, its inversion table is such a list; and given such a list, the corresponding permutation can be constructed from right to left: for i decreasing from N down to 1, set p_i to be the q_ith largest of the integers not yet used. Consider the example:

index	1	2	3	4	5	6	7	8	9	10	11	12	13	14	15
inversion table	0	0	2	3	1	4	2	1	5	5	3	9	6	0	8
permutation	9	14	4	1	12	2	10	13	5	6	11	3	8	15	7

The permutation can be constructed from the inversion table by moving right to left: 7 is the eighth largest of the integers from 1 to 15, 15 is the largest of the remaining integers, 8 is the sixth largest of what's left, and so forth. There are $N!$ inversion tables (and permutations!) since there are i possibilities for the ith entry.

This correspondence is important in analysis since a random permutation is equivalent to a "random" inversion table, built by making its jth entry a random integer in the range 0 to $j-1$. We will make use of this fact when setting up GFs for inversions and left-to-right maxima that nicely decompose in product form.

Exercise 6.10 Give an *efficient* algorithm for computing the inversion table corresponding to a given permutation, and another algorithm for computing the permutation corresponding to a given inversion table.

Exercise 6.11 Another way to define inversion tables is with q_i equal to the number of integers to the left of i in the permutation that are greater. Prove the one-to-one correspondence for this kind of inversion table.

Lattice representation. Figure 6.2 shows a two-dimensional representation that is useful for studying a number of properties of permutations: the permutation $p_1p_2\ldots p_N$ is represented by labelling the cell at row p_i and column i with the number p_i for each i. Reading these numbers from right to left gives back the permutation. There is one label in each row and in each column, so each cell in the lattice corresponds to a unique pair of labels: the one in its row and the one in its column. If one member of the pair is below and the other to the right, then that pair is an inversion in the permutation, and the corresponding cell is marked in Figure 6.2. Note in particular that the diagram for the permutation and its inverse are

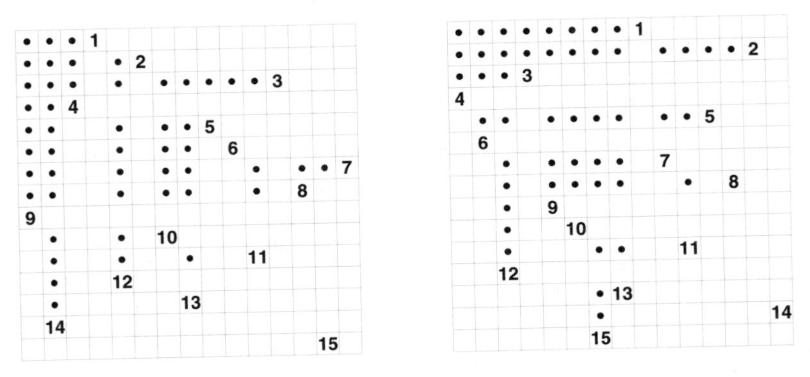

Figure 6.2 Lattice representation of a permutation and its inverse

simply transposes of one another—this is an elementary proof that every permutation has the same number of inversions as does its inverse.

Exercise 6.12 Show that the number of ways to place k mutually nonattacking rooks in an N-by-N chessboard is $\binom{N}{k}^2 k!$.

Exercise 6.13 Suppose that we mark cells whose marks are above and to the left in the lattice representation. How many cells are marked? Answer the same question for the other two possibilities ("above and right" and "below and left").

Exercise 6.14 Show that the lattice representation of an involution is symmetric about the main diagonal.

Binary search trees. A direct relationship between permutations and binary search trees is shown in Figure 6.3. Recall from §5.5 that each node in a binary search tree (BST) has a key, a (possibly null) left link that points to a BST comprised of smaller keys, and a (possibly empty) right link that points to a BST comprised of larger keys. In Chapter 5, we analyzed properties of trees built by using Program 5.3 to insert keys from a random permutation successively into an initially empty tree. Figure 6.3 illustrates a direct correspondence between lattice representations of permutations and BSTs: each label corresponds to a node with its row number as the key value, and left and right subtrees built from the parts of the lattice above and below (respectively) the label. Specifically, the binary search tree corresponding to rows $l, l+1, \ldots, r$, with the leftmost (lowest column number) mark in row k, is defined recursively by a node with key k, left subtree corresponding to rows $l, l+1, \ldots, k-1$, and right subtree

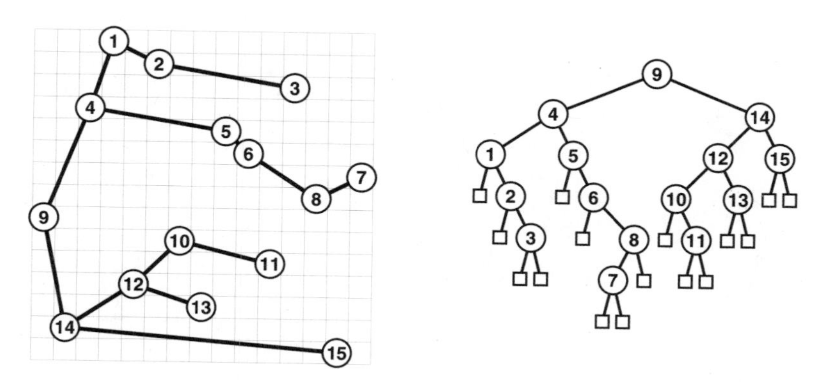

Figure 6.3 Binary search tree corresponding to a permutation

corresponding to rows $k+1$, $k+2$, ..., r. Note that many permutations might correspond to the same binary search tree: interchanging columns corresponding to a node above and a node below any node will change the permutation, not the tree. Indeed, in Chapter 3, we saw that the number of different binary tree structures is counted by the Catalan numbers, which are relatively small (about $4^N/N\sqrt{\pi N}$) compared to $N!$, so a large number of permutations certainly must correspond to each tree. The analytic results on BSTs in the previous chapter might be characterized as a study of the nature of this relationship.

Exercise 6.15 List five permutations that correspond to the BST in Figure 6.3.

Heap-ordered trees. A tree can also be built from the lattice representation in a similar manner involving columns, as illustrated in Figure 6.4. These trees, in which the key at the root has a smaller key than the keys in the subtrees, are called *heap-ordered* trees (HOTs). In the present context, they are important because properties of permutations that are of interest are easily seen to be tree properties. For example, a node with two nonempty subtrees in the tree corresponds to a valley in the permutation, and leaves correspond to peaks.

Such trees are also of interest as explicit data structures, to implement priority queues. The smallest key is at the root, so the "remove smallest" operation can be implemented by (recursively) replacing the node at the root with the node at the root of the subtree with the smaller key. The "insert" operation can be implemented by (recursively) inserting the new

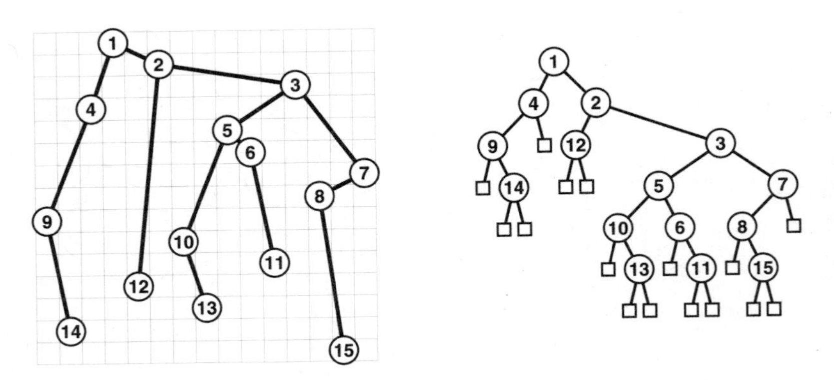

Figure 6.4 Heap-ordered tree corresponding to a permutation

node in the right subtree of the root, unless it has a smaller key than the node at the root, in which case it becomes the root, with the old root as its left subtree and a null right subtree.

Combinatorially, it is important to observe that an HOT is a complete encoding of a unique permutation (contrary to BSTs). See Vuillemin [17] for detailed information on HOTs, including other applications.

Direct counts of HOTs. To complete the cycle, it is instructive to consider the problem of enumerating HOTs directly (we already know that there are $N!$ of them). Let $\mathcal{H}$ be the set of HOTs and consider the EGF

$$H(z) = \sum_{t \in \mathcal{H}} \frac{z^{|t|}}{|t|!}.$$

Now, every HOT with $|t_L| + |t_R| + 1$ nodes can be constructed in a unique way by combining any HOT of size $|t_L|$ on the left with any HOT of size $|t_R|$ on the right, assigning the label "1" to the root, and assigning labels to the subtrees by dividing the $|t_L| + |t_R|$ labels into one set of size $|t_L|$ and one set of size $|t_R|$, sorting each set, and assigning them to the subtrees in order of their index. This is essentially a restatement of the labelled product construct described in Chapter 3. In terms of the EGF, this leads to the equation

$$H(z) = \sum_{t_L \in \mathcal{H}} \sum_{t_R \in \mathcal{H}} \binom{|t_L| + |t_R|}{|t_L|} \frac{z^{|t_L|+|t_R|+1}}{(|t_L| + |t_R| + 1)!}.$$

Differentiating both sides immediately gives

$$H'(z) = H^2(z) \qquad \text{or} \qquad H(z) = 1 + \int_0^z H^2(t)dt.$$

This formula is also available directly via the symbolic method for labelled objects (see Chapter 3 and [4]). Two basic operations explain the formula: labelling the root 1 corresponds to integration, and combining two subtrees corresponds to a product. Now, the solution to the differential equation is $H(z) = 1/(1 - z)$, which checks with our knowledge that there are $N!$ HOTs on N nodes.

Similar computations will give access to statistics on parameters of permutations that are characterized on the HOT representation (e. g., peaks, valleys, rises, and falls), as introduced in the exercises below and discussed further in §6.5.

Exercise 6.16 Characterize the nodes in an HOT that correspond to rises, double rises, falls, and double falls in permutations.

Exercise 6.17 How many permutations are strictly alternating, with p_{i-1} and p_{i+1} either both less or both greater than p_i for $1 < i < N$?

Exercise 6.18 List five permutations corresponding to the HOT in Figure 6.4.

Exercise 6.19 Let $K(z) = z/(1-z)$ be the EGF for nonempty HOTs. Give a direct argument showing that $K'(z) = 1 + 2K(z) + K^2(z)$.

Exercise 6.20 Use an argument similar to HOT enumeration by EGF to derive the differential equation for the exponential CGF for internal path length in binary search trees (see the proof of Theorem 5.5 and §6.5).

How many permutations correspond to a given binary tree shape via the HOT or BST construction? This turns out to be expressed with a simple formula. Given a tree t, let $f(t)$ be the number of ways to label it as an HOT. By the argument just given, this function satisfies the recursive equation

$$f(t) = \binom{|t_L| + |t_R|}{|t_L|} f(t_L) f(t_R).$$

The same formula holds if f is counting the number of permutations corresponding to a BST since there is a unique label for the root ($|t_L|+1$) and an unrestricted partition of the rest of the labels for the subtrees. Noting that the number of nodes in t is $|t_L| + |t_R| + 1$, and dividing both sides by that quantity, we get

$$\frac{f(|t_L| + |t_R| + 1)}{(|t_L| + |t_R| + 1)!} = \frac{1}{|t_L| + |t_R| + 1} \frac{f(t_L)}{t_L!} \frac{f(t_R)}{t_R!}.$$

This leads directly to:

Theorem 6.1 (*Frequency of HOTs and BSTs*) *The frequency of tree t, as either an HOT or BST shape, is*

$$f(t) = |t|!/(|u_1||u_2| \cdots |u_{|t|}|).$$

where $u_1, \ldots, u_{|t|}$ are the subtrees rooted at each of the nodes of $|t|$. In other words, $f(t)$ is the number of ways to label t as an HOT using the labels $1 \ldots |t|$ and the number of permutations of $1 \ldots |t|$ that lead to a BST with the shape of t when built with the standard algorithm.

Proof. Simply iterate the recursive formula given above, using the initial condition that $f(t) = 1$ for $|t| = 1$. ∎

For example, the number of ways to label the HOT in Figure 6.4 is $15!/(15 \cdot 3 \cdot 2 \cdot 11 \cdot 9 \cdot 5 \cdot 2 \cdot 2 \cdot 3) = 1223040$.

Notice that the fact that frequencies for HOTs and BSTs coincide is also to be expected combinatorially. The two correspondences exemplified by Figures 6.3 and 6.4 are structurally the same, with only the axes being interchanged. In other words, a stronger property holds: the BST corresponding to a permutation has the same shape as the HOT corresponding to the inverse permutation (but not the same labels).

Exercise 6.21 How many permutations correspond to the BST in Figure 6.3?

Exercise 6.22 Characterize the binary trees of size N for which the frequencies are smallest and those for which the frequencies are largest.

6.4 Enumeration Problems. Many of the problems listed in the introductory section of this chapter are enumeration problems. That is, we want to know the number of permutations that satisfy a certain property for various properties of interest. Equivalently, dividing by $N!$ gives the probability that a random permutation satisfies the property of interest. We work with the EGF that enumerates the permutations, which is equivalent to the OGF for the probability.

A variety of interesting properties of permutations can be expressed in terms of simple restrictions on the cycle lengths, so we begin by considering such problems in detail. We are interested in knowing, for a given parameter k, exact counts of the number of permutations having (*i*) cycles only of length equal to k, (*ii*) no cycles of length greater than k, and (*iii*)

cycle lengths	1	2	3	4	5	6	7	8	9
all $=1$	1	1	1	1	1	1	1	1	1
$=2$	0	1	0	3	0	15	0	105	0
$=3$	0	0	2	0	0	40	0	0	2240
$=4$	0	0	0	6	0	0	0	1260	0
<3 (*involutions*)	1	2	4	10	26	76	232	764	2620
<4	1	2	6	18	66	276	1212	5916	31068
<5	1	2	6	24	96	456	2472	14736	92304
>1 (*derangements*)	0	1	2	9	44	265	1854	14833	133496
>2	0	0	2	6	24	160	1140	8988	80864
>3	0	0	0	6	24	120	720	6300	58464
no restrictions	1	2	6	24	120	720	5040	40320	362880

Table 6.4 Enumeration of permutations with cycle length restrictions

no cycles of length less than k. In this section, we develop analytic results for each of these enumeration problems. Table 6.4 gives the counts for $N \le 10$ and $k \le 4$.

Cycles of equal length. How many permutations of size N consist solely of cycles of length k? We start with a simple combinatorial argument for $k = 2$. There are zero permutations consisting solely of doubleton cycles if N is odd, so we consider N even. We choose half the elements for the first element of each cycle, then assign the second element in each of $(N/2)!$ possible ways. The order of the elements is immaterial, so this counts each permutation $2^{N/2}$ times. This gives a total of

$$\binom{N}{N/2}(N/2)!/2^{N/2} = \frac{N!}{(N/2)!2^{N/2}}$$

permutations made up of cycles of length 2.

Multiplying by z^N and dividing by $N!$ we get the exponential generating function

$$\sum_{N \text{ even}} \frac{z^N}{(N/2)!2^{N/2}} = e^{z^2/2}.$$

As we saw in Chapter 3, the symbolic method also gives this EGF directly, using the "set of" construction and the observation that the EGF for cycles of length 2 is $z^2/2$. This generalizes to show that the EGF for the number of permutations consisting solely of cycles of length k is $e^{z^k/k}$. The reader is encouraged to review the discussion of the symbolic method for labelled objects in Chapter 3 and to contemplate this formula, even for $k = 1$ and $k = 2$, to appreciate how the "set of" construction works.

Involutions and upper bounds on cycle length. Since e^z is the EGF for permutations consisting only of singleton cycles and since $e^{z^2/2}$ is the EGF for permutations consisting only of doubleton cycles, the EGF for permutations consisting of cycles of length 1 or 2 is $e^{z+z^2/2}$. Similarly, the EGF for the number of permutations that consist only of cycles of length 1, 2, or 3 is $e^{z+z^2/2+z^3/3}$, and so on. As in Chapter 3, we can complete this analytic cycle by noting that the EGF for permutations with no restriction on cycle length is therefore

$$e^{z+z^2/2+z^3/3+z^4/4+\dots} = \exp\Bigl(\ln\frac{1}{1-z}\Bigr) = \frac{1}{1-z},$$

as expected.

Exercise 6.23 Find the EGF for the number of permutations that consist only of cycles of even length. Generalize to find the EGF for the number of permutations that consist only of cycles of length divisible by t.

As mentioned briefly in the previous section, involutions can be characterized by cycle length restrictions, and thus enumerated by the argument just given. If $p_i = j$ in a permutation, then $p_j = i$ in the inverse: both of these must hold for $i \neq j$ in an involution, or the cycle (i, j) must be present. This observation implies that involutions consist of cycles of length 2 ($p_{p_i} = i$) or 1 ($p_i = i$). Thus involutions are precisely those permutations comprised solely of singleton and doubleton cycles, and the EGF for involutions is $e^{z+z^2/2}$.

Theorem 6.2 (*Maximal cycle lengths*) *The EGF that enumerates the number of permutations with no cycles of length greater than k is*

$$\exp(z + z^2/2 + z^3/3 + \ldots + z^k/k).$$

In particular, the EGF that enumerates involutions is

$$B(z) = e^{z+z^2/2}$$

and

$$N![z^N]B(z) = \sum_{k\geq 0} \frac{N!}{(N-2k)!2^k k!} \sim \frac{1}{\sqrt{2\sqrt{e}}}\left(\frac{N}{e}\right)^{N/2} e^{\sqrt{N}}.$$

Proof. See the discussion above for the derivation of the EGFs. The number of involutions is obtained by expanding

$$e^{z+z^2/2} = \sum_{j\geq 0} \frac{1}{j!}\left(z + \frac{z^2}{2}\right)^j = \sum_{j,k\geq 0} \frac{1}{j!}\binom{j}{k} z^{j-k}\left(\frac{z^2}{2}\right)^k$$

and collecting $[z^N]$.

The asymptotic form of the number of involutions can be derived from the Laplace method of Chapter 4. Taking the ratio of successive terms in the sum, we have

$$\frac{N!}{(N-2k)!2^k k!} \Big/ \frac{N!}{(N-2k-2)!2^{k+1}(k+1)!} = \frac{2(k+1)}{(N-2k)(N-2k-1)},$$

which shows that the terms in the sum increase until k is approximately $(N - \sqrt{N})/2$, then decrease. Using Stirling's approximation to estimate the dominant contribution near the peak and a normal approximation to bound the tails, the result follows in the same way as in various examples in Chapter 4. Details are worked out in Knuth [10]. ■

It also instructive to derive the EGF for involutions directly. Let $B(z)$ be the exponential generating function for involutions, so that $b_N = N![z^N]B(z)$. By definition,

$$B(z) = \sum_{\substack{p \in \mathcal{P} \\ p \text{ involution}}} \frac{z^{|p|}}{|p|!}.$$

Now, every involution of length $|p|$ corresponds to (i) one involution of length $|p|+1$, formed by appending the singleton cycle consisting of $|p|+1$; and (ii) $|p|+1$ involutions of length $|p|+2$, formed by, for each k from 1 to $|p|+1$, adding 1 to permutation elements greater than k, then appending the doubleton cycle consisting of k and $|p|+2$. This implies that the generating function must satisfy

$$B(z) = \sum_{\substack{p \in \mathcal{P} \\ p \text{ involution}}} \frac{z^{|p|+1}}{(|p|+1)!} + \sum_{\substack{p \in \mathcal{P} \\ p \text{ involution}}} (|p|+1)\frac{z^{|p|+2}}{(|p|+2)!}.$$

Differentiating, this simplifies to

$$B'(z) = (1+z)B(z)$$

which has the solution

$$B(z) = e^{z+z^2/2}.$$

Exercise 6.24 Show that the number of involutions of size N satisfies the recurrence

$$b_{N+1} = b_N + Nb_{N-1} \qquad \text{for } N > 0 \text{ with } b_0 = b_1 = 1.$$

(This recurrence can be used, for example, to compute the entries on the row corresponding to involutions in Table 6.4.)

Exercise 6.25 Derive a recurrence that can be used to compute the number of permutations that have no cycle of length > 3.

Exercise 6.26 Use the methods from §4.10 to derive a bound involving $N^{N(1-1/k)}$ for the number of permutations with no cycle of length greater than k.

Derangements and lower bounds on cycle length. Perhaps the most famous enumeration problem for permutations is the *derangement problem*. Suppose that N people at the opera check their hats, then pick them up in random order. What is the probability that none of the hats go to their owners? For example, the derangements of 4 elements are the 6 permutations with a cycle of length 4

```
2 3 4 1   2 4 1 3   3 4 2 1   3 1 4 2   4 3 1 2   4 1 2 3
```

and the three permutations with two doubleton cycles

```
2 1 4 3   3 4 1 2   4 3 2 1.
```

All the other permutations of four elements have at least one singleton cycle, so the associated probability for $N = 4$ is $9/24 = .375$.

Solving this problem is straightforward with the methods we have been discussing. The probability in question is the coefficient of z^N in the EGF that enumerates permutations with no singleton cycles. As above, we can construct derangements from cycles of length $2, 3, 4, \ldots$, which gives the EGF

$$e^{z^2/2+z^3/3+\ldots} = \exp\Bigl(\ln\frac{1}{1-z} - z\Bigr) = \frac{e^{-z}}{1-z}.$$

An alternative derivation of this goes as follows. We construct the class of all permutations by taking the "product" of permutations consisting solely of singleton cycles and permutations containing no singleton cycles, as expressed by the symbolic equation

$$\mathcal{P} = \mathcal{C}^{[1]} \times \mathcal{D}^{[1]}.$$

This translates into an implicit equation defining the EGF $D(z)$ that enumerates derangements:

$$\frac{1}{1-z} = e^z D(z)$$

because $1/(1-z)$ enumerates all permutations and e^z enumerates singleton cycles. Thus

$$D(z) = \frac{e^{-z}}{1-z},$$

which is a simple convolution of generating functions that leads to the result

$$[z^N]D(z) = \sum_{0\le k\le N} \frac{(-1)^k}{k!}.$$

In §4.4 we showed this sum to be asymptotic to $1/e$.

Theorem 6.3 (*Minimal cycle lengths*) *The EGF for the number of permutations with no cycles of length k or less is*

$$D^{[k]}(z) = \frac{1}{1-z} e^{-z-z^2/2-z^3/3-\ldots-z^k/k}.$$

Asymptotically,

$$[z^N]D^{[k]}(z) \sim e^{-H_k}.$$

In particular, for derangements,

$$[z^N]D(z) = \sum_{0\le k\le N} \frac{(-1)^k}{k!} \sim 1/e \approx .36787944.$$

Proof. We can generalize either of the arguments above. For instance, starting with the symbolic equation

$$\mathcal{P} = \mathcal{C}^{[1]} \times \mathcal{C}^{[2]} \times \ldots \times \mathcal{C}^{[k]} \times \mathcal{D}^{[k]}.$$

we can transfer to the generating function equation

$$\frac{1}{1-z} = e^z e^{z^2/2} \cdots e^{z^k/k} D^{[k]}(z).$$

so that

$$D^{[k]}(z) = \frac{e^{-z-z^2/2-\ldots-z^k/k}}{1-z}.$$

The asymptotic result is a direct consequence of Theorem 4.12. ∎

For reference, the solutions to enumeration problems for permutations with cycle length restrictions that are discussed above are listed in Table 6.5. The exponential generating functions are listed, along with asymptotic estimates of their coefficients.

Exercise 6.27 By differentiating the relation $(1-z)D(z) = e^z$ and setting coefficients equal, obtain a recurrence satisfied by the number of derangements of N elements.

Exercise 6.28 Write a program to, given k, print a table of the number of permutations of N elements with no cycles of length $< k$ for $N < 20$.

Exercise 6.29 An *arrangement* of N elements is a sequence formed from a subset of the elements. Prove that the EGF for arrangements is $e^z/(1-z)$. Express the coefficients as a simple sum and interpret that sum combinatorially.

6.5 Analyzing Properties of Permutations with CGFs. In this section, we outline the basic method that we will use for the analysis of properties of permutations for many of the problems given in this chapter, using

	EGF	*asymptotic estimate of* $N![z^N]$
singleton cycles	e^z	1
cycles of length k	$e^{z^k/k}$	—
all permutations	$\dfrac{1}{1-z}$	$N! \sim \sqrt{2\pi N}\left(\dfrac{N}{e}\right)^N$
derangements	$\dfrac{e^{-z}}{1-z}$	$\sim N!e^{-1}$
all cycles $> k$	$\dfrac{e^{-z-z^2/2\ldots-z^k/k}}{1-z}$	$\sim N!e^{-H_k}$
involutions	$e^{z+z^2/2}$	$\sim \dfrac{1}{\sqrt{2\sqrt{e}}}e^{\sqrt{N}}\left(\dfrac{N}{e}\right)^{N/2}$
all cycles $\le k$	$e^{z+z^2/2+\ldots+z^k/k}$	—

Table 6.5 EGFs for permutations with cycle length restrictions

cumulative generating functions (CGFs). Introduced in Chapter 3, this method may be summarized as follows:

- Define an exponential CGF of the form $B(z) = \sum_{p \in \mathcal{P}} \text{cost}(p) z^{|p|}/|p|!$.
- Partition the sum by "decomposing" the permutations to find an alternate expression for $B(z)$.
- Derive a functional equation for $B(z)$.
- Solve the equation or use analytic techniques to find $[z^N]B(z)$.

The "partition" referred to in the second step actually is accomplished by finding a correspondence among permutations, most often one that partitions the $|p|!$ permutations of length $|p|$ into $|p-1|!$ sets of size $|p|$, each associated with one of the permutations of length $|p-1|$. Specifically, if $\mathcal{P}_q$ is the set of permutations of length $|q|+1$ that correspond to a given permutation q, then the second step above corresponds to rewriting the CGF as follows:

$$B(z) = \sum_{q \in \mathcal{P}} \sum_{p \in \mathcal{P}_q} \text{cost}(p) \frac{z^{|q|+1}}{(|q|+1)!}.$$

The permutations in $\mathcal{P}_q$ are typically closely related, and then the inner sum is easy to evaluate, which leads to an alternate expression for $B(z)$. Often, it is convenient to differentiate to be able to work with $z^{|q|}/|q|!$ on the right-hand side.

For permutations, the analysis is somewhat simplified because of the circumstance that the factorial for the exponential CGF also counts the total number of permutations, so the *exponential* CGF is also an *ordinary* GF for the average value sought. That is, if

$$B(z) = \sum_{p \in \mathcal{P}} \text{cost}(p) z^{|p|}/|p|!,$$

then it follows that

$$[z^N]B(z) = \sum_k k\{\#\text{ of perms of length } N \text{ with cost } k\}/N!,$$

which is precisely the average cost. For other combinatorial structures it is necessary to divide the cumulative count obtained from the CGF by the total count to get the average, though there are other cases where the cumulative count has a sufficiently simple form that the division can be incorporated into the generating function. We will see another example of this in Chapter 7.

The combinatorial argument involving the correspondence among permutations also often can be used to derive a recurrence or even a full BGF, which then gives a stronger result since explicit knowledge about the BGF for a parameter implies knowledge about the distribution of values. When working with CGFs, we are, however, working with average values, which can be manipulated without full knowledge of the distribution and thus often lead to simpler computations.

The following simple methods of partitioning permutations are the most important ones for use as the basis for this approach:

"Largest" or "smallest" correspondence. Given a permutation of length N, consider the permutation formed by simply removing the largest element. This permutation, of length $N - 1$, corresponds to exactly N different permutations of length N, one for each possible position of the largest element. For example,

```
5 4 1 2 3    4 5 1 2 3    4 1 5 2 3    4 1 2 5 3    4 1 2 3 5
```

all correspond to `4 1 2 3`. Or, working forwards, given any one of the $(N-1)!$ different permutations of length $N-1$, we can identify N different permutations of length N by putting the N in each possible position. We can do the same thing with any other element, not just the largest, by renumbering the other elements appropriately. For example, using the smallest element involves adding one to each other element, then placing 1 in each possible position.

"First" or "last" correspondence. Given a permutation of length N, consider the permutation formed by simply removing the first element, then renumbering the remaining elements, preserving their order, to make a proper permutation of length $N - 1$. This permutation corresponds to precisely N different permutations of length N, one for each possible value of the first element. For example,

```
1 5 2 3 4    2 5 1 3 4    3 5 1 2 4    4 5 1 2 3    5 4 1 2 3
```

all correspond to `4 1 2 3`. Or, working forwards, given any one of the $(N-1)!$ different permutations of length $N-1$, we can identify N different permutations of length N by, for each k from 1 to N, prepending k and then incrementing all numbers larger than or equal to k. This defines the "first" correspondence. We can do the same thing with any other element, not only the first. For example, if the last element is used as the basis for the correspondence, then

```
5 2 3 4 1    5 1 3 4 2    5 1 2 4 3    5 1 2 3 4    4 1 2 3 5
```

all correspond to `4 1 2 3`.

Binary search tree decomposition. Given two permutations p_l, p_r, we can create a total of

$$\binom{|p_l| + |p_r|}{|p_l|}$$

permutations of size $|p_l|+|p_r|+1$ by (*i*) adding $|p_l|+1$ to each element of p_r; (*ii*) intermixing p_l and p_r in all possible ways; and (*iii*) prefixing each permutation so obtained by $|p_l|+1$. As we saw in §6.3, all the permutations obtained in this way lead to the construction of the same binary search tree using the standard algorithm. Therefore this correspondence can be used as a basis for analyzing BST and related algorithms. (See Exercise 6.20.)

Heap-ordered tree decomposition. A permutation uniquely decomposes into "left" and "right" permutations, by taking those elements to the left of the smallest element and those to the right of the smallest element and renumbering. For example, `2 5 1 4 6 3` decomposes into `1 2` and `2 3 1`, and `6 2 4 3 1 5` decomposes into `4 1 3 2` and `1`. This decomposition, used recursively, corresponds to the HOT construction. It is useful for parameters that have a natural interpretation in terms of the HOT structure.

Note that all of these decompositions lead to differential equations in the CGFs because removing elements corresponds to shifting the counting sequences, which translates into integrating the generating function (see Table 3.4).

Runs and rises. For an example of the use of CGFs to analyze properties of permutations, we derive the average number of runs in a random permutation. Elementary arguments given above show that the average number of runs in a permutation of length N is $(N+1)/2$, but the full distribution is interesting to study, as discovered by Euler (see [10] and [1] for many details). Table 6.6 and Figure 6.5 illustrate this distribution for small values of N and k.

We start with the (exponential) CGF

$$A(z) = \sum_{p \in \mathcal{P}} \alpha(p) \frac{z^{|p|}}{|p|!}.$$

We use the "largest" correspondence: if the largest element is inserted at the end of a run in p, there is no change in the number of runs; otherwise, the number of runs is increased by 1. The total number of runs in the permutations corresponding to a given permutation p is

$$(|p|+1)\alpha(p) + |p| + 1 - \alpha(p) = |p|\alpha(p) + |p| + 1.$$

This leads to the alternate expression

$$A(z) = \sum_{p \in \mathcal{P}} (|p|\alpha(p) + |p| + 1) \frac{z^{|p|+1}}{(|p|+1)!},$$

which simplifies considerably if we differentiate:

$$\begin{aligned} A'(z) &= \sum_{p \in \mathcal{P}} (|p|\alpha(p) + |p| + 1) \frac{z^{|p|}}{|p|!} \\ &= zA'(z) + \frac{z}{(1-z)^2} + \frac{1}{1-z}. \end{aligned}$$

$N \downarrow$ $k \rightarrow$	1	2	3	4	5	6	7	8	9	10
1	1									
2	1	1								
3	1	4	1							
4	1	11	11	1						
5	1	26	66	26	1					
6	1	57	302	302	57	1				
7	1	120	1191	2416	1191	120	1			
8	1	247	4293	15619	15619	4293	247	1		
9	1	502	14608	88234	156190	88234	14608	502	1	
10	1	1013	47840	455192	1310354	1310354	455192	47840	1013	1

Table 6.6 Distribution of runs in permutations (Eulerian numbers)

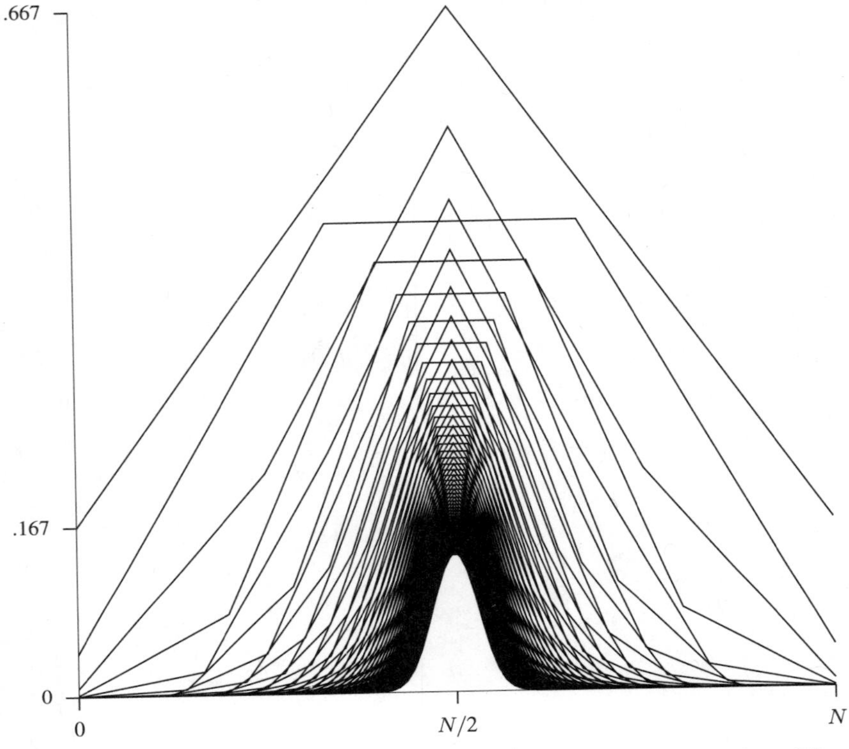

Figure 6.5 Distribution of runs, $3 \le N \le 60$ (k-axes scaled to N) (Eulerian numbers)

Therefore $A'(z) = 1/(1-z)^3$, so, given the initial conditions,

$$A(z) = \frac{1}{2(1-z)^2} - \frac{1}{2}$$

and we have the anticipated result $[z^N]A(z) = (N+1)/2$.

We will be doing several derivations of this form in this chapter. In some cases (including this one), it is possible to extend the argument or use symbolic methods to find the bivariate generating function (or a recurrence), but the CGF usually gives the average without much calculation, and we can use the BGF or recurrence to find the standard deviation and other moments of the distribution, if desired.

Theorem 6.4 (*Eulerian numbers*) *Permutations of N elements with k runs are counted by the Eulerian numbers, A_{Nk}, with exponential BGF*

$$A(u,z) \equiv \sum_{N\geq 0}\sum_{k\geq 0} A_{Nk}u^k \frac{z^N}{N!} = \frac{1-u}{1-ue^{z(1-u)}}.$$

The average number of runs in a permutation of size $N > 1$ is $(N+1)/2$ with variance $(N+1)/12$.

Proof. The argument given for the CGF generalizes to provide a partial differential equation for the BGF using the "largest" correspondence. We leave that for an exercise and consider the recurrence-based derivation, derived from the same correspondence. To get a permutation with k runs, there are k possibilities that the largest element is inserted at the end of an existing run in a permutation with k runs, and $N-k+1$ possibilities that the largest element "breaks" an existing run of a permutation with $k-1$ runs, thereby increasing the number of runs to k. This leads to

$$A_{Nk} = (N-k+1)A_{(N-1)(k-1)} + kA_{(N-1)k},$$

which, together with the initial conditions $A_{00} = 1$ and $A_{N0} = 0$ for $N \geq 0$ or $k > N$, fully specifies the A_{Nk}.

Multiplying by $z^N u^k$ and summing on N and k leads directly to the partial differential equation

$$A_z(u,z) = \frac{1}{1-uz}(uA(u,z) + u(1-u)A_u(u,z)).$$

It is then easily checked that the stated expression for $A(u,z)$ satisfies this equation.

Now, we calculate the mean and variance as in Table 3.6, but take into account that using an exponential BGF automatically includes division by $N!$, as mentioned above. Thus, the mean is given by

$$[z^N]\frac{\partial A(u,z)}{\partial u}\bigg|_{u=1} = [z^N]\frac{1}{2(1-z)^2} = \frac{N+1}{2},$$

and we can compute the variance in a similar manner. ∎

As noted above, all runs but the last in a permutation are terminated by a fall, so Theorem 6.4 also implies that the number of falls in a permutation has mean $(N-1)/2$ and variance $(N+1)/12$. The same result also applies to the number of rises.

Exercise 6.30 Give a simple noncomputational proof that the mean number of rises in a permutation of N elements is $(N-1)/2$. (*Hint*: For every permutation $p_1p_2\dots p_N$, consider the "complement" $q_1q_2\dots q_N$ formed by $q_i = N+1-p_i$.)

Exercise 6.31 Generalize the CGF argument above to show that the BGF $A(u,z) = \sum_{p\in\mathcal{P}} u^{\alpha(p)} z^{|p|}$ satisfies the partial differential equation given in the proof of Theorem 6.4.

Exercise 6.32 Prove that

$$A_{Nk} = \sum_{0\le j\le k} (-1)^j \binom{N+1}{j} (k-j)^N.$$

Exercise 6.33 Prove that

$$x^N = \sum_{1\le k\le N} A_{Nk} \binom{x+k-1}{N} \qquad \text{for } N \ge 1.$$

Increasing subsequences. Another way to develop an explicit formula for a CGF is to find a recurrence on the cumulative cost. For example, let

$$S(z) = \sum_{p\in\mathcal{P}} \{\#\text{ increasing subsequences in } p\} \frac{z^{|p|}}{|p|!} = \sum_{N\ge 0} S_N \frac{z^N}{N!}$$

so S_N represents the total number of increasing subsequences in all permutations of length N. Then, from the "largest" correspondence, we find that

$$S_N = NS_{N-1} + \sum_{0\le k<N} \binom{N-1}{k} (N-1-k)! S_k \qquad \text{for } N > 0 \text{ with } S_0 = 1.$$

This accounts for the N copies of the permutation of length $N-1$ (all the increasing subsequences in that permutation appear N times) *and* in a separate accounting, all the increasing subsequences ending in the largest element. If the largest element is in position $k+1$, then all the permutations for each of the choices of elements for the first k positions appear $(N-1-k)!$ times (one for each arrangement of the larger elements), each contributing S_k to the total. This argument assumes that the empty subsequence is counted as "increasing," as in our definition. Dividing by $N!$ and summing on N, we get the functional equation

$$(1-z)S'(z) = (2-z)S(z)$$

which has the solution

$$S(z) = \frac{1}{1-z}\exp\Bigl(\frac{z}{1-z}\Bigr).$$

Theorem 6.5 (*Increasing subsequences*) *The a erage number of increasing subsequences in a random permutation of N elements is*

$$\frac{S_N}{N!} = \sum_{0\le k\le N}\binom{N}{k}\frac{1}{k!} \sim \frac{1}{2\sqrt{\pi e}}e^{2\sqrt{N}}/N^{1/4}.$$

Proof. The exact formula follows directly from the discussion above, expanding the explicit formula for the generating function just given.

Again, the Laplace method can be used to derive the asymptotic estimate. Taking the ratio of successive terms, we have

$$\binom{N}{k}\frac{1}{k!}\Big/\binom{N}{k+1}\frac{1}{(k+1)!} = \frac{(k+1)^2}{N-k},$$

which shows that a peak occurs when k is about $\sqrt{N}$. Again, as in several examples in Chapter 4, Stirling's formula provides the local approximations and the tails are bounded via a normal approximation. Details may be found in Lifschitz and Pittel [12]. ∎

Exercise 6.34 Give a direct combinatorial derivation of the exact formula for S_N. (*Hint*: Consider all places at which an increasing subsequence may appear.)

Exercise 6.35 Find the EGF and an asymptotic estimate for the number of increasing subsequences of length k in a random permutation of length N (where k is fixed relative to N).

Exercise 6.36 Find the EGF and an asymptotic estimate for the number of increasing subsequences of length at least 3 in a random permutation of length N.

Peaks and valleys. As an example of the use of the heap-ordered tree decomposition of permutations, we now will derive results that refine the rise and run statistics. The nodes in an HOT are of three types: leaves (nodes with both children external), unary nodes (with one child internal and one external), and binary nodes (with both children internal). The study of the different types of nodes is directly relevant to the study of peaks and valleys in permutations (see Exercise 6.19). Moreover, these statistics are of independent interest because they can be used to analyze the storage requirements for HOTs and BSTs.

Given a heap-ordered tree, its associated permutation is obtained by simply listing the node labels in infix (left-to-right) order. In this correspondence, it is clear that a binary node in the HOT corresponds to a peak in the permutation: in a left-to-right scan, a binary node is preceded by a smaller element from its left subtree and followed by another smaller element from its right subtree. Thus the analysis of peaks in random permutations is reduced to the analysis of the number of binary nodes in random HOTs.

A random HOT of size N is composed of a left subtree of size k and a right subtree of size $N-k-1$, where all values of k between 0 and $N-1$ are equally likely and hence have probability $1/N$. This can be seen directly (the minimum of a permutation assumes each possible rank with equal likelihood) or via the HOT-BST equivalence. Mean values are thus computed by the same methods as those developed for BSTs in Chapter 5.

For example, the average number of binary nodes in a random HOT satisfies the recurrence

$$V_N = \frac{1}{N}\sum_{0\le k\le N-1}(V_k + V_{N-k-1}) + \frac{N-2}{N} \qquad \text{for } N \ge 3$$

since the number of binary nodes is the sum of the number of binary nodes in the left and right subtrees plus 1 unless the minimal element is the first or last in the permutation (an event that has probability $2/N$). We have seen this type of recurrence on several occasions before, starting in §3.3. Multiplying by z^{N-1} and summing leads to the differential equation

$$V'(z) = 2\frac{V(z)}{1-z} + \frac{z^2}{(1-z)^2},$$

which has the solution

$$V(z) = \frac{1}{3}\frac{z^3}{(1-z)^2} \qquad \text{so that} \qquad V_N = \frac{N-2}{3}.$$

Thus, the average number of valleys in a random permutation is $(N-2)/3$, and similar results about related quantities follow immediately.

Theorem 6.6 (*Local properties of permutations and nodes in trees*) *The average number of valleys, peaks, double rises, and double falls in a random permutation of N elements is, respectively,*

$$\frac{N-2}{3}, \qquad \frac{N-2}{3}, \qquad \frac{N+1}{6}, \qquad \frac{N+1}{6}.$$

The average number of binary nodes, leaves, left-branching, and right-branching nodes in a random HOT or BST of size N is, respectively,

$$\frac{N-2}{3}, \qquad \frac{N+1}{3}, \qquad \frac{N+1}{6}, \qquad \frac{N+1}{6}.$$

Proof. These results are straightforward by arguments similar to that given above (or just applying Theorem 5.7) and using simple relationships among the various quantities. See also Exercise 6.16.

For example, a fall in a permutation is either a valley or a double fall, so the average number of double falls is

$$\frac{N-1}{2} - \frac{N-2}{3} = \frac{N+1}{6}.$$

For another example, we know that the number of leaves in a random BST is $(N+1)/3$ (or a direct proof such as the one above for HOTs could be used) and the average number of binary nodes is $(N-2)/3$ by the argument above. Thus the average number of unary nodes is

$$N - \frac{N-2}{3} - \frac{N+1}{3} = \frac{N+1}{3},$$

with left- and right-branching nodes equally likely. ■

Exercise 6.37 Prove that valleys and peaks have the same distribution for random permutations.

Exercise 6.38 Suppose that the space required for leaf, unary, and binary nodes is proportional to c_0, c_1, c_2, respectively. Show that the storage requirement for random HOTs and for random BSTs is $\sim (c_0 + c_1 + c_2)N/3$.

Exercise 6.39 Under the assumption of the previous exercise, prove that the storage requirement for random binary Catalan trees is $\sim (c_0 + 2c_1 + c_2)N/4$.

Exercise 6.40 Show that a sequence of N random real numbers between 0 and 1 (uniformly and independently generated) has $\sim N/6$ double rises and $\sim N/6$ double falls, on the average. Deduce a direct continuous-model proof of this asymptotic result.

Exercise 6.41 Generalize Exercise 6.19 to show that the BGF for right-branching nodes and binary nodes in HOTs satisfies

$$K_z(u,z) = 1 + (1+u)K(u,z) + K^2(u,z)$$

and therefore

$$K(u,z) = \frac{1 - e^{(u-1)z}}{u - e^{(u-1)z}}.$$

(*Note*: This provides an alternate derivation of the BGF for Eulerian numbers, since $A(u,z) = 1 + uK(u,z)$.)

Table 6.7 summarizes the results derived above and some of the results that we will derive in the next three sections regarding the average values of various parameters for random permutations. Permutations are sufficiently simple combinatorial objects that we can derive some of these results in several ways, but, as the above examples make clear, combinatorial proofs with BGFs and CGFs are particularly straightforward. Next, we apply these techniques to analyze a number of quantities that play an essential role in the analysis of several basic algorithms.

6.6 Inversions and Insertion Sorts. Program 6.2 is an implementation of *insertion sort*, a simple sorting method that is easily analyzed. In this method, we "insert" each element into proper position among those previously considered, moving larger elements over one position to make room.

	exponential CGF	*average* ($[z^N]$)
left-to-right minima	$\frac{1}{1-z}\ln\frac{1}{1-z}$	H_N
cycles	$\frac{1}{1-z}\ln\frac{1}{1-z}$	H_N
singleton cycles	$\frac{z}{1-z}$	1
cycles $= k$	$\frac{z^k}{k}\frac{1}{1-z}$	$\frac{1}{k} \quad (N \ge k)$
cycles $\le k$	$\frac{1}{1-z}\left(z+\frac{z^2}{2}+\ldots+\frac{z^k}{k}\right)$	$H_k \quad (N \ge k)$
runs	$\frac{1}{2(1-z)^2}-\frac{1}{2}$	$\frac{N+1}{2}$
inversions	$\frac{z^2}{2(1-z)^3}$	$\frac{N(N-1)}{4}$
incr. subsequences	$\frac{1}{1-z}\exp(\frac{z}{1-z})$	$\sim \frac{1}{2\sqrt{\pi e}}e^{2\sqrt{N}}/N^{1/4}$
peaks, valleys	$\frac{z^3}{3(1-z)^2}$	$\frac{N-2}{3}$

Table 6.7 Analytic results for properties of permutations (average case)

Figure 6.6 shows the operation of Program 6.2 on a sample permutation. The highlighted elements in the ith line in the figure are the elements moved to do the ith insertion.

The running time of insertion sort is proportional to $c_1N + c_2B + c_3$, where c_1, c_2, c_3 are appropriate constants that depend on the implementation and B, a function of the input permutation, is the number of times `a[j+1] := a[j]` is executed. The number of elements moved to insert each element is the number of larger elements to the left, so we are led directly to consider inversion tables. The right portion of Figure 6.6 is the inversion table for the permutation as the sort proceeds. After the ith insertion (shown on the ith line), the first i elements in the inversion table are zero (because the first i elements of the permutation are sorted), and the next element in the inversion table specifies how many elements are going to be moved in the next insertion, because it specifies the number of larger elements to the left of the $(i+1)$st element. The only effect of the ith insertion on the inversion table is to zero its ith entry. This implies that the value of the quantity B when insertion sort is run on a permutation is equal to the sum of the entries in the inversion table—the total number of inversions in the permutation.

Exercise 6.42 How many permutations of N elements have exactly one inversion? Two? Three?

Exercise 6.43 Show how to modify insertion sort to also compute the inversion table for the permutation associated with the original ordering of the elements.

As mentioned above, there is a one-to-one correspondence between permutations and inversion tables. In any inversion table $q_1q_2 \dots q_N$, each entry q_i must be between 0 and $i-1$ (in particular, q_1 is always 0). There

```
a[0] := infinity;
for i := 2 to N do
  begin
  v := a[i]; j := i-1;
  while a[j] > v  do
    begin a[j+1] := a[j]; j := j-1 end;
  a[j+1] := v;
  end
```

Program 6.2 Insertion sort

```
 9 14  4  1 12  2 10 13  5  6 11  3  8 15  7     0 0 2 3 1 4 2 1 5 5 3 9 6 0 8
 9 14  4  1 12  2 10 13  5  6 11  3  8 15  7     0 0 2 3 1 4 2 1 5 5 3 9 6 0 8
 4  9 14  1 12  2 10 13  5  6 11  3  8 15  7     0 0 0 3 1 4 2 1 5 5 3 9 6 0 8
 1  4  9 14 12  2 10 13  5  6 11  3  8 15  7     0 0 0 0 1 4 2 1 5 5 3 9 6 0 8
 1  4  9 12 14  2 10 13  5  6 11  3  8 15  7     0 0 0 0 0 4 2 1 5 5 3 9 6 0 8
 1  2  4  9 12 14 10 13  5  6 11  3  8 15  7     0 0 0 0 0 0 2 1 5 5 3 9 6 0 8
 1  2  4  9 10 12 14 13  5  6 11  3  8 15  7     0 0 0 0 0 0 0 1 5 5 3 9 6 0 8
 1  2  4  9 10 12 13 14  5  6 11  3  8 15  7     0 0 0 0 0 0 0 0 5 5 3 9 6 0 8
 1  2  4  5  9 10 12 13 14  6 11  3  8 15  7     0 0 0 0 0 0 0 0 0 5 3 9 6 0 8
 1  2  4  5  6  9 10 12 13 14 11  3  8 15  7     0 0 0 0 0 0 0 0 0 0 3 9 6 0 8
 1  2  4  5  6  9 10 11 12 13 14  3  8 15  7     0 0 0 0 0 0 0 0 0 0 0 9 6 0 8
 1  2  3  4  5  6  9 10 11 12 13 14  8 15  7     0 0 0 0 0 0 0 0 0 0 0 0 6 0 8
 1  2  3  4  5  6  8  9 10 11 12 13 14 15  7     0 0 0 0 0 0 0 0 0 0 0 0 0 0 8
 1  2  3  4  5  6  8  9 10 11 12 13 14 15  7     0 0 0 0 0 0 0 0 0 0 0 0 0 0 8
 1  2  3  4  5  6  7  8  9 10 11 12 13 14 15     0 0 0 0 0 0 0 0 0 0 0 0 0 0 0
```

Figure 6.6 Insertion sort and inversions

are i possible values for each of the q_i, so there are $N!$ different inversion tables. Inversion tables are simpler to use in the analysis because their entries are independent: each q_i takes on its i different values independent of the values of the other entries.

Theorem 6.7 (*Inversion distribution*) *The number of permutations of size N with k inversions is*

$$[u^k] \prod_{1\le k\le N} \frac{1-u^N}{1-u} = [u^k](1+u)(1+u+u^2)\cdots(1+u+\ldots+u^{N-1}).$$

A random permutation of N elements has $N(N-1)/4$ inversions on the average, with standard deviation $N(N-1)(2N+5)/72$.

Proof. We present the derivation using PGFs; a combinatorial derivation would follow along (almost) identical lines.

In the inversion table for a random permutation, the ith entry can take on each value between 0 and $i-1$ with probability $1/i$, independently of the other entries. Thus, the probability generating function for the number of inversions involving the Nth element is $(1+u+u^2+\ldots+u^{N-1})/N$, independent of the arrangement of the previous elements. As discussed in Chapter 3, the PGF for the sum of independent random variables is the product of the individual PGFs, so the generating function for the total

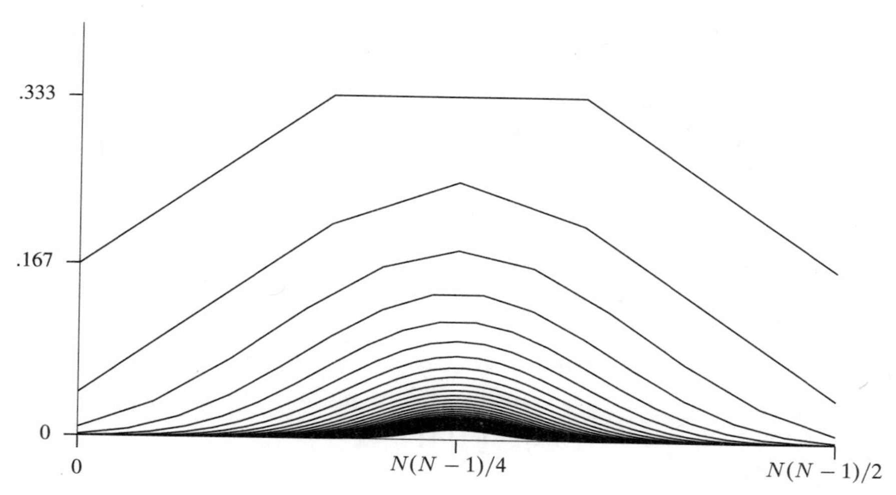

Figure 6.7 Distribution of inversions, $3 \le N \le 60$ (k-axes scaled to $\binom{N}{2}$)

number of inversions in a random permutation of N elements satisfies

$$b_N(u) = \frac{1 + u + u^2 + \ldots + u^{N-1}}{N} b_{N-1}(u).$$

That is, the number of inversions is the sum, for j from 1 to N, of independent uniformly distributed random variables with OGF $(1 + u + u^2 + \ldots + u^{j-1})/j$. The counting GF of the theorem statement equals $N!$ times $b_N(u)$. The average is the sum of the individual averages $(j-1)/2$, and the variance is the sum of the individual variances $(j^2-1)/12$. ■

The full distribution $[u^k]b_N(u)$ is shown in Figure 6.7. The curves are symmetric about $N(N-1)/4$, and they shrink towards the center (albeit slowly) as N grows. This curve can be characterized as the distribution for the sum of independent random variables. Though they are not identically distributed, it can be shown by the classical Central Limit Theorem of probability theory that the distribution is normal in the limit (see, for example, David and Barton [2]). This is not atypical in the analysis of algorithms, but we stop short of such a thorough analysis.

Corollary *Insertion sort performs* $\sim N^2/4$ *key comparisons and moves* $\sim N^2/4$ *records, on the average, to sort a file of* N *records with randomly ordered distinct keys.*

Solution with CGFs. It is also instructive to use a cumulative generating function to find the average number of inversions, since it serves as a model for more difficult problems. Consider the CGF

$$B(z) = \sum_{p \in \mathcal{P}} \sigma(p) \frac{z^{|p|}}{|p|!}.$$

As mentioned above, the coefficient of $z^N/N!$ in $B(z)$ is the total number of inversions in all permutations of length N, so that $B(z)$ is the OGF for the average number of inversions in a permutation. The argument given above is equivalent to calculating the cumulated cost from the "horizontal" generating functions for inversions; we now consider an alternate derivation that uses the CGF directly.

Using the "largest" correspondence, every permutation of length $|p|$ corresponds to $|p|+1$ permutations of length $|p|+1$, formed by putting element $|p|+1$ between the kth and $(k+1)$st element, for k between 0 and $|p|$. Such a permutation has $|p|-k$ more inversions than p, which leads to the expression

$$B(z) = \sum_{p \in \mathcal{P}} \sum_{0 \le k \le |p|} (\sigma(p) + |p| - k) \frac{z^{|p|+1}}{(|p|+1)!}.$$

The sum on k is easily evaluated, leaving

$$B(z) = \sum_{p \in \mathcal{P}} \sigma(p) \frac{z^{|p|+1}}{|p|!} + \sum_{p \in \mathcal{P}} \binom{|p|+1}{2} \frac{z^{|p|+1}}{(|p|+1)!}.$$

The first sum is $zB(z)$, and the second is simple to evaluate because it depends only on the length of the permutation, so the $k!$ permutations of length k can be collected for each k, leaving

$$\begin{aligned} B(z) &= zB(z) + \frac{z}{2} \sum_{k \ge 0} k z^k \\ &= zB(z) + \frac{1}{2} \frac{z^2}{(1-z)^2}, \end{aligned}$$

so $B(z) = z^2/(2(1-z)^3)$, the generating function for $N(N-1)/4$, as expected.

We will be studying other properties of inversion tables later in the chapter, since they can describe other properties of permutations that arise in the analysis of some other algorithms. In particular, we will be concerned with the number of zeros in the inversion table, and the value of the largest element.

Exercise 6.44 Derive a recurrence relation satisfied by p_{Nk}, the probability that a random permutation of N elements has exactly k inversions.

Exercise 6.45 Find the CGF for the total number of inversions in all involutions of length N. Use this to find the average number of inversions in an involution.

Exercise 6.46 Show that $N!p_{Nk}$ is a fixed polynomial in N for any fixed k, when N is sufficiently large.

Shellsort. Program 6.3 gives a practical improvement to insertion sort, called Shellsort, which reduces the running time well below N^2 by making several passes through the file, each time sorting h independent subfiles (each of size about N/h) of elements spaced by h. The "increments" `h[t],h[t-1],...,h[1]` that control the sort must form a decreasing sequence that ends in 1. Considerable effort has gone into finding the best sequence of increments, with few analytic results: though it is a simple extension to insertion sort, Shellsort has proved to be extremely difficult to analyze. The full treatment of the average-case performance of Shellsort remains an unsolved problem. Yao [19] has done an analysis of $(h, k, 1)$ Shellsort using techniques similar to those above, but the results and methods become much more complicated. For general Shellsort, even the functional form apparently depends on the increment sequence.

Two-ordered permutations. The analysis of Shellsort for the case where `h` takes on only the values `2` and `1` is interesting to consider because it is

```
for h := h[t], h[t-1], ...  , h[1] do
  for i := h+1 to N do
    begin
    v := a[i]; j := i-1;
    while a[j] > v  do
      begin a[j+1] := a[j]; j := j-1 end;
    a[j+1] := v;
    end
```

Program 6.3 Shellsort

closely related to the analysis of path length in trees in Chapter 5. This is equivalent to a merging algorithm: the files in odd- and even-numbered positions are sorted independently (with insertion sort), then the resulting permutation is sorted with insertion sort. Such a permutation, which consists of two interleaved sorted permutations, is said to be *2-ordered.* Properties of 2-ordered permutations are of interest in the study of other merging algorithms as well. Since the final pass of Shellsort, with `h=1`, is just insertion sort, its average running time will depend on the average number of inversions in a 2-ordered permutation. Three sample 2-ordered permutations, and their inversion tables, are given in Table 6.8.

Let $S(z)$ be the OGF that enumerates 2-ordered permutations. It is obvious that

$$S(z) = \sum_{N \ge 0} \binom{2N}{N} z^N = \frac{1}{\sqrt{1-4z}},$$

but we will consider an alternate method of enumeration to expose the structure. Figure 6.8 illustrates the fact that 2-ordered permutations correspond to paths in an N-by-N lattice, similar to those described for the "gambler's ruin" representation of trees in Chapter 5. Starting at the upper left corner, move right if i is in an odd-numbered position, down if i is in an even-numbered position. Since there are N moves to the right and N moves down, we end up in the lower right corner.

Now, the lattice paths that do not touch the diagonal correspond to trees, as discussed in Chapter 5, and are enumerated by the generating function

$$zT(z) = G(z) = (1 - \sqrt{1-4z})/2.$$

For 2-ordered permutations, the restriction on touching the diagonal is removed. However, any path through the lattice must touch the diagonal

4	1	5	2	6	3	9	7	10	8	13	11	15	12	16	14	19	17	20	18
0	1	0	2	0	3	0	1	0	2	0	1	0	2	0	2	0	1	0	2

1	4	2	5	3	6	8	7	9	12	10	13	11	14	17	15	18	16	19	20
0	0	1	0	2	0	0	1	0	0	1	0	2	0	0	1	0	2	0	0

4	1	5	2	6	3	7	8	12	9	13	10	14	11	15	17	16	18	20	19
0	1	0	2	0	3	0	0	0	1	0	2	0	3	0	0	1	0	0	1

Table 6.8 Three 2-ordered permutations, with inversion tables

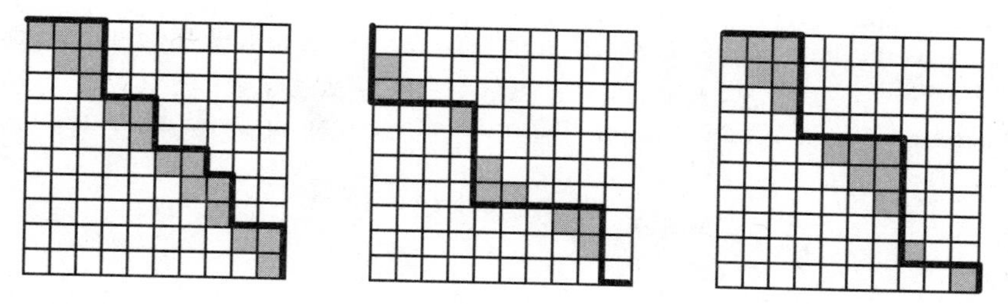

Figure 6.8 Lattice paths for 2-ordered permutations in Table 6.8

for the first time, which leads to the symbolic equation

$$S(z) = 2G(z)S(z) + 1$$

for the enumerating OGF for 2-ordered permutations. That is, any path through the lattice can be uniquely constructed from an initial portion that does not touch the diagonal except at the endpoints, followed by a general path. The factor of 2 accounts for the fact that the initial portion may be either above or below the diagonal. This simplifies to

$$S(z) = \frac{1}{1 - 2G(z)} = \frac{1}{1 - (1 - \sqrt{1 - 4z})} = \frac{1}{\sqrt{1 - 4z}},$$

as expected. Knuth [10] (see also Vitter and Flajolet [16]) shows that this same general structure can be used to write explicit expressions for the BGF for inversions, with the eventual result that the cumulative cost (total number of inversions in all 2-ordered permutations of length $2N$) is simply $N4^{N-1}$. The argument is based on the observation that the number of inversions in a 2-ordered permutation is equal to the number of lattice squares between the corresponding lattice path and the "down-right-down-right..." diagonal.

Theorem 6.8 (*Inversions in 2-ordered permutations*) *The average number of inversions in a random 2-ordered permutation of length* $2N$ *is*

$$N4^{N-1} \Big/ \binom{2N}{N} \sim \sqrt{\pi/128}(2N)^{3/2}.$$

Proof. The calculations that lead to this simple result are straightforward but intricate and are left as exercises. We will address this problem again, in a more general setting, in §7.5. ∎

Exercise 6.47 Show that the number of inversions in a 2-ordered permutation is equal to the number of lattice squares between the path and the "down-right-down-right..." diagonal.

Exercise 6.48 Let $\mathcal{T}$ be the set of all 2-ordered permutations, and define the BGF

$$P(u, z) = \sum_{p \in \mathcal{T}} u^{\{\text{\# inversions in } p\}} \frac{z^{|p|}}{|p|!}.$$

Define $Q(u, z)$ in the same way, but restricted to the set of 2-ordered permutations whose corresponding lattice paths do not touch the diagonal except at the endpoints. Moreover, define $S(u, z)$ and $T(u, z)$ similarly, but restricted to 2-ordered permutations whose corresponding lattice paths lie entirely above the diagonal except at the endpoints. Show that $P(u, z) = 1/(1 - Q(u, z))$ and $S(u, z) = 1/(1 - T(u, z))$.

Exercise 6.49 Show that $T(u, z) = uzS(u, uz))$ and $Q(u, uz) = T(u, uz) + T(u, z)$.

Exercise 6.50 Using the result of the previous two exercises, show that

$$S(u, z) = uzS(u, z)S(u, uz) + 1$$

and

$$P(u, z) = (uzS(u, uz) + zS(u, z))P(u, z) + 1.$$

Exercise 6.51 Using the result of the previous exercise, show that

$$P_u(1, z) = \frac{z}{(1 - 4z)^2}.$$

Corollary *The average number of comparisons used by* $(2, 1)$ *Shellsort on a file of* N *elements is* $N^2/8 + \sqrt{\pi/128}N^{3/2} + O(N)$.

Proof. Assume that N is even. The first pass consists of two independent sorts of $N/2$ elements and therefore involves $2((N/2)(N/2 - 1)/4) = N^2/8 + O(N)$ comparisons, and leaves a random 2-ordered file. Then an additional $\sqrt{\pi/128}N^{3/2}$ comparisons are used during the second pass.

The same asymptotic result follows for the case when N is odd. Thus, even though it requires two passes over the file, $(2, 1)$ Shellsort uses a factor of 2 fewer comparisons than insertion sort. ■

Exercise 6.52 Give an asymptotic formula for the average number of inversions in a 3-ordered permutation, and analyze Shellsort for the case when the increments are 3 and 1. Generalize to estimate the leading term of the cost of $(h, 1)$ Shellsort, and the asymptotic cost when the best value of h is used (as a function of N).

Exercise 6.53 Analyze the following sorting algorithm: Given an array to be sorted, sort the elements in odd positions and in even positions recursively, then sort the resulting 2-ordered permutation with insertion sort. For what values of N does this algorithm use fewer comparisons, on the average, than the pure recursive Quicksort of Chapter 1?

6.7 Left-to-Right Minima and Selection Sort. The trivial algorithm for finding the minimum element in an array is to scan through the array, from left to right, keeping track of the minimum found so far. By successively finding the minimum, we are led to another simple sorting method called *selection sort*, shown in Program 6.4. The operation of selection sort on our sample file is diagrammed in Figure 6.9: again, the permutation is shown on the left and the corresponding inversion table on the right.

To analyze selection sort, we first need to analyze the algorithm for "finding the minimum" in a random permutation: the first (`j = 1`) iteration of the outer loop of Program 6.4. As for insertion sort, the running time of this algorithm can be expressed in terms of N and a quantity whose value depends on the particular permutation, in this case the number of times the "current minimum" is updated (the number of times the value of the variable `v` is changed in Program 6.4). This is exactly the number of left-to-right minima in the permutation.

This quantity is easily analyzed with the help of the inversion table: as observed above, each entry in the inversion table $q_1 q_2 \ldots q_N$ for which $q_i = i - 1$ corresponds to a left-to-right minimum, since all elements to the left are larger. Therefore, each entry in the inversion table is a left-to-right minimum with probability $1/i$, independent of the other entries, so

```
for j := 1 to N do
  begin
  v := infinity; k := j;
  for i := j to N do
    if a[i] < v then
      begin v := a[i]; k := i end;
  t := a[j]; a[j] := a[k]; a[k] := t;
  end;
```

Program 6.4 Selection sort

9	14	4	1	12	2	10	13	5	6	11	3	8	15	7
9	14	4	1	12	2	10	13	5	6	11	3	8	7	15
9	7	4	1	12	2	10	13	5	6	11	3	8	14	15
9	7	4	1	12	2	10	8	5	6	11	3	13	14	15
9	7	4	1	3	2	10	8	5	6	11	12	13	14	15
9	7	4	1	3	2	10	8	5	6	11	12	13	14	15
9	7	4	1	3	2	6	8	5	10	11	12	13	14	15
5	7	4	1	3	2	6	8	9	10	11	12	13	14	15
5	7	4	1	3	2	6	8	9	10	11	12	13	14	15
5	6	4	1	3	2	7	8	9	10	11	12	13	14	15
5	2	4	1	3	6	7	8	9	10	11	12	13	14	15
3	2	4	1	5	6	7	8	9	10	11	12	13	14	15
3	2	1	4	5	6	7	8	9	10	11	12	13	14	15
1	2	3	4	5	6	7	8	9	10	11	12	13	14	15
1	2	3	4	5	6	7	8	9	10	11	12	13	14	15

0	0	2	3	1	4	2	1	5	5	3	9	6	0	8
0	0	2	3	1	4	2	1	5	5	3	9	6	7	0
0	1	2	3	0	4	1	0	5	5	2	9	5	0	0
0	1	2	3	0	4	1	3	5	5	1	9	0	0	0
0	1	2	3	3	4	0	2	4	4	0	0	0	0	0
0	1	2	3	3	4	0	2	4	4	0	0	0	0	0
0	1	2	3	3	4	2	1	4	0	0	0	0	0	0
0	0	2	3	3	4	1	0	0	0	0	0	0	0	0
0	0	2	3	3	4	1	0	0	0	0	0	0	0	0
0	0	2	3	3	4	0	0	0	0	0	0	0	0	0
0	1	1	3	2	0	0	0	0	0	0	0	0	0	0
0	1	0	3	0	0	0	0	0	0	0	0	0	0	0
0	1	2	0	0	0	0	0	0	0	0	0	0	0	0
0	0	0	0	0	0	0	0	0	0	0	0	0	0	0
0	0	0	0	0	0	0	0	0	0	0	0	0	0	0

Figure 6.9 Selection sort and left-to-right minima

the average is $\sum_{1\le i\le N} 1/i = H_N$. A slight generalization of this argument gives the PGF.

Theorem 6.9 (*Left-to-right minima distribution*) *Permutations of N elements with k left-to-right minima are counted by the Stirling numbers of the first kind:*

$$\begin{bmatrix} N \\ k \end{bmatrix} = [u^k]u(u+1)\ldots(u+N-1).$$

A random permutation of N elements has H_N left-to-right minima on the average, with variance $H_N - H_N^{(2)}$.

Proof. Consider the probability generating function $P_N(u)$ for the number of left-to-right minima in a random permutation of N elements. As above, we can decompose this into two independent random variables: one for a random permutation of $N-1$ elements (with PGF $P_{N-1}(u)$) and one for the contribution of the last element (with PGF $(N-1+u)/N$, since the last element adds 1 to the number of left-to-right minima with probability $1/N$, 0 otherwise). Thus we must have

$$P_N(u) = \frac{N-1+u}{N} P_{N-1}(u),$$

and, as above, we find the mean and variance of the number of left-to-right minima by summing the means and variance from the simple probability generating functions $(z+k-1)/k$. The counting GF equals $N!p_N(u)$. ∎

Solution with CGFs. As usual, we introduce the exponential CGF

$$B(z) = \sum_{p \in \mathcal{P}} \lambda(p) \frac{z^{|p|}}{|p|!}$$

so that $[z^N]B(z)$ is the average number of left-to-right minima in a random permutation of N elements.

As before, we can directly derive a functional equation from the combinatorial definition, in this case using the "last" correspondence from above. Of the $|p| + 1$ permutations of size $|p| + 1$, corresponding to a given permutation p, one ends in 1 (and so has one more left-to-right minimum than p), and $|p|$ do not end in 1 (and so have the same number of left-to-right minima as p). This leads to the formulation

$$\begin{aligned} B(z) &= \sum_{p \in \mathcal{P}} (\lambda(p) + 1) \frac{z^{|p|+1}}{(|p| + 1)!} + \sum_{p \in \mathcal{P}} |p| \lambda(p) \frac{z^{|p|+1}}{(|p| + 1)!} \\ &= \sum_{p \in \mathcal{P}} \lambda(p) \frac{z^{|p|+1}}{|p|!} + \sum_{p \in \mathcal{P}} \frac{z^{|p|+1}}{(|p| + 1)!} \\ &= zB(z) + \sum_{k \geq 0} \frac{z^{k+1}}{(k + 1)}. \\ &= zB(z) + \ln \frac{1}{1 - z}. \end{aligned}$$

which leads to the solution

$$B(z) = \frac{1}{1 - z} \ln \frac{1}{1 - z},$$

the generating function for the harmonic numbers, as expected.

Next, we consider how this derivation can be extended, with just slightly more work, to give an explicit expression for the exponential BGF describing the full distribution.

Exercise 6.54 Let p_{Nk} be the probability that a random permutation of N elements has k left-to-right minima. Give a recurrence relation satisfied by p_{Nk}.

Stirling numbers of the first kind. Continuing this discussion, we start with

$$B(u,z)=\sum_{p\in\mathcal{P}}\frac{u^{\lambda(p)}z^{|p|}}{|p|!}=\sum_{N\geq 0}\sum_{k\geq 0}p_{Nk}u^k z^N$$

where p_{Nk} is the probability that a random permutation of N elements has k left-to-right minima. The same combinatorial construction as above leads to the formulation

$$B(u,z)=\sum_{p\in\mathcal{P}}\frac{u^{\lambda(p)+1}z^{|p|+1}}{(|p|+1)!}+\sum_{p\in\mathcal{P}}\frac{|p|u^{\lambda(p)}z^{|p|+1}}{(|p|+1)!}.$$

Differentiating with respect to z, we have

$$\begin{aligned}B_z(u,z)&=\sum_{p\in\mathcal{P}}\frac{u^{\lambda(p)+1}z^{|p|}}{|p|!}+\sum_{p\in\mathcal{P}}\frac{u^{\lambda(p)}z^{|p|}}{(|p|-1)!}\\&=uB(u,z)+zB_z(u,z).\end{aligned}$$

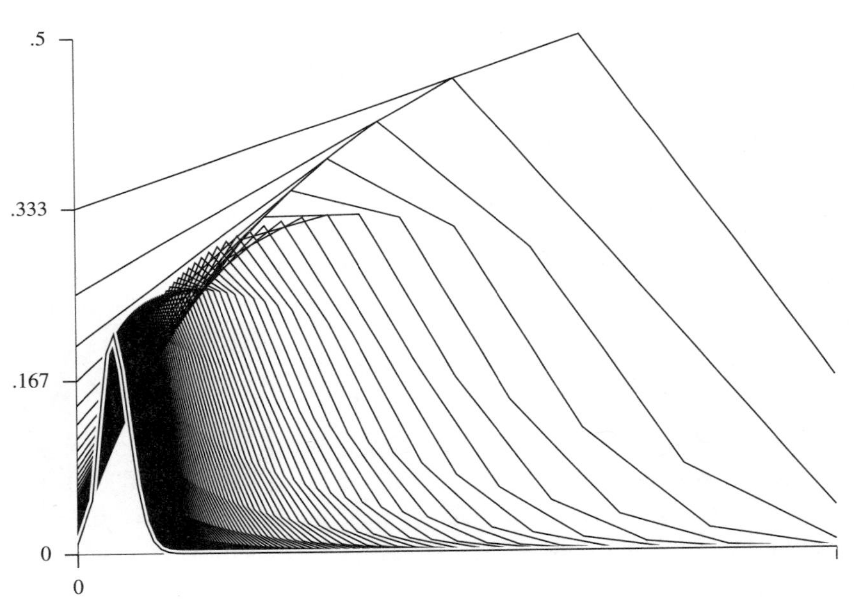

Figure 6.10 Distribution of left-to-right minima and cycles (Stirling numbers of the first kind)

Solving for $B_z(u,z)$, we get a simple first-order differential equation

$$B_z(u,z) = \frac{u}{1-z}B(u,z)$$

which has the solution

$$B(u,z) = \frac{1}{(1-z)^u}$$

(since $B(0,0) = 1$). Differentiating with respect to u, then evaluating at $u = 1$ gives the OGF for the harmonic numbers, as expected. Expanding

$$B(u,z) = 1 + \frac{u}{1!}z + \frac{u(u+1)}{2!}z^2 + \frac{u(u+1)(u+2)}{3!}z^3 + \ldots$$

gives back the expression for the Stirling numbers of the first kind in the statement of Theorem 6.9.

The BGF $B(u,z) = (1-z)^{-u}$ is a classical one that we have seen in Chapter 3. As we will see below, the number of permutations of N elements with exactly k left-to-right minima is the same as the number of permutations of N elements with exactly k cycles. Both are counted by the Stirling numbers of the first kind, which are therefore sometimes called the Stirling "cycle" numbers. This distribution is shown in Figure 6.10 and Table 6.9.

Exercise 6.55 Prove directly that $\sum_k k{N \brack k} = N!H_N$.

N ↓ $k \rightarrow$	1	2	3	4	5	6	7	8	9	10
1	1									
2	1	1								
3	2	3	1							
4	6	11	6	1						
5	24	50	35	10	1					
6	120	274	225	85	15	1				
7	720	1764	1624	735	175	21	1			
8	5040	13068	13132	6769	1960	322	28	1		
9	40320	109584	118124	67284	22449	4536	546	36	1	
10	362880	1026576	1172700	723680	269325	63273	9450	870	45	1

Table 6.9 Distribution of left-to-right minima and cycles (Stirling numbers of the first kind)

Selection sort. In Figure 6.9, it is obvious that the rightmost i elements of the inversion table are 0 after the ith step, but the effect on the rest of the inversion table is more difficult to explain. The reason for this is that the passes in selection sort are not independent: for example, if we have a low number of left-to-right minima on one iteration, we can expect a low number on the next. The "leading" term in the running time is the number of times the `if` statement is executed, which is easily shown to be $\binom{N+1}{2}$ for every input permutation; or, if the size of the records is very large, the number of times two records are exchanged, which is obviously $N-1$ for every input permutation.

In applications where the records are very large, the cost of exchanging records can dominate the running time. Since it performs the minimum possible number of exchanges, selection sort is the method of choice for such applications.

Theorem 6.10 (*Selection sort*) *Selection sort performs* $\sim N^2/2$ *key comparisons, saves key values* $\sim N \ln N$ *times, and moves* $\sim N$ *records, on the average, to sort a file of N records with randomly ordered distinct keys.*

Proof. See the above discussion. The only "variable" (quantity dependent on the permutation) in the running time of Program 6.4 is the total number of right-to-left maxima encountered during the life of the sort: the number of times the `if` statement succeeds. For large records, this code would be modified to save a key value and a record index, so the cost is not properly accounted for as either a key comparison or a record move.

We can derive the average value of this quantity by defining the following correspondence between permutations: given a permutation of $N-1$ elements, create N permutations of N elements by incrementing each element and then exchanging each element with a prepended 1. For example,

```
1 5 2 3 4   5 1 2 3 4   2 5 1 3 4   3 5 2 1 4   4 5 2 3 1
```

all correspond to `4 1 2 3`. That is, if any of these permutations is the initial input to the selection sort algorithm, the result will be `1 5 2 3 4` after one iteration, which is equivalent to `4 1 2 3` for subsequent iterations. This correspondence immediately implies that

$$B_N = B_{N-1} + H_N = (N+1)H_N - N.$$

More specifically, let cost(p) denote this cost for a given permutation p, and consider the CGF

$$B(z) = \sum_{N\geq 0} B_N z^N = \sum_{p\in\mathcal{P}} \text{cost}(p)\frac{z^{|p|}}{|p|!}.$$

The correspondence above says that the algorithm has uniform behavior in the sense that each permutation costs $\lambda(p)$ for the first pass; then, if we consider the result of the first pass (applied to all $|p|!$ possible inputs), each permutation of size $|p| - 1$ appears the same number of times. This leads to the solution

$$\begin{aligned} B(z) &= \sum_{p\in\mathcal{P}} \lambda(p)\frac{z^{|p|}}{|p|!} + \sum_{p\in\mathcal{P}} (|p|+1)\text{cost}(p)\frac{z^{|p|+1}}{(|p|+1)!} \\ &= \frac{1}{1-z}\ln\frac{1}{1-z} + zB(z). \end{aligned}$$

Therefore, $B(z) = \ln(1/(1-z))/(1-z)^2$, the generating function for partial sums of the harmonic numbers. ■

Note that we do *not* have independence among passes here, and the technique above cannot be used to get the variance or other properties of this distribution. This is a subtle but important point. For right-to-left minima, we were able to transform the CGF derivation easily into a derivation for the BGF (which yields the variance), but the above argument does not extend in this way. The lack of independence seems to make this problem nearly intractable: it remained open until 1988, when a delicate analysis by Yao [18] showed the variance to be $O(N^{3/2})$.

Exercise 6.56 Specify and analyze an algorithm that determines, in a left-to-right scan, the *two* smallest elements in an array.

Exercise 6.57 Consider a situation where the cost of accessing records is 100 times the cost of accessing keys, and both are large by comparison with other costs. For what values of N is selection sort preferred over insertion sort?

Exercise 6.58 Answer the previous question for Quicksort versus selection sort, assuming that an "exchange" costs twice as much as a "record access."

Exercise 6.59 Consider an implementation of selection sort for linked lists, where on each interation, the smallest remaining element is found by scanning the "input" list, but then it is *removed* from that list and appended to an "output" list. Analyze this algorithm.

Exercise 6.60 Suppose that the N items to be sorted actually consist of arrays of N words, the first of which is the sort key. Which of the four comparison-based methods that we have seen so far (Quicksort, Mergesort, insertion sort, and selection sort) adapts best to this situation? What is the complexity of this problem, in terms of the amount of input data?

6.8 Cycles and in Situ Permutation. In some situations, an array might need to be permuted "in place." As described in §6.2, a sorting program can be organized to refer to records indirectly, computing a permutation that specifies how to do the arrangement instead of actually rearranging them. Here, we consider how the rearrangement might be done *in place*, in a second phase. Here is an example:

index	1	2	3	4	5	6	7	8	9	10	11	12	13	14	15
input keys	29	41	77	26	58	59	97	82	12	44	63	31	53	23	93
permutation	9	14	4	1	12	2	10	13	5	6	11	3	8	15	7

That is, to put the array in sorted order, `a[9]` has to be moved to position `1`, `a[14]` to position `2`, `a[4]` to position `3`, and so on. One way to do this is to start by saving `a[1]` in a register, replace it by `a[p[1]]`, set `j` to `p[1]`, and continue until `p[j]` becomes `1`, when `a[j]` can be set to the saved value. This process is then repeated for each element not yet moved, but if we permute the `p` array in the same way, then we can easily identify elements that need to be moved, as in Program 6.5.

In the example above, first `a[9] = 12` is moved to position `1`, then `a[5] = 58` is moved to position `9`, then `a[12] = 31` is moved to po-

```
for i := 1 to N do
  if p[i] <> i then
    begin
    t := a[i]; k := i;
    repeat
      j := k; a[j] := a[p[j]];
      k := p[j]; p[j] := j;
    until k = i;
    a[j] := t
    end;
  end;
```

Program 6.5 In situ permutation

sition 5, then `a[3] = 77` is moved to position 12, then `a[4] = 26` is moved to position 3, then the 29 that was originally in position 1 is put in position 4. At the same time, `p[1]` is set to 1, `p[9]` is set to 9, and so on, to reflect these moves in the permutation. Note that when it is the case that `p[i] = i` the loop does nothing, so this program moves no element more than once.

How many times is the inner loop of this program iterated? Clearly, this quantity depends on the cycle structure of the permutation—the program itself actually demonstrates the concept of cycles in a rather succinct manner. The running time of Program 6.5 depends on the number of cycles, since a certain amount of extra bookkeeping is associated with each cycle. Thus, this quantity can range from 1 (for example, in the permutation `2 3 4 ... N 1`) to N (in the permutation `1 2 3 ... N`), but it turns out that the average is not very large.

Theorem 6.11 (*Cycle distribution*) *The distribution of the number of cycles in a random permutation is the same as the distribution of the number of left-to-right minima, and is gi en by the Stirling numbers of the first kind. The a erage number of cycles in a random permutation is H_N, with standard de iation $H_N - H_N^{(2)}$.*

Proof. We have already discussed, in §6.1, the fact that the distributions are the same by the fundamental correspondence. To complete an analytic verification of this, we give a direct analysis based on the bivariate generating function

$$B(w,z) = \sum_{p \in \mathcal{P}} w^{|p|} z^{\lambda(p)}$$

where $\lambda(p)$ is the number of cycles in p.

As before, we can directly derive a functional equation from the combinatorial definition. Given a permutation p, we can create $|p|+1$ permutations of size $|p|+1$ by adding element $|p|+1$ at every position in every cycle (including the "null" cycle). Of these permutations, one has one more cycle than p and $|p|$ have the same number of cycles as p. This correspondence is structurally the same as the correspondence that we established for left-to-right minima. Using precisely the same argument as given above, we of course find that the generating function is identical to the generating function for the number of left-to-right minima:

$$B(u,z) = \frac{1}{(1-z)^u}.$$

Therefore the distributions are identical: the average is as stated; the number of permutations of N elements with exactly k cycles is given by the Stirling numbers of the first kind, and so on. ∎

Corollary *A file can be arranged in place using* $\sim N + \ln N$ *data moves, on the average.*

Proof. See above discussion. ∎

Cycle lengths. Knowledge about the lengths of the cycles in a permutation is useful in analyzing Program 6.5 in more detail. For example, we might wish to know whether it might be worthwhile to modify the program to take no action at all when `p[i] = i`. We know from the enumeration results on permutations with cycle length restrictions in §6.4 that the probability that this will happen at least once for a random permutation is $1 - 1/e$, but how many times might we expect it to happen? It turns out that the number of singleton cycles in a random permutation is 1, on the average, and that we can analyze other facts about the cycle length distribution.

Singleton cycles. For comparison with other derivations above, we find the average number of singleton cycles using the combinatorial construction above and the CGF

$$B(z) = \sum_{p \in \mathcal{P}} \tau(p) \frac{z^{|p|}}{|p|!}$$

where $\tau(p)$ is the number of singleton cycles in a permutation p, so that the desired answer is $[z^N]B(z)$. By the construction above, the permutations of length $|p|$ can be grouped into groups of size $|p|$, each of which correspond to a permutation q of size $|p| - 1$. In the group corresponding to q, one has $\tau(q) + 1$ singleton cycle, $\tau(q)$ have $\tau(q) - 1$ singleton cycles, and the rest have $\tau(q)$ singleton cycles, for a total of

$$\tau(q) + 1 + \tau(q)(\tau(q) - 1) + (|p| - 1 - \tau(q))\tau(q) = 1 + |q|\tau(q)$$

singleton cycles for all of the permutations corresponding to q. Therefore,

$$B(z) = \sum_{q \in \mathcal{P}} (1 + |q|\tau(q)) \frac{z^{|q|+1}}{(|q| + 1)!}.$$

Differentiating this formula leads to the simple form

$$\begin{aligned}B'(z) &= \sum_{q\in\mathcal{P}} \frac{z^{|q|}}{|q|!} + \sum_{q\in\mathcal{P}} |q|\tau(q)\frac{z^{|q|}}{|q|!}\\ &= \frac{1}{1-z} + zB'(z),\end{aligned}$$

so $B'(z) = 1/(1-z)^2$ and $B(z) = 1/(1-z)$, as expected.

Cycles of length k. A more general argument using BGFs can be constructed to find the average number of cycles of length k in a random permutation. By adapting the arguments in §6.4, we can write down the (exponential) BGF for the number of cycles of length k:

$$\exp\Bigl(z + \frac{z^2}{2} + \frac{z^3}{3} + \ldots + \frac{z^{k-1}}{k-1} + \frac{z^k}{k}u + \frac{z^{k+1}}{k+1} + \ldots\Bigr).$$

If this is expanded, each term represents a permutation, where the exponent of u counts the number of times the term z^k/k is used, or the number of cycles of length k in the corresponding permutation. Now, the BGF can be rewritten in the form

$$\exp\Bigl(z + \frac{z^2}{2} + \ldots + \frac{z^k}{k} + \ldots\Bigr)\exp\Bigl((u-1)\frac{z^k}{k}\Bigr) = \frac{1}{1-z}\exp((u-1)z^k/k).$$

This form allows calculation of the quantities of interest,

Theorem 6.12 (*Singleton cycle distribution*) *The probability that a permutation of N elements has j singleton cycles is asymptotic to $e^{-1}/j!$. The average number of cycles of length k in a random permutation of size $N \ge k$ is $1/k$, with variance $1/k$.*

Proof. The probability sought is given by the coefficients of the BGF derived in the above discussion:

$$[u^j z^N]\frac{e^{(u-1)z}}{1-z} = \frac{1}{j!}[z^{N-j}]\frac{e^{-z}}{1-z} \sim \frac{e^{-1}}{j!},$$

by Theorem 6.3.

The computation of the average is a simple application of Theorem 3.6: differentiating with respect to u and evaluating at 1 gives

$$[z^N]\frac{z^k}{k}\frac{1}{1-z} = \frac{1}{k} \quad \text{for } N \ge k.$$

and the variance follows from a similar calculation. ∎

We can also sum to generalize Theorem 6.11 and derive the result that the average number of cycles of length $\le k$ in a random permutation of N elements is H_k. Of course, this holds only as long as k is not larger than N.

Exercise 6.61 Use asymptotics from generating functions (see §4.10) or a direct argument to show that the probability for a random permutation to have j cycles of length k is asymptotic to the Poisson distribution $e^{-\lambda}\lambda^j/j!$ with $\lambda = 1/k$.

Exercise 6.62 For a permutation of length 100, what is the probablility that the loop in Program 6.5 never iterates more than 50 times?

Exercise 6.63 [Knuth] Consider a situation where the permutation array cannot be modified and no other extra memory is available. An algorithm to perform in situ permutation can be developed as follows: the elements in each cycle will be permuted when the smallest index in the cycle is encountered. For `j` from `1` to `N`, test each index to see if it is the smallest in the cycle by starting with `k = j` and setting `k = p[k]` while `k > j`. If it is, then permute the cycle as in Program 6.5. Show that the BGF for the number of times this `k = p[k]` instruction is executed satisfies the functional equation

$$B_u(u, z) = B(u, z)B(uz, z).$$

From this, find the mean and variance for this parameter of random permutations. (See [11].)

9	14	4	1	12	2	10	13	5	6	11	3	8	15	7
9	4	1	12	2	10	13	5	6	11	3	8	14	7	15
4	1	9	2	10	12	5	6	11	3	8	13	7	14	15
1	4	2	9	10	5	6	11	3	8	12	7	13	14	15
1	2	4	9	5	6	10	3	8	11	7	12	13	14	15
1	2	4	5	6	9	3	8	10	7	11	12	13	14	15
1	2	4	5	6	3	8	9	7	10	11	12	13	14	15
1	2	4	5	3	6	8	7	9	10	11	12	13	14	15
1	2	4	3	5	6	7	8	9	10	11	12	13	14	15
1	2	3	4	5	6	7	8	9	10	11	12	13	14	15
1	2	3	4	5	6	7	8	9	10	11	12	13	14	15
1	2	3	4	5	6	7	8	9	10	11	12	13	14	15
1	2	3	4	5	6	7	8	9	10	11	12	13	14	15
1	2	3	4	5	6	7	8	9	10	11	12	13	14	15
1	2	3	4	5	6	7	8	9	10	11	12	13	14	15

0	0	2	3	1	4	2	1	5	5	3	9	6	0	8
0	1	2	0	3	1	0	4	4	2	8	5	0	7	0
0	1	0	2	0	0	3	3	1	7	4	0	6	0	0
0	0	1	0	0	2	2	0	6	3	0	5	0	0	0
0	0	0	0	1	1	0	5	2	0	4	0	0	0	0
0	0	0	0	0	0	4	1	0	3	0	0	0	0	0
0	0	0	0	0	3	0	0	2	0	0	0	0	0	0
0	0	0	0	2	0	0	1	0	0	0	0	0	0	0
0	0	0	1	0	0	0	0	0	0	0	0	0	0	0
0	0	0	0	0	0	0	0	0	0	0	0	0	0	0
0	0	0	0	0	0	0	0	0	0	0	0	0	0	0
0	0	0	0	0	0	0	0	0	0	0	0	0	0	0
0	0	0	0	0	0	0	0	0	0	0	0	0	0	0
0	0	0	0	0	0	0	0	0	0	0	0	0	0	0
0	0	0	0	0	0	0	0	0	0	0	0	0	0	0

Figure 6.11 Bubble sort (permutation and associated inversion table)

6.9 Extremal Parameters. In Chapter 5, we found that tree height was much more difficult to analyze than path length because calculating the height involves taking the maximum subtree values, whereas path length involves just enumeration and addition, and the latter operations correspond more naturally to operations on generating functions. In this section, we consider analogous parameters on permutations. What is the average length of the longest or shortest cycle in a permutation? What is the average length of the longest run? The longest increasing subsequence? What is the average value of the largest element in the inversion table of a random permutation? This last question arises in the analysis of yet another elementary sorting algorithm, to which we now turn.

Bubble sort. This method is simple to explain: to sort an array, pass through it repeatedly, exchanging each element with the next to put them in order, if necessary. When a pass through the array is completed without any exchanges (each element is not larger than the next), the sort is completed. An implementation is given in Program 6.6. To analyze this algorithm, we need to count the exchanges and the passes.

Exchanges are straightforward: each exchange is with an adjacent element (as in insertion sort), and so removes exactly one inversion, so the total number of exchanges is exactly the number of inversions in the permutation. The number of passes used is also directly related to the inversion table, as shown in Figure 6.11: each pass actually reduces each nonzero entry in the inversion table by 1, and the algorithm terminates when there are no more nonzero entries. This implies immediately that the number of passes required to bubblesort a permutation is precisely equal to the largest element in the inversion table. The distribution of this quantity is shown in Table 6.10 and Figure 6.12.

```
i := N+1;
repeat
  t := a[1]; i := i-1;
  for j := 2 to i do
    if a[j-1] > a[j] then
      begin t := a[j-1]; a[j-1] := a[j]; a[j] := t end
until (t = a[1]);
```

Program 6.6 Bubble sort

Theorem 6.13 (*Maximum inversion table entry*) *The largest element in the inversion table of a random permutation has mean value* $\sim N - \sqrt{\pi N/2}$.

Proof. The number of inversion tables of length N with all entries less than k is simply $k!k^{N-k}$ since the ith entry can be anything between 0 and $i-1$ for $i \le k$ and anything between 0 and $k-1$ for $i > k$. Thus, the probability that the maximum entry is less than k is $k!k^{N-k}/N!$, and the average value sought is

$$\sum_{0 \le k \le N} \left(1 - \frac{k!k^{N-k}}{N!}\right).$$

The second term in this sum is the "Ramanujan P-function" whose asymptotic value is given in Table 4.11. ■

Corollary *Bubble sort does* $\sim N^2/2$ *key comparisons and moves* $\sim N^2/2$ *records (in* $\sim N - \sqrt{\pi N/2}$ *passes), on the average, to sort a file of N records with randomly ordered distinct keys.*

Proof. See above discussion. ■

Exercise 6.64 Consider a modification of bubble sort where the passes through the array alternate in direction (right to left, then left to right). What is the effect of two such passes on the inversion table?

$N \downarrow$ $k \rightarrow$	0	1	2	3	4	5	6	7	8	9
1	1									
2	1	1								
3	1	3	2							
4	1	7	10	6						
5	1	15	38	42	24					
6	1	31	130	222	216	120				
7	1	63	422	1050	1464	1320	720			
8	1	127	1330	4686	8856	10920	9360	5040		
9	1	255	4118	20202	50424	80520	91440	75600	40320	
10	1	511	12610	85182	276696	558120	795600	851760	685440	362880

Table 6.10 Distribution of maximum inversion table entry

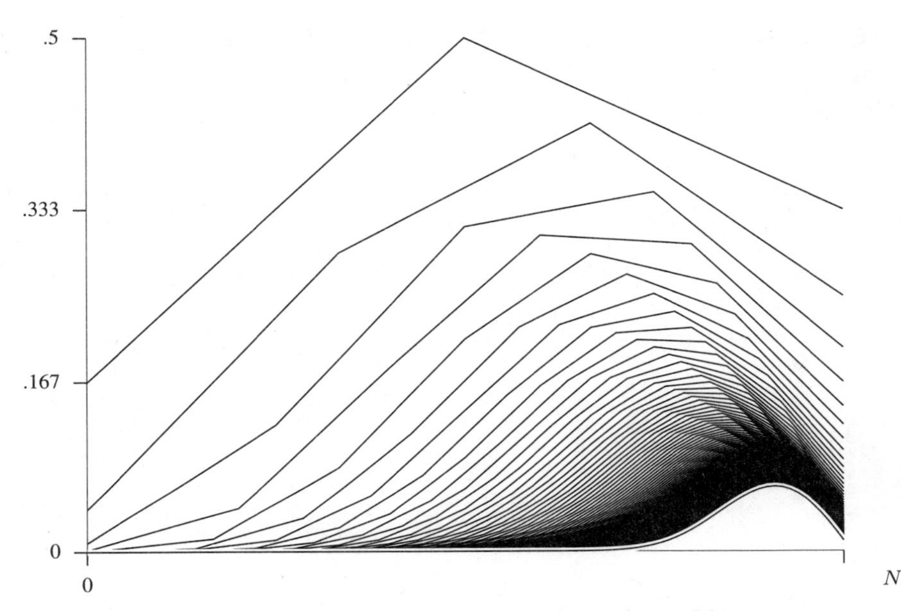

Figure 6.12 Distribution of maximum inversion table entry

Longest and shortest cycles. What is the average length of the longest cycle in a permutation? We can immediately write down an expression for this. Earlier in this chapter, we derived the exponential GFs that enumerate permutations with no cycle of length $> k$ (see Theorem 6.2):

$$
\begin{aligned}
e^{z} &= 1 + z + \frac{z^2}{2!} + \frac{z^3}{3!} + \frac{z^4}{4!} + \frac{z^5}{5!} + \frac{z^6}{6!} + \cdots \\
e^{z+z^2/2} &= 1 + z + 2\frac{z^2}{2!} + 4\frac{z^3}{3!} + 10\frac{z^4}{4!} + 26\frac{z^5}{5!} + 76\frac{z^6}{6!} + \cdots \\
e^{z+z^2/2+z^3/3} &= 1 + z + 2\frac{z^2}{2!} + 6\frac{z^3}{3!} + 18\frac{z^4}{4!} + 66\frac{z^5}{5!} + 276\frac{z^6}{6!} + \cdots \\
e^{z+z^2/2+z^3/3+z^4/4} &= 1 + z + 2\frac{z^2}{2!} + 6\frac{z^3}{3!} + 24\frac{z^4}{4!} + 96\frac{z^5}{5!} + 456\frac{z^6}{6!} + \cdots \\
&\ \ \vdots \\
e^{-\ln(1-z)} = \frac{1}{1-z} &= 1 + z + 2\frac{z^2}{2!} + 6\frac{z^3}{3!} + 24\frac{z^4}{4!} + 120\frac{z^5}{5!} + 720\frac{z^6}{6!} + \cdots .
\end{aligned}
$$

From these, we can write down the generating functions for the permutations with at least one cycle of length $> k$, or, equivalently, those for which the maximum cycle length is $> k$:

$$
\begin{aligned}
\frac{1}{1-z} - e^0 &= z + 2\frac{z^2}{2!} + 6\frac{z^3}{3!} + 24\frac{z^4}{4!} + 120\frac{z^5}{5!} + 720\frac{z^6}{6!} + \ldots \\
\frac{1}{1-z} - e^z &= \frac{z^2}{2!} + 5\frac{z^3}{3!} + 23\frac{z^4}{4!} + 119\frac{z^5}{5!} + 719\frac{z^6}{6!} + \ldots \\
\frac{1}{1-z} - e^{z+z^2/2} &= 2\frac{z^3}{3!} + 14\frac{z^4}{4!} + 94\frac{z^5}{5!} + 644\frac{z^6}{6!} + \ldots \\
\frac{1}{1-z} - e^{z+z^2/2+z^3/3} &= 6\frac{z^4}{4!} + 54\frac{z^5}{5!} + 444\frac{z^6}{6!} + \ldots \\
\frac{1}{1-z} - e^{z+z^2/2+z^3/3+z^4/4} &= 24\frac{z^5}{5!} + 264\frac{z^6}{6!} + \ldots \\
&\vdots
\end{aligned}
$$

From Table 3.6, the average length of the longest cycle in a random permutation is found by summing these and may be expressed as follows:

$$[z^N]\sum_{k\geq 0}\Bigl(\frac{1}{1-z} - e^{z+z^2/2+z^3/3+\ldots+z^k/k}\Bigr).$$

As is typical for extremal parameters, derivation of an asymptotic result from this information is rather intricate. We can compute the exact value of this quantity for small N by summing the equations above to get the initial terms of the exponential CGF for the length of the longest cycle:

$$1\frac{z^1}{1!} + 3\frac{z^2}{2!} + 13\frac{z^3}{3!} + 67\frac{z^4}{4!} + 411\frac{z^5}{5!} + \ldots.$$

It turns out that the length of the longest cycle in a random permutation is $\sim \lambda N$ where $\lambda \approx .62433\cdots$. This result was first derived by Golomb, Shepp, and Lloyd in 1966 [15].

Exercise 6.65 Find the average length of the shortest cycle in a random permutation of length N, for all $N < 10$. (*Note*: Shepp and Lloyd show this quantity to be $\sim e^{-\gamma}\ln N$, where γ is Euler's constant.)

PERMUTATIONS are well studied as fundamental combinatorial objects, and we would expect that knowledge of their properties could help in the understanding of the performance characteristics of sorting algorithms. The direct correspondence between fundamental properties such as cycles and inversions and fundamental algorithms such as insertion sort, selection sort, and bubble sort confirms this expectation.

Research on new sorting algorithms and the analysis of their performance is quite active. Variants on sorting such as priority queues, merging algorithms, and sorting "networks" continue to be of practical interest. New types of computers and new applications demand new methods and better understanding of old ones, and the kind of analysis outlined in this chapter is an essential ingredient in designing and using such algorithms.

As suggested throughout this chapter, general tools are available [4] that can answer many of the more complicated questions raised in this chapter. We have emphasized the use of cumulative generating functions to analyze properties of permutations because they provide a straightforward "systematic" path to the average value of quantities of interest. For analysis of properties of permutations, the cumulative approach can often yield results in a simpler, more direct manner than available with recurrences or BGFs. As usual, extremal parameters (those defined by a "maximum" or "minimum" rule as opposed to an additive rule) are more difficult to analyze, though "vertical" GFs can be used to compute small values and to start the analysis.

Despite the simplicity of the permutation as a combinatorial object, the wealth of analytic questions to be addressed is often quite surprising to the uninitiated. However, the fact that we can use a standard methodology to answer basic questions about the properties of permutations is encouraging, not only because many of these questions arise in important applications, but also because we can hope to be able to study more complicated combinatorial structures as well.

References

1. L. COMTET. *Advanced Combinatorics*, Reidel, Dordrecht, 1974.
2. F. N. DAVID AND D. E. BARTON. *Combinatorial Chance*, Charles Griffin, London, 1962.
3. W. FELLER. *An Introduction to Probability Theory and Its Applications*, John Wiley, New York, 1957.

4. P. FLAJOLET AND R. SEDGEWICK. *Analytic Combinatorics*, in preparation.
5. G. H. GONNET AND R. BAEZA–YATES. *Handbook of Algorithms and Data Structures*, 2nd edition, Addison-Wesley, Reading, MA, 1991.
6. I. GOULDEN AND D. JACKSON. *Combinatorial Enumeration*, John Wiley, New York, 1983.
7. R. GRAHAM, D. E. KNUTH, AND O. PATASHNIK. *Concrete Mathematics*, Addison-Wesley, Reading, MA, 1989.
8. D. E. KNUTH. *The Art of Computer Programming. Volume 1: Fundamental Algorithms*, Addison-Wesley, Reading, MA, 1968.
9. D. E. KNUTH. *The Art of Computer Programming. Volume 2: Seminumerical Algorithms*, Addison-Wesley, Reading, MA, 1969.
10. D. E. KNUTH. *The Art of Computer Programming. Volume 3: Sorting and Searching*, Addison-Wesley, Reading, MA, 1973.
11. D. E. KNUTH. "Mathematical Analysis of Algorithms," *Information Processing 71*, Proceedings of the IFIP Congress, Ljubljana, 1971, 19–27.
12. V. LIFSCHITZ AND B. PITTEL. "The number of increasing subsequences of the random permutation," *Journal of Combinatorial Theory (Series A)* **31**, 1981, 1–20.
13. B. F. LOGAN AND L. A. SHEPP. "A variational problem from random Young tableaux," *Ad ances in Mathematics* **26**, 1977, 206–222.
14. R. SEDGEWICK. *Algorithms*, 2nd edition, Addison-Wesley, Reading, MA, 1988.
15. L. SHEPP AND S. P. LLOYD. "Ordered cycle lengths in a random permutation," *Transactions of the American Mathematical Society* **121**, 1966, 340–357.
16. J. S. VITTER AND P. FLAJOLET. "Analysis of algorithms and data structures," in *Handbook of Theoretical Computer Science A: Algorithms and Complexity*, J. van Leeuwen, ed., Elsevier, Amsterdam, 1990, 431–524.
17. J. VUILLEMIN. "A unifying look at data structures," *Communications of the ACM* **23**, 4, 1980, 229–239.
18. A. YAO. "Analysis of selection sort," to appear.
19. A. YAO. "An analysis of $(h, k, 1)$ Shellsort," *Journal of Algorithms* **1**, 1980, 14–50.

CHAPTER SEVEN

STRINGS AND TRIES

SEQUENCES of characters or letters drawn from a fixed alphabet are called *strings*. Algorithms that process strings range from fundamental methods at the heart of the theory of computation to practical text-processing methods with a host of important applications. In this chapter, we study basic combinatorial properties of strings, some fundamental algorithms for searching for patterns in strings, and related data structures.

We use the term *bitstring* to refer to strings comprised of just two characters; if the alphabet is of size $M > 2$, we refer to the strings as *bytestrings*, or *words*, or M-ary strings. In this chapter, we assume that M is a small fixed constant, a reasonable assumption given our interest in text- and bit-processing algorithms. If M can grow to be large (for example, increasing with the length of the string), then we have a somewhat different combinatorial object, the subject of the next chapter. This is an important distinction, which we will discuss in more detail in Chapter 8. In this chapter, our primary interest is in potentially long strings made from constant-size alphabets, and in their properties as sequences.

From an algorithmic point of view, not much generality is lost by focusing on bitstrings rather than on bytestrings: a string built from a larger alphabet corresponds to a bitstring built by encoding the individual characters in binary. Conversely, when an algorithm, data structure, or analysis of strings built from a larger alphabet depends in some way on the size of the alphabet, that same dependence can be reflected in a bitstring by considering the bits in blocks. This particular correspondence between M-ary strings and bitstrings is exact only when M is a power of 2. It is also often very easy to generalize an algorithm or analysis from bitstrings to M-ary strings (essentially by changing "2" to "M" throughout), so we do so when appropriate.

Random bitstrings correspond precisely to sequences of independent Bernoulli trials, which are well studied in classical probability theory; in the analysis of algorithms such results are of interest because many algorithms naturally depend explicitly on properties of binary strings. We review some relevant classical results in this chapter and the next. As we have been doing for trees and permutations in the previous two chapters, we consider the problems from a computational standpoint and use generating functions as tools for combinatorial analysis. This approach yields simple solutions to some classical problems and gives a very general framework within which a surprising range of problems can be considered.

We consider basic algorithms for searching for the occurrence of a fixed pattern in a given string, which are best described in terms of pattern-specific finite-state automata (FSAs). Not only do FSAs lead to uniform, compact and efficient implementations, but also it turns out that the automata correspond precisely to generating functions associated with the patterns. In this chapter, we study some examples of this in detail.

Certain computational tasks involve explicit manipulation of *sets* of strings. Sets of strings (generally, infinite sets) are called *languages* and are the basis of an extensive theory of fundamental importance in computer science. Languages are classified according to the difficulty of describing their constituent strings. In the present context, we will be most concerned with *regular* languages and *context-free* languages, which describe many interesting combinatorial structures. In this chapter, we give many examples that illustrate the utility of generating functions in analyzing properties of languages. Remarkably, generating functions for both regular and context-free languages can be fully characterized and shown to be essentially different in nature.

A fundamental data structure called the *trie* is often used by algorithms that process strings and finite sets of strings. Tries are treelike objects with structure determined by bit values in a set of bitstrings. If the bitstrings are independent and randomly chosen, the trie is a combinatorial object with a wealth of interesting properties. In this chapter, we look at basic trie algorithms, properties of tries, and associated generating functions. Not only are tries useful in a wide range of applications, but also their analysis exhibits and motivates many of our most important tools for the analysis of algorithms.

7.1 String Searching. We begin by considering a basic algorithm for "string searching:" given a pattern of length k and some text of length N, look for occurrences of the pattern in the text. Program 7.1 gives the straightforward solution to this problem. For each position in the text, the program checks if there is a match by comparing the text, starting at this position, character-by-character with the pattern, starting at the beginning. The program assumes that two different sentinel characters are used, one at the end of the pattern (the $(k+1)$st pattern character) and one at the end of the text (the $(N+1)$st text character). Thus, all string comparisons end on a character mismatch, and we tell whether the pattern was present in the text simply by checking whether the sentinel(s) caused the mismatch.

Depending on the application, one of a number of different variations of the basic algorithm might be of interest:

- Stop when the *first* match is found.
- Print out the position of *all* matches.
- Count the number of matches.
- Find the longest match.

These are easily implemented in Program 7.1 by adding appropriate code at the indicated point, where matches are found. In some applications, partial matches at the end of the text string may be of interest; if not, the program could be improved by terminating the loop when fewer than k text characters are left in the text. Similar improvements may be appropriate in various other specific circumstances. The basic implementation given in Program 7.1 is a reasonable general-purpose method for many string-searching applications, though we will see better methods later in the chapter.

For the moment, we assume an arbitrary, but fixed, pattern even though trivial improvements to the basic method are available for some patterns. For example, we could search for a string of k consecutive 0s (a *run*) simply by maintaining a counter and scanning through the text, resetting the counter when a 1 is encountered, incrementing it when a 0

```
procedure stringsearch;
  var i, j:  integer;
  begin
  for i := 1 to N do
    begin
    j := 0;
    repeat j := j+1 until a[i+j-1] <> p[j];
    if j = k+1 then << match found >>
    end
  end;
```

Program 7.1 Basic method for string searching

is encountered, and stopping when the counter reaches k. By contrast, consider the action of Program 7.1 when searching for a string of k consecutive zeros (assume that k is large) and it encounters a small run of, say, five 0s followed by a 1. It examines all five 0s, determines there is a mismatch on finding the 1, then increments the text pointer *just by one* so that it finds a mismatch by checking four 0s and a 1, then it checks three 0s and a 1, and so on. The algorithm ends up checking $(t+1)(t+2)/2$ bits for every run of t 0s. Later in the chapter, we will be examining improvements to the basic algorithm that avoid such rechecking. For the moment, our interest is to examine how to analyze the basic method.

Analysis of "all matches" variant. We are interested in finding the average running time of Program 7.1 when searching for a given pattern in random text. Clearly, the running time is proportional to the number of characters examined during the search. Since each string comparison ends on a mismatch, its cost is 1 plus the number of characters that match the pattern at that text position. Table 7.1 shows this for each of the patterns of four bits in a sample text string. With each position in the text string we associate an integer, the number of character positions that match the pattern, starting at that text position. The total of these plus N (for the mismatches) is

	0	1	1	1	0	1	0	0	0	1	0	0	0	0	0	1	0	0	1	0	0	0	0	0	1	1	*total*
0000	1	0	0	0	1	0	3	2	1	0	4	4	3	2	1	0	2	1	0	4	4	3	2	1	0	0	39
0001	1	0	0	0	1	0	4	2	1	0	3	3	4	2	1	0	2	1	0	3	3	4	2	1	0	0	39
0010	1	0	0	0	1	0	2	4	1	0	2	2	2	4	1	0	4	1	0	2	2	2	3	1	0	0	35
0011	1	0	0	0	1	0	2	3	1	0	2	2	2	3	1	0	3	1	0	2	2	2	4	1	0	0	33
0100	2	0	0	0	4	0	1	1	4	0	1	1	1	1	4	0	1	4	0	1	1	1	1	2	0	0	31
0101	2	0	0	0	3	0	1	1	3	0	1	1	1	1	3	0	1	3	0	1	1	1	1	2	0	0	27
0110	3	0	0	0	2	0	1	1	2	0	1	1	1	1	2	0	1	2	0	1	1	1	1	3	0	0	22
0111	4	0	0	0	2	0	1	1	2	0	1	1	1	1	2	0	1	2	0	1	1	1	1	3	0	0	25
1000	0	1	1	2	0	4	0	0	0	4	0	0	0	0	0	3	0	0	4	0	0	0	0	0	1	1	21
1001	0	1	1	2	0	3	0	0	0	3	0	0	0	0	0	4	0	0	3	0	0	0	0	0	1	1	19
1010	0	1	1	2	0	2	0	0	0	2	0	0	0	0	0	2	0	0	2	0	0	0	0	0	1	1	14
1011	0	1	1	2	0	2	0	0	0	2	0	0	0	0	0	2	0	0	2	0	0	0	0	0	1	1	14
1100	0	2	3	1	0	1	0	0	0	1	0	0	0	0	0	1	0	0	1	0	0	0	0	0	2	1	13
1101	0	2	4	1	0	1	0	0	0	1	0	0	0	0	0	1	0	0	1	0	0	0	0	0	2	1	14
1110	0	4	2	1	0	1	0	0	0	1	0	0	0	0	0	1	0	0	1	0	0	0	0	0	2	1	14
1111	0	3	2	1	0	1	0	0	0	1	0	0	0	0	0	1	0	0	1	0	0	0	0	0	2	1	13

Table 7.1 Cost of searching for 4-bit patterns (basic method)

the number of times the inner loop in Program 7.1 is iterated, clearly the dominant term in the running time of the program. Using the cumulative method, we can calculate this with a simple counting argument.

Theorem 7.1 (*Pattern occurrence enumeration*) *The expected number of occurrences of an arbitrary fixed pattern of length k in a random bitstring of length N is $(N-k+1)/2^k$.*

Proof. Using cumulative counting, we count the total number of occurrences of the pattern in all of the 2^N bitstrings of N bits. The k bits can start in any one of $N-k+1$ positions, and, for each position, there are 2^{N-k} bitstrings with the pattern at that position. Collecting all these terms gives the desired total $(N-k+1)2^{N-k}$, and dividing by 2^N gives the stated result. ■

Corollary *The expected number of bit comparisons made by the basic string-searching algorithm when seeking all occurrences of an arbitrary fixed pattern of length k in a text string of length N is $N(2-2^{-k})+O(1)$.*

Proof. To find the number of bits examined by the algorithm in the search, we note that we can interpret the numbers in Table 7.1 another way: they count the number of *prefixes* of the pattern that occur starting at the corresponding position in the text. Now we can use the above formula to count the prefixes as well. This gives the expression

$$\sum_{1\le j\le k}(N-j+1)2^{N-j}$$

for the total number of occurrences of prefixes of the pattern in all of the 2^N bitstrings of N bits. Evaluating this sum, dividing by 2^N, and adding N (for the mismatch comparisons) gives the stated result. ■

Corollary *The average number of bits examined by the basic string-searching algorithm to find the longest match with an arbitrary infinitely long pattern in a random bitstring is $\sim 2N$.*

These results are independent of the pattern. This seems to run counter to the intuition just given, where we know that a search for a long string of 0s will examine $O(t^2)$ bits for every run of t 0s in the text, whereas a search for a 1 followed by a long string of 0s does not have such evident "quadratic" behavior. This is explained by noting that prefixes of the latter pattern are *somewhere* in the text, but not bunched together as for strings of 0s. Since we use cumulated totals, we need not worry about independence among different instances of prefixes; we count them all. By contrast, the time required to find the *first* match does depend on the pattern, even for random text. This is directly related to another quantity of interest, the probability that the pattern does not occur in the text. In the next section, we will look at details of these analytic results.

To reiterate this distinction, we consider the use of OGFs and the symbolic method for this problem. The OGF enumerating occurrences of an arbitrary fixed pattern of length k is

$$\frac{1}{1-2z} z^k \frac{1}{1-2z},$$

since such an occurrence is constructed by concatenating an arbitrary word, the pattern, and another arbitrary word. A particular bitstring may be counted several times in this enumeration (once for each occurrence of the pattern), which is precisely what we seek. Thus, the number of occurrences of a fixed pattern of length k in all bitstrings of length N is

$$[z^N]\frac{1}{1-2z} z^k \frac{1}{1-2z} = [z^{N-k}]\frac{1}{(1-2z)^2} = (N-k+1)2^{N-k},$$

as in Theorem 7.1. Again, this is *not* the same as the number of bitstrings of length N containing (one or more occurrences of) an arbitrary fixed pattern.

Later in the chapter, we will look at algorithmic improvements to the basic method. First we will look at the Knuth-Morris-Pratt algorithm, a method that uses preprocessing time proportional to the length of the pattern to get an "optimal" search time, examining each character in the text at most once. At the end of the chapter, we will see that with (much) more investment in preprocessing, the text can be built into a data structure related to a general structure known as a *trie* that allows searches for patterns to be done in time proportional to the length of the pattern. Tries also provide efficient support for a number of other algorithms on bitstrings, but we postpone considering those until after covering basic analytic results.

7.2 Combinatorial properties of bitstrings. We are interested in studying the properties of random strings of 0 and 1 values (bitstrings) with each of the 2^N bitstrings of length N equally likely. Bitstrings are enumerated by the OGF

$$S(z) = \sum_{s \in \mathcal{S}} z^{|s|} = \sum_{N \geq 0} \{\text{\# of bitstrings of length } N\} z^N$$

where $\mathcal{S}$ denotes the set of all bitstrings. Bitstrings are either empty or begin with a 0 or a 1, so

$$S(z) = 1 + 2\sum_{s \in \mathcal{S}} z^{|s|+1} = 1 + 2zS(z)$$

and therefore $S(z) = (1 - 2z)^{-1}$ and the number of bitstrings of length N is 2^N as expected. As with permutations and trees in the previous two chapters, we can modify this basic argument to study more interesting properties of bitstrings.

For example, we have already encountered the problem of enumerating the 1s in a random bitstring as an example in §3.12: the associated bivariate generating function involves the binomial distribution

$$P(u, z) = \sum_{s \in \mathcal{S}} u^{\nu(s)} z^{|s|} = \frac{1}{1 - z(1 + u)} = \sum_{N} \sum_{k} \binom{N}{k} u^k z^N.$$

We used Theorem 3.11 to calculate that the average number of 1 bits in a random N-bit string is

$$[z^N] P_u(1, z)/2^N = N/2,$$

and so forth. We will consider "global" properties like this in much more detail in Chapter 8; in this chapter our focus is more on "local" properties involving bits that are near one another in the string.

Studying properties of random bitstrings is equivalent to studying properties of independent Bernoulli trials (perhaps coin flips), so classical results from probability theory are relevant. Our specific focus in this chapter is not just on the trials, but also on the *sequence* of events. There are also classical results related to this. In probability theory, we consider properties of a sequence of random trials and study "waiting times" (see Feller [6], for example); in the analysis of algorithms, we consider the equivalent problem of searching for patterns in strings by taking the bits in sequence, a natural way to think about the same problem. As we will see, it turns out that formal language theory and generating functions combine to provide a clear explanation of analytic phenomena relating to the study of sequences of Bernoulli trials.

Runs of 0s. We begin by considering the following basic question: Where should we expect to find the first run of k consecutive 0s in a random bitstring? Table 7.2 gives ten long random bitstrings and the position where one, two, three, and four 0s first occur. It turns out that generating functions lead to a simple solution to this problem, and that it is representative of a host of similar problems.

Theorem 7.2 (*Runs of 0s*) *The generating function enumerating the number of bitstrings with no runs of k consecutive 0s is given by*

$$S_k(z) = \frac{1 - z^k}{1 - 2z + z^{k+1}}.$$

Proof. Let $\mathcal{S}_k$ be the number of bitstrings with no runs of k consecutive 0s. Then

$$\begin{aligned} S_k(z) &= \sum_{s \in \mathcal{S}_k} z^{|s|} \\ &= \sum_{N \geq 0} \{\#\text{ of bitstrings of length } N \text{ with no runs of } k \text{ 0s}\} z^N. \end{aligned}$$

	1	2	3	4
01010011101010000110011100010111011000110111111010	0	4	13	13
01110101010001010010011001010000100001010110100101	0	10	10	28
010111010110111100100011100000001010110010011110000	0	16	19	25
10101000010100111010101011110000111110000111001001	1	5	5	5
1111111100100000010010011001001100000000100000110001	8	8	11	11
00100010001100101110011100001100101000001011001111	0	0	3	24
01011011110110010110000100101001010000101001111110	0	13	19	19
10011010000010011001010010100011000001111010011010	1	1	7	7
01100010011001101100010111110001001000111001111010	0	3	3	—
01011001000110000001000110010101011100111100100110	0	5	8	13
average	1.0	6.5	9.8	—

Table 7.2 Position of first runs of 0s on sample bitstrings

Now, any bitstring without k consecutive 0s is either (*i*) null or consisting of from zero to $k-1$ 0s; or (*ii*) a string of from zero to $k-1$ 0s, followed by a 1, followed by any bitstring without k consecutive 0s. Establishing this correspondence based on the initial number of 0s in the bitstring gives a functional equation and then an explicit expression for the OGF:

$$\begin{aligned} S_k(z) &= 1 + z + \ldots + z^{k-1} + \sum_{s \in \mathcal{S}_k} \sum_{0 \le j < k} z^{|s|+j+1} \\ &= \frac{1-z^k}{1-z}(1 + zS_k(z)). \end{aligned}$$

Solving this, we find that

$$S_k(z) = \frac{\dfrac{1-z^k}{1-z}}{1 - z\dfrac{1-z^k}{1-z}} = \frac{1-z^k}{1-2z+z^{k+1}}.$$

■

These are rational functions and can thus be expanded if desired. Checking small values, we have the following expansions for $k = 1, 2, 3$:

$$\begin{aligned} \frac{1-z}{1-2z+z^2} &= 1 + z + z^2 + z^3 + z^4 + z^5 + z^6 + z^7 + \ldots \\ \frac{1-z^2}{1-2z+z^3} &= 1 + 2z + 3z^2 + 5z^3 + 8z^4 + 13z^5 + 21z^6 + 34z^7 + \ldots \\ \frac{1-z^3}{1-2z+z^4} &= 1 + 2z + 4z^2 + 7z^3 + 13z^4 + 24z^5 + 44z^6 + 81z^7 + \ldots . \end{aligned}$$

For $k = 1$, this checks with the fact that there is one string of length N with no runs of one 0 (the string that is all 1s). For $k = 2$, we have

$$S_2(z) = \frac{1+z}{1-z-z^2} \qquad \text{so} \qquad [z^N]S_2(z) = F_{N+1} + F_N = F_{N+2},$$

the Fibonacci numbers (see §2.4). Indeed, the representation

$$S_k(z) = \frac{1 + z + z^2 + \ldots + z^{k-1}}{1 - z - z^2 - \ldots - z^k}$$

shows that $[z^N]S_k(z)$ satisfies the same recurrence as the generalized Fibonacci numbers of Exercise 4.18, but with different initial values. Thus, Theorem 4.1 can be used to find asymptotic estimates for $[z^N]S_k(z)$.

Corollary *The number of bitstrings of length N containing no runs of k consecutive 0s is asymptotic to $c_k\beta_k^N$, where β_k is the root of largest modulus of the polynomial $z^k - z^{k-1} - \ldots - z - 1 = 0$ and $c_k = (\beta^k + \beta^{k-1} + \ldots + \beta)/(\beta^{k-1} + 2\beta^{k-2} + 3\beta^{k-3} + \ldots + (k-1)\beta + k)$.*

Proof. Immediate from Exercise 4.18 and Theorem 4.1. Approximate values of c_0 and β for small values of k are given in Table 7.3. ■

Exercise 7.1 Give two recurrences satisfied by $[z^N]S_k(z)$.

Exercise 7.2 How long a string of random bits should be taken to be 99% sure that there are at least three consecutive 0s?

Exercise 7.3 How long a string of random bits should be taken to be 50% sure that there are at least 32 consecutive 0s?

Exercise 7.4 Show that

$$[z^N]S_k(z) = \sum_i (-1)^i 2^{N-(k+1)i}\left(\binom{N-ki}{i} - 2^{-k}\binom{N-k(i+1)}{i}\right).$$

First run of 0s. A shortcut to computing the average position of the first run of k 0s is available because the OGF that enumerates bitstrings with no runs of k consecutive 0s is very closely related to the PGF for the position of the last bit (the end) in the first run of k consecutive 0s in a

k	$S_k(z)$	c_k	β_k
2	$\dfrac{1-z^2}{1-2z+z^3}$	$1.17082\cdots$	$1.61803\cdots$
3	$\dfrac{1-z^3}{1-2z+z^4}$	$1.13745\cdots$	$1.83929\cdots$
4	$\dfrac{1-z^4}{1-2z+z^5}$	$1.09166\cdots$	$1.92756\cdots$
5	$\dfrac{1-z^5}{1-2z+z^6}$	$1.05753\cdots$	$1.96595\cdots$
6	$\dfrac{1-z^6}{1-2z+z^7}$	$1.03498\cdots$	$1.98358\cdots$

Table 7.3 Count of bitstrings with no runs of k 0s ($[z^N]S_k(z) \sim c_k\beta_k^N$)

random bitstring, as shown by the following manipulations:

$$
\begin{aligned}
S_k(z) &= \sum_{s \in \mathcal{S}_k} z^{|s|} \\
&= \sum_{N \ge 0} \{\#\text{ of bitstrings of length } N \text{ with no runs of } k \text{ 0s}\} z^N \\
S_k(1/2) &= \sum_{N \ge 0} \{\#\text{ of bitstrings of length } N \text{ with no runs of } k \text{ 0s}\}/2^N \\
S_k(1/2) &= \sum_{N \ge 0} \Pr\{\text{1st } N \text{ bits of a random bitstring have no runs of } k \text{ 0s}\} \\
&= \sum_{N \ge 0} \Pr\{\text{position of end of first run of } k \text{ 0s is} > N\}.
\end{aligned}
$$

This sum of cumulative probabilities is equal to the expectation.

Corollary *The average position of the end of the first run of k 0s in a random bitstring is* $S_k(1/2) = 2^{k+1} - 2$.

Generating functions simplify the computation of the expectation considerably; any reader still unconvinced of this fact is welcome, for example, to verify the result of Corollary 7.4 by developing a recurrence on the probability p_j that the first run of k 0s occurs at position j, then calculating $\sum_j jp_j$. For permutations, we found that the count $N!$ of the number of permutations on N elements led us to EGFs; for bitstrings, the count 2^N of the number of bitstrings of N elements will lead us to functional equations involving $z/2$, as above.

Existence. The proof of the second corollary to Theorem 7.2 also illustrates that finding the first occurrence of a pattern is roughly equivalent to counting the number of strings that do *not* contain the pattern, and tells us that the probability that a random bitstring contains no run of k 0s is $[z^N]S_k(z/2)$. For example, for $k = 1$ this is $1/2^N$, since only the bitstring that is all 1s contains no runs of k 0s. For $k = 2$ the probability is $O\big((\phi/2)^N\big)$ (with $\phi = (1+\sqrt{5})/2 = 1.61803\cdots$), exponentially decreasing in N. For fixed k, this is always the case because the β_k's in Table 7.3 remain strictly less than 2. A slightly more detailed analysis reveals that once N increases past 2^k, it becomes increasingly unlikely that some k-bit pattern does not occur. For example, a quick calculation from Table 7.3 shows that there is a 92% chance that a 10-bit string does not contain a run of six 0s, a 44% chance that a 100-bit string does not contain a run of six 0s, and a .02% chance that a 1000-bit string does not contain a run of six 0s.

Longest run. What is the average length of the longest run of 0s in a random bitstring? The distribution of this quantity is shown in Figure 7.1. As we did for tree height in Chapter 5 and cycle length in permutations in Chapter 6, we can sum the "vertical" GFs given above to get an expression for the average length of the longest string of 0s in a random N-bit string:

$$\frac{1}{2^N}[z^N]\sum_{k\geq 0}\Bigl(\frac{1}{1-2z}-\frac{1-z^k}{1-2z+z^{k+1}}\Bigr).$$

Knuth [18] studied a very similar quantity for the application of determining carry propagation time in an asynchronous adder, and showed this quantity to be $\lg N + O(1)$. The constant term has an oscillatory behavior; close inspection of Figure 7.1 will give some insight into why this might be so. The function describing the oscillation turns out to be the same as one that we will study in detail for the analysis of tries at the end of this chapter.

Exercise 7.5 Find the bivariate generating function associated with the number of leading 1 bits in a random bitstring and use it to calculate the average and standard deviation of this quantity.

Exercise 7.6 By considering bitstrings with no runs of two consecutive 0s, evaluate the following sum involving Fibonacci numbers: $\sum_{j\geq 0} F_j/2^j$.

Exercise 7.7 Find the BGF for the length of the longest run of 0s in bitstrings.

Exercise 7.8 What is the standard deviation of the random variable marking the first occurrence of a run of k 0s in a random bitstring?

Exercise 7.9 Use a computer algebra system to plot the average length of the longest run of 0s in a random bitstring of N bits, for $2 < N < 100$.

Exercise 7.10 How many bits are examined by the basic algorithm given in the previous section to find the first string of k 0s in a random bitstring?

Arbitrary patterns. At first, we might suspect that the above results hold for *any* fixed pattern of k bits, but it is simply not true: the average position of the first occurrence of a fixed bit pattern in a random bitstring depends very much on the pattern itself. For example, it is easy to see that a pattern like 0001 tends to appear before 0000, on the average, by the

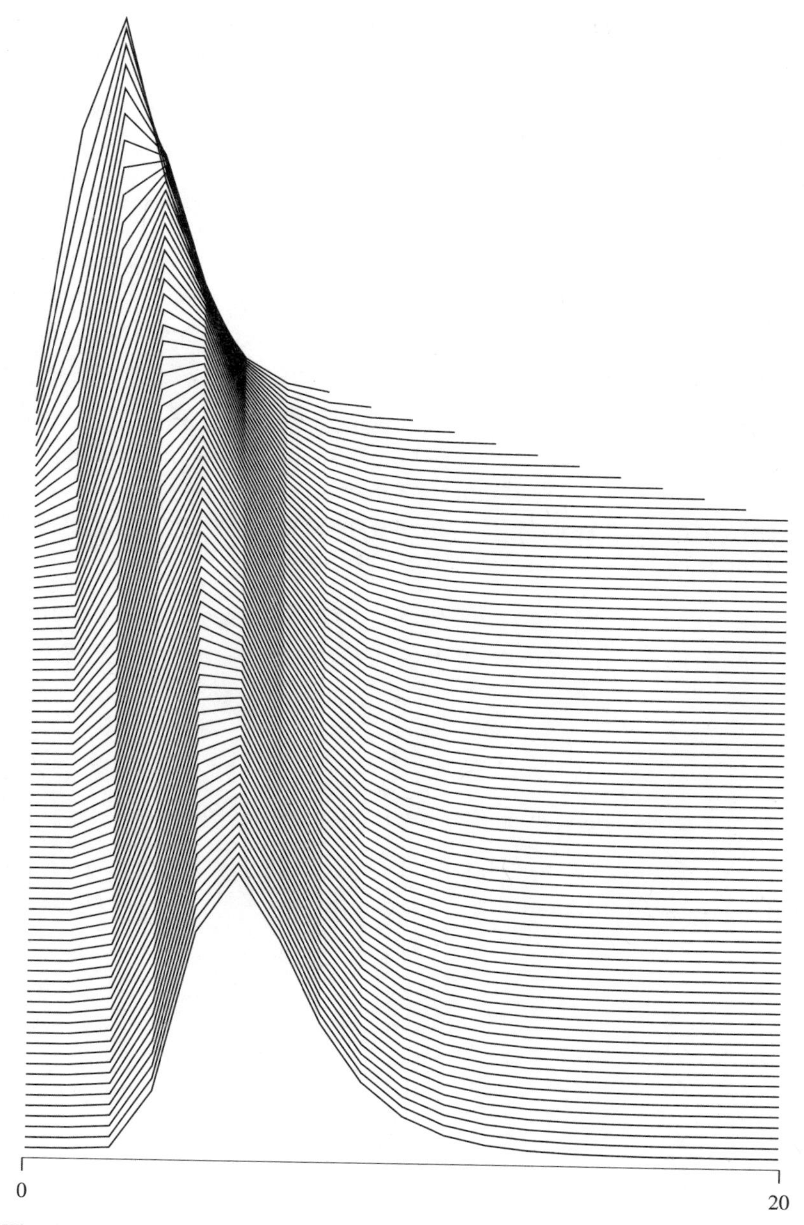

Figure 7.1 Distribution of longest run of 0s in a random bitstring (horizontal axes translated to separate curves)

following observation: once 000 has already been matched, in both cases a match occurs on the next character with probability $1/2$, but a mismatch for 0000 means that 0001 was in the text and no match is possible for four more characters, but a mismatch for 0001 means that 0000 is in the text and a match can happen on the next 1-bit. The dependence on the pattern turns out to be easily expressed in terms of a function matching the pattern against itself:

Definition *The* autocorrelation *of a bitstring* $b_0b_1\ldots b_{k-1}$ *is the bitstring* $c_0c_1\ldots c_{k-1}$ *with* c_i *defined to be* 1 *if* $b_j = b_{i+j}$ *for* $0 \le j \le k-1-i$, 0 *otherwise. The corresponding* autocorrelation polynomial *is obtained by taking the bits as coefficients:* $c(z) = c_0 + c_1z + \ldots + c_{k-2}z^{k-2} + c_{k-1}z^{k-1}$.

The autocorrelation is easily computed: the ith bit is determined by shifting left i positions, then putting 1 if the remaining bits match the original pattern, 0 otherwise. For example, Table 7.4 shows that the autocorrelation of `101001010` is `100001010`, and the corresponding autocorrelation polynomial is $1 + z^5 + z^7$. Note that c_0 is always 1.

Theorem 7.3 (*Pattern autocorrelation*) *The generating function for the number of bitstrings not containing a pattern* $p_0p_1\ldots p_{k-1}$ *is given by*

$$S(z) = \frac{c(z)}{z^k + (1-2z)c(z)},$$

where $c(z)$ *is the autocorrelation polynomial for the pattern.*

Proof. We use the symbolic method to generalize the proof given above for the case where the pattern is k consecutive 0s. We start with the OGF

								1	0	1	0	0	1	0	1	0	
								1	0	1	0	0	1	0	1	0	1
							1	0	1	0	0	1	0	1	0		0
						1	0	1	0	0	1	0	1	0			0
					1	0	1	0	0	1	0	1	0				0
				1	0	1	0	0	1	0	1	0					0
			1	0	1	0	0	1	0	1	0						1
		1	0	1	0	0	1	0	1	0							0
	1	0	1	0	0	1	0	1	0								1
1	0	1	0	0	1	0	1	0									0

Table 7.4 Autocorrelation of `101001010`

for $\mathcal{S}_p$, the set of bitstrings with no occurrence of p:

$$\begin{aligned} S(z) &= \sum_{s \in \mathcal{S}_p} z^{|s|} \\ &= \sum_{N \ge 0} \{\text{\# of bitstrings of length } N \text{ with no occurrence of } p\} z^N. \end{aligned}$$

Similarly, we define $\mathcal{T}_p$ to be the class of bitstrings of length N that end with p but have no other occurrence of p, and name its associated generating function $T(z)$.

Now, we consider two symbolic relationships between $\mathcal{S}_p$ and $\mathcal{T}_p$ that translate to simultaneous equations involving $S(z)$ and $T(z)$. First, $\mathcal{S}_p$ and $\mathcal{T}_p$ are disjoint, and if we remove the last bit from a bitstring in either, we get a bitstring in $\mathcal{S}_p$ (or the empty bitstring). Expressed symbolically, this means that

$$\mathcal{S}_p + \mathcal{T}_p = \epsilon + \mathcal{S}_p \times \{0, 1\},$$

which, since the OGF for $\{0, 1\}$ is $2z$, translates to

$$S(z) + T(z) = 1 + 2zS(z).$$

Second, consider the set of strings consisting of a string from $\mathcal{S}_p$ followed by the pattern. For each position i in the autocorrelation for the pattern, this gives a string from $\mathcal{T}_p$ followed by an i-bit "tail." Expressed symbolically, this gives

$$\mathcal{S}_p \times \texttt{<pattern>} = \mathcal{T}_p \times \sum_{c_i \ne 0} \texttt{<tail>}_i,$$

which, since the OGF for $\texttt{<pattern>}$ is z^k and the OGF for $\texttt{<tail>}_i$ is z^i, translates to

$$S(z)z^k = T(z) \sum_{c_i \ne 0} z^i = T(z)c(z).$$

The stated result follows immediately as the solution to the two simultaneous equations relating the OGFs $S(z)$ and $T(z)$. ■

For patterns consisting of k 0s (or k 1s), the autocorrelation polynomial is $1 + z + z^2 + \ldots + z^{k-1} = (1 - z^k)/(1 - z)$, so Theorem 7.3 matches our previous result in Theorem 7.2.

Corollary *The expected position of the end of the first occurrence of a bitstring with autocorrelation polynomial $c(z)$ is given by $2^k c(1/2)$.*

Table 7.5 shows the generating functions for the number of bitstrings not containing each of the 16 patterns of four bits. The patterns group into four different sets of patterns with equal autocorrelation. For each set, the table also gives the dominant root of the polynomial in the denominator of the OGF, and the expected "wait time" (position of the first occurrence of the pattern), computed from the autocorrelation polynomial. We can develop these approximations using Theorem 4.1 and apply them to approximate the wait times using the corollaries to Theorem 7.2 in the same way we did for Table 7.3. That is, the probability that an N-bit string has no occurrence of the pattern 1000 is about $(1.83929/2)^N$, and so forth. Thus, for example, there is about a 43% chance that a 10-bit string does not contain 1000, as opposed to the 69% chance that a 10-bit string does not contain 1111.

It is rather remarkable that such results are so easily accessible through generating functions. Despite their fundamental nature and wide applicability, it was not until systematic analyses of string-searching algorithms were attempted that this simple way of looking at such problems became apparent. These and many more related results are developed fully in papers by Guibas and Odlyzko [14][15].

Exercise 7.11 Calculate the expected position of the first occurrence of each of the following patterns in a random bitstring: *(i)* $k-1$ 0s followed by a 1; *(ii)* a 1

pattern	*autocorrelation*	*OGF*	*dominant root*	*wait*
`0000 1111`	`1111`	$\dfrac{1-z^4}{1-2z+z^5}$	$1.92756\cdots$	30
`0001 0011 0111` `1000 1100 1110`	`1000`	$\dfrac{1}{1-2z+z^4}$	$1.83929\cdots$	16
`0010 0100 0110` `1001 1011 1101`	`1001`	$\dfrac{1+z^3}{1-2z+z^3-z^4}$	$1.86676\cdots$	18
`0101 1010`	`1010`	$\dfrac{1+z^2}{1-2z+z^2-2z^3+z^4}$	$1.88320\cdots$	20

Table 7.5 Generating functions and wait times for 4-bit patterns

followed by $k-1$ 0s; *(iii)* alternating 0-1 string of length $2k$; *(iv)* alternating 0-1 string of length $2k+1$.

Exercise 7.12 Which bit patterns of length k are likely to appear the earliest in a random bitstring? Which patterns are likely to appear the latest?

Exercise 7.13 Does the standard deviation of the random variable marking the first position of a bit pattern of length k in a random bitstring depend on the pattern?

Larger alphabets. The methods above apply directly to larger alphabets. For example, a proof virtually identical to the proof of Theorem 7.3 will show that the generating function for strings from an M-character alphabet that do not contain a run of k consecutive occurrences of a particular character is

$$\frac{1-z^k}{1-Mz+(M-1)z^{k+1}},$$

and the average position of the end of the first run of k occurrences of a particular character in a random string on an M-character alphabet is $M(M^k-1)/(M-1)$.

Exercise 7.14 Suppose that a monkey types randomly at a 32-key keyboard. What is the expected number of characters typed before the monkey hits upon the phrase `TO BE OR NOT TO BE`?

7.3 Regular expressions. The basic method using generating functions above generalizes considerably. To determine properties of random strings, we ended up deriving generating functions that count the cardinality of sets of strings with well-defined properties. But developing specific descriptions of sets of strings falls within the domain of *formal languages*, the subject of a vast literature. We use only basic principles, as described in any standard text, for example, Eilenberg [5].

The simplest concept from formal language theory is the *regular expression*, a way to describe sets of strings based on the union, concatenation, and "star" operations, which are described below. A set of strings (a language) is said to be regular if it can be described by a regular expression. For example, a regular expression describing all bitstrings with no run of four consecutive 0s is given by

$$S_4 = \texttt{(1 + 01 + 001 + 0001)}^*\texttt{(}\epsilon\texttt{ + 0 + 00 + 000)}.$$

In this expression, + denotes unions of languages; the product of two languages is to be interpreted as the language of strings formed by concatenating a string from the first with a string from the second; and * is shorthand for concatenating a language with itself an arbitrary number of times (including zero). As usual, ϵ represents the empty word. Above, we derived the corresponding OGF

$$S_4(z) = \sum_{s \in \mathcal{S}_4} z^{|s|} = \frac{1 - z^4}{1 - 2z + z^5}$$

and deduced basic properties of the language by manipulating the generating functions. Other languages that we have considered to this point are also easily described with regular expressions and thus analyzed with OGFs, as we shall see.

There is a relatively simple mechanism for transforming the formal description of the sets of strings (the regular expression) into the formal analytic tool for counting them (the OGF). This is due to Chomsky and Schützenberger [2]. The sole requirement is that the regular expression be *unambiguous*: there must be only one way to derive any string in the language. It is known from formal language theory that any regular language can be specified by an unambiguous regular expression.

Theorem 7.4 (*OGFs for regular expressions*) *Let $\mathcal{A}$ and $\mathcal{B}$ be unambiguous regular expressions and suppose that $\mathcal{A} + \mathcal{B}$, $\mathcal{A} \times \mathcal{B}$, and $\mathcal{A}^*$ are also unambiguous. If $A(z)$ is the OGF that enumerates $\mathcal{A}$ and $B(z)$ is the OGF that enumerates $\mathcal{B}$, then*

$A(z) + B(z)$ *is the OGF that enumerates $\mathcal{A} + \mathcal{B}$;*

$A(z)B(z)$ *is the OGF that enumerates $\mathcal{A}\mathcal{B}$; and*

$\dfrac{1}{1 - A(z)}$ *is the OGF that enumerates $\mathcal{A}^*$.*

Moreover, OGFs that enumerate regular languages are rational functions.

Proof. The first part is essentially the same as our basic theorem on the symbolic method for OGFs (Theorem 3.3), but it is worth restating here because of the fundamental nature of this application.

If a_N is the number of strings of length N in $\mathcal{A}$ and b_N is the number of strings of length N in $\mathcal{B}$, then $a_N + b_N$ is the number of strings of length N in $\mathcal{A} + \mathcal{B}$, since the requirement that the languages are unambiguous implies that $\mathcal{A} \cap \mathcal{B}$ is empty.

Similarly, we can use a simple convolution to prove the translation of $\mathcal{AB}$, and the symbolic representation

$$\mathcal{A}^* = \epsilon + \mathcal{A} + \mathcal{A}^2 + \mathcal{A}^3 + \mathcal{A}^4 + \ldots$$

implies the rule for $\mathcal{A}^*$, exactly as for Theorem 3.3. Again, the requirement that the languages are unambiguous ensures that the strings in the language are generated as distinct combinatorial objects and thus counted uniquely.

The second part of the theorem results from the remark above that every regular language can be specified by an unambiguous regular expression. For the reader with knowledge of formal languages: if a language is regular, it can be recognized by a deterministic FSA, and the classical proof of Kleene's theorem associates an unambiguous regular expression to a deterministic automaton. We explore some algorithmic implications of associations with FSAs below. ■

Thus, we have a simple and direct way to transform a regular expression into an OGF that counts the strings described by that regular expression, provided only that the regular expression is unambiguous. Furthermore, an important implication of the fact that the generating function that results when successively applying Theorem 7.4 is always rational is that asymptotic approximations for the coefficients are available, using general tools such as Theorem 4.1.

Strings with no runs of k 0s. Above, we gave a regular expression for $\mathcal{S}_k$, the set of bitstrings with no occurrence of k consecutive 0s. Consider, for instance, $\mathcal{S}_4$. From Theorem 7.4, we find immediately that the OGF for

$$\texttt{1 + 01 + 001 + 0001} \quad \text{is} \quad z + z^2 + z^3 + z^4$$

and the OGF for

$$\epsilon\ \texttt{+ 0 + 00 + 000} \quad \text{is} \quad 1 + z + z^2 + z^3$$

so we have

$$S_4(z) = \frac{1 + z + z^2 + z^3}{1 - (z + z^2 + z^3 + z^4)} = \frac{\dfrac{1 - z^4}{1 - z}}{1 - z\dfrac{1 - z^4}{1 - z}} = \frac{1 - z^4}{1 - 2z + z^5}$$

as before.

Multiples of three. The regular expression

$$\texttt{(1(01}^{*}\texttt{0)}^{*}\texttt{10}^{*}\texttt{)}^{*}$$

generates the set of strings `11`, `110`, `1001`, `1100`, `1111`, ..., that are binary representations of multiples of 3. Applying Theorem 7.4, we find the generating function for the number of such strings of length N:

$$\frac{1}{1 - \dfrac{z^2}{1 - \dfrac{z^2}{1-z}}\left(\dfrac{1}{1-z}\right)} = \frac{1}{1 - \dfrac{z^2}{1-z-z^2}} = \frac{1-z-z^2}{1-z-2z^2}$$

$$= 1 - \frac{z^2}{(1-2z)(1+z)}.$$

This is very similar to one of the first GFs encountered in §3.3: it expands by partial fractions to give the result $(2^{N-1} + (-1)^N)/3$. All the bitstrings start with 1: about a third of all such strings represent numbers that are divisible by 3, as expected.

Height of a random walk. Taking 0 to mean "up" and 1 to mean "down," we draw a correspondence between bitstrings and random walks. Three examples of random walks are illustrated in Figure 7.2. If we restrict the walks to terminate when they first reach the start level (without ever going below), we get walks that correspond to the gambler's ruin sequences of §5.11. We can then easily count these walks according to height (maximum value achieved) with regular expressions:

	regular expression	*generating function*
height ≤ 1	$\texttt{(10)}^{*}$	$\dfrac{1}{1-z}$
height ≤ 2	$\texttt{(1(10)}^{*}\texttt{0)}^{*}$	$\dfrac{1}{1 - \dfrac{z}{1-z}} = \dfrac{1-z}{1-2z}$
height ≤ 3	$\texttt{(1(1(10)}^{*}\texttt{0)}^{*}\texttt{0)}^{*}$	$\dfrac{1}{1 - \dfrac{z}{1 - \dfrac{z}{1-z}}} = \dfrac{1-2z}{1-3z+z^2}$

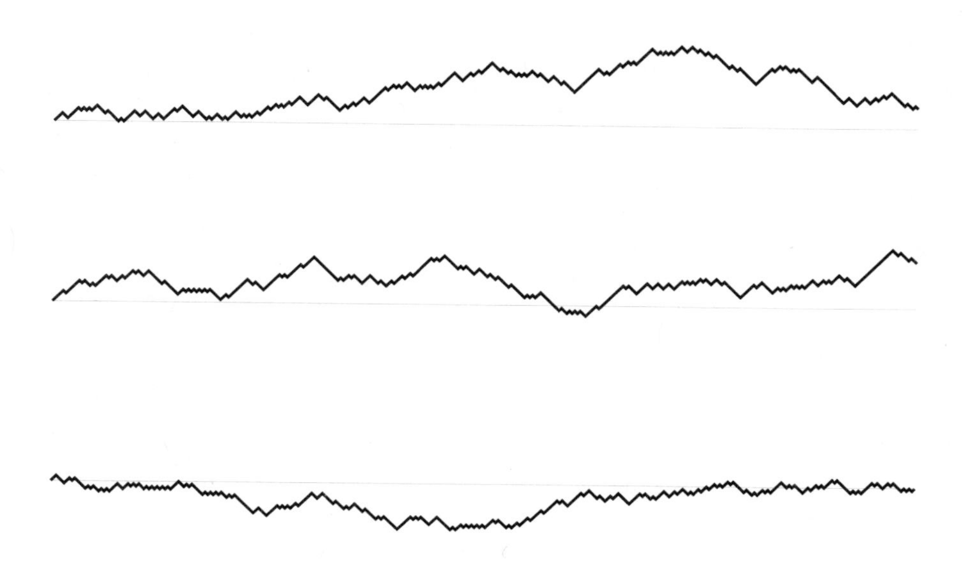

Figure 7.2 Three random walks

Since 1s and 0s are paired, we only translate one of them to z. These GFs match those derived in §5.9 and the average height is $\sim \sqrt{\pi N}$ by the corollary to Theorem 5.9. This is the same as the gambler's ruin correspondence discussed in §5.11, and this is equivalent to the height of Catalan forests (see Exercise 5.44).

Exercise 7.15 Give a regular expression for the set of all strings having no occurrence of the pattern `101101`. What is the corresponding generating function?

Exercise 7.16 What is the average position of the *second* disjoint string of k 0s in a random bitstring?

Exercise 7.17 Find the number of different ways to derive each string of N 0s with the regular expression `0*00`.

Exercise 7.18 Find the number of different ways to derive each string of N 0s with the regular expression `0*00*`.

Exercise 7.19 Find the average number of 0s appearing before the first occurrence of each of the bit patterns of length 4 in a random bitstring.

Exercise 7.20 Suppose that a monkey types randomly at a 2-key keyboard. What is the expected number of bits typed before the monkey hits upon a string of $2k$ alternating 0s and 1s?

7.4 Finite-State Automata and the Knuth-Morris-Pratt Algorithm. The brute-force algorithm for string matching is quite acceptable for many applications, but, as we saw above, it can run slowly for highly self-repetitive patterns. Eliminating this problem leads to an algorithm that not only is of practical interest, but also links string matching to basic principles of theoretical computer science and leads to more general algorithms.

For example, when searching for a string of k 0s, it is very easy to overcome the obvious inefficiency in the basic algorithm of §7.1: When a 1 is encountered at text position i, reset the "pattern" pointer j to the beginning and start looking again at position $i+1$. This is taking advantage of specific properties of the all-0s pattern, but it turns out that the idea generalizes to give an optimal algorithm for all patterns, which was developed by Knuth, Morris, and Pratt in 1977 [19].

The idea is to build a pattern-specific finite-state automaton that begins at an initial state, examining the first character in the text; scans text characters; and makes state transitions based on the value scanned. Some of the states are designated as *final* states, and the automaton is to terminate in a final state if and only if the associated pattern is found in the text. The implementation of the string search is a simulation of the FSA, based on a table indexed by the state. This makes the implementation extremely simple, as shown in Program 7.2. The key to the algorithm is the computation of the transition table, which depends on the pattern.

For example, the proper table for the pattern `10100110` is shown at the right in Table 7.6, and a graphic representation of this FSA is given in Figure 7.3. When this automaton is run on the sample piece of text given

```
procedure fsasearch;
  begin
  state := 0;
  for i := 1 to N do
    begin
    state := next(state, a[i]);
    if (state = k) then << match found >>
    end;
  end;
```

Program 7.2 String searching with an FSA (KMP algorithm)

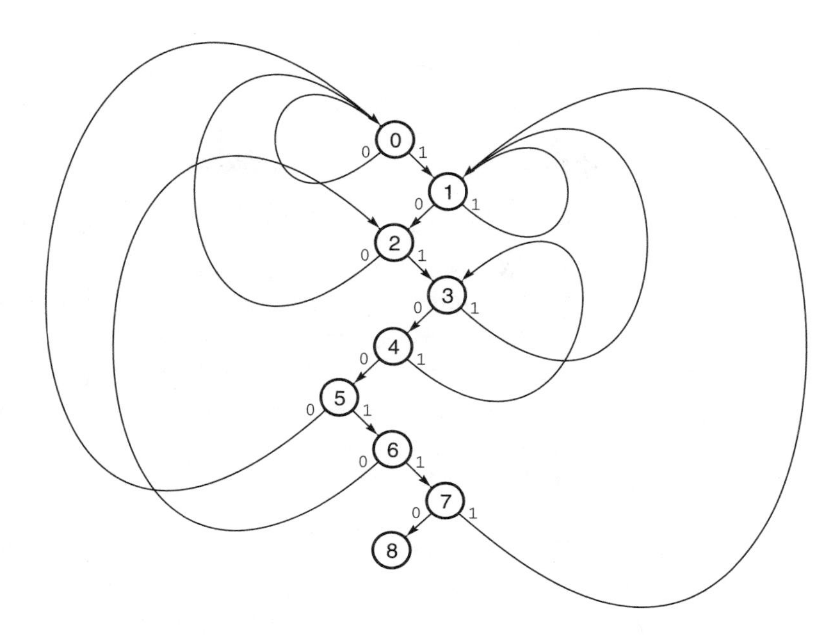

Figure 7.3 Knuth-Morris-Pratt FSA for `10100110`

below, it takes the state transitions as indicated. (Below each character is given the state the FSA is in when that character is examined.)

```
01110101110001110010000011010011000001010111010001
00111234311200111201200000112345678
```

Exercise 7.21 Give a text string of length 25 that maximizes the number of times the KMP automaton from Figure 7.3 reaches step 2.

This is an example of an algorithm that is sufficiently sophisticated that it is trivial to analyze, since it just examines each character in the text once.

Theorem 7.5 (*KMP string matching*) *The Knuth-Morris-Pratt algorithm does N bit comparisons when seeking a pattern of length k in a binary text string of length N.*

Proof. See the discussion above. ∎

The construction of the `next` table depends on correlations of prefixes of the pattern, as shown in Table 7.5. We define state i to correspond to this situation where the first $i-1$ characters in the pattern have been matched in the text, but the ith character does not match. That is, state i corresponds to a specific i-bit pattern in the text. For example, for the pattern in Table 7.5, the FSA is in state 4 if and only if the previous four bits in the text were 1010. If the next bit is 0, we would go on to state 5; if the next bit is 1, we know that this is not the prefix of a successful match *and* that the previous five bits in the text were 10101. What is required is to go to the state corresponding to the first point at which this pattern matches itself when shifted right, in this case state 3. In general, this is precisely the position (measured in bits from the right) of the second 1 in the correlation of this bitstring (0 if the first 1 is the only one).

Exercise 7.22 Give the KMP state transition table for the pattern `110111011101`.

Exercise 7.23 Give the state transitions made when using the KMP method to determine whether the text `01101110001110110111101100110111011101` contains the pattern in the previous exercise.

Exercise 7.24 Describe the state transition table for a string of $2k$ alternating 0s and 1s.

The "string-searching" problem that we have been considering is equivalent to determining whether the text string is in the language described by the (ambiguous) regular expression

```
(0+1)* <pattern> (0+1)*.
```

This is the *recognition* problem for regular expressions: given a regular expression and a text string, determine if the string is in the language described by the regular expression. In general, regular expression recognition can be done by building a FSA, and properties of such automata

10100110			0 1
0	1	0	0 1
11	11	1	2 1
100	100	0	0 3
1011	1001	1	4 1
10101	10101	3	5 3
101000	100000	0	0 6
1010010	1000010	2	2 7
10100111	10000001	1	8 1
mismatch	*autocorrelation*	*first match*	*table*

Table 7.6 Example of KMP state transition table

can be analyzed using algebraic techniques as we have been doing. As is usually the case, however, more specialized problems can be solved effectively with more specialized techniques. The KMP finite-state automaton is a prime example of this.

Generalization to larger alphabets involves a transition table of size proportional to the size of the pattern times the size of the alphabet, though various improvements upon this have been studied. Details on such issues and on text searching applications may be found in Gonnet and Baeza-Yates [12].

Exercise 7.25 For $M = 4$, give the KMP state transition table for the pattern `313131`. Give the state transitions made when using the KMP method to determine whether the text `1232032313230313131` contains this pattern.

Exercise 7.26 Prove directly that the language recognized by a deterministic FSA has an OGF that is rational.

Exercise 7.27 Write a computer algebra program that computes the standard rational form of the OGF that enumerates the language recognized by a given deterministic FSA.

7.5 Context-Free Grammars. Regular expressions allow us to concisely describe properties of languages in a formal way that turns out to be amenable to analysis. Next in the hierarchy of languages comes the *context-free* languages. For example, we might wish to know:

- How many bitstrings of length $2N$ have N 0s and N 1s?
- Given a random bitstring of length N, how many of its prefixes have equal numbers of 0s and 1s, on the average?
- At what point does the number of 0s in a random bitstring first exceed the number of 1s, on the average?

All these problems can be solved using *context-free grammars*, which are more expressive than regular expressions. Though the first question is trivial combinatorially, it is known from language theory that such a set cannot be described with regular expressions, and context-free languages are needed. As we will see, we also can develop automatic mechanisms involving generating functions to enumerate unambiguous context-free languages and thus open the door to studying a host of interesting questions.

First, we briefly summarize some basic definitions from formal language theory. A context-free grammar is a collection of *productions* relating *nonterminal symbols* and letters (also called *terminal symbols*) by means of unions and concatenation products. The basic operations are similar to those for regular expressions (the "star" operation is not needed), but the introduction of nonterminal symbols creates a more powerful descriptive mechanism because of the possibility of nonlinear recursion. A language is context-free if it can be described by a context-free grammar. Indeed, we have actually been using mechanisms equivalent to context-free grammars to define some of the combinatorial structures that we have been analyzing.

Perhaps the most important example of this is our definition of binary trees, in Chapter 5, which can be recast formally as the following simple unambiguous grammar:

```
<bin tree>:= <ext node> | <int node><bin tree><bin tree>
<int node>:= 0
<ext node>:= 1
```

Nonterminal symbols are enclosed in angle brackets. Each nonterminal can be considered as representing a context-free language, defined by direct assignment to a letter of the alphabet, or by the union or concatenation product operations. Alternatively, we can consider each equation as a *rewriting rule* indicating how the nonterminal can be rewritten with the vertical bar denoting alternate rewritings and juxtaposition denoting concatenation. This grammar generates bitstrings associated with binary trees according to the one-to-one correspondence introduced in Chapter 5: visit the nodes of the tree in preorder, writing 0 for internal nodes and 1 for external nodes. Now, recall that the generating function that counts binary trees satisfies

$$G(z) = z + G(z)G(z).$$

This equation, which defines the Catalan OGF, is virtually identical to the formal definition of binary trees, written using a different notation.

Note that variable assignments correspond to the index for counting. We translated <external node> to z and ignored <internal node> to get the functional equation above where $[z^N]G(z)$ is the number of binary trees with N external nodes. Alternatively, we could translate <internal node> to z and ignore <external node> to get the functional equation

$$T(z) = 1 + zT(z)T(z)$$

for the OGF where $[z^N]T(z)$ is the number of binary trees with N internal nodes, or we could translate both terminals to z to get

$$U(z) = z + zU(z)U(z),$$

which enumerates trees by the total number of nodes.

This relationship between CFGs and OGFs is essential, and it holds in general. We view each nonterminal as representing the set of strings that can be derived from it using rewriting rules in the grammar. Then, just as with regular expressions, we have a general approach for translating unambiguous context-free grammars into functional equations on generating functions:

- Define an OGF corresponding to each nonterminal symbol.
- Translate occurrences of terminal symbols to variables.
- Translate concatenation in the grammar to multiplication of OGFs.
- Translate union in the grammar to addition of OGFs.

When this process is carried out, there results a system of polynomial equations on the OGFs. A function $f(z)$ that is the root of a polynomial equation $P(z, f(z)) = 0$ is said to be an *algebraic* function. We have thus proved a result first observed by Chomsky and Schützenberger [2].

Theorem 7.6 (*OGFs for context-free grammars*) *Let* `<A>` *and* `<B>` *nonterminal symbols in an unambiguous context-free grammar and suppose that* `<A> | <B>` *and* `<A><B>` *are also unambiguous. If $A(z)$ is the OGF that enumerates the strings that can be derived from* `<A>` *and $B(z)$ is the OGF that enumerates* `<B>`*, then*

$A(z) + B(z)$ *is the OGF that enumerates* `<A> | <B>` *and*

$A(z)B(z)$ *is the OGF that enumerates* `<A><B>`.

Moreover, OGFs that enumerate unambiguous context-free languages are algebraic functions.

Proof. See the above discussion, and the comments below on Groebner basis elimination. ■

This theorem relates basic operations on languages to OGFs using the symbolic method in the same way as Theorem 7.4, but the expressive power of context-free grammars by comparison to regular expressions leads to differences in the result in two important respects. First, a more general type of recursive definition is allowed (it can be nonlinear) so that the resulting OGF has a more general form—the system of equations is in general nonlinear. Second, ambiguity plays a more essential role. Not every context-free language has an unambiguous grammar (the ambiguity problem is even undecidable), so we can claim the OGF to be algebraic only for languages that have an unambiguous grammar. By contrast, as mentioned above, it is known that there exists an unambiguous regular expression for every regular language, so we can make the claim that OGFs for all regular languages are rational.

Theorem 7.6 gives a system of polynomial equations corresponding to a given unambiguous context-free grammar. Once we have the system of equations, we obtain the solution of a "context-free" counting problem by these last two steps:

- Solve to get an algebraic equation for the OGF.
- Solve, expand, and/or develop asymptotic estimates for coefficients.

Solving for the OGF may be achieved by an *elimination* process that reduces a polynomial system to a unique equation relating the variable z and the OGF under consideration. For instance, *Groebner basis* algorithms that are implemented in some computer algebra systems can be used for this purpose (see Geddes, et. al. [11]). Specifically, Theorem 7.6 says that if $L(z)$ is the OGF of an unambiguous context-free language, then $P(z, L(z)) = 0$ for some bivariate polynomial $P(z, y)$. In some cases, the solution of that equation admits to explicit forms that can be expanded, as we see in an example below. In other cases, more advanced tools may be necessary to develop an asymptotic form for the coefficients (see [9]).

2-ordered permutations. The discussion in §6.6 about enumerating 2-ordered permutations corresponds to developing the following unambiguous context-free grammar for strings with equal numbers of 0s and 1s:

```
<S>:= <U>1<S> | <D>0<S> | ϵ
<U>:= <U><U>1 | 0
<D>:= <D><D>0 | 1
```

The nonterminals in this grammar may be interpreted as follows: <S> corresponds to all bitstrings with equal numbers of 0s and 1s; <U> corresponds to all bitstrings with precisely one more 0 than 1, with the further constraint that no prefix has equal numbers of 0s and 1s; and <D> corresponds to all bitstrings with precisely one more 1 than 0, with the further constraint that no prefix has equal numbers of 0s and 1s.

Now, by Theorem 7.5, each production in the grammar translates to a functional equation on the generating functions:

$$\begin{aligned} S(z) &= zU(z)S(z) + zD(z)S(z) + 1 \\ U(z) &= z + zU^2(z) \\ D(z) &= z + zD^2(z). \end{aligned}$$

In this case, of course, $U(z)$ and $D(z)$ are familiar generating functions from tree enumeration, so we can solve explicitly to get

$$U(z) = D(z) = \frac{1}{2z}(1 - \sqrt{1 - 4z^2})$$

then substitute to find that

$$S(z) = \frac{1}{\sqrt{1 - 4z^2}} \qquad \text{so} \qquad [z^{2N}]S(z) = \binom{2N}{N}$$

as expected.

Groebner basis elimination. In general, explicit solutions might not be available, so we sketch for this problem how the Groebner basis elimination process will systematically solve this system. First, we note that $D(z) = U(z)$ because both satisfy the same (irreducible) equation. Thus, what is required is to eliminate U from the system of equations

$$\begin{aligned} P_1 &\equiv S - 2zUS - 1 = 0 \\ P_2 &\equiv U - zU^2 - z = 0. \end{aligned}$$

The general strategy consists of eliminating higher-degree monomials from the system by means of repeated combinations of the form $AP - BQ$, with A, B monomials and P, Q polynomials subject to elimination. In this case, forming $UP_1 - 2SP_2$ cross-eliminates the U^2 to give

$$P_3 \equiv -US - U + 2zS = 0.$$

Next, the US term can be eliminated by forming $2zP_3 - P_1$, so we have

$$P_4 \equiv -2Uz + 4Sz^2 - S + 1 = 0.$$

Finally, the combination $P_1 - SP_4$ completely eliminates U, and we get

$$P_5 \equiv S^2 - 1 - 4S^2z^2 = 0$$

and therefore $S(z) = 1/\sqrt{1-4z^2}$ as before.

We have included details for this example to illustrate the fundamental point that Theorem 7.5 gives an "automatic" way to enumerate unambiguous context-free languages. This is of particular importance with the advent of computer algebra systems that can perform the routine calculations involved.

Ballot problems. The final result above is elementary, but context-free languages are of course very general, so the same techniques can be used to solve a diverse class of problems. Perhaps the most prominent such example is the classical *ballot problem*: Suppose that, in an election, candidate 0 receives $N + k$ votes and candidate 1 receives N votes. What is the probability that candidate 0 is always in the lead during the counting of the ballots? In the present context, this problem can be solved by enumerating the number of bitstrings with $N + k$ 0s and N 1s that have the property that no prefix has an equal number of 0s and 1s. This is also the number of paths through an $(N + k)$-by-N lattice that do not touch the main diagonal. For $k = 0$ the answer is zero, because, if both candidates have N votes, they must be tied somewhere during the counting, if only at the end. For $k = 1$ the count is precisely $[z^{2N+1}]U(z)$ from our discussion of 2-ordered permutations above. For $k = 3$, we have the grammar

```
<B>:= <U><U><U>
<U>:= <U><U>1 | 0
```

and the answer is is $[z^{2N+3}](U(z))^3$. This immediately generalizes to give the result for all k.

Theorem 7.7 (*Ballot problem*) *The probability that a random bitstring with k more 0s than 1s has the property that no prefix has an equal number of 0s and 1s is* $k/(2N + k)$.

Proof. By the discussion above, this result is given by

$$\frac{[z^{2N+k}]U(z)^k}{\binom{2N+k}{N}} = \frac{k}{2N+k}.$$

Here, the coefficients are extracted by a direct application of Lagrange inversion (see §3.10). ■

The ballot problem has a rich history, dating back to 1887. For detailed discussions and numerous related problems, see the books by Feller [6] and Comtet [3].

Beyond the direct relationship to trees, this type of result arises frequently in the analysis of algorithms in connection with so-called *history* or *sequence of operations* analysis of dynamic algorithms and data structures. For example, the ballot problem is equivalent to determining the probability that a random sequence of "push" and "pop" operations on an initially empty pushdown stack is "legal" in the sense that it never tries to pop an empty stack and leaves k items on the stack. Other applications may involve more operations and different definitions of legal sequences—examples are given in the exercises below. Such problems typically can be approached via context-free grammars. A number of applications of this type are discussed in an early paper by Pratt [21]; see also Knuth [17].

Exercise 7.28 Given a random bitstring of length N, how many of its prefixes have equal numbers of 0s and 1s, on the average?

Exercise 7.29 What is the probability that the number of 0s in a random bitstring never exceeds the number of 1s?

Exercise 7.30 Given a random bitstring of length N, how many of its prefixes have k more 0s than 1s, on the average? What is the probability that the number of 0s in a random bitstring never exceeds the number of 1s by k?

Exercise 7.31 Suppose that a stack has a fixed capacity M. What is the probability that a random sequence of N push and pop operations on an initially empty pushdown stack never tries to pop the stack when it is empty or push when it is full?

Exercise 7.32 [Pratt] Consider a data structure with one "insert" and two different types of "remove" operations. What is the probability that a random sequence of operations of length N is legal in the sense that the data structure is empty before and after the sequence, and "remove" is always applied to a nonempty data structure?

Exercise 7.33 Answer the previous exercise, but replace one of the "remove" operations with an "inspect" operation, which is applied to a nonempty data structure but does not remove any items.

Exercise 7.34 Suppose that a monkey types randomly at a 32-key keyboard that has 26 letters `A` through `Z`, the symbols `+`, `*`, `(`, and `)`, a space key, and a period. What is the expected number of characters typed before the monkey hits upon a legal regular expression? Assume that spaces can appear anywhere in a regular expression and that a legal regular expression must be enclosed in parentheses and have exactly one period, at the end.

7.6 Tries. Any set of N distinct bitstrings (which may vary in length) uniquely corresponds a *trie*, a labelled binary tree structure. Tries can be used to represent sets of strings, including the set of all patterns in a text string, so they provide a fast method for searching for patterns in a text *and* an alternative to binary trees for conventional key-searching applications. Tries also arise in many other applications in computer science.

First, we can associate sets of strings to binary trees. Given a binary tree, label the left links `0` and the right links `1` and identify each external node with the labels of the links on the path from the root to that node. This gives a mapping from binary trees to sets of bitstrings. For example, the tree on the left in Figure 7.4 maps to the set of strings

`000 001 01 10 11000 11001 11010 11011 11100 11101 1111,`

the tree in the middle to

`0 100 10100 1010100 101010100 1010101010 1010101011`

`10101011 101011 1011 11,`

and the tree on the right to

`0000 0001 0010 0011 0100 0101 011 100 101 110 111.`

All the sets of bitstrings that are obtained in this way have by construction the *prefix-free* property: no string is the prefix of another.

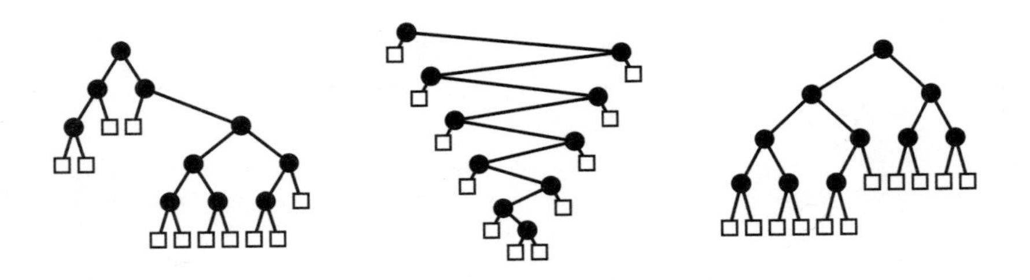

Figure 7.4 Three tries, each representing 11 bitstrings

Conversely, given a set of bitstrings, the associated binary tree structure can be built recursively by dividing the set according to the leading bit of the strings, as in the following formal definition. It is assumed that none of the bitstrings is a (strict) prefix of another. This assumption is justified, for example, if the strings are infinitely long, which is also a convenient assumption to make when analyzing properties of tries.

Definition *Given a set $\mathcal{B}$ of bitstrings that is prefix-free, the associated trie is a binary tree defined recursively as follows. If $\mathcal{B}$ is empty, the trie is null and represented by a void external node. If $|\mathcal{B}| = 1$, the trie consists of one external node corresponding to the bitstring. Otherwise, define $\mathcal{B}_0$ (respectively, $\mathcal{B}_1$) to be the set of bitstrings obtained by taking all the members of $\mathcal{B}$ that begin with 0 (respectively, 1) and removing the initial bit from each. Then the trie for $\mathcal{B}$ is an internal node connected to the trie for $\mathcal{B}_0$ on the left and the trie for $\mathcal{B}_1$ on the right.*

It is possible to handle prefix strings by associating extra information with the internal nodes, though tries are most commonly defined and used as above.

A trie for N bitstrings has N nonvoid external nodes, one corresponding to each bitstring, and may have an arbitrary number of void external nodes. As above, by considering 0 as "left" and 1 as "right," we can reach the external node corresponding to any bitstring by starting at the root and proceeding down the trie, moving left or right according to the bits in the string read from right to left. This process ends at the external node corresponding to the bitstring as soon as it can be distinguished from all the other bitstrings in the trie.

This mapping is not one-to-one. Many sets of bitstrings can map to the each tree structure, for two reasons:

- Not all external nodes necessarily correspond to a bitstring.
- Adding more bits to the bitstrings does not change the structure.

We consider these in turn.

The void external nodes correspond to situations where bitstrings have bits in common that do not distinguish them from other members of the set. For example, if all the bitstrings start with a 0-bit, then the right child of the root of the associated trie would be such a node, not corresponding to any bitstring in the set. Such nodes can appear throughout the trie.

For example, Figure 7.5 shows three tries with 11 external nodes, of which 3, 9, and 1 are void, respectively. In the figure, the void nodes are represented by small black squares and the nonvoid nodes (which each correspond to a string) are represented by larger open squares. The tree on the left represents the set of bitstrings

```
000 001 11000 11001 11010 11011 11100 11101,
```

the tree in the middle represents the set

```
1010101010 1010101011,
```

and the tree on the right represents the set

```
0000 0001 0010 0011 0100 0101 100 101 110 111.
```

It is possible to do a precise analysis of the number of void external nodes needed for random bitstrings. It is also possible to arrange matters so that unneeded bits do not directly correspond to unneeded nodes in the trie structure but are represented otherwise. We discuss these matters in some detail below.

The fact that adding more bits to the bitstrings does not change the structure follows from the "if $|\mathcal{B}| = 1$" clause in the definition, which is there because in many applications it is convenient to stop the trie branching as soon as the bitstrings are distinguished. For finite bitstrings, this condition could be removed, and the branching could continue until

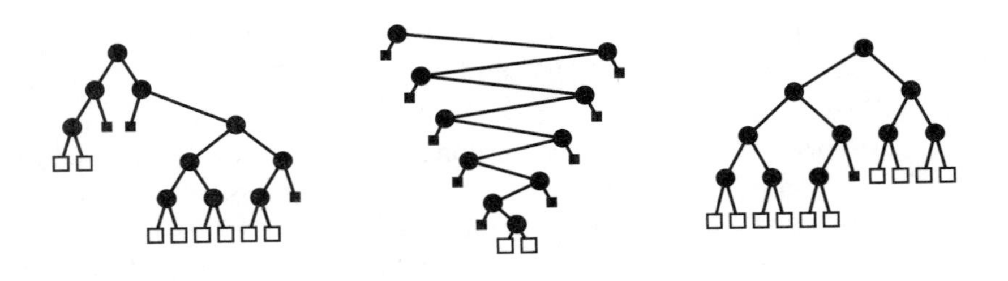

Figure 7.5 Three tries, representing 8, 2, and 10 bitstrings (respectively)

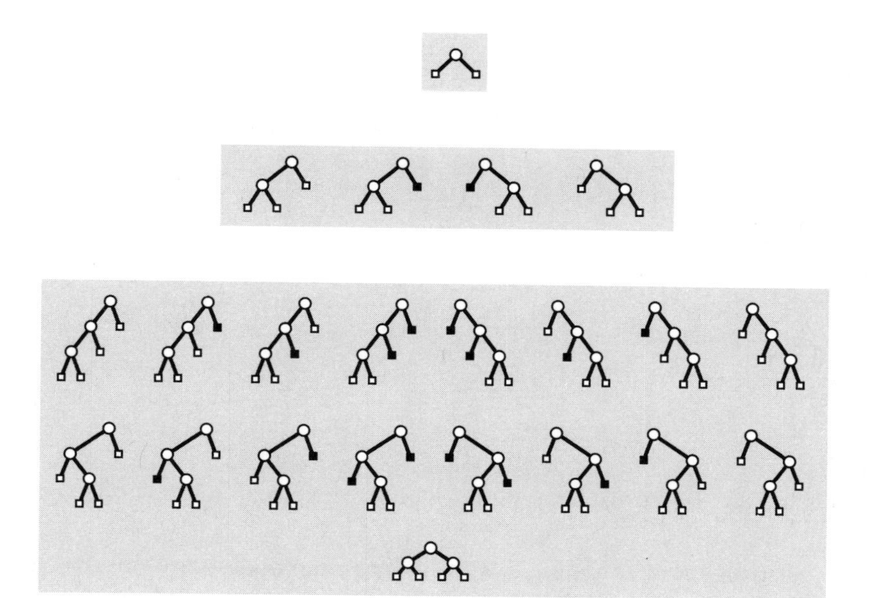

Figure 7.6 Tries with two, three, and four external nodes

the end of each bitstring is reached. We refer to such a trie as a *full* trie for the set of bitstrings. Conversely, we refer to the *minimal* set of bitstrings for a trie. These are nothing more than encodings of the paths from the root to each nonvoid external node. For example, the bitstring sets that we have given for Figure 7.4 and for Figure 7.5 are thus both minimal.

The recursive definition that we have given gives rise to binary tree structures with the additional properties that (*i*) external nodes may be void; and (*ii*) children of leaves must be nonvoid. That is, we never have two void nodes that are siblings, or a void and a nonvoid node as siblings. Figure 7.6 shows all the different tries with two, three, and four external nodes.

Figure 7.7 gives the minimal bitstring sets associated with each of the tree shapes with five external nodes (each of the tries with five external nodes, all of which are nonvoid). This figure also specifies the minimal bitstring sets associated with any trie with five external nodes: simply delete

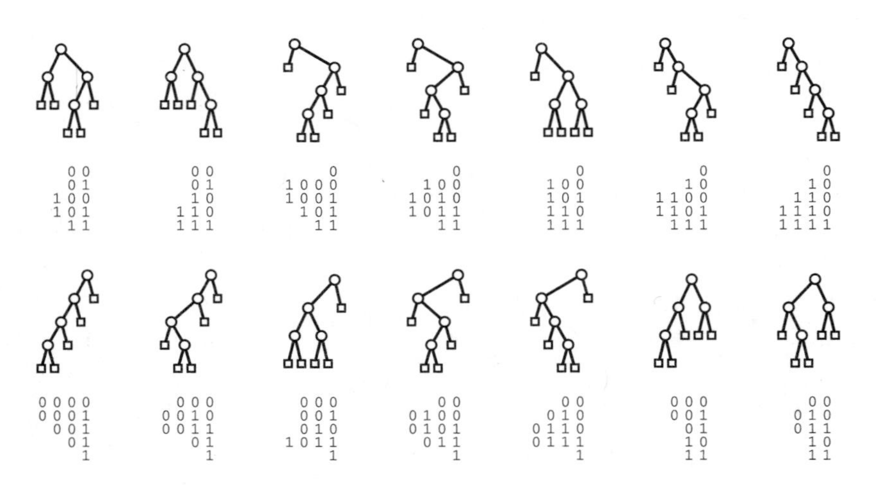

Figure 7.7 Bitstring sets for tries with five external nodes (none void)

the bitstrings corresponding to any void external nodes (any external node that is not the child of a leaf might be void) in the associated tree structure in the figure.

We could analyze properties of trie structures assuming each to be equally likely (in a manner analogous to Catalan trees in Chapter 5); we leave such questions for the exercises below. Instead, in the context of the analysis of algorithms, we focus on bitstrings and bitstring algorithms—where tries are most often used—and concentrate on viewing tries as mechanisms to efficiently *distinguish* among a set of strings, and as structures to efficiently *represent* sets of strings and work with probability distributions induced when the strings are random. Next, we consider several algorithmic applications of tries.

Exercise 7.35 Give the three tries corresponding to the sets of strings given above for Figure 7.5, but reading each string in right-to-left order.

Exercise 7.36 There are $\binom{8}{5} = 56$ different sets of five three-bit bitstrings. Which trie is associated with the most of these sets? The least?

Exercise 7.37 How many different tries are there with N external nodes?

Exercise 7.38 What proportion of the external nodes are void in a "random" trie (assuming each different trie structure to be equally likely to occur)?

Exercise 7.39 Given a finite set of strings, devise a simple test to determine whether there are any void external nodes in the corresponding trie.

7.7 Trie Algorithms. Binary strings are ubiquitous in digital computing, and trie structures are naturally associated with sets of binary strings, so it should not be surprising that there are a number of important algorithmic applications of tries. In this section, we survey a few such algorithms, to motivate the detailed study of the properties of tries to be undertaken in the next section.

Tries and digital searching. Tries can be used as the basis for algorithms for searching through a collection of binary data in a manner similar to binary search trees, but with bit comparisons replacing key comparisons.

Search tries. Treating bitstrings as keys, we can use tries as the basis for a conventional search algorithm such as Program 5.2: Set `x` to the root and `b` to 0, then proceed down the trie until an external node is encountered, incrementing `b` and setting `x` to `x^.l` if the `b`th bit of the key is `0`, or setting `x` to `x^.r` if the `b`th bit of the key is `1`. If the external node that terminates the search is void, then the bitstring is not in the trie; otherwise the corresponding bitstring can be compared to the key. This can be a very efficient search algorithm under proper conditions on the set of keys involved; for details see Knuth [17] or Sedgewick [24]. The analysis below can be used to determine how the performance of tries might compare with that of binary search trees for a given application. As discussed in Chapter 1, the first consideration in attempting to answer such a question is to consider properties of the implementation. This is especially important in this particular case, because accessing individual bits of keys can be very expensive on some computers if not done carefully.

Exercise 7.40 Explain how to modify a trie to reflect the addition of a new bitstring to the set of bitstrings represented (corresponding to insertion into a binary search tree).

Patricia tries. We will see below that about 44% of the external nodes in a random trie are void. This factor may be unacceptably high. The problem can be avoided by "collapsing" one-way internal nodes and keeping the index of the bit to be examined with each node. The external path length of this trie is somewhat smaller, though some extra information has to be associated with each node. The critical property that distinguishes Patricia tries is that there are no void external nodes, or, equivalently, there are $N-1$ internal nodes. Various techniques are available for implementing search and insertion using Patricia tries. Details may be found in Knuth [17] or Sedgewick [24].

Radix exchange sort. As mentioned in Chapter 1, a set of bitstrings of equal length can be sorted by partitioning them to put all those beginning with 0 before all those beginning with 1 (using a process similar to the partitioning process of Quicksort) then sorting the two parts recursively. This method, called *radix exchange sort*, bears the same relationship to tries as Quicksort does to binary search trees. The time required by the sort is essentially proportional to the number of bits examined. For keys comprised of random bits, this turns out to be the same as the "nonvoid external path length" of a random trie, that is the sum of the distances from the root to each of the nonvoid external nodes.

Trie encoding. Any trie with labelled external nodes defines a *prefix code* for the labels of the nodes. For example, if the external nodes in the trie on the left in Figure 7.4 are labelled, left to right, with the letters

C E F I L M N O P R S

then the bitstring

0110110001100111001110100111111111011010

encodes the phrase

FILE COMPRESSION.

Decoding is simple: starting at the root of the trie and the beginning of the bitstring, travel through the trie as directed by the bitstring (left on 0, right on 1), and, each time an external node is encountered, output the label and restart at the root. If frequently used letters are assigned to nodes with short paths, then the number of bits used in such an encoding will be significantly fewer than for the standard encoding. The well-known *Huffman encoding* method finds an optimal trie structure for given letter frequencies (see Sedgewick [24]).

Tries and pattern matching. Tries can also be used as a basic data structure for searching for multiple patterns in text files. For example, tries have been used successfully in the computerization of large dictionaries for natural languages and other similar applications. Depending upon the application, the trie can contain the patterns or the text, as described below.

String searching with suffix tries. In an application where the text string is fixed (as for a dictionary), and many pattern lookups are to be handled, the search time can be dramatically reduced by preprocessing the text string, as follows: Consider the text string to be a set of N strings, one starting at each position of the text string and running to the end of the string (stopping k characters from the end, where k is the length of the shortest pattern to be sought). Build a trie from this set of strings (such a trie is called the *suffix trie* for the text string). To find out whether a pattern occurs in the text, proceed down the trie from the root, going left on `0` and right on `1` as usual, according to the pattern bits. If a void external node is hit, the pattern is not in the text; if the pattern exhausts on an internal node, it is in the text; and if an external node is hit, compare the remainder of the pattern to the text bits represented in the external node as necessary to determine whether or not there is a match.

The analysis below shows that this process requires $O(\lg N)$ bit inspections on the average, a very substantial improvement over the $O(N)$ cost of the basic algorithm, though the initial cost of building the tree makes the method most useful when many patterns are to be sought in the same text. An implementation of this procedure is given in Program 7.3. This program uses the simple procedures `prefix`, which returns a true value if the first argument is a prefix of the second, false otherwise; `firstbit`, which returns the first bit of the argument; and `otherbits`, which removes the first bit from the argument. There are a number of ways to implement these procedures in a very efficient manner on most computers.

```
function search(v:  integer, x:  link):  link;
  begin
  if x = NIL << no match >> else
  if prefix(v, x^.key) << match found >> else
  if firstbit(v)  = 0 then search(otherbits(v), x^.left)
                      else search(otherbits(v), x^.right)
  end;
```

Program 7.3 String searching with a suffix trie

Searching for multiple patterns. Tries can also be used to find multiple patterns in one pass through a text string, as follows: First, build a full trie from the pattern strings. Then, for each position i in the text string, start at the top of the trie and match characters in the text while proceeding down the trie, going left for 0s in the text and right for 1s. Such a search must terminate at an external node. If the external node is not void, then the search was successful: one of the strings represented by the trie was found starting at position i in the text. If the external node is void, then none of the strings represented by the trie start at i, so that the text pointer can be incremented to $i + 1$ and the process restarted at the top of the trie. The analysis below implies that this requires $O(N \lg M)$ bit inspections, as opposed to the $O(NM)$ cost of applying the basic algorithm M times.

Trie-based finite-state automata. When the search process just described terminates in a void external node, we can do better than going to the top of the trie and backing up the text pointer, in precisely the same manner as with the Knuth-Morris-Pratt algorithm. A termination at a void node tells us not just that the sought string is not in the database, but also the characters in the text that precede this mismatch. These characters show exactly where the next search will require us to examine a text character where we can totally avoid the comparisons wasted by the backup, just as in the KMP algorithm. Indeed, Program 7.2 can be used for this application with no modification; we need only build the FSA corresponding to a set of strings rather than to a single string. For example, the automaton

0	1	2	3	4	5	6
1	3	5	7	5	3	9
2	4	2	4	8	6	8

corresponds to the set of strings `000 011 1010`. Figure 7.8 is a graphical representation of this FSA. For example, when this automaton is run on the sample piece of text given below, it takes the state transitions as indicated. (Below each character is given the state the FSA is in when that character is examined.)

```
11110010010010111010000011010011000001010111010001
02222534534534568
```

In this case, the FSA stops in state 8, having found the pattern `011`. The process of building a automaton for a given set of patterns is described by Aho and Corasick [1].

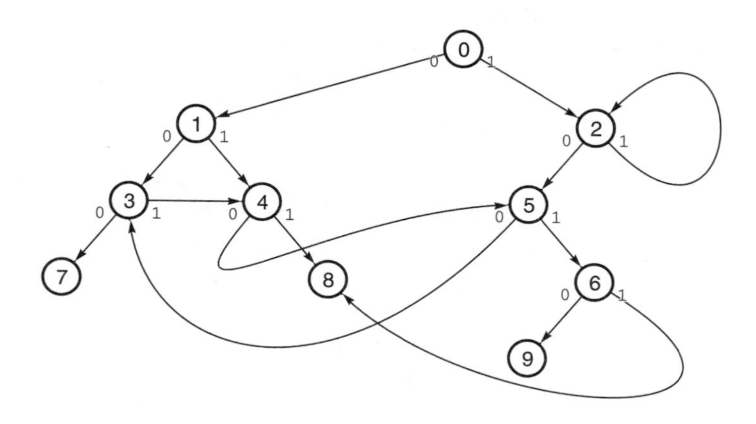

Figure 7.8 Aho-Corasick FSA for `000`, `011`, and `1010`

This list of algorithms and applications is representative, and demonstrates the fundamental importance of the trie data structure in computer applications. Not only are tries important as explicit data structures, but also they arise implicitly in algorithms based on bits, or in algorithms where truly "binary" decisions are made. Thus, analytic results describing properties of random tries have a variety of applications.

Exercise 7.41 How many bits are examined when using the trie in the middle in Figure 7.5 to search for one of the patterns `1010101010` or `1010101011` in the text string `10010100111110010101000101010100010010`?

Exercise 7.42 Given a set of pattern strings, describe a method for counting the number of times one of the patterns occurs in a text string.

Exercise 7.43 Build the suffix trie for patterns of eight bits or longer from the text string `10010100111110010101000101010100010010`.

Exercise 7.44 Give the suffix tries corresponding to all four-bit strings.

Exercise 7.45 Give the Aho-Corasick FSA for the set of strings `01 100 1011 010`.

7.8 Combinatorial Properties of Tries. As combinatorial objects, tries have been studied only recently, especially by comparison with classical combinatorial objects such as permutations and trees. As we will see, full understanding of even the most basic properties of tries requires the full array of analytic tools that we consider in this book.

Certain properties of tries naturally present themselves for analysis. How many void external nodes might be expected? What is the average external path length or the average height? As with binary search trees, knowledge of these basic properties gives the information necessary to analyze string searching and other algorithms that use trees.

A related, more fundamental, point to consider is that the model of computation used in the analysis needs to differ in a fundamental way: for binary search trees, only the relative order of the keys is of interest; for tries, the binary representation of the keys as bitstrings must come into play. What exactly is a random trie? Though several models are possible, it is natural to consider a random trie to be one built from a set of N random infinite bitstrings. This model is appropriate for many of the important trie algorithms, such as digital searching. It is *not* the same as a suffix trie built from a random bitstring, though it does appear to approximate that adequately, as well.

Thus, we will consider the analysis of properties of tries under the assumption that each bit in each bitstring is independently `0` or `1` with probability $1/2$.

Theorem 7.8 (*Trie path length and size*) *The trie corresponding to N random bitstrings has external path length $\sim N \lg N$, on the average. The mean number of internal nodes is asymptotic to $(1/\ln 2 \pm 10^{-5})N$.*

Proof. We start with a recurrence: for $N > 0$, the probability that exactly k of the N bitstrings begins with a 0 is the Bernoulli probability $\binom{N}{k}/2^N$, so if we define C_N to be the average external path length in a trie corresponding to N random bitstrings, we must have

$$C_N = N + \frac{1}{2^N}\sum_k \binom{N}{k}(C_k + C_{N-k}) \qquad \text{for } N > 1 \text{ with } C_0 = C_1 = 0.$$

This is precisely the recurrence describing the number of bit inspections used by radix-exchange sort that we examined for Theorem 4.9 in §4.9, where we showed that

$$C_N = N![z^N]C(z) = N\sum_{j\geq 0}\Bigl(1 - \Bigl(1 - \frac{1}{2^j}\Bigr)^{N-1}\Bigr)$$

and then we used the exponential approximation to deduce that

$$C_N \sim N\sum_{j\geq 0}(1-e^{-N/2^j}) \sim N\lg N.$$

A more precise estimate exposes a periodic fluctuation in the value of this quantity as N increases. As we saw in Chapter 4, the terms in the sum are exponentially close to 1 for small k and exponentially close to 0 for large k, with a transition when k is near $\lg N$ (see Figure 4.5). Accordingly, we split the sum:

$$\begin{aligned}
C_N/N &\sim \sum_{0\leq j<\lfloor\lg N\rfloor}(1-e^{-N/2^j}) + \sum_{j\geq\lfloor\lg N\rfloor}(1-e^{-N/2^j})\\
&= \lfloor\lg N\rfloor - \sum_{0\leq j<\lfloor\lg N\rfloor}e^{-N/2^j} + \sum_{j\geq\lfloor\lg N\rfloor}(1-e^{-N/2^j})\\
&= \lfloor\lg N\rfloor - \sum_{j<\lfloor\lg N\rfloor}e^{-N/2^j} + \sum_{j\geq\lfloor\lg N\rfloor}(1-e^{-N/2^j}) + O(e^{-N})\\
&= \lfloor\lg N\rfloor - \sum_{j<0}e^{-N/2^{j+\lfloor\lg N\rfloor}} + \sum_{j\geq 0}(1-e^{-N/2^{j+\lfloor\lg N\rfloor}}) + O(e^{-N}).
\end{aligned}$$

Now, separating out the fractional part of $\lg N$ as we did earlier in Chapter 2 (see Figures 2.3 and 2.4), we have

$$\lfloor\lg N\rfloor = \lg N - \{\lg N\} \quad\text{and}\quad N/2^{\lfloor\lg N\rfloor} = 2^{\lg N-\lfloor\lg N\rfloor} = 2^{\{\lg N\}}.$$

This leads to the expression

$$C_N/N \sim \lg N - \epsilon(N)$$

where

$$\epsilon(N) \equiv \{\lg N\} + \sum_{j<0}e^{-2^{\{\lg N\}-j}} - \sum_{j\geq 0}(1-e^{-2^{\{\lg N\}-j}}).$$

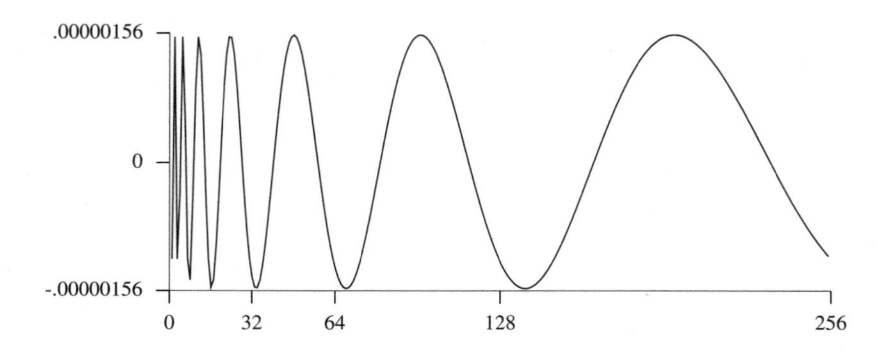

Figure 7.9 Periodic fluctuation in trie path length

Now, $\epsilon(N)$ is clearly a periodic function, with $\epsilon(2N) = \epsilon(N)$ because its dependence on N is solely in terms of $\{\lg N\}$.

This does not immediately rule out the possibility that $\epsilon(N)$ might be constant, but it is easy to check that it is not: $(C_N - N \lg N)/N$ does not approach a limit, but it fluctuates as N grows. Figure 7.9 is a plot of the function after subtracting its mean value for $N < 256$, and Table 7.7 shows exact values of $\epsilon(N)$ for $4 \le N \le 16$ (also for any power of 2 times these values). The function $\epsilon(N)$ is very close to 1.332746 numerically; and the amplitude of the fluctuating part is less than 10^{-5}.

This result is due to Knuth [17], who derived explicit expressions for the mean value and for $\epsilon(N)$ through Mellin transform analysis. This and related problems have been studied in detail by Guibas, Ramshaw, and Sedgewick [16] and by Flajolet, Gourdon, and Dumas [7] (see also [26] and [9]).

A similar analysis can be used to analyze the number of internal nodes in a trie on N bitstrings, which is described by the recurrence

$$A_N = 1 + \frac{1}{2^N} \sum_k \binom{N}{k} (A_k + A_{N-k}) \qquad \text{for } N > 1 \text{ with } A_0 = A_1 = 0.$$

In this case, the periodic fluctuation appears in the leading term: it turns out that

$$A_N \sim \frac{N}{\ln 2}(1 + \hat{\epsilon}(N))$$

where $\hat{\epsilon}(N)$ has absolute value less than 10^{-5}. The details of this analysis are similar to the above, and are left as an exercise. ■

Thus, the average number of bits inspected during a trie search is $\sim \lg N$, which is optimal. Knuth also shows that this is true for both Patricia and digital tree searching. It is possible to get accurate asymptotics and explicit expressions for the constants involved and for the oscillating term; see the references mentioned above for full details. As noted in the proof, this result also applies to the analysis of the radix-exchange variant of Quicksort discussed in Chapter 1.

Corollary *Radix-exchange sort uses $\sim N \lg N$ bit comparisons to sort an array of N random bitstrings.*

Proof. See the discussion above. We assume that the bitstrings are sufficiently long (say, much more than $\lg N$ bits) that we can consider them to be "infinite." Figure 7.10 shows the distribution of costs, for comparison with Figure 1.3. ■

Exercise 7.46 Show that A_N/N is equal to $1/\ln 2$ plus a fluctuating term.

Exercise 7.47 Write a program to compute A_N to within 10^{-9} for $N < 10^6$ and explore the oscillatory nature of A_N/N.

N	$\{\lg N\}$	$\sum_{j<0} e^{-2^{\{\lg N\}-j}}$	$\sum_{j\geq 0}(1 - e^{-2^{\{\lg N\}-j}})$	$-\epsilon(N)$
4	0.000000000	0.153986497	1.486733879	1.332747382
5	0.321928095	0.088868348	1.743543002	1.332746559
6	0.584962501	0.052271965	1.969979089	1.332744624
7	0.807354922	0.031110097	2.171210673	1.332745654
8	0.000000000	0.153986497	1.486733879	1.332747382
9	0.169925001	0.116631646	1.619304291	1.332747643
10	0.321928095	0.088868348	1.743543002	1.332746559
11	0.459431619	0.068031335	1.860208218	1.332745265
12	0.584962501	0.052271965	1.969979089	1.332744624
13	0.700439718	0.040279907	2.073464469	1.332744844
14	0.807354922	0.031110097	2.171210673	1.332745654
15	0.906890596	0.024071136	2.263708354	1.332746622
16	0.000000000	0.153986497	1.486733879	1.332747382

$\gamma/\ln 2 + 1/2 \approx 1.332746177$

Table 7.7 Periodic term in trie path length

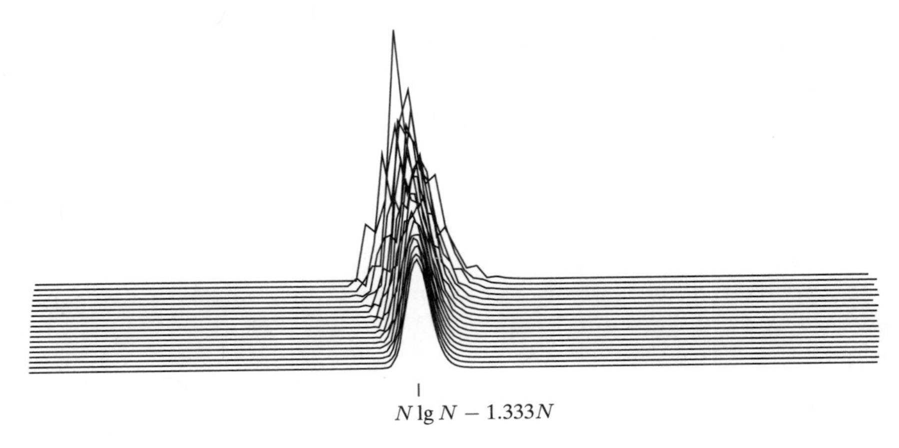

Figure 7.10 Distributions for path length in tries, $10 < N \le 50$ (scaled and translated to center and separate curves)

Exercise 7.48 Multiply both sides of the functional equation for $C(z)$ by e^{-z} to transform into a simpler equation on $\hat{C}(z) \equiv e^{-z}C(z)$. Use this equation to find $\hat{C}_N = [z^N]\hat{C}(z)$. Then apply the convolution implied by $C(z) = e^z\hat{C}(z)$ to show that

$$C_N = \sum_{2 \le k \le N} \binom{N}{k} \frac{k(-1)^k}{1 - 1/2^{k-1}}.$$

Exercise 7.49 Show directly that the sum given in the previous exercise is equivalent to the expression for C_N given in the proof of Theorem 7.8.

Distributed leader election. The random trie model is, as pointed out above, very general. It corresponds to a general probabilistic process where "individuals" (records, in the case of trie search) are recursively separated by coin flippings. That process can be taken as the basis of various resource allocation strategies, especially in a distributed context. As an example, we will consider a distributed algorithm for electing a leader among N individuals sharing a distributed access channel.

The method proceeds by rounds; individuals are selected or eliminated according to coin flips. Given a set of individuals:

- if the set is empty, then report failure;
- if the set has one individual, then declare that individual the leader;

- if the set has more than one individual, flip independent `0-1` coins for all members of the set and invoke the procedure recursively for the subset of individuals who got 1.

If we start with N individuals, then we expect N to be reduced roughly to $N/2$, $N/4$, ... in the course of the execution of the algorithm. Thus, we expect the procedure to terminate in about $\lg N$ steps, and a more precise analysis may be desirable. Also, the algorithm may fail (if everyone flips 0 and is eliminated with no leader elected), and we are also interested in knowing the probability that the algorithm is successful.

Theorem 7.9 (*Leader election*) *The average number of rounds used by the randomized algorithm to seek a leader out of N contenders is* $\lg N + O(1)$, *with probability of success asymptotic to* $1/(2\ln 2) \pm 10^{-5} \approx .72135$.

Proof. By representing an execution of the algorithm as a trie, it is clear that the average number of rounds is the expected length of the rightgoing branch in a trie built from N random bitstrings, and satisfies the recurrence

$$R_N = 1 + \frac{1}{2^N}\sum_k \binom{N}{k} R_k \qquad \text{for } N > 1 \text{ with } R_0 = R_1 = 0.$$

Similarly, the probability of success satisfies the recurrence

$$p_N = \frac{1}{2^N}\sum_k \binom{N}{k} p_k \qquad \text{for } N > 1 \text{ with } p_0 = 0 \text{ and } p_1 = 1.$$

These recurrences are quite similar to the path length recurrence that is considered in detail above. Solving them is left for exercises. As above, the stated result for p_N is accurate to within an oscillating term of mean 0 and amplitude less than 10^{-5}. ■

If the method fails, it can be executed repeatedly to yield an algorithm that succeeds with probability 1. On average, this will require about $2\ln 2 \approx 1.3863$ iterations, for a grand total of $\sim 2\ln N$ rounds. This algorithm is a simplified version of an algorithm of Prodinger that succeeds in an average of $\lg N + O(1)$ rounds [22].

Exercise 7.50 Solve recurrence for R_N given in the proof of Theorem 7.9, to within the oscillating term.

Exercise 7.51 Solve recurrence for p_N given in the proof of Theorem 7.9, to within the oscillating term.

Exercise 7.52 Analyze the version of the leader election algorithm that repeats rounds until a success occurs.

7.9 Larger alphabets. The results of this chapter generalize to strings comprising characters from alphabets of size M with $M > 2$. None of the combinatorial techniques used depends in an essential way on the strings' being binary. In practice, it is reasonable to assume that the alphabet size M is a constant that is not large: values such as 26, 2^8, or even 2^{16} are what might be expected in practice. We will not examine results for larger alphabets in detail, but we will conclude with a few general comments.

In §7.2 we noted that the first run of k 0s in a random M-bytestring ends at position $M(M^k - 1)/(M - 1)$. This makes it seem that the alphabet size can be a very significant factor: for example, we expect to find a string of ten 0s within the first few thousand bits of a random bitstring, but a string of ten identical characters would be extremely unlikely in a random string composed of eight-bit bytes, since the expected position of the first such string is about at the 2^{80}th byte. But this is just looking at the results of the analysis in two ways, since we can transform a bitstring into a string of bytes in the obvious way (consider eight bits at a time). That is, the alphabet size is less of a factor than it seems, because it intervenes only through its logarithm.

From both practical and theoretical standpoints, it generally suffices to consider bitstrings instead of bytestrings, since the straightforward encoding can transform any effective algorithm on bytestrings into an effective algorithm on bitstrings, and vice-versa.

The primary advantage of considering bits as groups is that they can be used as indices into tables or treated as integers, in essence using the computer addressing or arithmetic hardware to match a number of bits in parallel. This can lead to substantial speedups for some applications.

Multiway tries. An M-ary trie built from a random set of M-bytestrings has about $N/\ln M$ internal nodes and external path length asymptotic to $N \log_M N$, on the average. That is, using an alphabet of size M can save a factor of $\ln M$ in search time. But this comes at a cost of about $M/\ln M$ times more storage, since each internal node must have M links, most of which will be null if M is large.

Right-left string searching. Consider the problem of searching for a (relatively short) pattern in a (relatively long) text when both are bytestrings.

Extending the example above, we test the Mth character in the text with the last character in the pattern. If it matches, we then test the $(M-1)$st text character against the next-to-last pattern character and so on until a mismatch is found or a full match is verified. One approach to this process is to develop an "optimal shift" based on the mismatch, in much the same way as for the KMP algorithm. But a simpler idea is probably more effective in this case. Suppose that the text character does not appear in the pattern. Then this one character is evidence that we can skip M more characters, because any positioning of the right end of the pattern over any of those characters would necessitate matching the "current" character, which doesn't appear in the pattern. For many reasonable values of the relevant parameters, this event is likely, so this takes us close to the goal of examining N/M text characters when searching for a pattern of length M in a text string of length N. Even when the text character does appear in the pattern, we can precompute the appropriate shift for each character in the alphabet (distance from the right end of the pattern) to line up the pattern with its "next possible" match in the text. Details of this method, which originates from ideas of Boyer and Moore, are discussed by Gonnet and Baeza-Yates [12].

There are still a broad range of options to be considered. Should the pattern be bitshifted or byteshifted? How big a byte size is appropriate? Is some mix of right-to-left and left-to-right searching workable? Another approach is to use trie string searching to check for all possible prefixes and all possible suffixes at every Mth byte position. Many similar questions naturally arise—this is an area of active research where the kind of analysis that we have discussed in this chapter plays an active role.

Exercise 7.53 How many bits are examined, on the average, by an algorithm that searches for runs of M 0s in a text string (M not small) by, for $k = 1, 2, 3$, and higher, checking the t bits ending at kM and, if they are all 0, checking the bits on each side to determine the length of the run? Assume that the text string is random except for a run of M 0s hidden somewhere within it.

Exercise 7.54 Give a way to adapt the method of the previous exercise to find the longest string of 0s in a random bitstring.

BITSTRINGS are arguably *the* fundamental combinatorial object for computer science, and we certainly have touched on a number of basic paradigms in considering the combinatorics of strings and tries. Some of the results that we have examined relate to classical results from probability theory, but many others relate both to fundamental concepts of computer science and to important practical problems.

We considered a number of basic string-searching algorithms. These are quite interesting from the standpoint of algorithm design and analysis, though they have not been as widely studied as sorting and searching algorithms. Some of the algorithms, especially trie search, are quite adaptable to more general situations, and practical applications of string-searching algorithms are numerous.

Considering sets of strings leads to the study of *formal languages*, and the useful result that there is a specific connection between fundamental theoretical properties of formal language systems and analytic properties of the generating functions. Not the least of the implications of this is that it is possible to analyze a wide class of problems in an "automatic" fashion, particularly with the aid of modern computer algebra systems.

The *trie* is a combinatorial structure and a data structure that is of importance in all of these contexts. It is a practical data structure for classical search problems and it models a basic sort procedure; it is a natural representation for fixed sets of strings and applicable to string-search problems; as a type of tree, it directly relates to the basic divide-and conquer paradigm; and association with bits relates it directly to low-level representations and processes.

Finally, analysis of the basic properties of tries presents a significant challenge that cannot be fully met with elementary methods. Detailed analysis requires describing oscillatory functions. Advanced mathematical techniques to deal with the kinds of functions that arise in such problems (principally the Mellin transform) are discussed in detail by Flajolet, Gourdon, and Dumas [7] (see also [9]). This kind of function arises in a variety of algorithms, because many algorithms process binary strings either implicitly or explicitly.

References

1. A. V. AHO AND M. J. CORASICK. "Efficient string matching: An aid to bibliographic search," *Communications of the ACM* **18**, 1975, 333–340.
2. N. CHOMSKY AND M. P. SCHÜTZENBERGER. "The algebraic theory of context-free languages," in *Computer Programming and Formal Lan-*

guages, P. Braffort and D. Hirschberg, eds., North Holland, 1963, 118–161.

3. L. COMTET. *Advanced Combinatorics*, Reidel, Dordrecht, 1974.
4. H. DELANGE. "Sur la fonction sommatoire de la fonction somme des chiffres," *L'enseignement Mathématique* **XXI**, 1975.
5. S. EILENBERG. *Automata, Languages, and Machines*, Volume A, Academic Press, New York, 1974.
6. W. FELLER. *An Introduction to Probability Theory and Its Applications*, John Wiley, New York, 1957.
7. P. FLAJOLET, X. GOURDON, AND P. DUMAS. "Mellin transforms and asymptotics: harmonic sums," *Theoretical Computer Science* **144**, 1995, 3–58.
8. P. FLAJOLET, M. REGNIER, AND D. SOTTEAU. "Algebraic methods for trie statistics," *Annals of Discrete Math.* **25**, 1985, 145–188.
9. P. FLAJOLET AND R. SEDGEWICK. *Analytic Combinatorics*, in preparation.
10. P. FLAJOLET AND R. SEDGEWICK. "Digital search trees revisited," *SIAM Journal on Computing* **15**, 1986, 748–767.
11. K. O. GEDDES, S. R. CZAPOR, AND G. LABAHN. *Algorithms for Computer Algebra*, Kluwer Academic Publishers, Boston, 1992.
12. G. H. GONNET AND R. BAEZA–YATES. *Handbook of Algorithms and Data Structures*, 2nd edition, Addison-Wesley, Reading, MA, 1991.
13. I. GOULDEN AND D. JACKSON. *Combinatorial Enumeration*, John Wiley, New York, 1983.
14. L. GUIBAS AND A. ODLYZKO. "Periods in strings," *Journal of Combinatorial Theory, Series A* **30**, 1981.
15. L. GUIBAS AND A. ODLYZKO. "String overlaps, pattern matching, and nontransitive games," *Journal of Combinatorial Theory, Series A* **30**, 1981, 19–42.
16. L. GUIBAS, L. RAMSHAW, AND R. SEDGEWICK. Unpublished work, 1979.
17. D. E. KNUTH. *The Art of Computer Programming. Volume 3: Sorting and Searching*, Addison-Wesley, Reading, MA, 1973.
18. D. E. KNUTH. "The average time for carry propagation," *Indagationes Mathematicae* **40**, 1978, 238–242.
19. D. E. KNUTH, J. H. MORRIS, AND V. R. PRATT. "Fast pattern matching in strings," *SIAM Journal on Computing*, 1977, 323–350.

20. M. LOTHAIRE. *Combinatorics on Words*, Addison-Wesley, Reading, MA, 1983.
21. V. PRATT. "Counting permutations with double-ended queues, parallel stacks and parallel queues," in *Proceedings 5th Annual ACM Symposium on Theory of Computing*, 1973, 268–277.
22. H. PRODINGER. "How to select a loser," *Discrete Mathematics* **120**, 1993, 149–159.
23. A. SALOMAA AND M. SOITTOLA. *Automata-Theoretic Aspects of Formal Power Series*, Springer-Verlag, Berlin, 1978.
24. R. SEDGEWICK. *Algorithms*, 2nd edition, Addison-Wesley, Reading, MA, 1988.
25. L. TRABB-PARDO. Ph.D. thesis, Stanford University, 1977.
26. J. S. VITTER AND P. FLAJOLET, "Analysis of algorithms and data structures," in *Handbook of Theoretical Computer Science A: Algorithms and Complexity*, J. van Leeuwen, ed., Elsevier, Amsterdam, 1990, 431–524.

CHAPTER EIGHT

WORDS AND MAPS

STRINGS of characters from a fixed alphabet, or *words*, are of interest in a broad variety of applications beyond the types of algorithms considered in the previous chapter. In this chapter, we consider the same family of combinatorial objects studied in Chapter 7 (where we called them "bytestrings"), but from a different point of view.

A word may be viewed as a mapping taking an integer i in the interval 1 to N (the character position) into another integer j in the interval 1 to M (the character value, from an M-character alphabet). In the previous chapter, we primarily considered "local" properties, involving relationships among values associated with successive indices (correlations and so forth); in this chapter, we consider "global" properties, including the frequency of occurrence of values in the range and more complex structural properties. In Chapter 7, we generally considered the alphabet size M to be small constant and the string size N to be large (even infinite); in this chapter, we consider various other possibilities for the relative values of these parameters.

As basic combinatorial objects, words arise often in the analysis of algorithms. Of particular interest are *hashing* algorithms, a fundamental and widely used family of algorithms for information retrieval. We analyze a number of variations of hashing, using the basic generating function counting techniques of Chapter 3 and asymptotic results from Chapter 4. Hashing algorithms are very heavily used, and they have a long history in which the analysis of algorithms has played a central role. Conversely, the ability to accurately predict performance of this important class of practical methods has been an impetus to the development of techniques for the analysis of algorithms. Indeed, Knuth mentions that the analysis of a hashing algorithm had a "strong influence" on the structure of his pioneering series of books [20][21][22].

The elementary combinatorial properties of words have been heavily studied, primarily because they model sequences of independent Bernoulli trials. The analysis involves properties of the binomial distribution, many of which we have already examined in detail in Chapters 3 and 4. Some of the problems we consider are called *occupancy problems*, because they can be cast in a model where N balls are randomly distributed into M urns, and the "occupancy distribution" of the balls in the urns is to be studied. Many of these classical problems are elementary, though, as usual, simple algorithms can lead to variations that are quite difficult to analyze.

If the alphabet size M is small, the normal approximation to the binomial distribution is appropriate for studying occupancy problems; if M grows with N, then we use the Poisson approximation. Both situations arise in the analysis of hashing algorithms and in other applications in the analysis of algorithms.

Finally, we introduce the concept of a *map*: a functional mapping from a finite domain into itself. This is another fundamental combinatorial object that arises often in the analysis of algorithms. Maps are related to words in that they might be viewed as N-letter words in an N-letter alphabet, but it turns out that they are also related to trees, forests, and permutations; analysis of their properties unveils a rich combinatorial structure that generalizes several of those that we have studied. The symbolic method is particularly effective at helping us study the basic properties of maps. We conclude with an application of the principles of random maps in an algorithm for factoring integers.

8.1 Hashing with Separate Chaining. Program 8.1 shows a standard method for information retrieval that cuts the search time through a table of N keys by a factor of M. By making M sufficiently large, it is often possible to make this basic algorithm outperform the search algorithms based on trees and tries that we examined in §5.5 and §7.7.

We transform each key into an integer between 1 and M using a so-called *hash* function, assuming that, for any key, each value is equally likely to be produced by the hash function. When two keys hash to the same value (we refer to this as a *collision*), we keep them in separate data structure. To find out if a given key is in the table, we use the hash function to allow a secondary search among keys with the same hash value. Perhaps the simplest data structure for the secondary search—the one used in Program 8.1—is an unordered linked list, which is easy to build and search. This implementation uses a sentinel node z that is initialized with the value sought. An unsuccessful search is one that finds z.

The performance of a hashing algorithm depends on the effectiveness of the hash function, which converts arbitrary keys into values in the range 1 to M with equal likelihood. A typical way to do this is to use a prime M, then convert keys to large numbers in some natural way and use that number modulo M for the hash value. More sophisticated schemes have also been devised. Hashing algorithms are used widely for a broad variety of applications, and experience has shown that, if some attention is paid to the process, it is not difficult to ensure that hash functions transform keys into hash values that appear to be random. Analysis of algorithms is thus particularly effective for predicting performance because a straightforward randomness assumption is justified, being built into the algorithm.

The performance of a hashing algorithm also depends on the data structures that are used for the secondary search. For example, we might consider using an "ordered linked list," where the elements are kept in increasing order. Or, we might consider using a binary search tree for keys that hash to the same value. Of course, analysis of algorithms can help us choose among these variations.

If N is large by comparison to M and the hash function produces random values, we expect that each list will have about N/M elements, cutting the search time by a factor of M. Though we cannot make M arbitrarily large because increasing M implies the use of extra space to maintain the secondary data structure, we perhaps could make $M = O(N)$, which gives constant search time. Many variations of hashing that can achieve this have been proposed.

```
procedure insert(v:  integer);
  var x:  link;
  begin
  new(x); x^.next = table[hash(v)];
  table[hash(v)] = x;
  end;
function search(v:  integer):  link;
  var t:  link;
  begin
  t := table[hash(v)]; z^.key = v;
  while t^.next^.key <> v do t := t^.next;
  if t = z then t = NIL;
  search := t;
  end;
```

Program 8.1 Hashing with separate chaining

We are interested in analyzing hashing algorithms not only to determine how they compare to one another, but also to determine how they compare to other methods for the search problem and how best to set parameters (such as hash table size). To focus on the mathematics, we adopt the normal convention of measuring the performance of hashing algorithms by counting the number of *probes* used, or key comparisons made with elements in the data structure, for successful and unsuccessful search. As usual, more detailed analysis involving the cost of computing the hash function, the cost of accessing and comparing keys, and so forth is necessary to make definitive statements about the relative performance of algorithms. For instance, even though hashing can involve only a constant number of probes, it might be slower than a search based on tries (for example) if keys are very long, because computing the hash function involves examining the whole key, while a trie-based method might distinguish among keys after examining relatively few bits.

A sequence of N hash values into a table of size M is nothing more than a word of length N comprising letters from an alphabet of size M. Thus, the analysis of hashing corresponds directly to the analysis of the combinatorial properties of words. We consider the basic combinatorial properties of words next, including the analysis of hashing with separate chaining, then we look at some other hashing algorithms.

8.2 Basic Properties of Words.

Definition *An* M-word *of length* N *is a function* f *mapping integers from the interval* $[1 \ldots N]$ *into the interval* $[1 \ldots M]$.

As with permutations and trees, we specify a word by writing down its functional table:

index	1	2	3	4	5	6	7	8	9
word	1	8	2	8	4	5	9	0	4

We drop the index and specify the function by writing $f(1)f(2)\ldots f(N)$, which makes it plain that an M-word of length N is equivalent to a bytestring of length N (bytesize M). When studying words, we normally concentrate on properties of the *set* of values in the word (for example, how many 1s are there?). When studying bytestrings in Chapter 7, we concentrated on properties of the *sequence* of integers in the bytestring (how many *consecutive* 1s are there?).

In discrete probability, these combinatorial objects are often studied in the context of a *ball-and-urn* model. We imagine N balls to be randomly distributed among M urns, and we ask questions about the result of the distribution. This directly corresponds to words: N balls correspond to the N letters in a word, and M urns correspond to the M different letters in an alphabet, so we specify which urn each ball lands in. The "word" and "ball-and-urn" terminology are used interchangeably, and here we add the term "hash table," the basic data structure just described. Figure 8.1 illustrates a typical distribution of a relatively large number of balls into a relatively small number of urns.

The relative growth rates of M and N are of central importance in the analysis, and a number of different situations arise in practice. For strings of text or other kinds of "words," we normally think of M as being fixed and N as being the variable of interest. We make words of varying

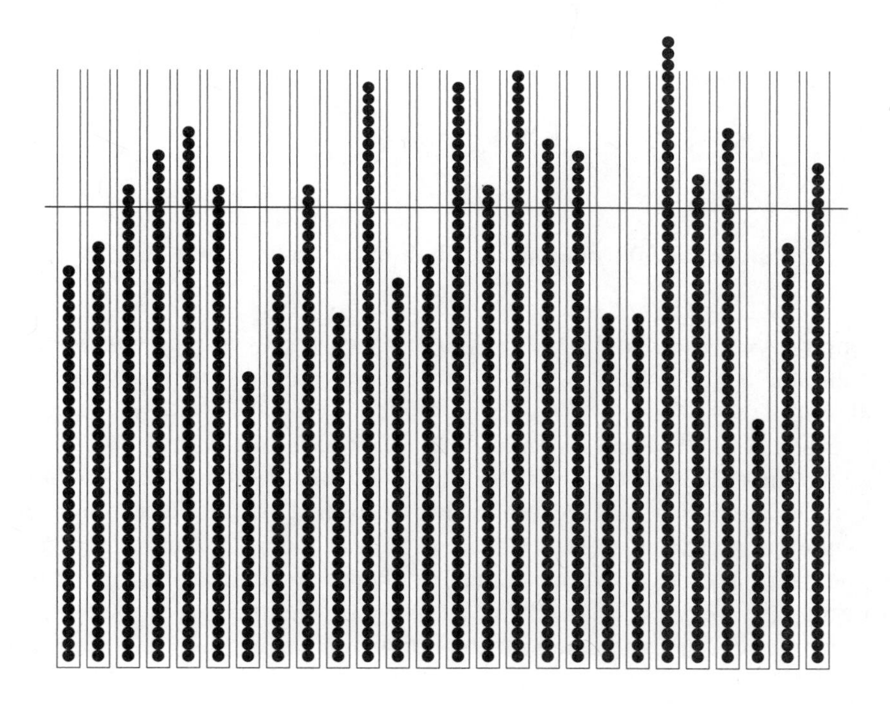

Figure 8.1 Random distribution of 1024 balls into 26 urns

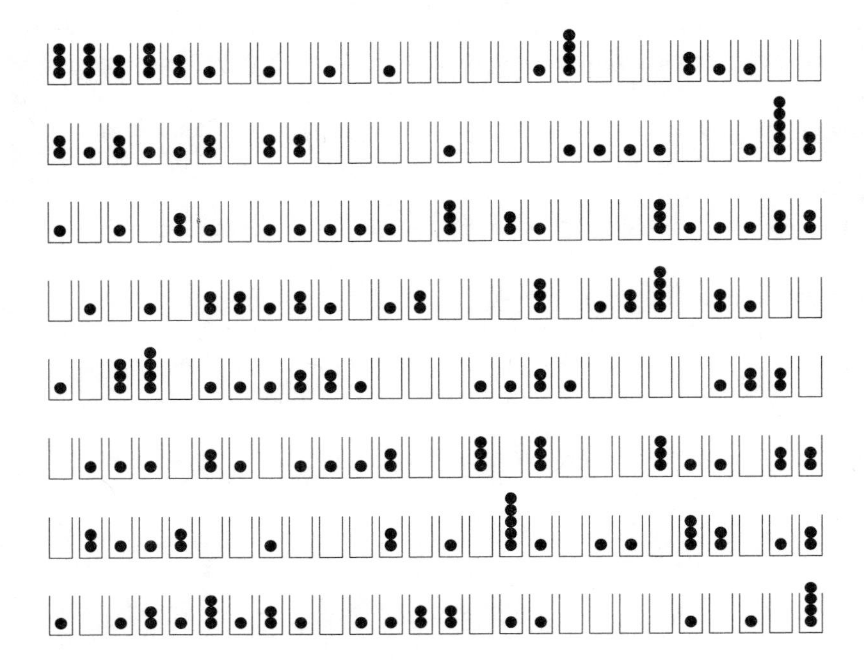

Figure 8.2 Eight random distributions of 26 balls into 26 urns

length from letters in a fixed alphabet, or we throw varying numbers of balls at a fixed number of urns. For other applications, particularly hashing algorithms, we think of M growing with N, typically $M = \alpha N$ with α between 0 and 1. Figure 8.2 illustrates eight examples with $\alpha = 1$: many of the urns tend to be empty, some have just one ball, and very few have several balls. As we will see, our analysis leads to a precise characterization of the "occupancy distributions" illustrated in Figure 8.1 and Figure 8.2. The distribution in question is of course the binomial distribution, and the results that we consider are classical (nearly two centuries old); we already covered them in some detail in Chapter 4.

Table 8.1 gives all the 3-words of length 4 (or all the ways to distribute 4 balls into 3 urns), along with the occupancy counts showing the number of letters that are used 0, 1, 2, 3, and 4 times (or the number of urns that

word	0	1	2	3	4	*word*	0	1	2	3	4	*word*	0	1	2	3	4
1111	2	0	0	0	1	2111	1	1	0	1	0	3111	1	1	0	1	0
1112	1	1	0	1	0	2112	1	0	2	0	0	3112	0	2	1	0	0
1113	1	1	0	1	0	2113	0	2	1	0	0	3113	1	0	2	0	0
1121	1	1	0	1	0	2121	1	0	2	0	0	3121	0	2	1	0	0
1122	1	0	2	0	0	2122	1	1	0	1	0	3122	0	2	1	0	0
1123	0	2	1	0	0	2123	0	2	1	0	0	3123	0	2	1	0	0
1131	1	1	0	1	0	2131	0	2	1	0	0	3131	1	0	2	0	0
1132	0	2	1	0	0	2132	0	2	1	0	0	3132	0	2	1	0	0
1133	1	0	2	0	0	2133	0	2	1	0	0	3133	1	1	0	1	0
1211	1	1	0	1	0	2211	1	0	2	0	0	3211	0	2	1	0	0
1212	1	0	2	0	0	2212	1	1	0	1	0	3212	0	2	1	0	0
1213	0	2	1	0	0	2213	0	2	1	0	0	3213	0	2	1	0	0
1221	1	0	2	0	0	2221	1	1	0	1	0	3221	0	2	1	0	0
1222	1	1	0	1	0	2222	2	0	0	0	1	3222	1	1	0	1	0
1223	0	2	1	0	0	2223	1	1	0	1	0	3223	1	0	2	0	0
1231	0	2	1	0	0	2231	0	2	1	0	0	3231	0	2	1	0	0
1232	0	2	1	0	0	2232	1	1	0	1	0	3232	1	0	2	0	0
1233	0	2	1	0	0	2233	1	0	2	0	0	3233	1	1	0	1	0
1311	1	1	0	1	0	2311	0	2	1	0	0	3311	1	0	2	0	0
1312	0	2	1	0	0	2312	0	2	1	0	0	3312	0	2	1	0	0
1313	1	0	2	0	0	2313	0	2	1	0	0	3313	1	1	0	1	0
1321	0	2	1	0	0	2321	0	2	1	0	0	3321	0	2	1	0	0
1322	0	2	1	0	0	2322	1	1	0	1	0	3322	1	0	2	0	0
1323	0	2	1	0	0	2323	1	0	2	0	0	3323	1	1	0	1	0
1331	1	0	2	0	0	2331	0	2	1	0	0	3331	1	1	0	1	0
1332	0	2	1	0	0	2332	1	0	2	0	0	3332	1	1	0	1	0
1333	1	1	0	1	0	2333	1	1	0	1	0	3333	2	0	0	0	1
												total	48	96	72	24	3

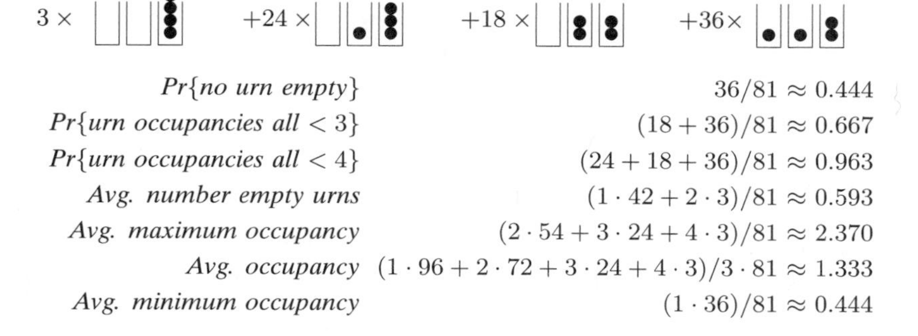

Pr{no urn empty} $36/81 \approx 0.444$

Pr{urn occupancies all < 3*}* $(18+36)/81 \approx 0.667$

Pr{urn occupancies all < 4*}* $(24+18+36)/81 \approx 0.963$

Avg. number empty urns $(1\cdot 42 + 2\cdot 3)/81 \approx 0.593$

Avg. maximum occupancy $(2\cdot 54 + 3\cdot 24 + 4\cdot 3)/81 \approx 2.370$

Avg. occupancy $(1\cdot 96 + 2\cdot 72 + 3\cdot 24 + 4\cdot 3)/3\cdot 81 \approx 1.333$

Avg. minimum occupancy $(1\cdot 36)/81 \approx 0.444$

Table 8.1 Occupancy distribution and properties of 3-words of length 4
or configurations of 4 balls in 3 urns
or hash sequences of length 4 (table size 3)

contain 0, 1, 2, 3, and 4 balls). A few other statistics of the type we are considering are also included.

Generally speaking, when N balls are randomly distributed among M urns, we are interested in the following sorts of questions:

- What is the probability that no urn will be empty?
- What is the probability that no urn will contain more than one ball?
- How many of the urns are empty?
- How many balls are in the urn containing the most balls?
- How many balls are in the urn containing the fewest balls?

These are immediately relevant to practical implementations of hashing and other algorithms: we want to know how long we may expect the lists to be when using hashing with separate chaining, how many empty lists we might expect, and so on. Some of the questions are enumeration problems akin to our enumeration of permutations with cycle length restrictions in Chapter 6; others require analysis of properties of words in more detail. These and related questions depend on the *occupancy distribution* of the balls in the urns, which we study in detail below.

Table 8.2 gives the values of some of these quantities for three urns with the number of balls ranging from 1 to 10, calculated using the results given in the next section. The fourth column corresponds to Table 8.1, which illustrates how these values are calculated. As the number of balls grows, we have a situation similar to that depicted in Figure 8.1, with balls distributed about equally into urns, about N/M balls per urn. Other

balls →	1	2	3	4	5	6	7	8	9	10
Probability										
urn occ. all < 2	1	.667	.222	0	0	0	0	0	0	0
urn occ. all < 3	1	1	.889	.667	.370	.123	0	0	0	0
urn occ. all < 4	1	1	1	.963	.864	.700	.480	.256	.085	0
urn occ. all > 0	0	0	.222	.444	.617	.741	.826	.883	.922	.948
urn occ. all > 1	0	0	0	0	0	.123	.288	.448	.585	.693
urn occ. all > 2	0	0	0	0	0	0	0	0	.085	.213
Average										
# empty urns	2	1.33	.889	.593	.395	.263	.176	.117	.0780	.0520
max. occupancy	1	1.33	1.89	2.37	2.78	3.23	3.68	4.08	4.50	4.93
min. occupancy	0	0	.222	.444	.617	.864	1.11	1.33	1.59	1.85

Table 8.2 Occupancy parameters for balls in three urns

phenomena that we expect intuitively are exhibited in this table. For example, as the number of balls increases, the number of empty urns becomes small, and the probability that no urn is empty becomes large.

The relative values of M and N dictate the extent to which the answers to the various questions posed above are of interest. If there are many more balls than urns ($N \gg M$), then it is clear that the number of empty urns will be very low; indeed, we expect there to be about N/M balls per urn. This is the case illustrated in Figure 8.1. If there are many fewer balls than urns ($N \ll M$), most urns are empty. Some of the most interesting and important results describe the situation when N and M are within a constant factor of each other. Even when $M = N$, urn occupancy is relatively low, as illustrated in Figure 8.2.

Table 8.3 gives the values corresponding to Table 8.2, but for the larger value $M = 8$, again with N ranging from 1 to 10. When the number of balls is small, we have a situation similar to that depicted in Figure 8.2, with many empty urns and few balls per urn generally. Again, we are able to calculate exact values from the analytic results given in the next section.

As with permutations, we can develop combinatorial correspondences among words for use in deriving functional relationships among CGFs that yield analytic results of interest. Many such correspondences are potentially useful; choosing among them for a particular application is part of the art of analysis. For words there are more possibilities than for permutations, because there are two parameters: our correspondences for M-words of length N are to words with smaller values of N *and* M.

balls →	1	2	3	4	5	6	7	8	9	10
Probability										
urn occ. all < 2	1	.875	.656	.410	.205	.077	.019	.002	0	0
urn occ. all < 3	1	1	.984	.943	.872	.769	.642	.501	.361	.237
urn occ. all < 4	1	1	1	.998	.991	.976	.950	.910	.855	.784
urn occ. all > 0	0	0	0	0	0	0	0	.002	.011	.028
urn occ. all > 1	0	0	0	0	0	0	0	.000	.000	.000
Average										
# empty urns	7	6.13	5.36	4.69	4.10	3.59	3.14	2.75	2.41	2.10
max. occupancy	1	1.13	1.36	1.65	1.93	2.18	2.39	2.60	2.81	3.02
min. occupancy	0	0	0	0	0	0	0	.002	.011	.028

Table 8.3 Occupancy parameters for balls in eight urns

Exercise 8.1 Give a table like Table 8.1 for three balls in four urns.

Exercise 8.2 Give a table like Tables 8.1 and 8.3 for two urns.

Exercise 8.3 Give necessary and sufficient conditions on N and M for the average number of empty urns to equal the average minimum urn occupancy.

"First" or "last" correspondence. Given an M-word of length N, consider the word formed by simply removing the first element, to make a word of length $N-1$. This corresponds to precisely M different words of length N, one for each possible value of the first element. Or, working forwards, given any M-word of length $N-1$, we can identify M different M-words of length N simply by, for each k from 1 to M, prepending k. For example,

`1 2 1 3 3    2 2 1 3 3    3 2 1 3 3`

all correspond to `2 1 3 3`. This defines the "first" correspondence; one can obviously do the same thing with any other element, not only the first. This correspondence says that the number of M-words of length N is M times the number of M-words of length $N-1$, a restatement of the obvious fact that the count is M^N.

"Largest" correspondence. Given an M-word of length N, consider the $(M-1)$-word formed by simply removing all occurrences of M. If there were k such occurrences (k could range from 0 to N), this word is of length $N-k$, and corresponds to exactly $\binom{N}{k}$ different words of length N, one for every possible way to add k elements. For example,

`3 3 2 1    3 2 3 1    3 2 1 3    2 3 3 1    2 3 1 3    2 1 3 3`

all correspond to `2 1`. This correspondence leads to the recurrence

$$M^N = \sum_{0\le k\le N}\binom{N}{k}(M-1)^{N-k},$$

a restatement of the binomial theorem.

8.3 Birthday Paradox and Coupon Collector Problem. We know that the distribution of balls in urns is the binomial distribution, and we discuss properties of that distribution in detail later in this chapter. Before doing so, however, we consider two classical problems about ball-and-urn configurations that have to do with the dynamics of the process of the urns filling up with balls. As N balls are randomly distributed, one after another, among M urns, we are interested in knowing how many balls are thrown, on the average, before

- a ball falls into a nonempty urn for the first time; and
- no urns are empty for the first time.

These are called the *birthday problem* and the *coupon collector problem*, respectively. Again, they are immediately relevant to practical implementations of hashing and other algorithms. For example, the solution to the birthday problem will tell us how many keys we should expect to insert before we find the first collision; and the solution to the coupon collector problem will tell us how many keys we should expect to insert before finding that there are no empty lists.

Birthday problem. Perhaps the most famous problem in this realm is the *birthday problem* which is often stated as follows: How many people should one gather in a group for it to be more likely than not that two of them have the same birthday? Taking people one at a time, the probability that the second has a different birthday than the first is $(1 - 1/M)$; the probability that the third has a different birthday than the first two is (independently) $(1 - 2/M)$, and so on, so the probability that N people have different birthdays is

$$\Bigl(1 - \frac{1}{M}\Bigr)\Bigl(1 - \frac{2}{M}\Bigr)\ldots\Bigl(1 - \frac{N-1}{M}\Bigr) = \frac{N!}{M^N}\binom{M}{N}.$$

This distribution for $M = 365$ is plotted in Figure 8.3.

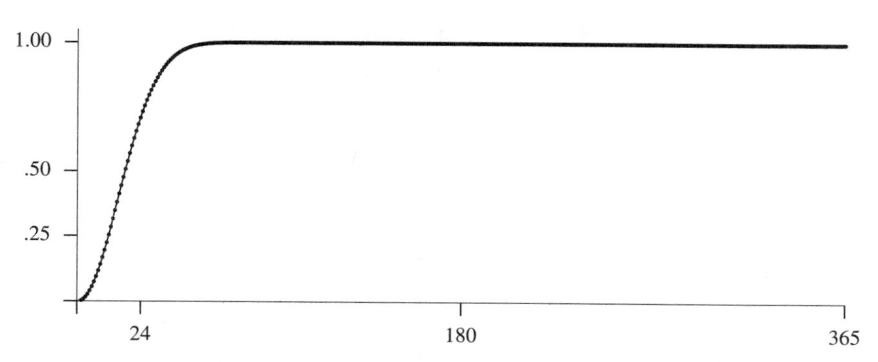

Figure 8.3 Probability that two people have the same birthday

Theorem 8.1 (*Birthday problem*) *The probability that there are no collisions when N balls are thrown into M urns is given by*

$$\Bigl(1-\frac{1}{M}\Bigr)\Bigl(1-\frac{2}{M}\Bigr)\dots\Bigl(1-\frac{N-1}{M}\Bigr).$$

The expected number of balls thrown until the first collision occurs is

$$1+Q(M)=\sum_k \binom{M}{k}\frac{k!}{M^k}\sim\sqrt{\frac{\pi M}{2}}+\frac{2}{3}$$

where $Q(M)$ is the Ramanujan Q-function.

Proof. See the above discussion for the probability distribution. To find the expected value, let X denote the random variable for the number of balls until the first collision occurs. Then the given probability is precisely $\Pr\{X>N\}$. Summing these, we get an expression for the expectation:

$$\sum_{N\ge 0}\Bigl(1-\frac{1}{M}\Bigr)\Bigl(1-\frac{2}{M}\Bigr)\dots\Bigl(1-\frac{N-1}{M}\Bigr),$$

which is precisely $1+Q(M)$ by the definition of $Q(M)$ (see §4.7). The asymptotic form follows from Theorem 4.8. ∎

The value of $1+Q(365)$ is between 24 and 25—this is the average number of people we would expect to ask to find two with the same birthday. This is often referred to as the "birthday paradox" because one might expect the number to be much higher.

It is also of interest to find the median value: the value of N for which the probability given above is closest to $1/2$. This could be done with a quick computer calculation, or an asymptotic calculation can also be used. Asymptotically, the cutoff point is determined by

$$\Bigl(1-\frac{1}{M}\Bigr)\Bigl(1-\frac{2}{M}\Bigr)\dots\Bigl(1-\frac{N-1}{M}\Bigr)\sim\frac{1}{2}$$

$$\sum_{1\le k<N}\ln\Bigl(1-\frac{k}{M}\Bigr)\sim\ln(1/2)$$

$$\sum_{1\le k<N}\frac{k}{M}\sim\ln 2$$

$$\frac{N(N-1)}{2M}\sim\ln 2$$

$$N\sim\sqrt{2M\ln 2},$$

which slightly underestimates the answer $N = 23$ for $M = 365$.

The coefficient of $\sqrt{M}$ for the mean number of people to be gathered before a birthday collision occurs is $\sqrt{\pi/2} \approx 1.2533$, and the coefficient of $\sqrt{M}$ for the median (the number of people to be gathered to be 50% sure that a birthday collision will occur) is $\sqrt{2\ln 2} \approx 1.1774$. These give rise to the approximate values 24.6112 and 22.4944, respectively, for $M = 365$, and it is interesting to note that the mean and median are *not* asymptotically equivalent in this case.

Exercise 8.4 For $M = 365$, how many people are needed to be 99% sure that two have the same birthday?

Exercise 8.5 Estimate the variance associated with the birthday distribution in Theorem 8.1, and explain the apparent discrepancy concerning the asymptotic values of the mean and the median.

Coupon collector problem. Another famous problem in this realm is the classical *coupon collector* problem: if each box of a product contains one of a set of M coupons, how many boxes must one buy, on the average, before getting all the coupons? This is equivalent to the expected number of balls thrown until all urns have at least one ball or the expected number of keys added until all the chains in a hash table built by Program 8.1 have at least one key.

To solve this problem, we define a *k-collection* to be a word that consists of k different letters, with the last letter in the word being the only time that letter occurs, and $\mathcal{W}_{Mk}$ to be the set of k-collections of M possible coupons. The number of k-collections of length N divided by M^N is the probability that N coupons need to be collected to get k different ones. In the ball-and-urn model, this is the probability that the last ball falls into an empty urn, making the number of nonempty urns equal to k. Now, the OGF

$$P_k(z) \equiv \sum_{w \in \mathcal{W}_{Mk}} z^{|w|}$$

satisfies

$$P_k(z) = (k-1) \sum_{w \in \mathcal{W}_{Mk}} z^{|w|+1} + (M-(k-1)) \sum_{w \in \mathcal{W}_{M(k-1)}} z^{|w|+1}$$

by the "first" correspondence: either the first coupon is in the collection of $(k-1)$ coupons (not including the last one) in w, in which case the rest of the word is a k-collection, or it is not, in which case the rest of the word is a $(k-1)$-collection. Therefore,

$$\begin{aligned}P_k(z) &= (k-1)zP_k(z) + (M-(k-1))zP_{k-1}(z)\\ &= \frac{(M-(k-1))z}{1-(k-1)z}P_{k-1}(z),\end{aligned}$$

with $P_0(z) = 1$. Note that $P_k(z/M)$ is the PGF for the length of k-collections, so we have $P_k(1/M) = 1$ and the average length is $P_k'(z/M)|_{z=1}$. Differentiating both sides of the equation

$$P_k(z/M) = \frac{(M-(k-1))z}{M-(k-1)z}P_{k-1}(z/M),$$

evaluating at $z = 1$, and simplifying gives the recurrence

$$\frac{d}{dz}P_k(z/M)|_{z=1} = 1 + \frac{(k-1)}{M-(k-1)} + \frac{d}{dz}P_{k-1}(z/M)|_{z=1},$$

which telescopes to the solution

$$\frac{d}{dz}P_k(z/M)|_{z=1} = \sum_{0\le j<k}\frac{M}{M-j} = M(H_M - H_{M-k}).$$

Theorem 8.2 (*Coupon collector problem*) *The average number of balls thrown until all M urns are filled is*

$$MH_M = M\ln M + M\gamma + O(1)$$

with variance

$$M^2H_M^{(2)} - MH_M \sim M^2\pi^2/6.$$

The probability that the Nth ball fills the last empty urn is

$$\frac{M!}{M^N}\left\{{N-1 \atop M-1}\right\}.$$

Proof. The mean is derived in the discussion above. Alternatively, telescoping the recurrence on the OGF for k-collections gives the explicit form

$$P_k(z) = \frac{M(M-1)\dots(M-k+1)}{(1-z)(1-2z)\dots(1-(k-1)z)}z^k$$

which leads immediately to the PGF

$$P_M(z/M) = \frac{M!z^M}{M(M-z)(M-2z)\ldots(M-(M-1)z)}.$$

It is easily verified that $P_M(1/M) = 1$ and that differentiating with respect to z and evaluating at $z = 1$ gives MH_M, as above. Differenting a second time and applying Theorem 3.10 leads to the stated expression for the variance. The distribution follows immediately by extracting coefficients from the PGF using the identity

$$\sum_{N\geq M} \left\{ {N \atop M} \right\} z^N = \frac{z^M}{(1-z)(1-2z)\ldots(1-Mz)},$$

from Table 3.7 in §3.13. ∎

Exercise 8.6 Find all the 2-collections and 3-collections in Table 8.1, then compute $P_2(z)$ and $P_3(z)$ and check the coefficients of z^4.

Stirling numbers of the second kind. As pointed out already in §3.13, the Stirling "subset" numbers $\left\{ {N \atop M} \right\}$ also represent the number of ways to partition an N-element set into M nonempty subsets. We will see a derivation of this fact later in this section. Starting with this definition leads to an alternate derivation of the coupon collector distribution, as follows. Consider a set of $N-1$ balls and $M-1$ urns. The order of the urns is not significant, so $\left\{ {N-1 \atop M-1} \right\}(M-1)!$ is the number of ways for the $N-1$ balls to fall into $M-1$ different urns. Any of the urns could be the last urn to be filled, so the number of ways for the last of N balls to fill the last of M urns is $M\left\{ {N-1 \atop M-1} \right\}(M-1)!$, and dividing by M^N gives the same result as given in Theorem 8.2.

The classical derivation of the mean given in Theorem 8.2 (see, for example, Feller [9]) proceeds as follows. Once k coupons have been collected, the probability that j or more additional boxes are needed to get the next coupon is

$$\sum_{j\geq 0} \left(\frac{k}{M}\right)^j = \frac{1}{1-k/M} = \frac{M}{M-k},$$

and summing on k gives the result MH_M, as above. This requires less computation than the derivation above, but the generating functions capture the full structure of the problem, making it possible to calculate the variance without explicitly worrying about dependencies among the random variables involved, and also giving the complete probability distribution.

Exercise 8.7 Expand the PGF by partial fractions to show that the probability that the Nth ball fills the last empty urn can also be expressed as the alternating sum

$$\sum_{0\le j<M}\binom{M}{j}(-1)^j\Big(1-\frac{j}{M}\Big)^{N-1}.$$

Exercise 8.8 Give an expression for the probability that collecting *at least* N boxes gives a full collection of M coupons.

Direct enumeration of surjections. Ball-and-urn sequences with no empty urns (words with at least one occurrence of each letter) are called *surjections*. Surjections arise in many contexts, since they correspond to dividing N items into exactly M distinguished nonempty groups. We consider here an approach to enumerating them that is similar to several arguments we saw in Chapters 5 and 6. Every M-surjection of length $|f|$ corresponds to M different M-surjections of length $|f|+1$, obtained by appending one of the integers between 1 and M, and every $(M-1)$-surjection of length $|f|$ corresponds to M different M-surjections of length $|f|+1$, obtained by inserting M in any one of the M possible positions between elements. Every M-surjection is generated in this way (if there is a single M, remove it to get the corresponding $(M-1)$ surjection; otherwise remove the last element). Thus the EGF

$$F_M(z)=\sum_{\substack{f\in\mathcal{F}_M\\ f\text{ surjection}}}\frac{z^{|f|}}{|f|!}.$$

satisfies

$$F_M(z)=\sum_{\substack{f\in\mathcal{F}_M\\ f\text{ surjection}}}M\frac{z^{|f|+1}}{(|f|+1)!}+\sum_{\substack{f\in\mathcal{F}_{M-1}\\ f\text{ surjection}}}M\frac{z^{|f|+1}}{(|f|+1)!}.$$

Differentiating, this simplifies to

$$F'_M(z)=MF_M(z)+MF_{M-1}(z),$$

which has the solution

$$F_M(z)=(e^z-1)^M.$$

This is an exponential generating function for the Stirling numbers of the second kind (see Table 3.7), so we have proved that the number of M-surjections of length N is $M!\{{N \atop M}\}$. Again, starting with the combinatorial definition that Stirling numbers of the second kind enumerate partitions of N elements into M subsets gives a direct proof of this same result, since each of the $M!$ orderings of the sets yields a surjection.

Exercise 8.9 Consider the "largest" correspondence among surjections: given an M-surjection of length N, consider the $(M-1)$-surjection formed by removing all occurrences of M. Find the EGF for surjections using this correspondence.

Exercise 8.10 Write a program to print out all M-surjections of length N whenever the number of such objects is less than 1000.

Exercise 8.11 Expand $(e^z - 1)^M$ by the binomial theorem to show that

$$N![z^N]F_M(z) = \sum_j \binom{M}{j}(-1)^{M-j}j^N = M!\left\{{N \atop M}\right\}.$$

(See Exercise 8.7.)

Exercise 8.12 Show that the number of partitions of N elements into nonempty subsets is

$$N![z^N]e^{e^z-1}.$$

(This defines the so-called *Bell numbers*.)

Exercise 8.13 Show that

$$N![z^N]e^{e^z-1} = \frac{1}{e}\sum_{k\geq 0}\frac{k^N}{k!}.$$

Exercise 8.14 Prove that the bivariate EGF for the Stirling numbers of the second kind is $\exp(u(e^z - 1))$.

Exercise 8.15 Applying the "largest" correspondence to find the number of M-words of length N might lead to the recurrence

$$F_{NM} = \sum_{0\leq k\leq M}\binom{N}{k}F_{(N-k)(M-1)}.$$

Show how to solve this recurrence using BGFs.

Caching algorithms. Coupon collector results are classical, and they are of direct interest in the analysis of a variety of useful algorithms. For example, consider a "demand paging" system where a k-page cache is used to increase the performance of an M-page memory by keeping the k most recently referenced pages in the cache. If the "page references" are random, then the coupon collector analysis gives the number of references until the cache fills up.

Corollary *The average number of page references until a cache of size k fills up in an M-page memory system, assuming page references are independent and uniformly distributed, is $M(H_M - H_{M-k})$.*

Proof. This follows directly from the computation of $P_k(z)$ given in the proof of Theorem 8.2. ■

Note that, although it takes $\sim M \ln M$ references before all the pages are hit, a cache of size αM fills up after about $M \ln(1/(1-\alpha))$ references. For instance, a cache of size $M/2$ will fill after about $M \ln 2 \approx .69M$ page references, resulting in a 19% savings. In practice, references are not random, but correlated and nonuniform. For example, recently referenced pages are likely to be referenced again, resulting in much higher savings from caching. The analysis thus should provide lower bounds on cache efficiency in practical situations. In addition, the analysis provides a starting point for more "realistic" analysis under nonuniform probabilistic models. (See Flajolet, Gardy, and Thimonier [10].)

The birthday problem and the coupon collector problem appear at opposite ends of the process of filling cells with balls. In the birthday problem, we add balls and look at the first time some cell gets more than one ball, which takes about about $\sqrt{\pi M/2}$ steps, on the average. Continuing to add the balls, we eventually fill each cell with at least one ball, after about $M \ln M$ steps on the average, by the coupon collector result. In between, when $M = N$, we will see in the next section that about $1 - 1/e \approx 36\%$ of the cells are empty, and, furthermore, one of the cells should have about $\ln N / \ln\ln N$ balls.

These results have various practical implications for hashing algorithms. First, the birthday problem implies that collisions tend to occur early, so a collision resolution strategy must be designed. Second, the filling tends to be rather uneven, with a fair number of empty lists and a few long lists (almost logarithmic in length). Third, empty lists do not completely disappear until after a rather large number of insertions.

Many more details on the birthday problem, coupon collector problems, and applications are given by Feller [9] and by Flajolet, Gardy, and Thimonier [10].

8.4 Occupancy Restrictions and Extremal Parameters. Solving the birthday problem involves enumerating arrangements (the number of words with no letter occurring twice) and solving the coupon collector problem involves enumerating surjections (the number of words with at least one occurrence of each letter). In this section, we describe generalizations of these two enumeration problems on words.

In Chapter 6 we discussed enumeration of permutations with restrictions on cycle length; in Chapter 7 we discussed enumeration of bitstrings with restrictions on patterns of consecutive bits. Here we use similar techniques to discuss enumeration of words with restrictions on frequency of occurrence of letters, or, equivalently, ball-and-urn configurations with occupancy restrictions, or hash sequences with collision frequency restrictions, or functions with range frequency restrictions.

Table 8.4 shows the situation for 3-words. The top four rows in Table 8.4 give the numbers of 3-words with no more than 1, 2, 3, and 4 occurrences of any letter, and the bottom four rows give the number of 3-words with at least 1, 2, 3, and 4 occurrences of every letter (thus the fifth row corresponds to surjections). The numbers given are frequency

frequency / *balls* →	1	2	3	4	5	6	7	8	9	10	11	12
< 2	3	6	6									
< 3	3	9	24	54	90	90						
< 4	3	9	27	78	210	510	1050	1680	1680			
< 5	3	9	27	81	240	690	1890	4830	11130	22050	34650	34650
> 0			6	36	150	540	1806	5796	18150	55980	171006	519156
> 1						90	630	2940	11508	40950	125100	445896
> 2									1680	12600	62370	256410
> 3												34650

Table 8.4 Enumeration of 3-words with letter frequency restrictions or configurations of balls in 3 urns with occupancy restrictions or hash sequences (table size 3) with collision restrictions

counts, so dividing each entry by M^N yields Table 8.2. The fourth column corresponds to Table 8.1. There are many relationships among these numbers, which are most easily uncovered through systematic application of the symbolic method, in a very similar manner to our treatment of permutations in Chapter 6.

Maximal occupancy. The EGF for a word comprising at most k occurrences of a given letter is $1 + z + z^2/2! + \ldots + z^k/k!$. Therefore,

$$(1 + z + z^2/2! + \ldots + z^k/k!)^M$$

is the EGF for words comprising at most k occurrences of each of M different letters. This is a straightforward application of the symbolic method for labelled objects (see Theorem 3.8). Removing the restriction on k gives the EGF

$$(1 + z + z^2/2! + \ldots + z^k/k! + \ldots)^M = e^{zM}$$

so the total number of M-words of length N is $N![z^N]e^{zM} = M^N$ as expected.

Taking $k = 1$ gives the EGF

$$(1 + z)^M,$$

which says that the number of words with at most one occurrence of each letter (no duplicates) is

$$N![z^N](1 + z)^M = M(M-1)(M-2)\ldots(M-N+1) = N!\binom{M}{N}.$$

This quantity is also known as the number of *arrangements*, or ordered combinations, of N elements chosen among M possibilities. Dividing the number of arrangements by M^N gives the probability distribution in Theorem 8.1 for the birthday problem, and the use of the symbolic method provides a straightforward generalization.

Theorem 8.3 (*Maximal occupancy*) *The number of words of length N with at most k occurrences of each letter is*

$$N![z^N]\left(1 + \frac{z}{1!} + \frac{z^2}{2!} + \ldots + \frac{z^k}{k!}\right)^M.$$

In particular, the number of arrangements ($k = 1$) is $N!\binom{M}{N}$.

Proof. See the above discussion. ∎

The numbers in the top half of Table 8.4 correspond to computing coefficients of these EGFs for $1 \le k \le 4$. For example, the second line corresponds to the expansion

$$\begin{aligned}\left(1+z+\frac{z^2}{2!}\right)^3 &= 1+3z+\frac{9}{2}z^2+4z^3+\frac{9}{4}z^4+\frac{3}{4}z^5+\frac{1}{8}z^6\\ &= 1+3z+9\frac{z^2}{2!}+24\frac{z^3}{3!}+54\frac{z^4}{4!}+90\frac{z^5}{5!}+90\frac{z^6}{6!}.\end{aligned}$$

Exercise 8.16 Find the EGF for M-words with all letter frequencies even.

Exercise 8.17 Prove that the number of ways to distribute $M(k+1)$ balls among M urns with all urns having $> k$ balls is equal to the number of ways to distribute $M(k+1)-1$ balls among M urns with all urns having $< (k+2)$ balls, for all $k \ge 0$. (See Table 8.4.) Give an explicit formula for this quantity as a quotient of factorials.

Exercise 8.18 What is the expected number of balls thrown in N urns before the *second* collision occurs? Assume that "collision" here means the event "ball falling into nonempty urn."

Exercise 8.19 What is the expected number of balls thrown in N urns before the second collision occurs, when we assume that "collision" means the event "ball falling into urn with exactly one ball in it?"

Exercise 8.20 Give an explicit expression for the number of M-words with no three occurrences of the same letter.

Exercise 8.21 Give a plot like Figure 8.3 for the probability that *three* people have the same birthday.

Exercise 8.22 For $M = 365$, how many people are needed to be 50% sure that three have the same birthday? Four?

Minimal occupancy. By arguments similar to those used above for maximal occupancy, the EGF for words comprising more than k occurrences of each letter is

$$(e^z - 1 - z - z^2/2! - \ldots - z^k/k!)^M.$$

In particular, taking $k = 1$ gives the EGF for the number of words with at least one occurrence of each letter (the number of ball-and-urn sequences with no empty urns):

$$(e^z - 1)^M.$$

This constitutes another direct way to enumerate surjections, and we are considering a generalization of the coupon collector problem of the previous section.

Theorem 8.4 (*Minimal occupancy*) *The number of words of length N with at least k occurrences of each letter is*

$$N![z^N]\Bigl(e^z - 1 - \frac{z}{1!} - \frac{z^2}{2!} - \ldots - \frac{z^{k-1}}{(k-1)!}\Bigr)^M.$$

In particular, the number of M-surjections of length N is

$$N![z^N](e^z - 1)^M = M!\left\{ {N \atop M} \right\}.$$

Proof. See the above discussion. ■

The numbers in the bottom half of Table 8.4 correspond to computing coefficients of these EGFs. For example, the third line from the bottom corresponds to the expansion

$$\begin{aligned}(e^z - 1 - z)^3 &= (\frac{z^2}{2} + \frac{z^3}{6} + \frac{z^4}{24} + \frac{z^5}{120} + \ldots)^3\\ &= \frac{1}{8}z^6 + \frac{1}{8}z^7 + \frac{7}{96}z^8 + \frac{137}{4320}z^9 + \frac{13}{1152}z^10 + \ldots\\ &= 90\frac{z^6}{6!} + 630\frac{z^7}{7!} + 2940\frac{z^8}{8!} + 11508\frac{z^9}{9!} + 40958\frac{z^{10}}{10!} + \ldots.\end{aligned}$$

As for maximal occupancy, generating functions succinctly describe the computation of these values.

Table 8.5 gives a summary of the generating functions from Theorems 8.3 and 8.4, for enumerating words with letter frequency restrictions. These theorems are the counterparts to Theorems 6.2 and 6.3 for permutations with cycle length restrictions. These four theorems, containing the analysis of arrangements, surjections, involutions, derangements, and their generalizations, are worthy of review, as they account for a number of basic combinatorial structures and classical enumeration problems in a uniform manner.

Characterizing the asymptotic values of the functions in Theorems 8.3 and 8.4 involves addressing multivariate asymptotic problems, each with different asymptotic regimes according to the ranges considered. This may be viewed as a generalization of our treatment of the binomial distribution (see Chapter 4 and the discussion below), where different approximations are used for different ranges of the parameter values. For instance, for fixed M, the coefficients $[z^N](1+z+z^2/2)^M$ are eventually 0, as $N \to \infty$. At the same time, for fixed M, the coefficients sum to $(5/2)^M$, with a peak near $5M/4$, and a normal approximation near the peak can be developed for the coefficients. Thus, there are interesting regions when M and N are proportional. Similarly, consider $[z^N](e^z - 1 - z)^M$, and fixed M, as $N \to \infty$. Here, we are counting functions that assume each value at least twice. But it is probabilistically obvious that all but a very small fraction of these functions will assume all values at least twice (actually about N/M times). Thus, for fixed M, this coefficient is asymptotic to $[z^N](e^z)^M$. Again, there will be an interesting transition when N grows and becomes $O(M)$. Such asymptotic results are best quantified by saddle point methods, as discussed in detail by Kolchin [23] (see also [12]).

Exercise 8.23 Find the average number of balls thrown before each urn is filled at least twice.

Expected maximum occupancy. What is the average of the *maximum* number of balls in an urn, when N balls are distributed randomly among M urns? This is an extremal parameter similar to several others that we have encountered. As we have done for tree height, maximum cycle length in permutations, and other parameters, we can use generating functions to compute the maximum occupancy.

From Theorem 8.4, we can write down the generating functions for the ball-and-urn configurations with at least one urn with occupancy $> k$,

one urn, occupancy k	$z^k/k!$
all words	e^{zM}
all occupancies > 1 *(surjections)*	$(e^z - 1)^M$
all occupancies $> k$	$(e^z - 1 - z - z^2/2! \ldots - z^k/k!)^M$
no occupancies > 1 *(arrangements)*	$(1+z)^M$
no occupancies $> k$	$(1 + z + z^2/2! + \ldots + z^k/k!)^M$

Table 8.5 EGFs for words with letter frequency restrictions or ball-and-urn configurations with occupancy restrictions or hash sequences with collision frequency restrictions

or, equivalently, those for which the maximum occupancy is $> k$:

$$\begin{aligned}
e^{3z} - (1)^3 &= 3z + 9\frac{z^2}{2!} + 27\frac{z^3}{3!} + 81\frac{z^4}{4!} + 243\frac{z^5}{5!} + \dots \\
e^{3z} - (1+z)^3 &= 3\frac{z^2}{2!} + 21\frac{z^3}{3!} + 81\frac{z^4}{4!} + 243\frac{z^5}{5!} + \dots \\
e^{3z} - \Bigl(1 + z + \frac{z^2}{2!}\Bigr)^3 &= 6\frac{z^3}{3!} + 27\frac{z^4}{4!} + 153\frac{z^5}{5!} + \dots \\
e^{3z} - \Bigl(1 + z + \frac{z^2}{2!} + \frac{z^3}{3!}\Bigr)^3 &= 3\frac{z^4}{4!} + 33\frac{z^5}{5!} + \dots \\
e^{3z} - \Bigl(1 + z + \frac{z^2}{2!} + \frac{z^3}{3!} + \frac{z^4}{4!}\Bigr)^3 &= 3\frac{z^5}{5!} + \dots \\
&\vdots
\end{aligned}$$

and so on, and we can sum these to get the exponential CGF

$$= 3z + 12\frac{z^2}{2!} + 54\frac{z^3}{3!} + 192\frac{z^4}{4!} + 675\frac{z^5}{5!} + \dots$$

for the (cumulative) maximum occupancy when balls are distributed in three urns. Dividing by 3^N yields the average values given in Table 8.2. In general, the average maximum occupancy is given by

$$\frac{N!}{M^N}[z^N]\sum_{k\ge 0}\Bigl(e^{Mz} - \Bigl(\sum_{0\le j\le k}\frac{z^j}{j!}\Bigr)^M\Bigr).$$

This quantity was shown by Gonnet [14] to be $\sim \ln N/\ln\ln N$ as $N, M \to \infty$ in such a way that $N/M = \alpha$ with α constant (the leading term is independent of α). Thus, for example, the length of the longest list when Program 8.1 is used will be $\sim \ln N/\ln\ln N$, on the average.

Exercise 8.24 Derive an expression for the exponential CGF for the expected *minimal* occupancy when N balls are distributed into M urns. Tabulate the values for M and N less than 20.

Exercise 8.25 What is the average number of blocks of contiguous equal elements in a random word?

Exercise 8.26 Analyze "rises" and "runs" in words (cf. §6.1).

8.5 Occupancy Distributions. The probability that an M-word contains exactly k instances of a given value is

$$\binom{N}{k}\left(\frac{1}{M}\right)^{k}\left(1-\frac{1}{M}\right)^{N-k}.$$

This is established by a straightforward calculation: $\binom{N}{k}$ (pick the positions) times $(1/M)^k$ (probability that those letters have the value) times $(1-1/M)^k$ (probability that the other letters do not have the value). We studied this distribution, the familiar *binomial* or *Bernoulli* distribution, in detail in Chapter 4. and have already encountered it on several different occasions throughout this book. For example, Table 4.6 gives values for $M = 2$. Another example is given in Table 8.6, which gives corresponding values for $M = 3$; the fourth line in this table corresponds to Table 8.1.

Involvement of two independent variables (number of balls and number of urns) and interest in different segments of the distribution mean that care needs to be taken to characterize it accurately for particular applications. The intuition behind the ball-and-urn model is often quite useful for this purpose.

In this section, we will be examining precise formulae and asymptotic estimates of the distributions for many values of the parameters. A few sample values are given in Table 8.7. For example, when 100 balls are distributed in 100 urns, we expect that about 18 of the urns will have 2 balls, but the chance that any urn has as many as 10 balls is negligible. On the other hand, when 100 balls are distributed in 10 urns, 1 or 2 of the urns

$N \downarrow$ $k \rightarrow$	0	1	2	3	4	5	6
1	0.666667	0.333333					
2	0.444444	0.444444	0.111111				
3	0.296296	0.444444	0.222222	0.037037			
4	0.197531	0.395062	0.296296	0.098765	0.012346		
5	0.131687	0.329218	0.329218	0.164609	0.041152	0.004115	
6	0.087791	0.263375	0.329218	0.219479	0.082305	0.016461	0.001372

Table 8.6 Occupancy distribution for $M = 3$: $\binom{N}{k}(1/3)^k(2/3)^{N-k}$
Pr{an urn has k balls after N balls are distributed in 3 urns}

are likely to have 10 balls (the others are likely to have between 7 and 13), but very few are likely to have 2 balls. As we saw in Chapter 3, these results can be described with the normal and Poisson approximations, which are accurate and useful for characterizing this distribution for a broad range of values of interest.

The above derivation of the distribution is straightforward, but it is worthwhile to develop it in a slightly different manner, using cumulative counting. With N balls and M urns, the total number of ball-and-urn sequences (M-words of length N) that have k balls in an urn is given by:

$$\begin{aligned} C_{Nk}^{[M]} &= \sum_{u \text{ urn}} \{\# \text{ of } M\text{-words of length } N \text{ with } k \text{ occurrences of } u\} \\ &= \sum_{u \text{ urn}} \binom{N}{k}(M-1)^{N-k} = M\binom{N}{k}(M-1)^{N-k}. \end{aligned}$$

This leads to the BGF, which we can use to compute moments, as usual. Dividing by M^N leads us to the classical formulation of the distribution. which we restate here along with asymptotic results summarized from Chapter 4.

urns M	*balls* N	*occupancy* k	*average # urns with k balls* $M\binom{N}{k}\left(\frac{1}{M}\right)^k\left(1-\frac{1}{M}\right)^{N-k}$
2	2	2	0.500000000
2	10	2	0.087890625
2	10	10	0.001953125
10	2	2	0.100000000
10	10	2	1.937102445
10	10	10	0.000000001
10	100	2	0.016231966
10	100	10	1.318653468
100	2	2	0.010000000
100	10	2	0.415235112
100	10	10	0.000000000
100	100	2	18.486481882
100	100	10	0.000007006

Table 8.7 Occupancy distribution examples

Theorem 8.5 (*Occupancy distribution*) *The a erage number of urns with k balls, when N balls are randomly distributed in M urns, is*

$$M\binom{N}{k}\Big(\frac{1}{M}\Big)^k\Big(1-\frac{1}{M}\Big)^{N-k}.$$

For M fixed and $k = N/M + x\sqrt{N/M - N/M^2}$ with $x = O(1)$, this is

$$M\frac{e^{-x^2}}{\sqrt{2\pi}} + O\Big(\frac{1}{\sqrt{N}}\Big) \qquad \textit{(normal approximation)},$$

and for $N/M = \alpha > 0$ fixed and $k = O(1)$, this is

$$M\frac{\alpha^k e^{-\alpha}}{k!} + o(M) \qquad \textit{(Poisson approximation)}.$$

Proof. See above discussion. The stated approximations to the binomial distribution are from Chapter 4 (Exercise 4.66 and Theorem 4.7). ■

Corollary *When $N/M = \alpha$ (constant), the a erage number of empty urns is asymptotic to $Me^{-\alpha}$.*

Corollary *The a erage number of balls per urn is N/M, with standard de iation $\sqrt{N/M - N/M^2}$.*

Proof. Multiplying the cumulative cost given above by u^k and z^N, we get the BGF

$$\begin{aligned} C^{[M]}(u,z) &= \sum_{N\ge0}\sum_{k\ge0} C^{[M]}_{Nk}u^k z^N = \sum_{N\ge0}\sum_{k\ge0}\binom{N}{k}(M-1)^{N-k}u^k z^N \\ &= \sum_{N\ge0}(M-1+u)^N z^N \\ &= \frac{1}{1-(M-1+u)z}. \end{aligned}$$

Dividing by M^N or, equivalently, replacing z by z/M converts this cumulative BGF into a PGF that is slightly more convenient to manipulate. The cumulated cost is given by differentiating this with respect to u and evaluating at $u = 1$, as in Table 3.6.

$$[z^N]\frac{\partial C^{[M]}(u,z/M)}{\partial u}\Big|_{u=1} = [z^N]\frac{1}{M}\frac{z}{(1-z)^2} = \frac{N}{M}$$

and

$$[z^N]\frac{\partial^2 C^{[M]}(u, z/M)}{\partial u^2}|_{u=1} = [z^N]\frac{1}{M^2}\frac{z^2}{(1-z)^3} = \frac{N(N-1)}{M^2}$$

so the average is N/M and the variance is $N(N-1)/M^2 + N/M - (N/M)^2$, which simplifies to the stated result. ∎

We have presented these calculations along familiar classical lines, but the symbolic method of course provides a quick derivation. For a particular urn, the BGF for a ball that misses the urn is $(M-1)z$ and the BGF for a ball that hits the urn is uz; therefore the ordinary BGF for a sequence of balls is

$$\sum_{N\geq 0}((M-1+u)z)^N = \frac{1}{1-(M-1+u)z},$$

as before.

Alternatively, the exponential BGF

$$F(u, z) = \left(e^z + (u-1)\frac{z^k}{k!}\right)^M$$

gives the cumulated number of urns with k balls:

$$N![z^N]\frac{\partial F(u, z)}{\partial u}\Big|_{u=1} = N![z^N]Me^{(M-1)z}\frac{z^k}{k!} = M\binom{N}{k}(M-1)^{N-k}$$

as before. (See §6.4 for a similar derivation.)

The occupancy and binomial distributions have a broad variety of applications and have been very widely studied, so many other ways to derive these results are available. Indeed, it is important to note that the average number of balls per urn, which would seem to be the most important quantity to analyze, is completely independent of the distribution. *No matter how* the balls are distributed in the urns, the cumulative cost is N: counting the balls in each urn, then adding the counts, is equivalent to just counting the balls. The average number of balls per urn is N/M, whether or not they were distributed randomly. The variance is what tells us whether the number of balls in a given urn can be expected to be near N/M.

Figures 8.4 and 8.5 show the occupancy distribution for various values of M. The bottom series of curves in Figure 8.4 corresponds precisely to Figure 4.2, the binomial distribution centered at $1/5$. For large M, illustrated in Figure 8.5, the Poisson approximation is appropriate. The limiting curves for the bottom two families in Figure 8.5 are the same as the limiting curves for the top two families in Figure 4.3, the Poisson distribution for $N = 60$ with $\lambda = 1$ and $\lambda = 2$. (The other limiting curves in Figure 4.3, for $N = 60$, are the occupancy distributions for $M = 15$ and $M = 12$.) As M gets smaller with respect to N, we move into the domain illustrated by Figure 8.4, where the normal approximation is appropriate.

Exercise 8.27 What is the probability that one urn will get all the balls when 100 balls are randomly distributed among 100 urns?

Exercise 8.28 What is the probability that each urn will get one ball when 100 balls are randomly distributed among 100 urns?

Exercise 8.29 What is the standard deviation for the average number of empty urns?

Exercise 8.30 What is the probability that each urn will contain an even number of balls when N balls are distributed among M urns?

Exercise 8.31 Prove that

$$C_{Nk}^{[M]} = (M-1)C_{(N-1)k}^{[M]} + C_{(N-1)(k-1)}^{[M]}$$

for $N > 1$ and use this fact to write a program that will print out the occupancy distribution for any given M.

Analysis of hashing with separate chaining. Properties of occupancy distributions are the basis for the analysis of hashing algorithms. For example, an unsuccessful search in a hash table using separate chaining involves accessing a random list, then following it to the end. The cost of such a search thus satisfies an occupancy distribution.

Theorem 8.6 (*Hashing with separate chaining*) *Using a table of size M for N keys, hashing with separate chaining requires N/M probes for unsuccessful search and $(N+1)/(2M)$ probes for successful search, on the average.*

Proof. The result for unsuccessful search follows directly from the discussion above. The cost of accessing a key that is in the table is the same

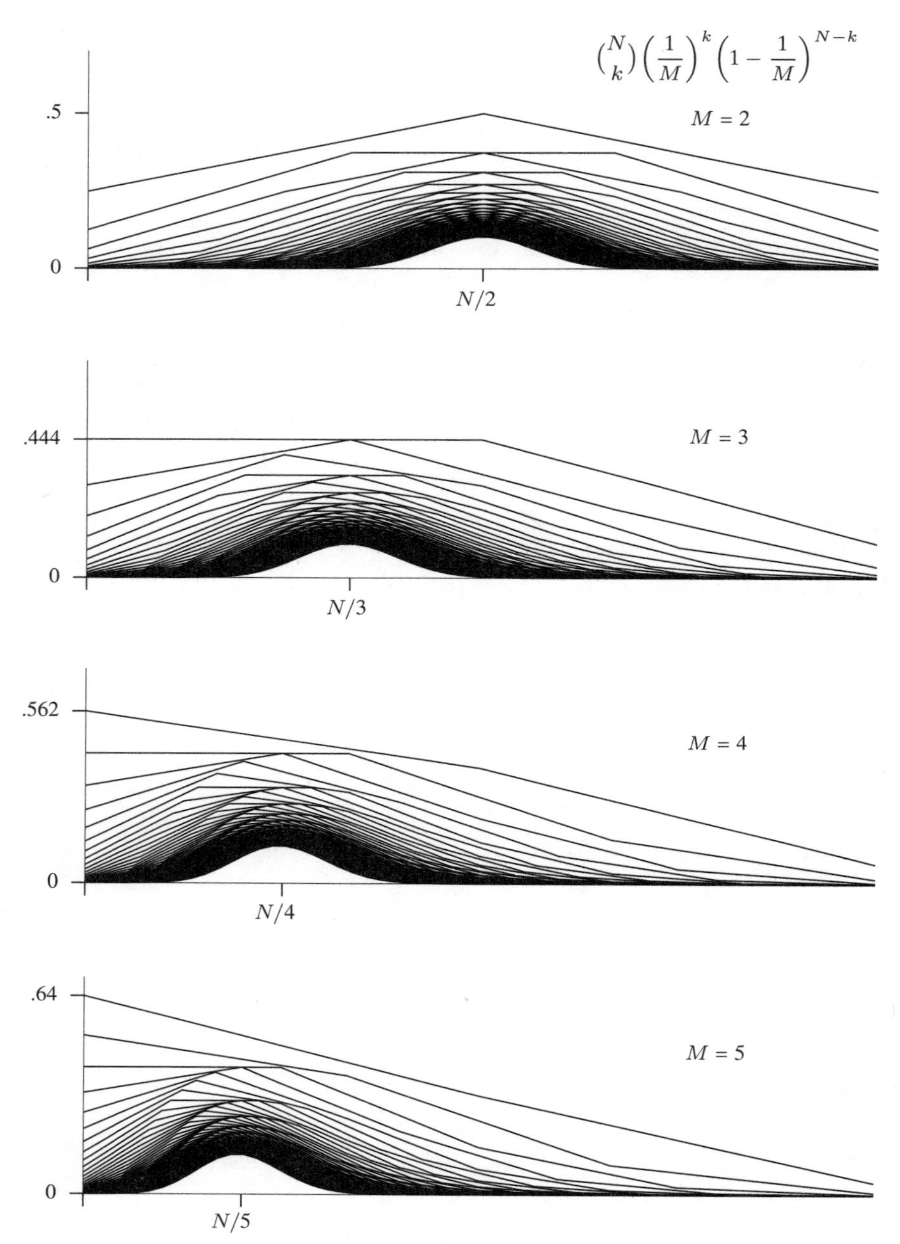

Figure 8.4 Occupancy distributions for small M and $2 \leq N \leq 60$ (k-axes scaled to N)

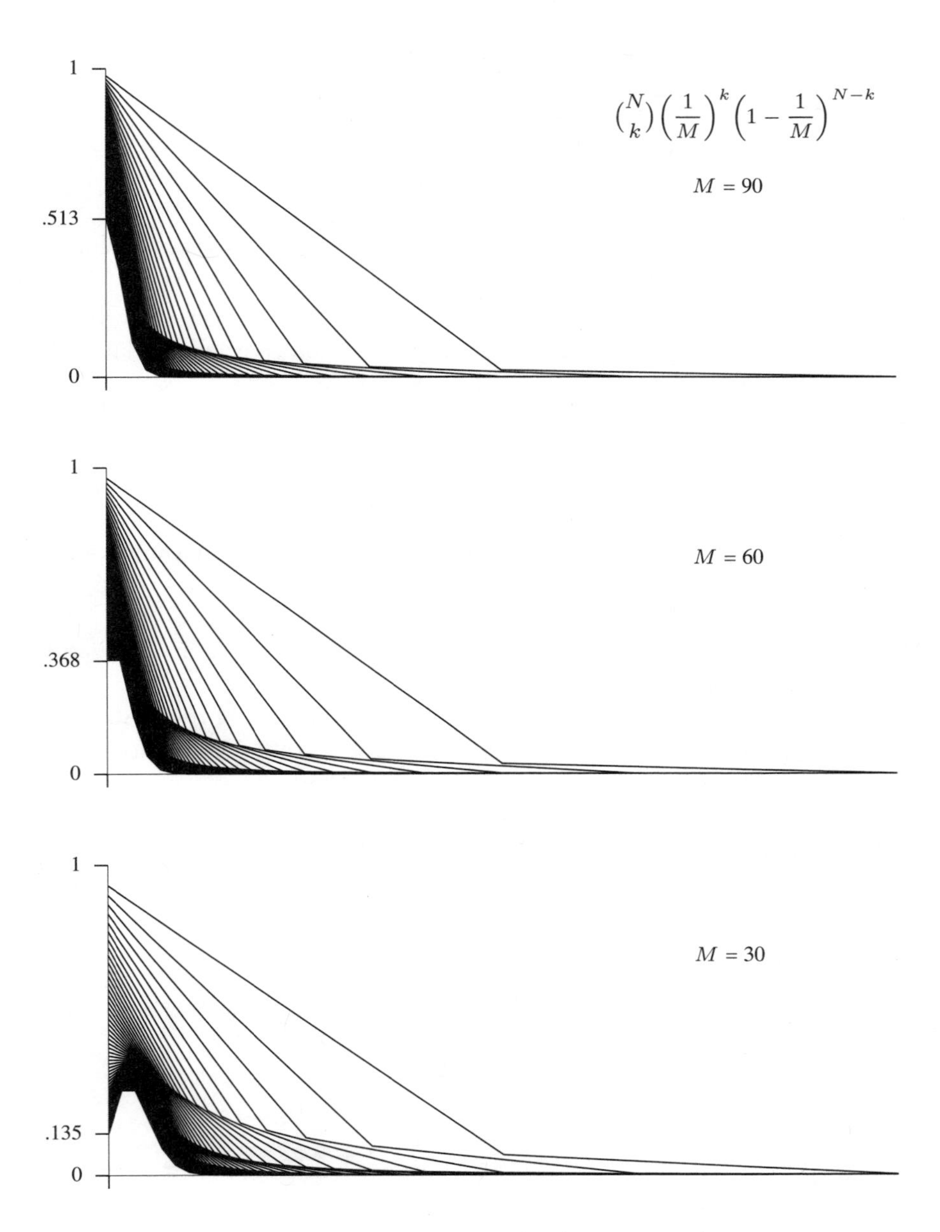

Figure 8.5 Occupancy distributions for large M and $2 \le N \le 60$ (k-axes scaled to N)

as the cost of putting it into the table, so the average cost of a successful search is the average cost of all the unsuccessful searches used to build the table, in this case

$$\frac{1}{N}\sum_{1\le k\le N}\frac{k}{M}=\frac{N+1}{2M}.$$

This relationship between unsuccessful and successful search cost holds for many searching algorithms, including binary search trees. ∎

The Chebyshev inequality say that with with a thousand keys, we could use a hundred lists and expect about ten items per list, with at least 90% confidence that a search will examine no more than twenty items. With a million keys, one might use a thousand lists, and the Chebyshev inequality says that there is at least 99.9% confidence that a search will examine no more than two thousand items. Though generally applicable, the Chebyshev bounds are actually quite crude in this case, and we can show through direct numerical computation or through use of the Poisson approximation that for a million keys and a table size of a thousand, the probability that more than 1300 probes are needed is on the order of 10^{-20}, and the probability that more than 2000 probes are needed is around 10^{-170}.

Furthermore, we can know many other properties of the hash structure that may be of interest. For example, Figure 8.6 is a plot of the function $e^{-\alpha}$, which tells us the percentage of empty lists as a function of the ratio of the number of keys to the number of lists. Such information can be instrumental in tuning an algorithm to best performance. For

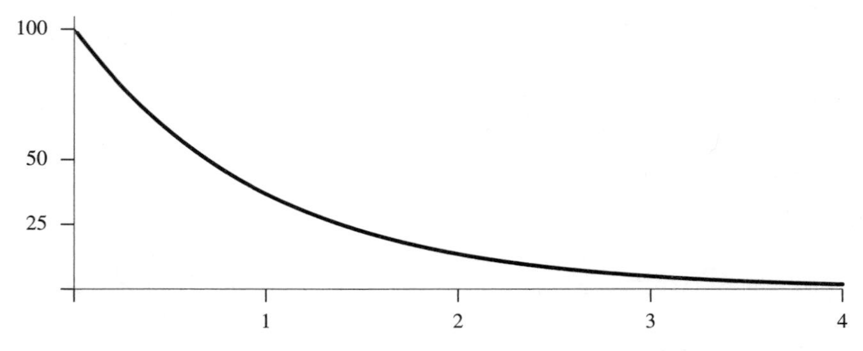

Figure 8.6 Percentage of empty urns as a function of load factor N/M

example, in applications with large numbers of keys, proper accounting of memory requirements involves taking note that space overhead may be associated with each list and that all keys are eventually stored in the same "table" (the computer memory).

A number of variants to the basic separate chaining scheme have been devised to economize on space in light of these two observations. The most notable of these is *coalesced hashing*, which has been analyzed in detail by Vitter and Chen [29] (see also Knuth [22]). This is an excellent example of the use of analysis to set values of performance parameters in a practical situation.

Exercise 8.32 For a thousand keys, what value of M will make hashing with separate chaining access fewer keys than a binary tree search? For a million keys?

Exercise 8.33 Find the standard deviation of the number of comparisons required for successful search in hashing with separate chaining.

Exercise 8.34 Determine the average and standard deviation of the number of comparisons used for a search when the lists in the table are kept in sorted order (so that a search can be cut short when a key larger than the search key is found).

Exercise 8.35 [Broder and Karlin] Analyze the following variant of Program 8.1: compute two hash functions and put the key on the shorter of the two lists.

8.6 Open Addressing Hashing. If we take $M = O(N)$ in hashing with separate chaining, then our search time is $O(1)$, but a significant amount of extra space, in the form of pointers, is used to maintain the secondary data structure. So-called open addressing methods do not use pointers and directly address a set of N keys within a table of size M with $M \geq N$.

The birthday paradox tells us that the table does not need to be very large for some keys to have the same hash values, and a *collision resolution* strategy is needed to decide how to deal with such conflicts.

Linear probing. Perhaps the simplest such strategy is *linear probing*: if, when inserting a key into the table, the addressed position (given by the hash value) is occupied, then simply examine the previous position. If that is also occupied, examine the one before that, continuing until an empty position is found. (If the beginning of the table is reached, simply cycle back to the end.) In the ball-and-urn model, we might imagine linear probing to be a sort of pachinko machine, where one ball fills up an urn and new balls bounce to the left until an empty urn is found.

An implementation of search and insertion for linear probing is given in Program 8.2. The program assumes that the has function does not return zero, so that zero can be used to mark empty positions in the hash table.

We will see below that linear probing performs badly for a nearly full table but reasonably well for a table with enough empty space. As the table fills up, the keys tend to "cluster" together, producing long chains that must be searched to find an empty space. Figure 8.7 shows an example of a table filling up with linear probing, with a cluster developing in the last two insertions. An easy way to avoid clustering is to look not at the previous but at the tth previous position each time a full table entry is found, where t is computed by a second hash function. This method is called *double hashing*.

Uniform hashing. Linear probing and double hashing are difficult to analyze because of interdependencies among the lists. A simple approximate model is to assume that each occupancy configuration of N keys in a table of size M is equally likely to occur. This is equivalent to the assumption that a hash function produces a random *permutation* and the positions in the hash table are examined in random order (different for different keys) until an empty position is found.

```
procedure insert(v:  integer);
  var x:  integer;
  begin
  x = hash(v);
  while table[x] <> 0 do x := (x-1) mod M;
  table[x] = v;
  end;
function search(v:  integer):  integer;
  var x:  integer;
  begin
  x = hash(v);
  while (table[x] <> 0) and (table[x] <> v) do
    x := (x-1) mod M;
  if t = z then t = NIL;
  search := t;
  end;
```

Program 8.2 Hashing with linear probing

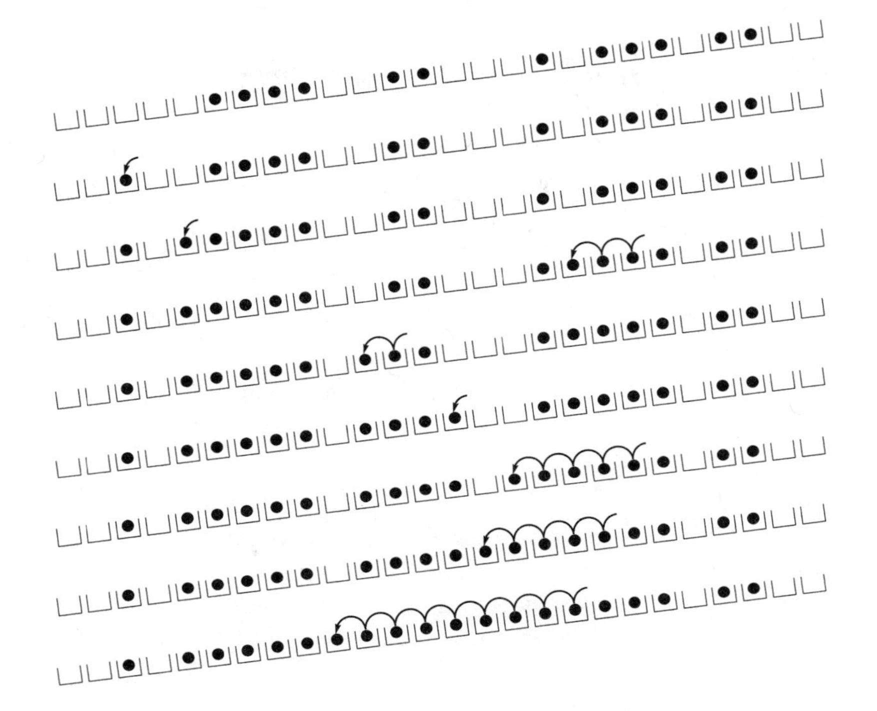

Figure 8.7 Hashing with linear probing

Theorem 8.7 (*Uniform hashing*) *Using a table of size M for N keys, the number of probes used for successful and unsuccessful search with uniform hashing is*

$$\frac{M+1}{M-N+1} \quad \textit{and} \quad \frac{M+1}{N}(H_{M+1}-H_{M-N+1}),$$

(respectively), on the average.

Proof. An unsuccessful search will require k probes if $k-1$ table locations starting at the hashed location are full and the kth empty. With k locations and $k-1$ keys accounted for, the number of configurations for which this holds is the number of ways to distribute the other $N-k+1$ keys among the other $M-k$ locations. The total unsuccessful search cost in all the occupancy configurations is therefore

$$\begin{aligned}
\sum_{1\le k\le M} k\binom{M-k}{N-k+1} &= \sum_{1\le k\le M} k\binom{M-k}{M-N-1}\\
&= \sum_{0\le k<M} (M-k)\binom{k}{M-N-1}\\
&= (M+1)\binom{M}{N} - \sum_{0\le k<M} (k+1)\binom{k}{M-N-1}\\
&= (M+1)\binom{M}{N} - (M-N)\sum_{0\le k<M} \binom{k+1}{M-N}\\
&= (M+1)\binom{M}{N} - (M-N)\binom{M+1}{N}\\
&= \frac{M+1}{M-N+1}\binom{M}{N}.
\end{aligned}$$

and the average cost for unsuccessful search is obtained by dividing this by the total number of configurations $\binom{M}{N}$.

The average cost for successful search is obtained by averaging the unsuccessful search cost, as in the proof of Theorem 8.6. ∎

Thus, for $\alpha = N/M$, the average cost for successful search is asymptotic to $1/(1-\alpha)$. Intuitively, for small α, we expect that the probability that the first cell examined is full to be α, the probability that the first two cells examined are full to be α^2, and so on, so the average cost should be asymptotic to

$$1 + \alpha + \alpha^2 + \alpha^3 + \ldots.$$

This analysis validates that intuition under the uniformity assumption. The cost for successful search can be calculated by averaging the average costs for unsuccessful searches, as in the proof of Theorem 8.6.

The uniform hashing algorithm is impractical because of the cost of generating a random permutation independently for each key, but the corresponding model does provide a performance goal for other collision resolution strategies. Double hashing is an attempt at approximating such a "random" collision resolution strategy, and it turns out that its performance approximates the results given above for uniform hashing, though this is a difficult result that was some years in the making (see Guibas and Szemeredi [18] and Lueker and Molodowitch [25]).

Analysis of linear probing. Linear probing is a fundamental searching method, and an analytic explanation of the clustering phenomenon is clearly of interest. The algorithm was first analyzed by Knuth, who states that this derivation had a strong influence on the structure of his books. His books certainly have had a strong influence on the structure of research in the mathematical analysis of algorithms. This derivation is a prototype example showing how a simple algorithm can lead to nontrivial and interesting mathematical problems.

Following Knuth, we define three quantities that we will use to develop an exact expression for the cumulative cost for unsuccessful search:

$$\begin{aligned} f_{NM} &= \{\#\text{ words where 0 is left empty}\} \\ g_{NMk} &= \{\#\text{ words where 0 and } k+1 \text{ are left empty, 1 through } k \text{ full}\} \\ p_{NMj} &= \{\#\text{ words where inserting the } (N+1)\text{st key takes } j+1 \text{ steps}\}. \end{aligned}$$

As usual, by *word* in this context, we mean "sequence of hashed values."

First, we get an explicit expression for f_{NM} by noting that position 0 is equally likely to be empty as any other table position. The M^N hash sequences each leave $M-N$ empty table positions, for a grand total of $(M-N)M^N$, and dividing by M gives

$$f_{NM} = (M-N)M^{N-1}.$$

Second, we can use this to get an explicit expression for g_{NMk}. The empty positions divide each hash sequence to be included in the count into two independent parts, one containing k elements hashing into positions 0 through k leaving 0 empty, and the other containing $N-k$ elements hashing into positions $k+1$ through $M-1$ leaving $k+1$ empty. Therefore,

$$\begin{aligned} g_{NMk} &= \binom{N}{k} f_{k(k+1)} f_{(N-k)(M-k-1)} \\ &= \binom{N}{k}(k+1)^{k-1}(M-N-1)(M-k-1)^{N-k-1}. \end{aligned}$$

Third, a word will involve $j+1$ steps for the insertion of the $(N+1)$st key whenever the hashed position is in the kth position of a block of k consecutive occupied cells (with $k \ge j$) delimited at both ends by unoccupied cells. Again by circular symmetry, the number of such words is g_{NMk}, so

$$p_{NMj} = \sum_{j \le k \le N} g_{NMk}.$$

Now, we can use the cumulated counts p_{NMj} to calculate the average search costs, just as above. The cumulated cost for unsuccessful search is

$$\begin{aligned}\sum_{j\geq 0}(j+1)p_{NMj} &= \sum_{j\geq 0}(j+1)\sum_{j\leq k\leq N} g_{NMk} = \sum_{k\geq 0} g_{NMk}\sum_{0\leq j\leq k}(j+1)\\ &= \frac{1}{2}\sum_{k\geq 0}(k+1)(k+2)g_{NMk}\\ &= \frac{1}{2}\sum_{k\geq 0}((k+1)+(k+1)^2)g_{NMk}.\end{aligned}$$

Thus the average cost for unsuccessful search in linear probing is

$$\frac{1}{2}(S^{[1]}_{NM1}+S^{[2]}_{NM1})$$

where

$$S^{[i]}_{NMt} \equiv \frac{M-t-N}{M^N}\sum_k \binom{N}{k}(k+t)^{k-1+i}(M-k-t)^{N-k-i}.$$

This rather daunting function is actually rather easily evaluated with Abel's identity (Exercise 3.66 in §3.11). This immediately gives the result

$$tS^{[0]}_{NMt} = 1-\frac{N}{M}.$$

For larger i it is easy to prove (by taking out one factor of $(k+t)$) that

$$S^{[i]}_{NMt} = \frac{N}{M}S^{[i]}_{(N-1)M(t+1)} + tS^{[i-1]}_{NMt}.$$

Therefore,

$$S^{[1]}_{NMt} = \frac{N}{M}S^{[1]}_{(N-1)M(t+1)} + 1 - \frac{N}{M},$$

which has the solution

$$S^{[1]}_{NMt} = 1.$$

This is to be expected, since, for example, $S^{[1]}_{NM1} = \sum_k p_{NMk}$, a sum of probabilities. Finally, for $i=2$, we have

$$S^{[2]}_{NMt} = \frac{N}{M}S^{[2]}_{(N-1)M(t+1)} + t,$$

which has the solution

$$S^{[2]}_{NM1} = \sum_{0\le i\le N} i\frac{N!}{M^i(N-i)!}.$$

Theorem 8.8 (*Hashing with linear probing*) *Using a table of size M for N keys, linear probing requires*

$$\frac{1}{2}+\frac{1}{2}\sum_{0\le i<N}\frac{(N-1)!}{M^i(N-i-1)!}=\frac{1}{2}\Bigl(1+\frac{1}{1-\alpha}\Bigr)+O\Bigl(\frac{1}{N}\Bigr)$$

probes for successful search and

$$\frac{1}{2}+\frac{1}{2}\sum_{0\le i\le N} i\frac{N!}{M^i(N-i)!}=\frac{1}{2}\Bigl(1+\frac{1}{(1-\alpha)^2}\Bigr)+O\Bigl(\frac{1}{N}\Bigr)$$

for unsuccessful search, on the average. The asymptotic forms hold for $\alpha = N/M$ with $\alpha < 1$.

Proof. See the discussion above. The expression for successful search is obtained by averaging the result for unsuccessful search, as usual.

If α is strictly less than 1, the sum is similar to the Ramanujan Q-function of Theorem 4.8, and it is not difficult to estimate using the Laplace method. We have

$$\sum_{0\le i\le N}\frac{N!}{M^i(N-i)!}=\sum_{0\le i\le N}\Bigl(\frac{N}{M}\Bigr)^i\frac{N!}{N^i(N-i)!}.$$

Splitting the sum into two parts, we can use the fact that terms in this sum begin to get negligibly small after $i > \sqrt{N}$ to prove that this sum is

$$\sum_{i\ge 0}\Bigl(\frac{N}{M}\Bigr)^i\Bigl(1+O\Bigl(\frac{i^2}{N}\Bigr)\Bigr)=\frac{1}{1-\alpha}+O\Bigl(\frac{1}{N}\Bigr).$$

Adding 1 and dividing by 2 gives the stated result for successful search. A similar calculation gives the stated estimate for unsuccessful search. ∎

Corollary *The average number of table entries examined by linear probing during a successful search in a full table is* $\sim \sqrt{\pi N/2}$.

Proof. Taking $M = N$ in the expression above gives precisely the Ramanujan Q-function, whose approximate value is proved in Theorem 4.8. ▪

Despite the relatively simple form of the solution, a derivation for the average cost of linear probing using generating functions and the symbolic method has not yet been worked out. There are many interesting relationships among the quantities that arise in the analysis. For example, if we multiply the expression for successful search in Theorem 8.8 by z^{N-1}, divide by $(N-1)!$, and sum for all $N > 0$, we get the rather compact explicit result

$$\frac{1}{2}\Big(e^z + \frac{e^M}{1 - z/M}\Big).$$

This is not directly meaningful for linear probing because the quantities are defined only for $N \le M$ but it would seem a fine candidate for a combinatorial interpretation.

The asymptotic performance of the hashing methods we have discussed is summarized in Table 8.8. This table includes the asymptotic cost as a function of the load factor $\alpha \equiv N/M$ as the table size M and the number of keys N grow; an expansion of the cost function that estimates the cost for small α; and approximate values of the functions for typical values of α. The table shows that all the methods perform roughly the same for small α; that linear probing begins to degrade to an unacceptable level when the table gets 80–90% full; and that the performance of double hashing is quite close to "optimal" (same as separate chaining) unless the table is very full. These and related results can be quite useful in the application of hashing in a practical situation.

Exercise 8.36 How many keys can be inserted into a linear probing table of size M before the average search cost gets to be greater than $\ln N$?

Exercise 8.37 Compute the exact cost of an unsuccessful search using linear probing for a full table.

Exercise 8.38 Give an explicit representation for the EGF for the cost of unsuccessful search.

Exercise 8.39 Use the symbolic method to derive the EGF of the number of probes required by linear probing in a successful search, for fixed M.*

---

* The temptation to include one footnote at this point can't be resisted: we don't know the answer to this exercise!

Exact costs for N keys in a table of size M

	successful search	*unsuccessful search*
separate chaining	$1+\dfrac{N}{2M}$	$1+\dfrac{N}{M}$
uniform hashing	$\dfrac{M+1}{M-N+1}$	$\dfrac{M+1}{N}(H_{M-1}-H_{M-N+1})$
linear probing	$\dfrac{1}{2}\Big(1+\sum_k \dfrac{k!}{M^k}\binom{N-1}{k}\Big)$	$\dfrac{1}{2}\Big(1+\sum_k k\dfrac{k!}{M^k}\binom{N}{k}\Big)$

Asymptotic costs as $N, M \to \infty$ with $\alpha \equiv N/M$

	average	.5	.9	.95	*small* α
unsuccessful search					
separate chaining	$1+\alpha$	2	2	2	$1+\alpha$
uniform hashing	$\dfrac{1}{1-\alpha}$	2	10	20	$1+\alpha+\alpha^2+\ldots$
double hashing	$\dfrac{1}{1-\alpha}$	2	10	20	$1+\alpha+\alpha^2+\ldots$
linear probing	$\dfrac{1}{2}\Big(1+\dfrac{1}{(1-\alpha)^2}\Big)$	3	51	201	$1+\alpha+\dfrac{3\alpha^2}{2}+\ldots$
successful search					
separate chaining	$1+\dfrac{\alpha}{2}$	1	1	1	$1+\dfrac{\alpha}{2}$
uniform hashing	$\dfrac{1}{\alpha}\ln(1+\alpha)$	1	3	4	$1+\dfrac{\alpha}{2}+\dfrac{\alpha^2}{3}+\ldots$
double hashing	$\dfrac{1}{\alpha}\ln(1+\alpha)$	1	3	4	$1+\dfrac{\alpha}{2}+\dfrac{\alpha^2}{3}+\ldots$
linear probing	$\dfrac{1}{2}\Big(1+\dfrac{1}{1-\alpha}\Big)$	2	6	11	$1+\dfrac{\alpha}{2}+\dfrac{\alpha^2}{2}+\ldots$

Table 8.8 Analytic results for hashing methods

8.7 Maps. The study of hashing into a full table leads naturally to looking at properties of mappings from the set of integers between 1 and N onto itself. The study of these leads to a remarkable combinatorial structure that is simply defined, but it encompasses much of what we have studied in this book.

Definition *An* N-map *is a function* f *mapping integers from the interval* $[1\ldots N]$ *into the interval* $[1\ldots N]$.

As with words, permutations and trees, we specify a map by writing down its functional table:

index	1	2	3	4	5	6	7	8	9
map	9	6	4	2	4	3	7	8	6

As usual, we drop the index and specify a map simply as a sequence of N integers in the interval 1 to N (the *image* of the map). Clearly, there are N^N different N-maps. We have used similar representations for permutations (Chapter 6) and trees (Chapter 5)—maps encompass both of these as special cases. For example, a permutation is a map where the integers in the image are distinct.

Naturally, we define a *random map* to be a sequence of N random integers in the range 1 to N. We are interested in studying properties of random maps. For example, the probability that a random map is a permutation is $N!/N^N \sim \sqrt{2\pi N}/e^N$.

Image cardinality. Some properties of maps may be deduced from properties of words derived in the previous section. For example, by Theorem 8.5, we know that the average number of integers that appear k times in the map is $\sim Ne^{-1}/k!$, the Poisson distribution with $\alpha = 1$. A related question of interest is the distribution of the number of different integers that appear, the cardinality of the image. This is N minus the number of integers that do not appear, or the number of "empty urns" in the occupancy model, so the average is $(1 - 1/e)N$ by the corollary to Theorem 8.5. A simple counting argument says that the number of maps with k different integers in the image is given by $\binom{N}{k}$ (choose the integers) times $k!\left\{ {N \atop k} \right\}$ (count all the surjections with image of cardinality k). Thus,

$$C_{Nk} = k!\binom{N}{k}\left\{ {N \atop k} \right\}.$$

This distribution is plotted in Figure 8.8.

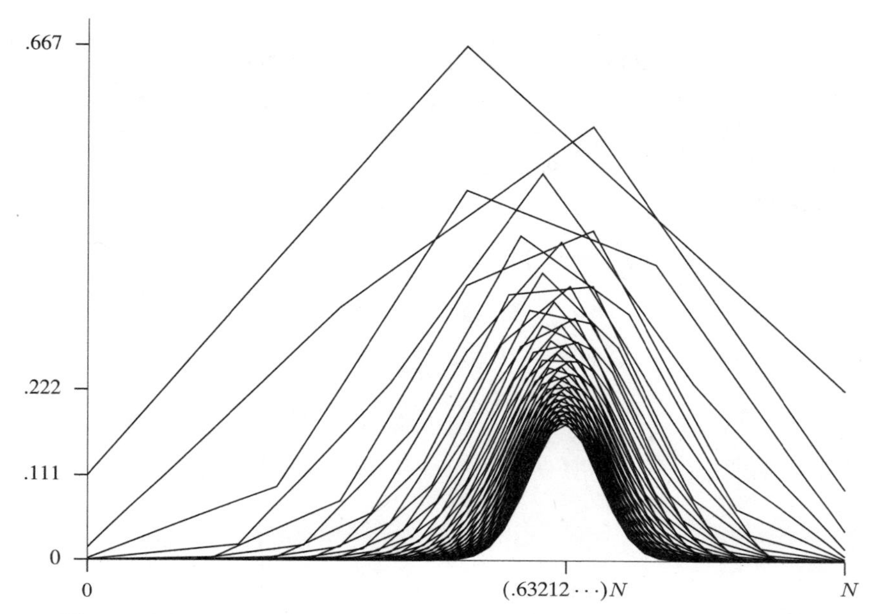

Figure 8.8 Image cardinality of random maps for $3 \leq N \leq 50$ (k-axes scaled to N)

Exercise 8.40 Find the exponential BGF for the image cardinality distribution.

Exercise 8.41 Use a combinatorial argument to find the exponential BGF for the image cardinality distribution.

Exercise 8.42 Give a recurrence relationship for the number of maps of size N with k different integers in the image, and use that to obtain a table of values for $N < 20$.

Exercise 8.43 Give an explicit expression for the number of M-words of length N having k different letters.

Random number generators. A random N-map is any function f with the integers 1 to N as both domain and range, where all N^N such functions are taken with equal likelihood. For example, the following map is defined by the function $f(i) \equiv 1 + i^2 \bmod 9$:

index	1	2	3	4	5	6	7	8	9
map	2	5	1	8	8	1	5	2	1

One application of such functions is to model *random number generators*: subroutines that return sequences of numbers with properties as similar as possible to those of random sequences. The idea is to choose a function that is an N-map, then produce a (pseudo) random sequence by iterating $f(x)$ starting with an initial value called the *seed*. Given a seed u_0, we get the sequence

$$\begin{aligned} &u_0 \\ &u_1 = f(u_0) \\ &u_2 = f(u_1) = f(f(u_0)) \\ &u_3 = f(u_2) = f(f(f(u_0))) \\ &\vdots \end{aligned}$$

For example, *linear congruential* random number generators are based on

$$f(x) = (ax + b) \bmod N,$$

and *quadratic* random number generators are based on

$$f(x) = (ax^2 + bx + c) \bmod N.$$

Quadratic random number generators are closely related to the *middle square* method, an old idea that dates back to von Neumann's time: Starting with a seed u_0, repeatedly square the previously generated value and extract the middle digits. For example, using four-digit decimal numbers, the sequence generated from the seed $u_0 = 1234$ is $u_1 = 5227$ (since $1234^2 = 01522756$), $u_2 = 3215$ (since $5227^2 = 27321529$), $u_3 = 3362$ (since $3215^2 = 10336225$), and so forth.

It is easy to design a linear congruential generator so that it produces a permutation (that is, it goes through N different values before it repeats). A complete algebraic theory is available, for which we refer the reader to Knuth [21].

Quadratic random number generators are harder to analyze mathematically. However, Bach [2] has shown that, on average, quadratic functions have characteristics under iteration that are essentially equivalent to those of random maps. Bach uses deep results from algebraic geometry; as we are going to see, properties of random maps are somewhat easier to analyze given all the techniques developed so far in this book. There are

N^3 quadratic trinomials modulo N, and we are just asserting that these are representative of the N^N random maps, in the sense that the average values of certain quantities of interest are asymptotically the same. The situation is somewhat analogous to the situation for double hashing described above: in both cases, the practical method (quadratic generators, double hashing) is studied through asymptotic equivalence to the random model (random maps, uniform hashing).

In other words, quadratic generators provide one motivation for the study of what might be called *random random number generators*, where a randomly chosen function is iterated to produce a source of random numbers. In this case, the result of the analysis is negative, since it shows that linear congruential generators might be preferred to quadratic generators (because they have longer cycles), but an interesting outcome of these ideas is the design and analysis of the *Pollard rho method* for integer factoring, which we discuss at the end of this section.

Exercise 8.44 Prove that every random map must have at least one cycle.

Exercise 8.45 Explore properties of the random maps defined by $f(i) \equiv 1 + (i^2 + 1) \bmod N$ for $N = 100$, 1000, 10000, and primes near these values.

Path length and connected components. Since the operation of applying a map to itself is well defined, we are naturally led to consider what happens if we do so successively. The sequence

$$f(k),\ f(f(k)),\ f(f(f(k))),\ f(f(f(f(k)))),\ \ldots$$

is well defined for every k in a map: what are its properties? It is easy to see that, since only N distinct values are possible, the sequence must

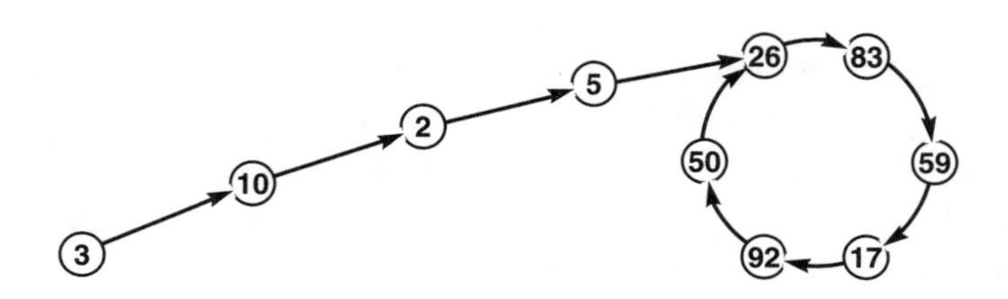

Figure 8.9 Tail and cycle iterating $f(x) = x^2 + 1 \bmod 99$ from $x_0 = 3$

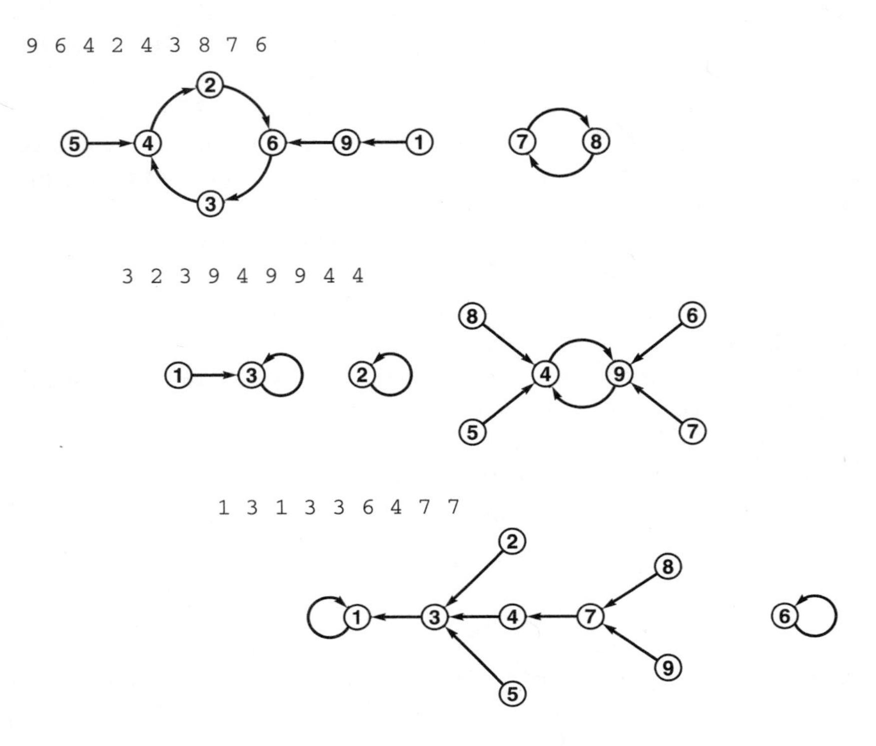

Figure 8.10 Tree-cycle representation of three random maps

ultimately repeat a value, at which point it becomes cyclic. For example, as shown in Figure 8.9, if we start at $x_0 = 3$ in the map defined by $f(x) = x^2 + 1 \bmod 99$, we have the ultimately cyclic sequence 3, 10, 2, 5, 26, 83, 59, 17, 92, 50, 26, ... The sequence always has a cycle preceded by a "tail" of values leading to the cycle. In this case, the cycle is of length 6 and the tail of length 4. We are interested in knowing the statistical properties of both cycle and tail lengths for random maps.

Cycle and tail length depend on the starting point. Figure 8.10 is a graphical representation showing i connected to $f(i)$ for each i for three sample maps. For example, in the top map, if we start at `7` we immediately get stuck in the cycle `7 8 7 ...`, but if we start at `1` we encounter a two-element tail followed by a four-element cycle. This representation more clearly exposes the structure: every map decomposes into a set of connected components, also called *connected maps*. Each component consists of the set of all points that wind up on the same cycle, with each point on the cycle attached to a tree of all points that enter the cycle at that point. From the point of view of each individual point, we have a tail-cycle as in Figure 8.9, but the structure as a whole is certainly more informative about the map.

As noted above, maps generalize permutations, where we have the restriction that each element in the range must appear once, which leads to a set of cycles. All tail lengths are 0 for maps that correspond to permutations. If all the cycle lengths in the map are 1, we have maps that correspond to forests. We are naturally led to consider the idea of path length:

Definition *The* path length *or* rho length *for an index k in a map f is the number of distinct integers obtained by iterating*

$$f(k),\ f(f(k)),\ f(f(f(k))),\ f(f(f(f(k)))),\ \ldots .$$

The cycle length *for an index k in a map f is the length of the cycle reached in the iteration, and the* tail length *for an index k in a map f is the rho length minus the cycle length or, equivalently, the number of steps taken to connect to the cycle.*

The path length of an index is called the "rho length" because the shape of the tail plus the cycle is reminiscent of the Greek letter ρ (see Figure 8.9). Beyond these properties of the map as seen from a single point, we are also interested in global measures that involve all the points in the map.

Definition *The* rho length *of a map f is the sum, over all k, of the rho length for k in f. The* tree path length *of a map f is the sum, over all k, of the tail length for k in f.*

Thus, from Figure 8.9, it is easy to verify that `9 6 4 2 4 3 8 7 6` has rho length 36 and tree path length 4; `3 2 3 9 4 9 9 4 4` has rho length 20 and tree path length 5; and `1 3 1 3 3 6 4 7 7` has rho length 27 and tree path length 18. In these definitions, tree path length does not include costs for any nodes on cycles while rho length includes the whole length of the cycle for each node in the structure. Both definitions give the standard notion of path length for maps that are trees.

map	cycles	trees	rho length	longest cycle	longest path
123	3	0	3	1	1
113	2	1	4	1	2
121	2	1	4	1	2
122	2	1	4	1	2
133	2	1	4	1	2
223	2	1	4	1	2
323	2	1	4	1	2
112	1	1	6	1	3
131	1	1	6	1	3
221	1	1	6	1	3
322	1	1	6	1	3
233	1	1	6	1	3
313	1	1	6	1	3
111	1	2	5	1	2
222	1	2	5	1	2
333	1	2	5	1	2
213	2	0	5	2	2
321	2	0	5	2	2
132	2	0	5	2	2
211	1	1	7	2	3
212	1	1	7	2	3
232	1	1	7	2	3
311	1	1	7	2	3
331	1	1	7	2	3
332	1	1	7	2	3
231	1	0	9	3	3
312	1	0	9	3	3

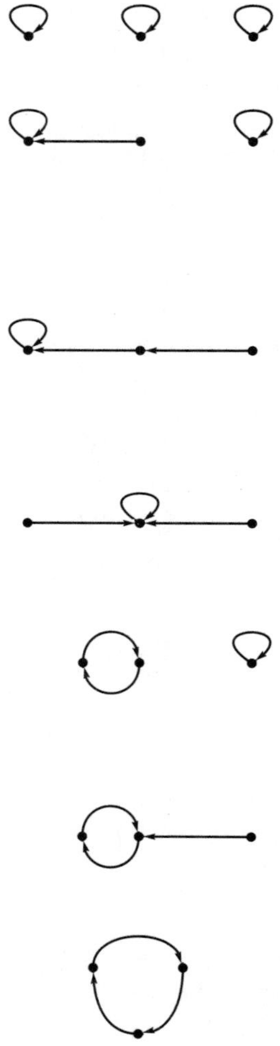

Table 8.9 Basic properties of all maps of three elements

We are interested in knowing basic properties of the kinds of structures shown in Figure 8.10:

- How many cycles are there?
- How many points are on cycles, and how many on trees?
- What is the average cycle size?
- What is the average rho length?
- What is the average length of the longest cycle?
- What is the average length of the longest path to a cycle?
- What is the average length of the longest rho-path?

Table 8.9 gives an exhaustive list of the basic measures for all 3-maps, and Table 8.10 gives six random 9-maps. On the right in Table 8.9 are drawn the seven different tree-cycle structures that arise in 3-maps, reminding us that our tree-cycle representations of maps are labelled and ordered combinatorial objects.

As with several other problems that we have seen in this chapter, some properties of random maps can be analyzed with a straightforward probabilistic argument. For example, the average rho length of a random map is easily derived.

Theorem 8.9 (*Rho length*) *The rho length of a random point in a random map is* $\sim \sqrt{\pi N/2}$, *on the average. The rho length of a random map is* $\sim N\sqrt{\pi N/2}$, *on the average.*

Proof. Suppose that we start at x_0. The probability that $f(x_0) \neq x_0$ is clearly $(N-1)/N$. This is the same as the probability that the rho length is greater than or equal to 1. Similarly, the probability that the rho length is greater than or equal to 2 is the probability that the first two elements are different ($f(x_0) \neq x_0$) and the third is different from both of the first two

map	*occupancy*	*dist.*	*cycles*	*trees*	*rho length*	*longest cycle*	*longest path*
323949944	012300003	5112	3	3	19	2	3
131336477	203101200	4221	2	1	27	1	5
517595744	100230201	4221	2	4	29	3	5
215681472	220111110	2520	1	2	42	2	8
213693481	212101011	2520	3	2	20	2	4
964243786	011212111	1620	2	1	34	4	6

Table 8.10 Basic properties of some random 9-maps

$(f(f(x_0)) \neq x_0$ and $f(f(x_0)) \neq f(x_0))$, or $(N-1)/N$ times $(N-2)/N$. Continuing, we have

$$\Pr\{\text{rho length} \geq k\} = \frac{N-1}{N}\frac{N-2}{N}\cdots\frac{N-k}{N}.$$

Thus, the average rho length of a random point in a random map is the sum of these cumulative probabilities, which is precisely the Ramanujan Q-function, so the approximation of Theorem 4.8 provides our answer. The same argument holds for each of the N points in the map, so the expected rho length of the map is obtained by multiplying this by N. ■

This problem is equivalent to the birthday problem of §8.3, though the models of randomness are not formally identical.

Exercise 8.46 Show that the analysis of the rho length of a random point in a random map is equivalent to that for the birthday problem.

Generating functions. Many other properties of maps depend more upon global structural interactions. They are best analyzed with generating functions. Maps are sets of cycles of trees, so their generating functions are easily derived with the symbolic method. We proceed exactly as for counting "sets of cycles" when we introduced the symbolic method in Chapter 3, but with trees as the basic object.

We begin, from Chapter 5, with the EGF for Cayley trees:

$$C(z) = ze^{C(z)}.$$

As in Chapter 3, the EGF that enumerates cycles of trees (connected maps) is

$$\sum_{k\geq 1}\frac{C(z)^k}{k} = \ln\frac{1}{1-C(z)}$$

class	*EGF*	*coefficient*
trees	$C(z) = ze^{C(z)}$	$(N-1)![u^{N-1}]e^{Nu} = N^{N-1}$
cycles of trees	$\ln\dfrac{1}{1-C(z)}$	$(N-1)![u^{N-1}]\dfrac{1}{1-u}e^{Nu} \sim N^N/\sqrt{\pi N}$
maps	$\exp\Bigl(\ln\dfrac{1}{1-C(z)}\Bigr)$	$(N-1)![u^{N-1}]\dfrac{1}{(1-u)^2}e^{Nu} = N^N$

Table 8.11 Exponential generating functions for maps

and the EGF that enumerates sets of connected maps is

$$\exp\left(\ln\frac{1}{1-C(z)}\right)=\frac{1}{1-C(z)}.$$

The functional equations involve the implicitly defined Cayley function $C(z)$, and the Lagrange inversion theorem applies directly. For example, applying the theorem to the EGF just derived leads to the following computation:

$$\begin{aligned}[z^N]\frac{1}{1-C(z)}&=\frac{1}{N}[u^{N-1}]\frac{1}{(1-u)^2}e^{Nu}\\&=\sum_{0\le k\le N}(N-k)\frac{N^{k-1}}{k!}=\sum_{0\le k\le N}\frac{N^k}{k!}-\sum_{1\le k\le N}\frac{N^{k-1}}{(k-1)!}\\&=\frac{N^N}{N!}.\end{aligned}$$

This is a check on the fact that there are N^N maps of size N.

It is convenient to summarize these calculations involving the application of the Lagrange inversion theorem to functions of the Cayley function as follows:

Lemma *For the Cayley function $C(z)$, we have*

$$[z^N]g(C(z))=\sum_{0\le k<N}(N-k)g_{N-k}\frac{N^{k-1}}{k!}\quad \textit{when}\quad g(z)\equiv\sum_{k\ge 0}g_kz^k.$$

Proof. Immediate from Theorem 3.9. ■

Thus, the number of connected maps of N nodes is given by

$$N![z^N]\ln\frac{1}{1-C(z)}=N!\sum_{0\le k<N}(N-k)\frac{1}{N-k}\frac{N^{k-1}}{k!}=N^{N-1}Q(N).$$

The Ramanujan Q-function again makes an appearance.

The above results imply that the probability that a random map is a tree is exactly $1/N$ and the probability that a random map is a single connected component is asymptotically $\sqrt{\pi/(2N)}$. We can use BGFs in a similar manner to analyze other properties of random maps.

Theorem 8.10 (*Components and cycles*) *A random N-map has* $\sim \frac{1}{2}\ln N$ *components and* $\sim \sqrt{\pi N}$ *nodes on cycles, on the average.*

Proof. By the discussion above, the BGF for the distribution of the number of components is given by

$$\exp\Bigl(u \ln \frac{1}{1-C(z)}\Bigr) = \frac{1}{(1-C(z))^u}.$$

The average number of components is then given by

$$\begin{aligned}\frac{1}{N^N}[z^N]\frac{\partial}{\partial u}\frac{1}{(1-C(z))^u}\Big|_{u=1} &= \frac{1}{N^N}[z^N]\frac{1}{1-C(z)}\ln\frac{1}{1-C(z)}\\ &= \sum_{0\le k\le N}(N-k)H_{N-k}\frac{N^{k-1}}{k!}\end{aligned}$$

by the lemma given above. The stated asymptotic result is a straightforward calculation in the manner of the proof of Theorem 4.8.

The BGF for the number of nodes on cycles is

$$\exp\Bigl(\ln\frac{1}{1-uC(z)}\Bigr) = \frac{1}{1-uC(z)},$$

from which coefficients can be extracted exactly as above. ■

Other properties. Various other properties can be handled similarly. Also, proceeding just as for permutations in Chapter 6 and for words earlier in this chapter, we find that the number of maps having exactly k components has EGF $C(z)^k/k!$; the number of maps having at most k components has EGF $1 + C(z) + C(z)^2/2! + \ldots + C(z)^k/k!$; and so forth. These can be used to give explicit expressions for extremal parameters, as we have done several times before. Asymptotic methods for estimating these quantities are discussed in detail by Flajolet and Odlyzko [11] and by Kolchin [23] (see also [12]). The results given in [11] are summarized in Table 8.12. The various constants in the extremal parameters can be expressed explicitly, though with rather complicated definite integrals. It is interesting to note that cycle length plus tail length equals rho length for the averages, but not for the extremal parameters. This means that the tallest tree is not attached to the longest cycle for a significant number of maps.

Average as seen from a random point	
rho length	$\sqrt{\pi N/2}$
tail length	$\sqrt{\pi N/8}$
cycle length	$\sqrt{\pi N/8}$
tree size	$N/3$
component size	$2N/3$
Average number of	
k-nodes	$\frac{Ne^{-1}}{k!}$
k-cycles	$\frac{1}{k}$
k-components	$\frac{e^{-k}}{k!}\{\#\ k\text{-node connected maps}\}$
k-trees	$(\sqrt{\pi N/2})\frac{e^{-k}}{k!}\{\#\ k\text{-node trees}\}$
Extremal parameters (expected number of nodes in)	
longest tail	$\sqrt{2\pi N}\ln 2 \approx 1.74\sqrt{N}$
longest cycle	$\approx 0.78\sqrt{N}$
longest rho-path	$\approx 2.41\sqrt{N}$
largest tree	$\approx 0.48N$
largest component	$\approx 0.76N$

Table 8.12 Asymptotic properties of random maps

Exercise 8.47 Which N-maps have maximal and minimal rho length? Tree path length?

Exercise 8.48 Write a program to find the rho length and tree path length of a random map. Generate 1000 random maps for N as large as you can and compute the average number of cycles, rho length, and tree path length.

Exercise 8.49 Write a program to find the rho length and tree path length of a random map *without* using any extra storage.

Exercise 8.50 A map with no repeated integers is a permutation. Give an efficient algorithm for determining whether a map is a tree.

Exercise 8.51 Compute the average size of the largest component in a random N-map, for all $N < 10$.

Exercise 8.52 Prove Theorem 8.9 using BGFs.

Exercise 8.53 What is the average number of different integers in the image when a random map is iterated *twice*?

Exercise 8.54 Consider the N^N tree-cycle structures that correspond to all the N-maps. How many of these are different when considered as unlabelled, unordered objects, for $N \leq 7$? (These are called *random mapping patterns.*)

Exercise 8.55 Describe the graph structure of *partial* maps, where the image of a point may be undefined. Set up the corresponding EGF equations and check that the number of partial maps of size N is $(N+1)^N$.

Exercise 8.56 Analyze "path length" in sequences of $2N$ random integers in the range 1 to N.

Exercise 8.57 Generate 100 random maps of size 10, 100, and 1000 and empirically verify the statistics given in Table 8.12.

8.8 Integer Factorization and Maps. In this section we will examine *Pollard's rho method*, an efficient algorithm for factoring integers (in the "intermediate" range of 10 to 30 decimal digits) that relies on structural and probabilistic properties of maps. The method is based on exploiting the following two facts:

- A point on some cycle can be found quickly (in time proportional to the rho length of a starting point), using $O(1)$ memory.
- A random point on a random map has rho length $O(\sqrt{N})$ on the average.

First, we will consider the cycle detection problem, then we look at the Pollard rho method itself.

Cycle detection. The naive method for finding a point on a cycle of a map is to iterate the map, storing all the function values in a search structure and looking up each new value to see if some value already in the structure has been reached again. This algorithm is impractical for large maps because one cannot afford the space to save all the function values.

Program 8.3 gives a method due to Floyd (cf. Knuth [21]) for finding cycle points in an arbitrary map using only constant space without sacrificing time. In the program, we can view the point `a` as moving along the rho-graph (see Figure 8.9) at speed 1 and the point `b` as moving along the rho-graph at speed 2. The algorithm depends on the fact that the two points must collide at some point once they are on the cycle. For example, suppose that the method is used for the map of Figure 8.9 with the starting point 10. Then the cycle is detected in 7 steps, as shown by the following trace of the values taken on by `a` and `b`:

```
a    10  2   5  26  83  59  17
b    10  5  83  17  50  83  17
```

Theorem 8.11 (*Cycle detection*) *Given a map and a starting point x, the Floyd method finds a cycle point on the map using constant space and time proportional to the rho length of x.*

Proof. Let λ be the tail length of x, μ the cycle length, and $\rho = \lambda + \mu$ the rho length. After λ steps of the loop, point `a` reaches the cycle, while point `b` is already on the cycle. We now have a race on the cycle, with a speed differential of 1. After at most μ steps, `b` will catch up with `a`.

```
a := x; b := x; t := 0;
repeat
  a := f(a);
  b := f(f(b));
  t := t+1;
until (a = b);
```

Program 8.3 Floyd method for cycle detection

Let t be the value of the variable `t` when the algorithm terminates. We also must have

$$t \le \rho \le 2t.$$

The inequality on the left holds because t is the position of point `a`, and the algorithm terminates before `a` starts on a second trip around the cycle. The inequality on the right holds because $2t$ is the position of point `b`, and the algorithm terminates after `b` has been around the cycle at least once. Thus, the algorithm gives not only a point on the cycle (the value of the variables `a` and `b` on termination), but also an estimate of the rho length of the starting point to within a factor of 2. ■

By saving some more function values, it is possible to virtually eliminate the extra factor of 2 in the time taken by the algorithm (and the estimate of the rho length), while still using a reasonable amount of space. This issue is studied in detail by Sedgewick, Szymanksi, and Yao [28].

Exercise 8.58 Use Floyd's method to test the random number generators on your machine for short cycles.

Exercise 8.59 Use Floyd's algorithm to test the middle square random number generator.

Exercise 8.60 Use Floyd's method to estimate the rho length associated with various starting values, c, and N for the function

$$f(x) = (x^2 + c) \bmod N.$$

Pollard's rho method. The rho method is a randomized algorithm that factors integers with high probability. An implementation is given in Program 8.4, with the caveat that it assumes that arithmetic operations on very large integers are available. The method is based on choosing a value `c` at random, then iterating the quadratic function

$$f(x) = (x^2 + c) \bmod N$$

from a randomly chosen starting point until a cyclic point is found.

For simplicity, assume that $N = pq$ where p and q are primes to be found by the algorithm. By the Chinese remainder theorem, any integer y modulo N is determined by its values mod p and mod q. In particular, the function f is determined by the pair

$$f_p(x) = x^2 + c \bmod p \quad \text{and} \quad f_q(x) = x^2 + c \bmod q.$$

If the cycle detection algorithm were applied to f_p starting at an initial value x, then a cycle would be detected after t_p steps where t_p is at most twice the rho length of x (modulo p). Similarly, a cycle (modulo q) for t_q would be detected after t_q steps. Thus, if $t_p \neq t_q$, which should occur with a very high probability for large integers) we find after $\min(t_p, t_q)$ steps that the values a and b of the variables a and b in the algorithm satisfy

$$a \equiv b \pmod{p} \quad \text{and} \quad a \not\equiv b \pmod{p}, \qquad \text{if} \quad t_p < t_q$$

$$a \not\equiv b \pmod{p} \quad \text{and} \quad a \equiv b \pmod{p}, \qquad \text{if} \quad t_p > t_q.$$

In either case, the greatest common divisor of $a - b$ and N is a nontrivial divisor of N.

Connection with random maps. Assume that quadratic functions of the form $x^2 + c \bmod N$ have path length properties that are asymptotically equivalent to path lengths in random maps. This heuristic assumption asserts that properties of the N quadratic maps (there are N possible choices for c) are similar to properties of the N^N random maps. In other words, quadratic functions are assumed to be a "representative sample" of random maps. This assumption is quite plausible and has been extensively validated by simulations, but it has only been partially proven [2]. Nevertheless, it leads to a useful approximate analysis for Pollard's method.

```
function factor(N: integer):  integer;
  var a, b, c, d:  integer;
  begin
    a := randominteger(0, N-1);
    b := a;
    c := randominteger(0, N-1);
    repeat
      a := (a*a + c) mod N;
      b := (b*b + c)*(b*b + c) + c mod N;
      d := gcd(a-b mod N, N);
    until (d <> 1);
  factor := d;
  end;
```

Program 8.4 Pollard rho method for factoring

The discussion above shows that the number of steps taken by the algorithm is $\min(t_p, t_q)$, where t_p and t_q are the rho lengths of f_p and f_q, respectively. By Theorem 8.9, the rho length of a random point on random N-map is $O(\sqrt{N})$, so under the assumption discussed in the previous paragraph we should expect the algorithm to terminate in $O(\min(\sqrt{p}, \sqrt{q}))$ steps, which is $O(N^{1/4})$. This argument obviously generalizes to the situation where N has more than two factors.

Theorem 8.12 (*Pollard rho method*) *Under the heuristic assumption that path length in quadratic functions is asymptotic to path length in random maps, Pollard's rho method factors a composite integer number N in an expected number of steps that is $O(\sqrt{p})$ where p is the smallest prime factor of N. In particular, N is factored in $O(N^{1/4})$ steps, on the average.*

Proof. See the discussion above. The global bound follows from the fact that $p \le \sqrt{N}$. ■

In 1980, Brent [26] used Pollard's method to factor the 8th Fermat number for the first time. Brent discovered that

$$F_8 = 2^{2^8} + 1 \approx 1.11579 \cdot 10^{77}$$

has the prime factor

$$1238926361552897$$

(also see Knuth [21]). The fact that the approximate analysis currently rests on a partly unproven assumption does not detract from the utility

N	*number of steps*
13·23	4
127·331	10
1237·4327	21
12347·54323	132
123457·654323	243
1234577·7654337	1478
12345701·87654337	3939
123456791·987654323	11225
1234567907·10987654367	23932

Table 8.13 Sample execution of Pollard's algorithm ($c = 1$)

of the algorithm. Indeed, knowledge of properties of random maps gives confidence that the method should factor efficiently, and it does.

Table 8.13 shows the number of steps used by Pollard's method to factor numbers of the form $N = pq$ where p and q are chosen to be primes near numbers of the form $1234\cdots$ and $\cdots 4321$, respectively. Though c and the starting points are supposed to be chosen at random, the value $c = 1$ and starting points $a = b = 1$ work sufficiently well for this application (and make it easy to reproduce the results). From the table, we can see that the cost rises roughly by a factor of 3 when N rises by a factor of about 100, in excellent agreement with Theorem 8.12. The method factors the last number on the list, which is $\approx 1.35 \cdot 10^{19}$, in less than $24,000$ steps, while exhaustive trials would have required about 10^9 operations.

WORDS and maps relate directly to classical problems in combinatorics and "classical" problems in the analysis of algorithms. Many of the methods and results that we have discussed are well known in mathematics (Bernoulli trials, occupancy problems) and are widely applicable outside the analysis of algorithms. They are directly relevant to modern applications such as predicting the performance of hashing algorithms, and detailed study of problems in this new domain leads to new problems of independent interest.

Hashing algorithms were among the first to be analyzed mathematically, and they are still of paramount practical importance. New types of applications and changes of fundamental characteristics in hardware and software contribute to the continued relevance of the techniques and results about hashing algorithms presented here and in the literature.

The analysis of random maps succinctly summarizes our general approach to the analysis of algorithms. We develop functional equations on generating functions corresponding to the underlying combinatorial structure, then use analytic tools to extract coefficients. The symbolic method is particularly effective for the former in this case, and the Lagrange inversion theorem is an important tool for the latter.

Maps are characterized by the fact that each element maps to precisely one other element. In the graphical representation, this means that there are precisely N edges and that each element has exactly one edge pointing "from" it, though many elements might point "to" a particular element. The next generalization is to *graphs*, where this restriction is removed and each element can point "to" any number of other elements.

Graphs are more complicated than maps or any of the other combinatorial structures that we have examined in this book because they are more difficult to decompose into simpler substructures, normally our basis for analysis by solving recurrences or exploiting structural decomposition to develop relationships among generating functions.

Random graphs have a wealth of interesting properties. A number of books have been written on the subject, and it is an active research area. (See, for example, Bollobás [3] for a survey of the field.) Analysis of random graphs centers on the "probabilistic method," where the focus is not on exactly enumerating properties of *all* graphs, but rather on developing suitable inequalities that relate complex parameters to tractable ones. There are many important fundamental algorithms for processing graphs, and there are many examples in the literature of the analysis of such algorithms. Different models of randomness are appropriate for different applications, making analysis along the lines we have been studying appropriate in many cases. Learning properties of random graphs is a fruitful area of study in the analysis of algorithms.

Random maps are an appropriate topic on which to close for many reasons. They generalize basic and widely structures (permutations and trees) that have occupied so much of our attention in this book; they are of direct practical interest in the use of random number generators and random sequences; their analysis illustrates the power, simplicity, and utility of the symbolic enumeration method and other tools that we have been using; and they represent the first step towards studying random graphs (for example, see Janson, Knuth, Luczak, and Pittel [19]), which are fundamental and widely applicable structures. It is our hope that the basic tools and techniques that we have covered in this book will provide readers with the interest and expertise to attack these and other problems in the analysis of algorithms that arise in the future.

References

1. M. ABRAMOWITZ AND I. STEGUN. *Handbook of Mathematical Functions*, Dover, New York, 1970.
2. E. BACH. "Toward a theory of Pollard's rho method," *Information and Computation* **30**, 1989, 139–155.
3. B. BOLLOBÁS. *Random Graphs*, Academic Press, London, 1985.
4. R. P. BRENT AND J. M. POLLARD. "Factorization of the eighth Fermat number," *Mathematics of Computation* **36**, 1981, 627–630.
5. B. CHAR, K. GEDDES, G. GONNET, B. LEONG, M. MONAGAN, AND S. WATT. *Maple V Library Reference Manual*, Springer-Verlag, New York, 1991.
6. L. COMTET. *Advanced Combinatorics*, Reidel, Dordrecht, 1974.
7. T. H. CORMEN, C. E. LEISERSON, AND R. L. RIVEST. *Introduction to Algorithms*, MIT Press, New York, 1990.
8. F. N. DAVID AND D. E. BARTON. *Combinatorial Chance*, Charles Griffin, London, 1962.
9. W. FELLER. *An Introduction to Probability Theory and Its Applications*, John Wiley, New York, 1957.
10. P. FLAJOLET, D. GARDY, AND L. THIMONIER. "Birthday paradox, coupon collectors, caching algorithms and self-organizing search," *Discrete Applied Mathematics* **39**, 1992, 207–229.
11. P. FLAJOLET AND A. M. ODLYZKO. "Random mapping statistics," in *Advances in Cryptology*, J.-J. Quisquater and J. Vandewalle, eds., Lecture Notes in Computer Science No. 434, Springer-Verlag, New York, 1990, 329–354.
12. P. FLAJOLET AND R. SEDGEWICK. *Analytic Combinatorics*, in preparation.
13. D. FOATA AND J. RIORDAN. "Mappings of acyclic and parking functions," *Aequationes Mathematicae* **10**, 1974, 10–22.
14. G. H. GONNET. "Expected length of the longest probe sequence in hash code searching," *Journal of the ACM* **28**, 1981, 289–309.
15. G. H. GONNET AND R. BAEZA–YATES. *Handbook of Algorithms and Data Structures* (second edition), Addison-Wesley, Reading, MA, 1991.
16. I. GOULDEN AND D. JACKSON. *Combinatorial Enumeration*, John Wiley, New York, 1983.
17. R. GRAHAM, D. E. KNUTH, AND O. PATASHNIK. *Concrete Mathematics*, Addison-Wesley, Reading, MA, 1989.

18. L. GUIBAS AND E. SZEMEREDI. "The analysis of double hashing," *Journal of Computer and Systems Sciences* **16**, 1978, 226–274.
19. S. JANSON, D. E. KNUTH, T. LUCZAK, AND B. PITTEL. "The birth of the giant component," *Random Structures and Algorithms* **4**, 1993, 233–358.
20. D. E. KNUTH. *The Art of Computer Programming. Volume 1: Fundamental Algorithms*, Addison-Wesley, Reading, MA, 1968.
21. D. E. KNUTH. *The Art of Computer Programming. Volume 2: Seminumerical Algorithms*, Addison-Wesley, Reading, MA, 1969.
22. D. E. KNUTH. *The Art of Computer Programming. Volume 3: Sorting and Searching*, Addison-Wesley, Reading, MA, 1973.
23. V. F. KOLCHIN. *Random Mappings*, Optimization Software, New York, 1986.
24. V. F. KOLCHIN, B. A. SEVASTYANOV, AND V. P. CHISTYAKOV. *Random Allocations*, John Wiley, New York, 1978.
25. G. LUEKER AND M. MOLODOWITCH. "More analysis of double hashing," in *Proceedings 20th Annual ACM Symposium on Theory of Computing*, 1988, 354–359.
26. J. M. POLLARD. "A Monte Carlo method for factorization," *BIT* **15**, 1975, 331–334.
27. R. SEDGEWICK. *Algorithms*, 2nd edition, Addison-Wesley, Reading, MA, 1988.
28. R. SEDGEWICK, T. SZYMANSKI, AND A. YAO. "The complexity of finding cycles in periodic functions," *SIAM Journal on Computing* **11**, 1982, 376–390.
29. J. S. VITTER AND W. CHEN. *Design and analysis of coalesced hashing*, Oxford University Press, New York, 1987.
30. J. S. VITTER AND P. FLAJOLET, "Analysis of algorithms and data structures," in *Handbook of Theoretical Computer Science A: Algorithms and Complexity*, J. van Leeuwen, ed., Elsevier, Amsterdam, 1990, 431–524.

LIST OF THEOREMS

INDEX

RELATED TITLES FROM ADDISON-WESLEY

Robert Sedgewick

Algorithms in C++	© 1992	0-201-51059-6
Algorithms in C	© 1990	0-201-51425-7
Algorithms in Modula-3	© 1993	0-201-53351-0
Algorithms, 2/e [*in Pascal*]	© 1988	0-201-06673-4

Robert Sedgewick is the author of a popular series of books on algorithms. The books each cover the same broad range of fundamental algorithms and more advanced methods: sorting, search, string-processing, geometric, graph, and mathematical algorithms. Each book offers concise implementations of these algorithms in a particular programming language.

Donald E. Knuth

The Art of Computer Programming

Volume 1: Fundamental Algorithms, 2/e	© 1973	0-201-03809-9
Volume 2: Seminumerical Algorithms, 2/e	© 1981	0-201-03822-6
Volume 3: Sorting and Searching	© 1973	0-201-03803-X

Gaston Gonnet and Ricardo Baeza-Yates

Handbook of Algorithms and Data Structures in Pascal and C, 2/e © 1991 0-201-41607-7

Ronald L. Graham, Donald E. Knuth, and Oren Patashnik

Concrete Mathematics: A Foundation for Computer Science, 2/e © 1994 0-201-55802-5

Ralph Grimaldi

Discrete and Combinatorial Mathematics, 3/e © 1994 0-201-54983-2

Stephen B. Mauer and Anthony Ralston

Discrete Algorithmic Mathematics © 1991 0-201-15585-0

---

text fonts : Times Ten
math fonts : Computer Modern
typesetting : TEX
figures : PostScript
symbolic mathematics : Maple
operating system : UNIX
text editor : emacs